Evidentiary Foundations

Twelfth Edition

EDWARD J. IMWINKELRIED
Edward L. Barrett, Jr. Professor of Law Emeritus,
University of California at Davis School of Law

2023

 LexisNexis®

QUESTIONS ABOUT THIS PUBLICATION?

For questions about the **Editorial Content** appearing in these volumes or reprint permission, please call:

Mark Landis, J.D. at .... (415) 908-3300
Email: .... mark.a.landis@lexisnexis.com
Outside the United States and Canada, please call . . . . (973) 820-2000

For assistance with replacement pages, shipments, billing or other customer service matters, please call:

Customer Services Department at . . . . (800) 833-9844
Outside the United States and Canada, please call . . . . (518) 487-3385
Fax Number . . . . (800) 828-8341
Customer Service Website . . . . http://www.lexisnexis.com/custserv/

For information on other Matthew Bender publications, please call

Your account manager or . . . . (800) 223-1940
Outside the United States and Canada, please call . . . . (937) 247-0293

Library of Congress Cataloging-in-Publication Data

Names: Imwinkelried, Edward J., author.
Title: Evidentiary foundations / Edward J. Imwinkelried, Professor of Law Emeritus, University of California at Davis School of Law.
Description: Twelfth edition. | New York : LexisNexis, 2023. | Includes bibliographical references and index. | Summary: "Evidentiary Foundations provides sample lines of questioning that demonstrate how to lay the foundation for admitting various kinds of evidence. It also includes a brief discussion of the underlying legal principles, based on modern common law and the applicable Federal Rules of Evidence"—Provided by publisher.
Identifiers: LCCN 2022046845 (print) | LCCN 2022046846 (ebook) | ISBN 9781663351388 (hardcover) | ISBN 9781663351395 (ebook)
Subjects: LCSH: Evidence (Law)—United States.
Classification: LCC KF8935 .I45 2023 (print) | LCC KF8935 (ebook) | DDC 347.73/6—dc23/eng/20221123
LC record available at https://lccn.loc.gov/2022046845
LC ebook record available at https://lccn.loc.gov/2022046846

LCCN: 2022046845 (print)
ISBN: 978-1-6633-5138-8 (print)

Cite as:

Edward J. Imwinkelreid, *Evidentiary Foundations*, § [000.00] (Matthew Bender [ ] ed. [date])

Example:

Edward J. Imwinkelreid, *Evidentiary Foundations*, § 4.02[6] (Matthew Bender 12th ed. 2023)

Editorial Office
230 Park Ave., 7th Floor, New York, NY 10169 (800) 543-6862
www.lexisnexis.com

MATTHEW◆BENDER

Dedication

I would like to dedicate my work on this text to:
Cindy, Marie, Ken, Kindra, and Danielle; my parents, the late Enes and John Imwinkelried; and my parents-in-law, the late Lyman (Brownie) and Mary Jane Clark.

Acknowledgements

The author would like to express his thanks to: Ms. Nichelle Walker, who helped prepare the 11th edition; Mr. Jay Paik, class of 2003, University of California, at Davis Law School, who proofread the manuscript for the fifth edition; Ms. Ryan Hall, class of 1998, University of California, at Davis Law School, who proofread the manuscript for the fourth edition; Ms. Kristin Lucey, class of 1996, University of California, at Davis Law School, who researched and proofread the manuscript for the third edition; Mr. Ronald Richards, class of 1989, University of California, at Davis Law School, who researched and proofread the manuscript for the first edition; Jennifer Angeles, Glenda McGlashan, Jessica Drushell, Cynthia Coble, Kristi Case, Diane Monheit, Helen Forsyth, Berta Lewin, Paula Buchignani, and Kathy Houston, who typed the manuscript; and his colleagues, Richard C. Wydick, James E. Hogan, Michael Graham, John O'Brien, David Schlueter, Thomas Stewart, Sam Stonefield, and Dr. Marty Greer, DVM. In 1988, Professors Wydick and Hogan helped the author prepare a special California edition of *Evidentiary Foundations*; and in 1994 and 2000, we prepared the second and third editions of that text. Professor Leach has coauthored the fourth and fifth editions of that text. Their comments on the manuscripts for *California Evidentiary Foundations* were instrumental in preparing this edition of *Evidentiary Foundations*. Professor Graham led the teams which prepared the special Florida and Illinois editions. Whenever the technology advances, Professor Graham prods me to keep this text at the cutting edge. He has inspired many of the improvements in this text. Professor Schlueter leads the teams which prepared the Texas and military editions. He was especially helpful in drafting the new foundation for STR DNA typing. Professor Stonefield was kind enough to give the fifth edition of this text a very close read and made several acute suggestions for improving the text. Dr. Greer made several excellent suggestions for improving and expanding the X-ray foundation in the seventh edition. Professor David Schlueter, my coauthor on *Texas* and *Military Evidentiary Foundations*, made several suggestions for additions to the eighth edition. Professors O'Brien and Stewart prepared the new edition of *Missouri Evidentiary Foundations*, which included several revised foundations.

Table of Contents

A DETAILED SYNOPSIS FOR EACH CHAPTER APPEARS AT THE BEGINNING OF THE CHAPTER

Chapter 1	**INTRODUCTION**
§ 1.01	Introduction
§ 1.02	Laying a Foundation—In General
[1]	Legal Rules
[2]	Practical Rules
§ 1.03	Laying a Foundation on Direct Examination
[1]	In General
[2]	Legal Rules
[3]	Practical Rules
§ 1.04	Laying a Foundation on Cross-Examination
[1]	In General
[2]	Legal Rules
[3]	Practical Rules

Chapter 2	**RELATED PROCEDURES**
§ 2.01	Introduction
§ 2.02	Pretrial Motion *In Limine* by the Opponent
[1]	The Doctrine
[2]	Elements of a Motion *In Limine*
[3]	Sample Motion *In Limine*
§ 2.03	Objections at the Trial by the Opponent
[1]	The Doctrine
[2]	Elements of an Objection
[3]	Sample Objections
§ 2.04	Motions to Strike at Trial by the Opponent
[1]	The Doctrine
[2]	Elements of a Motion to Strike
[3]	Sample Motion to Strike
§ 2.05	Request by the Opponent to Take a Witness on Voir Dire
[1]	The Doctrine
[2]	Sample Request to Take a Witness on Voir Dire
§ 2.06	Offer of Proof by the Proponent
[1]	The Doctrine
[2]	Elements of an Offer of Proof
[3]	Sample Offer of Proof

Table of Contents

Chapter 3	THE COMPETENCY OF WITNESSES
§ 3.01	Introduction
§ 3.02	The Voir Dire of a Child by the Witness's Proponent
[1]	The Doctrine
[2]	Elements of the Foundation
[3]	Sample Foundation
§ 3.03	The Questioning of a Lay Witness by the Proponent to Demonstrate Personal Knowledge
[1]	The Doctrine
[2]	Elements of the Foundation
[3]	Sample Foundation
§ 3.04	The Opponent's Presentation of Psychiatric Testimony Attacking a Prospective Witness's Competency
[1]	The Doctrine
[2]	Elements of the Foundation
[3]	Sample Foundation
§ 3.05	The Witness Spouse
[1]	The Doctrine
[2]	Elements of the Foundation
[3]	Sample Foundation
§ 3.06	Dead Persons' Statutes or Survivors' Evidence Acts
[1]	The Doctrine
[2]	Elements of the Foundation
[3]	Sample Foundations

Chapter 4	AUTHENTICATION
§ 4.01	Authentication in General
[1]	Introduction
[2]	Authentication in Traditional Courtrooms
[3]	Authentication in Computerized Courtrooms
[a]	In General
[b]	The Presentation of an Unmarked Hard Copy by Using a Document Camera
[c]	The Presentation of a Premarked Exhibit by Using a Document Camera
[d]	The Presentation of Digitized Exhibits Loaded Onto a Computer
§ 4.02	The Authentication of Private Writings
[1]	Writings also Raise Issues of Best Evidence and Hearsay
[2]	Testimony of a Witness Who Observed the Document's Execution
[3]	Testimony of a Witness Familiar With the Author's Handwriting Style
[4]	The Reply Letter Doctrine

Table of Contents

[5]   A Comparison by an Expert Questioned Document Examiner

[6]   A Printout From a Social Media Profile Page

[7]   Text Messages

[8]   Ancient Writings

§ 4.03   The Authentication of Business Writings

[1]   Conventional Business Writings

[2]   Computer Records

[3]   "Faxed" Documents

[4]   E(lectronic)-Mail

 [a]   Overview

 [b]   Evidentiary Doctrines and Foundational Elements

 [c]   Sample Foundations

  [i]   In General

  [ii]   Chain of Custody Handling Testimony by an Employee of an E-Mail Service

  [iii]   Testimony about a Digital Signature

[5]   Scanned Writings

[6]   Information Posted at A Business' Web Site

[7]   Self-Authenticating Business Records

[8]   Self-Authenticating Printouts of Records Automatically Generated by an Electric Process or System

[9]   Self-Authenticating Printouts of Data Copies from an Electronic Device, Storage Medium, or File

[10]   The Authentication of Printouts of Records Maintained on a Blockchain

[11]   The Authentication of Records Stored in the Cloud

§ 4.04   The Authentication of Official Writings

[1]   The Doctrine

[2]   Elements of the Foundation

[3]   Sample Foundation

§ 4.05   The Authentication of Oral Statements

[1]   In General

[2]   Lay Opinion Testimony of a Witness Familiar with the Speaker's Voice

[3]   The Telephone Directory Doctrine

[4]   Testimony by a Voiceprint or Sound Spectrography Expert

[5]   Caller Identification

 [a]   The Doctrine

 [b]   Elements of the Foundation

 [c]   Sample Foundation

Table of Contents

§ 4.06		Audio Recordings
	[1]	The Doctrine
	[2]	Elements of the Foundation
	[3]	Sample Foundations
§ 4.07		Demonstrative Evidence
	[1]	In General
	[2]	Verification of a Diagram
	[3]	Marking a Diagram
	[4]	Models
§ 4.08		The Identification of Real or Original Physical Evidence
	[1]	The Doctrine
	[2]	Elements of the Foundation
	[3]	Sample Foundations
§ 4.09		The Verification of Photographs
	[1]	Still Photographs
	[2]	Motion Pictures and Videotapes
	[3]	X-Rays
	[4]	Automated Surveillance Cameras
	[5]	Computer Animations and Simulations
	[a]	In General
	[b]	Illustrative Evidence
	[c]	Substantive Evidence
	[6]	Enhanced Photographs
§ 4.10		The Validation of Scientific Evidence
	[1]	The Doctrine
	[2]	Elements of the Foundation
	[3]	Sample Foundation

Chapter 5   **RULE 403 AND LEGAL IRRELEVANCE LIMITATIONS ON CREDIBILITY EVIDENCE**

PART A.	Introduction	
§ 5.01		Overview
§ 5.02		The Stages of Credibility Analysis
PART B.	Bolstering Witnesses Before Impeachment	
§ 5.03		Prior Identification
	[1]	The Doctrine
	[2]	Elements of the Foundation
	[3]	Sample Foundation
§ 5.04		Fresh Complaint
	[1]	The Doctrine
	[2]	Elements of the Foundation

Table of Contents

[3]   Sample Foundation

PART C.   Impeachment of Witnesses
§ 5.05   Bad Acts That Have Not Resulted in a Conviction
[1]   The Doctrine
[2]   Elements of the Foundation
[3]   Sample Foundation
§ 5.06   Proof of the Character Trait of Untruthfulness
[1]   The Doctrine
[2]   Elements of the Foundation
[3]   Sample Foundations
§ 5.07   Proof That the Witness Has Failed a Polygraph Examination
[1]   The Doctrine
[2]   Elements of the Foundation
[3]   Sample Foundation
§ 5.08   Proof that Another Witness Specifically Contradicts the Testimony of the Witness to Be Impeached
§ 5.09   Proof that the Witness Made a Prior Inconsistent Statement
[1]   In General
[2]   Cross-Examination to Elicit a Witness's Concession that the Witness Earlier Made an Inconsistent Statement
[3]   Extrinsic Evidence of a Prior Inconsistent Statement
[4]   Evidence of the Witness's Failure to Mention a Fact in a Prior Statement
§ 5.10   Proof that the Witness has Suffered a Conviction
[1]   The Doctrine
[2]   Elements of the Foundation
[3]   Sample Foundations
§ 5.11   Proof that the Witness Is Biased
[1]   The Doctrine
[2]   Elements of the Foundation
[3]   Sample Foundations
§ 5.12   Proof that the Witness Is Deficient in an Element of Competency
[1]   The Doctrine
[2]   Elements of the Foundation
[3]   Sample Foundations

PART D.   Rehabilitation of Witnesses After Impeachment
§ 5.13   Prior Consistent Statement
[1]   The Doctrine
[2]   Elements of the Foundation
[3]   Sample Foundation

Table of Contents

§ 5.14   Proof of the Character Trait of Truthfulness

  [1]   The Doctrine

  [2]   Elements of the Foundation

  [3]   Sample Foundation

Chapter 6   **LEGAL IRRELEVANCE LIMITATIONS ON EVIDENCE THAT IS RELEVANT TO THE HISTORICAL MERITS OF THE CASE**

§ 6.01   Introduction

§ 6.02   Character Evidence

  [1]   Overview

  [2]   Reputation Character Evidence

  [3]   Opinion Character Evidence

  [4]   Proof of Character by Specific Instances of Conduct

  [5]   Cross-Examination of a Character Witness

§ 6.03   Habit or Routine Practice Evidence

  [1]   The Doctrine

  [2]   Elements of the Foundation

  [3]   Sample Foundation

§ 6.04   Other Crimes or Uncharged Misconduct Evidence

  [1]   The Doctrine

  [2]   Elements of the Foundation

  [3]   Sample Foundation

§ 6.05   Uncharged Misconduct Evidence in Civil Actions

  [1]   The Doctrine

  [2]   Elements of the Foundation

  [3]   Sample Foundation

§ 6.06   Similar Happenings Evidence

  [1]   The Doctrine

  [2]   Elements of the Foundation

  [3]   Sample Foundation

§ 6.07   In-Court Exhibitions

§ 6.08   In-Court Demonstrations

§ 6.09   Liability Insurance

Chapter 7   **PRIVILEGES AND SIMILAR DOCTRINES**

§ 7.01   Introduction

§ 7.02   Privileges for Confidential Relations—In General

§ 7.03   Privileges for Confidential Information—Invoking a Privilege

  [1]   Elements of the Foundation

  [2]   Sample Foundation

Table of Contents

§ 7.04   Privileges for Confidential Relations—Defeating a Privilege by Proving Waiver

  [1]   In General

  [2]   In-Court Waiver

  [3]   Out-Of-Court Waiver

§ 7.05   Privileges for Confidential Relations—Defeating a Privilege by Proving a Special Exception

  [1]   In General

  [2]   At the Time of the Communication, the Holder Sought the Information to Facilitate a Future Crime or Fraud

  [3]   The Joint Consultation Situation

  [4]   The Patient-Litigant Exception

§ 7.06   The Work Product Protection

  [1]   The Conditional Work Product Protection

  [2]   The Absolute Work Product Protection

§ 7.07   Government Privileges—Military and State Secrets

  [1]   The Doctrine

  [2]   Elements of the Foundation

  [3]   Sample Foundation

§ 7.08   Government Privileges—Minor Government Secrets

  [1]   The Doctrine

  [2]   Elements of the Foundation

  [3]   Sample Foundations

§ 7.09   Government Privileges—An Informant's Identity

  [1]   The Doctrine

  [2]   Elements of the Foundation

  [3]   Sample Foundation

§ 7.10   Subsequent Repairs

  [1]   The Doctrine

  [2]   Elements of the Foundation

  [3]   Sample Foundations

§ 7.11   Compromise Statements

  [1]   Statements During Civil Settlement Negotiations

  [2]   Statements During Plea Bargaining Negotiations

Chapter 8   **THE BEST EVIDENCE RULE**

§ 8.01   Introduction

§ 8.02   The Object Involved Is Not a "Writing"

§ 8.03   The Writing's Terms Are Not "In Issue"

§ 8.04   The Writing's Terms Are Only Collaterally "In Issue"

Table of Contents

§ 8.05		The Evidence Offered Is an "Original"
	[1]	The Doctrine
	[2]	Elements of the Foundation
	[3]	Sample Foundation
§ 8.06		The Evidence Offered Is a "Duplicate"
	[1]	The Doctrine
	[2]	Elements of the Foundation
	[3]	Sample Foundations
§ 8.07		Admissible Types of Secondary Evidence
	[1]	In General
	[2]	An Authenticated Copy
	[3]	Oral Recollection Testimony
§ 8.08		Excuses for Non-Production
	[1]	In General
	[2]	The Proponent Lost the Original
	[3]	The Proponent Innocently Destroyed the Original
	[4]	The Original Is in Official Custody
	[5]	The Original Is in the Possession of a Third Party Beyond the Reach of the Court's Compulsory Process
	[6]	The Party-Opponent has Possession of the Original and Fails to Produce It After Notice to Produce
	[7]	Voluminous or Bulky Records

Chapter 9		**OPINION EVIDENCE**
§ 9.01		Introduction
§ 9.02		Lay Opinion Testimony
	[1]	In General
	[2]	Collective Fact Opinions
	[3]	Skilled Lay Observer Testimony
	[4]	Owners' Opinions about the Value of Their Property
§ 9.03		Expert Opinion Testimony
	[1]	In General
	[2]	The Expert's Qualifications to Form the Opinion
	[3]	The General Methodology (The Theory or Technique) the Expert Relies On
	[4]	The Case-Specific Factual Bases of the Expert's Opinion
	[a]	Overview
	[b]	Facts the Expert Personally Knows or That Are Otherwise Independently Admissible
	[c]	Secondhand Reports From Third Parties
	[d]	Hypothetically Assumed Facts

Table of Contents

[e]   The Sufficiency of the Facts or Data to Support the Opinion

[5]   The Proper Application of the General Methodology to the Case-Specific Information

[6]   The Statement of the Opinion Itself

[7]   The Explanation of the Opinion

§ 9.04   Evidence of an Out-of-Court Experiment

[1]   The Doctrine

[2]   Elements of the Foundation

[3]   Sample Foundation

Chapter 10   **THE HEARSAY RULE, ITS EXEMPTIONS, AND ITS EXCEPTIONS**

PART A.   Introduction

§ 10.01   Overview

PART B.   Hearsay

§ 10.02   The Definition of Hearsay

[1]   In General

[2]   The Evidence Is an Assertive Statement or Act

[a]   Assertive Statements

[b]   Assertive Acts

[c]   Nonassertive Acts

[3]   The Statement Is Offered for a Hearsay Purpose

[a]   Overview

[b]   The Statement Is Circumstantial Proof of the Declarant's State of Mind—Mental Output

[c]   The Statement Is an Operative Fact or Verbal Act

[d]   The Effect of the Statement on the Mind of the Hearer or Reader—Mental Input

[4]   The Statement Was Not Made by a Human Declarant

[5]   The Statement Was Made or the Act Performed by a Person Still Considered an Out-Of-Court Declarant

PART C.   The Admissions Exemption Requiring a Showing of Neither Reliability Nor Necessity

§ 10.03   The Exemption for Statements or Admissions of A Party-Opponent

[1]   In General

[2]   Personal Admissions

[a]   Overview

[b]   In Civil Cases

[c]   In Criminal Cases

Table of Contents

[3]   Adoptive Admissions

  [a]   Overview

  [b]   Express Adoption

  [c]   Implied Adoption by Silence—"Tacit Admission"

[4]   Vicarious Admissions

  [a]   In Civil Cases

  [b]   In Criminal Cases

PART D.   Hearsay Exceptions Based Primarily on a Showing of Reliability

§ 10.04   In General

§ 10.05   Business Entries

  [1]   The Doctrine

  [2]   Elements of the Foundation

  [3]   Sample Foundation

§ 10.06   Official Records

  [1]   The Doctrine

  [2]   Elements of the Foundation

  [3]   Sample Foundations

§ 10.07   Past Recollection Recorded and Present Recollection Refreshed or Revived

  [1]   Past Recollection Recorded

  [2]   Present Recollection Refreshed or Revived

§ 10.08   Learned Treatises

  [1]   The Doctrine

  [2]   Elements of the Foundation

  [3]   Sample Foundation

§ 10.09   Excited or Startled Utterances

  [1]   The Doctrine

  [2]   Elements of the Foundation

  [3]   Sample Foundation

§ 10.10   Present Sense Impressions or Contemporaneous Statements

  [1]   The Doctrine

  [2]   Elements of the Foundation

  [3]   Sample Foundation

§ 10.11   Declarations of State of Mind or Emotion

  [1]   Offered to Prove State of Mind or Emotion

  [2]   Offered to Prove Subsequent Conduct

§ 10.12   Declarations of Bodily Condition

  [1]   Present Bodily Condition

  [2]   Past Bodily Condition

  [3]   External Cause or Source

Table of Contents

PART E.   Hearsay Exceptions Based on a Showing of Unavailability

§ 10.13   In General
§ 10.14   The Unavailability of the Declarant at Trial
  [1]   At Common Law and by Statute
  [2]   As a Matter of Constitutional Law
§ 10.15   Declarations Against Interest
  [1]   The Doctrine
  [2]   Elements of the Foundation
  [3]   Sample Foundation
§ 10.16   Dying Declarations
  [1]   The Doctrine
  [2]   Elements of the Foundation
  [3]   Sample Foundation
§ 10.17   Former or Prior Testimony
  [1]   The Doctrine
  [2]   Elements of the Foundation
  [3]   Sample Foundation
§ 10.18   Forfeiture by Wrongdoing
  [1]   The Doctrine
  [2]   Elements of the Foundation
  [3]   Sample Foundation

PART F.   The Residual Hearsay Exception Based on Showings of Reliability and Necessity

§ 10.19   The Residual Hearsay Exception
  [1]   The Doctrine
  [2]   Elements of the Foundation
  [3]   Sample Foundation

Chapter 11   SUBSTITUTES FOR EVIDENCE

§ 11.01   Introduction
§ 11.02   Stipulations
  [1]   The Doctrine
  [2]   Elements of the Foundation
  [3]   Sample Foundations
§ 11.03   Judicial Notice
  [1]   The Doctrine
  [2]   Sample Foundations
§ 11.04   Jury Views
  [1]   The Doctrine
  [2]   Elements of the Foundation
  [3]   Sample Foundation

Table of Contents

Index

CHAPTER 1

INTRODUCTION

§ 1.01   INTRODUCTION

I have taught both Evidence and Trial Techniques for almost five decades. During that time I have identified some recurring complaints by my students. The primary complaint of the Evidence students is that they find it difficult to develop a working understanding of the evidentiary doctrines we discuss in class. The students say that their Evidence casebooks and hornbooks do not explain how the doctrines operate in the courtroom. For their part, the Trial Techniques students complain that although they think they understand the abstract evidentiary doctrines, they cannot apply the doctrines. Specifically, they cannot convert the classroom theories into concrete lines of questioning for the courtroom.

Given those complaints, I began an experiment in the late 1970s. I browsed through such texts as the AMERICAN JURISPRUDENCE PROOF OF FACTS set (Bancroft-Whitney Publishing Co.) and THE TRIAL MANUAL OF PREDICATE QUESTIONS (National District Attorneys Association). I selected a set of sample foundations from these texts and encouraged my students to read the sample foundations during the course. At the end of the course, I solicited the students' comments on the experiment. On the one hand, the students responded that a set of sample foundations was an excellent idea. Several students remarked that as soon as they read a sample foundation, the abstract evidentiary doctrine came to life and made much more sense. On the other hand, most students felt that some of the sample foundations I had collected were too sophisticated or lengthy. That feeling is understandable. After all, the available sets of sample foundations are designed primarily for practitioners rather than law students.

At this point, I resolved to prepare a comprehensive set of sample foundations for law students and young trial attorneys. That set became the first edition of EVIDENTIARY FOUNDATIONS (1980). The second edition was released in 1989, the third in 1993, the fourth in 1998, the fifth in 2002, the sixth in 2005, the seventh in 2008, the eighth in 2012, the ninth in 2015, the tenth in 2018, and the eleventh in 2020. I have used those editions in my own classes since the release of the first. I think that the level of student performance in both Evidence and Trial Practice has improved since I began using the text, and I hope that the improvement is due in some small part to the use of the text. It has become clear to me that it is time for a new edition of EVIDENTIARY FOUNDATIONS. Developments in Evidence law have rendered some passages of the earlier editions inaccurate or misleading. This edition mentions more proposed amendments to the Federal Rules of Evidence that are scheduled to take effect in late 2023 and late 2024. In addition, this edition not only adds a new authentication foundation for records stored in "the cloud" but also expands on the foundation for expert opinions, notably the requirements of Rules 702(b) and (d).

Most sections of the text use the following format. First, at the beginning of each section, there is a discussion of an evidentiary doctrine. The text discusses the modern common law and usually cites the applicable Federal Rule of Evidence as well. Since the principal purpose of this text is to teach trial technique rather than the evidentiary doctrine, the textual discussion of the doctrine is relatively short; and there are few case citations. The reader can find ample authority for this text's propositions of Evidence law in such hornbooks as MCCORMICK ON EVIDENCE (West Publishing Co., 8th ed. 2020) and E. IMWINKELRIED, P. GIANNELLI, F. GILLIGAN, F. LEDERER & L. RICHTER, COURTROOM CRIMINAL EVIDENCE (LEXIS Law Pub., 7th ed. 2022). Second, the text breaks the doctrine down into a list of foundational, predicate, or preliminary elements. These elements are the historical facts and events which constitute the foundation. Each element is numbered. Finally, the section contains a sample foundation for the evidentiary doctrine. Each question in the body of the sample foundation is numbered; the number corresponds to the element of the foundation the question relates to. Thus, the numbered foundation shows how each element in the doctrine converts into concrete questions in the courtroom. In the sample foundations, "J" means judge, "W" means witness, "P" the proponent of the evidence, "O" the opponent of the evidence, and "B" the bailiff or court reporter. "YR" signifies the current year while "YR-1" indicates the prior year. Thus, if YR is 2023, YR-1 would be 2022. The foundations assume that a jury is present. The procedure would be a bit more informal in a bench trial (a trial by judge alone). In some cases, to help the reader better appreciate limited admissibility doctrines such as non-character and non-hearsay, the text also includes illustrative limiting instructions and closing arguments.

Most previous new editions have added new foundations, statutory amendments, and relevant cases. However, since the fifth edition, some of the sample foundation sections contain a different type of material: limiting instructions and closing arguments for certain types of evidence. Law students and young litigators commonly have difficulty with doctrines such as character evidence. In particular, young litigators often overreach and attempt to elicit improper opinions from the foundational witness. The root cause may be that beginners do not fully appreciate (a) what the judge will tell the jury about the evidence in his or her instructions or (b) what the attorney himself or herself can say about the evidence during summation. The beginner might mistakenly feel compelled to have the witness verbalize the inference because they do not realize that either the judge or the attorney can later articulate the inference for the jury. The new summations are not offered as models of effective trial advocacy. Rather, the limited objective is to help the beginner understand what can be said about the evidence by both judges and attorneys *after* the witness lays the foundation for the admission of the evidence.

§ 1.02 LAYING A FOUNDATION—IN GENERAL

[1] LEGAL RULES

For our purposes, the most important procedural rule is that the proponent of an item of evidence must ordinarily lay the foundation before formally offering the item into evidence. For example, the proponent of a letter must present proof of its authenticity before offering the letter into evidence. Proof of the letter's authenticity is part of the letter's "foundation" or "predicate." Substantive Evidence law makes proof of authenticity a condition precedent to the letter's admission into evidence. Whenever Evidence law makes proof of a fact or event a condition to the admission of an item of evidence, that fact or event is part of the foundation for the evidence's admission.

In most jurisdictions, the trial judge has discretion to deviate from this procedural rule; the judge may vary the order of proof and admit the evidence subject to the subsequent proof of the foundation. However, judges are reluctant to use this discretion. Proof of the foundation before the evidence's admission is usually the more logical order of presentation. Moreover, if the judge admits the evidence subject to subsequent proof of the foundation and the proponent later fails to present the proof, the judge will be in an awkward position. At the very least, the judge will have to instruct the jurors to disregard the evidence they have already heard.[1] If the judge believes that the curative instruction will be ineffective[2] and the jurors will be unable to put the evidence out of mind, the judge may have to declare a mistrial. Hence, whenever possible, the proponent should lay the foundation or predicate before formally offering the item of evidence.

[2] PRACTICAL RULES

There are three cardinal rules for drafting a line of questioning: simplicity, brevity, and preparation.

---

[1] As Professor Ronald Carlson of the University of Georgia tells his students, the judge must instruct the jurors to remember to forget the stricken evidence. *But see* Wenner, *Under the Surface,* 53 TRIAL, Apr. 2017, at 22, 26 (the article is an interview with Professor Daniel Kahneman, the psychologist who won the 2002 Nobel Prize in Economics and coauthored the popular text, THINKING FAST AND SLOW (2011); Professor Kahneman explains that collectively, the jury may be better able to follow the instruction than an individual juror; people use two types of thought in decision-making, System 1 (fast and intuitive) and System 2 (slow and reflective); to begin with, "[t]here is more System 2 thought . . . with juries than with [individual] jurors"; jurors ordinarily vote after some discussion of the evidence, and that delay gives System 1 thought time to come into play; moreover, one conscientious, attentive juror "may remind fellow jurors that they are not supposed to consider certain evidence" or use it in a certain manner); David Sklansky, *Evidentiary Instructions and the Jury as Other,* 65 STAN. L. REV. 407 (2013) (the article reviews 33 published studies of the effectiveness of jury instructions; the author concludes that the negative assessments of jury instructions are "at best greatly exaggerated"; "the conventional wisdom about evidentiary instructions—'of course they don't work' is unduly pessimistic").

[2] The Advisory Committee Note to Rule 105 specifically states that Rule 105 "repel[s] any implication that limiting or curative instructions are sufficient in all situations." The Note to Rule 403 adds that "[i]n reaching a decision whether to exclude on grounds of unfair prejudice, consideration should be given to the probable effectiveness of lack of effectiveness of a limiting instruction."

First, always use the simplest, most easily understood term. R. WYDICK & A. SLOAN, PLAIN ENGLISH FOR LAWYERS Ch. 7 (6th ed. 2019). The trial attorney must communicate effectively with lay witnesses and jurors. Effective communication with laypersons requires that the trial attorney use lay diction. Jonathan Swift quite properly condemned the attorneys of his day for using "a peculiar Cant and Jargon of their own that no other mortal can understand." Sadly, many modern trial attorneys are guilty of the same literary sin. There is no need to resort to "prior" and "subsequent" if "before" and "after" will do quite nicely. There is no need to refer to "motor vehicle" when the word "car" is available. There is no justification for using "altercation" when the attorney could say "fight." Trial attorneys should realize that the examination of witnesses is a test of communicative skill rather than vocabulary.

Second, always make each question as short as possible. Rudolph Flesch has pointed out that there is an inverse relation between the length of a sentence and its comprehensibility; the longer the sentence is, the lower the level of reader or hearer comprehension. Leading psychology studies document that as a general proposition, the maximum length of a written sentence should be 25 words; if the sentence is any longer, reader comprehension drops off markedly. It is more difficult for a hearer to absorb a spoken sentence than it is for a reader to absorb a written sentence. Consequently, many experienced trial attorneys strive to limit their questions to 10 or 15 words in length. If the spoken question exceeds 15 words, it can be very difficult for the witness and jurors to follow.

The third cardinal rule is preparation. Both the attorney and the witness must be well prepared for trial. If the attorney falters or pauses too long during direct examination, the examination loses its flow and rhythm. If the witness appears uncertain during questioning, at the very least the jurors will doubt the quality of the witness's memory. The attorney must review the contemplated testimony with the witness before trial; in particular, the attorney should have the witness review the witness's own deposition transcript and other pretrial statements to refresh the witness's recollection.

§ 1.03 LAYING A FOUNDATION ON DIRECT EXAMINATION

[1] IN GENERAL

The general rules for laying foundations apply to direct examination. The direct examiner should lay a foundation before offering the evidence, and the examiner should observe the cardinal rules of simplicity and brevity. However, there are some additional rules the direct examiner must be familiar with.

[2] LEGAL RULES

In many jurisdictions, the technical evidentiary rules do not apply to some foundational questions. For instance, restyled Federal Rule of Evidence 104(a) provides: "The court must decide any preliminary question about whether a witness is qualified, a privilege exists, or evidence is admissible. In so deciding, the court is not bound by evidence rules, except those on privileges." The judge finally resolves the question of the existence of facts falling under Rule 104(a). As the Advisory Committee Note to Rule 104(a) states, the technical evidentiary rules are generally viewed as "the child of the jury system," and there is no need to apply those rules when the judge is the factfinder. Suppose that the proponent is offering a witness's former testimony at a prior trial. Part of the foundation for the former testimony exception to the hearsay rule is proof that the witness is unavailable at the present trial. In a jurisdiction where the hearsay rule does not apply to foundational evidence, the proponent could ask an investigator on the witness stand to relate a third party's statement that the former witness had said she was moving to Sweden. If the proponent attempted to present the third party's statement to the jury during the trial on the merits, the judge might rule that the statement was inadmissible hearsay; the third party was outside the courtroom when he or she made the statement, and the proponent is offering the statement for the truth of its assertion. However, when the judge rules on foundational facts under Rule 104(a), the hearsay rule is inapplicable.

The examiner must also bear in mind that under restyled Rule 611(c), leading questions are generally forbidden on direct examination. Leading questions suggest the desired answer to the witness. Since the witness is presumably friendly to the direct examiner, the witness will probably follow the lead. Suppose that the plaintiff's brother was a witness to the accident. The plaintiff alleges that the defendant was speeding. The plaintiff calls her brother as a witness. It would be impermissibly leading for the plaintiff's attorney to ask, "Isn't it true that the defendant was going 80 miles an hour?" There is a serious risk that the witness, the plaintiff's brother, will simply follow the attorney's lead rather than attempt to give the most accurate testimony. On direct examination, the law prefers that the attorney use the non-leading question, "In your opinion, what was the defendant's speed?"

In addition to knowing the general prohibition of leading questions on direct examination, the direct examiner must realize that the prohibition is merely a norm rather than an absolute rule. It is true that Rule 611(c) announces that "[l]eading questions should not be used on direct examination except as necessary to develop the witness's testimony," but the Advisory Committee Note explains that the drafters deliberately chose the weaker verb "should" to phrase the norm "in words of suggestion rather than command." Furthermore, there are numerous exceptions to the norm. D. CAPRA & E. GREENBERG, THE FORM OF THE QUESTION 66-81 (West Publishing Co., 2014). One notable exception is that the direct examiner may use leading questions on preliminary matters. Most judges limit the scope of this exception to such matters as the witness's occupation and setting the scene for events. However, some judges construe "preliminary" very broadly and liberally permit leading questions on foundational matters. Another exception is that the direct examiner may use mildly leading questions to refresh the memory of a forgetful witness. Further, the direct examiner may employ leading questions to assist witnesses who may have difficulty testifying, such as children, the disabled, and persons who are not fluent in English.

[3] PRACTICAL RULES

Notwithstanding Rule 104(a), whenever possible, comply with the technical evidentiary rules. Even if the local law permits you to disregard those rules in laying a foundation, your disregard of the rules will often prompt an objection. The opponent may not realize that the technical rules are inapplicable, or in bad faith the opponent may be searching for any pretext or excuse to disrupt your direct examination. The ideal direct examination is flowing and uninterrupted; without distracting objections, the direct examiner gives the witness an opportunity to tell a story to the jurors. You want to minimize the risk that the opponent will interrupt your foundation with an objection. Every time you disregard the technical rules in your foundational questions, you risk a distracting objection.

The same practical considerations lead to the conclusion that whenever possible, you should use non-leading questions on direct examination. You want to reduce the risk that your foundation will be interrupted by a leading question objection. Moreover, if you have a good witness, you want the witness to do the talking. By using leading questions which must be answered "Yes" or "No," you restrict the witness's opportunity to speak; and the jurors may suspect that you are putting words in the witness's mouth. If the witness projects honesty and intelligence, you want to use open-ended,[3] non-leading questions. Put the witness on display for the jury. The witness should be center stage. Juror psychology studies suggest a further reason to avoid leading the witness. One study found that the more acute jurors note the difference between leading and non-leading questioning. More importantly, when the jurors note that the attorney is leading a particular witness, they tend to infer that the attorney is doing so because the attorney lacks faith in the witness. Understandably, after drawing that inference, the jurors discount the witness's credibility. Why should they have faith in the witness if the attorney lacks faith? If you have a good witness, non-leading questions are tactically preferable on direct examination.

To ensure that your questions are non-leading, begin as many as possible with the natural interrogatory words, "who," "what," "which," "when," "where," "how," and "why." If you begin a question with one of these words, you will find that it is very difficult to make the question leading. Indeed, many trial judges use the rule of thumb that questions beginning with these words are not leading. In this text, I have made a conscious effort to begin virtually every question in the sample foundations for direct examination with one of these words. In the sample foundations, the word is in capital letters. My hope is that reading questions beginning with these words will help the student develop the skill and habit of phrasing non-leading questions.

I am not advocating beginning every sentence of direct examination with one of these words; that practice would make your direct examination annoyingly monotonous. As professional writers say, you want "elegant variation" in the phrasing of your questions.

---

[3] Ideally, most of the witness's answers should be a short paragraph, not a single word or sentence. The reader might wonder whether such phrasing is objectionable on the ground that it "calls for a narrative." However, there is no such prohibition in the Federal Rules of Evidence. Rather, Rule 611(a) gives the trial judge discretionary control over the "mode" or form of questioning. Most judges prefer that the witness answer in the form of short paragraphs. To begin with, that type of questioning provides greater assurance that the jury hears the witness's version of the events, not the attorney's. Moreover, presenting the testimony in that manner is usually less time-consuming. The judge will begin insisting that the attorney resort to more narrowly worded questions if (a) the witness cannot keep the chronology straight or (b) the witness makes repeated references to inadmissible matter. As previously stated, the third cardinal rule is preparation. In preparing a witness to testify, you must ensure that the witness knows the timeline and also knows what *not* to refer to unless the question specifically calls for it.

Sometimes you will not want an interrogatory sentence. When you elicit background information about your witness, you can use imperative sentences; for example, you may command the witness to "Please tell us where you work." To highlight the subdivisions of your direct examination, you may use declarative sentences such as "Now I want to ask you a few questions about what happened at the hospital." Strictly speaking, during the examination of a witness, the only thing you have a right to do is ask questions; but judges tolerate such declarative sentences to help the jury follow the testimony. Even when you use interrogatory sentences, as we have seen, Evidence law sometimes permits you to use gently leading questions. However, most law students and new trial attorneys pay insufficient attention to the phrasing of their questions on direct examination. This text uniformly uses non-leading phrasing to help the reader develop a habit of consistently phrasing non-leading questions.

§ 1.04 LAYING A FOUNDATION ON CROSS-EXAMINATION

[1] IN GENERAL

The general rules for laying a foundation also apply here. Most of the general rules apply with even greater force on cross-examination. On cross-examination, many judges are very reluctant to permit the examiner to introduce an item of evidence before presenting the foundational proof. On cross-examination, the witness is often hostile to the examiner; and the judge is more skeptical of the examiner's assurance that the witness will give favorable testimony at a later point in the examination. The norms of simplicity and brevity also apply with greater force on cross-examination. The hostile witness will often strain to misinterpret the question. The cross-examiner wants to frame questions that are so clear and so short that they cannot be misinterpreted. Box the witness in; the witness's only options should be to give you the concession you want or to commit perjury. However, in addition to knowing the general rules for laying foundations, the cross-examiner must be cognizant of several special legal rules for cross.

[2] LEGAL RULES

You will occasionally encounter a trial judge who firmly believes that an attorney may not introduce an exhibit during the cross-examination of an opposing witness. That belief is erroneous. J. TANFORD, THE TRIAL PROCESS: LAW, TACTICS AND ETHICS 292 (Carolina Academic Press, 4th ed. 2009). It is true that Federal Rule of Evidence 611(b) confines cross-examination to "the subject matter of the direct examination." But if the exhibit relates to a matter raised on direct examination, "new exhibits properly may be introduced during cross-examination." TANFORD, *supra*. Rule 611(a) gives the judge discretionary control over the order of proof; the permissibility of introducing exhibits during the cross-examination "lies in the discretion of the trial judge." TANFORD, *supra*. If you are trying a case before a judge whom you do not know and you contemplate introducing an exhibit during cross-examination, attempt to learn beforehand whether this judge permits the cross-examiner to proffer exhibits.

Since the witness is frequently hostile to the cross-examiner,[4] the law permits leading questions on cross-examination. While leading questions are permissible on cross-examination, argumentative questions are objectionable. D. CAPRA & E. GREENBERG, THE FORM OF THE QUESTION Ch. 10 (West Publishing Co., 2014). An argumentative question challenges the witness about an inference from the facts in the case. Assume that the witness testifies on direct examination that the defendant's car was going 80 miles an hour just before the collision. You want to impeach the witness with a prior inconsistent statement. It would be permissible, leading cross-examination to ask, "Isn't it true that you told your neighbor, Mrs. Ashton, at a party last Sunday that the defendant's car was going only 50 miles an hour?" The cross-examiner may legitimately attempt to force the witness to concede the historical fact of the prior inconsistent statement. Now assume that the witness admits the statement. It would be impermissibly argumentative to next ask, "How can you reconcile that statement with your testimony on direct examination?" The cross-examiner is not seeking any additional facts; rather, the cross-examiner is challenging the witness about an inference from the facts. Questions such as "How can you expect the jury to believe that?" are similarly argumentative and objectionable. The attorney may argue the inferences during summation or closing argument, but the attorney must ordinarily restrict his or her questions to those calculated to elicit facts.

[3]　PRACTICAL RULES

Negatively, as a tactical matter the cross-examiner should generally avoid argumentative questions. If a hostile witness is intelligent, the witness usually will not easily concede the favorable inference you want to draw. An argumentative question often prompts a heated exchange between the cross-examiner and the witness. The lay jurors usually sympathize with the lay witness, and you can antagonize the jurors by arguing with the witness. Unless the witness has a particularly abrasive personality, arguments between the attorney and witness are usually "no-win" situations for the attorney. If the attorney appears to dominate the exchange, the jurors may infer that the attorney does not want the witness to tell the whole truth; but if the witness appears to dominate, the jurors may conclude that the attorney is diffident—perhaps because the attorney lacks faith in his or her case. Elicit the historical facts you are morally certain the witness will concede, and draw your inferences later during closing argument.

Affirmatively, as a general proposition, you should consistently use leading questions on cross-examination. You ordinarily do not want to give a hostile witness any opening. Do not give that witness an opportunity to explain by asking "Why?" If you want to impeach a witness with a conviction, ask, "Isn't it true that in YR-3, a New York court convicted you of perjury?" If you want to prove a prior inconsistent statement, ask, "Isn't it a fact that right after the fight, you told the officer that the hallway was so dark

---

[4] Some witnesses are deemed hostile as a matter of law. Rule 611(c)(2) refers to "a witness identified with an adverse party." Thus, if the defendant is a corporation and the witness to be cross-examined is the corporation's president, the witness's legal relationship to the defendant renders the witness hostile as a matter of law. In other cases in which the witness being cross-examined engages in conduct such as refusing to answer, the witness can be deemed hostile in fact.

that you couldn't identify your attacker?" You can preface your questions with "Isn't it true . . . ?", "Isn't it correct . . . ?" or "Isn't it a fact . . . ?" to maintain control over the witness; or you can make a declarative statement and add a tag sentence such as "Isn't that true?" at the very end of your question.

I have attempted to begin every question in the sample foundations for cross-examination with such prefatory language. The preface is in capital letters. My purpose is to help the reader develop the habit of consistently using leading questions on cross-examination. Again, I do not advocate beginning virtually every question with blatantly[5] leading introductory language. Sometimes you will want to use non-leading questions. For instance, you may suspect that an adverse child witness has a memorized story. As the cross-examiner, you might want to pose an open-ended, non-leading question to the witness to give the child another opportunity to repeat the story verbatim. You can then argue in summation that the jury has heard a script rather than the truth. In other cases, if the topic is safe, you can use gently leading questions, beginning with such words as "Is," "Was," and "Did." However, the primary failing of neophyte cross-examiners is that they do not lead enough. I have deliberately exaggerated and begun every cross-examination question with blatantly leading language to underscore the importance of maintaining witness control. The late Albert Krieger, a former president of the National Association of Criminal Defense Lawyers, remarked that under the guise of asking questions, a good cross-examiner actually makes factual assertions and forces the witness to express assent on the record. By using leading, non-argumentative phrasing, the cross-examiner can virtually testify for the witness.

Finally, remember that your demeanor and tone should ordinarily be friendly even when you are using narrowly phrased, leading questions. You want the opposing witness to cooperate. At least early in the cross, your objective is usually to elicit helpful concessions from the witness; and to achieve that objective, you need a modicum of the witness's cooperation. You will not get that cooperation if your demeanor is combative or offensive. Quite to the contrary, if your demeanor is aggressive, the witness will put up his or her defenses, and you will have a very difficult time eliciting favorable information. You will sometimes want to make a show of righteous indignation at an opposing witness caught in an obvious lie; but when you are using the opposing witness to lay a foundation, the wisest tactic is to be friendly, polite, and low-key.

---

[5] There are degrees of leading.

— Questions that begin with words such as "Is," "Are," "Do," "Did," "Was," or "Were" are mildly leading. They refer to events or facts, and the reference itself suggests that the event occurred or that the fact is true.

— If the examiner uses more negative phrasing such as "Isn't" or "Didn't," the phrasing is fairly leading because the suggestion to the witness is even clearer.

— Finally, the phrasing can be brutally leading. The examiner can make the phrasing brutally leading by (a) beginning the questioning with expressions such as "Isn't is true" or "Won't you admit" or (b) making a declarative statement about a fact or event and adding a short, second "tag" sentence such as "Correct?" or "Right?"

CHAPTER 2

RELATED PROCEDURES

§ 2.01 INTRODUCTION

Most law students realize the importance of learning the procedures the proponent uses to present evidence. The subsequent chapters outline those procedures. However, there are two other sets of procedural rules a trial attorney must master: (1) the procedures the opponent uses to object to the admission of the proponent's evidence; and (2) the procedures the proponent uses if the trial judge sustains the opponent's objection. The purpose of this chapter is to familiarize the student with these two sets of procedural rules. §§ 2.02 through 2.05 describe the procedures the opponent must invoke to exclude evidence. § 2.06 illustrates the procedures the proponent resorts to if the judge sustains an objection by the opponent.

§ 2.02 PRETRIAL MOTION *IN LIMINE* BY THE OPPONENT

[1] THE DOCTRINE

If the opponent anticipates an evidentiary issue arising at trial, the opponent need not wait until trial to voice the objection. The opponent may raise the objection by a pretrial motion *in limine*. The proponent may make a motion *in limine* to obtain an advance ruling of the evidence's admissibility. With the benefit of a favorable advance ruling, the proponent can safely refer to the item of evidence during opening statement. An advance favorable ruling eliminates the risk that the judge will later rule the evidence inadmissible and that the opponent will subsequently move for a mistrial due to the jury's exposure to inadmissible evidence.[1] However, such motions are more frequently used by the opponent to suppress evidence before the trial begins. The opponent may use the motion for such purposes as preventing any mention of a wrongful death plaintiff's re-marriage, a civil defendant's liability insurance, or a criminal accused's prior convictions.

There are several tactical reasons why the opponent may employ a motion *in limine*. The most obvious reason is that the objectionable evidence might be highly prejudicial. If the opponent delays objecting until trial, during trial the jurors may at least hear some mention of the evidence. It would be preferable to litigate the issue before trial and preclude the proponent from even mentioning the evidence during trial. If the jurors hear any mention of the evidence, they may conclude that the opponent is attempting

---

[1] It is especially advisable for the proponent to move *in limine* if he or she believes that convincing the judge will be an uphill battle. For example, proponents often use this tactic when they intend to offer a novel type of expert testimony that no court has previously admitted.

to hide the truth from them. Further, the opponent may need an advance ruling to make strategic decisions for trial. Should the criminal defense attorney advise his or her client to take the stand? The defense attorney must consider the risk that if the client testifies, the judge may permit the prosecutor to impeach the client with prior convictions. If the judge grants a pretrial motion *in limine* to exclude the convictions, the defense attorney can confidently place the client on the stand. Without the benefit of the pretrial ruling, the defense attorney must gamble that the judge will exclude the convictions on objection.

How does the opponent make a motion in limine? Some jurisdictions require that the opponent give the proponent advance notice of the motion. In any case, as a matter of fairness, the opponent should give advance notice. Some jurisdictions also require or strongly prefer that the opponent reduce the motion to writing. However, perhaps the majority still permits oral motions. The opponent often makes the motion at the in-chambers conference before the trial begins; the attorneys and the judge meet in the judge's chambers before they walk into open court and meet the jurors. The trial judge generally has discretion whether to entertain the motion,[2] and the judge may prefer to rule on the issue during trial. If the judge entertains the motion and reaches its merits, there are several possible rulings: (1) The judge may deny the motion; (2) the judge may grant the motion and enter an absolute order prohibiting the proponent from mentioning the evidence during the trial; or (3) the judge may enter a preliminary or tentative order. On the one hand, a preliminary order prohibits the proponent from mentioning the evidence to the jury without the judge's consent. The order can be worded to apply not only to witnesses' testimony but also to any reference to the evidence by the attorney during voir dire examination and opening statement.[3] On the other hand, a preliminary order permits the proponent to request a hearing out of the jury's presence during the trial. At the hearing, the proponent may attempt to persuade the judge to admit the evidence; the proponent can point to some development during trial and argue that that development justifies the introduction of the evidence. A preliminary order is appropriate when the judge finds that the evidence is prejudicial but does not want to rule finally until he or she knows the final state of the record at trial.

If the judge denies the motion, there is a split of authority over the question of whether the moving party must renew the objection at trial to preserve the issue for appeal. As amended effective December 1, 2000, Federal Rule of Evidence 103(a)(2) stated that "[o]nce the court makes a definitive ruling on the record admitting . . . evidence, either at or before trial, a party need not renew an objection . . . to preserve a claim of error for appeal." Restyled Rule 103(b) reads: "Once the court rules definitively on the record—either before or at trial—a party need not renew an

---

[2] A few jurisdictions require the trial judge to rule pretrial on a defense motion to preclude the use of convictions to impeach a defendant's credibility if the defendant decides to testify. People v. Patrick, 233 Ill. 2d 62, 330 Ill. Dec. 149, 908 N.E.2d 1 (2009) (collecting cases).

[3] If the judge is inclined to grant relief, the opponent should ask the judge to order the proponent to admonish the witness to avoid referring to the evidence. If the proponent fails to do so, the witness might inadvertently refer to the evidence and perhaps necessitate a mistrial.

objection . . . to preserve a claim of error for appeal." The Advisory Committee Note accompanying the 2000 amendment indicates that the moving party has the burden to ensure that the judge makes it clear on the record that the ruling is final in nature. However, some states take a contrary view; according to this view, even if the ruling purports to be final, the opponent must renew the objection at trial in order to preserve the appellate issue. There is an additional requirement to preserve the objection when the objection challenges convictions offered as impeachment evidence under Federal Rule of Evidence 609. The requirement was announced in *Luce v. United States*, 469 U.S. 38, 105 S. Ct. 460, 83 L. Ed. 2d 443 (1984). In that case, the defense moved *in limine* to exclude the defendant's conviction on the ground that the prejudicial character of the evidence outweighed its probative value. The defense argued that the prospect of the admission of the conviction would deter the accused from even testifying and thereby deprive the jury of the accused's valuable testimony. The trial judge denied the motion, and the accused elected not to testify. On appeal, the defense challenged the denial of the motion. The Court held that the alleged error will not be reviewed unless the accused actually testifies at trial. Writing for the majority, former Chief Justice Burger asserted that without the benefit of the accused's trial testimony, "[a]ny possible harm flowing from a district court's *in limine* ruling permitting impeachment by a prior conviction is wholly speculative." Under *Luce*, in order to preserve the issue for purposes of appeal, the accused must both move *in limine* (or object at trial) and testify. Although the original *Luce* case involved conviction impeachment under Federal Rule of Evidence 609, many lower courts have extended *Luce* to other types of evidence such as untruthful acts impeachment under Rule 608(b), uncharged misconduct offered under Rule 404(b), and testimony from the accused's witnesses.[4]

[2] ELEMENTS OF A MOTION *IN LIMINE*

The following are the elements of a motion *in limine* to exclude evidence:

1. The opponent states his or her intent to move *in limine* to exclude certain evidence.

2. The opponent has reason to believe that the proponent possesses the evidence and will offer the evidence at trial. The motion should identify the objectionable evidence as specifically as possible.

3. The opponent briefly states the ground on which the evidence is inadmissible. The opponent must state the ground with at least the same degree of specificity with which he or she would make a trial objection. *See* § 2.03, *infra*. Many courts demand greater specificity in this setting. At trial, objections can arise unexpectedly; and it can be unreasonable to insist on greater specificity. However, in the pretrial setting, the opponent has much more time to formulate the objection; the opponent makes the motion precisely because he or she can anticipate that the proponent will later offer the evidence at trial.

---

[4] However, some states reject *Luce*. These jurisdictions allow the defendant to challenge the ruling on appeal even if the defendant elects against testifying at least when the defense makes a detailed offer of proof as to what the defendant's testimony would have been.

4. The opponent explains why an ordinary trial objection would be inadequate protection for the opponent. The opponent might state that they need an early decision to make a strategic decision such as whether the defendant should testify or that the evidence in question is so highly prejudicial that a curative instruction to disregard at trial is likely to be ineffective.

5. The opponent presents the legal argument in favor of the motion.

After the proponent's response, the judge rules.

[3] SAMPLE MOTION *IN LIMINE*

The fact situation is a criminal prosecution in the hypothetical State of El Dorado. The accused is charged with armed robbery. The accused has a prior, YR-3 conviction for armed robbery in Alabama. The judge has already begun the in-chambers conference before trial. The opponent is the defense counsel.

J   Are there any other matters either of you think we should take up before trial begins?

O   Yes, Your Honor. I would like to make a motion *in limine* to absolutely preclude the prosecutor from mentioning my client's YR-3 armed robbery conviction. (1) When the prosecutor gave me the discovery file, the file contained a certified copy of the judgment of conviction. I assume that if my client takes the stand, the prosecutor will attempt to use the conviction to impeach my client. (2) I have given the prosecutor a week's advance notice of my intention to make this motion. I have given her a copy of the memorandum of law, citing the cases I'm relying on as authority.

J   (*To the prosecutor*) Did you receive the advance notice?

P   Yes.

J   And is it your intention to use the conviction?

P   Yes, Your Honor. It is well-settled in El Dorado that you can use a felony conviction to impeach a witness, even a criminal accused. In Alabama, this type of armed robbery is a felony.

O   Your Honor, I'm aware of the usual rule in El Dorado. However, our position is that since the YR-3 conviction is for the very same type of crime my client is now charged with, the conviction is too prejudicial; there's too great a risk that the jurors will disregard any limiting instruction, misuse this impeachment evidence, and treat it as evidence of the accused's bad character.

J   I normally defer ruling on this type of issue until trial.

O   I'm aware of that, Your Honor. However, I think that you should dispose of this issue before trial begins; a trial objection won't adequately protect my client. In this case, the charged crime and the crime my client was previously convicted of are absolutely identical. If there's any mention of this conviction at trial, the jurors simply won't be able to

** **   follow any curative instruction you give to disregard the evidence. Moreover, I'm trying to decide whether to advise my client to take the stand. It's vital that he do so because he's the only witness with personal knowledge of several exculpatory facts. Your ruling is going to be a major factor in my decision. (4)

J   Do you have any authority to support your motion?

O   I've cited the most important cases in my memorandum of law. *Luck*,[5] on page two of my memo, is authority that as trial judge, you have discretion to balance a conviction's probative value against its prejudicial character. If the prejudicial character outweighs the probative value, you may exclude an otherwise admissible conviction. *Rist*,[6] on page four, emphasizes the extreme potential prejudice when the charged crime is identical to the crime of which the accused was previously convicted. *Rist* establishes a norm that identical offenses are inadmissible. This case falls squarely within *Rist*.

P   Your Honor, all you have to do is give the jurors a limiting instruction under Rule 105. Tell them affirmatively that they are to consider the conviction solely as impeachment evidence. And you can tell them negatively that they're not to use the conviction as evidence of the accused's bad character on the historical merits; they're not to infer that he committed the charged robbery because he committed a previous robbery or because he is a bad person.

O   As the cases point out, we can't trust a limiting instruction here. The crimes are identical, and we consequently can't naively assume that the jurors will follow the limiting instruction. The Advisory Committee Notes to both Rule 105 and Rule 403 state that you should realistically consider the likely effectiveness of any limiting instruction. (5)

P   My last point, your Honor, is that we have a substantial need for this evidence. There's only one eyewitness, the victim. This trial is going to be a classic swearing contest. The outcome is going to turn on whom the jury believes. We need all the impeaching evidence at our disposal.

J   I think that this is an appropriate case for a preliminary rather than an absolute order. I agree that since the crimes are identical, the conviction has tremendous potential for prejudice. Yet I don't want to absolutely preclude any use of the conviction; if the trial becomes the swearing contest the prosecutor predicts, the prosecution's need for the impeaching evidence may outweigh its prejudicial character. Hence, I'm going to enter a preliminary order. I don't want any mention of the conviction in the jury's hearing without my prior permission. Ms. Prosecutor, please admonish your witnesses accordingly. This order applies during voir

[5] Luck v. United States, 348 F.2d 763 (D.C. Cir. 1965).

[6] People v. Rist, 16 Cal. 3d 211, 127 Cal. Rptr. 457, 545 P.2d 833 (1976).

dire and opening. However, Ms. Prosecutor, if at any point during the trial you think that the record establishes your need for the evidence, I want you to request a hearing out of the jurors' presence. You can make an offer of proof at the hearing, and then I'll finally rule whether you can use the conviction.

§ 2.03 OBJECTIONS AT THE TRIAL BY THE OPPONENT

[1] THE DOCTRINE

If the opponent does not move *in limine* or the judge refuses to entertain the pretrial motion, the opponent must object at trial. When the opponent objects, the opponent in effect asserts that it is improper to admit the proponent's evidence. The American litigation system is patterned after an adversary model: the burden of presenting evidence is on the proponent, and the onus of excluding evidence is on the opponent. In rare cases, an error can be so plain and prejudicial that the judge will exclude the evidence on his or her own motion. However, given our adversary model, the opponent must ordinarily assume the responsibility for excluding evidence by objecting.

An objection must be courteous, timely, and specific. The opponent owes a duty of courtesy to the trial judge. The opponent should stand to state any objection and preface the objection with "Your Honor." By standing, you alert the witness not to answer until the judge has ruled on the objection.

An objection must also be timely. The objection must be neither too early nor too late. Suppose that there has been no *in limine* ruling and that the trial objection relates to a foundational issue such as authentication, best evidence, or hearsay. Foundational objections are premature until the questioning attorney attempts to elicit the objectionable testimony itself. Thus, if the opposing attorney believes that there is an inadequate authentication foundation for a letter, the attorney must reserve the objection until the questioning attorney offers the letter into evidence or asks the witness to read from the letter. Similarly, when the opposing attorney believes that there is an inadequate hearsay foundation for an out-of-court statement, the attorney must reserve the objection until the questioning attorney asks the witness to state the contents of the out-of-court statement. In contrast, if the objection relates to a form problem such as leading or argumentative questioning, the opponent should state the objection immediately after the improper question and before the witness begins the answer. If the opponent delays a form objection, the opponent has waived the objection.

Finally, to be effective, an objection must be specific; opponents must specify both what they are objecting to and why they are objecting. Opponents should identify the word, phrase, or question they are objecting to. In addition, they must state the legal ground for the objection. Federal Rule of Evidence 103(a)(1) requires that the opponent state "the specific ground [of objection] unless it was apparent from the context." There is a minority view that to be sufficiently specific, the objection must identify the missing foundational element. Under this view, if the opponent were objecting to a hearsay document being proffered as a business entry, the objection would have to specify that there was no foundational evidence that it was a regular practice of the business to prepare that type of record. However, the overwhelming majority view is that it is sufficient to cite the generic evidentiary doctrine the opponent claims the proponent is violating; the opponent names the violated rule by stating "inadequate authentication," "not the best evidence," or "incompetent hearsay." As a rule of thumb, the wording of the objection should be at the same level of specificity of the titles of the Articles in the Federal Rules. Thus, the title of Article VIII is "Hearsay," and it is sufficient to object that the question calls for inadmissible "hearsay." Likewise, part of the title of Article IX is "Authentication." "Inadequate authentication" is a sufficiently specific objection.

In the presence of the jury, the opponent should slightly vary the objection's wording to ensure that the jury does not gain the impression that the opponent is invoking technical rules to suppress or hide the truth. For example, the opponent should state that the proponent is "unfairly" leading, "putting words in the witness's mouth." Similarly, the opponent might state that the proponent is attempting to introduce "unreliable" hearsay, "a statement from a person we've never had a chance to question." While tailoring the objection's phrasing for the jury, the opponent must not make a "speaking objection." That expression refers to long-winded objections; the opponent makes a speech rather than briefly stating the legal ground for the objection. Trial judges will not tolerate speaking objections. Moreover, after you have embellished an objection such as leading once or twice, there is no need to do so during the balance of the trial. By then you have taught the jury the meaning of the objection; and the judge will no longer permit you to embellish the wording of the objection.

[2]   ELEMENTS OF AN OBJECTION

A proper objection includes the following elements:

1.   The opponent addresses the judge.

2.   The opponent indicates that he or she is raising an objection.

3.   The opponent specifies what he or she is objecting to, e.g., the particular word, phrase, clause, or question.

4.   The opponent specifies the legal ground for the objection, that is, the generic evidentiary doctrine the proponent is violating.

[3]   SAMPLE OBJECTIONS

Some of the opponent's objections will claim violations of substantive evidentiary doctrines. These objections are illustrative.

- Your Honor (1), I object (2) to any testimony by this proposed witness (3) on the ground that this person is incompetent to be a witness. (4) (*See* Chapter 3, *infra*.)

- Your Honor (1), I object (2) to the admission of that exhibit (3) on the ground that there has been insufficient authentication. (4) (*See* Chapter 4, *infra*.)

- Your Honor (1), I object (2) to the admission of that copy (3) on the ground that it is not the best evidence. (4) (*See* Chapter 8, *infra*.)

- Your Honor (1), I object (2) to that question (3) on the ground that it calls for improper opinion. (4) (*See* Chapter 9, *infra*.)

- Your Honor (1), I object (2) to that question (3) on the ground that it calls for incompetent hearsay. (4) (*See* Chapter 10, *infra*.)

- Your Honor (1), I object (2) to that question (3) on the ground that it calls for a privileged (attorney-client) (doctor-patient) (psychotherapist-patient) (penitent-clergy) (spousal) communication. (4) (*See* Chapter 7, *infra*.)

However, most of the objections made during the typical trial relate to matters of form rather than substance. The following are examples of form objections:

- Your Honor (1), I object (2) to that question (3) on the ground that it is vague, indefinite, and ambiguous. (4)

- Your Honor (1), I object (2) to that question (3) on the ground that it is leading. (4)

- Your Honor (1), I object (2) to that question (3) on the ground that it is compound. (4)

- Your Honor (1), I object (2) to that question (3) on the ground that it has already been asked and answered. (4)[7]

- Your Honor (1), I object (2) to that question (3) on the ground that it is argumentative. (4)[8]

- Your Honor (1), I object (2) to that question (3) on the ground that it calls for a narrative answer. (4)

- Your Honor (1), I object (2) to that question (3) on the ground that it assumes facts not in evidence. (4)[9]

§ 2.04   MOTIONS TO STRIKE AT TRIAL BY THE OPPONENT

[1]   THE DOCTRINE

In most cases, when the opponent desires to exclude the proponent's evidence, the opponent uses the procedural device of an objection. However, in three situations, the opponent must use the procedural device of a motion to strike. The first situation is the case in which the question is proper, but the witness's answer is improper at least in the sense that the answer exceeds the scope of the question asked. Second, the witness answers so rapidly that the opponent did not have a fair opportunity to interpose an objection. In that event, the opponent should move to strike the answer "for the purpose of interposing an objection to the question." If the judge grants the motion, the opponent then makes the objection. Finally, after the witness has given apparently proper testimony, it develops that the testimony was improper. For example, on direct examination, the lay witness purports to testify from personal knowledge; but on cross-examination, the witness makes the surprise concession that he was actually relating what he was told by third parties. In all three instances, the opponent should "move to strike" rather than "object."

---

[7] In some jurisdictions, the accepted phrasing is that "the question is repetitive" or "cumulative."

[8] In some jurisdictions, the accepted phrasing is that "the attorney is badgering the witness."

[9] In some jurisdictions, the accepted phrasing is "misleading."

Like an objection, a motion to strike must be courteous, timely, and specific. The general requirements for objections apply to motions to strike. If the witness's answer is improper, the opponent should move to strike immediately after the answer and before the next question. If the judge grants the motion, the opponent should then request a curative instruction to disregard; the judge informs the jury that the answer was improper and orders the jurors to disregard the answer.

[2] ELEMENTS OF A MOTION TO STRIKE

The elements of a motion to strike are roughly the same as those of an objection:

1. The opponent addresses the judge.

2. The opponent indicates that he or she is moving to strike.

3. The opponent specifies what he or she is moving to strike.

4. The opponent specifies the legal ground for the motion.

5. If the judge grants the motion, the opponent requests a curative instruction to disregard.

If the improper evidence was highly inflammatory, the opponent should seriously consider moving for a mistrial. If the evidence is likely to leave an indelible impression on the jurors, a curative instruction will be ineffective. Realistically, the instruction might be ineffective if the stricken evidence is directly relevant to a key issue in the case and the jury will probably assume that the source of the evidence had firsthand, personal knowledge of the facts. R. CARLSON & E. IMWINKELRIED, DYNAMICS OF TRIAL PRACTICE: PROBLEMS AND MATERIALS § 15.3(A), at 539–41 (6th ed. 2020) (collecting the relevant Supreme Court decisions).

[3] SAMPLE MOTION TO STRIKE

The fact situation is a burglary prosecution. The accused has a number of previous burglary arrests. The prosecution witness is the arresting officer. The officer is testifying that he observed the burglary in progress. The proponent is the prosecutor.

P   Officer Jordan, WHERE were you when the accused left the building?

W   I was standing across the street—maybe 50 feet away.

P   WHAT did you observe the accused do?

W   I saw him place a bag in the truck, look all around, and then enter the car to start the engine. Knowing the accused's long arrest record for burglaries, I immediately concluded that he had just completed a burglary.

O   Your Honor (1), I move to strike (2) that last sentence (3) on two grounds. First, the answer is nonresponsive.[10] Second, the answer is

---

[10] Although a minority of states permit both parties to move to strike on the ground of nonresponsiveness (CAL. EVID. CODE § 766), the prevailing view in the United States is that only the questioner has standing to move on that ground. Of course, if the answer is objectionable on another ground such as hearsay, the opponent has standing to urge that objection.

clearly improper character evidence. (4)

J   Motion granted. Officer, I want to caution you very strongly just to answer the questions asked.

O   Your Honor, would you please instruct the jury to disregard the answer? (5)

J   Certainly. Ladies and gentlemen of the jury, the officer just made a reference to the accused's arrest record. I have stricken that statement from the record, and I instruct you to completely disregard it. The only testimony you may consider is the officer's testimony about what he personally saw the defendant do.

§ 2.05 REQUEST BY THE OPPONENT TO TAKE A WITNESS ON VOIR DIRE

[1] THE DOCTRINE

There are two types of preliminary facts which condition the admissibility of evidence. One type of fact conditions only the basic logical relevance of the evidence. For example, if the item of evidence is a letter, one preliminary fact conditioning its admissibility is its authenticity; the letter is inadmissible unless it is authentic. That preliminary fact conditions the relevance of the letter in a fundamental sense. If the letter is not genuine, it has no logical relevance or probative value in the case. When the fact falls within this category, the judge uses the following procedure. The judge listens to only the proponent's evidence and decides the question of law whether, on its face, that evidence has sufficient probative value to support a rational jury finding of the fact's existence. Federal Rule of Evidence 104(b) states that "[w]hen the [logical] relevance of evidence depends on whether a fact exists, proof must be introduced sufficient to support a finding that the fact does exist." The judge accepts the testimony at face value and conducts a limited inquiry: Is there enough evidence to support a rational finding that the letter is authentic? If there is enough evidence, the judge submits the letter to the jury. The opponent submits any controverting evidence to the jury; and, on instruction by the judge, the jury finally decides whether the letter is genuine. In essence, this is a two-step procedure: The judge initially plays a limited, screening role, and then the jury decides whether the fact exists. Rule 104(b) applies to such foundational facts as whether a letter is genuine, whether lay witnesses have personal knowledge of the facts they intend to testify about, and whether the accused is the person who committed an act offered as uncharged misconduct under Rule 404(b). *Huddleston v. United States*, 485 U.S. 681, 108 S. Ct. 1496, 99 L. Ed. 2d 771 (1988). Again, these facts condition the logical relevance of the evidence, and they do so in such a fundamental way that even lay jurors without legal training will readily understand that if the fact is false, the item of evidence has no probative value at all in the case. We entrust these decisions to the jury because we are confident that if the jury decides that the letter is a fake ("It isn't worth the paper it's written on") or that the witness lacks firsthand knowledge ("The witness doesn't know what he's talking about") or that another person committed the act, common sense will naturally lead the jury to disregard the testimony during deliberations. Even if the jury decides that the item of evidence is inadmissible, the jury's exposure to the foundational testimony will not distort the balance of their deliberations.

The other type of preliminary fact conditions the application of "competence" doctrines which exclude logically relevant evidence: the best evidence, hearsay, opinion, and privilege rules. These rules exclude relevant evidence either because the evidence presumably is unreliable, such as hearsay, or to promote social policies, such as the protection of confidential relations. If the fact falls within this category, the judge listens to the evidence on both sides, passes on the credibility of the foundational evidence, and finally decides whether the fact exists. This is a one-step procedure; Federal Rule of Evidence 104(a) provides that when the fact falls within this category, the trial judge makes the final decision. Thus, the judge finally decides whether the original document was destroyed, whether a witness qualifies as an expert, whether a communication was intended to be confidential, whether an out-of-court declarant was excited when he made a hearsay statement, or whether at the time of the statement the declarant was a member of the same criminal conspiracy to which the defendant belonged. *Bourjaily v. United States*, 483 U.S. 171, 107 S. Ct. 2775, 97 L. Ed. 2d 144 (1987). The rationale for assigning these decisions to the judge is that the jury cannot be trusted to make these determinations. For instance, realistically it would be unsound to allocate to the jury the decision as to whether an allegedly privileged conversation had occurred in private. Once the jury had heard that the client had admitted his or her liability or criminal responsibility to the attorney, at a subconscious level it would be difficult for the jurors to set that testimony aside even if they concluded that the conversation was technically privileged. For that reason, the decision is assigned to the judge; and the judge has plenary power to find the facts.

When the fact falls within the second category, the opponent has the right to take the witness on voir dire examination before the judge rules on the evidence's admissibility.[11] As previously stated, the judge must listen to both sides' evidence—the evidence pro and con—before ruling. How does the opponent interrupt the proponent's direct examination to present the contrary evidence? The opponent interrupts by requesting the judge's permission to take the witness on voir dire. For example, the opponent might say: "Your Honor, I object on the ground that the question calls for inadmissible hearsay; and I request permission to conduct a brief voir dire in support of my objection." In one respect, the voir dire is functionally a cross-examination during the

---

[11] Strictly speaking, the opponent should have no right to voir dire under Rule 104(b). The Advisory Committee Note to Rule 104(b) indicates that the drafters used California Evidence Code § 403 as their model. Section 403 expressly provides that the judge "[s]hall instruct the jury to disregard the proffered evidence if the court subsequently [after hearing the opponent's evidence] determines that a jury could not reasonably find that the preliminary fact exists." Thus, § 403 contemplates that the opponent will present any contrary evidence after the judge admits the proponent's evidence and that the judge will administer the specified instruction if the opponent's evidence later turns out to be overwhelming. However, either out of an excess of caution or on the theory that they possess discretion to permit voir dire on a Rule 104(b) issue, trial judges occasionally allow the voir dire. Michael Graham, *Self-Authentication Generally: Certifications Under the Confrontation Clause: Confrontation Clause Application Summary*, 55 CRIM L. BULL. 71, 72 (2019).

proponent's direct examination: the opponent conducting the voir dire may ordinarily use leading questions. However, the opponent must remember that the voir dire's only purpose is to test the competency of the witness or evidence. The voir dire has a limited scope, and the opponent may not conduct a general, broad-ranging cross-examination on the case's merits under the guise of voir dire. Under Federal Rule 103(d), the judge might conduct the voir dire out of the jury's hearing.

[2]   SAMPLE REQUEST TO TAKE A WITNESS ON VOIR DIRE

The fact situation is a homicide prosecution. The prosecution witness is an ambulance attendant. The prosecutor hopes to elicit the ambulance attendant's testimony that he heard the decedent identify the accused as the assailant. The prosecutor's theory is that the decedent's statement falls within the dying declaration exception to the hearsay rule. The proponent is the prosecutor.

P	WHAT is your occupation?
W	I am an ambulance attendant employed by the emergency ward of General Hospital.
P	WHAT were you doing on the evening of January 19, YR-3?
W	I was on duty when we received a call about a shooting at the Senator Hotel downtown.
P	WHAT did you do then?
W	We responded to the call.
P	WHAT did you find when you arrived at the scene?
W	We found Mr. Jones there.
P	WHAT was his condition?
W	He had a very serious gunshot wound. He'd lost a lot of blood. You could hardly make out what he was talking about.
P	WHAT, if anything, did he talk about?
W	He talked about the fight in which he received the wound.
P	WHO did he say had shot him?
O	Your Honor, I object to that question on the ground that it calls for incompetent hearsay. I request permission to take the witness on voir dire before you rule on my objection.
J	Very well.
O	ISN'T IT TRUE THAT before he died, Mr. Jones said he was going to get the person who had shot him?
W	Yes.
O	ISN'T IT ALSO A FACT THAT he wanted to be rushed into surgery as soon as possible?
W	Right.

O   Your Honor, I renew my objection. The witness's testimony shows that
                  the decedent did not believe that imminent death was certain. The
                  declarant had not abandoned all hope of recovery. For that reason, the
                  dying declaration exception is inapplicable.

J   Objection sustained.

§ 2.06   OFFER OF PROOF BY THE PROPONENT

[1]   THE DOCTRINE

Assume that the judge grants the opponent's pretrial motion *in limine* or sustains an
objection at trial. The trial judge thus precludes the proponent from pursuing the line
of inquiry. What should the proponent do at this point? The general rule is that to
preserve the issue for appeal, the proponent should make an offer of proof. There are
two senses of the expression, "offer of proof" or "avowal." The first is the broad,
nontechnical meaning; the proponent "offers" proof whenever he or she presents
evidence. However, we are now using the expression in the second, technical sense; for
the record, the proponent states what the witness would have testified to and why the
proponent wanted to elicit that testimony. Federal Rule of Evidence 103(a)(2) requires
that the proponent "inform the court of . . . [the] substance" of the evidence.

Why should the proponent make an offer of proof? There are several reasons. When
the proponent makes the offer of proof, the judge may reconsider and change the ruling.
The judge may have little familiarity with the facts of the case. Until the offer of proof,
the judge may not have realized where the line of questioning was leading. The offer
of proof is also important if there is an appeal. If there is no offer of proof, the appellate
court will have a difficult time evaluating the propriety and effect of the judge's ruling.
With an offer of proof in the record of trial, the appellate court can make much more
intelligent decisions whether there was error, whether the error was prejudicial, and
whether the appropriate disposition of the case is to simply remand or enter judgment
for a party.

The proponent should make the offer of proof out of the jury's hearing. If the
proponent anticipated the unfavorable ruling, the proponent can prepare a written offer
of proof for insertion in the record. Otherwise, the proponent usually makes an oral
statement at a sidebar conference. If the expected testimony is complex, the proponent
may make the offer in question-and-answer form; the proponent actually elicits the
testimony out of the jury's hearing. The judge may insist that the proponent do so if the
judge doubts that the witness's testimony will match the proponent's description of the
expected testimony in the offer of proof. It might be advisable for the proponent to
make the offer in this fashion when the tenor of the testimony is almost too good to be
believed. As a practical matter, the appellate court might be skeptical that the offer was
accurate unless the proponent at least offered to put the witness on the stand under oath
and elicit the favorable testimony on the record.

[2]   ELEMENTS OF AN OFFER OF PROOF

An offer of proof contains the following elements:

1.   The proponent asks for permission to approach the bench or for an out-of-court

hearing.

2.   The proponent states that he or she intends to make an offer of proof.

3.   The proponent states what the witness would have testified to if the judge had permitted the proponent to pursue the line of inquiry. The statement should be factual and neutral. The proponent should avoid embellishing or editorializing.

4.   The proponent states the purpose for which he or she wants to offer the testimony. The proponent explains the testimony's logical relevance under Rule 401.

5.   If the judge sustained the objection on the ground of a competence doctrine, such as hearsay, the proponent explains why the evidence is admissible. This additional element is necessary whenever the judge sustains the objection on a ground other than the logical relevance doctrine.

When you move to sidebar, make certain that the court reporter is in a position to hear the conference. Unless the court reporter records the conference, the appellate court will never learn the tenor of the offer of proof at trial.

[3]   SAMPLE OFFER OF PROOF[12]

The fact situation is a rape prosecution. The accused denies the rape. The accused denies any intercourse with the alleged victim. The accused calls Ms. Gerhard as his next witness.

P	WHAT is your name?
W	Jane Gerhard.
P	WHAT is your address?
W	I live at 4502 New Hampshire Street in Morena, El Dorado.
P	WHAT is your occupation?
W	I am a physician.
P	WHERE did you attend medical school?
W	I attended Washington University Medical School in Missouri.
P	WHERE are you licensed?
W	In California, New York, Missouri, and here in El Dorado.
P	WHAT, if anything, is your specialty?
W	I specialize in the treatment of venereal disease.
P	HOW many cases of venereal disease have you treated in your practice?
O	Your Honor, I object to this line of questioning on the ground that it is irrelevant.
J	I'm inclined to agree. Objection sustained.

---

[12] This hypothetical is based on DEPARTMENT OF THE ARMY PAMPHLET 27-10: MILITARY JUSTICE HANDBOOK 205 (1969).

P   Your Honor, may we approach the bench? (1)

J   Yes.

P   I would like to make an offer of proof for the record. (2)

J   Very well.

P   If Dr. Gerhard is permitted to testify, she will state that: She examined the alleged victim last week; the victim is now suffering from an advanced stage of syphilis chancroids, a venereal disease; at the time of the alleged rape, the disease would undoubtedly have been in a highly infectious and communicable stage; anyone who had intercourse with the alleged victim at that time would probably contract the disease; and the doctor examined the accused yesterday and found no evidence of the disease. (3) This testimony would be logically relevant to support my client's denial that he had intercourse with the alleged victim. (4)

J   Now I can see what you're driving at. I'm going to change my ruling and permit you to pursue this line of inquiry. Now I can appreciate its logical relevance. Objection overruled.

P   Dr. Gerhard, let me repeat the question.[13] HOW many cases of venereal disease have you treated in your practice?

---

[13] Whenever there is an extended argument over the objection, the proponent should repeat the question after the judge overrules the objection. The jurors may have forgotten the wording of the question. In some cases, the witness may have forgotten.

CHAPTER 3

THE COMPETENCY OF WITNESSES

§ 3.01 INTRODUCTION

Some evidentiary doctrines can keep a prospective witness off the stand altogether; the doctrines can prevent the person from giving any testimony at all in the case. These doctrines govern the competency of the person to be a witness in the case. The application of these doctrines ordinarily turns on the prospective witness's status rather than the content of his or her contemplated testimony. Thus, as we shall soon see, one of the common-law doctrines requires that the prospective witness possess perceptual ability. Furthermore, in some jurisdictions, one spouse is incompetent to testify against the other spouse in a criminal prosecution if the other spouse is the accused and objects. The prospective witness's status as the spouse of the accused spouse is determinative. The accused spouse can preclude the witness spouse from testifying at all. Even if the witness is competent, other evidentiary doctrines may prevent the witness from testifying to certain facts. Thus, even when the witness spouse is competent to testify, he or she may not be able to testify to privileged, confidential communications with the other spouse. In this chapter, we are concerned with competency doctrines that have the more drastic effect of keeping the witness completely off the stand.

Federal Rule of Evidence 601 purports to abolish most of the traditional requirements for competency. It is true that some courts have balked at reading Rule 601 literally; these courts construe the Rule as merely creating a rebuttable presumption of the person's competency as a witness. Some trial judges seem to believe that Rule 603 permits them to continue to enforce the traditional competency requirements. That Rule requires the prospective witness to testify under oath or affirmation, and these judges reason that the Rule impliedly authorizes them to determine, as a foundational fact, whether the proposed witness is capable of understanding and complying with the oath. However, the better view is that the plain meaning of the text of Rule 601 is that the Rule sweeps away the traditional requirements, and the Advisory Committee Note to Rule 601 confirms that the drafters intended that result; the Note declares that "[s]tandards of mental capacity have proved elusive in actual application." Under this view, the witness must have personal or firsthand knowledge under Rule 602, but the proponent need not demonstrate that the prospective witness satisfies the other common-law requirements. (Some commentators believe that even assuming that Rule 601 abolishes the traditional competency requirements, a judge can sometimes bar a witness from the stand. These commentators argue that the judge has the power to do so under Rule 403 when it is clear as a matter of law that the prospective witness lacks one of the testimonial abilities required at common law. Alternatively, a prospective witness's mental disorder might render his or her testimony so incoherent and garbled that the risk of confusing the jury would clearly outweigh the minimal probative value of the testimony. Chapter 5 discusses Rule 403.).

However, in some jurisdictions, the common-law requirements are still in effect. At common law, to prove that the prospective witness is competent, the proponent must show that the person possesses the following abilities: (1) to observe—the testimonial quality of perception; (2) to remember—the testimonial quality of memory; (3) to relate—the testimonial quality of narration; and (4) to recognize a duty to tell the truth—the testimonial quality of sincerity. These abilities ensure that the witness's testimony will have at least some minimal credibility and reliability. If the person lacks one or more of these capacities, the person is incompetent to be a witness.

Even when the person is competent in the sense that he or she possesses these four capacities, the law may render the person incompetent as a witness. The law may do so to promote some social policy such as protecting the stability of marriages. Hence, as previously stated, even if a witness spouse has all four capacities, the witness may be disqualified from testifying against his or her spouse.

How does the opponent challenge the prospective witness's competency? In most jurisdictions, the opponent must raise the objection as soon as the person is called to the stand. The opponent objects before the person is even sworn as a witness. The opponent both objects and requests a voir dire of the person concerning his or her qualifications to be a witness. In some jurisdictions, the person then takes a special oath to truthfully answer the voir dire questions about his or her competency. The bailiff or reporter might administer this oath: "Do you swear the answers you will give to these questions about your competency to be a witness shall be the truth, the whole truth, and nothing but the truth?" In other jurisdictions, the voir dire examination is unsworn.

In most jurisdictions, the judge has discretion to determine who shall examine the person and the order of the examinations. Competency doctrines do not simply condition the testimony's logical relevance; rather, they fall within the category of doctrines designed to ensure the reliability of concededly relevant evidence. For that reason, the procedure prescribed in Federal Rule of Evidence 104(a) governs; the trial judge finally decides the question of the witness's competency and may permit the opponent to present extrinsic evidence such as a psychiatrist's testimony. If at the end of the presentation of the evidence the judge decides that the person is incompetent, the judge sustains the objection and directs the person to leave the witness stand. If the judge finds that the person is competent, the judge overrules the objection; and the person then takes the normal oath in the case. In many jurisdictions, the opponent not only has the burden of raising the issue of the prospective witness's competency; the opponent may also have the burden of proof on the issue. At least in the case of adult witnesses, at common law many jurisdictions recognize a rebuttable presumption of competency.

§ 3.02   THE VOIR DIRE OF A CHILD BY THE WITNESS'S PROPONENT

[1]   THE DOCTRINE

In some jurisdictions, there are presumptions concerning children's competency to serve as witnesses. For example, the dividing line might be 7, 10, or 12 years of age;

if the child is 12, the child is presumed competent, but if the child is younger, the child is presumed incompetent. The presumption is usually rebuttable; even when the child is presumed incompetent, the proponent may attempt to show that, in fact, the child possesses the four requisite abilities. *See* 18 U.S.C. § 3509(c)(2).

Most jurisdictions have no presumptions. In these jurisdictions, it is a question of fact whether the person has the requisite capacities. The trial judge finally decides the question.

Some jurisdictions have enacted statutes declaring that child witnesses are competent in child abuse prosecutions or at least that the child who is the alleged victim is a competent witness. In such a jurisdiction, the proponent calling a child witness would not need to demonstrate the child's competency as a witness.

[2] ELEMENTS OF THE FOUNDATION

When the opponent challenges the proponent's witness's competency, the proponent must lay a foundation showing that the person possesses the four capacities. The proponent must demonstrate that:

1. The child has the capacity to observe.
2. The child has the capacity to remember.
3. The child has the capacity to relate.
4. The child recognizes a duty to tell the truth.

[3] SAMPLE FOUNDATION

The fact situation is a personal injury action arising from a traffic accident at an intersection. The plaintiff, the proponent, calls a child as a witness. The child witnessed the collision.

P	As his next witness, the plaintiff calls Master James Giannelli.
O	Your Honor, we object to any testimony by this child on the ground that the child is incompetent to be a witness. We request a voir dire examination of the child concerning his competency.
J	Request granted.
P	Your Honor, may I conduct the initial voir dire of Master Giannelli?
J	You may.
P	Master Giannelli, do you swear that the answers you will now give concerning your competency to be a witness will be the truth, the whole truth, and nothing but the truth? So help you God. (*Please remember that in many jurisdictions, the voir dire examination is unsworn, especially when the prospective witness is a child. In those jurisdictions, this oath would not be administered.*)
W	I do.
P	WHAT is your name and address?
W	My name is Jim Giannelli. I live at 12 Frontage Road in town with my parents.

P	James, HOW well do you see? (1)
W	I have no problems. I can see real well.
P	WHEN do you need to wear glasses? (1)
W	Never. I don't wear glasses for my eyes.
P	HOW well do you hear? (1)
W	Just great.
P	HOW old are you? (2)
W	I'm six. I had my birthday last month.
P	WHAT day is your birthday? (2)
W	It's September 28, just after my mommy's birthday.
P	WHERE do you live? (2)
W	Like I said, on Frontage Road with my folks.
P	HOW long have you lived there? (2)
W	Gee. I guess as long as I can remember.
P	HOW many brothers and sisters do you have? (2)
W	I have one sister.
P	WHAT is her name? (2)
W	Amy.
P	HOW old is Amy? (2)
W	She's older than me. She's almost 15.
P	WHAT school do you go to? (2)
W	Horace Mann.
P	WHERE is that school located? (2)
W	On Fourth Street.
P	WHAT grade are you in? (2)
W	I'm in the first grade.
P	WHO is your teacher? (2)
W	Her name is Mrs. Lederer. She's real nice.
P	WHAT courses do you take? (3)
W	We take arithmetic and English.
P	WHAT do you learn in English? (3)
W	We learn about words and sentences and stuff.
P	WHAT grades do you get in English? (3)
W	I do real well. I got an A on the last paper.

P	WHAT does "car" mean? (3)
W	My dad has one. You drive around in them. They take you places.
P	WHAT does "fast" mean? (3)
W	Well, when you drive, you should go slow. You can get hurt if you don't go slow, if you go too fast.
P	James, WHAT is an "intersection"? (3)
W	That's where two streets meet. They sort of come together.
P	WHAT is the truth? (4)
W	The truth is what really happens—not a story you come up with.
P	WHAT is a lie? (4)
W	That's when you don't tell the truth.
P	WHAT happens when you don't tell the truth? (4)
W	Your parents can get real mad at you, and God won't love you.
P	HOW do you know that? (4)
W	I learned that at Sunday School.
P	WHERE do you go to Sunday School? (4)
W	At our church.
P	WHICH church is that? (4)
W	Holy Comforter on 12th Avenue.
P	WHAT do you learn at Sunday School? (4)
W	We learn that you have to be good. You gotta obey your parents and tell the truth and stuff like that.
P	WHAT is an oath? (4)
W	I promise to tell the truth to the judge.
P	WHAT happens if you don't tell the judge the truth? (4)
W	He can punish you.
P	I have no further questions of Master Giannelli about his competency. Your witness.
O	I have no questions. I renew my objection on the ground that this child is simply too young to be a witness.
P	Your Honor, I think the child's answers demonstrate the basic capacities to observe, remember, and relate as well as his recognition of a duty to tell the truth.
J	I agree. The objection will be overruled. (*To the court reporter*) Please administer the oath to Master Giannelli.

§ 3.03   THE QUESTIONING OF A LAY WITNESS BY THE PROPONENT TO DEMONSTRATE PERSONAL KNOWLEDGE

[1]   THE DOCTRINE

All courts agree that a lay witness must have personal or firsthand knowledge of facts or events to testify about them at trial. Personal knowledge is a common-law requirement. Although the Federal Rules generally abolish the traditional competency requirements, Rule 602 still insists on personal or firsthand knowledge. Before questioning a lay witness about an event, the proponent should show that the witness has personal knowledge of the event. The standard for showing personal knowledge is lax, since the Federal Rule of Evidence 104(b) applies to the fact of the witness's firsthand knowledge. However, as a matter of sound trial advocacy, the proponent often goes far beyond the minimal showing needed to satisfy Rule 104(b). The jury's evaluation of the witness's testimony and its verdict might turn on whether the jury is convinced that the witness accurately observed and recalls the event in question, and the proponent consequently attempts to make a persuasive showing of the witness's personal knowledge

[2]   ELEMENTS OF THE FOUNDATION

The proponent should show that:

1. The witness was in a physical position to perceive the event. The witness normally observes the event by the sense of sight, but the witness may use any sense to perceive the event.

2. The witness actually perceived the event. If the occurrence of the event is a central, disputed issue, the proponent can question in detail about such matters as what the lighting conditions were, how close the witness was, and whether anything obstructed the witness's view.

3. The witness currently remembers the perceived event. To establish this element in convincing fashion, the proponent often elicits the witness's explanation of why the event is so memorable to the witness. For example, the proponent might elicit the witness's testimony that she remembers the event so clearly because the event is the one and only traffic accident she has ever personally witnessed.

[3]   SAMPLE FOUNDATION

We can continue the hypothetical in § 3.02, *supra*. Assume that the judge rules that the child is a competent witness. The child takes the oath and begins testifying. Now the plaintiff wants to elicit the testimony about the accident. The accident occurred at the intersection of Fourth and Main Streets.

P   James, WHERE did you go on Monday, January 21, YR-3? (1)

W   I went to school.

P   WHERE is your school located? (1)

W   It's on Fourth Street.

P	WHERE on Fourth Street? (1)
W	Right at Main Street. There's a big intersection there. There's lots of cars.
P	WHAT happened at the intersection that day at about noon? (1)
W	There was this big crash.
P	WHERE were you at the time of the crash? (1)
W	I was standing at that corner.
P	WHAT crashed? (2)
W	Two cars.
P	WHO was driving the cars? (2)
W	The man over there in green and that lady over there in yellow.
P	Please let the record reflect that the witness has pointed to the plaintiff and defendant.
J	It will so reflect.
P	HOW do you know they were driving the cars? (2)
W	I ran up right after the big noise, and I saw them get out of their cars.
P	HOW well could you see the cars? (2)
W	I got a good look. They were real close to me when they crashed. I was real scared.
P	HOW well could you see the drivers? (2)
W	Gee. I got right up close to them. I ran up right after the big noise, and I saw them get out of their cars.
P	HOW much time passed between the crash and the time when you ran up to see the drivers? (2)
W	Only a couple of seconds.
P	HOW well do you remember the crash? (3)
W	Real well.
P	WHY do you remember the crash so well? (3)
W	It's the only crash I've ever seen. It stands out real well in my mind.
P	James, now I want to ask some questions about how the crash occurred. . . .

§ 3.04 THE OPPONENT'S PRESENTATION OF PSYCHIATRIC TESTIMONY ATTACKING A PROSPECTIVE WITNESS'S COMPETENCY

[1] THE DOCTRINE

Trial judges rarely sustain objections to prospective witnesses' competency; a judge will sustain an objection in only an extreme case. The Advisory Committee Note to Rule 601 states that even prior to the enactment of the Federal Rules, "few [prospective] witnesses [were] disqualified on [the] ground" of lack of mental capacity. The opponent may prove recent adjudications of incompetency such as civil commitments. These adjudications are relevant to prove incompetency; but, as a practical matter, the opponent must present expert, psychiatric testimony attacking the witness's competency. The psychiatrist will have to testify that the person is suffering from a full-fledged psychosis and that the psychosis grossly interferes with one of the testimonial qualities such as perception or memory.

[2]   ELEMENTS OF THE FOUNDATION

The opponent should demonstrate that:

1. The witness is a qualified psychiatrist.

2. The psychiatrist has examined the prospective witness.

3. The prospective witness has certain symptoms.

4. The symptoms lead to the conclusion that the prospective witness is suffering from a psychosis.

5. The psychosis grossly interferes with one or more of the prospective witness's testimonial qualities such as perception or memory.

[3]   SAMPLE FOUNDATION

The fact situation is a rape prosecution. The prosecution calls Ms. Janet Lincoln as a witness. Ms. Lincoln has told the police that she witnessed the rape; her window overlooks the park, and she saw the accused attack the alleged victim. The defense counsel objects to any testimony by Ms. Lincoln; the counsel contends that she is incompetent to be a witness. The defense counsel has already taken Ms. Lincoln on voir dire and questioned her.

J	Do you have anything further you'd like to present on the issue of Ms. Lincoln's competency?
O	Yes, Your Honor. At this point, I would like to call Dr. Kenneth Rogers.
J	Proceed.
B	Do you swear that the evidence you will give in the case now in hearing will be the truth, the whole truth, and nothing but the truth? So help you God.
W	I do.
O	WHAT is your name?
W	Kenneth Rogers.
O	WHERE do you live?
W	I reside at 1774 Club Center Drive.
O	WHAT is your occupation? (1)
W	I am a physician.

O	WHERE are you licensed to practice medicine? (1)
W	Here in El Dorado and in California and New York as well.
O	WHEN did you obtain your license in El Dorado? (1)
W	Approximately 10 years ago.
O	WHAT medical school did you attend? (1)
W	Washington University in Missouri. I received my M.D. degree in YR-12.
O	WHERE did you intern? (1)
W	I interned at U.S.C. Medical Center in California.
O	HOW long did you intern there? (1)
W	Approximately one year.
O	WHAT field of medicine, if any, is your specialty? (1)
W	Psychiatry.
O	WHAT is the subject matter of that specialty? (1)
W	A psychiatrist studies the diseases and disorders of the mind.
O	WHAT special training have you had in psychiatry? (1)
W	I spent three years as a resident in psychiatry.
O	WHERE did you take this residency? (1)
W	At Bellevue in New York City.
O	WHAT other special training have you had in psychiatry? (1)
W	I'm a diplomate of the American Board of Psychiatry. I passed the oral and written examinations for the diploma. I've taught psychiatry at two medical schools, and I've written 13 articles for psychiatric journals.
O	WHO is Janet Lincoln? (2)
W	She's a woman I've had occasion to interview several times.
O	WHY have you interviewed her? (2)
W	One of the local judges, Judge Lopardo, asked me to do so. It was a court appointment.
O	HOW many times did you interview her? (2)
W	Three times.
O	WHEN was the first interview? (2)
W	Approximately three months ago.
O	HOW long did this interview last? (2)
W	Roughly two and a half hours.
O	WHAT was her appearance at the time of the interview? (3)

W	It was rather unkempt. She was rather dirty.
O	WHAT was her general attitude? (3)
W	At first, she seemed rather detached and distant. She became excited and angry whenever I tried to question her about sexual subjects.
O	WHAT, if anything, did she say during the interview? (3)
W	Initially she just told me to keep my distance.
O	WHAT did she say then? (3)
W	She said that all men were sex fiends and could not be trusted. She said that as long as she could remember, at least once a day a man had attempted to assault her.
O	HOW would you characterize her statements? (3)
W	They were delusional. A delusion is a belief that a rational person would not entertain under the same circumstances. The person persists in the belief although all the evidence is to the contrary.
O	WHY did she have this belief? (3)
W	She said that voices told her to distrust all men. Not just some men, but all men.
O	WHO were the voices? (3)
W	She didn't know.
O	HOW would you characterize those statements? (3)
W	They are hallucinations; she has auditory experiences when in fact there is no voice or sound.
O	WHAT did you do after you interviewed Ms. Lincoln? (3)
W	I tried to gather her history.
O	WHAT is a history? (3)
W	The background of an illness. You trace it through the years and its various stages.
O	HOW did you gather Ms. Lincoln's history? (3)
W	I spoke with her brother, Vance Lincoln.
O	WHO is he? (3)
W	He's a certified public accountant in town.
O	WHAT was her background or history? (3)
W	Evidently she had made numerous rape complaints to the police. In each case, the police or medical investigation had shown the complaint was groundless. She had spent almost a year in a hospital in the East for mental illness.
O	WHAT did you do then? (3)

W   I conducted further interviews with Ms. Lincoln.

O   WHAT happened during those interviews? (3)

W   She repeated her beliefs. She told me about some incidents in her life—sometimes giving me very conflicting stories about the same incident. On several occasions she accused me of making advances towards her. She again became quite restless and agitated.

O   WHAT, if anything, did you do to lead her to believe that you were making an advance against her? (3)

W   Nothing, as far as I could tell. My mere physical presence in the same room seemed to trigger that belief.

O   WHAT, if any, diagnosis have you reached of Ms. Lincoln's psychiatric condition? (4)

W   I would diagnose her condition as a schizophrenic reaction of the paranoid type.

O   WHAT does that mean? (4)

W   A schizophrenic person has a sort of split personality. They live in two worlds—one the world of fantasy, the other the world of reality. They have lost contact with reality to a severe extent. Her disorder manifests itself in paranoid beliefs that men are persecuting and constantly attacking her. It's a disorder recognized in *DSM-V*, the latest edition of the American Psychiatric Association's DIAGNOSTIC AND STATISTICAL MANUAL.

O   WHAT leads you to this diagnosis? (4)

W   The irrational content of her statements for one thing. I also consider her appearance and attitude. Finally, I attach particular importance to her delusions and hallucinations. Her history confirms the diagnosis. Cumulatively, these symptoms satisfy the diagnostic criteria set out in the *DSM-V.*

O   Doctor Rogers, in this case Ms. Lincoln wants to testify about a sexual assault she allegedly observed. WHAT effect, if any, would her psychosis have on her ability to accurately observe an encounter between a man and a woman? (5)

W   The psychosis grossly interferes with that capacity. She's going to see things that didn't really happen—just as she hears voices when they're not there. Every male-female encounter tends to become an assault in her mind. Again, she thinks that all men are sex fiends.

O   WHAT effect, if any, would her psychosis have on her ability to accurately remember a male-female encounter she had observed? (5)

W   It's going to severely distort the memory process. A psychosis of this magnitude is going to distort her abilities to perceive and remember. Her purported recollections will be untrustworthy. In the process of remembering, she'll almost always add sexually assaultive aspects to the encounter.

O   Thank you, Doctor. Your witness.

§ 3.05   THE WITNESS SPOUSE

[1]   THE DOCTRINE

Modernly, there are four views of the competency of one spouse to testify against another. The first view, followed in approximately 10 jurisdictions, is that the spouse is as competent as any other witness. Even if the accused and witness spouses object, the witness spouse may be called as a witness against the accused spouse. Although in these 10 states the witness spouse is fully competent, most jurisdictions recognize a disqualification in criminal cases. However, even the majority jurisdictions differ over the scope of the disqualification. The second view, the traditional common-law position, is that if the marriage exists when the witness spouse is called to the stand, the accused spouse can object and keep the witness spouse off the stand altogether. Under this view, the disqualification belongs to the accused spouse. In contrast, the third view is that the witness spouse is the holder of the disqualification. The witness spouse may testify if he or she desires. The accused spouse may not prevent the witness spouse from testifying. The United States Supreme Court opted for this view in *Trammel v. United States*, 445 U.S. 40, 100 S. Ct. 906, 63 L. Ed. 2d 186 (1980), and the trend is toward this view. The proponents of this view argue that the rationale for the witness spouse's disqualification is the protection of the marriage and that in the typical case in which the witness spouse is willing to testify against the party spouse, there is little left to the marriage. The fourth and final view is that both the accused and witness spouses have privileges. They each have a privilege and may exercise the disqualification independently. The courts often refer to the doctrine as the spousal testimonial privilege to distinguish it from the more limited spousal communications privilege.

There are two important exceptions to the scope of the disqualification. The first exception is the so-called injured spouse doctrine: The disqualification is inapplicable when the charged offense is a crime against the other spouse. For example, if the criminal accused is charged with a battery against his wife, he cannot invoke the disqualification to bar her from testifying. Many courts have expanded the scope of the exception to apply to offenses against the family's children. It would be difficult to prosecute these offenses if the disqualification silenced the victim. Some jurisdictions recognize a second exception; they do not apply the disqualification if the witness spouse's testimony relates to an event that occurred before the marriage. These jurisdictions sometimes refer to the disqualification as the marital facts privilege. Since events that occurred before the marriage cannot be considered "marital facts," the disqualification cannot operate to bar testimony about such events. However, a number of courts bar testimony even about such events if the other spouse knew about the event at the time of marriage. These courts reason that if the other spouse entered into the marriage despite such knowledge, they condoned any prior offense and that subsequent testimony about the offense would amount to a betrayal.

[2]   ELEMENTS OF THE FOUNDATION

The party attempting to invoke the disqualification must show that:

1.   The witness spouse married the party spouse.

2.   The marriage is still in existence when the witness is called to the stand.

The party attempting to invoke the exceptions to the disqualification must show that:

3.   The witness spouse was the victim of the charged crime; or

4.   The witness spouse's expected testimony relates to an event occurring before the marriage.

[3]   SAMPLE FOUNDATION

The fact situation is a criminal prosecution. George Nerney, the accused, is charged with two batteries. The indictment first alleges that on January 1, YR-3, the accused committed a battery against Grenda Kuhns. The second count of the indictment alleges that on July 1, YR-3, the accused committed a battery against Susan Grace. The proponent of the witness is the prosecutor.

P	As its next witness, the State calls Ms. Susan Grace.
O	Your Honor, I object to any testimony by this witness on the ground that she is incompetent. The witness is married to my client, and my client invokes the spousal disqualification to keep her off the witness stand. May I voir dire the witness in support of my objection?
J	You may.
O	Ms. Grace, ISN'T IT TRUE THAT on March 1, YR-3, you married a George Nerney? (1)
W	Yes.
O	ISN'T IT A FACT THAT George Nerney is the accused in this case, seated at this table? (1)
W	Yes.
O	ISN'T IT CORRECT THAT there has been no divorce proceeding since the marriage? (2)
W	Yes.
O	ISN'T IT TRUE THAT there hasn't been any annulment proceeding since the marriage? (2)
W	Yes.
O	Your Honor, I have no further questions. We renew our objection.
P	Your Honor, may I voir dire Ms. Grace?
J	Yes. Proceed.
P	WHEN did you marry the defendant? (4)
W	I think it was March 1, YR-3.

P	WHO is Grenda Kuhns? (4)
W	She's a desk clerk at a hotel in a town which the defendant and I once visited.
P	WHEN did you visit that hotel? (4)
W	In early January of YR-3.
P	WHAT, if anything, happened between the accused and Ms. Kuhns? (4)
W	Unfortunately, they got into an argument, and the defendant punched Ms. Kuhns.
P	WHICH came first—the defendant's argument with Ms. Kuhns or your marriage to the defendant? (4)
W	The argument with Ms. Kuhns. It came first by several months.
P	WHAT, if anything, happened on July 1, YR-3? (3)
W	That's when George and I had an argument.
P	WHAT happened during the argument? (3)
W	He slashed me with a knife.
P	WHOM did he slash? (3)
W	Me.
P	WHO else was involved in this argument? (3)
W	No one else. I was the only other person there, and I was the only one George attacked.
P	Thank you, Ms. Grace. Your Honor, this voir dire examination demonstrates that Ms. Grace is competent to testify about both counts in the indictment. The first count alleges a battery that occurred before her marriage to the accused. In the second count, she is the victim, and the injured spouse exception obviously applies. The marital disqualification shouldn't preclude Ms. Grace from testifying about either count.
J	I concur. Objection overruled. (*To the court reporter*) You may administer the oath to the witness.

§ 3.06   DEAD PERSONS' STATUTES OR SURVIVORS' EVIDENCE ACTS

[1]   THE DOCTRINE

Suppose that two parties enter into a contract. One dies, and the other files suit for breach of contract against the decedent's estate. The decedent can no longer testify to rebut any false claims. Is it fair to permit the survivor to testify against the estate? Roughly half the state legislatures have enacted dead persons' or survivors' evidence statutes. These statutes represent a judgment that it is unfair to permit the survivors to testify in these circumstances. The survivor possesses the four capacities requisite at common law, but the argument runs that fairness dictates the exclusion of the witness's testimony. The statute's coverage varies from state to state, and there is no such thing as a "typical" statute. However, many provide that in actions defended by the decedent's personal representative, the survivor or any interested person may not testify adversely to the estate about a transaction with a decedent.

The coverage of a particular statute is a problem of statutory construction. Most statutes address four questions: (1) To what types of actions does the statute apply? As previously stated, the statutes usually apply at least to civil actions filed or defended by the decedent's personal representative. The statute might also apply to wrongful death actions brought by the decedent's heirs. (2) Whom does the statute disqualify from testifying? The survivor is ordinarily disqualified. "Interested persons" are also frequently disqualified. In some jurisdictions, a person is deemed interested only if the judgment in the case will have a direct legal operation against that person. Other jurisdictions use a broader definition of interest and consider a person interested if the person has a significant economic stake in the case's outcome. (3) What type of incompetence does the statute impose? The dead persons' statutes impose a peculiar type of "incompetence." The statutes usually do not keep the witness off the stand altogether. Rather, they have the limited effect of precluding the witness from testifying *against* the estate *about* certain topics. (4) What topics is the witness precluded from testifying about? The statute typically uses the expression, "transactions with the decedent." A contract with the decedent is obviously a transaction with the decedent. Moreover, many courts use an expansive definition of transaction: A witness's testimony is testimony about a transaction with the decedent if the decedent might have contradicted the testimony from personal or firsthand knowledge. This is a broad, purposive interpretation of "transaction." The purpose of the statute is to remedy the unfairness which arises because the estate has lost the decedent's testimony based on personal knowledge, and it effectuates the purpose of the statute to apply the statute to any fact or event of which the decedent had personal knowledge.

These same four questions indicate how the proponent of the witness can defeat a dead persons' statute objection: The opponent need show only that one element of the statute is missing. The proponent can argue that the statute does not apply to this type of action, *or* the witness is neither a survivor nor an interested person, *or* the statute does not impose this type of incompetence, *or* the witness is not testifying about a transaction with the decedent. Even when the statute applies, the statute can be waived; and there are often special exceptions to the scope of the statute. The law on waiver and special exceptions varies from state to state; and ultimately, the resolution of these issues is a question of statutory interpretation. As a general proposition, the courts are hostile to these statutes and construe the statutes narrowly, since the statutes exclude relevant evidence. Some courts manifest that hostility by holding that the opponent waives the statute by deposing a covered witness. The antipathy to the statutes also accounts for the tendency of most courts to broadly construe the exceptions to the scope of the statutes.

[2] ELEMENTS OF THE FOUNDATION

To invoke a dead persons' or survivors' evidence statute, the opponent of the evidence must show that:

    1.   The statute applies to this type of action.

2.   The witness is a survivor or an interested person.

3.   The witness is testifying about a forbidden topic, *e.g.*, a transaction with the decedent.

The first element presents a question of law; the judge construes the statute and compares the statute's coverage to the pleadings on file in the case. However, the opponent may have to voir dire the witness to develop factual support for the second and third elements of the foundation.

[3] SAMPLE FOUNDATIONS

The first hypothetical is a contract action against the decedent's estate. The decedent is John Grant. The plaintiff is Miles Dalton. Dalton alleges that the decedent breached a contract with Dalton. Dalton calls his brother, William, as a witness. William will testify about the conversation in which Dalton and Grant formed the contract. The plaintiff is the proponent of the witness.

P   WHAT did the two men say during this conversation?

O   Your Honor, I object to the last question on the ground that under the dead persons' statute, this witness is incompetent to testify on that topic.

P   Your Honor, may I be heard?

J   Yes.

P   It's true that the statute applies to contract actions against the decedent's estate (1) and that a conversation with the decedent is a transaction. (3) However, this witness isn't the plaintiff. Moreover, although he's the plaintiff's brother, he doesn't have any direct economic stake in the case. He's not an interested person. (2)

O   May I voir dire the witness in support of my objection?

J   Yes. Proceed.

O   ISN'T IT TRUE THAT on January 1, YR-3, you gave your brother, Miles, $90,000 as an investment in his business? (2)

W   Yes.

O   ISN'T IT A FACT THAT in exchange for that $90,000, Miles gave you a quarter share in the business? (2)

W   Yes.

O   ISN'T IT CORRECT THAT you are Miles' silent partner? (2)

W   Yes.

O   ISN'T IT TRUE THAT you expect to receive a share of whatever money your brother recovers in this suit? (2)

W   Yes.

O   Your Honor, the witness's answers demonstrate that he has a direct economic stake in the case's outcome. I renew my objection.

J   Objection sustained.

The second hypothetical is a wrongful death action brought by the decedent's heirs. They allege that the defendant, Steven Pollet, negligently caused the death of the decedent, Kathryn Manning, in a traffic accident. The defense attorney calls the defendant as a witness. The defense attorney is the proponent. The defendant has already testified about what happened earlier in the day. The defendant has just testified that he reached a narrow curve in the road. The collision occurred as he rounded the curve.

P   WHAT happened when you rounded the curve?

W   I saw this other car coming.

P   HOW did you maneuver your car after you saw this other car coming?

O   Your Honor, I object to that question on the ground that under the dead persons' statute, the witness is incompetent to testify about that topic.

P   Your Honor, may I be heard?

J   Yes.

P   It's true that in this jurisdiction, the statute applies to actions filed by the heirs (1) and that the witness is the surviving party. (2) However, the witness isn't testifying about any transaction with the decedent; he's testifying about how he maneuvered his own car. (3)

O   May I voir dire the witness?

J   Yes. Proceed.

O   ISN'T IT TRUE THAT when you rounded the curve, you had an unobstructed view of the decedent's car? (3)

W   Yes.

O   ISN'T IT A FACT THAT it was a clear day? (3)

W   Yes.

O   ISN'T IT CORRECT THAT the stretch of road just past the curve was straight and level? (3)

W   Yes.

O   ISN'T IT TRUE THAT from the time you rounded the curve until the time of the collision, you had a clear view of the decedent's car? (3)

W   Yes.

O   Your Honor, the witness's testimony shows that the decedent also must have had a clear view of the manner in which the defendant's car maneuvered. If she had survived, the decedent might have contradicted the defendant's testimony from firsthand, personal knowledge. Thus, this testimony is testimony about a "transaction" with the decedent. I renew my objection.

J   Objection sustained.

CHAPTER 4

AUTHENTICATION

§ 4.01 AUTHENTICATION IN GENERAL

[1] INTRODUCTION

This chapter deals with the authentication of evidence. The common law generally requires that the proponent of evidence prove the evidence's authenticity as a condition precedent to the admission of the evidence. To authenticate an item of evidence, the proponent must present proof that the article is what the proponent claims that it is. Federal Rule of Evidence 901(a) states: "To satisfy the requirement of authenticating or identifying an item of evidence, the proponent must produce sufficient evidence to support a finding that the item is what the proponent claims it is." Thus, if the proponent claims that the decedent signed a letter, the proponent must prove that the document is a genuine letter signed by the decedent. If the proponent offers a photograph of an intersection, the proponent must show that the photograph accurately depicts the intersection. Or if the prosecutor alleges that a pistol is the accused's pistol, the prosecutor must present evidence tracing the pistol to the accused's possession.

In addition to stating the requirement for authentication, Federal Rule of Evidence 901(a) outlines the procedure for determining the evidence's authenticity. Rule 901(a) prescribes the same procedure as Rule 104(b). It is the conditional relevance procedure described in § 2.05[1]. The test is whether the proponent has presented sufficient evidence to support a rational jury finding that the letter is genuine or the photograph is accurate. The issue of the rational sufficiency of the foundational evidence is in the nature of a question of law. The trial judge looks only to the proponent's evidence and asks that question of law. Of course, the opponent may have controverting evidence. For example, although the proponent has a lay witness prepared to identify a friend's handwriting on a letter, the opponent may have an expert questioned document examiner ready to testify that the letter is a forgery. In this circumstance, the trial judge would admit the letter, and the opponent would later present his or her controverting evidence to the jury. The trial judge would instruct the jurors that they must finally decide by a preponderance of the evidence whether the letter is genuine. Thus, as is generally true under Rule 104(b), there is a two-step procedure; the judge initially plays a limited, screening role, and the jury then makes the final decision on the question of fact.

[2] AUTHENTICATION IN TRADITIONAL COURTROOMS

What are the mechanics of presenting physical or documentary evidence in a traditional courtroom? As a matter of legal ethics, until the proponent is ready to use the evidence, the proponent should keep the evidence out of the sight of the jury. In many courts today, the trial judge permits or encourages attorneys to premark exhibits before the trial in open court begins.[1] Otherwise, when the proponent wants to use the evidence, the proponent should first request that the item be marked "for identification." Many jurisdictions insist that the proponent ask only that "this" be marked for identification. To make the record of trial clearer to the appellate court, some trial judges permit the proponent to use a short description of the exhibit. For example, these judges would allow the proponent to request that "this letter" or "this knife" be marked for identification. The court reporter or bailiff handles the marking of the exhibits. In many jurisdictions, plaintiffs and prosecutors use numbers to identify their exhibits ("plaintiff's exhibit number two for identification") while defense attorneys use letters ("defense exhibit C for identification"). After marking the exhibit for identification, the proponent hands the exhibit to the opposing attorney for inspection. In some jurisdictions, it is customary at this point for the proponent to ask that the record reflect that the opposing attorney is examining the exhibit. If the opposing attorney later fails to raise an objection evident on the face of the exhibit, there is a stronger argument that the opposing attorney has waived the objection.

The proponent then hands the exhibit to the witness. The proponent should describe the exhibit as an exhibit for identification: "I now hand you prosecution exhibit number seven for identification." In most jurisdictions, it is improper to state, "I now hand you a letter purportedly signed by the defendant"; the proponent's attorney is not a witness, and that description would both be leading and amount to unsworn testimony by the attorney. Once the exhibit is in the witness's hands, the proponent asks the witness to identify the article. The proponent now lays all the foundations necessary for the exhibit's admission. At the very least, the foundation usually includes proof of the item's authenticity. As § 4.02[1] notes, hearsay and best evidence foundations might also be necessary. When all the required foundations have been laid, the proponent formally offers the exhibit into evidence. The proponent can "move" the item's admission or "offer defense exhibit G for identification into evidence as defense exhibit G." Some judges prefer a simpler style; rather than insisting that the proponent "offer defense exhibit G for identification into evidence as defense exhibit G," these judges permit the proponent to simply "offer defense exhibit G for identification into evidence."

At first blush, the procedures might sound complex. However, as the accompanying diagram indicates, you can easily visualize the mechanics. In effect, the proponent walks—and talks—a triangle. The proponent starts the first leg of the triangle by presenting the exhibit to the court reporter to be marked "for identification." The proponent next turns and walks the first leg of the triangle. At that end of this leg of the triangle, the proponent shows the exhibit to the opposing counsel. Then the proponent walks the second leg of the triangle and approaches the witness. At the end of the

---

[1] Many judges have adopted this practice in order to save time at trial. However, practical problems can arise if later during trial, the attorney chooses not to offer the exhibit. If so, some jurors might be confused by the non-consecutive numbering of the exhibits. However, the judge can instruct the jurors that they should draw no inference from the fact that an exhibit marked before trial was not offered during the trial.

second leg, the proponent hands the exhibit to the witness and elicits the foundational testimony. Finally, the proponent turns again and walks the third, short leg toward the judge. The proponent formally tenders the exhibit into evidence. If the judge agrees that the foundation is complete, the court reporter strikes "for identification" from the title of the exhibit.

Fig. 4-1

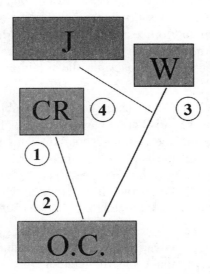

If there is no objection or the trial judge overrules the objection, the item is received in evidence. In the case of a letter, the proponent should then request the judge's permission to read all or part of the document to the jury. When the proponent makes this request, the opposing attorney occasionally objects on best evidence grounds and states that "the document speaks for itself." This objection is bogus. W. BROCKETT & J. KEKER, EFFECTIVE DIRECT AND CROSS-EXAMINATION § 11.11 (1986). The best evidence rule may require that the proponent produce the document in court; but once the proponent has done so, under Rule 611(a) the trial judge has discretion as to how best to present the document to the jury. The judge has discretion to permit the witness or the attorney to quote from a document which has already been admitted into evidence. In the case of any documentary or physical evidence, the proponent may request the judge's permission to hand the item to the jurors for their inspection. In some courts, it is customary to request permission to "publish" the exhibit to the jury. When the proponent has completed using the exhibit, the proponent should hand the exhibit back to the court reporter or bailiff. The proponent could later request that the judge permit the jurors to have the exhibit in the jury room during their deliberations.

[3]   AUTHENTICATION IN COMPUTERIZED COURTROOMS

[a]   IN GENERAL

A growing number of courtrooms incorporate computer technology. The use of such technology requires an adaptation of the traditional procedures described in § 4.01[2], *supra.* Visualize a courtroom with multiple monitors—one for the judge, one for the technologist or court reporter, one for each counsel table, one for the witness, and several for the jurors.

Whenever you intend to use computerized technology to present an exhibit, check out all the equipment before the trial begins. Do not merely check the equipment at your office; more importantly, check it in the courtroom. The courtroom may have a different type of electrical connection than your office, an extension cord that is long enough in your office may prove to be too short in the courtroom, or the equipment may be damaged in transit between your office and the courtroom. Moreover, have a hard copy available as a backup. If for any reason you cannot use more sophisticated technology to present the exhibit, you may fall back on the traditional procedure described in § 4.01[2], *supra.*

In addition, before trial check to learn how the exhibit must be preserved for purposes of appeal. Even if the jurisdiction permits the use of sophisticated technology to present the exhibit at trial, the appellate court may require that a hard copy be inserted in the record of trial. Further, the jurisdiction may have a rule or at least a preference as to how digitized exhibits are preserved for appeal. For instance, Fifth Circuit Rule 25.2 states that "[i]f electronic filing is permitted, the clerk shall advise the parties of acceptable formats and procedures. Adobe Acrobat PDF format is the preferred standard."

Consider the following three variations of the procedure. In these illustrations, assume that the court reporter doubles as the technologist.

[b] THE PRESENTATION OF AN UNMARKED HARD COPY BY USING A DOCUMENT CAMERA

In this variation, the proponent is attempting to introduce a hard copy exhibit that has not been previously marked.

P	Your Honor, may I approach the technologist?
J	Yes.
P	I request that this be marked plaintiff's exhibit number one for identification.
J	It will be so marked.
P	Your Honor, I request that the technologist (display *or* release *or* show) the exhibit to the opposing counsel.
O	I see it, Your Honor.
P	Your Honor, I now request that the technologist (display *or* release *or* show) the exhibit to the witness.
J	Granted.
P	Ms. Holguin, do you see plaintiff's exhibit number one for identification on your screen?
W	Yes, I do.

P   WHAT is it?

          (*At this point, the proponent lays whatever foundations are necessary.*)

P   Your Honor, we now offer plaintiff's exhibit number one for identification into evidence as plaintiff's exhibit number one.

J   (*To the opponent*) Any objections?

O   No, Your Honor.

J   Very well. The exhibit will be received.

P   Your Honor, I now request that the technologist (display *or* release *or* show) the exhibit to the jurors.

J   Granted.

While this procedure involves more sophisticated technology than the traditional procedure, in some respects it is simpler than the traditional method. In the traditional procedure, the proponent must walk: from the court reporter to the opposing counsel's table, from that table to the witness stand, and finally from the witness stand back to the judge's bench. In this procedure, after marking the exhibit for identification, the proponent can assume a position at the end of the jury box. From that position, he or she can request that the judge issue all the necessary directions to the technologist.

[c]   THE PRESENTATION OF A PREMARKED EXHIBIT BY USING A DOCUMENT CAMERA

In many cases, the proponent will have premarked the exhibit before the trial begins. If so, the exhibit may already be in the technologist's possession. Consequently, it will not even be necessary for the proponent to walk to the court reporter/technologist's table to submit the exhibit for marking.

P   Your Honor, at this point I intend to refer to the exhibit which was previously marked as plaintiff's exhibit number one for identification. I request that the technologist (display *or* release *or* show) the exhibit to opposing counsel.

J   Fine.

O   I see it, Your Honor.

P   Your Honor, I now request that the technologist (display *or* release *or* show) the exhibit to the witness.

J   Granted.

P   Ms. Holguin, do you have plaintiff's exhibit number one for identification on your screen?

W   Yes, I do.

P   WHAT is it?

          (*Again, the proponent lays any necessary foundations for the introduction of the exhibit.*)

P	Your Honor, we now offer plaintiff's exhibit number one for identification into evidence as plaintiff's exhibit number one.
J	(*To the opponent*) Any objections?
O	None, Your Honor.
J	Very well. The exhibit will be received.
P	Your Honor, I now request that the technologist (display *or* release *or* show) the exhibit to the jurors.
J	Granted.

[d] THE PRESENTATION OF DIGITIZED EXHIBITS LOADED ONTO A COMPUTER

The prior two scenarios involved relatively simple technology, that is, a document camera. The camera is used to project an image of a hard copy exhibit to various persons in the courtroom. In this third scenario, the exhibit has been digitized. It might be loaded onto the proponent's laptop computer which, in turn, is connected to the courtroom's own technology. At the beginning of the procedure, the proponent calls the image up on his or her laptop screen.

P	Your Honor, I have called up what has been previously been marked as plaintiff's exhibit number one for identification on the computer. I request permission to have the technologist (display *or* release *or* show) the exhibit to opposing counsel.
J	Granted.
O	I see it, Your Honor.
P	Your Honor, I now request permission to (display *or* release *or* show) the exhibit to the witness.
J	Granted.
P	Ms. Holguin, do you see plaintiff's exhibit number one for identification on your screen?
W	Yes, I do.
P	WHAT is it?
	(*Again, at this juncture the plaintiff lays any necessary evidentiary foundations.*)
P	Your Honor, I now offer plaintiff's exhibit number one for identification into evidence as plaintiff's exhibit number one.
J	(*To the opponent*) Any objections?
O	No, Your Honor.
J	All right. The exhibit will be received.
P	Your Honor, I now request that the technologist (display *or* release *or* show) the exhibit to the jurors.

J   Granted.

§ 4.02   THE AUTHENTICATION OF PRIVATE WRITINGS

[1]   WRITINGS CAN ALSO RAISE ISSUES OF BEST EVIDENCE AND HEARSAY

There are several well-settled techniques for authenticating private writings. These techniques are alternative methods of establishing the writing's authenticity.

The reader should develop the habit of automatically thinking of a trilogy of doctrines—authentication, best evidence, and hearsay—whenever a document is used in the courtroom. Whenever a document is used, the proponent will have to authenticate it. If the document's terms are in issue, the proponent will also have to comply with the best evidence rule. Finally, when the proponent wants to use the document's contents as substantive evidence, the proponent will probably have to show that the document falls within a hearsay exception. In short, the proponent offering a document will often have to lay three separate foundations—authenticity, best evidence, and hearsay. The proponent should thus consult Chapters 8 and 10 as well as this chapter.

[2]   TESTIMONY OF A WITNESS WHO OBSERVED THE DOCUMENT'S EXECUTION

The proponent can use direct evidence. If a witness previously observed the writing's execution and presently recognizes the document executed, the witness's testimony is sufficient authentication. Federal Rule of Evidence 901(b)(1) sanctions authentication by "[t]estimony that an item is what it is claimed to be."

This technique is ideal for writings such as letters, promissory notes, and checks that bear only a single signature.

The following are the elements of the foundation:

1. Where the witness previously observed the document's execution.

2. When the witness observed the execution.

3. Who was present.

4. What happened—the writing's execution.

5. The witness presently recalls and recognizes the exhibit as the document previously executed.

6. How the witness recognizes the document.

Assume that one issue in a commercial case is whether the defendant signed a certain check. The defendant's acquaintance, Mr. Bucher, observed the defendant sign the check. The plaintiff is the proponent.

P   WHERE were you on the afternoon of February 4, YR-3? (1), (2)

W   I was at the defendant's house.

P   WHO was there? (3)

W   It was just me, the defendant, and his wife, Ruth.

P	WHAT, if anything, happened while you were there? (4)
W	The defendant was writing out some checks to pay his month's bills.
P	Your Honor, I request that this be marked plaintiff's exhibit number seven for identification.
J	It will be so marked.
P	Please let the record reflect that I am showing the exhibit to the opposing counsel.
J	It will so reflect.
P	I request permission to approach the witness.
J	Permission granted.
P	Mr. Bucher, I now hand you plaintiff's exhibit number seven for identification. WHAT is it? (5)
W	It's one of the checks the defendant signed that afternoon.
P	HOW do you recognize it? (6)
W	Well, the defendant handed it to me and asked me to take a look at it. I recognize the signature and other writing on it.
P	HOW long did you have to examine it? (6)
W	About a minute or so.
P	HOW carefully did you examine it? (6)
W	Closely enough to recognize it now.
P	WHAT characteristics of the exhibit are you relying on as the basis for your identification? (6)
W	I remember the amount of the check, the payee, the defendant's rather peculiar signature, and the color of the check.
P	Your Honor, I now offer plaintiff's exhibit number seven for identification into evidence as plaintiff's exhibit number seven.
J	It will be received.
P	I request permission to hand the exhibit to the jurors for their inspection.
J	Permission granted. Ladies and gentlemen of the jury, plaintiff's exhibit number seven has been admitted into evidence. I have determined that at this point in the proceeding, you may view the exhibit. I am going to hand the exhibit to Mr. Asture, the bailiff. He is going to hand it to Ms. Grant, the first juror in front. She may now view the exhibit, and then in turn all of you may inspect it as well.

[3] TESTIMONY OF A WITNESS FAMILIAR WITH THE AUTHOR'S HANDWRITING STYLE

Even if the proponent cannot locate a person who observed the writing's execution, the proponent may be able to find someone familiar with the author's handwriting style.

It is true that courts usually prohibit opinion testimony by lay witnesses; but, as we shall see in Chapter 9, the admissibility of lay opinion testimony on handwriting style is a recognized exception to the general prohibition. The primary problem of proof for the proponent is establishing that the witness is sufficiently familiar with the author's handwriting style to recognize that style. If the witness possesses the requisite familiarity, the witness qualifies as a skilled lay observer as to the author's handwriting. Ideally, the witness will have observed the author sign his or her name on several previous occasions. It is sufficient, though, if the witness has seen the author's signature under reliable circumstances. For example, one corporate executive's secretary may have seen documents bearing the signature of another executive of the same corporation on hundreds of prior occasions. Even if the witness has never seen that second corporate executive sign a document, the witness is sufficiently acquainted with the executive's handwriting style. Federal Rule of Evidence 901(b)(2) recognizes this authentication technique. The Rule permits authentication by means of "[a] nonexpert's opinion that handwriting is genuine, based on familiarity with it that was not acquired for the current litigation."

The foundation is very simple; the elements are:

1. The witness recognized the author's handwriting on the document.
2. The witness is familiar with the author's handwriting style.
3. The witness has a sufficient basis for familiarity.
4. The witness did not acquire the familiarity specifically for purposes of the current litigation.

Like Rule 901(b)(1), Rule 901(b)(2) can readily be applied to writings such as letters, checks, and promissory notes that bear only one signature.

Now vary the original hypothetical. Assume that the witness, Mr. Bucher, did not observe the check's execution but is familiar with the author's handwriting style:

P	Your Honor, I request that this be marked plaintiff's exhibit number seven for identification.
J	It will be so marked.
P	Please let the record reflect that I am showing the exhibit to the opposing counsel.
J	It will so reflect.
P	I request permission to approach the witness.
J	Request granted.
P	Mr. Bucher, I now hand you plaintiff's exhibit number seven for identification. WHAT is it?
W	It seems to be a check.
P	WHO signed the check? (1)
W	I'd say that the defendant signed it.
P	WHY do you say that? (2)

W	I recognize the defendant's handwriting style on the check.
P	HOW well do you know the defendant's handwriting style? (3)
W	Very well.
P	HOW did you become familiar with his handwriting style? (3)
W	We've been friends for years.
P	HOW many years? (3)
W	About 10.
P	HOW often have you seen the defendant sign his name? (3)
W	Tens, maybe hundreds. We work for the same company, and I've often been present when he's written out a note and put his signature on it.
P	WHY did you happen to see those signatures? (4)
W	In the normal course of work.
P	Your Honor, I now offer plaintiff's exhibit number seven for identification into evidence as plaintiff's exhibit number seven.
J	It will be received.
P	I request permission to hand the exhibit to the jurors for their inspection.
J	Permission granted.

[4] THE REPLY LETTER DOCTRINE

The courts assume that the mails are reliable. Given that assumption, the courts have developed the so-called reply letter doctrine. Although the text of the Federal Rules of Evidence does not expressly codify the doctrine, there is a reference to the doctrine in the Advisory Committee Note to Rule 901(b)(4). Suppose that the witness sent a letter to a certain person. In the due course of mail, the witness receives a letter. The letter purports to be signed by the person to whom the witness sent the first letter, and the contents of the second letter refer to or purport to respond to the first letter. The courts generally hold that this fact pattern creates a sufficient circumstantial inference that the second letter is authentic.

This foundation contains several elements:

1. The witness prepared the first letter.

2. The witness placed the letter in an envelope and properly stamped the envelope.

3. The witness addressed the letter to the author.

4. The witness mailed the letter to the author.

5. The witness received a letter.

6. The letter arrived in the due course of mail—the time that it would normally take for a letter to travel from the place of dispatch to the intended destination.

7. The second letter referred to the first letter or was responsive to it.

8.   The second letter bore the name of the author.

9.   The witness recalls and recognizes the exhibit as the second letter.

10.   The witness specifies the basis on which he or she recognizes the exhibit.

Our fact situation is a contract case. The plaintiff wants to prove that the defendant, a sole proprietor, sent a letter containing an express warranty of the goods' condition. The plaintiff had not had previous dealings with the defendant, and, hence, cannot recognize the defendant's handwriting style. The witness is the plaintiff. The plaintiff has just testified that he had a telephone conversation with the defendant. The plaintiff's attorney is the proponent.

P   WHAT did you do after this telephone conversation? (1)

W   I decided to send the defendant a letter requesting some specific assurances and warranties about the goods.

P   HOW did you do that? (1)

W   I typed it up on my computer, printed it out, and then signed it.

P   WHAT did you do with it after you signed it? (2), (3), (4)

W   I stuck it in an envelope. I stamped the envelope, addressed it, and stuck it in the mail.

P   WHERE did you get the defendant's address? (3)

W   Out of the telephone book.

P   WHEN did you mail the letter? (4)

W   I think it was that afternoon. Yes, it was Monday afternoon.

P   WHAT happened then? (5)

W   I got a reply letter.

P   WHEN did the letter arrive? (6)

W   The following Monday.

P   HOW often have you exchanged letters with people in Atlantic City? (6)

W   I've done it hundreds of times in the course of business.

P   HOW long does it usually take to get a reply from Atlantic City? (6)

W   About a week.

P   HOW much time passed between the time you mailed your letter and the time when you received this second letter? (6)

W   About a week. The reply letter was right on time.

P   WHY did you refer to the letter as a "reply letter"? (8)

W   Well, it referred to my letter. It said it was going to answer my questions.

P   WHOSE name appeared on this second letter? (8)

W   The defendant's.

P	Your Honor, I request that this be marked plaintiff's exhibit number eight for identification.
J	It will be so marked.
P	Please let the record reflect that I am showing the exhibit to the opposing counsel.
J	It will so reflect.
P	I request permission to approach the witness.
J	Permission granted.
P	I now hand you plaintiff's exhibit number eight for identification. WHAT is it? (9)
W	It's the letter I just referred to.
P	HOW can you recognize it? (10)
W	I remember the contents, and the signature on the bottom is rather unique.
P	Your Honor, I now offer plaintiff's exhibit number eight for identification into evidence as plaintiff's exhibit number eight.
J	It will be received.
P	I request permission to have the witness read the last paragraph and signature block.
J	Permission granted.
P	(*To the witness*) Please read this passage to the jurors.
W	It reads: "I guarantee that it's a first-rate product. Nobody makes a better shingle. They'll last at least 15 years. Sincerely yours, John Bettencourt."
P	Your Honor, I now request permission to hand the exhibit to the jurors for their inspection.
J	Permission granted.

[5]   A COMPARISON BY AN EXPERT QUESTIONED DOCUMENT EXAMINER

Subsection 4.02[3] analyzed nonexpert lay opinion testimony about the author's handwriting style. The proponent may use expert testimony rather than lay testimony. Federal Rule of Evidence 901(b)(3) allows authentication based on "[a] comparison with an authenticated specimen by an expert witness." Before presenting the expert questioned document examiner, the proponent must authenticate the other specimens or exemplars. The proponent may use any authentication technique other than expert comparison to establish the exemplars' genuineness. The traditional practice is that the trial judge rules finally on the authenticity of the exemplars. However, as we shall see, in federal practice the authenticity of the exemplars is considered a Rule 104(b) issue. The judge admits the exemplars so long as there is sufficient evidence to support a permissive inference of their genuineness, and the jury finally decides whether the exemplars are authentic. The expert will compare the questioned document with these exemplars. The proponent then calls the expert to the stand.

It is true that there is authority that expert questioned document examination (QD) does not qualify as "scientific knowledge" under *Daubert v. Merrell Dow Pharms.*, 509 U.S. 579, 113 S. Ct. 2786, 125 L. Ed. 2d 469 (1993). *United States v. Starzecpyzel*, 880 F. Supp. 1027 (S.D.N.Y. 1995). Moreover, a few cases have gone to the length of excluding some types of QD testimony even when it has been offered as non-scientific expertise. *United States v. Fujii*, 152 F. Supp. 2d 939 (N.D. Ill. 2000) (the identification of the author of Japanese handprinting). However, there is an argument that Rule 901(b)(3) constitutes a legislative recognition of the validity of questioned document expertise, obviating the need for a normal foundation. In any event, assuming that a normal foundation is necessary, most authorities hold that testimony about questioned document examination is still admissible at least as nonscientific expertise—perhaps with a cautionary instruction that this type of expertise does not amount to full-fledged science. 2 P. GIANNELLI, E. IMWINKELRIED, A. ROTH, J. CAMPBELL MORIARTY & V. BEETY, SCIENTIFIC EVIDENCE § 14.07 (Matthew Bender, 6th ed. 2020). After qualifying as an expert, the witness compares the exemplars with the questioned document. On the basis of this comparison, the expert may testify whether in his or her opinion, the same person who wrote the exemplars authored the questioned document. In most cases, the expert has viewed all the documents before trial; pretrial comparison makes the in-court testimony more reliable and credible.

The elements of the foundation are:

1. The proponent authenticates the exemplars. At common law in many jurisdictions, the judge decided the authenticity of the exemplars. However, the Advisory Committee Note to Rule 901(b)(3) states that the rule rejects "the reservation to the judge of the question of the genuineness of the exemplars . . . . Consequently, [the question is] to be governed by Rule 104(b)."

2. The witness qualifies as an expert questioned document examiner.

3. The witness compares the exemplars and the questioned document.

4. After the comparison, the witness concludes that the same person who wrote the exemplars authored the questioned document.

5. The witness specifies the basis for his or her opinion, namely, the similarities between the exemplars and the questioned document.

Assume that the proponent has already authenticated the exemplars. Someone who saw the defendant sign two letters authenticated the letters. The letters are marked plaintiff's exhibits number three and four. The plaintiff will mark the disputed check as plaintiff's exhibit number five for identification. The plaintiff is the proponent. The next witness is the questioned document examiner. The witness has already identified himself as John Glenn and stated his address.

P   WHAT is your occupation? (2)

W   I am a technician with Richard Whaley and Associates.

P   WHAT line of business is that firm in? (2)

W	It is a private forensic laboratory. We do all sorts of scientific work for legal cases.
P	HOW long have you worked there? (2)
W	For about 12 years.
P	WHAT are your duties there? (2)
W	I do mainly questioned document examination.
P	WHAT does a questioned document examiner do? (2)
W	Among other things, we attempt to determine who signed writings.
P	WHAT is your formal education? (2)
W	I have a Bachelor of Science degree from Pennsylvania State University.
P	WHAT other training, if any, have you had? (2)
W	I attended several two-week courses on questioned document examination at Northwestern University. I've also attended many seminars on the subject sponsored by the Federal Bureau of Investigation.
P	HOW long have you been a questioned document examiner? (2)
W	The whole time I've had my present position—roughly seven years.
P	WHAT part of your working time do you devote to questioned document examination? (2)
W	All of it. It's my specialty.
P	HOW often have you testified as an expert questioned document examiner? (2)
W	At least one hundred times.
P	WHERE have you testified? (2)
W	Mainly in the courts in this state.
P	WHEN was the last time you testified as a questioned document examiner? (2)
W	Last month.
P	WHERE was that? (2)
W	In another courtroom in this same building.
P	Your Honor, permission to approach the witness?
J	Granted.
P	Mr. Glenn, I now hand you plaintiff's exhibits number three and four and plaintiff's exhibit number five for identification. WHAT are they?
W	They're handwriting specimens.
P	HOW many times have you seen these documents? (3)
W	Once before.

P	WHEN was that? (3)
W	An investigator brought them to my office.
P	WHAT happened when the investigator came to your office? (3)
W	Well, I examined them. I studied them under an optical microscope to determine whether they had a common authorship.
P	HOW long did you study them? (3)
W	I spent the better part of the afternoon, maybe three hours, working on the comparison.
P	HOW did you make the comparison? (3)
W	I studied the documents. I had some blown up into enlarged photographs and studied the enlargements as well.
P	HOW can you recognize these documents as the ones you previously examined? (3)
W	I noted the peculiarities of the handwriting style. They were uniform throughout each document. In my personal experience as an examiner, they're quite rare and distinctive.
P	Do you have an opinion on the question whether the author of exhibits number three and four also wrote plaintiff's exhibit number five for identification?
W	Yes.
P	WHAT is that opinion? (4)
W	In my opinion, it was the same author.
P	WHAT is the basis for your opinion? (5)
W	In all, I detected five unique writing characteristics common to all three documents. There was a common misspelling, a spacing peculiarity, the large tail on each y, the pronounced loop on each o, and the rather unique way or style in which they are written. These characteristics all point to common authorship.
P	Your Honor, I now offer plaintiff's exhibit number five for identification into evidence as plaintiff's exhibit number five.
J	It will be received.
P	I now request permission to hand exhibits number three, four, and five to the jurors for their inspection.
J	Permission granted.

[6] A PRINTOUT FROM A SOCIAL MEDIA PROFILE PAGE

Increasingly, Americans are using social media such as Facebook, MySpace, and Twitter to circulate information to friends and the public. Predictably, social media postings are becoming an important source of evidence. Apart from any related best evidence or hearsay issues, if a proponent offers a printout from a social media profile page as evidence, two authentication issues arise. One is whether the exhibit is an authentic printout from the social media site. In many cases, though, there is a second, more important issue, that is, whether the posting is attributable to a particular source such as a certain party to the lawsuit. Although the issue arises in the novel setting of social media, it is governed by the normal authentication standard of Rule 104(b).

The following are the elements of the foundation:

1.   The exhibit is a genuine printout or screen capture from the social media profile page. There is certainly sufficient authentication when the witness testifies that: He or she personally printed out the posting, they recall the appearance of the printout, and they recognize the exhibit as the printout. Alternatively, assuming that the proponent can satisfy the best evidence rule, a witness could testify to the contents of the profile page if he or she is willing to swear that they visited the page, read the contents, and currently remember the contents. There is no invariable requirement that the proponent call a representative from the social media company to lay this element of the foundation.[2]

2.   The posting is attributable to a certain person. Some of the early cases applied an enhanced burden of proof such as clear and convincing evidence on this element. However, the better and emerging view is that the normal standard prescribed by Rules 104(b) and 901(a) governs. To lay this element of the foundation, the proponent could present a forensic computer expert's testimony that he or she recovered copies of the postings sent to the social media site from the hard drive of a computer owned by the person.[3] However, in most cases the proponents have presented neither such testimony nor testimony by a representative of the social media company. Standing alone, the fact that the profile page bears the person's name is not sufficient. Even under Rules 104(b) and 901, without more, the self-authentication of the author of a letter or the caller on a voicemail message is not enough; and by parity of reasoning, self-identification is insufficient here. In one case, a state court ruled that the facts that a MySpace page displayed a person's photograph and correct birthdate were insufficient to attribute the page to that person.[4] In the cases upholding the adequacy of the showing of authentication, the courts have typically relied on a combination of circumstances, including:

   • The person in question had adopted the user name shown on the profile page. That fact could be established by stipulation or circumstantial

---

[2]   State v. Bell, 2009 Ohio 2335, 2009 Ohio App. LEXIS 2112 (May 18, 2009); Dockery v. Dockery, 2009 Tenn. App. LEXIS 717 (Oct. 29, 2009).

[3]   People v. Clevenstine, 68 A.D.3d 1448, 891 N.Y.S.2d 511 (2009).

[4]   Griffin v. State, 419 Md. 343, 19 A.3d 415 (2011). *See also* State v. Eleck, 23 A.3d 818 (2011), *appeal granted*, 302 Conn. 945, 2011 Conn. LEXIS 458 (2011) (the court states that the possibility of hacking "highlights the general lack of security of the medium").

evidence.

- The person in question had not shared his or her social media password with other persons. More broadly, the judge should consider the privacy settings protecting the posting. Those settings might make it very difficult for a third party to hack the person's account.

- The photograph on the profile page was that of the person in question.[5]

- Personal information stated on the profile page such as the person's birthday, children's names, hometown, occupation, or nickname matched the corresponding facts in that person's background.

There are no hard-and-fast rules governing the sufficiency of the foundation. Under Rule 104(b), the dispositive question is whether, as a matter of logic, the combination of circumstances supports a permissive inference that the person made or authorized the posting.

The prosecution contends that the defendant committed a crime in Dallas on February 27, YR-3. The defendant claims that he spent the entire day in San Antonio. The prosecution calls a witness, Ms. Janice Adbal, to testify that she printed out a posting from the defendant's MySpace profile page. The posting is dated February 26, YR-3 and states that the person making the posting intended "to drive to Big D tomorrow and spend the entire day there with buds." The prosecution intends to offer the printout as an exhibit during Ms. Abdal's testimony.

P	Please state your name and current address.
W	My name is Janice Abdal, and I live at 4240 Running Ridge Road in San Antonio.
P	Ms. Abdal, do you know the defendant in this case, John Grant?
W	Yes.
P	Do you see him in the courtroom?
W	Yes.
P	Could you please state where he is sitting and describe his clothing?
W	He's sitting at the table closest to the court reporter, and he's wearing a blue suit with a gold tie.
P	Your Honor, please let the record reflect that the witness has identified the defendant, John Grant.
J	The record will so reflect.
P	Ms. Abdal, how did you come to know the defendant?
W	We've worked together at the same Agricultural Cooperative agency for the past seven years.

---

[5] People v. Beckley, 185 Cal. App. 4th 509, 110 Cal. Rptr. 3d 362, *modified*, 2010 Cal. App. LEXIS 963 (June 24, 2010).

P	WHAT is the nature of your relationship with the defendant? Is it purely professional?
W	It's also social. We don't date, but we hang out together a lot. We have mutual interests such as country and western music.
P	Do you recall the evening of February 26, YR-3?
W	Yes.
P	WHAT were you doing that night?
W	I wanted to go out, and I was checking to see which of my friends might be available to hit a club later that evening.
P	WHICH friends did you attempt to reach?
W	Three or four, including the defendant.
P	HOW did you try to reach the defendant? (2)
W	I visited his MySpace page.
P	WHY did you do that? (2)
W	I know that while John rarely answers his cell phone, he often posts his plans in advance on his MySpace profile page. It makes it easier for his friends like me to track him down.
P	WHICH account did you visit at MySpace? (2)
W	I went to "doit3cowboy."
P	WHY did you go to that account? (2)
W	Because it's John's account.
P	HOW do you know that? (2)
W	Well, to begin with, he told me that that's his account.
P	You said "to begin with." WHY else? (2)
W	I've found that I can trust his postings there. Even when he doesn't reply to my messages or pick up his cell, I've learned that if I go to the places he's indicated he's heading on the profile page, I can usually run into him there.
P	WHO, besides the defendant, knows the MySpace password to access that profile page? (2)
W	As far as I know, no one else.
P	HOW do you know that? (2)
W	He's told me that. He once said that in the past, he's had some problems with identity theft and that he consequently doesn't share information like PINs and passwords.
P	In general terms, WHAT type of information is posted on that profile page? (2)

W   Basic stuff like John's birthday and place of birth.

P   HOW accurate is the information posted there? (2)

W   Very accurate.

P   HOW do you know that? (2)

W   John's told me. I give him a birthday card on that date, and he's never
        told me that I've gotten the date wrong. I also kid him about growing up
        in Lubbock. He takes the ribbing in good nature.

P   In addition to the basic information, WHAT else, if anything, is posted
        on the profile page? (2)

W   There are a bunch of photographs.

P   WHAT do these photographs depict? (2)

W   They're lots of photos of John and his friends, including a couple with
        me.

P   HOW positive are you that those are photographs of the defendant? (2)

W   I'm confident of that. I've known him for years, I recognize him, and I
        certainly recognize myself in the shots that I'm in with him. I remember
        when they were taken. In fact, he told me that he was going to post
        those.

P   WHAT, if anything, happened on March 1, YR-3? (1)

W   I was contacted by some police.

P   WHAT, if anything, did the police ask you to do? (1)

        (*Since this question inquires about what the police "ask[ed]," the
        question relates to an interrogatory sentence that is not an assertion
        under Federal Rule of Evidence 801(a). The question is therefore not
        objectionable on the ground that it calls for hearsay.*)

W   They wanted to know what I knew about John's whereabouts on
        February 26 and 27.

P   HOW did you answer them? (1)

W   I told them that all I knew was what I had found posted on his MySpace
        account.

        (*This statement is logically relevant to explain why the police then
        requested the witness to locate and printout the posting on the
        defendant's social media page. Therefore, it is logically relevant for a
        nonhearsay purpose under Federal Rule of Evidence 801(c)(2).*)

P   After you told them that, WHAT other questions, if any, did they ask
        you? (1)

        (*This question is designed to elicit the witness's testimony that the police
        requested that the witness visit the defendant's account. The testimony*

thus relates to an imperative sentence that is not an assertion under Federal Rule of Evidence 801(a).)

W   They asked if I could pull up the same posting on my computer.

P   HOW did you answer that question? (1)

W   I said that I'd cooperate and try to do so.

P   WHAT happened next? (1)

W   I did what they asked me to do—I went to John's MySpace account.

P   WHAT did you find there? (1)

W   I found the same posting about John's plans for February 27th.

P   HOW did you know that it was the same posting? (1)

W   I recognized it. It had been only a short time since I'd last read it.

P   HOW, if at all, had the posting changed? (1)

W   As far as I could tell, it hadn't changed. It seemed to be exactly the same, and no one had taken it down or changed it.

P   WHAT, if anything, did the police ask you to do after you found the posting? (1)

W   They asked me to print it out.

P   WHAT did you do then? (1)

W   I printed it out and handed it to the officers.

P   Your Honor, I request that this be marked as prosecution exhibit number five for identification.

J   It will be so marked.

P   Your Honor, please let the record reflect that I am showing the exhibit to the defense counsel.

J   The record will so reflect.

P   (*To the judge*) Permission to approach the witness?

J   Granted.

P   Ms. Abdal, I now hand you what has been marked as prosecution exhibit number five for identification. Do you recognize it? (1)

W   Yes.

P   Please tell the ladies and gentlemen of the jury WHAT this exhibit is.

W   It's the printout that I gave the police that day.

P   HOW can you recognize it? (1)

W   Well, I recognize the contents—the dates and some of the statements in particular. In addition, at the officers' suggestion I placed my initials on the printout. I see them right here.

P   Your Honor, I now offer prosecution exhibit number five for identification into evidence as prosecution exhibit number five.

J   (*To the defense counsel*) Any objection?

O   Yes, Your Honor. Hearsay.

P   Your Honor, we've laid a sufficient foundation that this is a statement posted by the defendant himself. Therefore, it's a personal admission or statement of a party-opponent under Rule 801(d)(2)(A). We want to use it to show that the defendant carried out his announced plan to go to Dallas the next day, February 27. That's a permissible use of the evidence under Rule 803(3).

J   Objection overruled. The exhibit will be received.

P   Ms. Abdal, I'd now like to have you read the next to last line on the printout to the jury.

[7] TEXT MESSAGES

Like social media posts and e-mails, text messages from cell phones are a very common modern means of communication. In some respects, given a choice of means of communication, a person will prefer a text message because the communication occurs in real time. As we shall soon see, text messages pose questions similar to those posted by social media posts, discussed in [6], supra: the authentication of the testimony about the contents of the message and, in most cases, the identification of the person sending the message. Moreover, the same Federal Rules of Evidence, namely, Rules 104(b) and 901(a), prescribe the governing standard of authentication.

However, there are differences between this setting and setting of social media posts and e-mails. To begin with, cellphone carriers periodically purge their records of customers' texts. Some carriers do so after relatively short periods of time. Thus, it may be more difficult for the proponent to produce a physical exhibit to present at trial to the witness who allegedly received the message. The purging, though, may supply an excuse for non-production under the best evidence rule. In that event, Rule 602 on personal knowledge can come into play because the proponent may have to rely on the witness's present recollection of the substance of the earlier message. Moreover, it can be more difficult to attribute the message to a particular person because more persons may have access to the phone. Typically, to make a social media post or send an e-mail, a person must know the username and password for the account. However, unless a cell phone is locked by, for example, a biometric identifier, anyone near the phone could pick it up and send a text message. A third party would need at least some technical expertise to hack a social media or e-mail account, but the third party does not need any special background or training to pick up a phone and punch in a phone number. Understandably, in applying the authentication requirement to text messages, many courts tend to apply Rules 104(b) and 901(a) in a more demanding fashion when the testimony indicates that in the past, multiple persons have used the cell phone in question.

The foundation for introducing a text message is strikingly similar to that for introducing testimony about a social media post:

1.   The message had certain relevant contents. As previously stated, in some cases, if the carrier has purged its copy of the message and the message has been deleted from the cell phone, the proponent will be unable to offer a physical exhibit, a printout of the message, at trial. In that case, the sponsoring witness will have to testify that he or she previously received a certain message and that at trial, they can recall the substance of the message. The witness does not have to be able to quote the message verbatim, but he or she must testify that they remember the basic contents of the message. In other cases, though, the message will still be available. Ideally, the message will still be present on both the sending phone and the receiving phone. The witness might even be able to produce his or her phone and still call up the message in question on the witness stand. Or a forensic expert could prepare a spreadsheet of the relevant messages on the phone. Or the cell phone carrier might provide a printout of the message. If a certificate complying with Rule 902(11) is attached, the carrier's printout will be self-authenticating.

2.   The message is attributable to a certain person. On the one hand, without more, proof that the person in question owns the cell phone that sent the message is insufficient. Again, even third parties with little or no technical expertise could use a person's cell phone to send a text message. On the other hand, as in the case of social media posts, there is sufficient authentication under Rules 104(b) and 901(a) when a combination of circumstances is logically adequate to support a rational, permissive inference that that person sent the message. The published opinions have approved myriad combinations of circumstances, including the following facts, inter alia:

•   The person had the phone in his or her physical possession shortly before or after the time stamp on the message. This evidence could take the form of testimony that the person called the witness during a text message exchange; of course, under Rules 701 and 901(b)(5) the witness would have to testify that he or she was familiar with the person's voice and recognized the caller's voice as that of the person;

•   The contacts on the phone list individuals associated with the person, such as family members and friends;

•   Other messages on the phone have attached photographs of individuals associated with the person;

•   Prior to the time stamp on the message, either in person or during a telephone call in which the witness recognized the caller's voice as that of the person, the person said that he or she would soon be sending the witness a text on the topic discussed in the message. Under Rule 803(3), the person's statement of then-existing plan would be admissible as evidence that the person later carried out the plan and sent the message.

•   The contents of the message referred to the earlier conversation in which the person had stated the plan to send the message. More broadly, the contents of the message disclose information likely to be known only by that person. For example, the message might be signed with a nickname known only to the person and the person's very close friends. Or the message might refer to a prior in-person or telephone conversation between the person and the witness;

- After the time stamp on the message, the person engaged in conduct consistent with the intentions stated in the message. This evidence could take the form of testimony that in a later in-person or telephonic conversation, the person mentioned the prior message to the witness.

There are no firm, rigid rules as to the sufficiency of the foundational testimony to satisfy this element. The bottom line is whether, as a matter of logic, the combination of circumstances gives rise to the sort of permissive inference demanded by Rules 104(b) and 901(a).

The prosecution alleges that the defendant, James Grantham, was a member of a drug trafficking conspiracy between February YR-2 and January YR-1. The indictment names Sheldon Lanaster as one of the defendant's coconspirators. The defendant pleads not guilty. Before trial and in opening statement, the defendant has claimed that he does not even know Lanaster. Earlier in the prosecution case-in-chief, the following has occurred: A police officer testified that she arrested the defendant; the officer adds that when she arrested the defendant, the officer found a cell phone on the defendant's person; the defendant told the officer that he owned the phone; the officer finally testifies that she later delivered the phone to a forensic expert at the local crime laboratory; the expert then testifies; she states that she recalls receiving the phone from the officer and immediately proceeding to examine the phone; she adds that during the examination, she discovered and printed out a text message bearing a December 23, YR-2 time stamp; and when the prosecutor presents her with an exhibit marked People's Exhibit #3 for identification, she recognizes it as the printout. (The message reads:

"Dear Cindy,

Please tell the boss I'll be a little late getting in to work. I know it's the Christmas crush, but I went out clubbing with my good buddy Shelly Lan last night, and we both got pretty plastered. It's going to take me a little while to get moving this morning. Be in as soon as I can. Sorry mucho.

The Scone King"). The prosecution and defense have stipulated that the number assigned to the defendant's cell phone is (715) 934-8763.

The next witness is Ms. Cindy Chandler.

P	Please state your name and current address.
W	My name is Cynthia-Cindy-Chandler. I live at Unit 107 at the Winds Apartments, 10350 Historyland Lane here in Duluth.
P	Do you know the defendant in this case, Mr. Grantham?
W	I do.

P　　HOW did you come to know him?

W　　We're coworkers. We work together at a small bakery in downtown Duluth, Carlson's on B Street.

P　　HOW many people work at Carlson's?

W　　Just three of us—the owner, Mrs. Carlson, the defendant, and myself.

P　　WHAT electronic communications devices, if any, do you own?

W　　Not many. I've got a small computer in my apartment, and then I have my cell phone.

P　　WHAT do you use the cell phone for?

W　　I can't afford a bunch of apps. So I just do basic stuff, telephone calls and texts messages, on the phone.

P　　HOW often, if ever, have you exchanged text messages with the defendant?

W　　A few times. Not many. We don't hang out socially outside work, but sometimes I end up exchanging texts with him, especially work-related stuff.

P　　Ms. Chandler, I now hand you what has previously been marked as People's Exhibit Number 3 for identification. Do you recognize it? (1)

W　　Yes.

P　　HOW do you recognize it? (1)

W　　I received this message on my phone, and I remember it well.

P　　WHY do you remember it well? (1)

W　　I received the message just before Christmas. The message tells me that he's going to be late for work that day. Quite frankly, I was angry. Christmas is our busiest time. Again, we're a small business. It's just the owner, the defendant, and me. Everyone wants their cakes and cookies around Christmas time. The bakery is packed with customers, and he's letting me know that he's going to be late coming into work that day. And he wants me to tell the boss rather than calling her himself. I was none too pleased.

P　　Without going into the rest of the message, WHAT phone number is listed as the source of the text message? (2)

W　　Right there on top it says (715) 934-8763.

P　　WHOSE phone number is that? (2)

W　　The defendant's.

P　　HOW do you know that? (2)

W　　Again, we don't hangout a lot outside work. But several times I've had to call him at that number, and he's called me from that number.

P	When you called that number, WHO answered? (2)
W	The defendant.
P	HOW do you know that? (2)
W	I recognized his voice.
P	HOW well do you know his voice? (2)
W	Very well. We worked together six days a week for almost three years.
P	When you called that number in the past, HOW many people other than the defendant have ever answered? (2)
W	None. If someone answered, it was always the defendant.
P	HOW regularly does the defendant carry his phone? (2)
W	All the time. You can always see it sticking out of his back pocket. He's almost never without it.
P	HOW often does the defendant simply put down his phone and leave it laying around? (2)
W	Almost never. He's one of those guys who's basically tied to his phone. Again, the phone's either sticking out of his back pocket, or he's on it to talk or text.
P	WHAT is the name at the very bottom of this message? (2)
W	"The Scone King."
P	WHO is "the Scone King"? (2)
W	The defendant. It's his nickname.
P	HOW did he get that nickname? (2)
W	He gave himself that nickname. Again, we're a bakery. His specialty is making scones, and I have to say that he's really good at that. He's proud of that.
P	HOW many people use that nickname for the defendant? (2)
W	The three of us—Mrs. Carlson, the defendant, and me.
P	HOW many other persons, if any, have you ever heard refer to the defendant by that nickname? (2)
W	I can't recall of anyone else doing that.
P	WHAT happened after you received this message that morning? (2)
W	I went to work, and together with Mrs. Carlson I did the best I could to hold down the fort with all the Christmas customers without the defendant's help.
P	WHEN, if at all, did the defendant come into work that day? (2)
W	He didn't grace us with his presence until about 2:00 p.m.
P	WHAT, if anything, did he say to you when he showed up for work? (2)

W	He said he was sorry. He added that like he'd said in his message, he was just too hung over that morning. He could tell that I was really upset with him
P	Your Honor, I now offer People's Exhibit number three for identification into evidence as People's number three.
J	(*To the defense counsel*) Any objection?
O	Yes, Your Honor. Lack of authentication. No one saw the defendant write that message and send it to the witness. Someone else could easily have just picked up the phone and sent it.
P	Your Honor, we've laid a more than adequate foundation. To begin with, the witness clearly recognizes the message as one she received that day. She remembers it so well because it made her angry. In addition, although no one saw the defendant send the text, in combination the circumstances support a strong inference that the defendant is the one who sent the message. It's his phone, he almost always has it on him, the message is signed with his nickname that very few people knew, and he even referred to the message when he subsequently apologized to the witness for showing up late that day. Cumulatively, that's more than enough to satisfy Rules 104(b) and 901(a).
J	I agree. The objection will be overruled, and the exhibit will be received.
P	Ms. Chandler, let's go back to the text message. I'd like to direct your attention to the second sentence in the message. WHAT reason does the defendant give for being late that day?
W	He said that he got drunk going out with a buddy the night before.
P	In that sentence, HOW does he describe that person?
W	He refers to him as "my good buddy Shelly Lan."
P	Your Honor, I now request permission to circulate People's number three to the jury.
J	Granted.

[8] ANCIENT WRITINGS

Especially in property and estate litigation, it is sometimes necessary to introduce a rather old writing. The difficulty is that if the writing is decades old, it may be impossible to find either witnesses to the writing's execution or witnesses familiar with the handwriting style of the purported author. The common law recognized a special technique for authenticating old writings. Federal Rule of Evidence 901(b)(8) codifies a version of the common-law doctrine. The statute provides that there is sufficient authentication

[f]or a document or data compilation, [when there is] evidence that it:

(A) Is in a condition that creates no suspicion about its authenticity;

(B) Was in a place where, if authentic, it would likely be; and

(C) Is at least 20 years old.

In light of the statute, the foundation consists of the following elements:

1. The writing was found in a certain place;

2. That location is a place where the writing would likely be found if it were authentic (the trial judge decides whether the location is appropriate for that type of document);

3. The writing was in a certain condition;

4. The condition does not raise any serious questions about the authenticity of the writing. As in the case of element #4, the judge exercises discretion in determining whether the condition of the writing was suitable; and

5. The writing is at least 20 years old when the proponent offers the writing into evidence at the time of trial. At common law, the requisite period was 30 years, but the Federal Rules shorten that period to 20 years. Some jurisdictions such as California have a statutory presumption that a writing is properly dated. CAL. EVID. CODE § 640. There is also case law recognizing a presumption or permissive inference to the same effect. 9 WIGMORE, EVIDENCE § 2520 (Chadbourn rev. 1981).

The fact situation is a hearing in an estate proceeding. The proponent claims that a certain person, John Ferguson, was in possession of a particular house, 1440 Stevick Street, Champaign, Illinois, in YR-27. The proponent offers a letter that is dated March 17, YR-27 and purportedly signed by Ferguson. The letter is addressed to Ferguson's sister, Rachel Roust, who is now deceased. The letter states that at the time of the letter, Ferguson was residing at 1440 Stevick Street in Champaign. The witness is Benjamin Roust, Rachel's son.

P	Your Honor, I request that this be marked plaintiff's exhibit number three for identification.
J	It will be so marked.
P	Please let the record reflect that I am showing the exhibit to opposing counsel.
J	It will so reflect.
P	Permission to approach the witness?
J	Granted
P	Mr. Roust, I now show you what has been marked as plaintiff's exhibit three for identification.
W	Yes.
P	WHAT is it? (1), (2)
W	It's a letter that my wife and I found in the attic of our house.
P	WHO currently lives in that house? (1), (2)
W	We do—that is, my wife and I with our three kids.

P   WHO previously lived in the house? (1), (2)

W   My parents.

P   HOW long did they live there? (1), (2)

W   In total forty years. My dad died in YR-25, and my mom passed away in YR-21. Mom left the house to me when she died.

P   WHERE did you find the letter in your house? (1), (2)

W   In an old trunk in the attic.

P   WHY were you looking in the attic? (1), (2)

W   Some attorney called us and asked us to search for any letters that my mom might have received from John Ferguson in that period of time. (*Although the witness is referring to an out-of-court statement by the attorney, the statement was a request, not an assertion under Rule 801(a). The witness's testimony is consequently nonhearsay.*)

P   WHO was John Ferguson? (1), (2)

W   He was my mom's brother and therefore my uncle. (*If the opponent objected that the witness lacked personal knowledge, the proponent could invoke one or both of the hearsay exceptions for family matters set out in Rules 803(19) and 804(b)(4).*)

P   Again, WHY were you looking in the attic? (1), (2)

W   My mom was a real pack rat. She kept lots of letters from her family members, including Uncle John. She kept the correspondence in a trunk in the guest bedroom. When she passed away and we moved in, I put the trunk in the attic. I remember that the trunk was up there, and that's why I searched the attic.

P   WHEN you searched the attic, did you find the trunk? (1), (2)

W   Yes. It was right where I remembered putting it years before.

P   WHAT condition was the trunk in? (3), (4)

W   Incredibly dusty. No one had touched it since I had moved to the attic years before. We rarely go up there, and I previously had had no occasion to open the trunk.

P   WHAT, if anything, did you find in the trunk? (1), (2)

W   I found a whole stack of letters from Uncle John, including this one.

P   Was the letter sitting by itself in the trunk? (1), (2)

W   No. There were several stacks of letters from various relatives—my mom was really organized. I found the stack from Uncle John and then searched through it until I found this one.

P   HOW can you recognize this exhibit as the letter you found in the trunk?

W   Well, I recognize both its condition and its contents.

P	WHAT condition was the letter in? (3), (4)
W	To begin with, the whole stack—in fact everything in the trunk—was pretty dusty.
P	WHAT about the letter itself? (3), (4)
W	The original stationery had been white, but over the years it had turned sort of yellow, as you can see. In addition, the edges had become a bit brittle. It's still in one piece, but it certainly looks like a letter written decades ago.
P	WHY do you think that the letter was written decades ago? (5)
W	All you have to do is check the date.
P	WHAT is the date on the letter? (5)
W	March 17, YR-27.
P	Your Honor, I now offer plaintiff's exhibit number four for identification into evidence as plaintiff's exhibit number four.
J	Any objection?
O	Yes, Your Honor, my first objection is lack of authentication. The witness hasn't testified that he is familiar with his uncle's handwriting style.
J	Any response?
P	Yes, Your Honor. I'm not relying on skilled lay observer opinion under Rule 701 to authenticate the letter. Rather, it's been adequately authenticated under Rule 901(b)(8). It was found in the attic of the house where Mr. Ferguson's sister lived in YR-27. In addition, its condition is evidence of its age. The trunk was dusty, and the letter itself has turned yellow. Finally, the letter is dated in YR-27—well beyond the 20 year period specified in Rule (b)(8). It's true that we don't have a statutory presumption that writings are properly dated, but at common law many cases recognize at least a permissive inference of authenticity.
J	I agree. The authentication objection is overruled. Any further objections?
O	Yes, Your Honor. Hearsay.
J	Any response?
P	Your Honor, just as Rule 901(b)(8) recognizes a special authentication technique, Rule 803(16) carves out a hearsay exception for statements in documents that are more than 20 years old.
J	I'm familiar with that provision. Objection overruled.
P	Your Honor, I request your permission to have the witness read the second paragraph of the letter to the jury.
J	Permission granted.

The 2017 amendments to the Federal Rules modified Rule 803(16), the hearsay exception for ancient writings, but left Rule 901(b)(8), the authentication provision, untouched.

§ 4.03 THE AUTHENTICATION OF BUSINESS WRITINGS

[1] CONVENTIONAL BUSINESS WRITINGS

Authenticating an ordinary business record is a very simple matter. The cases teach that proper custody is sufficient authentication for business records. It is sufficient if the witness is familiar with the business' filing system, took the record from the right file, and recognizes the exhibit as the record removed from the files.

The foundation is brief; the elements are:

1. The witness has personal knowledge of the business' filing system.

2. The witness removed a record from a certain file.

3. It was the right file.

4. The witness recognizes the exhibit as the record he or she removed from the files.

5. The witness specifies the basis on which he or she recognizes the exhibit.

In a contract action, the plaintiff's business, Collegiate Clothing Manufacturers, wants to authenticate a bill it prepared in December YR-3. The plaintiff calls Ms. Peters as its witness.

P	WHAT is your occupation? (1)
W	I am a chief bookkeeper.
P	WHERE do you work? (1)
W	I work at the main office of the plaintiff.
P	HOW long have you worked there? (1)
W	About seven years.
P	WHAT are your duties? (1)
W	As chief bookkeeper, I ensure that we have proper records of all the money and goods flowing into and out of the company. To some extent we're still old school; we actually keep some written records. I supervise the records' preparation, maintenance, and eventual destruction.
P	HOW well do you know the plaintiff's filing system? (1)
W	I know it backwards and forwards. In fact, I helped design the system.
P	Ms. Peters, WHERE were you this morning? (3)
W	I was picking up the records I thought we would need for the trial today.
P	WHERE did you go to get the files? (4)
W	I went to the file cabinet for our YR-3 records. I was particularly interested in the records for December of that year.

P	WHAT did you find in the file? (3)
W	I located all the bills and invoices we needed.
P	Your Honor, I request that this be marked as plaintiff's exhibit number three for identification.
J	It will be so marked.
P	I request permission to approach the witness.
J	Permission granted.
P	Ms. Peters, I now hand you plaintiff's exhibit number three for identification. WHAT is it? (4)
W	It's one of the bills I removed from the file for December YR-3.
P	HOW can you recognize it? (5)
W	I recognize the handwriting of the clerk, John Winters; I've known him for years. In addition, I can generally recall the contents of each of the bills I took out of the file cabinet.
P	Your Honor, I now offer plaintiff's exhibit number three for identification into evidence as plaintiff's exhibit number three.
J	It will be received.
P	I now request permission to hand the exhibit to the jurors for their inspection.
J	Permission granted.

In 2000, Rule 902 was amended to provide that a copy of a business record accompanied by a proper attesting certificate is self-authenticating. Thus, as we shall later see in subsection [7], if the exhibit included a proper 902(11) certificate, there is no need for live, sponsoring testimony.

[2] COMPUTER RECORDS

Computer-generated evidence is a species of scientific evidence. The scientific process of generating data by computer is beyond the knowledge of most laypersons. As § 4.10 of this chapter explains, the presentation of scientific evidence usually requires proof of the validity of the underlying theory and the reliability of the instrument. However, computers are so widely accepted and used that the proponent of computer evidence need not prove those two elements of the foundation; under Federal Rule of Evidence 201, the trial judge will judicially notice the validity of the theory underlying computers and the general reliability of computers.

In the past, many courts have been lax in applying the authentication requirement to computer records; they have been content with foundational evidence that the business has successfully used the computer system in question and that the witness recognizes the record as output from the computer. S. MASON & D. SENG, ELECTRONIC EVIDENCE AND ELECTRONIC SIGNATURES (5th ed. 2021); Rudolph J. Peritz, *Computer Data and Reliability: A Call for Authentication of Business Records Under the Federal Rules of Evidence*, 80 NW. U.L. REV. 956 (1986). However, following the recommendations of the Federal Judicial Center's, *Manual for Complex Litigation*, many courts now require a more extensive foundation. *Id.* These courts require the proponent to authenticate a computer record by proving the reliability of the particular computer used, the dependability of the business's input procedures for the computer, the use of proper procedures to obtain the document offered in court, and the witness's recognition of that document as the readout from the computer.

It is important to remember that a layperson might be unable to interpret the readout. The readout may use symbols and terminology only an expert can understand. If that is the case, after introducing the record, the proponent will have to have the expert explain the contents of the record to the trier of fact.

In general, the elements of the foundation are these:

1.   The business uses a computer.

2.   The computer is reliable.

3.   The business has developed a procedure for inserting data into the computer.

4.   The procedure has built-in safeguards to ensure accuracy and identify errors.

5.   The business keeps the computer in a good state of repair.

6.   The witness had the computer readout certain data.

7.   The witness used the proper procedures to obtain the readout.

8.   The computer was in working order at the time the witness obtained the readout.

9.   The witness recalls and recognizes the exhibit as the readout.

10.   The witness explains how he or she recognizes the readout.

11.   If the readout contains strange symbols or terms, the witness explains the meaning of the symbols or terms for the trier of fact.

The immediately following foundation is for a computer system that used traditional punch card technology. Some older jurors may be familiar with this technology. Although very few businesses employ this technology today, in a given case the proponent might have to introduce business records that were prepared decades before. If so, the proponent could conceivably have to lay a foundation based on the old punch card methodology. That foundation is followed by a second foundation for a more modern computer system in which each employee has a computer that is part of a network, so that each employee can directly input information to the business' central databases.

Suppose that Acme Corporation brings an antitrust suit against Bechtor, Inc. To prove its damages, Acme wants to show that its gross sales declined from YR-8 to YR-3. Acme wants to use a computer printout to show its gross sales in those five years. As its witness, Acme calls Mr. Schons. Acme is the proponent.

Traditional Foundation for Punch Card Technology

P   Mr. Schons, WHAT is your occupation?

W	I am one of the accountants from Acme Corporation.
P	HOW long have you worked for Acme Corporation?
W	Roughly 10 years.
P	HOW long have you worked for Acme Corporation as an accountant?
W	Again, roughly 10 years.
P	WHAT are your duties with Acme Corporation?
W	My specialty is the maintenance of our computer records.
P	HOW does Acme maintain its business records? (1)
W	We maintain the overwhelming majority of our data in our computer.
P	WHICH computer do you use? (1)
W	We use an IBM 720.
P	HOW long have you used that computer? (2)
W	For the last eight years.
P	HOW widely used is that model computer? (2)
W	There are hundreds—maybe thousands—in use throughout the country. When it was first marketed, it was the top of the line. There's a somewhat more sophisticated model available now, but the 720 is still regarded as one of the most dependable models on the market.
P	WHAT procedure does Acme have for using the computer to maintain its records? (3)
W	When an order comes in from a customer, we ship it straight to the sales department. They check it to ensure that the order has the correct spelling of the product name.
P	WHAT does the sales department do with the order then? (3)
W	They send it to the computer center. The center personnel punch the information onto cards. We use the cards to feed the data into the computer. The computer tries to make certain that the merchandise is available and that the purchaser's credit is good. If the order passes those tests, the computer then makes entries on the customer's account and stores data for statistical and management reports.
P	HOW do you know that that is the procedure? (3)
W	I helped design the procedure. As I said, computer record maintenance is my specialty.
P	WHAT safeguards, if any, do you use to ensure that your records are accurate? (4)
W	There are double checks at several points. We have a program that automatically checks each sales invoice against the online order. Perhaps the most important safeguard is the customers' review of the bills we

print out and send them. If anything's wrong, they usually let us know right away.

P HOW is the computer maintained? (5)

W We have an IT contractor who visits the department every two weeks. She thoroughly checks the computer.

P WHERE were you yesterday afternoon? (6)

W I was at my office.

P WHAT were you doing there? (6)

W I was trying to get the data I thought we'd need today in court.

P WHAT data was that? (6)

W I knew we'd need the total sales figures for YR-8 and YR-3.

P HOW did you obtain the data? (6)

W I had the computer print it out.

P HOW did you obtain the printout? (7)

W I went to the terminal, set it in the printout mode, and then requested the sales figures.

P HOW many times did you request the data from the computer? (7)

W Twice.

P WHY did you do it twice? (7)

W I wanted to make certain I had the right figures.

P WHAT was the result of your double-check? (7)

W The computer read out the same data both times.

P WHAT condition was the computer in at the time? (8)

W It seemed to be O.K. There were certainly no obvious problems. It had been checked the night before, and we'd used it several times already that day without any difficulty.

P Your Honor, may this be marked plaintiff's exhibit number ten for identification?

J It will be so marked.

P May the record reflect that I am showing exhibit number ten to the opposing attorney?

J It will so reflect.

P Request permission to approach the witness.

J Permission granted.

P Mr. Schons, I now hand you plaintiff's exhibit number ten for identification. WHAT is it? (9)

W	It's the second printout I just referred to.
P	HOW can you recognize it? (10)
W	I put my initials and the date in that corner. I can easily recognize them.
P	Your Honor, I now offer plaintiff's exhibit number ten for identification into evidence as plaintiff's exhibit number ten.
J	It will be received.
P	Now, Mr. Schons, directing your attention to this notation on the exhibit, WHAT does it say there? (11)
W	It reads "MER S."
P	WHAT does that mean? (11)
W	It means sales of merchandise.
P	HOW do you know that? (11)
W	I helped select the symbols and terminology the computer would use in printouts.
P	WHAT are these figures? (11)
W	They're the dollar amounts of sales for the years indicated, for example, $2,675,334 in YR-8.
P	Your Honor, may exhibit number ten be handed to the jurors for their inspection?
J	Yes.

Modern Foundation for Networked Computers

P	Mr. Schons, WHAT is your occupation?
W	I am one of the accountants for Acme Corporation.
P	HOW long have you worked for Acme Corporation?
W	Roughly 10 years.
P	HOW long have you worked for Acme Corporation as an accountant?
W	Again, roughly 10 years.
P	WHAT are your duties with Acme Corporation?
W	My specialty is the maintenance of our computer records.
P	HOW does Acme create and maintain its business records? (1)
W	We use a modern system of networked computers.
P	WHAT do you mean by that expression? (1)
W	In the old days, companies like ours typically had a single, large computer. It was sometimes called the "mainframe." The employees generated paper records of the transactions they conducted. They would send the paper records to the office where the central computer was kept.

At that office, other personnel would prepare punch cards and transfer the information from the paper records to the computer database. We abandoned that system a long time ago.

P   WHY did you abandon that system? (1)

W   There are several reasons. To begin with, there was a huge waste of time. In essence, the personnel who input the data to the computer duplicated the work of the employees who generated the paper records. Moreover, every time some person has to write a document or prepare a punch card, there's another possibility for human error. Finally, computers became much less expensive. As the price came down, it became feasible to have a computer at the workstation for every salesperson. That's where networking comes in.

P   WHAT is "networking"? (1)

W   As I just indicated, today you have individual computers at each workstation. However, they're networked—in essence, they're wired together. That means that an employee at a sales desk on the first floor can enter information about a sale directly into the central company sales database. It also means that a few seconds later in accounting on the seventh floor, I can immediately use the computer at my desk to access the same information. It's a much more efficient way of doing business.

P   Please describe the network at your company. (1)

W   The three components of our network are the hardware, the software, and the personnel.

P   WHICH hardware do you use? (1)

W   We use Niello 45A computers. All the employees linked into the network have one at their workstation. I have one sitting on my desk.

P   HOW long have you used that computer? (2)

W   For the last three years.

P   HOW widely used is that model computer? (2)

W   There are thousands in use throughout the world. Since I'm the computer specialist in accounting, I go to the business technology shows. The technology moves so fast that the 45A is no longer the state of the art, but it's still one of the most widely used and certainly one of the most dependable.

P   WHAT software do you use? (2)

W   All the computers have Microquality BDB business data base. The software is specially designed for businesses with networks.

P   HOW long have you used that software? (2)

W   For the same period of time, roughly three years.

P   HOW widely is that software used by businesses? (2)

W   My impression is that it's one of the most popular not just in the United States but throughout the world. And we buy the upgrades to the software. The last upgrade was only about three months ago.

P   Finally, WHAT about the personnel? (3)

W   We give them training.

P   WHICH employees receive training? (3)

W   Any employee who might have occasion to make a sale and input sales data into the database receives a full day's training in the use of the hardware and software.

P   WHO conducts the training? (3)

W   At first, we hired an outside computer consultant. However, within a year I learned the ropes of the system well enough to do the training. For the past two years, I've personally trained every new employee. In addition, since we keep buying the upgrades, on a yearly basis every employee gets refresher training.

P   WHAT procedures does Acme have for using these computers to create and maintain its records? (3)

W   As I've indicated, the employee who makes the sale actually inputs the data directly into the networked system. At the same time, at the workstation they're printing out a partial paper copy for the transaction.

P   WHAT happens to the paper copies? (4)

W   At the end of each work day, they're sent to accounting.

P   WHAT does accounting do with them? (4)

W   At the end of each week, we randomly select a few paper copies from each workstation and double check them against the electronic data. That way we can ensure that the entries are correct. Of course, perhaps the most important safeguard is the customers' review of the bills we ultimately print out and send them. If anything's wrong, they usually let us know right away.

P   HOW is the computer network maintained? (5)

W   Whenever an employee encounters any mechanical problem, he or she calls accounting immediately; and in turn, we call the Niello service representative. We have an IT service contract with Niello. In addition, pursuant to the same service contract, on a bimonthly basis Niello stops by and does preventative maintenance on the network.

P   WHERE were you yesterday afternoon? (6)

W   I was at my office.

(The rest of the questioning proceeds in roughly the same manner as in

the immediately preceding foundation based on older punch card technology.).

[3] "FAXED" DOCUMENTS

Recent decades have witnessed a communications revolution. To a significant degree modern, faster technologies have superseded snail mail as a means of business communication. Much of the business correspondence that had been conducted by snail mail was instead transmitted by fax machine or later by e-mail. Therefore, counsel must know how to authenticate faxed documents and e-mails. See [4], *below*, for authentication of e-mails. E-mails have eclipsed fax as the primary means of business communication, but many, if not most, businesses still have a fax or a machine with fax capability. Even when the testimony is based on a new technology, however, the pertinent evidentiary principles are old and well settled. The introduction to this chapter pointed out that whenever the proponent offers an exhibit into evidence, he or she must lay a preliminary showing that the exhibit "is what its proponent claims it is." Federal Rule of Evidence 901(a) provides that when the preliminary question is the authenticity of an exhibit, the test is whether the proponent has presented sufficient foundational proof "to support a finding that the item is what the proponent claims it is."

The application of these principles depends on the nature of the proponent's claim about the faxed document. The following two fact patterns illustrate the more common claims which the proponent might make.

When the Proponent Is Trying to Prove Receipt of the FAX

Suppose that the issue is whether a purported recipient, a company, received a fax setting out certain information transmitted by an alleged sender. The pivotal issue is the receipt of the fax. In a lawsuit involving an allegation of breach of a warranty of fitness for a specific purpose, the plaintiff might claim that the plaintiff informed the defendant of the intended use of the product before the defendant agreed to sell the product to the plaintiff. The essential question is thus *whether a fax transmitted by a certain sender reached the alleged recipient*. In this variation of the hypothetical, the witness is an employee of the company that *sent* the fax rather than the company *receiving* the fax. The employee might give the following foundational testimony: The employee's company uses a fax machine; the machine is capable, when operating properly, of transmitting and receiving a fax; the machine was in proper working order on the occasion in question; before using the machine, the employee looked up the addressee company's fax number in a reliable directory or obtained the fax number from another reliable source; the employee dialed that number on the machine; the sheet of paper containing the facts passed through the machine; and the machine generated a confirmation or transmission report listing the dialed number and indicating that the attempted transmission has succeeded. Then show an exhibit to the witness, who identifies the same as the sheet which passed through the originating fax machine.

In the above hypothetical, the proponent claims that: (1) the exhibit is the paper which the witness passed through the fax machine at the transmitting end, and (2) the paper is an accurate copy of the document which the other company received at its end. The foregoing foundation is adequate to establish that twofold claim. The witness is certainly competent to prove the initial claim. With respect to the second claim, an adequate foundation is presented by evidence that the fax machine employed to send the fax is capable of transmitting an accurate reproduction when properly employed and that, in the particular case, the fax machine was properly employed. Under Federal Rule 201, a trial judge could judicially notice the general reliability of fax machines. Furthermore, an analogy may be drawn between this "faxed document doctrine" and the telephone directory doctrine discussed in § 4.05[3] of this chapter. Just as the use of a telephone directory number identifies the speaker at the other end as the person dialed under Federal Rule 901(b)(6), the use of a fax number from a trustworthy directory identifies the recipient of the fax. Absent such a directory, the fax number would have to be shown to have been obtained from a similar reliable source.

When the Proponent Is Trying to Prove the Identity of the Sender of a FAX

Now consider a second fact situation in which the issue is the identity of the sender of a fax. The essential question is *whether a fax which reached a certain recipient was transmitted by the alleged sender*. The addressee or recipient company is the plaintiff in a contract action alleging that the defendant company sent it an offer which the plaintiff accepted. The plaintiff is the proponent, and the witness is one of the plaintiff's employees. The employee testifies that she received the fax in question, and the proponent claims that the fax is an accurate copy of an offer transmitted by the defendant. This fact pattern differs from the preceding versions. In the first fact pattern, the source of the fax was irrelevant; here the source is critical—if the defendant company was not the source, the defendant has no contract liability to the plaintiff. In the second fact pattern, the witness was an employee of the sending or transmitting entity; here the witness is an employee of the recipient. Does the employee's testimony sufficiently lay the foundation for the exhibit?

Under the Rule 104(b) standard, faxed documents are properly authenticated by the introduction of evidence sufficient to support a finding that the documents received accurately reflect the documents "faxed"; this requires evidence that the machine employed to send and receive the fax is capable of producing an accurate reproduction when properly employed and that, in the particular case, the machine was properly employed. In addition, it will be necessary to establish that the faxed document originated with the alleged sender. A proponent could identify the sender of a fax in several fact situations. For example, in one situation the fax received might disclose information known only to the alleged sender. Or in a second fact situation if the recipient of the fax in question had earlier contacted the alleged sender by letter, phone, or fax, and the fax in question was obviously responsive to the previous contact, the fax could be authenticated by analogy to the reply letter doctrine. For that matter, if the fax in question bore the sender's fax number automatically imprinted on each page and the imprinted digits are sufficiently established to be the sender's fax number, an adequate foundation has arguably been presented.

Suppose that the case falls into the last variation of the second fact situation. The following foundation would suffice to authenticate the fax as originating from the alleged sender:

1. The receiving business uses a facsimile machine.

2. The facsimile machine is standard equipment that can both send and receive documents by telephone. The trial judge could judicially notice this proposition.

3. The machine accurately transmits copies of original documents.

4. A procedure exists for checking for mechanical and human error.

5. The facsimile machine accurately and automatically records the time and date of transmittal.

6. A cover sheet, faxed with the document, shows the phone number of the originating machine and the name of the person to whom the document is directed, as well as the fax number of that person.

7. Each fax page received is automatically imprinted with the fax number of the originating machine.

8. The fax number stated on the cover sheet and on the fax pages is the number of the alleged sender.

9. The witness identifies the exhibit as the cover sheet received on the addressee's fax machine.

The following fact situation concerns litigation involving an order placed by Acme Widget Company with one of its suppliers, Pesotum Widget Frames, Inc., for 3,000 widget frames. As part of its case, Pesotum wishes to show that a Ms. Baker, a Pesotum employee, received a "faxed" letter from Acme containing an order for 3,000 widget frames. Pesotum's lawyer is the proponent, and Ms. Baker is the witness in the following scenario.

P	WHERE do you work?
W	At Pesotum Widget Frames, Inc.
P	WHAT is your position there?
W	I am the executive secretary and assistant to the president of Pesotum, George Clinton.
P	As of September 11, YR-3, the date in question here, DID Pesotum own a facsimile machine? (1)
W	Yes.
P	As of the date, for HOW long had Pesotum had the facsimile machine?
W	At least three or four years before that date.
P	HOW often, if ever, did you have occasion to use that machine to both fax documents and receive documents that others had faxed to Pesotum? (4)
W	Many dozens, perhaps hundreds, of times, both sending and receiving.
P	WHAT procedure did you use in September YR-3 when you wished to fax a document to someone? (2), (3), (5), (6), (7)
W	I fill out a cover sheet indicating the person to whom the document was

directed and that person's phone number. The cover sheet would also contain other information, such as the total number of pages being transmitted, the date and time of the transmission, any additional routing information, and a statement that in case of poor transmission the party receiving the document should call me at the number written on the cover sheet so that I could fax the document again. I would then feed the cover sheet and the document to be transmitted into the facsimile machine. The machine would transmit them to the number I dialed. The machine automatically recorded the time and date of transmittal on the documents being faxed. Our model of machine also automatically imprints the fax number on the top of each page.

P   WHAT was the procedure for documents which you received by fax?

W   The same as I described, only in reverse. We get the cover sheet that the person faxing the documents filled out. If the sender uses a fax machine like ours, the originating fax number is automatically imprinted somewhere on the page, either on the very top or the bottom.

P   HAVE you ever had occasion to compare original documents that you have sent by fax with the documents received by the other fax machine? (4)

W   Oh, sure. During the course of my handling the paperwork regarding Pesotum's contracts, I often see documents that I have faxed to some third party that are being returned to me by mail with some additional writing on them.

P   HOW closely do the faxed documents resemble original documents? (4)

W   They're exact copies. There are no deviations of any kind. In all instances, the machine has accurately transmitted just what appears on the original document to be faxed.

P   To your knowledge, HOW can you alter the fax machine to create a difference between the document being faxed and the document received? (3)

W   Maybe some computer whiz could, but I sure don't know of any way that I could do that.

P   More specifically, HOW, if at all, could your facsimile machine be set to alter in any way a document that someone had faxed to you? (3)

W   I don't know how that could be done. Absolutely not.

P   Directing your attention to September 11, YR-3, WHAT, if any, fax transmission did you receive that day?

W   I received a fax transmission from Acme on that date.

P   Your Honor, I request that this be marked as plaintiff's exhibit number four for identification.

J	It will be so marked.
P	Please let the record reflect that I am showing the exhibit to opposing counsel.
J	The record will so reflect.
P	May I approach the witness?
J	Yes.
P	I show you what has been marked as "Plaintiff's Exhibit 4 for Identification." Can you tell me WHAT that is?
W	This is the four-page document and the cover sheet that I received on our fax machine on September 11, YR-3, that indicated it was being sent from Acme Widget Company. Our machine had been called, and this document had been transmitted to it.
P	HOW, if at all, does the present condition of this document differ from its condition when you received it on September 11, YR-3? (9)
W	As far as I can tell, it's in exactly the same condition.
P	WHAT date, time, and telephone number, if any, are imprinted on plaintiff's exhibit number four for identification?
W	September 11, YR-3, 10:15 A.M., and (804) 456-7890.
P	WHERE, if anywhere, does the fax number appear on those pages? (7)
W	To begin with, it's on the originating cover sheet. Moreover, it's been imprinted on each page.
P	WHAT is the significance of the date and time—September 11, YR-3, 10:15 A.M.? (3), (5), (6)
W	That's the date and approximate time I can recall receiving the documents from Acme.
P	WHOSE telephone or fax number is (804) 456-7890? (8)
W	It is the telephone and fax number of Acme Widget Company.
P	HOW do you know that? (8)
W	I've faxed documents back and forth with them several times. On some occasions, I pick up the phone and talk to one of their people minutes after getting or sending a fax. I'm positive that that's their number.
P	Your Honor, I now offer plaintiff's exhibit number four for identification into evidence.
J	It will be received.
P	I request permission to publish this exhibit by reading it to the jury.
J	Permission granted.

[4]　E(LECTRONIC)-MAIL

[a]　OVERVIEW

Although businesses once relied heavily on fax to replace snail mail, they later turned to electronic mail delivery systems. The systems include simple e-mail (electronic mail), text messaging, Google chat, and instant messaging. Like faxes, discussed in § 4.03[3], electronic mail (e-mail) poses evidentiary issues.[6] To appreciate the authentication problem posed by e-mail, we must first understand e-mail technology. E-mail is more versatile than fax; it can be sent over a variety of network links, ranging from dialup to fiber optic lines. E-mail is ordinarily text, but other formats can be sent, including graphic images.

The mechanics of a simple e-mail system are straightforward. To send e-mail, the person first opens the e-mail application. The user next sees the e-mail screen. The screen consists of two parts: the header and the body. The visible part of a typical heading includes at least three lines, and sometimes four. One is a line for the sender's e-mail address. In most modern e-mail applications, that line is not manually completed by the sender; instead, the e-mail application inserts the sender's e-mail address when the message is sent. There is a second line for the primary recipient's address, and an optional third "cc" line for additional recipients' e-mail addresses. An Internet e-mail address consists of a local part and a host part: username@hostname. The local part is the mailbox, login name, or user identification of the intended recipient. The host name indicates the network serving that person. Professor Imwinklelried's address is "ejimwinkelried@ucdavis.edu"; his host is U.C. Davis in the educational domain. There are Internet online directory service databases of varying reliability—"white pages"—for locating e-mail addresses. A final line is provided for a brief summary or title of the message.

After completing the heading, the sender composes the body of the message. Once the sender completes the message, he or she ordinarily types "send" or clicks on a "send" button. Alternatively, the user might press a "queue" button and later send queued messages before signing off. The program routes the message through the computer networks connecting the source (the sender) and the destination (the intended recipient). Service providers (servers) intervene between the sender and recipient to transmit the message. After traveling through various servers and networks, the message reaches the recipient's inbox. When that person logs on and checks for mail, he or she will learn that they have new mail. At that point, the recipient can open the message and read it. After reading it, the recipient may decide to reply. Most e-mail programs have a reply feature. To use this feature, the recipient types "reply" or clicks a "reply" button. Depending on the program, the recipient then types the reply immediately above or below the message received. When the recipient clicks the "send" button, the program automatically forwards the reply to the original sender. The original sender usually receives an e-mail string consisting of both his or her message and the

---

[6] Note, Anthony J. Dreyer, *When the Postman Beeps Twice: The Admissibility of Electronic Mail Under the Business Records Exception to the Federal Rules of Evidence*, 64 FORDHAM L. REV. 2285 (1996).

recipient's reply, although some e-mail programs give the replying party the option of omitting the original message from the reply message.

As noted above, in nearly all modern e-mail applications, when a sender logs into the e-mail application and composes a new message, there is no need or even an option to insert a "from" line indicating the sender's e-mail address. Instead, when the sender dispatches the e-mail message, the "from" line is automatically added to the message. Thus, one might think that it is reasonable to assume that an e-mail message purportedly from a particular e-mail address in fact came from the person owning that address; there is an arguable inference of authenticity because in the ordinary operation of an e-mail program it is not possible to alter the "from" line. However, in some circumstances, with the right information and computer skills, it is possible to "fake" an e-mail message—that is, a message that appears to be from a certain person but is not from that person. Those circumstances include the following:

- A person who has somehow obtained access to another person's user ID and password could log into that person's e-mail account and send a message purporting to be from that person.

- By various means such as viruses, spyware, and other malicious software devices, a computer hacker might be able to hack into or hijack another person's e-mail account to send messages purporting to come from that person.

- Although it is impossible to directly change the "from" line when composing an original message, the "from" line in the original message can be altered when forwarding or replying to that message. Hence, it is possible for a person to change the name and e-mail address in a message that originally came from person A to make it appear that it came from person B when forwarding the message to person C.

Given these possibilities, a trial judge might insist on a substantial foundation to authenticate an e-mail message.

[b]   EVIDENTIARY DOCTRINES AND FOUNDATIONAL ELEMENTS FOR AUTHENTICATING E-MAIL

Although e-mail is a relatively new technology, in many instances the proponent can authenticate an e-mail message by adapting a traditional doctrine:

Reply letter doctrine. § 4.02[4] discusses the reply doctrine. This doctrine can also be applied by analogy to e-mail. The proponent makes a foundational showing that he or she obtained the address from an online directory or other reliable source, sent an e-mail message to an address obtained from such a source, and in due course received a message responsive in terms to the earlier message. In the context of e-mail, "due course" will ordinarily be a much shorter period of time than in the case of conventional "snail" mail. When the doctrine is applied to letters, it might take several days for the response to reach the original sender. When the doctrine is applied to e-mail, it might require only a few minutes or hours.

Content. Adapting still another traditional technique, the proponent can authenticate an e-mail by showing that only the purported author was likely to know the information reflected in the message. There are several fact situations in which that technique would come into play. First, the substantive content of the message might be information known only to the purported sender. Second, if the recipient used the reply feature to respond, the new message will include the sender's original message. If the sender dispatched that message to only one person, its inclusion in the new message indicates that the new message originated with the original recipient.

Subsequent action consistent with the message. Suppose that after the receipt of the message, the purported sender takes action consistent with the content of the message. In a business context, the action might be the delivery of merchandise mentioned in the message. That conduct could provide circumstantial authentication of the source of the method. The common law recognized this method of authentication in the past, and the method is still valid in the e-mail setting.

While the above three authentication methods are traditional techniques, other methods of authenticating e-mail are more avant-garde. The latter methods involve testimony about cryptography, e-mail servers, and digital signatures.

Cryptography

The proponent can sometimes lay a foundation to authenticate an e-mail message by presenting testimony about the cryptography used in transmitting the message. While it is true that cryptography is employed in only a very small percentage of e-mail communication, that percentage is growing. Moreover, many important electronic transactions—the kinds of transactions likely to generate litigation—utilize cryptography. In most cryptography, the communicating parties use a key which encrypts or scrambles the message. There are two basic types of key cryptography. One is single-key cryptography. In that system, the communicating parties use the same key; the sender utilizes the key to encrypt the message, and the recipient employs the same key to decipher or decrypt it. One difficulty with single-key cryptography is that before using the key, the parties must have a secure communication channel to exchange the key. It can be difficult to obtain access to such a channel. Sending the private key under secure channels can be expensive and slow.

The other type of cryptography, the public/private two-key system, provides an additional level of security at the price of some computational complexity. One key is the public key, and the other is the private or secret key. The keys are complementary; each unlocks the code which the other key makes. A person can employ commercially available software called Viacrypt which uses PGP (Pretty Good Privacy) to create the two keys.[7] The person, the key owner, will then publish one key and keep the other private. The person can use the private key to send messages which could be sent only by that person;[8] since those messages can be decrypted only by using that person's

---

[7] Technically, PGP is a "hybrid" system: the program uses public/private key encryption to encrypt a session key—a one-time, disposable key—which is then used by IDEA, a strong single-key algorithm, to encrypt the actual message. PGP employs this two-step process because public/private key encryption can be very slow when utilized on long messages.

[8] A. Michael Froomkin, *Flood Control on the Information Ocean: Living with Anonymity, Digital Cash*

public key, the fact that the recipient successfully opened the message by employing that public key identifies the key owner as the sender.

However, there is a problem: How can the recipient determine that the purported sender is indeed the owner of that public key?

> The problem facing [the recipient] in this scenario . . . is that there is no more reason to trust an e-mail message purporting to be from Bob that says "here is my public key" than there is to trust any other e-mail message purporting to come from Bob.[9]

To overcome that problem, a new industry emerged—the business of certification authorities or CAs.[10] These companies are in the business of verifying that a particular person owns a certain public key. Thus, after receiving a request from the person owning the public key, the company would conduct an inquiry to verify the identity of the key owner. Having done so, the company can provide third parties with assurance of the person's ownership of the key by issuing identifying certificates to this effect.[11] A person can request that the CA verify his or her ownership of the public key. After receiving the request, the CA conducts an inquiry to verify the identity of the key owner. Having verified the owner's identity, the CA issues an identifying certificate.[12] In effect, the certificate notarizes the connection between the owner and the public key.

> The CA might publish the resulting certificate on a World Wide Web site available to anyone with Internet access, or give the certificate to [the owner], or contract with [the owner] to honor e-mailed requests for the certificate from all comers.[13]

Given this cryptography technology, the proponent could generally authenticate an e-mail message by laying the following foundation:

1. There is a certain CA. In Utah, there is a state statute regulating CAs.[14] However, in most states CAs are unregulated. The proponent can call a representative of the CA as a witness, introduce the relevant part of a transcript of the representative's deposition, or proffer a stipulation as to the existence and operation of the CA.

2. The CA received a request to verify that a particular person owned a specified public key. The request itself, a weak imperative sentence, is nonhearsay under Federal Rule of Evidence 801(a). The request is not a declarative sentence

---

and Distributed Databases, 15 J.L. & COM. 395, 419 n.74 (1996) [hereinafter Froomkin I]; A. Michael Froomkin, *Symposium: Innovation and the Information Environment: The Essential Role of Trusted Third Parties in Electronic Commerce*, 75 OR. L. REV. 49, 52 (1996) [hereinafter Froomkin II].

9 Froomkin II, 75 OR. L. REV. 49, 52 (1996).

10 *Id.* at 49.

11 *Id.* at 60.

12 *Id.*

13 *Id.*

14 Utah Code Ann. § 46-3-309 (1996).

asserting any facts. The CA's record reflecting receipt of the request qualifies as a business entry under Rule 803(6).

3. The CA conducted an inquiry to verify that the person in question owned that public key. The CA might conduct varying levels of inquiry. For instance, VeriSign offers four classes of certificates corresponding with differing levels of inquiry. "Class 1 certificates . . . certify only 'the uniqueness of a name or e-mail address.' In contrast, VeriSign will issue a Class 2 certificate, which is more expensive, after receiving 'third party proofing of name, address and other personal information.' "[15] If the CA has retained the records reflecting the inquiry, the records themselves are admissible under Rule 803(6). If the CA no longer has those records, under Rule 406 the proponent can elicit the representative's testimony about the CA's routine practices for conducting inquiries.

4. As a result of the inquiry, the CA issued an identifying certificate verifying that the person in question owns the specified public key. There are various types of certificates,[16] but for our purpose an identifying certificate is of greatest interest. An identifying certificate establishes the connection or link between a specified public key and a particular person. In essence, the certificate vouches that that person is the key owner. Like the records reflecting the CA's receipt of the request (element #2) and its inquiry (element #3), the certificate itself will qualify as a business entry under Rule 803(6). The CA is not only in the business of conducting the inquiries; another essential part of its business is issuing the certificates and thereby giving third parties assurance of the key owner's identity. (The proponent could dispense with the preceding foundational elements if the opponent were willing to stipulate that the person in question was the owner of the specified public key.).

5. The recipient of the message to be authenticated had previously learned of the person's identity as the owner of the specified public key. The recipient might have obtained the information from any of many sources, including a telephone call or a page on the World Wide Web. In many cases, in an earlier e-mail message, the recipient received the plain text of the person's public key.[17] The recipient's testimony about his or her discovery of the key owner's identity is not subject to a hearsay objection. The testimony is proffered only for the nonhearsay purpose of explaining the recipient's subsequent conduct under Rule 801(c)(2), namely, later using that public key to decrypt the message in question. On request by the opponent, the trial judge would give the jury a Rule 105 limiting instruction about the nonhearsay status of the recipient's testimony. Of course, the proponent must present independent,

---

[15] Froomkin II, 75 OR. L. REV. 49, 58–59 (1996).

[16] *Id.* at 59–65 (identifying certificates, authorizing certificates, transactional certificates, and digital time-stamping devices).

[17] *Id.* at 52.

admissible evidence of the person's identity as the key owner. However, the prior four foundational elements furnish that evidence.

6. The recipient received the message in question.

7. When the recipient received the message, the recipient used the person's public key to decrypt or decipher the message.

8. When the recipient used the specified public key, the key successfully unscrambled the message.

9. The message identified the key owner as the sender. Standing alone, foundational elements numbers 1–8 support this inference. However, when the message itself identifies the originator, the proponent should elicit this additional testimony to strengthen the inference.

The proponent would use the above foundation to authenticate an encrypted e-mail message.

Digital Signature

In the previous discussion of cryptography, we assumed that the Sender encrypted the message itself. A variation of this foundation is presenting foundational testimony about a digital signature to authenticate an unencrypted message.[18] Although the body of the message itself is unencrypted, the sender can use his or her private key to encrypt the digital signature.[19] If the recipient can successfully use the person's public key to decrypt the signature, the circumstances "uniquely identif[y] the sender and connect [] the sender to the exact message."[20]

To authenticate a message on the basis of a digital signature, the proponent could lay a foundation including the following elements. This foundation is based in part on key cryptography. However, this foundation also relies on a CA's certificate with a DS (digital signature). The foundational elements relate to three parties—the CA, the Sender of a message, and the Recipient of the message. The assumption is that the CA, Sender, and Recipient use compatible public-key cryptographic software.

THE CA (THE CERTIFYING AUTHORITY)

1. There is a CA which is in the business of certifying, inter alia, the identity of the holders of public keys.

2. The CA itself has a public key and a private key.

3. The CA makes its public key accessible. For example, a bank might include some sort of key "fingerprint" in its bank statements. Alternatively, a CA can publish its own public key at its World Wide Web site available to anyone with Internet access.

4. A person (Sender) requests a certificate from the CA.

---

[18] *Id.* at 54.

[19] *Id.*

[20] *Id.*

5. The CA requests certain proof of identity from Sender.

6. Sender furnishes the requested proof.

7. CA:

   a. generates a certificate attesting that Sender has a certain public key;

   b. digitally signs its certificate. A hash function is used to produce the DS. The hash function utilizes the text of the certificate as an input and produces a hash number, for instance, a 500-digit number which is probabilistically unique. A hash function is a one-way function. In other words, knowing the text, the function allows you to determine the hash number, but knowing the number does not allow you to reproduce the text; and

   c. uses its private key to encrypt the DS.
   THE END RESULT of this step is both CA's message with unencrypted text and the appended CA's DS, an encrypted hash number.

8. CA can make the certificate accessible by the following means, inter alia:

   a. publishing the certificate on its World Wide Web site;

   b. giving the certificate to Sender who requested the certificate; or

   c. contracting with Sender to honor e-mailed requests for the certificate from all comers.

SENDER

9. Sender later generates a message to Recipient. Just as CA can use its private key to digitally sign its certificate, Sender can use its private key to digitally sign the message to Recipient. Sender uses a hash function to produce its DS. The hash function utilizes the text of the message as an input and produces a hash number. Sender uses its private key to encrypt the DS.
THE END RESULT of this step is both a message from Sender with unencrypted message and an associated DS.

10. Sender sends Recipient both Sender's message and the DS. (If Sender has CA's certificate, Sender can send the CA certificate as well. Alternatively, Sender might inform Recipient that CA has posted the certificate at its Web site or will honor Recipient's request for the certificate.).

RECIPIENT

11. One way or another, Recipient obtains CA's digitally signed certificate.

12. Recipient knows or learns CA's public key. (Again, by way of example, Recipient might have previously contacted CA, Recipient might find CA's public key on an Internet directory, or Recipient can go to CA's Web site.).

13. *CA's Certificate.* Recipient uses CA's public key to decrypt the DS appended to CA's certificate (the end result of #7). The decryption reveals the hash number for the certificate. Recipient then independently hashes the text of the

certificate, yielding a hash number. If the two numbers match, the CA certificate is presumed valid when created. (If anyone had altered the text of the certificate, in all probability the two numbers would not match.). This step establishes that CA is the source of the certificate stating that Sender owns a particular public key.

14. *Sender's Message.* Again, CA's certificate states that Sender owns a certain public key. Recipient next uses that public key to decrypt the Sender's DS appended to Sender's message. The decryption reveals the hash number for the message. Recipient then independently hashes the text of the message, yielding a hash number. If the two numbers match, the message is presumed authentic. (If anyone had altered the text of the message, in all probability the two numbers would not match.).

15. Recipient checks CA's certificate revocation list (CRL). In its CRL, CA lists any certificates that have expired or been compromised. If the certificate in question is not on the list, Recipient has reason to believe that the certificate was in effect and valid at the time Sender sent the message.

Chain of Custody Handling by E-mail Servers

The chain of custody technique can also be used to authenticate a document.[21] Even if a person did not read the letter within an envelope, the person's testimony about the physical handling of the envelope can help establish a chain of custody for the enclosed letter. Suppose, for instance, that B testifies that she received an envelope from A and that she later handed it to C. In turn, C testifies that he received the envelope from B and later delivered it to D. D testifies that he accepted the envelope from C, opened it, and found a letter purportedly signed by A. Even though neither B nor C saw the contents of the envelope, their testimony suffices to establish that the letter D received was in fact authored by A.

Analogously, the proponent of an e-mail message may authenticate the message by showing its electronic handling. The proponent can use the business records of all the systems which transmitted the message to trace the message back to the source computer. So long as those records show that each system handled a message originating from the purported sender's computer, it is immaterial that no one at the intermediate systems actually opened and read the message. At the recipient's end, using proper commands, the computer can print out a complete heading, setting out the information indicating the handling of the message between its dispatch and receipt. For example, the computer might print out the following:

From aamerson@oxy.edu Fri June 7 16:51:49 YR-3
  Received: from guilder.ucdavis.edu by peseta.ucdavis.edu (8.76/UCD3.5.6)
  id QAA24323; Fri, 7 June YR-3 16:31:30-0700 (PDT)
  Received: from bobcat.cc.oxy.edu by guilder-ucdavis.edu (8.7.5/UCD3.5.4)
  id QAA24807; Fri, 7 June YR-3 16:31:26-0700 (PDT)

---

[21] United States v. Thomas, 54 F.3d 73 (2d Cir. 1995).

Received (from aamerson@localhost) by bobcat.cc.oxy.edu (8.61.11/8.6.11)
id QAAA21403 for sdlangford@ucdavis.edu; Fri, 7 June YR-3 16:31:22-0700
From Andy Amerson aamerson@oxy.edu.

This string traces a message from Andy Amerson (aamerson@oxy.edu) to Steve Langford (sdlangford@ucdavis.edu). The message initially went from Amerson's computer to bobcat, the e-mail server for Amerson's organization, Occidental College. In turn, the bobcat server routed the message to guilder, the e-mail hub for Langford's organization, the University of California at Davis. Next, guilder routed the message to the peseta network on the Davis campus. Peseta is the e-mail server for that campus. Finally, peseta routed the message to the recipient's e-mail account. Each server in this chain is maintained by a regularly conducted activity such as a department of a college or business. That department generates records documenting the receipt and transmittal of the message in question. When the server receives the message, it assigns the message an identification number and notes the time and date of its processing of the message. Those records qualify as business entries admissible under Rule 803(6) when testified to by the appropriate custodians or other qualified witnesses or properly certified under Rule 902(11). Unless the server's administrator has "flushed" or disposed of the records, the records should still be available to help lay the foundation for an e-mail passage which was handled by the server. Thus, if every other authentication technique fails, the proponent can lay the foundation for an e-mail message by:

1. having the recipient print out the entire routing of the message;

2. introducing the routing records for each server which handled the message to verify that the message was processed as the recipient's printout indicates; and

3. establishing that the alleged author had primary or exclusive access to the computer which, according to the records, originated the message.

[c] SAMPLE FOUNDATIONS

[i] IN GENERAL

The following foundations illustrate two popular techniques for authenticating e-mail messages, that is, proof of a chain of custody for the message and the use of a digital signature.

[ii] CHAIN OF CUSTODY HANDLING TESTIMONY BY AN EMPLOYEE OF AN E-MAIL SERVICE

The case involves an order placed by the University of California, Davis Purchasing Office with one of its suppliers, Intel Company, for computer parts. As part of its case, the University of California wishes to show that Mr. Langford, its employee, received an e-mail message. The message purportedly came from Intel and contained an offer to sell the computer components in question. The university's lawyer is the proponent.

Langford has already taken the stand. During his testimony, he testifies that: On September 12, YR-3, he received an e-mail message on his personal computer at work; the university hub is "guilder.undavis.edu"; the university server is "peseta.ucdavis.edu";

the message purported to come from Mr. Mishkin, a representative of Intel; the message was an offer to sell the computer parts; at the attorney's request, Langford printed out all the routing information for the message; and he recognizes an exhibit as the printout. (The printout includes seven entries. Three entries represent Langford's address and the identifications for the university's hub and server. A fourth line of the printout indicates that the message in question was routed by "orgmail.intel.com." That line lists OAA23641 as the identification number for the message and indicates that the message was routed on September 17, YR-3 at 2:02 p.m. in the afternoon. That line represents Organization Mail, the external server intermediate between the plaintiff's e-mail system and the defendant's. The other three lines correspond to the Internet address and identification identified in the stipulation, *infra*.) The printout is marked as plaintiff's exhibit number eight for identification.

In addition, the plaintiff introduces a stipulation of fact between the parties. The stipulation is to the effect that: On September 12, YR-3, Jerome Mishkin was one of the defendant's employees; he is now deceased; as of September YR-3, though, he had been assigned the Internet address "jeromemishkin@ccm.jf.intel.com"; the identification for Intel's server is "ccm.jf.intel.com"; and the identification for Intel's hub is "relay.jf.intel.com." (That address and those identifications correspond with three lines on the heading which Langford printed out.)

The next witness is Ms. Carlton, the employee in charge of records for the Organization Mail company. Organization Mail is an e-mail server for users in the commercial, government, and educational domains. The proponent will use Organization Mail's record (exhibit 9) to establish part of the foundation for the university's printout (exhibit 8).

P	WHAT is your name?
W	My name is Elise Carlton.
P	WHO do you work for?
W	I work for Organization Mail.
P	WHAT is the nature of your company's business?
W	We are an Internet service provider. We're sometimes called an external server. We get e-mail messages from one company or agency and transmit them to another. We take the message from the sender's mail system and transmit it to the intended recipient's system.
P	WHAT is your job title there?
W	I'm chief of records for serving operations.
P	WHAT are your responsibilities as chief?
W	I oversee the generation and maintenance of our records of all the messages which we receive and send on to destination.
P	WHAT kinds of messages do you handle?
W	All kinds—government, commercial, and educational.

P   When your company handles an e-mail message, HOW, if at all, will your firm's handling be reflected at the message's final destination?

W   Well, when they print out the heading at the final destination, the word "orgmail" will include an entry indicating that we were a server.

P   When you receive a message for transmission, WHERE, if at all, would the word "orgmail" appear on the message?

W   It automatically becomes part of the larger heading. It shows that we handled the message.

P   Specifically, WHAT would the heading say about the message?

W   It gives it an identification number and notes the date and time of handling the message.

P   Your Honor, I request that this be marked as plaintiff's exhibit number nine for identification.

J   It will be so marked.

P   Please let the record reflect that I am showing the exhibit to the defense attorney.

J   The record will so reflect.

P   Permission to approach the witness.

P   Ms. Carlton, I now hand you plaintiff's exhibit number nine for identification. WHAT is it?

W   It's one of our logs of e-mail messages.

P   WHAT is a "log"?

W   It's a printout of the information relevant to the handling of a message. At the end of every 12-hour period, someone in my office prints out the log listing all the messages received or sent on our server system.

P   WHAT does this log show?

W   It documents the handling of messages on a particular date.

P   WHICH date?

W   September 12, YR-3.

P   WHAT types of messages does this log list?

W   As I said just a while ago, it lists all the outgoing and incoming messages routed by our server "orgmail" on that date.

P   WHY does your company prepare these logs?

W   For quality control and business reasons. To begin with, the logs help us determine whether our equipment is working properly—that is, whether we're sending messages to the right destinations. Moreover, we obviously have to monitor the volume of traffic for each customer for billing purposes. That's how we determine how much to charge each customer.

	These logs are absolutely essential in our business.
P	HOW do you prepare these logs?
W	As I said, at the end of each day, we print out our e-mail records and store them.
P	WHO prepares them?
W	One of our employees, one of the people I supervise.
P	HOW often do you prepare this type of record?
W	We do it every day—in fact—twice every day. Again, we do it at the end of every 12-hour period.
P	HOW do you recognize this record?
W	I recognize the contents. You told me that you were interested in the e-mail log for a particular day. I personally went to the file to pull the log. I went to the file cabinet in my office where we store the logs for September YR-3. I can vouch that this is the log I took out of the file for that date.
P	Your Honor, I now offer plaintiff's exhibit number nine for identification into evidence as plaintiff's exhibit number nine.
J	Any objection?
O	None, Your Honor.
J	Very well, the exhibit will be received as plaintiff's exhibit number nine.
P	Ms. Carlton, I'd like to take a look at the third entry on the second page of the log.
W	Yes.
P	According to that entry, WHAT message did your server handle on September 12, YR-3?
W	According to that entry, we routed a September 12 message from the computer used by one of Intel's employees, a person named Jerome Mishkin. The entry is "jeromemishkin@ccm.jf.intel.com."
P	According to your log, WHO was the intended recipient of that message?
W	The log says that the recipient's e-mail address was "sdlangford@ucdavis.edu."

It is true that neither Carlton nor any other Organization Mail employee read the content of the e-mail message handled by her company. However, cumulatively the stipulation and Langford's and Carlton's testimony support a permissive inference that the message Langford received on September 12, YR-3 (reflected in exhibit 9) originated from Mishkin, Intel's employee. Based on the stipulation and the testimony, the plaintiff can now successfully introduce exhibit number eight. The information in a heading can be faked, but the possibility of fabrication goes to the weight of the evidence rather than its admissibility.

[iii] TESTIMONY ABOUT A DIGITAL SIGNATURE

This alternative sample foundation is annotated to the previous list of elements for a digital signature foundation. To lay the foundation, the proponent of the e-mail message would initially call an expert to educate the judge and jury about certificates and digital signatures:

P   WHAT is your name? Please state your full name and spell your last name for the record.

W   Gina Martinez. My surname is spelled M-A-R-T-I-N-E-Z.

P   Ms. Martinez, WHAT is your current address?

W   4502 Shenandoah Place here in El Dorado.

P   WHERE do you work?

W   I'm on the faculty of El Dorado State University.

P   WHAT do you teach?

W   Computer science. I'm the assistant chair of that department.

P   WHAT, if any, specialties do you have?

W   My specialty has been electronic commerce.

P   WHAT does that specialty involve?

W   I study the way in which computers are used to conduct commerce, including the way messages are authenticated.

P   WHAT do you mean by "the way messages are authenticated"?

W   Suppose that you are a seller. You receive a message that purports to come from a potential buyer. Before you rely on that message and ship goods, you want to be sure that the message really came from that person. You could be shipping the goods to an imposter, and you might not get your money. In short, you have to "authenticate" the message—in other words, you have to establish that that person was really the individual who sent the message. If that person cannot prove his or her identity to your satisfaction, you're not going to supply them with goods or services.

P   HOW can you do that?

W   There are several ways, but the one I've studied most intensively is the use of digital signatures.

P   HOW is a digital signature used to authenticate an electronic message?

W   It's a complicated process involving several parties.

P   WHICH parties?

W   There are basically three—you have a certifying authority, a sender, and a recipient.

P   Your Honor, I request that this be marked plaintiff's exhibit number one for identification.

J   It will be so marked.

P   Your Honor, I request that the record reflect that I am showing the exhibit to the opposing counsel.

J   The record will so reflect.

P   Permission to approach the witness?

J   Granted.

P   Ms. Martinez, I now hand you what has been marked as plaintiff's exhibit number one for identification. WHAT is it?

Fig. 4-2

W   It's a simple chart depicting the relationship among a certifying authority, the sender of a message, and the recipient of a message. Using the chart will help me explain the process.

P   All right. I notice that this chart three times uses the expression, "public key," and twice uses the expression, "private key." WHAT do those expressions mean?

W   The basic problem is this. You're in business in the market place; and when you send messages to other businesses such as orders for supplies, you want them to believe that you're really the sender. Again, if they can't trust those messages when you send them, you can't do business with them. You have to be able to provide these other businesses with proof that you are who you say you are in your messages—you are in fact ABC Software at 123 Adams Street in San Francisco. If you can't prove that to them, they're not going to respond to your messages and give you the goods and services you need. Pardon my pun, but the key to understanding how you prove your identity to other businesses is key cryptography.

P   I think we can excuse the pun, but please explain WHAT you mean by "key cryptography."

W   "Cryptography" is a term which used to be associated only with military codes. One military unit would use code or cryptography to send a message to another military unit. The first platoon on the west side of the hill uses the code to send a message to the second platoon on the east side. Today cryptography is used extensively by civilians, especially businesses. In most cases key cryptography involves the use of a public and a private key. One key is public; you make it available to everyone. The other key is private or secret. The relationship between the two keys has special properties or characteristics. Special software programs create the keys. The two keys are created by a single process and have a complementary property.

P   WHAT do you mean by the expression, "a complementary property"?

W   The complementary characteristic is that each unlocks the code that the other key makes. The two keys match up. If I have a private key and I send you a message encoded with my private key, there's only one way you can open and read my message—you have to have my public key. That's the sense in which they complement each other.

P   You just mentioned this businessperson "creating" a public and a private key. HOW does someone get these keys?

W   There are commercially available software programs specially designed to create these keys. You buy the program, and the program will create for you a public key and a complementary private key. The programs use algorithms to create the keys.

P   Professor, I vaguely recall the term, "algorithm," from high school. However, could you refresh my memory as to WHAT that term means?

W   Sure. Simply stated, it's a type of mathematical concept or formula. The software uses this formula to generate a long number—which probabilistically and for all practical purposes is unique—and it programs that number into both the public and the private key. When someone attempts to use the public key to open a message coded with the private key, the private key recognizes the number, opens, and allows you to read it. But if you don't have the right public key, there's no way to open the message without destroying it.

P   But couldn't someone just get a person's public key, figure out what the number is, and then open messages coded with the private key?

W   No.

P   WHY not?

W   As I said, there's a very special relationship between the public and private keys. This works only one way. There's no way to just extract the number from the public key. You can use the public key to open messages coded with the private key; but even if you know someone's public key, you can't determine what number the public and private key share. Again, that sort of key cryptography is the key to understanding this process.

P   Now let's take the parties one by one. Let's start in the middle of the chart by talking about a certifying authority or CA. To begin with, WHY is that person in the middle of the chart? (1)

W   The chart shows the CA positioned between the sender and the recipient. They allow the sender and the recipient to communicate with confidence. In a sense, the CA intervenes between the two and serves as an intermediary, enabling the recipient to trust the messages the sender sends the recipient. Again, in the market the basic problem facing a businessperson is to get the recipient to trust his or her messages. If the recipient can't trust the messages, they won't do business with the sender. The CA or certifying authority enables the recipient to trust the sender's message.

P   WHAT does the term "certifying authority" mean? (1)

W   A certifying authority is a company which is in the business of certifying or attesting to the identity of holders or owners of public keys.

P   Again, WHAT do you mean by a public key? (2)

W   This is the core concept, so it probably bears repeating. During a war, each combatant uses cryptography or codes to "encrypt" or scramble important messages. Today businesses also use cryptography to protect their messages. The public key is part of a technique—the public key/private key technique—used in modern cryptography. The public and private keys are complementary; each unlocks the codes which the other key makes. The key owner makes one key publicly available and keeps the other key secret. The first key is the public one, and the second is the private key. The owner can use the private key to send messages which could be sent only by that person. Messages coded with that person's private key can be decoded only by using that person's public key. Therefore, the fact that the recipient can successfully open the message by employing that public key helps identify the key owner as the sender. Certifying authorities establish that a particular person owns a certain public key and issue certificates to that effect.

P   HOW can someone trust the certificate and know that the certificate actually came from the certifying authority?

W   You can trust it because of the way the certifying authority generates and issues the certificate.

P   Specifically, HOW does the certifying authority do that?

W   Well, the certifying authority or CA itself has a public and private key.

P	Again, WHY do you call it a public key? (2)
W	It's accessible to the public.
P	HOW does the CA make it accessible to the public? (3)
W	There are a number of ways it can be done. For example, a bank might include the key in the bank statements it sends out. Alternatively, a CA can publish the public key at its World Wide Web site available to anyone with Internet access.
P	HOW does the process of certification begin? (4)
W	The CA receives a request from someone who wants to send messages. We'll call them Sender. Sender requests that CA issue a certificate to the effect that Sender owns or holds a certain public key.
	(The request is an imperative sentence and, hence, nonhearsay under Federal Rule of Evidence 801(a).)
P	WHAT does CA do after receiving the request? (5)
W	The CA requests certain proof of identity from Sender.
	(Like the sender's request, the CA's request is nonhearsay under Rule 801(a).)
P	WHAT happens next? (6)
W	If Sender supplies the requested proof of identity, CA generates a certificate that Sender owns that key.
	(Since the CA is in the business of issuing such certificates, the certificate qualifies as a business entry under Federal Rule of Evidence 803(6). The CA does not accept the sender's representation as to sender's identity at face value. Rather, CA demands independent proof of identity. The CA's inquiry arguably satisfies the requirement for personal knowledge under Rule 803(6).)
P	WHAT does CA do next? (7)
W	CA digitally signs its certificate. As the chart shows, at the end of this part of the process CA generates and issues a digitally signed certificate.
P	WHAT do you mean by the expression, "CA digitally signs its certificate"? (7)
W	CA uses a hash function to produce the digital signature.
P	WHAT does "a hash function" do? (7)
W	It takes the text of its certificate as an input and uses it to produce a hash number.
P	WHAT do you mean by "hash number"? (7)
W	For instance, it might convert the wording of the certificate into a 500 digital number that is probabilistically unique.

P	WHAT do you mean by "probabilistically" unique? (7)
W	The number could include 500 digits. It's possible—in the same sense that virtually anything is possible—that just by chance that someone could come up with the same number. But when you're talking about a 500-digit number, the odds against that are absolutely astronomical. For all practical purposes, the number is unique to that message. If you have software using that hash function, you can convert the text of the certificate into that number; but if the text were changed in even the slightest—one letter in one word or even a comma—you'd come up with a different hash number. That's the way you generate the digital signature for the certificate.
P	WHAT does the CA do with this digital signature? (7)
W	It uses its own private key to encrypt the digital signature.
P	WHAT does the CA do with its certificate and the digital signature? (8)
W	It can do one of several things. It could publish the certificate on its World Wide Web site. Or it could contract with Sender to honor any requests from third parties for the certificate. Or it might give the certificate to Sender.
P	We've been talking about the role of the first person, the certifying authority. Now let's shift and talk in more detail about the second person shown on the left hand side of the chart, Sender.
W	Sure. This is the businessperson who needs to convince the recipient that the sender really is ABC Software on Adams Street in San Francisco. Sender needs to prove his or her identity to potential suppliers and customers.
P	WHAT does the Sender do after the CA generates its certificate with the digital signature? (9)
W	As I said at the outset, Sender will want to engage in some business transaction. So just as CA generated a certificate, Sender generates a message—perhaps an offer to buy some goods.
P	WHAT does Sender do with the message? (10)
W	Before sending it, Sender will digitally sign its message just as CA digitally signed its certificate. As the chart indicates, while CA generates and issues a digitally signed certificate, Sender is going to generate and send out a digitally signed message.
P	HOW does Sender digitally sign the message? (10)
W	In roughly the same way as CA digitally signs its certificate. Again, Sender uses a hash to produce a hash function. The hash function uses the text of Sender's message as an input and yields a hash number.
P	WHAT does Sender do next? (10)

W	There's another parallel to what the certifying authority does. As I said, the CA uses its private key to encrypt the digital signature on its certificate. For his or her part, Sender uses its private key to encrypt the digital signature on the message.
P	WHAT does Sender do next? (10)
W	Well, we call this person Sender because they send both their message and the digital signature to the third party, Recipient.
P	WHAT else, if anything, would Sender provide to Recipient? (10)
W	Sender might send Recipient the certificate from CA. Or, as I testified previously, Recipient could find the certificate on CA's World Wide Web site. Alternatively, CA might furnish the certificate in response to a specific request by Recipient.
P	Finally, let's consider the role of the third part shown on the right hand side of the chart, Recipient in this transaction. WHO is this person?
W	On the chart I've called that person the Recipient. In the business world, this is the person whom Sender has to convince of Sender's identity. For example, Recipient could be the supplier of goods or services that Sender needs to keep his or her business going. If Recipient doesn't trust the messages Sender sends, Sender can't do business.
P	WHAT does Recipient do after getting CA's certificate? (11), (15)
W	To begin with, as the chart shows, if it has any sense, the Recipient will check CA's CRL.
P	WHAT is a "CRL"? (15)
W	That's CA's certificate revocation list. In a CRL, a CA lists any of its certificates that have expired or been compromised.
	(*Since the CRL is prepared in the regular course of CA's business, the entries on the CRL also qualify as business entries under Federal Rule of Evidence 803(6).*)
P	WHAT do you mean by "compromised"? (15)
W	If CA learns that some third party has learned Sender's private key, the public key is compromised. Some impostor could then use the private key. If CA learns that the private key has been compromised, the CA should immediately announce that you can no longer rely on the certificate. The certificate stated that Sender owned that public key—and implied that Sender was the only one who knew the corresponding private key. If that's no longer true, CA will include the certificate on the CRL.
P	WHAT happens if Recipient checks the list and the certificate in question is not on the list? (15)
W	Recipient should then conclude that the certificate is still good. If the

certificate is good, Recipient has reason to conclude that Sender is still the owner and holder of that public key.

P   If Recipient reaches that conclusion, WHAT does Recipient do next? (12)

W   Recipient will use CA's public key to decrypt the digital signature on CA's certificate.

P   WHAT happens when Recipient does that? (13)

W   The decryption reveals the hash number for CA's certificate.

P   WHAT does Recipient do after it learns the hash number for the certificate? (13)

W   Using compatible software, Recipient independently hashes the text of CA's certificate.

P   WHAT happens when Recipient does that? (13)

W   Recipient gets another hash number. If the two hash numbers match, Recipient will conclude that CA's certificate is authentic. No one has tampered with the text of the certificate. Again, if you changed the text in any way, in all probability you'd get two different numbers.

P   WHAT does Recipient do if Recipient concludes that the CA's certificate is valid? (14)

W   Remember that the certificate states that Sender owns a certain public key. Recipient will next use that public key to decrypt the digital signature appended to Sender's message.

P   WHAT happens when Recipient does that? (14)

W   The decryption reveals the hash number for the message.

P   WHAT does Recipient do next? (14)

W   Just as Recipient independently hashed the text of CA's certificate, Recipient does the same thing to the wording of Sender's message.

P   WHAT happens when Recipient does that? (14)

W   You get another hash number. If the two numbers match, now Recipient can conclude that no one has tampered with the text of the message. If no one has tampered with the text of Sender's message and CA's certificate establishes that Sender holds that public key, Recipient will conclude that he or she has an authentic message from Sender. If that message is a purchase order for a certain number of goods, now Recipient can rely on the order and get ready to ship to Sender.

After the first expert has taught the judge and jury about the technology, the proponent calls a second witness to explain how the technology was used in the instant case.

P   WHAT is your name? Please state your full name and spell your last

	name for the record.
W	Jane Stevick. My last name is spelled S-T-E-V-I-C-K.
P	WHAT is your current address?
W	440 West Point Court in Morena.
P	WHERE do you work?
W	I work for the plaintiff, Furnish Company.
P	WHAT do you do for Furnish Company?
W	I'm in charge of monitoring all the messages we receive and send through the Internet. We conduct a large percentage of our business that way.
P	WHERE were you on the morning of January 13, YR-3?
W	I was at work.
P	WHAT were you doing?
W	I was in my office monitoring our Internet communications.
P	WHAT, if anything, happened at roughly 10:00 a.m. that morning?
W	We received a communication.
P	WHAT was in the communication? (10)
W	It consisted of two things—first an unencrypted message with an associated digital signature and secondly a certificate with a digital signature.
P	Your Honor, I request that these be marked as plaintiff's exhibits number two and three for identification.
J	They will be so marked.
P	Your Honor, please let the record reflect that I am showing the exhibits to the opposing counsel.
J	The record will so reflect.
P	Your Honor, may I have permission to approach the witness?
J	Yes.
P	Ms. Stevick, I now hand you what have been marked as plaintiff's exhibits numbers two and three for identification. WHAT are they? (10)
W	Two is the printout of the certificate, and three is the printout of the accompanying message.
P	HOW do you recognize them? (10)
W	They have distinctive contents. I've never seen any other message or certificate with the same appearance.

(This testimony suffices to satisfy Federal Rule of Evidence 901(b)(4).)

P	WHOM did the message, exhibit number three for identification, purport to come from? (10)
W	Martinez Construction.
P	WHOM did the certificate, exhibit number two for identification, purport to come from? (10)
W	Cyberspace Certification.
P	Now, Ms. Stevick, let me first ask you some questions about exhibit number two for identification, the certificate purportedly from Cyberspace. WHAT did you do after you received this certificate? (11)
W	I contacted Cyberspace.
P	HOW did you do that? (11)
W	I went to their Website.
P	HOW did you know the address of their Website? (11)
W	We've dealt with them on numerous prior occasions. Many of our customers use Cyberspace as the certifying authority. I have their address in my personal directory of Website addresses.
P	WHY did you go to Cyberspace's Website? (15)
W	I wanted to check their certificate revocation list or CRL.
P	WHY did you want to check the list? (15)
W	I wanted to see if their certificate for Martinez Construction was listed as having expired or been compromised.
P	WHAT did you learn when you checked the list? (15)
W	That certificate was not on the list. So I figured that the certificate in question was still good and in effect.
P	After learning that, WHAT did you do? (12)
W	I used Cyberspace Certificate's public key to decrypt the digital signature appended to the CA's certificate.
P	HOW did you learn their public key? (12)
W	As I said, we've dealt with them on numerous prior occasions. I also have that in my office records.
P	WHAT happened when you used their public key to decrypt the signature? (13)
W	It yielded a hash number.
P	WHAT did you do next? (13)
W	I independently hashed the text of the certificate.
P	WHAT happened when you did that? (13)
W	Again, I got a hash number.

P	HOW did the two numbers compare? (13)
W	They were identical.
P	So at that point, WHAT did you conclude? (13)
W	That exhibit number two for identification was the real McCoy, a genuine certificate from Cyberspace Certification.
P	Your Honor, I request that plaintiff's exhibit number two for identification be accepted into evidence as plaintiff's exhibit number two.
J	It will be received.
P	WHAT, if anything, did exhibit number two, the certificate, state? (14)
W	It identified Martinez Construction as the holder of a certain public key.
P	I've asked you some questions about what you did with exhibit number two, the certificate which purported to come from Cyberspace Certification. Now I'd like to shift topics and ask you some questions about what you did with exhibit number three for identification, the message that purported to come from Martinez Corporation. After you read Cyberspace's certificate, WHAT did you do? (15)
W	I used that public key—the public key for Martinez Construction—to decrypt the digital signature associated with the message.
P	WHICH message? (14)
W	The one that said that it came from Martinez Construction.
P	WHAT happened when you used that public key to do that? (14)
W	I got a hash number.
P	WHAT did you do next? (14)
W	I independently hashed the text of the message that purported to come from Martinez Construction.
P	WHAT happened when you did that? (14)
W	I got another hash number.
P	HOW did the two numbers compare? (14)
W	They were identical.
P	At that point, WHAT did you conclude? (14)
W	That the message had in fact come from Martinez Construction.
P	Your Honor, I now request that plaintiff's exhibit marked number three for identification be accepted into evidence as plaintiff's exhibit number three.
J	It will be received.
P	Ms. Stevick, I'd now like you to read plaintiff's exhibit number three to the jury.

[5] SCANNED WRITINGS

Section [3] pointed out that at one time, a business would routinely FAX documents to another company. Section [4] then noted that e-mail (electronic mail) overtook FAX as the most popular means of communication between businesses. However, it was to be expected that the technology would continue to improve. Today if a business wants to send information to another company or a government agency, in many cases it will neither FAX the writing nor set out all the information in the body of an e-mail message and send that message to the addressee. Rather, the business frequently scans[22] the document to convert it to an electronic file and sends the file as an attachment to an e-mail message. Doing so not only simplifies communication with the addressee. It also makes it easier for the recipient to circulate the information internally; the recipient can either place the attachment on a computer drive accessible to its employees or attach the file to an e-mail within its network.

Of course, the best practice is to check the electronic file against the original document that was scanned. If someone does that after scanning the document and before transmitting the file, the authentication of a printout from the file will be a simple matter. The person who compared the original document with the content of the electronic file has personal knowledge that the file is an accurate version of the original document. That person can provide authenticating testimony under Federal Rule 901(b)(1).

However, in some cases the person does not have the time to make the comparison before E-mailing the file to the recipient. Business transactions are sometimes hurried. In that event, the proponent will need to lay a different, more elaborate foundation. The foundation should include the following elements:

1. Scanning technology is reliable. Scanning has been in use for so many years now that the general reliability of the technology is now judicially noticeable under Rule 201(b).

2. The scanner used in the instant case is reliable. At one time flatbed scanners were popular. The scanner was a separate device which could be connected to a computer. The device sent the electronic file to the computer; and the computer user could either place the file on the computer's hard drive, send the file as an attachment to an E-mail message, or do both. Many businesses now have larger devices with multiple capabilities, including copying, FAXing, and scanning. It is ideal if the proponent calls a representative of the machine's manufacturer to explain the features that ensure the trustworthiness of the scanner. However, as previously stated, today scanning is in widespread use. Consequently, many judges will accept testimony from an employee of the sending company that the company has successfully used the scanner for a substantial period of time.

---

[22] A digital scanner divides each page into a grid of millions of picture elements or pixels. The scanner automatically measures the reflectivity of the pixels in dots. In turn, the dots are converted into a stream of bits (zeros and ones) that collectively represent a bit map. The bit map is an image of the original page.

3. On the occasion in question, the employee followed the proper procedure for scanning the document to produce an electronic file.

4. After the document was scanned, the employee input the e-mail address of the intended recipient and directed the machine to send the electronic file to the recipient.

5. On the occasion in question, the employee did not notice any indication that the machine was malfunctioning.

In the hypothetical fact situation, a company that purchased real estate from another business has sued the latter business for fraud. The plaintiff company alleges that the defendant did not disclose the existence of a subsoil condition that substantially reduces the fair market value of the property. In its answer, the defendant business alleges that the week before the parties signed the contract of sale, the defendant scanned and e-mailed to the plaintiff a soil expert's report disclosing the condition and describing it in detail. The defense has begun its case-in-chief. The defense witness is Ms. Chandler, the defendant's vice-president who hired the soil expert and claims to have sent the expert's report to the plaintiff. Earlier in her testimony she described the report; and based on Ms. Chandler's testimony, the defense attorney introduced the report as defense exhibit D. The direct examination continues.

P	After you received the report, exhibit D, from the soil expert on Monday, January 9th, WHAT did you do with it?
W	First, I shared it with our president. Then I sent it to the plaintiff's office.
P	HOW did you do that? (1)
W	I scanned the report to create an electronic file including the report and e-mailed it to the plaintiff.
P	WHAT equipment did you use? (2)
W	In our suite of offices at headquarters, we have a Xerox ColorQube 9300 in the work room.
P	WHAT does the ColorQube 9300 do? (2)
W	It has several capabilities. Years ago we had a separate small scanner, but now scanning is simply built in as one of the capabilities of the much larger 9300. The machine can copy, FAX, and scan.
P	HOW long has your business used the ColorQube? (2)
W	For several years now.
P	HOW reliable is the scanner in the ColorQube? (2)
W	Very.
P	HOW do you know that? (2)
W	I've often used it to generate electronic files, and it usually produces files with great, accurate copies.
P	Please be more specific. HOW do you know that it produces accurate copies? (2)

W　　　In many cases, I scanned the document and sent it to myself so that I could check it before circulating it internally or sending it out. On numerous occasions I've checked the original document against the file or printout of the electronic file, and in the overwhelming majority of cases the printout was a perfect copy.

P　　　You said in the "majority" of cases. WHEN did the machine fail to produce an accurate copy? (2)

W　　　It depends on the physical characteristics of the document you're scanning. If you have a messy document, you're going to get a messy file. Sometimes the original isn't very clear, or the words and numbers might be very close together on the page. When that happens, on very rare occasions there have been mistakes in scanning. However, if you properly place the document on the scanner bed, most of the time you get a very accurate copy.

P　　　Now I'd like to direct your attention to the afternoon of Monday, January 9th. WHERE were you at approximately 1:30 p.m.? (3)

W　　　I had just left the president's office. I went to the work room where we have the ColorQube 9300.

P　　　WHAT did you do after you entered the room? (3)

W　　　I used the machine to scan and send the soil report to the plaintiff.

P　　　WHAT procedure did you use? (3)

W　　　I followed the regular procedures. I've personally done it tens of times. It's so simple that in many cases I don't bother my administrative assistant. It's often faster just to do it myself.

P　　　Could you please describe those procedures for the jury? (3)

W　　　Sure. As I said before, the machine has several capabilities. The first screen you see on the top of the machine asks you to select a function or capability. So I selected the scanning icon. Then you get another screen with more options.

P　　　WHAT are those options? (3)

W　　　There are several. I guess the ones that are relevant here are either scanning for internal distribution or scanning in order to directly e-mail. I can directly e-mail to myself or send it to someone outside the business.

P　　　WHICH one did you choose? (3)

W　　　Since I was in sort of a rush and wanted to get the report to the plaintiff as soon as possible, I chose the option to scan for immediate e-mailing outside our company.

P　　　After you selected that option, WHAT happened? (4)

W　　　Well, I placed the report in the ColorQube's feeder. At this point, the machine asks you to input the e-mail address of the intended recipient.

P   WHOSE address did you input? (4)

W   The company e-mail address of the plaintiff's vice-president, Mr. Bermudez. He'd been handling their end of the negotiations over the real estate deal.

P   HOW did you know that that is his e-mail address? (4)

W   The negotiations over the sale of the property lasted almost five months. During the course of the negotiations, I've communicated with him several times by both e-mail and telephone. I'd scan a document and send it to him, and then we'd have a follow-up phone conversation. You could say that we were always on the same page. In other words, it became clear during each conversation that he was looking at exactly the same language or data that I had; the scanner had successfully sent him an exact copy of whatever document I had in my hands.

P   WHAT did you do after entering Mr. Bermudez' e-mail address? (4)

W   I pushed start.

P   WHAT did the machine do then? (4)

W   The feeder automatically pulled the two pages of the report into the machine, and I assume that it then properly scanned the report and sent it.

P   Ms. Chandler, FAX machines sometimes printout a confirmation or transmission report. HOW, if at all, does the ColorQube let you know whether the transmission has been successful? (4)

W   It doesn't printout a confirmation. However, after saying "Processing," the touchscreen says "Completed" when the transmission is successful. But again, there's no printout.

P   WHEN you used the ColorQube on January 9th, WHAT, if any, indication was that there the scanner didn't work properly? (5)

W   None. I didn't get any error message or, for that matter, any other sign that there was a problem.

P   Looking for a moment at exhibit D, HOW clear is the wording on the page? (5)

W   The quality's quite good. There are no ink smudges or blurs.

P   And, again looking at exhibit D, HOW close together are the letters and numbers on each page of the report? (5)

W   You can see for yourself. The soil expert even double spaced the report. I'm not an IT expert; but in my experience, when the spacing is that wide, the scanner almost always does its job and sends the recipient a pretty much perfect copy of the scanned document. Consequently, the plaintiff should have received an accurate copy of exhibit D.

[6] INFORMATION POSTED AT A BUSINESS WEB SITE

E-commerce has become one of the most important types of business activity. In order to participate in E-commerce, many businesses have established websites that customers can visit. The information posted at these sites can become relevant as evidence in litigation. In some cases, at trial the proponent may want to use assertions posted at a web site as substantive evidence and will hence need to lay a foundation for a hearsay exemption or exception. In other cases, though, the proponent can put the assertion to a nonhearsay use under Rule 801(c)(2). For example, in a suit for breach of warranty, the plaintiff customer might want to prove that in purchasing the defendant manufacturer's goods, the customer relied on an assurance posted on the defendant's web site. In that situation, the assurance would be admissible as nonhearsay, since it would be a verbal act; the assurance is the warranty. Or in a trade libel case, a plaintiff competitor might allege that an assertion posted on the defendant's web site defamed the plaintiff's product. Here again the assertion would be admissible as a nonhearsay verbal act; in this hypothetical trade libel action, the last thing the plaintiff wants to prove is the truth of the assertion defaming its product. Truth is a defense to liability for libel, and the plaintiff would be proving itself out of court.

Whatever the hearsay status of the proposed testimony about the information posted at the web site, in most cases the proponent must authenticate the information as posted on the business' site and emanating from the business. On the one hand, in the early cases some courts were quite skeptical about proffers of testimony about web site data:

> While some look to the Internet as an innovative vehicle for communication, the Court continues to warily . . . view it largely as one catalyst for rumor, innuendo, and misinformation . . . . Anyone can put anything on the Internet. No web-site is monitored for accuracy and nothing contained therein is under oath or even subject to independent verification absent underlying documentation. Moreover, the Court holds no illusions that hackers can adulterate the content of any web-site from any location at any time.

St. Clair v. Johnny's Oyster & Shrimp, Inc., 76 F. Supp. 2d 773, 774–75 (S.D. Tex. 1999). On the other hand, in the final analysis, like the other questions discussed in this chapter, this authentication issue is governed by the lax conditional relevance standard codified in Federal Rules of Evidence 104(b) and 901(a). The courts treat the problem of authenticating web site postings in roughly the same manner as they approach social media postings.

To authenticate testimony describing information allegedly posted at a web site, the proponent can lay the following foundation:

1. The Internet exists and is an effective medium for electronic communication. This proposition is so well known that it qualifies for judicial notice under Federal Rule of Evidence 201(b).

2. In the Internet, a person or entity can establish a web site that other persons can visit. This proposition is also so well established that it is judicially noticeable.

3. A certain person or entity operates a web site with a particular universal

resource locator (URL) address, usually prefaced with "www." If the site purports to be operated by a government entity, the documents posted there are arguably self-authenticating under Federal Rule of Evidence 902(5).[23] Likewise, if a site includes a company's "inscription" or "label," the self-authentication provision of Rule 902(7) might come into play. If the court demands extrinsic proof of the identity of the operator of the site and the alleged operator is the opposing litigant, an out-of-court statement or admission would be sufficient authentication. Moreover, circumstantial evidence will suffice. If only that person or entity is likely to possess the information posted at the site, that fact can establish the identity of the site's operator. Or if persons have visited that site, ordered merchandise from a particular company, and later received merchandise from that company, that course of conduct identifies the operator of the site.

4.   At a certain time, someone visited the web site.

5.   When they visited the site, they found certain information posted there. There are several methods of proving that the information was posted there. To begin with, the proponent could call the web master responsible for maintaining the site. If he or she recalled the posting of the information, he or she could testify to that from personal knowledge under Rule 602. Alternatively, if the web master maintained records of postings, the records would qualify as business records under Rule 803(6). (The records would have to be those of the web master rather than the Internet service provider.) The person who visited the site could also testify from firsthand knowledge if at trial he or she remembered the contents of the posting the person found at the site. Better still, if the person printed out the information, he or she could authenticate the printout as an accurate copy of the data he or she read at the site at that time.

6.   The information in question is attributable to the business. This element is similar to the problem that arises when the proponent attempts to attribute a social media posting to a particular person. In large part, the propriety of the attribution depends on the part of the web site where the information was posted. Some web sites feature chat rooms which third parties can visit and in which they can post messages. Without a manifestation of adoption by the business, a chat room posting cannot be imputed to the business. However, if the information appears in a part of the site purportedly maintained by the business itself, the information can be attributed to the business.[24]

The fact situation is a breach of warranty action. The Dothee Corporation alleges that: It purchased tires from the Carpeneti Corporation; in so doing, it relied on a

---

[23] Elliott Assocs., L.P. v. Banco de la Nacion, 194 F.R.D. 116, 121 (S.D.N.Y. 2000) (prime rates published on Federal Reserve Board web site); Sannes v. Jeff Wyler Chevrolet, Inc., 107 Ohio Misc. 2d 6, 736 N.E.2d 112 (1999) (FTC press releases printed from FTC's world wide web page).

[24] Gregory P. Joseph, MODERN VISUAL EVIDENCE § 15.02[1][a] (rev. 2016) (if the information appears in a part of the site where the postings are ordinarily made by the owner of the site, there should be a presumption that information appearing there was posted by the owner).

representation about the quality of the tires posted on the Carpeneti Corporation's web site; and the tires the defendant delivered did not live up to the representation. The witness is Ms. Stewart, the head of Dothee Corporation's Purchasing Department.

P WHAT is your name?

W Donarae Stewart.

P WHERE do you live?

W Right here in Sacramento.

P WHERE do you work?

W I've worked for Dothee Corporation for the past 15 years. We retail car supplies.

P WHAT are your job duties?

W I'm the head of our purchasing department. I'm responsible for ordering all the supplies from manufacturers and wholesalers.

P WHAT contact, if any, have you had with Carpeneti Corporation?

W They're one of our regular suppliers.

P WHAT do they supply you with?

W Primarily tires.

P When you want to contact Carpeneti Corporation, HOW do you reach them?

W In the old days, I used to phone them. However, for the past three years they've maintained a web site; and I ordinarily deal with them by visiting their site.

P WHAT is the address of their web site? (3)

W The address is "www.Carpenetitires.com."

P HOW do you know that? (3)

W As I testified a few moments ago, I've been dealing with them through their web site for the past three years. On numerous occasions I've ordered goods from them over the site and later received both their merchandise and their bills.

P HOW do you know it was their merchandise? (3)

W All the tires arrived in boxes with Carpeneti labels, and the tires themselves bore the company inscription.

(Under Federal Rule of Evidence 902(7), "[a]n inscription, sign, tab, or label purporting to have been affixed in the course of business and indicating origin, ownership, or control" is self-authenticating.)

P All right. WHAT contact, if any, did you have with Carpeneti Corporation on September 19, YR-3? (4)

W	My boss, Ms. Clark, told me to place an order for 500 tires for large pickup trucks, and I decided to order the tires from Carpeneti. Consequently, I visited the Carpeneti web site.
P	HOW did you do that? (4)
W	As usual, I just logged on to my computer, went to the Internet, and typed in the address of the Carpeneti site.
P	WHAT happened after you did that? (4)
W	Everything worked fine, and in a matter of moments I was at the site.
P	WHAT did you do after you reached the site? (5)
W	I went to their product list, particularly their tires suitable for large pickups.
P	HOW many parts of the web site are there? (6)
W	There are a number of parts. There's even a chat room where customers can exchange views or submit questions to company representatives. Then there are all the sections maintained by the Carpeneti Corporation itself, including the listing and description of products.
P	WHICH part of the web site did you go to? (6)
W	Well, I wasn't in a chatty mood. So I went straight to the listing and description of pickup truck tires.
P	HOW can you as a customer post anything there? (6)
W	Simply stated, you can't. You can post messages in the chat room, but in the part I visited all you can do is read the information the company has posted and print out what's posted.
P	When you went to that part of the web site, WHAT, if anything, did you find? (5)
W	I found a description of several types of pickup truck tires, including one that I was particularly interested in.
P	WHY were you particularly interested in that description? (5)
W	The description indicated that that particular model of tire was especially suitable for use by large pickups that go off road. We have a lot of customers who have that type of vehicle.
P	WHAT did you do when you came up upon that description? (5)
W	To begin with, I read it very carefully to make certain that the specifications would meet our needs.
P	WHAT else, if anything, did you do? (5)
W	I was confident that the boss, Ms. Clark, would be very interested in that model tire. However, since it was a little more expensive than the other models, I wanted her to make the final decision whether to order that

model. Consequently, I printed out the description from the web site.

P Your Honor, I request that this be marked as plaintiff's exhibit number three for identification. (5)

J It will be so marked.

P Your Honor, please let the record reflect that I am showing the exhibit to opposing counsel. (5)

J It will so reflect.

P Permission to approach the witness? (5)

J Granted.

P Ms. Stewart, I now hand you what has been marked as plaintiff's exhibit number three for identification. WHAT is it? (5)

W It's the printout of the description of that tire.

P HOW can you recognize the exhibit? (5)

W First, I remember the contents. They're pretty distinctive. The unique qualities of the tire are what caught my attention. In addition, immediately after printing it out and before showing it to Ms. Clark, I placed my initials and the date in the upper, right hand corner. They're still there. That's why I can recognize the printout so easily.

P Your Honor, I now offer plaintiff's exhibit number three for identification into evidence as plaintiff's exhibit number three.

J Any objection?

O No, Your Honor.

J In that event, the exhibit will be received.

P Ms. Stewart, I'm handing you plaintiff's exhibit number three. With Your Honor's permission, I'd like you to read the second full paragraph of the printout to the ladies and gentlemen of the jury. (5)

W Certainly.

[7] SELF-AUTHENTICATING BUSINESS RECORDS

As § 4.04 of this chapter explains, the courts have long treated copies of official records as self-authenticating so long as they are accompanied by certain types of certificates. Until late 2000, though, the federal courts refused to extend the same treatment to private business records. However, on December 1, 2000, an amendment to Federal Rule of Evidence 902 took effect. Rule 902 lists the types of documents that are considered self-authenticating in federal practice. The amendment added subdivisions (11) and (12) to Rule 902. Subdivision (11) renders self-authenticating

> [t]he original or a copy of a domestic record that meets the requirements of Rule 803(6)(A)–(C), as shown by a certification of the custodian or another qualified person that complies with a federal statute or a rule prescribed the Supreme Court. Before the trial or hearing, the proponent must give an adverse

party reasonable written notice of the intent to offer the record—and must make the record and certification available for inspection—so that the party has a fair opportunity to challenge them.

Subdivision (12) contains a similar provision for foreign business records. When the business record in question falls within either subdivision (11) or (12), at trial the record can be handled in the manner indicated in the next section devoted to official writing.

Under Rule 902(11), the elements of the foundation include:

1. The document purports to be a domestic business record.

2. The document is either an original or a duplicate. Rule 1001(d) defines "original" while Rule 1001(e) sets out a definition of "duplicate." The latter definition is especially broad.

3. A declaration, executed by the custodian of the document or another person familiar with the business' filing system, is attached to the document. 28 U.S.C. § 1746 prescribes the requirements for declarations in federal practice.

4. The declaration states that the document was made at or near the time of the occurrence of the matters set forth by, or from information transmitted by, a person with firsthand knowledge of the matters.

5. The declaration states that the document was kept in the course of the business.

6. The declaration states that it was a regular practice of the business to make that type of document.

The fact situation is a contract case. The plaintiff, a landowner, is suing a general contractor for the losses caused by a delay in completing a construction project. Under the prime contract, the landowner had the responsibility to have certain construction supplies delivered to the site before the general contractor began work. The plaintiff wants to establish that the construction supplies ordered by the landowner were delivered to the site on time. The plaintiff attempts to introduce a copy of the supplier's delivery records, indicating timely delivery.

P	Your Honor, I request that this be marked plaintiff's exhibit number three for identification.
J	It will be so marked.
P	Please let the record reflect that I am showing the exhibit to the opposing counsel.
J	The record will so reflect.
P	I now offer plaintiff's exhibit number three for identification into evidence as plaintiff's exhibit number three.
O	I object on the ground that there was been insufficient authentication. No sponsoring witness has come forward to verify the authenticity of this document.
J	(*To the plaintiff*) What is your response to the objection?
P	Your Honor, live testimony is unnecessary. As you can see, the

document purports to be an exact, Xerox copy (2) of a business record of Jiminez Construction Supply here in town. (2) The copy is accompanied by a declaration satisfying 28 U.S.C. § 1746. (3) The declaration states that: The declarant is the bookkeeper for Jiminez Construction Supply (3); it is that company's regular practice to prepare records of its deliveries (6); the delivery record is prepared by the employee who actually makes the delivery within 24 hours of the delivery (4); and the company maintains these records in the regular course of its business. (5) Thus, the declaration renders the attached copy of Jiminez' delivery records self-authenticating.

J   Objection overruled.

P   Your Honor, at this point I would like to read plaintiff's exhibit number three to the jury.

J   Permission granted.

[8]   SELF-AUTHENTICATING PRINTOUTS OF RECORDS AUTOMATICALLY GENERATED BY AN ELECTRONIC PROCESS OR SYSTEM

On December 1, 2017, the following amendment to Rule 902 took effect:

The following items of evidence are self-authenticating; they require no extrinsic evidence of authenticity in order to be admitted:

(13) Certified Records Generated by an Electronic Process or System. A record generated by an electronic process or system that produces an accurate result, as shown by a certification of a qualified person that complies with the certification requirements of Rule 902(11) or (12). The proponent must also meet the notice requirements of Rule 902(11).

The amendment deals with printouts of a specific category of records—records that have been have maintained of data automatically generated by electronic processes and systems. The records contain data created by the system, not records of reports created by human beings and merely stored on a computer. In the Evidence Advisory Committee's May 7, 2016 report to the Judicial Conference Committee on Rules of Practice and Procedure, the committee provided several examples of permissible uses of Rule 902(13):

- Proving that a USB device was connected or plugged into a particular computer. The issue is whether a person used his or her computer to access files stored on a particular USB thumb drive. The computer uses the Windows operating system. That system includes the Windows registry. The registry automatically records information about every USB device connected to the computer—the date of the connection and the manufacturer, model, and serial number of the connected device.

- Proving that a server was used to connect to a particular webpage. The issue is whether a hacker, who uses a certain IP address, attempted to attack the website. The website server includes an Internet Information Services (IIS) log. That log automatically records information about every internet connection routed to website server in order to view a page on the site. The recorded information includes the IP address attempting to access the page and what was requested from the website.

- Proving that a person was or was not near the scene of an event. The issue is whether the defendant was at the scene of a hit-and-run collision. The defendant has claimed alibi. The police seize the defendant's iPhone. The iPhone contains several photographs. The iPhone's software automatically generates and records metadata about the photographs: the dates, times, and GPS coordinates of each photograph. The date, time, and place of a photograph could corroborate or contradict the alibi.

- Proving association between alleged co-conspirators. The police seize a Samsung Galaxy phone belonging to the defendant, an alleged member of a conspiracy. The phone's software automatically records a log of text messages. The log contains the text content, the date and time of each text, and the number of the other phone involved. On the one hand, the 902(13) amendment itself does not authorize the introduction of the content of the text messages; the messages were created by human beings; and, as we shall discuss in § 4.03[9], the proponent might have to present extrinsic foundational testimony to overcome a hearsay objection to the admission of the content of the messages. On the other hand, the amendment applies to the information in the log that was automatically generated: the date and time of each text and the number of the other phone.

The common denominator in all these examples is that the data was generated and recorded by a reliable automatic system, not by a human declarant. The amendment applies to exhibits that are printouts of that specific type of data.

Drafting the Required Certificate Before Trial

According to the terms of the amendment, the printout is self-authenticating only if it is accompanied by a certain type of certificate. The Evidence Committee Note accompanying the proposed amendment states:

A proponent establishing authenticity under this Rule must present a certification containing information that would be sufficient to establish authenticity were that information provided by a witness at trial. If the certification provides information that would be insufficient to authenticate the record if the certifying person testified, then authenticity is not established under this Rule.

In that light, suppose that the proponent wanted to use a certificate to authenticate the printout of the Windows registry in the first example in the Evidence Advisory Committee's May 7, 2016 report. To render the printout self-authenticating, the certificate should include the following contents:

— The technician who printed out the exhibit identifies himself or herself.

— The technician describes his or her education and professional experience. The technician must set out sufficient credentials to qualify as an expert under

Federal Rule of Evidence 702. The testimony also shows that the technician is "a qualified person" within the meaning of that expression in 902(13).

— On a certain date and place, he or she received a computer. The technician should state the make, model, and serial number of the computer. The technician must link up with the prior links in the chain of custody for the computer in order to satisfy Rules 401 and 901.

— Someone—often the person who delivered the computer to the technician— requested that the technician examine the computer to determine, if possible, whether the computer was connected to a USB device. Since the request is a weak imperative sentence, it is not an assertion. Thus, under Federal Rule 801(a) the request is not hearsay.

— The technician is familiar with the operating system of the type of computer in question. This certification establishes that the technician possesses relevant "technical . . . knowledge" under Federal Rule of Evidence 702(a).

— The computer's operation system automatically generates and records data about any USB device connected to the computer.

— The system for generating and recording the data is accurate. The technician ought to provide sufficient detail about the system to satisfy Federal Rule of Evidence 702(c).

— At a particular date and place, the technician followed the proper procedure for outputting the automatically generated data in the form of a printout. This certification is necessary to satisfy Federal Rule of Evidence 702(d).

— The exhibit attached to the certificate is the printout.

Using the Certificate to Introduce the Printout at Trial

Before attempting to introduce the printout at trial, the proponent should present testimony tracing the chain of custody for the computer from the time of initial seizure to its delivery to the technician. For example, the proponent might call the police officer who seized the computer from the defendant or the defendant's apartment, house, or automobile. The defendant can still dispute whether he or she was the person who connected the computer to the USB device. To establish the relevance or provenance of the printout under Rule 401, to some extent the proponent must connect the defendant to the computer. A Rule 902(13) certificate does not demonstrate the relevance of the exhibit; the solitary, narrow purpose of 902(13) is to establish that the exhibit is an accurate printout of data that was automatically generated and recorded by the computer.

The fact situation is a variation of the first example in the Evidence Advisory Committee's May 7, 2016 report. The exhibit is a printout including such data as the make, model, and serial number of a USB device that was connected to the computer at a particular date and time. Assume that the proponent has already presented the other chain of custody testimony or that exercising discretion under Rule 611(a), the judge has permitted the proponent to introduce the exhibit before the presentation of the chain of custody testimony. The hypothetical continues.

P   Your Honor, I request that this be marked plaintiff's exhibit number three for identification.

J   It will be so marked.

P   Please let the record reflect that I am showing the exhibit to the opposing counsel.

J   The record will so reflect.

P   Your Honor, I now offer plaintiff's number three for identification into evidence as plaintiff's exhibit number three.

O   I object on the ground that there has been insufficient authentication. No sponsoring will has come forward to verify the authenticity of this exhibit.

J   *(To the plaintiff's counsel)* What is your response to the objection?

P   Your Honor, live testimony is unnecessary. As you can see, the document is a printout. The accompanying certificate shows that the data in the printout was accurately and automatically generated and recorded by a computer and that a qualified technician used proper procedure to output the data and create the printout. Under Rule 902(13), this certificate eliminates the need for live testimony. We satisfied Rule 902(13)'s procedural requirement by giving the defense pretrial notice of our intent to present the printout accompanied by this certificate rather than present the technician's live testimony.

J   *(To the defense counsel)* Did the plaintiff's counsel give you pretrial notice?

O   Yes, Your Honor. But I reiterate my authentication objection.

J   Objection overruled.

P   Your Honor, at this point I would like to read the contents of plaintiff's exhibit number three to the jury.

J   Permission granted.

[9] SELF-AUTHENTICATING PRINTOUTS OF DATA COPIES FROM AN ELECTRONIC DEVICE, STORAGE MEDIUM, OR FILE

On December 1, 2017, another amendment to Rule 902 took effect:

The following items of evidence are self-authenticating; they require no extrinsic evidence of authenticity in order to be admitted:

(14) Certified Data Copied from an Electronic Device, Storage Medium, or File. Data copied from an electronic device, storage medium, or file, if authenticated by a process of digital identification, as shown by a certification of a qualified person that complies with the certification requirements of Rule 902(11) or (12). The proponent must also meet the notice requirements of Rule 902(11).

Rule 902(14) is critical in the forensic examination of computer information. Almost all forensic examinations are conducted on copies from the original storage medium, for example, the hard drive of a computer or cell phone. Forensic analysts use copies because, for chain of custody purposes, they need to maintain the original without altering its contents or metadata.

Before going into more detail about 902(14), it is important to distinguish it from two other self-authentication provisions. To begin with, (14) differs fundamentally from (13). As § 4.03[8] explained, (13) is strictly limited to data that have been automatically generated and recorded. There is no human declarant, and the only issue is the reliability of the system for generating and recording the data. In sharp contrast, (14) applies to records of statements made by human declarants such as text messages or chats. Moreover, (14) must be distinguished from (11). We discussed 902(11) in § 4.03[7], dealing with the authentication of business writings. Suppose that Facebook has a copy of a chat on its servers. Why did we need to add 902(14) if Rule 902 already includes a provision, (11), permitting the self-authentication of business records? Facebook does possess certain information about the chat that constitutes Facebook's own business data, e.g., the data and time of the chat; Facebook is in the business of providing a platform for chats. However, the content of the chat itself does not represent a Facebook business record; "Facebook did not verify or rely upon the substance of the chats in the course of its business."[25] Since the chat itself is not Facebook's business data, a 902(11) certification from a Facebook employee would not suffice to authenticate a printout of the chat. The limited scope of 902(11) was one of the reasons for the promulgation of 902(14).

To understand the scope of 902(14), revisit the fourth example discussed in § 4.03[8]. Again, in its May 7, 2016 report, the Advisory Committee hypothesized a case in which the police have seized a Samsung Galaxy phone from a suspected co-conspirator. The phone contains a number of text messages. As § 4.03[8] pointed out, the prosecution could use 902(13) to authenticate the automatically generated metadata about the messages such as the date and time of each message and the number of the other phone involved. However, 902(13) cannot be utilized to authenticate the text messages themselves because they were generated by human beings. Since the prosecution could use neither 902(11) nor 902(13) for that purpose, the prosecution would resort to 902(14).

Under 902(14), how would a technician go about establishing that a copy is accurate? The text of 902(14) refers to "a process of digital identification." The Committee deliberately chose that broad language to permit technicians to capitalize on future advances in digital identification technology. However, today by a wide margin the most popular identification technique is the use of a hash value. § 4.03[4][b] contains a discussion of hash values. The Advisory Committee Note to Rule 902(14) states:

Today, data copied from electronic devices, storage media, and electronic files

---

[25] John M. Haried, *How Two New Rules for Self-Authentication Will Save You Time and Money,* 100 JUDICATURE, Wint. 2016, at 33, 40, citing United States v. Browne, 834 F.3d 403 (3d Cir. 2016).

are ordinarily authenticated by "hash value." A hash value is a number that is often represented by a sequence of characters and is produced by an algorithm based upon the digital contents of a drive, medium, or file. If the hash values for the original and copy are different, then the copy is not identical to the original. If the hash values for the original and copy are the same, it is highly improbable that the original and copy are not identical. Thus, identical values for the original and copy reliably attest to the fact that they are exact duplicates.

Like Rule 902(13), Rule 902(14) serves a limited function. The only thing that a (14) certificate establishes is that the printout is an accurate copy of the contents of the human statement contained on the electronic device, storage medium, or file. By itself, Rule 902(14) does not establish the relevance or provenance of the printout. As in [8], in our hypothetical the proponent would have to establish a chain of custody for the phone. The chain should run from the initial seizure of the phone to its delivery to the technician who executes the certification. The defendant can dispute whether it was his phone and whether he was the person who used the phone to send or receive messages. Moreover, the proffer of the printout will often raise hearsay issues. There are no hearsay issues under 902(13); since that data is automatically generated, there is no human declarant under Rule 801(b). Here, though, all the text messages on the phone were created by human declarants. If the proponent wants to use assertive statements in the messages to prove the truth of the assertions, the proponent will be putting the messages to a hearsay use under Rule 801(c)(2). In the hypothetical, the proponent might have to present extrinsic evidence to invoke the co-conspirator hearsay exemption codified in Rule 801(d)(2)(E).

Drafting the Required Certificate Before Trial

Like the Advisory Committee Note accompanying (13), the Note for (14) states:

A proponent establishing authenticity under this Rule must present a certificate containing information that would be sufficient to establish authenticity were that information provided by a witness at trial. If the certification provides information that would be insufficient to authenticate the record if the certifying person testified, then authenticity is not established under this Rule.

In that light, suppose that the proponent wanted to use a certificate to authenticate the printout of text message found on the defendant's phone. To render the printout self-authenticating, the certificate should include the following contents:

— The technician who printed out the exhibit identifies himself or herself.

— The technician describes his or her education and professional experience. The technician must set out sufficient credentials to qualify as an expert under Federal Rule of Evidence 702. The testimony also shows that the technician is "a qualified person" within the meaning of that expression in 902(14).

— On a certain date and time, he or she received a phone. The technician should state the make, model, and serial number of the phone. The technician must link up with the prior links in the chain of custody for the phone in order to satisfy Rules 401 and 901.

— Someone—often the person who delivered the device to the technician—requested that the technician examine the device to determine, if possible, whether the device contained text messages. Since the request is a weak imperative sentence, it is not an assertion. Thus, under Federal Rule 801(a) the request is not hearsay.

— The technician is familiar with the design of the type of phone in question. This certification establishes that the technician possesses relevant "technical . . . knowledge" under Federal Rule of Evidence 702(a).

— The phone's design permits it to maintain records of text messages sent from or received by the phone.

— When the technician examined the phone in question, he or she discovered text messages recorded on the phone.

— At a particular date and place, the technician used a certain methodology to make a copy of the text messages. The technician should provide sufficient detail about the methodology to satisfy Federal Rule of Evidence 702(c).

— After making the copy, the technician used hashing technology to compare the contents of the original and the copy. Under Rule 201(b)(2), the judge can judicially notice the general reliability of the hashing technique. The technician should state that the particular hashing software that the technician employed is industry standard and that he or she did not encounter any problems when they used the software to make the comparison. This certification is relevant to satisfying Federal Rule of Evidence 702(d).

— The comparison indicated that the contents of the copy were identical to the contents of the original. Simply stated, the hash values matched.

— The technician followed proper procedure in printing out the contents of the copy. This certification is also relevant to satisfying Rule 702(d).

— The exhibit attached to the certificate is the printout.

Using the Certificate to Introduce the Printout at Trial

Before attempting to introduce the printout at trial, the proponent should present testimony tracing the chain of custody for the phone from the time of initial seizure to its delivery to the technician. For example, the proponent might call the police officer who seized the phone from the defendant or the defendant's apartment, house, or automobile. The defendant can still dispute whether the phone is his or whether he was the person who used the phone to send or receive text message. To establish the relevance or provenance of the printout under Rule 401, to some extent the proponent must connect the defendant to the phone. A Rule 902(14) certificate does not demonstrate the relevance of the exhibit; the narrow purpose of Rule 902(14) is to establish that the exhibit is an accurate copy of the original contents stored on the device, medium, or file.

The fact situation is a variation of the fourth example in the Evidence Advisory Committee's May 7, 2016 report. The exhibit is a printout of the contents of several text messages. Assume that the proponent has already presented the other chain of custody testimony or that exercising discretion under rule 611(a), the judge has permitted the proponent to introduce the exhibit before the presentation of the chain of custody testimony. The hypothetical continues:

P Your Honor, I request that this be marked prosecution exhibit number four for identification.

J It will be so marked.

P Please let the record reflect that I am showing the exhibit to the opposing counsel.

J The record will so reflect.

P Your Honor, I now offer prosecution exhibit number four for identification into evidence as prosecution exhibit four.

O Your Honor, I object on two grounds. First, there has been insufficient authentication. No sponsoring witness will come forward to verify the authenticity of this exhibit. Second, I object on hearsay grounds. The printout purports to quote the content of some messages allegedly sent by third parties to my client.

J *(To the prosecutor)* Let's deal with these objections one at a time. First, let's talk about the defense's authentication objection. What is your response to that objection?

P Your Honor, live testimony is unnecessary. As you can see, the document is a printout. The accompanying certificate shows that the data in the printout is an accurate copy of the original text messages on the defendant's phone. Under Rule 902(14), this certificate eliminates the need for live testimony. We satisfied Rule 902(14)'s procedural requirement by giving the defense pretrial notice of our intent to present the printout accompanied by this certificate rather than present the technician's live testimony.

J *(To the defense counsel)* Did the prosecutor give you pretrial notice?

O Yes, Your Honor. But I reiterate both my authentication and hearsay objections.

J The authentication objection will be overruled. However, before I allow the messages to be read to the jury, we need to deal with the second, hearsay objection. *(To the prosecutor)* What is your response to the defense's hearsay objection.

P Your Honor, any messages that the defendant himself sent fall within the hearsay exemption for personal statements or admissions of a party-opponent under Rule 801(d)(2)(A). As for the messages originating from third parties, we believe that the extrinsic evidence shows that they are admissible as vicarious admissions by co-conspirators under Rule 801(d)(2)(E). To begin with, under Rule 902(13), you have already

> admitted a printout showing the extent of the contact between the alleged co-conspirators—all the messages flying back and forth between them immediately before and after the commission of the crime. In addition, ...

It is doubtful that standing alone, the fact of extensive contact among several persons would ever suffice to lay the foundation for the co-conspirator exemption. However, the prosecution could present additional foundational testimony to complete the foundation.

[10] THE AUTHENTICATION OF PRINTOUTS OF RECORDS MAINTAINED ON A BLOCKCHAIN

The notoriety of Bitcoin has raised the visibility of blockchain technology. There are numerous types of blockchains. Some are public and permissionless; anyone can download and run the open source software that enables one to participate in the blockchain. In permissionless blockchains such as Bitcoin, the participants often rely on pseudonyms and digital signatures. Other blockchains are private and permissioned; in this type of blockchain, an administrator or gatekeeper decides who will be granted access and allowed to participate. In permissioned blockchains, persons and entities frequently use their actual names. Blockchains can be used for a wide variety of purposes, including supporting cryptocurrencies such as Bitcoin or simple record keeping (accounting). The use of blockchain is spreading rapidly, especially in the finance sector. NASDAQ is developing a blockchain-based system to record trades in privately held companies, and the Bank of England is also contemplating utilizing blockchain. State statutes in Arizona, Delaware, and Ohio have already been amended to reflect the fact that many business entities are turning to blockchain technology.

Blockchain is essentially shared or Distributed Ledger Technology (DLT). The blockchain is a peer-to-peer (P2P) network. Previous systems relied on a centralized, trusted intermediary or middleman. For example, as a trusted intermediary a bank could act as a central authority for verifying financial transactions and as a centralized repository for records of transactions with multiple customers. However, there are disadvantages to reliance on trusted human intermediaries. Some, including the proponents of Bitcoin, have a libertarian bias against the consolidation of power in a central authority and favor decentralization. Others advance the practical argument that systems reliant on central authorities are more vulnerable to hacking. If there is one central authority, that authority becomes the obvious target; and the successful hack of that target's records poses a risk to all the persons and entities relying on the accuracy of those records. The 2008 economic downturn highlighted some of the pitfalls of centralization, both governmental and corporate.

Blockchain substitutes reliance on cryptography for reliance on human beings. Blockchain provides a safe basis for transactions between persons and entities—even prior strangers who do not know each other. As previously stated, there are various types of blockchains. However, most share several common denominators. The following is an admittedly oversimplified description of blockchain technology:

— The blockchain network consists of participating computers or nodes. In some blockchains, participating nodes can have different privileges. For example, some blockchains distinguish between "lightweight" modes with limited privileges and "full" nodes with full privileges. A lightweight node might not be able to printout the entire ledger; it might have only the more limited right to printout blocks directly relating to that node. In many blockchains, though, all nodes enjoy the same privileges.

— Suppose that a business creates a private, permissioned blockchain in which all participating nodes have equal privileges. Any node can therefore create the first or genesis block in the chain. Assuming that all the participants are full nodes, they all will receive a copy of that block. The first participant that concluded the initial business transaction posts that block.

— Now assume that there is a second transaction. In some blockchains, only designated miner nodes can propose an addition to the blockchain. However, in other blockchains, any node can serve as a miner. When a miner node conducts the second transaction, the node creates a header for the second block. That header will contain two things: a hash for the second transaction and a pointer with the hash of the preceding block, in this case the genesis block. Section 4.03[9] discusses hashing. As previously stated, a hash is a string of digits of fixed length that is probabilistically unique. By way of example, suppose that this blockchain uses SHA 256 (Secure Hashing Algorithm 256). No matter how long or short the input hashed, the algorithm produces a string that is 256 bits in length. It is theoretically possible that hashing a different input could yield the same hash value; but given the length of the string, the odds are astronomically against such a coincidence.

— Next, the miner broadcasts or propagates the proposed second block to the network. At this point, a consensus protocol comes into play. The protocol is a consensus algorithm that determines whether the proposed second block is added to the blockchain. There can be various protocols. In some protocols all nodes can participate in this step; the protocol might provide that there is consensus when a majority of the network agrees. The protocol may include other requirements for consensus, but at the very least the other nodes run a computation to determine whether the hash in the new block is valid. If all the nodes use SHA 256, all their hashes should yield the same 256 bit string.

— Once the consensus protocol has been satisfied, the second block is added to update the chain. Whenever subsequent blocks are proposed, the above steps are repeated. All the local versions of the blockchain should be consistent. Each local hard drive will contain the same sequentially organized, time-stamped chain; each version includes the blocks in chronological order with time stamps indicating when the block was added to the chain. In each version, each block is chained back to the previous block by cryptographic hashing.

— This chaining is critical to understanding why there is a strong inference of the integrity of each block in the chain. If a hacker were to make even the slightest change in one block—for example, the insertion or deletion of a single comma—it will change the hash for that block *and* all other subsequent blocks. This is the so-called Avalanche Effect. It is sometimes asserted that the blockchain is tamper proof because the chain is immutable and incorruptible. That assertion is overstated. It is not that the chain is absolutely tamper proof; rather, the point is that the chain is tamper resistant because tampering will be evident. The blockchain is cryptographically auditable. If a hacker succeeds in tampering with a block at one node, the next time another node attempts to add a block, the hashes will not match. Once the tampering is discovered, the hashes will enable the other nodes to trace the tampering back to the specific block tampered with. It is exceedingly difficult for the hacker to recalculate the hashes at all the other nodes before the discovery of the tampering; but as a practical matter it is virtually impossible to rewrite the blocks that quickly.[26] The very difficulty of revising all the hashes deters hacking. If an intelligent hacker has a choice—attacking a system with one central target or assaulting a blockchain—the former is a much more attractive target.

In this light, how would one go about authenticating records maintained on a blockchain? Consider first live authenticating testimony and then the use of a certificate rendering the printout self-authenticating.

Live Authenticating Testimony

A proper foundation would include the following elements:

1. The witness is qualified to both establish the general validity of blockchain technology and the reliability of the blockchain system used by the specific entity that maintained the records.

2. Blockchain methodology is valid. In some jurisdictions, the judge will judicially notice the general reliability of the technology. Again, a growing number of states is enacting legislation recognizing the widespread use of blockchain. Nevertheless, the witness should describe the technology in sufficient detail to enable the jury to understand why they should infer that the record is reliable.

3. The specific blockchain system that generated the record has proven to be trustworthy. In order to establish this element, the witness should be either an employee of a vendor servicing the entity's blockchain system or an employee of the entity with responsibility for overseeing the operation of the system.

4. The exhibit tendered to the witness on the stand is a relevant printout from the entity's blockchain.

---

[26] P. DE FILIPPI & A. WRIGHT, BLOCKCHAIN AND THE LAW: THE LAW OF CODE 25 (2018) ("The most plausible way to change a record in the Bitcoin blockchain would be for a group of attackers to engage in a '51% attack' and effectively take over the network so that they can approve transactions at a rate that outpaces the rest of the network. Given the scale of Bitcoin's distributed network, such an attack is becoming increasingly remote. Starting in 2015, Bitcoin miners . . . had '13,000 times more combined number-crunching power than the world's 500 biggest super-computers.' . . . [O]rchestrating such an attack today could . . . cost hundreds of millions of dollars, if not billions, an operation that would prove too costly for most private parties or independent hacking coalitions").

The fact situation is a lawsuit by Ms. Elise, the owner of an expensive painting, against her insurer. The plaintiff's complaint alleges that shortly after she purchased the painting, an accidental fire destroyed the painting that was insured by the defendant. The central issue at trial is the value of the painting that was destroyed. At this point in the trial, the plaintiff is attempting to establish the purchase price of the painting. The witness is the Director of Information Technology for a corporation that operates art galleries in 40 countries, including the United States where the plaintiff purchased the painting. The plaintiff purchased the painting in question from this corporation.

P   Please state your full name and spell your last name for the record. (1)

W   My name is Kindra Rosic. Rosic is spelled R-O-S-I-C.

P   Where do you currently live? (1)

W   I live here in Alexandria, Virginia.

P   WHERE do you work? (1)

W   I work for Eterna Art Galleries at its Washington, D.C. office.

P   WHAT line of business is Eterna in? (1)

W   As our name implies, we operate art galleries. To be specific, we own 40 galleries spread throughout the world. We specialize in high-end, high-value paintings.

P   WHAT do you mean by "high-value paintings"? (1)

W   Well, the asking price for the very cheapest painting in our Washington gallery is $50,000. Many of our paintings are priced at well more than $1,000,000.00.

P   WHAT is your position with Eterna? (1)

W   I'm the Director of IT—Information Technology—not just at the Washington gallery but for all our galleries throughout the world.

P   WHAT is your educational background? (1)

W   I was always interested in art, but I quickly discovered that I didn't have the talent to become an artist. Consequently, I decided to focus on the business aspects of operating art galleries. And as I was studying that subject, it became clear that computer systems would play a huge role in the future of galleries—just as they do in so many businesses. Consequently, in addition to minoring in Art History, I obtained both a B.S. and a Master's in Computer Science from the University of Virginia.

P   HOW long have you worked for Eterna? (1)

W   For fifteen years.

P   And HOW long have you held the position of IT Director for global operations? (1)

W   For ten years. I started working as an IT technician. Then I was made the director for the Washington gallery, and a decade ago they put me in charge of IT for all our galleries throughout the world.

P   HOW does Eterna maintain its records of sales of paintings? (2)

W   We use blockchain technology.

P   WHAT is blockchain technology? (2)

W   It's sometimes called Distributed Ledger Technology or DLT. We don't have a single central computer or database that maintains all the sales data. Every one of our 40 galleries is part of a computer network. It's called a peer-to-peer network because they're all in contact with each other rather than in contact only with some central authority. They all have complete copies of the ledger.

P   WHY don't you use one central authority or database? (2)

W   To be honest, about 11 or 12 years ago when we had one central computer authority at our Paris gallery, we suffered some terrible hacks—hacks that eventually cost our company tens of millions of dollars and Euros.

P   WHAT is the connection, if any, between having one central authority and the risk of hacking? (2)

W   If there's one central computer authority, there's one target that the hacker has to attack to get all the information. It's a much, much bigger challenge to successfully modify the records in a blockchain system. And that's not the only advantage.

P   WHAT are the other advantages to using blockchain? (2)

W   The primary one is that it's so easy to detect attempted hacking and tampering.

P   WHY is it so easy to do so? (2)

W   I'll give you an example. Let's say that our gallery in Paris makes a sale. They're one participating computer or "node" in our system. They create the first block for that sale. Then a short time later our gallery in London makes a sale. When they do, they propose adding a second block to the chain.

P   WHAT do they do when they want to propose adding the second block? (2)

W   They use hashing.

P   WHAT is hashing? (2)

W   It's a special type of computer program. One of the most popular is SHA-256. The "SHA" stands for Secure Hashing Algorithm. "256" indicates that when you process any input such as a record, the program produces a string that is 256 bits in length. As a practical matter, that hash is unique to that input, in my example the record of the sale. Whenever you use SHA-256 to process the same input, you should get exactly the same string of 256 bits. It's theoretically possible that you'd come up with the same string by sheer coincidence, but the odds against that are astronomical.

P   WHAT role does hashing play in blockchain? (2)

W   When our London gallery proposes adding the second block for its sale, it hashes both the information for the new block for sale #2 and the prior block for sale #1. Everyone in the network—the 40 nodes at the 40 galleries—can run the same computation to ensure that they come up with the same hash values. When they do that and reach consensus on the computation, the second block is added to the chain. And when our gallery in Mexico City makes a third sale a short time later and proposes a third block for that sale, they will hash the record for their sale and the prior sale in London. And again, they'll broadcast that throughout the network to give all the nodes the opportunity to check to ensure that their records are consistent, that is, that they produce the identical hash values. That helps makes it easy to detect any tampering.

P   HOW does it do that? (2)

W   All the blocks in the chain are linked. That interdependence creates the so-called Avalanche Effect. If you make the slightest change in any block at any node—even just adding or deleting a comma—it changes the hash value not only for that block but all the subsequent blocks. And the next time someone tries to add another block, the hash values won't match. It's sometimes said that blockchain is tamper proof and immutable. That's not quite true. It would be possible for a hacker to attack the same block and change the calculations for all the subsequent blocks at all the nodes, but again as a practical matter you wouldn't have enough time or computational power to pull that off. So it's not that blockchain is absolutely tamper proof. The point, though, is that it's highly tamper resistant because it's almost certain that any tampering will become evident to the other nodes. And that's why hackers would much rather attack a system with a central authority and depository of information.

P   HOW widespread is blockchain technology? (2)

W   It's rapidly growing in popularity. You may have heard of Bitcoin. Bitcoin used blockchain. They did so not only because they wanted to prevent tampering but also, frankly, because part of their political agenda was eliminating central authority such as government agencies and big banks. Now NASDAQ is using blockchain to record some types of trades, the Bank of England is following suit, and lots of government agencies both here and abroad are turning to blockchain.

P   Let's turn to the blockchain that Eterna uses. HOW long has Eterna relied on blockchain? (3)

W   It's been almost nine years. As I said, over a decade ago we experienced some bad, costly hacks. That's when as Director, I decided that we should shift to blockchain. Today it's still difficult to use blockchain for large scale operations. Think of all the processing time it would take Walmart to use a blockchain for all of its sales worldwide. However, the scale of our operations is much smaller. Consequently, it's feasible for us to employ blockchain.

P   HOW successful has Eterna's blockchain been? (3)

W   The bottom line is that we achieved what we really wanted. We didn't want a repetition of those successful hacks; and as far as I can tell, we haven't had a single hack since we shifted to blockchain. And we haven't had any instances in which different nodes had inconsistent records of a transaction.

P   WHERE were you on September 19th of this year? (4)

W   I was at our office in Washington.

P   WHAT telephone calls, if any, did you receive that morning? (4)

W   I received a call from your client, Ms. Elise.

P   HOW do you know that the caller was Ms. Elise? (4)

W   I'm familiar with her voice. I spent a good deal of time with her when she purchased the painting from our gallery. She has a pretty distinctive New England accent.

P   WHAT did she say during her call? (4)

W   She asked me to printout the record for her purchase of the painting to prove the purchase price. (*Ms. Elise's statement to the witness is not hearsay under Federal Rule of Evidence 801(a). The statement is a weak imperative sentence—a request, not an assertion. Moreover, under 801(c)(2), the statement will not be offered for the truth of any assertion in the statement. Rather, it will be offered for the nonhearsay purpose of showing the effect of the statement on the hearer's state of mind—it explains what she does after receiving the call.*)

P   WHAT, if anything, did you do after you received Ms. Elise's phone call? (4)

W   I went to our computer and printed the record reflecting the block in the chain for her purchase.

P   WHAT did you do with the printout after you printed it out? (4)

W   Immediately, I reviewed the contents of the record and noted my initials and the date on the record. I then kept the record in my office desk until I came to court today.

P   WHAT did you do with the record when you came to court? (4)

W   I gave it to you at your counsel table a short time ago.

P	Your Honor, I request that this be marked as Plaintiff's Exhibit Number 3 for identification.
J	It will be so marked.
P	Your Honor, please let the record reflect that I am showing the exhibit to the defense counsel.
J	The record will so reflect.
P	Ms. Rosic, I now hand you what has been marked Plaintiff's Exhibit Number 3 for identification.
	WHAT is it? (4)
W	It's the printout that I mentioned.
P	HOW do you recognize it? (4)
W	As I said, as soon as I printed it out, I carefully studied its contents. Plus, I noted my initials and the date. I recognize the contents as well as my initials and the date.
P	Your Honor, I now offer Plaintiff's Exhibit Number 3 for Identification into evidence as Plaintiff's Exhibit Number 3.
J	Any objection?
O	No, Your Honor.
J	Very well, the exhibit will be received.

The Use of a Certificate Rendering the Printout Self-Authenticating

Although blockchain technology is relatively new, if the company or agency maintaining the blockchain is a regularly conducted domestic or foreign entity, a certificate satisfying Rule 902(11) or (12) should arguably render the printout self-authenticating. Section 4.03[7] discusses the use of such certificates. The argument is particularly strong because, as § 4.03[9] points out, the Advisory Committee Note to Rule 902(14) specifically states that hashing is "a process of digital identification" within the meaning of that expression in 902(14).

However, perhaps out of an excess of caution, in 2019 the Vermont legislature adopted the following statute, 12 V.S.A. § 1913:

(a) As used in this section:

(1) "Blockchain" means a cryptographically secured, chronological, and decentralized consensus ledger or consensus database maintained via Internet, peer-to-peer network, or other interaction.

(2) "Blockchain technology" means computer software or hardware, or both, that utilize or enable a blockchain.

(b) Authentication, admissibility, and presumptions.

(1) A digital record electronically registered in a blockchain shall be self-authenticating pursuant to Vermont Rule of Evidence 902, if it is accompanied by a written declaration of a qualified person, made under oath, stating the qualification of the person to make the certification and:

(A) the date and time the record entered the blockchain;

(B) the date and time the record was received from the blockchain;

(C) that the record was maintained in the blockchain as a regularly conducted activity; and

(D) that the record was made by the regularly conducted activity as a regular practice.

While the above provision deals with self-authentication, a separate, subsequent provision in the legislation states that such blockchain records qualify for admission under the hearsay exception codified in Rule 803(6). The authentication provision is Vermont Rule of Evidence 902(13).

[11] THE AUTHENTICATION OF RECORDS STORED IN THE CLOUD

Increasingly, businesses, organizations, and individuals are using the "Cloud" (e.g., Amazon Web Services (AWS), MicrosoftAzure, IBMCloud, Gmail, Yahoo, and similar companies) to store vast amounts of electronic information (ESI) off-site. The information can be in the form of business records, photographs, and personal information such as family history documents. Doing so frees up storage space on the user's personal or company computers and smart phones. Once the information is stored on the cloud, the user can access that information from any device.

The volume of electronic records is becoming so large that many businesses no longer want to incur the expense of expanding the capacity of their company's server to maintain all their records. Instead, they are turning to cloud storage providers. The businesses transmit their records to the providers that maintain records on multiple servers often in multiple locations.

The providers not only maintain the business' records without altering their content; they also promise to grant the business ready access to the records whenever the business wants to retrieve the records. In some cases, the cloud service providers furnishes the business with software enabling the business itself to retrieve the records from storage without any assistance from the provider. In other instances, the provider requires that the business submit a request to the provider for the return of the records; after receiving the request, the provider sends the records back. For example, if the business becomes involved in litigation, the business may need to retrieve the records during pretrial discovery or introduce the records at trial.

It is conceivable that the trial judge might allow the business to use the simple custody technique, discussed in § 4.03[1], because the printouts purport to be the records of the business and are now back in the business' custody. Suppose, for instance, that a business maintained all its records in traditional written format but kept some of the records at a rented warehouse at a different location other than the business' headquarters. If the business proffered some of the writings into evidence, the business would not have to lay any special foundation merely because the business had to arrange to have the writings transferred from the warehouse to headquarters before trial. The proponent of an electronic record that had been stored in the cloud could analogize between physically transferring the record back from the warehouse and electronically retrieving the record back from the cloud. For that matter, relying on similar reasoning, the judge might permit the business to resort to Rule 902(11)'s self-authentication provision.

However, in a case in which the records are critical, the proponent may want to lay a more extensive foundation for the records. For that matter, given the relative novelty of introducing cloud-stored records into evidence, a cautious trial judge might insist that the proponent do so.

If the proponent intends to do so, the proponent can call the business' records custodian or deputy custodian to elicit foundational testimony. The proponent should establish the following elements:

1. The business entered into a contract with a particular cloud storage provider.[27]

2. The business' records reflect that at one time, the business possessed the original records in question, for example, the records relating to the purchase or sale of certain merchandise.

3. At a later point in time, the business transmitted the records to the cloud storage provider.[28]

4. The business' records indicate that before transmitting the records, the business hashed the records.[29]

5. The business' records reflect that at a still later point in time the business requested that the provider return the records to the business or the business used a program that enabled the business to retrieve the records without submitting a request.

6. The business' records indicate that certain records were returned to the business.

7. The business' records reflect that when the business received the records, it again hashed them; and the hash matched the value that the hashing yielded

---

[27] If at the relevant time during the litigation the provider has a website, the judge may judicially notice the existence of the website under Rule 201(b)(2). Moreover, Rule 902(7) can serve to establish the authenticity of the website. Under 902(7), self-authentication can be utilized by showing an inscription, sign, tag, or label purporting to have been affixed in the course of business and indicating origin, ownership, or control. The business could introduce its own records reflecting the entry into the contract. The business' records custodian or deputy custodian can qualify the underlying records as business entries under Rule 803(6). The reference in the records to the contract does not create a second hearsay level; the reference is nonhearsay under Rule 801(c)(2) because contracts are verbal acts or operative facts.

[28] The records reflecting the transmittal also qualify as business entries. In some cases, the business' computers automatically transmit such records on a regular basis, for example, daily, weekly, or monthly. In other cases, the business selectively sends some but not all of its records to the provider. If so, the business' records will reflect that the business requested the provider to store the records in question. The reference in the records to the request does not introduce a second hearsay level; the reference is nonhearsay under Rule 801(a), since requests and instructions are not assertions. They are weak or strong imperative sentences, not declarative sentences about events or facts.

[29] As previously stated, the Advisory Committee Note to Rule 902(14) recognizes hashing as a reliable method of establishing the identity of a record or set of records.

before the business sent the records to the cloud storage provider.

In the following foundation, European Autowerks is suing the defendant Ward for delinquent payments on an automobile he purchased from the plaintiff business. The proponent is the plaintiff, who has called Autowerks' records custodian to establish the defendant's failure to pay on the loan. The records in question have been maintained on the cloud at a site managed by UniversalStorage, which stores records of automobile dealerships nationwide. The plaintiff calls Ms. Peters to the stand.

P   Ms. Peters, WHAT is your occupation? (1)

W   I am the chief bookkeeper for European Autowerks here in Tampa.

P   HOW long have you worked there? (1)

W   About seven years.

P   WHAT are your duties? (1)

W   As chief bookkeeper, I ensure that we have proper records of all the money flowing into and out of the company. I supervise the records' preparation and maintenance.

P   HOW do you store the dealership's financial records? (1)

W   We don't keep all the records on-site. Years ago we shifted from written records to electronic records, And then the electronic records became so voluminous and took up so much space on the hard drive of our computers that we shifted to cloud storage. Virtually all big businesses are doing that today. So several years ago, we signed an agreement with UniversalStorage, a leading cloud provider, to keep all of our records on the cloud, which that company manages.

P   HOW does that filing system work? (2), (3), (4)

W   We initially prepare the documents in our offices. At first we prepare some written records, but eventually everything goes onto electronic files. Once an account has been established for loan on a car we sell, we send the electronic record in the form of a file, over the Internet, to the cloud storage maintained by UniversalStorage.

P   WHAT steps, if any, do you take to ensure that the documents you send to Universal are accurate and secure? (4)

W   Before we send Universal any files or sets of files, we create a hash code for that set of documents.

P   WHAT is hashing? (4)

W   Simply stated, you use a computer program that reviews the entire contents of the document and generates a very long string of numbers identifying that particular document. That long string of numbers is the hash value or identifier for the file.

P   HOW does a hash value "identify" a file? (4)

W   Any time you use the same program to hash the same file, you should get exactly the same string of numbers. If you change the file in the slightest way—even adding just one digit or deleting a single comma—it changes the hash value. That enables you to detect any changes that have been made to the file.

P And HOW do you retrieve one of those stored documents from UniversalStorage? (5)

W You use a computer to send a request to Universal to return a particular record to us.

P When the record is returned to you, WHAT, if anything, do you do to ensure that it is the same file in the same condition? (7)

W We hash it again. As I said, if you hash the same document twice with the same program, you'll always get the same string of numbers. If the hash values match, you can be confident that no one has changed or tampered with the file.

P Thank you.

[To the court reporter] Would you please mark this as plaintiff's exhibit number four for identification? *[The reporter marks the exhibit and hands it back to the counsel.]*

P Your Honor, please let the record reflect that I am now showing plaintiff's exhibit number four for identification to the defense counsel.

J It will so reflect.

P Your Honor, may I approach the witness?

J Yes.

P Ms. Peters, I am now handing you plaintiff's exhibit number four for identification. Do you recognize it?

W Yes.

P WHAT is it? (4)

W It's a copy of the loan payment records for the car that Mr. Ward purchased from us.

P HOW can you recognize it? (5)

W I recognize the contents, the name of the purchaser, and the date of the sale. Also, I personally requested that Universal send this document to us, after you requested a copy last week.

P HOW can you be sure that these are the same records you sent to the cloud? (6), (7)

W I checked my office for the hash value of that batch of records that we sent to Universal. When They returned the file, I printed out the file and then hashed it. I then compared the two hash values. They were identical. It's therefore the same records in the same condition.

P	Thank you, Ms. Peters. Your Honor, we offer plaintiff's exhibit number four for identification into evidence as plaintiff's number four.
J	Any objections?
O	None, Your Honor.
J	Then the exhibit is admitted.
P	Your Honor, may I hand exhibit number for to the jurors for their inspection?
J	Yes, you may.

§ 4.04 THE AUTHENTICATION OF OFFICIAL WRITINGS

[1] THE DOCTRINE

The government often possesses information relevant to the outcome of civil and criminal actions. Thus, it frequently becomes necessary for one of the parties to introduce an official record. It would obviously be inconvenient to require public officials to appear in court to authenticate official records; their appearance would not only divert them from their official duties but also create the risk of the record's loss.

Even before the enactment of statutes such as Rule 902(11) rendering some private business records self-authenticating, almost every jurisdiction adopted the rule that a properly attested copy of an official record is self-authenticating. The party obtains a copy of the official record from the official custodian, and the custodian attaches an attesting certificate. The certificate reads along these lines: "I, Robert Dondero, certify that I am the County Clerk of San Francisco, California, and that the attached document is a true and accurate copy of an original, official record in my custody." The certificate is signed and often bears the seal of the official's office. The courts have developed the doctrine that the purported signature or seal of an official is presumed to be authentic. Federal Rule of Evidence 902 treats domestic public documents under seal as self-authenticating.

[2] ELEMENTS OF THE FOUNDATION

The mechanics of introducing a properly attested copy of an official record are simple; the elements of the foundation include:

1. The document purports to be a copy of an official record.

2. A certificate is attached to the copy.

3. The certificate states that the signatory is a public custodian of official records.

4. The certificate states that the document is a true and accurate copy of an original, official record.

5. The certificate bears a presumptively authentic signature and/or seal.

[3] SAMPLE FOUNDATION

The fact situation is a probate contest. At one point in the trial, the contestant must prove that a Jean Simmons was born in San Francisco, California, in YR-20. The contestant is the proponent. The contestant is attempting to introduce a copy of a birth certificate in the custody of the San Francisco County Clerk. The hearing is a bench trial without a jury.

P   Your Honor, I request that this be marked contestant's exhibit number four for identification.

J   It will be so marked.

P   Please let the record reflect that I am showing the exhibit to the opposing counsel.

J   The record will so reflect.

P   I now offer contestant's exhibit number four for identification into evidence as contestant's exhibit number four.

O   I object on the ground that there has been insufficient authentication. No sponsoring witness has come forward to verify the authenticity of this document.

J   (*To the contestant*) What is your response to the objection?

P   Your Honor, live testimony is unnecessary. In this jurisdiction, the purported signatures and seals of public officials are presumed genuine. This document bears both a purported official signature and a seal. The signature and seal authenticate the certificate itself. In turn, the certificate states that the attached document is a true and accurate copy of an official record in Mr. Dondero's custody. Thus, the certificate serves to authenticate the attached copy.

J   Objection overruled.

P   Your Honor, at this point I would like to invite the court's attention to the body of exhibit number four.

J   Yes.

P   I would like to point out that it states that a Jean Simmons was born in San Francisco, California, on September 19, YR-20.

J   I have noted that.

This hypothetical example is so short because the proponent needed only an attesting certificate to make the document self-authenticating. In an *attesting* certificate, the signatory writes that he or she is the custodian or deputy custodian of a set of official records and that the attached document is an original official record or a copy of an original official record in the official's custody. If the court can presume the authenticity of the signature or seal on the attesting certificate, that presumption authenticates the certificate; and in turn, the attesting certificate authenticates the attached document.

Suppose, however, that the document originates in a foreign country. The presumption of authenticity may not attach to a foreign official's signature, and consequently, a foreign official's attesting certificate will probably not suffice to authenticate the attached document. In that event, the proponent will need a chain of certificates, usually culminating in an authenticating certificate executed by an American official. In an *authenticating* certificate, one official writes that he or she is acquainted with the position and handwriting of another official and that the signature attached to another certificate in the chain is the signature of that other official. The chain used to authenticate a foreign record might include an attesting certificate by a local foreign official, an authenticating certificate by a national foreign official, and finally an authenticating certificate by an American consular officer. Such a chain would satisfy Federal Rules of Evidence 902(3)–(4).

§ 4.05   THE AUTHENTICATION OF ORAL STATEMENTS

[1]   IN GENERAL

Like written statements, oral statements must be authenticated. In the case of a written statement, authentication usually requires identifying the author. In the case of an oral statement, authentication ordinarily consists in identifying the speaker. To do so, the proponent may use several techniques.

[2]   LAY OPINION TESTIMONY OF A WITNESS FAMILIAR WITH THE SPEAKER'S VOICE

The proponent may use lay opinion testimony to authenticate an oral statement just as the proponent may use lay opinion testimony to authenticate a writing. In the case of a writing, the witness must testify that he or she is acquainted with the author's handwriting style. In the case of oral statements, the witness must testify that he or she is acquainted with the person's voice. Federal Rule of Evidence 901(b)(5) recognizes this method of voice identification.

The foundation contains these elements:

1.   At a specific time and place, the witness heard a voice.

2.   The witness recognized the voice as that of a certain person.

3.   The witness is familiar with that person's voice. Given that familiarity, under Federal Rule of Evidence 701, the witness can give a skilled lay observer opinion identifying the person's voice.

4.   The witness explains the basis for his or her familiarity with that person's voice.

5.   The person made a statement during the conversation.

The fact situation is a tort action for slander. The plaintiff, Brown, sues the defendant, Nolan. The plaintiff alleges that Nolan slandered the plaintiff during a telephone conversation with Parish. The plaintiff calls Parish to the stand.

P   Mr. Parish, WHERE were you on the evening of April 6th of this year? (1)

W   I was at home.

P   WHAT, if anything, happened while you were home? (1)

W   I received a phone call.

P	WHO was the caller? (2)
W	It was the defendant, Ms. Nolan.
P	HOW do you know that it was Ms. Nolan? (3)
W	I recognized her voice, and she said it was Ms. Nolan.
P	HOW did you become familiar with her voice? (4)
W	We've known each other for years.
P	HOW many years? (4)
W	Easily 15.
P	HOW often have you spoken with her? (4)
W	I can't answer; we've spoken thousands of times, I guess. We're neighbors. I see her at least a couple of times a week. Sometimes I bump into her several times in a single day.
P	WHAT condition was your telephone in when you received this call?
W	It was in good working condition. There was no static or anything.
P	HOW much noise was there in the background?
W	None that I could tell. I didn't have the stereo on or anything like that, and I couldn't hear any noise at the other end other than Ms. Nolan talking.
P	WHAT did Ms. Nolan say during this telephone conversation? (5)
W	She said that she had a hot item of news for me.
P	WHAT was that? (5)
W	She said that the plaintiff, Mr. Brown, had paid $10,000 to bribe one of the City Councilpeople to get favorable zoning on some commercial property Brown owns.

[3] THE TELEPHONE DIRECTORY DOCTRINE

The telephone directory doctrine parallels the reply letter doctrine. Under the reply letter doctrine, the courts trust the reliability of the Post Office. Under this doctrine, the courts place their faith in the accuracy of telephone directories. Federal Rule of Evidence 901(b)(6) describes the doctrine: The proponent may authenticate "a telephone conversation" by presenting

Evidence that a call was made to the number assigned at the time to:

  (A) a particular person, if circumstances, including self-identification, show that the person answering was the one called; or

  (B) a particular business, if the call was made to a business and the call related to business reasonably transacted over the telephone.

This fact pattern creates a circumstantial inference that the person answering was the person the telephone number is assigned to.

The foundation includes these elements:

1. A reliable telephone directory assigned a certain number to the person.

2. The witness called that number.

3. The witness asked for the person to whom the number is assigned.

4. The person answering identified himself or herself as the person to whom the number is assigned.

5. Any other circumstances indicating that the person answering was the person to whom the number was assigned.

The fact situation is a tort action arising from a crash. The expert testimony indicates that the failure of the defendant's brakes caused the crash. One issue is whether the defendant knew his brakes were defective. The plaintiff wants to elicit Mr. Martinez' testimony that he worked on the defendant's car, found the brakes defective, and notified the defendant by telephone. The telephone conversation was Mr. Martinez' only contact with the defendant, Mr. Jackson. The plaintiff is the proponent.

W	After examining the brakes, I concluded that they were in dangerous condition.
P	WHAT did you do then?
W	I decided to notify the owner, this fellow Jackson.
P	HOW did you notify him?
W	I wanted to phone him and let him know.
P	HOW did you do that? (1)
W	First I checked the telephone directory to get his number. (*If there is a hearsay objection to the reference to the telephone directory, the proponent can respond by citing Federal Rule of Evidence 803(17). That provision creates an exception for "directories . . . generally used and relied on by the public." The Advisory Committee Note gives "telephone directories" as an example.*)
P	WHAT did you do then? (2)
W	I called the number.
P	WHERE was the directory when you were dialing? (2) (*If there is a best evidence objection at this objection, the proponent could cite Federal Rule of Evidence 1004(d). While the contents of the telephone directory are relevant to lay this foundation, they are "not closely related to a controlling issue" on the merits of the case.*)
W	It was right in front of me. I was looking at it as I dialed.
P	WHAT happened next? (3)
W	It rang, and a man answered.
P	WHAT did you say? (3)
W	I asked to speak to Mr. Jackson, the owner of the purple Corvette.
P	HOW did the person answering the phone identify himself? (4)

W	He just said he was Jackson, the person I wanted to talk to.
P	WHAT, if anything, did he say about the Corvette? (5)
W	He told me that he realized that it had some problems.
P	WHAT problems? (5)
W	He mentioned a problem with the exhaust and the windshield wipers.
P	HOW accurate were those statements? (5)
W	The guy was right. I'd looked at the car, and I'd seen those problems, among others. The guy I was talking with sure sounded very familiar with the car.
P	WHAT did you say then?
W	I told him about the brakes.
P	Specifically, WHAT did you tell him?
W	I said that they were defective and dangerous. I told him that they could fail anytime and that he should have them repaired immediately.

[4] TESTIMONY BY A VOICEPRINT OR SOUND SPECTROGRAPHY EXPERT

Subsection [2] dealt with lay opinion testimony about voice identification. Now we turn to expert opinion. The sound spectrography (voiceprint) expert is to the identification of speakers what the questioned document examiner is to the identification of writers. The voiceprint witness is the supposed expert. There are two theoretical premises underlying sound spectrography. The first premise is that interspeaker variability exceeds intraspeaker variability; even though a person's voice pattern changes from time to time, the voice pattern differences among speakers are greater than the variations in a single speaker's voice pattern. The second premise is intraspeaker invariant speech; each voice has certain unique characteristics that it will invariably display under spectrographic analysis. Most speech scientists accept the first premise, but there is still a good deal of controversy in scientific circles over the second premise. Many critics of sound spectrography argue that there has been insufficient experimental verification of the theory of invariant speech. A 1979 report of a committee of the National Academy of Sciences found insufficient empirical verification.

The spectrograph instrument itself includes: (1) a magnetic recording device; (2) a variable electronic filter; (3) a paper-carrying drum coupled to the magnetic recording device; and (4) an electronic stylus that marks the paper as the drum rotates. The spectrograph operates in this fashion. The operator starts with a tape of certain, commonly used English cue words such as "the," "and," "me," "on," "is," "it," "I," "a," and "you." The cue words are static-state words; the words preceding and following them have little effect on their pronunciation and, hence, on the spectrograms they produce. The operator prepares the tape by having the suspect read the words into the tape or excerpting the words from a tape of the known suspect's speech. The operator plays the tape repeatedly on the magnetic recording device. The device is attached to the electronic filter; and each time the operator replays the tape, the filter lets another frequency pass through. The frequencies pass through to an electronic stylus; and as the frequencies pass through, the stylus marks the paper-carrying drum. The stylus thus produces a spectrogram, a graphic depiction of the voice pattern. The usual spectrogram is a bar spectrogram. The vertical axis is frequency, the horizontal axis is time, and the darkness is the voice's amplitude.

Fig. 4-3

BAR SPECTROGRAM

The operator then takes the unknown voice, for example, the recording of a bomb threat or obscene telephone call. The operator excerpts the same words from the recording of that voice and prepares another spectrogram in the same fashion. The operator then compares the two spectrograms and forms an opinion whether the same voice produced the two spectrograms. Experts vary on the number of points of similarity required for a match; some will accept as few as 16 while others insist upon as many as 33.

Given the division in the scientific community over sound spectrography, it is understandable that the courts are also split. The numerical majority of courts rejects the evidence. In *People v. Kelly*, 17 Cal. 3d 24, 130 Cal. Rptr. 144, 549 P.2d 1240 (1976), the California Supreme Court excluded sound spectrography evidence. Courts in the District of Columbia, Louisiana, Maryland, Michigan, New Jersey, and Pennsylvania have followed *Kelly*. Other courts accept such evidence. For example, the federal Courts of Appeals for the Second and Seventh Circuits, the Alaska Supreme Court, the Maine Supreme Judicial Court, and the Rhode Island Supreme Court have sustained the admission of sound spectrography evidence. 1 P. GIANNELLI, E. IMWINKELRIED, A. ROTH, J. CAMPBELL MORIARTY & V. BEETY, SCIENTIFIC EVIDENCE § 15.06 (Matthew Bender, 6th ed. 2020). There have been very few sound spectrography decisions since *Daubert*. One thing is clear: If the proponent is going to offer sound spectrography evidence, the proponent must lay a complete foundation. Since sound spectrography is a scientific technique, the proponent must lay the foundation outlined in § 4.10 of this chapter. As § 4.10 explains, the courts are currently split over the general test for admitting scientific evidence. That section notes that most jurisdictions now follow the *Daubert* test. However, the majority of the reported sound spectrography cases precede *Daubert*. For purposes of the following foundation, we shall assume that the court follows the traditional *Frye* general acceptance standard.

The elements of a foundation for sound spectrography evidence include:

1. The audio recordings used to produce the spectrograms are authentic. *See* § 4.06 of this chapter.

2. The witness has the qualifications to explain sound spectrography's underlying premises and to conduct the test.

3. The underlying premises of sound spectrography are interspeaker variability and invariant speech.

4. Those premises are generally accepted as valid in the relevant scientific circles.

5. The instrument is the sound spectrograph.

6. The instrument is generally accepted as reliable in the relevant scientific circles.

7. At a particular time and place, the witness conducted a voiceprint examination.

8. The witness used the audio recordings mentioned in element number 1.

9. The witness excerpted the cue words from both recordings.

10. The witness used a spectrograph to analyze the tapes of the cue words.

11. The spectrograph was in good working condition at the time.

12. The witness used the proper procedures.

13. The analysis produced two spectrograms.

14. The witness identifies the spectrograms.

15. There are several points of similarity between the two spectrograms.

16. In the witness's opinion, the same voice produced the two spectrograms.

The following is a sample foundation. The fact situation is a bomb threat prosecution. A police officer recorded the threat and authenticated the audio recording on a flash drive as prosecution exhibit number one. Another officer obtained a voice exemplar recording from the accused; the officer has authenticated that audio recording on another flash drive as prosecution exhibit number two. Thus, the two officers have laid the first element of the foundation. The prosecution now calls Ms. Janice Cottrell, a sound spectrography expert. The prosecution is the proponent. Ms. Cottrell has already identified herself and stated her address.

P	WHAT is your occupation? (2)
W	I am a member of the staff of the Pittsburgh Police Department Police Laboratory.
P	HOW long have you worked there? (2)
W	For the past six years—ever since I graduated from college.
P	WHERE did you attend college? (2)
W	I attended University of California, Berkeley.
P	WHAT was your undergraduate major? (2)

W	I was a Science major, specializing in speech science and acoustics.
P	WHAT are your present duties? (2)
W	I do all the sound spectrography or voiceprint analysis for the Pittsburgh Police Department.
P	WHAT is sound spectrography? (3)
W	It's a scientific technique for identifying a speaker.
P	WHAT is the basis of this technique? (3)
W	It has two premises. One is interspeaker variability.
P	WHAT does that mean? (3)
W	It means simply that the difference between your and my voice is greater than the fluctuations in my voice. Depending on whether I'm alert or sleepy, my voice pattern changes; but the differences between our two voices are still greater than the changes in my voice pattern from time to time. That's one of the two major premises of sound spectrography.
P	WHAT is the other premise? (3)
W	Invariant speech.
P	WHAT does that mean? (3)
W	Each person's voice has some unique characteristics, and you'll always be able to detect those characteristics with the instrument we use, the spectrograph.
P	WHAT experiments have been conducted to verify these theories? (3)
W	There has been extensive experimentation at Stanford, Michigan State, and a number of industrial laboratories.
P	WHAT has been the outcome of these experiments? (3)
W	They show that if you have a trained examiner, the examiner will ordinarily be able to determine whether the same voice produced two spectrograms, the charts of the voice patterns.
P	HOW high has the error rate been? (3)
W	It depends on the type of error you're talking about. If you're talking about false identifications, erroneously identifying a suspect as the person who produced the unknown spectrogram, it's pretty low. If you give the examiner a third option to say that a particular test is too close to call, the error rate is likely to be only one or two percent.
P	HOW widely are these theories accepted? (4)
W	There's still some controversy. However, I think that the people who are knowledgeable, who have read all the available data and studies, accept both premises.
P	HOW do you apply these theories to a particular case? (5)

W	As I said, you use a spectrograph. In our laboratory, we use a Series 700 Sound Spectrograph manufactured by Voiceprint Laboratories in New Jersey.
P	WHAT is a sound spectrograph? (5)
W	It has four basic components. First, there's a magnetic recording device. Then there's an electronic filter. Third, the machine has a stylus. Finally, it has a paper-carrying drum.
P	HOW does the spectrograph operate? (5)
W	You put a tape on the recording device. You play it again and again. Every time you play it, the filter lets a different frequency of the voice through. The frequencies activate the stylus, and the stylus marks the paper. The end result is a sort of chart that we call a spectrogram. In effect, it's a visual display of a voice pattern. You compare two charts; and if there are enough points of similarity, you conclude that the same voice produced the two spectrograms and, hence, the two audio recordings.
P	WHAT experiments have been conducted to verify the spectrograph's reliability? (5)
W	Basically the same ones I mentioned before. The researchers have tested both the theory and the instrument. The test results I mentioned before tend to validate the instrument as well.
P	HOW widely is the spectrograph accepted? (6)
W	I'd say that its reliability is accepted to the same extent as the underlying theories—generally accepted by the really knowledgeable people in the field.
P	Ms. Cottrell, WHERE were you on the morning of July 17 of this year? (7)
W	I was at my office at the lab.
P	WHAT happened while you were there? (7)
W	A police officer dropped by some audio recordings for spectrographic analysis.
P	I now hand you prosecution exhibits number one and two. WHAT are they? (8)
W	They're the flash drives with audio recordings I was given.
P	HOW can you recognize them? (8)
W	I remember the notations on the flash drives.
P	WHAT did you do with the recordings? (7)
W	I proceeded to conduct the analysis.
P	HOW did you do that? (9)

W	First I had to excerpt common words from both recordings. That took a little while.
P	Then WHAT did you do? (10)
W	One at a time, I put the new recordings of the excerpts on the spectrograph.
P	WHAT condition was your spectrograph in at the time? (11)
W	It was in good working condition.
P	HOW do you know that? (11)
W	I ran through the manufacturer's maintenance checklist before I used the spectrograph. The instrument checked out fine.
P	HOW are you supposed to operate the machine? (12)
W	You let it warm up a bit, input the recording you're analyzing, activate the machine, and then let it run until the spectrogram is complete.
P	WHAT procedure did you use on this occasion? (12)
W	I followed the proper procedure exactly. I did just what I outlined for you.
P	WHAT was the result of the test? (13)
W	At the end, I had two spectrograms, two visual displays of voice patterns.
P	Your Honor, I request that these be marked prosecution exhibits number three and four for identification.
J	They will be so marked.
P	Please let the record reflect that I am showing these exhibits to the opposing attorney.
J	It will so reflect.
P	Ms. Cottrell, I now hand you prosecution exhibit number three for identification. WHAT is it? (14)
W	It's the spectrogram of the recording from prosecution exhibit number one.
P	HOW can you recognize the spectrogram? (14)
W	As you can see, on the other side, I marked my initials, the date, and the number of the flash drive it corresponded to.
P	I now hand you prosecution exhibit number four for identification. WHAT is it? (14)
W	It's the spectrogram produced by analyzing the recording from prosecution exhibit number two.
P	HOW can you recognize it? (14)

W	I made the same sort of notations on the back here.
P	Your Honor, I now offer prosecution exhibits number three and four for identification into evidence as prosecution exhibits number three and four.
J	They will be received.
P	Ms. Cottrell, WHAT did you do with the spectrograms? (15)
W	I compared them.
P	WHAT was the result of your comparison? (15)
W	I found a large number of points of similarity between the two spectrograms.
P	HOW many points of similarity? (15)
W	32 in all.
P	Do you have an opinion on the question whether the same voice produced the two spectrograms? (16)
W	Yes.
P	WHAT is that opinion? (16)
W	In my opinion, it was the same voice.
P	WHAT is the basis of that opinion? (15)
W	Not just the number of points of similarity, but some of them were really unique. I'm fairly confident that the same person who phoned in this bomb threat made this other voice exemplar.
P	Request permission to hand exhibits number three and four to the jurors for their inspection.
J	Permission granted.

In both aural and spectrographic voice identification, the ultimate decision is made by a human being. However, there is a new generation of forensic voice comparison technology. Morrison & Thompson, *Assessing the Admissibility of a New Generation of Forensic Voice Comparison Testimony*, 18 COLUM. SCI. & TECH. L. REV. 326 (2017). In this technology, the decision is made by a computer based on an algorithm. There is a much smaller body of case on this methodology. *United States v. Arce Lopez*, 979 F. Supp. 2d 228 (D.P.R. 2013) (the defense was the proponent, and the judge barred the evidence on the ground that it would not be helpful to the jury); *United States v. Ahmed*, 94 F. Supp. 3d 394 (E.D.N.Y. 2015) (although the trial judge conducted a *Daubert* hearing, the defendant accepted a plea before a ruling on the admissibility of the expert testimony). A proponent of testimony based on this novel methodology would have to lay a foundation that would satisfy § 4.10, *infra*.

[5] CALLER IDENTIFICATION

[a] THE DOCTRINE

Caller identification technology is a means of identifying the telephone number of an incoming call and, thus, can furnish some evidence of the identity of the person who made the statements on the caller's side of the conversation. Caller ID units or boxes are widely available commercially from most vendors of telephones and telephone accessories. After purchasing a caller ID unit, the user installs the unit on the telephone line and requests caller ID service from the telephone company. The telephone company then activates the service for the user. The caller ID information is transmitted as a burst of a modem signal to the unit. Once service has been activated, whenever someone places a call to the user, the user's caller ID unit will automatically display the caller's telephone number.[30] More sophisticated caller ID units have the capability of timestamping and storing the number for later retrieval and printout.

Suppose that at trial, the proponent wants to prove that a certain call to the proponent's home or business originated from a certain number. In a contract action, the proponent might be the plaintiff contending that the telephone call (the alleged offer) came from the defendant's corporate headquarters.[31]

[b] ELEMENTS OF THE FOUNDATION

To lay a proper foundation, the proponent would be required to show the following:

1. In general, caller ID technology is reliable. Caller ID is already in such widespread use that many judges would be willing to judicially notice this proposition under Rule 201. The general reliability of the technology is both a matter of common knowledge and a matter capable of verification as beyond reasonable controversy. The problem facing the proponent is that to date, there are few published opinions upholding an authentication based on caller ID. Given the dearth of precedent, a cautious trial judge might insist that the proponent present live expert testimony to establish this element of the foundation. In that event, the proponent could call a telephone company representative. The representative would qualify as an expert, and the hypothesis of the reliability of the technology would undoubtedly qualify as both empirically validated under *Daubert* and generally accepted in the particular field to which it belongs under the *Frye* test.

2. Prior to the telephone call in question, the user acquired and installed a caller ID unit or box.

3. The caller ID unit in question is a reliable one. Even if the judge is willing to

---

[30] Some callers, though, have "blocking." They can block the transmission of their phone number either in all cases or for a particular call. If the caller has the latter type of blocking, he or she must dial a special code at the time of the call in order to prevent the transmission of his or her phone number.

[31] Some callers have PBX, private branch exchanges. If so, the number transmitted to the user might be the main number for the corporation, rather than the number of the specific phone that the call was actually originated from.

judicially notice the first element of the foundation, the judge will probably balk at noticing this proposition. To be on the safe side, as on element number 1, the proponent could call an expert witness. In this case, the ideal expert would be a representative of the manufacturer. A salesperson at a telephone store would also probably qualify as an expert if he or she had substantial experience with the make and model in question.

The judge might not demand the appearance of an expert to testify directly to the reliability of the caller ID unit installed at the plaintiff's office. Instead, the judge might well be content with circumstantial proof. For example, one of the plaintiff's agents could testify that: She has used the unit in question for several months or years; when the agent receives a telephone call, the unit regularly displays a telephone number; and on numerous occasions, the circumstances have indicated that the number displayed was in fact the number from which the call originated.

A myriad of circumstances could suffice. The circumstance might be that when the agent answered, she recognized the voice as that of the person whose number was displayed. Or the caller might have disclosed information known only to employees of the business whose number was displayed. Or at a later point in time, the user called the number previously displayed by the caller ID unit; and in that subsequent conversation, the respondent referred to the earlier telephone call.

4.   On the occasion in question, the caller ID unit displayed a particular telephone number. If the user recalls the number displayed, he or she can testify to that number on the basis of personal knowledge. If the unit has logging and printout capability, the proponent can offer the printout into evidence so long as the foundational witness provides a sufficient foundation by identifying the exhibit as the printout from the user's caller ID unit. If, as is often done in the business world, the user has connected the caller ID unit to a computer which stores a history of the telephone numbers, the proponent can offer the computer printout.

5.   The telephone number in question belongs to a particular person or business. The witness could testify from personal experience that that number belongs to that individual or business. Failing that, the proponent could introduce a telephone directory. Telephone directories fall within the hearsay exception for commercial publications,[32] and the inscription on the directory would make it self-authenticating.[33] In many cases, the two parties can reach a stipulation that the phone number has been assigned to a particular person or business.

[c]   SAMPLE FOUNDATION

The fact situation is a civil contract action. The plaintiff, Arnett Corporation, alleges that the defendant, Balantine Corporation, breached a contract with the plaintiff. The

---

[32] *See* Fed. R. Evid. 803(17); M. Graham, HANDBOOK OF ILLINOIS EVIDENCE § 803(17) (2017).

[33] *See* Fed. R. Evid. 902(6).

plaintiff contends that on June 15, YR-3, the defendant telephoned the plaintiff and purchased an order for custom merchandise to be manufactured by the plaintiff. Before trial, the parties stipulated that the main telephone number for the defendant's purchasing department is (916) 752-0727. At a pretrial hearing, the judge accepted the stipulation. In addition, at the same hearing, the judge granted the plaintiff's request that she judicially notice the general reliability of caller identification technology. The next witness is Ms. Amann. Just before calling her, the plaintiff's attorney states:

P   Your Honor, as you will recall, at our pretrial conference, you granted our request for judicial notice. I would ask that at this point, you instruct the jury on the judicially noticed proposition. (1)

J   Very well. Ladies and gentlemen, I am going to give you an instruction now. The instruction is that you are to assume that in general, caller identification units for telephones are reliable. You are to assume that when a unit is working properly, it correctly displays the number of the incoming telephone call. You must assume the truth of that fact even though you will not hear any live testimony about it. All right, let's proceed.

P   Thank you, Your Honor. As our next witness, we call Ms. Holly Amann.

J   Ms. Amann, please approach the witness stand.

           (*Ms. Amann is sworn and identifies herself. The plaintiff's direct examination continues.*)

P   Ms. Amann, WHERE do you work? (2)

W   I work for Arnett Corporation.

P   HOW long have you worked there? (2)

W   I've been employed there for 15 years.

P   WHAT is your current position with Arnett Corporation? (2)

W   I'm the head of the order department.

P   HOW long have you held that position? (2)

W   I've been in orders for 10 years, and I've headed the department for the past three years.

P   WHAT is the job of the order department? (2)

W   We take all the incoming orders for merchandise. We make sure that the order is sent on to records, bookkeeping, and the plant.

P   HOW do you receive these orders? (2)

W   Lots of ways.

P   Such as WHICH ways? (2)

W   We get them by personal contact, snail mail, e-mail, fax, telephone— basically, if the means of communication exists, we use it to get orders.

P	WHAT percent of your orders come over the telephone? (2)
W	A significant percentage of people—especially our older customers—still use the good old telephone rather than the fancier stuff like e-mail.
P	WHAT type of telephone equipment do you use in your department? (2)
W	We have a phone hooked to a caller identification unit.
P	HOW long have you had a caller ID unit in your department? (2)
W	We've used one for over three years now.
P	WHAT type of unit do you have? (2)
W	It's a standard caller ID box manufactured by AT&T.
P	WHAT does the unit do? (2)
W	Since we're a business, we use one of the more advanced models.
P	WHAT do you mean by "advanced"? (2), (4)
W	A basic caller ID unit—like the one I have at home—just displays the incoming call number. However, as a business, we need to keep a record of our calls. So we have a caller unit with a history capability.
P	WHAT do you mean by "history capability"? (2), (4)
W	It not only displays the incoming caller number. Moreover, it logs or records the number in memory and time stamps it, indicating the date and time the call came in. At a later point, you can retrieve the number and time stamp from memory; you can either display it again or print it out.
P	HOW reliable is your caller ID unit? (3)
W	It's very trustworthy.
P	HOW do you know that? (3)
W	On many occasions, the information I've gotten from the unit has checked out.
P	HOW has it checked out? (3)
W	Someone will tell me something over the phone, and it will turn out to be true.
P	WHAT would be an example? (3)
W	Well, I'll get a call, and someone will tell me to expect an order from their business. Then in a couple of days I'll get that order, and I'll recognize the handwriting on the order. Or they'll say that a check is on the way, and a check will shortly show up from that very company.
P	HOW often, if ever, has the caller ID unit malfunctioned? (3)
W	As I recall, there was one day in YR-4 when it went down. It's not that it malfunctioned in the sense of giving you the wrong number. It shorted and didn't work at all. We immediately called the repairman and got the

	unit fixed. Since then we've had no problems at all.
P	Ms. Amann, WHERE were you on June 15th of YR-3? (4)
W	I was at work at the office.
P	WHAT, if any, telephone calls did you receive that day? (4)
W	I got one from a person who said he was a buyer for Ballantine.
P	Before that telephone call, HOW much contact, if any, had you had with that person? (4)
W	I have to say honestly that I didn't recognize his voice.
P	WHO did the caller say he worked for? (4)
W	He said he was calling on behalf of Ballantine to place an order.
P	At the time of the call, WHAT telephone number was the caller ID unit displaying? (4)
W	It was displaying Ballantine's number.
P	WHAT is that number? (5)
W	It's (916) 752-0727.
P	HOW do you know that? (5)
W	I've dealt with them on dozens of occasions before.
P	HOW do you know that the caller ID unit displayed that number? (4)
W	As I said, I didn't recognize this person's voice. However, I always make it a practice to check the caller ID display whenever I don't recognize the voice. You have to make sure who you're dealing with. If it hadn't displayed that number, I'd remember that. That would have been a red flag for me.
P	WHERE were you before coming to court this afternoon? (4)
W	I was at the office.
P	WHY were you there? (4)
W	You asked me to stop by and print out the history log from the caller ID unit for June 15, YR-3.
P	WHAT did you do? (4)
W	I did as you asked. I went to the unit, called up the log for that date, and printed it out.
P	Your Honor, I request that this be marked plaintiff's exhibit number three for identification. (4)
J	It will be so marked.
P	Please let the record reflect that I am showing the exhibit to the opposing counsel. (4)
J	The record will so reflect.

P   Permission to approach the witness? (4)

J   Granted.

P   Ms. Amann, I now hand you what has just been marked as plaintiff's exhibit number three for identification. WHAT is it? (4)

W   It's the printout of the history log from the caller ID unit in my department.

P   HOW can you recognize it? (4)

W   To begin with, I read it as soon as it printed out. I recognize the contents. In addition, just to be on the safe side, I wrote my initials and today's date on the page. They're right here. I recognize them as well.

P   Your Honor, I now offer plaintiff's exhibit number three for identification into evidence as plaintiff's exhibit number three. (4)

J   Any objection?

O   No, Your Honor.

J   Very well, it will be received.

P   Ms. Amann, I'd like you to read to the jury the third entry on this page. (4)

W   Certainly. It reads: "June 15 0930 hours (916) 752-0727."

P   WHAT does that entry mean? (4)

W   It means that at 0930 hours—that is, 9:30 a.m. in the morning, we received a telephone call from that number.

P   Thank you, Ms. Amann. Your Honor, as you know, at the pretrial hearing, you accepted a stipulation between the parties. I would request that at this point, you inform the jury of the stipulation.

J   Certainly. Ladies and gentlemen, earlier today the parties "stipulated" to a fact. That term means that they agreed to that fact. You are to assume that that fact is true. The stipulated fact is that (916) 752-0727 is the main telephone number for the defendant's purchasing department. You are to assume the truth of the stipulated fact just as you are to accept as true the fact I judicially noticed earlier.

§ 4.06   AUDIO RECORDINGS

[1]   THE DOCTRINE

Like computers, digital and tape recorders present scientific evidence issues. However, the validity of the underlying theory and the reliability of recorders in general are so well accepted that the judge will judicially notice those elements of the foundation. Notwithstanding the courts' willingness today to notice those foundational elements, the courts have traditionally taken a strict attitude towards audio recordings. The courts realize that recordings, digital and tape, can be tampered with. For that reason, in the past the courts generally insisted on a very complete foundation: the operator's qualifications, the equipment's working condition, custody of the recording, an identification of the speakers on the recording, and finally testimony of someone who heard the conversation that the recording is an accurate reproduction of the conversation.

However, the courts have begun to liberalize the standards for the admission of audio recordings. There are two reasons for the liberalization. First, there are now electronic techniques for determining in many cases whether a recording has been altered. If the opponent seriously contests a recording's accuracy, the opponent can use an expert to detect the tampering. Secondly and more importantly, the courts have gone back to fundamentals and begun to treat the question of an audio recording's authenticity as a simple question of authentication under Federal Rule of Evidence 104(b). As § 4.01 of this chapter emphasizes, the test for authentication is lax: Has the proponent presented sufficient evidence to support a rational finding of fact that the audio recording is authentic? Given that test, many modern courts are no longer insisting on the traditional, strict foundation. In truth, the last element of the traditional foundation, standing alone, has sufficient probative value to authenticate the recording. If a witness testifies that he or she heard a conversation and that the audio recording accurately reproduces the conversation, there is a permissive inference of the recording's genuineness. Similarly, proof of the other elements of the traditional foundation is sufficient authentication without the last element. Proof of the operator's qualifications, the equipment's working condition, and the audio recording's custody shows that the recording is an accurate reproduction of some conversation; and in principle, testimony identifying the speakers (by any person familiar with their voices) suffices to complete the foundation to authenticate audio recording.

[2] ELEMENTS OF THE FOUNDATION

The strict, traditional foundation includes the following elements:

1. The operator of the equipment was qualified.
2. The operator recorded a conversation at a certain time and place.
3. The operator used certain equipment to record the conversation.
4. The equipment was in good working order.
5. The operator used proper procedures to record the conversation.
6. The recording is a good reproduction of the conversation.
7. The operator accounts for the recording's custody between the time of taping and the time of trial.
8. The operator recognizes the exhibit as the recording.
9. The recording is still an accurate reproduction of the conversation.

[3] SAMPLE FOUNDATIONS

A Traditional Foundation

The first foundation is an example of a strict, traditional foundation. The fact situation is a contract action. The contracting parties were rather suspicious of each other, and they had a private investigator record a key negotiating session.

P	WHAT is your occupation? (1)
W	I'm a private investigator.
P	WHO is your employer? (1)
W	I work for the Stead Detective Agency downtown.
P	HOW long have you worked there? (1)
W	For about 10 years now.
P	WHAT are your duties for your employer? (1)
W	My real specialty is electronic surveillance and tape recording.
P	HOW long have you worked in that field? (1)
W	About 15 years.
P	WHEN did you begin working in that field? (1)
W	When I was in the military service.
P	WHICH military service were you in? (1)
W	I was in the Army.
P	WHAT did you do while you were in the service? (1)
W	I specialized in radar.
P	WHAT training did you receive in that specialty? (1)
W	I took a four-month course and was even able to get a first-class license from the Federal Communications Commission.
P	WHAT additional training have you had in the field? (1)
W	Since leaving the service, I've taken 10 college-level courses in electronics. I've also attended a number of seminars on tape recording and electronic surveillance techniques.
P	WHERE were you on the morning of January 17, YR-3? (2)
W	I went to the offices of Atco Corporation.
P	WHY did you do that? (2)
W	The president of the corporation, Mr. Semegen, had asked me to come and record a negotiating session between him and a Mr. Heiser, the head of another corporation.
P	WHAT did you do while you were at the offices of Atco Corporation? (3)
W	I did what I'd been asked to do; I recorded this conversation.
P	WHAT equipment did you use to record the conversation? (4)
W	I used a Uher digital recorder and microphones.
P	WHAT does "Uher" mean? (3)
W	It's a trade name. It is one of the most dependable manufacturers in the field.

P	HOW often had you used that equipment in the past? (3)
W	Hundreds of times. I really trust their equipment; it's very reliable.
P	WHAT condition was the equipment in that morning? (4)
W	It was in good condition.
P	HOW do you know that? (4)
W	Well, I checked out the recorder and microphones. I test-recorded some conversation and replayed it; it was a good quality reproduction. I cleared the storage on the recorder so that it had plenty of capacity.
P	HOW did you use the equipment? (5)
W	I followed my standard procedure. First, I plugged the recorder into a wall outlet. Then I attached the mikes. After I'd test-recorded some sound, I was good to go.
P	WHAT did you do then? (5)
W	Before I started recording the conversation, I asked the parties, Messrs. Semegen and Heiser, to speak into the microphones. I got the right voice level, and then I was all set to record.
P	WHAT happened then? (5)
W	They spoke continuously for about half an hour. I then read my name, the date, and the address into the tape. After doing that, I turned off the recorder.
P	HOW well did the recorder work during the conversation? (6)
W	Very well.
P	HOW do you know that? (6)
W	In the first place, I didn't experience any technical or mechanical difficulties during the recording session. Secondly, right after the session, I reviewed it.
P	WHAT happened when you replayed the recording? (6)
W	I could hear the recording of the conversation.
P	WHAT was the quality of the recording? (6)
W	Excellent. As far as I could tell, the recorder picked up everything; and the recording was loud and clear.
P	WHAT did you do with the recording after you replayed it? (7)
W	I downloaded it as an audio file to a USB flash drive, placed it in an envelope, and wrote my name, the parties' names, the date, and address on it.
P	WHAT is a flash drive? (7)
W	It's a small portable electronic storage device, capable of holding a large amount of electronic data.

P	WHAT did you do with the envelope? (7)
W	I took it back to my office.
P	WHERE did you put it in your office? (7)
W	In my evidence locker.
P	HOW many people have access to the locker? (7)
W	Only me. I have a combination lock on it, and I'm the only one who knows the combination. Not even my secretary knows the combination.
P	WHAT happened to the flash drive after you placed it in your evidence locker? (7)
W	With one exception until today, it's been in the locker the whole time.
P	WHAT was that exception? (7)
W	You and I took it out several months ago and listened to it.
P	WHO was present during that playing of the electronic file? (7)
W	You and I were the only two persons there.
P	WHERE were you while the envelope containing the flash drive was out of the evidence locker? (7)
W	I was present the whole time. I took it out, played it for you, and then immediately put it back.
P	WHERE has the envelope with the flash drive been since then? (7)
W	In the locker the whole time.
P	Your Honor, I request that this flash drive be marked plaintiff's exhibit number ten for identification.
J	It will be so marked.
P	May the record reflect that I am showing plaintiff's exhibit number ten for identification to the opposing counsel?
J	It will so reflect.
P	I request permission to approach the witness.
J	Permission granted.
P	I now hand you plaintiff's exhibit number ten for identification. WHAT is it? (8)
W	It's the USB flash drive I've been talking about.
P	HOW can you recognize it? (8)
W	I recognize my handwriting. Those are my initials. I made those markings on the label on the side.
P	WHAT condition is the electronic file in? (9)
W	It's in excellent condition.

P	HOW do you know that? (9)
W	When I removed it from the locker this morning, I replayed it.
P	WHAT was the quality of the recording? (9)
W	It hasn't changed at all. It was and is an excellent reproduction of the conversation.
P	Your Honor, I now offer plaintiff's exhibit number ten for identification into evidence as plaintiff's exhibit number ten.
J	It will be received.
P	I request permission to have the bailiff play the exhibit for the jury.
J	Permission granted.

A Modern Foundation

The second foundation is a simple, modern foundation. Here the witness overheard the conversation. Suppose that Mr. Semegen's secretary, Ms. Grant, was present during the negotiating session. Ms. Grant is the witness.

P	WHAT is your occupation?
W	I'm a secretary at Atco Corporation.
P	WHOM do you work for?
W	I work directly for the president, Mr. Jason Semegen.
P	HOW long have you worked for him?
W	Easily three years.
P	WHERE were you on the morning of January 17, YR-3?
W	I was at the office at work.
P	WHAT happened that morning?
W	Mr. Semegen had a bargaining session with a Mr. Heiser.
P	WHERE were you when this session occurred?
W	I was in the room.
P	HOW close were you to them?
W	I was sitting right next to them to take notes.
P	HOW well could you hear the conversation?
W	Just fine.
P	Your Honor, I request that this be marked plaintiff's exhibit number ten for identification.
J	It will be so marked.
P	Please let the record reflect that I am showing plaintiff's exhibit number ten for identification to the opposing counsel.
J	It will so reflect.

P	I request permission to approach the witness.
J	Permission granted.
P	I now hand you plaintiff's exhibit number ten for identification. WHAT is it?
W	It's an audio recording on a flash drive of the conversation between Mr. Semegen and Mr. Heiser.
P	HOW do you know that?
W	I listened to the recording in the judge's chambers just a few hours ago.
P	WHAT is the quality of the audio recording?
W	It's an excellent reproduction of the conversation as far as I can tell.
P	HOW can you recognize this recording as the one you listened to in the judge's chambers?
W	I recognize the marking on the flash drive, and I've kept it in my possession ever since I listened to it.
P	WHERE have you kept it?
W	I've kept it on my person while I was sitting listening to this trial.
P	HOW long did you have it in your possession?
W	About two hours. I kept it until I put it on your counsel table as I walked to the witness stand just a few minutes ago.
P	Your Honor, I now offer plaintiff's exhibit number ten for identification into evidence as plaintiff's exhibit number ten.
J	It will be received.
P	I request permission to have the bailiff play the audio recording for the jury.
J	Permission granted.

In the above hypothetical, the proponent was content to play the audio recording to the jury. However, suppose that some of the statements on the recording are either soft or otherwise difficult to understand. In that event, the proponent might want to hand the jurors a transcript of the recording that they may read while they are listening to the recording. To do so, the proponent must lay a further foundation. The proponent should have the witness testify that: He or she listened carefully to the recording; while doing so, the witness compared the transcript to the recording; and, as best he or she can tell, the exhibit is an accurate transcription of the recording. There is no need to identify the person who prepared the transcript.[34] Even when the proponent lays this foundation,

---

[34] In fact, the transcript might not have been prepared by a human being. There are now programs that can generate transcripts from recordings. Moran, *Leveling the Playing Field,* 108 A.B.A.J., Feb./Mar. 2022, at 38 (describing Justice Text, a tool "which reviews . . . audio files and generates searchable transcripts of them").

though, the judge ordinarily gives the jury a limiting instruction under Rule 105. The instruction informs the jury that: The real evidence is the recording; they are being provided with the transcript only for the limited purpose of helping them determine what is on the tape recording; and if they believe that the transcript misstates the contents of the recording, they are to disregard that portion of the transcript.

§ 4.07   DEMONSTRATIVE EVIDENCE

[1]   IN GENERAL

The types of articles we have discussed to date are real or original evidence; the articles have an historical connection with the transaction giving rise to the suit. For example, the document is a will the decedent signed before death, or the item is the very pistol the defendant used during the assault. Sometimes the proponent may use an item even if the item has no historical connection with the case (§ 4.08). Suppose, for example, that the police never found the pistol used in the assault. The trial judge might permit an eyewitness to the assault to use another, similar pistol to illustrate his or her testimony. The courts often refer to this latter type of evidence as demonstrative; the article helps the witness to demonstrate or illustrate oral testimony. On request, the judge will administer a Rule 105 limiting instruction about the evidentiary status of a demonstrative exhibit. The only constraints on the use of demonstrative evidence are the trial judge's discretion and the trial attorney's imagination.[35] This category of evidence includes diagrams and models.

The current Federal Rules do not expressly regulate the use of demonstrative or illustrative aids. However, in its May 15, 2022 report the Advisory Committee has proposed an amendment to Rule 611. The new Rule 611(d) would read:

Illustrative Aids.

(1)   Permitted Uses. The court may allow a party to present an illustrative aid to help the finder of fact understand admitted evidence if:

    (A)   its utility in assisting comprehension is not [substantially] outweighed by the danger of unfair prejudice, confusing the issues, misleading the jury, undue delay, or wasting time; and

    (B)   all parties are given notice and a reasonable opportunity to object to its use, unless the court, for good cause, orders otherwise.

(2)   Use in Jury Deliberations. An illustrative aid must not be provided to the jury during deliberations unless:

    (A)   all parties consent; or

    (B)   the court, for good cause, orders otherwise.

---

[35] However, jurisdictions and judges vary over the procedures for handling these exhibits. Maureen A. Howard & Jeffrey C. Barnum, *Bringing Demonstrative Evidence in from the Cold: The Academy's Role in Developing Model Rules,* 88 TEMPLE L. REV. 513 (2016). They differ on such questions as: whether the exhibit should be formally admitted, whether the exhibit may be sent to the jury during deliberations, and what the judge should say about the exhibit in the final jury charge.

    (3)   Record. When practicable, an illustrative aid that is used at trial must be entered into the record.

The accompanying Note elaborates:

the Committee concluded that trial courts should have some discretion to allow the jury to consider an aid during deliberations; that discretion is most likely to be exercised in complex cases, or in cases where the jury has requested to see the illustrative aid.

The proposed amendment is tentatively scheduled to take effect in December 2024.

[2]   VERIFICATION OF A DIAGRAM

The verification of a diagram is very similar to the verification of a photograph. In most cases, the diagram need not be to scale. However, the sponsoring witness must testify that the diagram is generally a "true," "accurate," "good," or "fair" depiction of the scene or object shown. If the diagram is not to scale, the opposing counsel is entitled to a limiting instruction.

The elements of the foundation are:

1.   The diagram depicts a certain area or object.

2.   The witness is familiar with that area or object.

3.   The witness explains the basis for his or her familiarity with the area or object.

4.   In the witness's opinion, the diagram is an accurate depiction of that area or object.

The fact situation is an assault prosecution. The indictment alleges that the accused attacked the victim, Mr. Williams, in a bathroom in the Senator Hotel in San Diego. The prosecutor wants to use a chart to illustrate the victim's testimony. The witness is the victim. The prosecutor is the proponent. The victim has just testified that he was attacked.

P	WHERE did this attack occur?
W	As I said, it occurred in the bathroom on the second floor of the hotel.
P	Your Honor, I request that this be marked prosecution exhibit number three for identification.
J	It will be so marked.
P	Please let the record reflect that I am showing the exhibit to the defense attorney.
J	It will so reflect.
P	Request permission to approach the witness.
J	Permission granted.
P	Mr. Williams, I hand you prosecution exhibit number three for identification. WHAT is it? (1)
W	It's a chart of the bathroom I was just referring to.

P	HOW do you recognize it? (2)
W	I know that hotel very well.
P	HOW did you become familiar with the hotel? (3)
W	I've lived in it for two years. It's a boarding hotel.
P	HOW many times have you been in that bathroom? (3)
W	Lots of times. I couldn't give you a specific figure.
P	HOW accurate is the diagram? (4)
W	Well, it's not to scale. That's for sure.
P	Otherwise, HOW accurate is the diagram? (4)
W	It's correct. It shows everything in roughly the right place.
P	Your Honor, I now offer prosecution exhibit number three for identification into evidence as prosecution exhibit number three.
O	Your Honor, under Rule 105, may a limiting instruction be given that the diagram is not to scale?
J	Yes. The exhibit will be received. (*To the jurors*) Ladies and gentlemen of the jury, the prosecutor is now going to show you a diagram of the bathroom in the Senator Hotel. The witness has testified that the diagram is basically accurate, but the witness also stated that the diagram is not to scale. The diagram does not show exact distances or dimensions. In deciding what weight, if any, to attach to the diagram, you should consider the fact that the diagram is not to scale.
P	I now request permission to hand the diagram to the jurors for their inspection.
J	Permission granted.

[3] MARKING A DIAGRAM

To effectively use a chart, the proponent will sometimes have to have the witness mark on the chart. The marking will help the jury visualize the testimony. Moreover, the marking will help the appellate court understand the record of trial. Unless the diagram is marked, the record of trial may be positively confusing to the appellate court; the court will not know where "here" or "there" was on the map. The proponent should give the witness specific instructions as to how to mark the chart. In addition, in some jurisdictions, it is customary to have the record reflect that the witness complied with the proponent's instructions.

To illustrate these techniques, we shall use the original hypothetical:

P	Mr. Williams, using the chart, WHERE were you when the accused first walked into the bathroom?
W	I was standing over here.
P	Please take this red pen, place a circle where you were standing, and write the letter W in the circle.

W	*(The witness complied.)*
P	Please let the record reflect that the witness complied with my instruction.
J	The record will so reflect.
P	Now, Mr. Williams, WHAT direction was the defendant Dugan walking in when he first entered the room?
W	He was going that way.
P	Please use this blue pen, draw an arrow showing that direction, and write the letter D at the tip of the arrow.
W	*(The witness complied.)*
P	Please let the record reflect that the witness complied with my direction.
J	The record will so reflect.

The reader should bear in mind two important caveats. Many trial judges prefer that the chart be completely marked before it is formally offered into evidence. These judges will not permit any further marking after the exhibit has been received into evidence. If you contemplate using a chart during a trial, you should inquire about the judge's preference during the chambers conference before the trial begins. The second caveat is that if you ultimately want the judge to send the chart to the jury during deliberation, you may want to add a legend at the bottom of the chart. Of course, the jurors may remember that "W" represents Williams and "D" the defendant Dugan. However, days or weeks might elapse between the use of the chart during trial and the beginning of the jury deliberations. To ensure that the jury correctly interprets the markings on the chart, you can instruct the witness to indicate on the bottom of the chart the significance of each mark. For example, you might add, "Mr. Williams, would you please indicate on the bottom of the chart that the letter 'D' represents or equals the defendant?"

[4] MODELS

The use of models is becoming increasingly common in courtrooms. The proponent may use a skeletal model or a model of a house or machine. Models present more logistical problems for trial courts than simple diagrams. For that reason, some judges are more reluctant to permit the use of models. Indeed, in some jurisdictions, before resorting to a model, the proponent must affirmatively show that the witness needs the model to adequately explain his or her testimony.

The foundation for the use of a model should include the following elements:

1. The witness needs the visual aid to explain his or her testimony.

2. The aid depicts a certain scene or object.

3. The witness is familiar with the scene or object.

4. The witness explains the basis for his or her familiarity with the scene or object.

5. In the witness's opinion, the aid is a "true," "accurate," "good," or "fair" model of the scene or object.

The fact situation is a tort action for injuries. The plaintiff, Ms. Graham, suffered extensive bone damage. The next witness is Dr. Miller, a bone specialist. In general terms, Dr. Miller has already described the extensive nature of the bone damage.

P	Now, Doctor, in detail, WHAT are the injuries to Ms. Graham's bones? (1)
W	That question is really difficult to answer orally.
P	WHY? (1)
W	Well, in the first place, a large number of bones have been damaged. Secondly, it's sometimes difficult for me to explain the precise location of the bone. Finally, some of the damage is really to the way bones work and fit together. It's hard to put all that into words.
P	HOW could you explain the detailed injuries more effectively? (1)
W	It would be much better if I were permitted to use a skeletal model.
P	Your Honor, I request that this be marked plaintiff's exhibit number seven for identification.
J	It will be so marked.
P	Doctor, I now show you plaintiff's exhibit number seven for identification. WHAT is it? (2)
W	It's the sort of skeletal model I just mentioned.
P	HOW do you know that? (3), (4)
W	I'm not only a medical doctor; I'm a bone specialist. I've studied and used models such as this one for years. In fact, I've consulted with some of the art companies that manufacture these models.
P	HOW accurate is this skeletal model? (5)
W	It's quite good. It depicts the bone structure of a female of the approximate height and build of the plaintiff, Ms. Graham.
P	HOW helpful would this be to illustrate your testimony about the specific bone injuries? (1)
W	Very. I can point to the location of the bones, show you what they look like, and demonstrate how they're supposed to fit together with adjacent bones.

In some jurisdictions, models such as the one in the hypothetical are used without even marking them for identification. That practice makes it difficult for the appellate court to understand the record of trial. Perhaps the prevailing practice modernly is at least to mark the model as an exhibit for identification. However, in many jurisdictions, if an exhibit is merely marked for identification, it cannot be sent to the jury for use during deliberation. A few jurisdictions require the proponent to formally offer the model into evidence. In such a jurisdiction, the sample foundation would continue:

P	Your Honor, I now offer plaintiff's exhibit number seven for identifica-

tion into evidence as plaintiff's exhibit number seven.

J   It will be received.

P   I request permission to use the model to illustrate Dr. Miller's testimony.

J   Permission granted.

One final point is that the proponent does not always have to leave the model in the court's possession after trial. In most jurisdictions, the trial judge has discretion to permit the proponent to later substitute a photograph or written description for insertion in the record of trial. If the proponent wishes to do so, after the judge receives the exhibit into evidence, the proponent should state: "I request permission to later substitute a photograph of this model into the record of trial."

§ 4.08   THE IDENTIFICATION OF REAL OR ORIGINAL PHYSICAL EVIDENCE

[1]   THE DOCTRINE

Section 4.07 of this chapter discussed demonstrative physical evidence. Demonstrative evidence has two characteristics. On the one hand, it illustrates or demonstrates the witness's testimony. On the other hand, the exhibit itself has no historical connection with the facts of the case; it is not the actual pistol or knife used in the crime.

In contrast, real or original physical evidence has a connection with the case. For example, the prosecutor may contend that the exhibit is the very pistol or knife used. If the prosecutor makes that claim, the prosecutor must authenticate the evidence by proving the claim. The prosecutor must demonstrate the object's connection with the case. The process of demonstrating this historical connection is usually termed the identification of the physical evidence. There are two recognized methods of identifying physical evidence.

The first method is ready identifiability. If the article has a unique, one-of-a-kind characteristic or combination of characteristics, the characteristic or set of characteristics makes the article readily identifiable. The foundation is complete so long as the witness testifies that he or she previously observed the characteristic and presently recalls the characteristic. An identification resting on that characteristic is sufficient. The foundation is adequate to establish the exhibit's identity as the object the witness previously observed. Federal Rule of Evidence 901(b)(4) expressly permits identification of an object by its "distinctive characteristics."

Suppose, however, that one of the elements of the foundation for ready identifiability is missing; the object lacks a unique characteristic, the witness did not observe the characteristic on the previous occasion, or the witness cannot presently recall the characteristic. Or suppose that the proponent is interested in the object's condition rather than its simple identity; the proponent might want a laboratory technician to testify about a scientific analysis of the object. A ready identifiability foundation establishes the identity of the object, but the foundation for a scientific analysis of the object also necessitates proof that the object's condition was unchanged. In these circumstances, the proponent must establish a chain of custody from the time of seizure until at least the time of analysis. Chain of custody is the second method of identifying physical evidence.

Who are the links in the chain? The links are people who actually handle the object. Other persons who merely have access to the object are not considered links. Thus, even if two other laboratory technicians know the combination to the safe where the witness kept the object, the other technicians are not deemed links. The only link would be the technician who physically handled the object. The proponent would have to account for that technician's handling of the object. (If one custodian of the object mails the object to a laboratory for analysis, the postal employees who handle the object technically become links. However, the courts dispense with any need for proof of the postal employees' conduct by presuming that public officials properly discharge their duties.).

How does the proponent account for handling? The proponent must show the link's initial receipt of the object, ultimate disposition of the object (retention, destruction, or transfer), and safekeeping of the object between receipt and disposition. The witness can keep the object in a locked safe, a secure evidence container, or any other place where substitution and tampering are unlikely.

Ideally, the proponent should call each link to the stand in the sequence in which they handled the object. The proponent would mark the object for identification and hand it to the first link for identification. The proponent would also hand it to every intermediate link for identification. However, the proponent does not formally tender the exhibit into evidence until the last link's testimony; at that point, the foundation is complete. Alternatively, the proponent might be able to introduce chain-of-custody receipts as substantive evidence.

[2] ELEMENTS OF THE FOUNDATION

The foundation for ready identifiability is very short:

1. The object has a unique characteristic. The characteristic can be a single, peculiar feature or a unique combination of features.

2. The witness observed the characteristic(s) on a previous occasion.

3. The witness identifies the exhibit as the object. The witness testifies that he or she can presently recall the unique characteristic(s).

4. The witness rests the identification on his or her present recognition of the characteristic(s).

5. As best the witness can tell, the exhibit is in the same condition as it was when he or she initially received the object.

As previously stated, when the person who handled the exhibit was a public employee, some courts invoke the rebuttable presumption that public employees properly discharge their duties. Unless the proponent has the benefit of a presumption, the foundation for chain of custody must be laid during the testimony of each link in the chain:

1. The witness initially received the object at a certain time and place.

2. The witness safeguarded the object; the witness testifies to circumstances making it unlikely that substitution or tampering occurred. The admissibility standard is lax, since Federal Rule of Evidence 104(b) governs the adequacy of the proof of safeguarding. However, the proponent would go into more detail if he or she anticipated that the opponent will attack the weight of the evidence by suggesting that the handling of the physical evidence was sloppy.

3. The witness ultimately disposed of the object (retention, destruction, or transfer to another person).

4. As best the witness can tell, the exhibit is the same object he or she previously handled.

5. As best the witness can tell, the exhibit is in the same condition as it was when he or she initially received the object.

[3] SAMPLE FOUNDATIONS

The fact situation for the ready identifiability foundation is a civil tort case. The complaint alleges that the defendant assaulted the plaintiff with a knife. The witness is a police officer who investigated the complaint. The proponent is the plaintiff. The officer has just testified that he reported to the scene and began inspecting the scene.

P	WHAT did you do during this inspection?

W	I was looking for any evidence.

P	WHAT, if anything, did you find?

W	I found a knife answering the description the plaintiff, Mr. Brown, gave me.

P	WHERE did you find it?

W	Right at the corner of the building where the alleged assault occurred.

P	WHAT did you do with the knife? (1)

W	I followed standard operating procedure.

P	WHAT is that procedure? (1)

W	I marked it for identification.

P	HOW did you do that? (1)

W	In the case of a relatively inexpensive item such as this one, I tagged it and scratched my initials and the date onto the wooden handle.

P	WHEN did you do this? (2)

W	As soon as I found it.

P	HOW much time passed between your discovery of this knife and your marking it? (2)

W	No more than a couple of minutes.

P	Your Honor, I request that this be marked plaintiff's exhibit number two for identification.
J	It will be so marked.
P	Please let the record reflect that I am showing the exhibit to the opposing counsel.
J	It will so reflect.
P	I request permission to approach the witness.
J	Permission granted.
P	I now hand you plaintiff's exhibit number two for identification. WHAT is it? (3)
W	It's the knife I found.
P	HOW can you recognize it? (4)
W	As I testified, I marked my initials and the date on the handle. They're right there.
P	WHAT condition is the exhibit in? (5)
W	It's in good condition.
P	HOW, if at all, has it changed since you found it at the scene? (5)
W	It doesn't appear to have changed at all. It seems to be in exactly the same condition.
P	Your Honor, I now offer plaintiff's exhibit number two for identification into evidence as plaintiff's exhibit number two.
J	It will be received.
P	I request permission to hand the exhibit to the jurors for their inspection.
J	Permission granted.

The fact situation for the chain of custody foundation is a criminal assault prosecution. The government alleges that the accused, Mr. Morris, used his feet to kick and beat the victim, Mr. Navin. The government wants to show that the DNA of the blood stains on the accused's shoes matches the victim's DNA. As a predicate for that scientific analysis, the government must establish a chain of custody for the shoes; the government must demonstrate that the shoes were in the same condition at the time of analysis as they were when they were seized from the accused. The seizing police officer, Officer Stevens, has already testified. He testified that he seized the shoes from Morris, kept them safe, and then delivered them to the laboratory technician, Ms. Quinn. Ms. Quinn is the next witness. The prosecutor is the proponent. The shoes have been marked prosecution exhibit number four for identification.

P	WHAT is your occupation?
W	I am a laboratory technician with the Baltimore Police Department.
P	HOW long have you worked for the Baltimore Police Department?

W	About six years.
P	WHAT are your duties?
W	I specialize in blood and stain analysis, including DNA testing.
P	HOW long have you done that sort of work?
W	About six years—ever since I graduated.
P	WHAT school did you graduate from?
W	Oregon State.
P	WHAT was your major area of study?
W	Chemistry, especially organic chemistry.
P	Ms. Quinn, WHERE were you on the afternoon of November 12, YR-3? (1)
W	I was on duty at work at the laboratory.
P	WHAT, if anything, happened that afternoon? (1)
W	Officer Stevens delivered some shoes to me for analysis.
P	WHO is Officer Stevens? (1)
W	He was the last witness on this case.
P	HOW do you know that? (1)
W	I was sitting in the spectators' section over there when he testified.
P	WHAT did you do with the shoes when he delivered them to you? (2)
W	I followed standard practice. The very first thing I did was initial the evidence slip that's attached.
P	WHAT is an evidence slip? (2)
W	It's a chain of custody receipt. You sign off on it when you receive the attached object.
P	WHAT did you do with the shoes after you initialed the evidence slip? (2)
W	I immediately conducted an analysis of some stains on the soles of the shoes.
P	HOW much time passed between his delivery of the shoes and your analysis? (2)
W	Only about five minutes. I wasn't very busy when he walked in.
P	WHAT did you do after you conducted the analysis? (2)
W	I put the shoes in my evidence locker.
P	WHERE is this locker? (2)
W	It's in my work area in the lab.
P	HOW secure is this locker? (2)

W	Well, I have a combination lock on it.
P	WHO knows the combination? (2)
W	Just me and the head of the Fluids section of the lab, Ms. Guinn.
P	WHAT happened to the shoes after you put them in the locker? (3)
W	They've just been sitting there until today.
P	HOW often have you opened the locker between the time you placed the shoes there and today? (2)
W	Probably hundreds of times.
P	WHAT procedure do you use to open the locker? (2)
W	I use the combination to open it, remove what I want, and immediately close and lock it.
P	HOW, if at all, have the shoes changed since you placed them in the locker? (2)
W	They're certainly a little dustier than before, but otherwise they haven't changed.
P	Your Honor, I request permission to approach the witness.
J	Permission granted.
P	I now hand you prosecution exhibit number four for identification. WHAT is it? (4)
W	They seem to be the shoes I analyzed.
P	HOW can you recognize them? (4)
W	I notice my handwriting on the attached slip, and I recognize their general appearance, including the scrapes and the stains on the soles.
P	HOW did the shoes get out of the evidence locker? (4)
W	I removed them just before coming here to testify.
P	WHO has had possession of them since you removed them from the locker? (4)
W	I had possession until I got here.
P	WHAT did you do then? (4)
W	As I walked to the witness stand, I placed them on your counsel table so you could use them.
P	WHAT did you do then? (4)
W	I sat in the spectators' area and observed the trial and kept an eye on the shoes.
P	HOW often did you leave the room? (4)
W	I didn't. I've been here this entire morning, watching the trial and the shoes.

P	WHAT condition are the shoes in? (5)
W	They seem to be in the same condition as when Officer Stevens delivered them to me.
P	WHAT condition are the stains in? (5)
W	They're a bit changed because I had to scrape some off to analyze the stains. Otherwise they're in the same condition.
P	Your Honor, I now offer prosecution exhibit number four for identification into evidence as prosecution exhibit number four.
J	They will be received.
P	I request permission to hand the exhibit to the jurors for their inspection.
J	Request granted.

(The jurors inspect the shoes.)

P	Now, Ms. Quinn, I'd like to ask you a few questions about the results of your analysis of the shoes.

In the past, especially in the jurisdictions applying the Rule 104(b) procedure to determine the sufficiency of chain-of-custody foundations, the courts have been very liberal in ruling on the sufficiency of the foundation. In particular, the courts often remarked that questions about the quality of the safeguarding of the sample analyzed cut to the weight of the testimony, not its admissibility. However, in the near future in some cases that attitude may change. The sensitivity of forensic techniques is improving; that is, the techniques can detect and analyze smaller and smaller samples. For example, some laboratories now conduct Low Copy Number (LCN) or "touch" DNA testing of miniscule samples in the nanogram and picogram range. 2 P. GIANNELLI, E. IMWINKELRIED, A. ROTH, J. CAMPBELL MORIARTY & V. BEETY, SCIENTIFIC EVIDENCE § 18.03[d] (6th ed. 2020). The use of such tiny samples increases the risk of both substitution and contamination. Especially when the witness will testify to the analysis of such a small sample, the proponent should not be content with the type of minimal foundation that the courts have frequently accepted in the past. The proponent ought to go into more detail about the steps taken to prevent substitution and contamination.

§ 4.09   THE VERIFICATION OF PHOTOGRAPHS

[1]   STILL PHOTOGRAPHS

Like other articles, still photographs must be authenticated or verified. In the past, some courts insisted that the photographer appear as the sponsoring witness. Modernly, the prevailing view is that any person familiar with the scene or object depicted may verify the photograph.

The foundational elements are as follows:

1. The witness is familiar with the object or scene.
2. The witness explains the basis for his or her familiarity with the object or scene.

3.   The witness recognizes the object or scene in the photograph.

4.   The photograph is a "fair," "accurate," "true," or "good" depiction of the object or scene at the relevant time.

Our fact situation is a civil tort action arising from a collision. The collision occurred at the intersection of A and Third Streets. The plaintiff calls a witness to verify a photograph of the intersection. The witness has already identified himself as Mr. Donald Adams. The accident occurred in YR-4.

P	WHERE do you work? (2)
W	Downtown.
P	WHERE downtown? (2)
W	I'm a teller at the River City Bank branch on Third Street.
P	WHERE is the bank located on Third Street? (2)
W	I think it's the 400 block. The bank is between A and B Streets.
P	HOW long have you worked there? (2)
W	A good seven years.
P	Your Honor, I request that this be marked plaintiff's exhibit number three for identification.
J	It will be so marked.
P	Please let the record reflect that I am showing the exhibit to the opposing counsel.
J	The record will so reflect.
P	I request permission to approach the witness.
J	Permission granted.
P	I now hand you plaintiff's exhibit number three for identification. WHAT is it? (3)
W	It's a photograph of the intersection of A and Third Streets.
P	HOW can you recognize it? (2)
W	As I said, I've worked in that area for years.
P	HOW often have you passed that intersection? (2)
W	I couldn't give you a figure. I've been there hundreds of times.
P	WHAT perspective or viewpoint does this photograph show? (3)
W	Let's see. Third Street runs north-south. A Street runs east-west.
P	WHICH corner are you on? (3)
W	You're on the southwest corner.
P	In WHICH direction are you facing? (3)
W	You're facing north; you're looking up Third Street.

P	HOW accurate is this photograph? (4)
W	Very. It's a good, true depiction as far as I can tell.
P	HOW accurately does it show the intersection as it was in YR-4? (4)
W	Well. It's a good photograph for that purpose. I worked downtown then, and I think it shows roughly how the intersection looked then.
P	HOW, if at all, has the intersection changed since YR-4? (4)
W	Some of the business signs have changed; businesses come and go. However, the intersection itself really hasn't changed. As best I can recall, it's the same size, the street markings are the same, and traffic flows the same way.
P	Your Honor, I now offer plaintiff's exhibit number three for identification into evidence as plaintiff's exhibit number three.
J	It will be received.
P	I request permission to hand the exhibit to the jurors for their inspection.
J	Permission granted.

[2] MOTION PICTURES AND VIDEOTAPES

Like computers and audio recorders, motion pictures raise scientific evidence issues. Again, the validity of the underlying theory and the general reliability of motion picture and digital cameras are now so well accepted that the judge will judicially notice those two elements of the foundation. The Evidence law governing motion pictures parallels the law governing audio recorders in another respect; as in the case of audio recorders, the courts were initially very conservative in their treatment of motion pictures. The traditional view was that because of the possibility of distortion, the proponent had to lay a very strict foundation: the operator's qualifications, the good working condition of the equipment, the custody of the film, identification of the persons or objects depicted in the film, and testimony by someone present that the film accurately depicts the activity filmed. The law governing the admission of motion pictures has been liberalized in recent years. More and more courts have ruled that Federal Rule of Evidence 104(b) governs the sufficiency of the proof of the accuracy of films. Under Rule 104(b), the testimony of any person present when the activity occurred is sufficient to authenticate the film; and even without the testimony of such a person, the remaining foundation elements have sufficient probative value to verify the film.

A complete, traditional foundation includes these elements:

1. The operator was qualified to take a digital video movie.

2. The operator videoed a certain activity.

3. The operator used certain equipment to film the activity. Some trial attorneys prefer to present very detailed testimony about the equipment, such as the number of pixels per inch, the storage memory of the digital recorder, and the lens used. As the sample foundation indicates, a general description of the equipment is sufficient.

4.   The equipment was in good working order.

5.   The operator used proper procedures to video the activity. Here again some attorneys like to offer detailed testimony. Their foundation covers such technical matters as the lens used. General testimony is satisfactory.

6.   The operator accounts for the custody of the recorded video.

7.   The recorded video was a good reproduction of the activity.

8.   The operator recognizes the exhibit as the video he or she took.

9.   The video is still an accurate depiction of the activity.

The fact situation is a civil tort action. The plaintiff's theory is that the defendant, Polecat Motors, defectively designed the YR-3 Sport Sprint. The plaintiff wants to introduce films depicting impact experiments with a YR-3 Sport Sprint. The plaintiff calls the photographer who filmed the experiment. The photographer has already identified himself as Mr. Blair McIntosh.

P	WHAT is your occupation? (1)
W	I am a professional photographer.
P	WHERE do you work? (1)
W	I have my own studio at 1333 Front Street downtown.
P	HOW long have you been a professional photographer? (1)
W	For over 12 years now.
P	HOW did you become a professional photographer? (1)
W	I started working for another professional photographer in Denver right after graduation from high school.
P	WHAT training have you had as a photographer? (1)
W	I've taken 10 college level courses in photography and attended numerous seminars and training conferences.
P	HOW long have you had your own professional photography business? (1)
W	The last seven years.
P	Mr. McIntosh, WHERE were you on the morning of August 17th of this year? (2)
W	I was at Abbott Laboratories on C Street here in Fort Collins.
P	WHY did you go there? (2)
W	You asked me to go there to film some experiments.
P	WHAT experiments? (2)
W	It was an impact or crash experiment with a YR-3 Polecat Sport Sprint.
P	WHAT did you do when you arrived at Abbott Laboratories? (2)
W	I carried out my assignment. I introduced myself to the personnel

conducting the experiment and proceeded to film their experiment.

P WHAT equipment did you use? (3)

W I used a Sony PMW 320. It is a lower-end state of the art HD digital camera. The PMW shoots onto a solid state media card called an SKS, which is 16 GB and can hold 54 minutes of film.

P HOW widely is this equipment used? (3)

W Lots of professional photographers, especially television news photographers, use the very same set of equipment. It's a very reliable set.

P WHAT condition was the equipment in when you filmed the experiment? (4)

W Good operating condition.

P HOW do you know that? (4)

W I didn't experience any mechanical difficulty with the camera or lens during the filming, and I had just given my equipment complete maintenance a week before. I was able to check the video as I was recording, and it looked perfect.

P HOW did you film the experiment? (5)

W I checked my light meter to make certain that I had the right opening on the lens. Then I set the camera upon the tripod and focused until I had a clear image in my viewer.

P HOW long did it take you to film the experiment? (6)

W Only about 20 minutes.

P WHAT did you do after you filmed the experiment? (6)

W I disassembled my equipment and went back to my studio.

P WHAT did you do after you arrived there? (6)

W I downloaded the digital film from the SKS card onto a newly purchased flash drive.

P Did you view the digital video? (6)

W Yes. It turned out excellent. As far as I could tell, it was a fine, accurate depiction of the experiment.

P WHAT did you do after you viewed the video? (7)

W I burned the video onto a DVD and placed the DVD in its case. I marked the time and date of the video on the case, and placed it in my files.

P WHERE did you keep the DVD after that? (6)

W With one exception, it's been in my files the whole time.

P WHAT was that exception? (6)

W You and I viewed the DVD two weeks ago.

P	WHO was present during the viewing? (6)
W	Just the two of us. And the other attorney over there.
P	Your Honor, please let the record reflect that the witness pointed to and identified the defense attorney.
J	The record will so reflect.
P	WHERE were you during the viewing? (6)
W	I was present the whole time during this viewing.
P	WHAT did you do with the DVD after the viewing? (6)
W	I put it back in my files.
P	Your Honor, I request that this be marked plaintiff's exhibit number five for identification.
J	It will be so marked.
P	Please let the record reflect that I am showing the exhibit to the opposing counsel.
J	The record will so reflect.
P	I request permission to approach the witness.
J	Permission granted.
P	Mr. McIntosh, I now hand you plaintiff's exhibit number five for identification. WHAT is it? (8)
W	It's the DVD of the video of the experiment.
P	HOW do you recognize it? (8)
W	I recognize my handwriting on the label on the DVD.
P	HOW did the DVD get from your files to the courtroom today? (6)
W	I took it out of my files this morning and brought it here myself.
P	WHAT did you do with it after you arrived here? (9)
W	You, the other attorney, the judge, and I viewed the DVD in the judge's chambers.
P	WHAT condition was the DVD in? (9)
W	Fine. It's in the same excellent condition it previously was in.
P	WHAT happened to the DVD after we viewed it in the judge's chambers? (6)
W	I kept it in my possession.
P	WHEN did you surrender possession of it? (6)
W	I put it on your counsel table as I walked up to the witness stand.
P	Your Honor, I now offer plaintiff's exhibit number five for identification into evidence as plaintiff's exhibit number five.

J   It will be received.

P   I request permission to have the bailiff show the DVD to the jurors.

J   Permission granted.

When the proponent offers a videotape, the proponent must not only lay the normal foundation for a motion picture; he or she must also authenticate the noises, especially voices, heard on the videotape. If the proponent's sponsoring witness was present at the activity shown on the videotape, that witness can ordinarily identify the noises heard on the tape. If for some reason that witness cannot identify the voices heard on the tape, the proponent could call another witness or witnesses familiar with those voices to lay that element of the foundation.

The following example focuses on a videotape recording of a "sting" operation during which the defendant allegedly sold stolen goods to undercover police agents posing as pawnshop owners. The proponent is the prosecutor. The witness is Officer Jones, who operated a camcorder from behind a two-way mirror in an adjoining room. The officer just finished describing how the sting operation worked.

P   Officer Jones, HOW did you record the sting operation?

W   We set up a camcorder on a tripod in the backroom and pointed it straight at the two-way mirror. The people bringing the stolen goods to the store thought that they were dealing members of an organized crime family interested in buying stolen goods. They had no idea that they were being filmed.

P   Please describe WHAT type of camera equipment you used? (3)

W   It was a Canon Vixia HF S200 flash memory camcorder. We used a remote microphone to pick up all the voices in the room. This type of equipment is available in any neighborhood electronics store.

P   WHAT was the condition of the equipment? (4), (5)

W   It worked fine. I ran several trial recordings and sound checks before the defendant came in. The quality was excellent.

P   WHAT, if any, training have you had in operating the equipment? (1)

W   I haven't had any formal training as such. However, several of us have worked with one of our electronics people at the crime lab to familiarize ourselves with the equipment. I've used this equipment at least 15 times without any difficulty. The system is pretty straightforward to operate.

P   Your Honor, I am marking this DVD as prosecution exhibit three for identification.

J   It will be so marked.

P   Your Honor, please let the record reflect that I am showing the exhibit to opposing counsel.

J   It will so reflect.

P   May I have permission to approach the witness?

J   Yes.

P   Officer Jones, I now show you what has been marked as prosecution exhibit number three for identification. WHAT is this? (8)

W   It's the DVD recording of the camcorder video we ran on the defendant.

P   HOW do you know that?

W   My initials are on the DVD label. Right here.

P   WHAT, if any, changes have been made to the digital video since it was recorded? (7)

W   Absolutely none.

P   WHERE has the video been kept since the recording? (7)

W   In our police files under lock and key. We removed it only once, and that was to show it to you and the defense counsel last month.

P   WHO is shown on the video? (2)

W   Officers Mickey and Frances, the two undercover officers posting as the buyers, and then the defendant.

P   WHAT, if any, inducement did you offer the defendant to get him to participate in the recorded transaction?

W   The only thing we did was to spread the word on the street that we were offering cold cash for hot merchandise. Everything on this video was voluntarily done and said by the defendant and the two officers.

P   Officer Jones, HOW accurately does this video depict what took place when the defendant came into the store? (9)

W   It's absolutely true.

P   HOW can you be so sure? (9)

W   Well, for one thing, this equipment has a date and time feature on it. Once you turn it on, it runs continuously until the switch is turned off. By watching the DVD, you can see for yourself that the date and time indicator is on continuously from the second the defendant walked into the store until we arrested him 10 minutes later. There is no break in the action.

P   Thank you. Your Honor, we now move for the admission of prosecution exhibit number three for identification.

J   Any objections from the defense?

O   We have none, Your Honor.

J   Very well. The exhibit will be admitted as prosecution exhibit number three.

P   At this time, Your Honor, we would like to use the television monitors to show the DVD to the jury.

J   That will be fine. Bailiff, will you please get the lights?

[3] X-RAYS

X-rays are also photographs. In most cases, the counsel stipulate to the authenticity of X-rays in the case. However, occasionally, the proponent will have to authenticate the X-ray. The authentication of an X-ray is a rather peculiar process. No one can testify that he or she saw what the X-ray depicts and verify the X-ray on that theory.

Because of that peculiarity, the proponent must resort to some other authentication technique. Some judges treat X-rays as business records of the hospital; they accept authentication by the testimony of the hospital's X-ray librarian that he or she removed the X-ray from the right file. Other judges view X-ray evidence as presenting both scientific and physical evidence problems; the proponent must show the operator's qualifications, the working order of the X-ray, and a chain of custody for the X-ray film. The traditional X-ray is a thin piece of film with emulsions on both sides. The image of the patient's organs is exposed and saved on the film itself. A cassette holds the X-ray film. The cassette is a hard plastic case with intensifying screens. The cassette serves a number of functions. To begin with, it holds the X-ray film flat and straight and in the right position under or behind the patient. In addition, it protects the X-ray film from light. Finally, the intensifying screens vary the amount of energy that it takes to expose the X-ray film. Newer, better intensifying screens can both improve the quality of the image and reduce the patient's exposure to radiation. While the X-ray film is unique to a particular exposure of a particular patient, the cassette can be reused over and over.

In older X-ray techniques, the technician placed lead letters and numbers near the film during the patient's exposure. The letters and numbers identified the patient and the date of the X-ray; the final X-ray included images of the identifying letters and numbers. In effect, the letters and numbers made the film a readily identifiable article. However, today X-ray technicians rarely use such lead letters and numbers. Instead, they prepare a special label that is handwritten or typed, or has an impression from the patient's plastic hospital ID card. The label is attached to the X-ray cassette before the X-ray is exposed. When exposed, the X-ray emulsion captures a permanent, indelible patient identification. Again, these images convert the X-ray film into a readily identifiable object. There are more modern techniques, but even today you may encounter X-rays produced by the older technology.

In newer modalities such as digital radiography, the patient's name is typed onto a screen. When the images are printed out for the patient's file, the patient's name and other information appear on the images.

The complete foundation for the X-ray would include the following elements:

1. The operator was a qualified X-ray technician.
2. The operator filmed a certain part of a person's body at a certain time and place.
3. The operator used certain equipment.
4. The equipment was in good working condition.
5. The operator used the correct procedures.

6. In the past, the operator would explain the use of an identification assembly on the cassette. Alternatively, today the operator describes how the digital images are uploaded and stored.

7. The operator accounts for the X-ray's custody between exposure and trial. In the past, establishing this element entailed proof of the proper development of the film.

8. The witness recognizes the exhibit as the film.

The fact situation is a civil action. The plaintiff contends that as a result of the tort, she suffered severe personal injuries, including bone fractures. The plaintiff wishes to introduce an X-ray to depict some of the fractures. The plaintiff calls Mr. Paul Nesbitt. Mr. Nesbitt has already identified himself.

P	WHAT is your occupation? (1)
W	I am an X-ray technician at Sharp Hospital downtown.
P	HOW long have you worked as an X-ray technician? (1)
W	For seven years.
P	WHAT is your formal education? (1)
W	I have a degree from Cornell.
P	WHAT was your major field of study? (1)
W	Science.
P	WHAT other training have you had as an X-ray technician? (1)
W	I attended a three month course at U.C.L.A. Medical School, and I've also attended numerous seminars on the subject.
P	WHERE were you on the afternoon of July 7th, YR-3? (2)
W	As I recall, I was on duty at the X-ray lab.
P	WHAT, if anything, happened that afternoon? (2)
W	Doctor Bertrand asked me to take the plaintiff's X-ray, and the plaintiff stopped by for the X-ray.
P	WHO is the plaintiff? (2)
W	The woman at the table to the right over there.
P	WHAT is she wearing? (2)
W	The green dress and yellow scarf.
P	Your Honor, please let the record reflect that the witness has identified the plaintiff, Ms. Wohlmuth. (2)
J	It will so reflect.
P	WHAT did you do when Ms. Wohlmuth arrived at the lab? (3)
W	I showed her how to position herself on the table to enable me to get a good X-ray of her right leg.

P	WHAT happened then? (3)
W	Then I set up the equipment.
P	WHAT equipment? (3)
W	The X-ray machine and (the cassette with identification assembly) *or* (the digital cassette).
P	WHAT is the X-ray machine? (3)
W	It's the camera that you use to take an X-ray.
P	WHAT is the film? (3)
W	The X-rays make the impression on the film.
P	*(If the X-ray was taken in the traditional manner, the proponent asks the following question.)*
	WHAT is the identification assembly? (6)
W	It's a label identifying this patient and this exposure. It can be handwritten, typed, or an impression from the patient's plastic hospital ID card. It's applied to the X-ray cassette before the X-ray is exposed. When it is exposed, the film's emulsion captures a permanent, indelible patient identification.
P	Again, WHAT does the information on the label represent? (6)
W	It identifies the film as an image of a certain patient's organs at a particular time.
P	WHAT condition was the equipment in when you took these X-rays? (4)
W	It was in fine condition.
P	HOW do you know that? (4)
W	I had checked it myself the day before. I always check it Monday morning. I took this X-ray on a Tuesday.
P	HOW did you learn to check the equipment? (4)
W	That was one of the subjects we studied at U.C.L.A.
P	HOW did you take the plaintiff's X-ray? (5)
W	(I re-entered the room and removed the cassette.) *or* (I downloaded the images onto our computer system in Radiology).

The Traditional Technique

P	WHAT did you do then? (5)
W	I re-entered the room and removed the cassette.
P	WHAT did you do with the cassette? (7)
W	I put it in a corner in the room and developed it that afternoon.
P	WHAT happened to the cassette between the filming and development? (7)

W	As far as I know, nothing. It was just there in the room.
P	WHO handled the cassette between the filming and development? (7)
W	As far as I can tell, I was the only one.
P	HOW did you develop the X-ray? (7)
W	I went into the dark room, removed the film from the cassette, and then put it through the developing process.
P	HOW did you learn to develop X-rays? (7)
W	That was another subject we studied in detail at U.C.L.A.
P	WHAT did you do with the film after you developed it? (7)
W	I brought it down to our X-ray records library on the second floor.
P	WHAT happened then? (7)
W	I gave it to the clerk and asked her to file it under the plaintiff's name.

The Modern Technique

P	HOW can the doctors in Radiology view the images?
W	They have computer access and can view the images on the computer system where I stored them.
P	HOW, if at all, can you alter or manipulate the X-ray images once they are stored electronically?
W	No way that I know of. Once the images are saved, there is no way that I know of that the images can be changed.
P	Were you able to print a copy of the digital X-rays for use in court today?
W	Yes. I printed a positive image so we could view it without the need for a shadow box.
P	Your Honor, I request that this be marked plaintiff's exhibit number four for identification.
J	It will be so marked.
P	Please let the record reflect that I am showing the exhibit to the opposing counsel.
J	It will so reflect.
P	I request permission to approach the witness.
J	Permission granted.
P	Mr. Nesbitt, I now hand you plaintiff's exhibit number four for identification. WHAT is it? (8)
W	It's the X-ray I took of the plaintiff's leg.
P	HOW can you recognize it? (8)

W	I recognize this type of film, and (I see the plaintiff's information on the identification assembly. I also recognize the general appearance of the bones depicted) *or* (I see the plaintiff's name and the date just as they were recorded on the X-ray. It is a copy of the digital image that was stored for this patient).
P	HOW did the film get to court today? (7)
W	(I went to the file for that month and looked for the X-ray with the plaintiff's name and the date.) *or* (I went to the computer database and searched under the plaintiff's name and date. I then printed out this image.)
P	HOW many images were there? (7)
W	Only the one I took.
P	HOW many times have you used that (computer) filing system in the past? (7)
W	Hundreds.
P	WHO taught you how to use the system? (7)
W	The X-ray records librarian herself, Doctor Riley.
P	Your Honor, I now offer plaintiff's exhibit number four for identification into evidence as plaintiff's exhibit number four.
J	It will be received.

The proponent will use the X-ray later during a doctor's testimony. The doctor will testify about the extent of injury and use the X-ray to illustrate the injuries.

Today X-ray is only one of the many imaging technologies. The reader will find an excellent overview of these technologies in Samuel D. Hodge, Jr., *A Litigation Primer on Diagnostic Imaging*, 16 THE PRACTICAL LITIGATOR 7 (Sept. 2005) (discussing plain film X-ray, venography, angiogram, anthrogram, myelography, computed axial tomograph (CT), discogram, intravenous pyelogram (IVP), magnetic resonance imaging (MRI), bone scan, signal photon emission commuted tomography (SPECT), ultrasound, electromyography (EMG), and nerve conduction study). When the proponent offers an image produced by any of these techniques in court, the proponent faces the same two evidentiary issues: the validation of the scientific technique and the physical evidence problem of the identification of the particular image. In the case of a traditional technique such as X-ray, the trial judge can judicially notice the validity of the underlying scientific theory and the general reliability of the technique. In the case of more avant-garde imaging techniques, the proponent will have to lay a *Daubert* or *Frye* foundation. In either event, the proponent will also have to show that the exhibit proffered at trial is an authentic image of a particular person or object, taken at a particular time. To make that showing, the proponent can rely on a variation of the identification assembly testimony illustrated in the above X-ray foundation.

[4] AUTOMATED SURVEILLANCE CAMERAS

In the first two subsections, there was a witness competent to verify a photograph or video by testifying that he or she had seen the person, object, or activity depicted. However, in the last subsection devoted to X-rays, no witness was competent to testify that they saw what the X-ray depicts. Out of necessity, in the X-ray cases the courts developed a new theory, namely, the so-called "silent witness" method of authenticating a photograph. The courts accepted the photograph or film because the proponent validated the scientific process that had created the image. The proponent ordinarily invokes this approach when he or she wants to introduce an image produced by an automated surveillance camera.

To lay a "silent witness" foundation for a surveillance image, the proponent could elicit testimony establishing:

1. How the digital camera system works and is activated.

2. How the images were retrieved.

3. How the images were stored onto a computer, DVD disk, or flash drive; and

4. That the process produces accurate images.

In the following example, the exhibit is a surveillance video of the defendant attempting to break into a bank's automatic teller machine (ATM) at night when no one else was present. The proponent is the prosecutor. The witness is the bank security guard, Jay Morkes. Mr. Morkes has already described his position with the bank.

P   Mr. Morkes, WHAT, if any, photographic system does your bank use for recording what takes place at the teller machine in the parking lot? (2)

W   The system consists of a small video camcorder located behind protective plexiglass.

P   HOW does it work? (2)

W   The camcorder is set to record continuously whenever anyone comes within three feet of the machine. It continues to run until the person leaves. However, it does not record any sound.

P   WHO manufactures the camera? (2)

W   It's a Sony 2000 system.

P   WHAT type of digital storage capacity does the Sony have? (1)

W   It can record and store up to 12 hours of high-definition video footage with the built-in, embedded flash memory.

P   WHO checks the camcorder? (3)

W   Either I do, or one of the other two bank security personnel responsible for the computer system does. We download the digital images every eight hours and store them on our hard drive.

P   Your Honor, I request that this be marked as prosecution exhibit number six for identification?

J	It will be so marked.
P	Your Honor, please let the record reflect that I am showing the exhibit to the defense counsel.
J	It will so reflect.
P	May I approach the witness?
J	Certainly.
P	Mr. Morkes, I am handing you prosecution exhibit six for identification. Do you recognize it?
W	Yes.
P	WHAT is it?
W	This is the video of a person attempting to pry into the automatic teller machine in the parking lot on April 3, YR-3. I burned the video onto this DVD.
P	HOW do you know that?
W	I've watched the video several times during the past few months before trial. I recognize my initials right here on the plastic part of the DVD.
P	HOW accurate is the DVD video? (5)
W	Well, of course, I wasn't there. However, the quality of the DVD and recording is certainly very good. You can clearly see the person's face as well as the date and time stamp on the screen. You can even see small fragments of the machine go flying in the air when the person hit it with a hammer.
P	WHO retrieved this video? (4)
W	I did it. I marked my initials on the DVD to indicate that I had downloaded the information onto our hard drive for a particular date and then burned the images onto this DVD.
P	WHERE has this DVD been since you downloaded and burned it? (4)
W	It has been in our bank records section. I took it from there this morning just before coming to court. Oh, I should add that I believe that the police made a copy for their own investigation several months ago.
P	Your Honor, I now offer prosecution exhibit number six for identification into evidence as prosecution exhibit six.
J	It will be received.
P	I now request permission to play exhibit six to the jury on the electronic equipment that we have here in court.
J	Permission granted.

[5]　COMPUTER ANIMATIONS AND SIMULATIONS (CGA)

[a]　IN GENERAL

Rather than offering motion pictures or videotapes of historical events, attorneys frequently offer computer animations of the events. A computer animation is the display of a sequence of computer-generated images. There are several reasons for the growing use of computer animations. To begin with, when there is no movie or video of the event being litigated, a computer animation is a superior method of communicating the relevant information to the trier of fact. Absent a movie or video, the proponent might have to rely on static charts or oral testimony to convey a large amount of complex information to the trier of fact. When the proponent relies solely on oral expert testimony, the details may be presented one at a time; but an animation can piece all the details together for the jury. A computer animation in effect condenses the information into a single evidentiary package. In part due to television, the typical American is a primarily visual learner; and for that reason, in the short term, many jurors find the animation more understandable than charts or oral testimony. Use of an animation can also significantly increase long-term juror retention of the information.

In part, computer animations are so popular because the medium is so flexible. The animation can adopt almost any conceivable vantage point or angle. For instance, the animation can depict the perspective of the person behind the wheel of a car or portray an aerial overview of two cars approaching each other. The animation can pan or zoom in. The animation can even display an impossible perspective, that is, the inner workings of a piece of machinery. The split-screen capability permits the simultaneous display of several perspectives; one perspective can be that of the airplane pilot, and the other that of a ground observer watching the airplane descend for landing. The technology is also flexible in a temporal sense; the animation can be real time, time lapse (accelerated), slow motion (decelerated), or freeze frame. Finally, the animation can be combined with other media. The trial exhibit can begin with a photograph of the actual object involved in the case and then fade or dissolve into a photorealistic animation. Given this flexibility, animations have already been employed in court to depict a wide range of events, including plane crashes, highway accidents, murders, gas well explosions, product failures, the movement of contaminating particles in the soil, and the progress of diseases.

The foundation depends upon the purposes for which the proponent proffers the animation. The animation can be offered either as illustrative demonstrative evidence or as a substantive computer simulation.

[b]　ILLUSTRATIVE EVIDENCE

Suppose that a lay or expert witness is prepared to describe an event and that the witness did not initially obtain his or her information about the event by viewing any computer animation. A lay witness might simply have seen the accident. For his or her part, a scientist might have derived an opinion about the event by sitting down, reading the police report describing the accident, and applying the laws of physics to the data in the report. Assume further, though, that after hearing the witness's description of the event before trial, the attorney has a computer animation prepared to depict that description. In that event, the attorney could offer the animation as purely demonstrative evidence to illustrate the witness's description. When that is the proponent's theory of admissibility, the foundation is minimal. It suffices if the witness testifies that he or she has viewed the animation and that the animation fairly and accurately depicts the witness's version of the event. *People v. Mitchell*, No. 12462 (Cal. Marin County Super. Ct. Feb. 19, 1992) is illustrative. In that case, the prosecution introduced an animation of a shooting. Crime scene reconstruction expert Lucien Haag testified that the animation accurately illustrated his testimony. In the words of *People v. McHugh*, 124 Misc. 2d 559, 476 N.Y.S.2d 721 (N.Y. Sup. Ct. 1984):

> The [illustrative computer animation] sought to be introduced here is more akin to a chart or diagram than a scientific device. Whether a diagram is hand drawn or mechanically drawn by means of a computer is of no importance. What is important is [that] the presentation . . . fairly and accurately reflect the oral testimony offered and that it be an aid to the jury's understanding of the issue.

As a practical matter, it may be safer to call the animator as well as the lay or expert witness to overcome any objections under Rule 403; but if the proponent offers the animation strictly as illustrative evidence, the lay or expert witness can give sufficient sponsoring testimony to authenticate the animation. For instance, after establishing her firsthand knowledge of an event, the witness could testify that she has viewed the animation in question and that the animation accurately depicts the event which she observed. That testimony should satisfy Federal Rule of Evidence 104(b) when the proponent is content to introduce the animation as demonstrative evidence to illustrate testimony by a lay or expert witness.

There are procedural downsides to proffering the animation purely as an illustrative, demonstrative exhibit. Under Rule 105, on the opponent's request the trial judge will have to give the jury a limiting instruction as to the evidentiary status of the animation. Moreover, in many jurisdictions, illustrative exhibits cannot accompany the jury into the deliberation room. However, offering the animation for such a limited purpose obviates the necessity for testimony validating the scientific assumptions programmed into the software which generates the animation.

[c]   SUBSTANTIVE EVIDENCE

Conventional Substantive CGA

In other cases, though, the proponent will want to offer the animation as substantive evidence. In these cases, it is often said that the proponent is proffering a computer "simulation." Computer simulation software includes scientific equations and principles, such as the laws of Newtonian physics, which predict the behavior of, for example, automobiles. Such software applies those equations and principles as follows: (1) it accepts input of the data, such as skidmark length, required to apply the scientific principles and equations; (2) it converts mathematic predictions based on the equations and principles into still images; and (3) it subsequently records those images in a medium, such as a videotape, that can be played back on the computer's screen. When the proponent offers an animation as an accurate computer simulation, the inference of accuracy does not arise from the simulation's correspondence with a description of the same event by any lay or expert witness. Rather, the bases of the inference are the validity of the pertinent scientific principles and the trustworthiness of the input data. Consequently, the foundation for a simulation differs from that for a merely demonstrative, illustrative exhibit; the simulation foundation must include a showing of the principle's validity and the data's trustworthiness. If the proponent can lay the necessary foundation, there will be no need for a limiting instruction under Rule 105. As substantive evidence, the simulation could be taken into the jury room and viewed during deliberation.

Unfortunately, the published cases offer little firm, specific guidance as to the foundational requirements for computer simulations. However, in principle the following foundation should suffice:

1. There are certain valid scientific equations and principles, such as the Newtonian laws of motion. Depending on the jurisdiction, these equations and principles will have to pass muster under either the *Frye* general acceptance test or the *Daubert* validation standard. § 4.10 of this chapter describes the *Frye* and *Daubert* tests. If the principle or equation in question is widely accepted, it may be judicially noticeable under Federal Rule 201(b).

2. Computer technology is capable of producing simulations or models based on scientific equations and principles. In some jurisdictions, this proposition is judicially noticeable.

3. The equations and principles mentioned in foundational element number one have been programmed into a particular computer software.

4. To generate a mathematical representation, the equations and principles require certain input. The program may require numerical data about measurements of dimensions of objects, human beings, and the environment in which the objects and human beings are moving or acting. For example, to produce a virtual reality (VR) simulation of a room, "everything in the room is measured, and each object's position relative to all other objects—including the VR user—is calculated." Dilworth, *Virtual Reality: Coming Soon to a Courtroom Near You?*, 29 TRIAL 13, 14 (July 1993).

5. The software in question is capable of converting its mathematical predictions of behavior into accurate images. Some programs produce a picture—an individual computer graphic—every thirtieth of a second. When the software is in widespread, commercial use, the judge may treat its widespread acceptance as circumstantial evidence of its accuracy. If a defective program were used widely, presumably the defect would have caused problems for its users; and the program would have been corrected or withdrawn. When the software has not yet come into widespread use, the proponent should present expert testimony vouching for the program's accuracy. For instance, one of the computer experts who helped develop an accident reconstruction program could testify that she had verified the program's accuracy by comparing its output with data from test crashes of automobiles.

6. Someone input all the data needed to use the principles or equations

programmed into the software.

7. The data input was trustworthy. This foundational element reflects "the GIGO principle: garbage in, garbage out." The sources of the data should qualify under Federal Rule of Evidence 703.

8. The computer operator checked to ensure that the data was properly input. The operator could simply call the data up on the screen and double-check the accuracy of the input data against the police reports which were the source of the data.

9. After inputting the data, the operator asked the computer to perform the function of generating a simulation or model of the relevant behavior.

10. The computer recorded the images of the simulation on videotape or laser disc. Videotape is more popular. However, many practitioners prefer laser disc; laser disc tends to yield better definition, and the use of bar codes enables the proponent during trial to jump to any sequence in the animation.

11. The witness on the stand recognizes the videotape or laser disc as the output produced when the operator asked the computer to perform the function of generating a simulation of the relevant behavior.

In some cases, a single witness is qualified to lay the entire foundation. However, in a given case, multiple witnesses might be necessary: one to validate the pertinent scientific principles and equations, another to verify the part of the program that generates the mathematical representation of behavior, still another to vouch for part of the program converting the mathematical prediction into visual images, a further witness to describe the collection of the input data, and a final witness to testify to the inputting of the data and the production of the videotape or laser disc.

The fact situation is a civil tort action. The plaintiff alleges that the defendant negligently lost control of her auto and allowed the auto to drift into a bike lane where the auto struck and killed the plaintiffs' daughter. The proponent is the defense. The defense calls Professor Ernest Kamisar as its next witness. Professor Kamisar will lay the foundation for a computer animation tending to show that the accident occurred in a manner relieving the defendant from fault.

P   Please state your full name and spell your last name for the record.

W   My name is Ernest Kamisar. My last name is spelled K-A-M-I-S-A-R.

P   WHERE do you live?

W   I live and work in East Lansing, Michigan.

P   WHAT is your place of work?

W   I teach in the Engineering Department of Michigan State University.

P   WHAT is your educational background?

W   I obtained my Bachelor of Science degree in engineering from Iowa State University in YR-18.

P   In general terms, WHAT is engineering?

W	Engineers are specialists in using the laws of physics to create machines for human use.
P	WHAT did you do after you obtained your bachelor's degree?
W	We moved to Ann Arbor, Michigan, so that I could begin my graduate studies at the University of Michigan. I wanted to get my Master's degree and then a doctorate. I got the Master's in YR-16 and the doctorate in YR-14.
P	WHAT subjects did you study in the course of obtaining those degrees?
W	I pretty much specialized in vehicle dynamics and computer graphics related to vehicle dynamics.
P	WHAT do you mean by the expression, "vehicle dynamics"?
W	That's the study of how automobiles like cars behave as they move and travel down a highway.
P	WHAT do you mean by "computer graphics"?
W	That's the use of computer programs to create sequences of images which depict the movement of automobiles such as trucks on a road or highway.
P	WHAT licenses do you hold in this state?
W	I'm registered as an engineer.
P	HOW many professional papers, if any, have you had published?
W	Approximately 20.
P	WHAT topics did those papers relate to?
W	They all deal with vehicle dynamics, and the vast majority of them relate more specifically to computer animation of vehicle dynamics.
P	WHAT professional engineering organizations, if any, do you belong to?
W	For years I've been a member of the Society of Automotive Engineers and the American Society of Mechanical Engineers. I've served as the president of the state chapter of the SAE, the Society of Automotive Engineers.
P	WHAT practical experience, if any, do you have in vehicle dynamics?
W	I've consulted with major manufacturers such as General Motors and Subaru on a number of design projects. My contribution was determining how a design change would affect the dynamics of the vehicles in question.
P	HOW many times, if ever, have you qualified as an expert witness in a court of law?
W	On over 40 occasions.
P	WHAT topics did you testify about as an expert witness?

W   On each occasion, the testimony related to some aspects of vehicle dynamics.

P   HOW many times, if ever, did you testify about computer animation of vehicle dynamics?

W   The majority of the time.

P   WHAT do these computer animations do? (1)

W   The ones that I prepare do more than simply illustrate a version of an accident. The ones I develop are intended to use the laws of physics to accurately recreate and portray accidents.

P   WHAT laws of physics are you referring to? (1)

W   To begin with, you have Newton's laws of motion. Those are fundamental tenets of modern physics. In addition, there are other rules of auto dynamics physics which have been empirically derived.

P   WHAT do you mean by "empirically derived"? (1)

W   People have conducted controlled experiments to establish that these other propositions are true. You run tests with autos, trucks, and bicycles to prove that the proposition is valid.

P   HOW well accepted are these propositions? (1)

W   They're almost universally accepted by engineers in my specialty.

P   HOW thoroughly have these propositions been established by the experiments you referred to? (1)

W   There are some that are still in the experimental, debatable stage, but the ones which I use in my computer programs have been validated beyond any real doubt. They have held up in all the experiments which I know of.

P   HOW can a computer apply these propositions? (2)

W   You simply program the principle or equation into the source code for the software. The software's code contains the instructions for the computer, and you include the various principles and equations as part of the instructions. Using these principles and equations, the computer can create a mathematical representation of an auto such as a truck. The simulation program utilizes an "icon" of the vehicle, and the computer simulates the motion of the icon.

P   WHAT experience, if any, do you have programming these principles and equations into computer software? (2)

W   In large part, that's what I did during my Master's and doctoral work at Michigan. I know several programming languages, and over the years I've developed dozens of programs based on the principles of auto dynamics.

P   WHAT is "Autodynam"? (3)

W   That's the name of a program which I've developed for computer simulations of auto dynamics.

P   WHAT laws and equations is that program based on? (3)

W   It's one of my most conservative programs.

P   WHAT do you mean by "conservative"? (3)

W   As I said a little while ago, some propositions about vehicle dynamics are still debatable; the research into the validity of those propositions is still incomplete and inconclusive. None of those propositions is included in Autodynam. It's a conservative program in the sense that it rests on the original laws of motion, propositions deduced directly from those laws, and further propositions which have clearly been established by ample research.

P   HOW accurately does Autodynam program state those propositions? (3)

W   Not just accurately, but perfectly.

P   HOW do you know that? (3)

W   To begin with, I have access to a number of databases on actual and test auto crashes. I've checked the results of the program against the databases, and on each occasion the result of using the program has checked out and been confirmed. More importantly, I periodically print out the program itself and review the portion of the program setting out the propositions. I can read programming language; and as a scientist, I also know the propositions. I can personally vouch that the program is very accurate in that regard. If you input the right information about an accident, you're going to get an accurate reconstruction of the event.

P   WHAT do you mean by "input"? (4)

W   The laws and equations are general propositions about vehicle dynamics. If you're going to make some findings about a specific accident, you need some of the case-specific data about that accident—where the vehicles came to rest, the extent of the damage to the vehicles, the length and direction of skidmarks and yaw marks, the drag factor of the road surface—that sort of thing.

P   Suppose that you wanted to use Autodynam to create a computer animation of an accident involving a truck and a bicycle and you wanted to use Autodynam to determine how fast the truck was going. WHAT case-specific input would you have to give the computer to determine that? (4)

W   I'd need to tell the computer the final resting place of the truck, bicycle and the rider, the extent and nature of any personal injuries suffered by the bicyclist, the extent and location of the damage to the truck and bicycle, the road drag factor, the point where the rider's body first struck the ground, the relative angle of the bicycle and truck at impact, and the length and direction of any skidmarks. Given that information, the computer can create a valid, mathematical representation of the dynamics of the two vehicles.

P   All right. You have this mathematical representation in the computer. HOW does the computer convert that into an image on the screen? (5)

W   The program also does that. The program creates a sequence of images on the screen. It creates a new picture every thirtieth of a second. Autodynam is a sophisticated program, and its images are photorealistic—they look awfully close to the real thing.

P   HOW accurate are these images? (5)

W   They're quite accurate.

P   HOW do you know that? (5)

W   I previously mentioned test crashes. We have a lot of test crashes on videotape. I've often used Autodynam to generate a computer animation and then compared it to a videotape of the same accident. The computer simulation produces amazingly accurate images of the crash.

P   Professor, WHERE were you on January 19, YR-3? (6)

W   I was at my office at the university in Ann Arbor.

P   WHAT happened that day? (6)

W   That's the day I received the Federal Express package with Xerox copies of all the police reports and depositions in this case.

P   WHAT do you mean by "this case"? (6)

W   This lawsuit. You had phoned me the week before, and during our telephone conversation I had agreed to use Autodynam to generate a computer simulation of the truck-bicycle collision involved in this lawsuit.

P   WHAT reports and depositions did you receive on January 13? (6)

W   The stack included the official police report on the accident, the truck driver's deposition, and the deposition of two eyewitnesses to the accident.

P   WHAT did you do with the reports? (6)

W   I carefully reviewed every page of every document and then extracted the information which Autodynam needs.

P   HOW much of the necessary information did you find in the reports? (6)

W   They contained all the information the program requires.

P   In particular, WHICH reports did you take the information from? (7)

W   I gathered all the information from the police report and the eyewitness accounts.

P   WHY didn't you take any information from the truck driver's deposition? (7)

W   You instructed me not to.

P   WHAT reason did I give you? (7)

W   You said that you didn't want the simulation to represent simply your client's driver's version of the accident; you said that there might be questions about his bias. So you expressly instructed me to use the police report and the depositions given by the two eyewitnesses who had no connection with either party.

P   WHAT did you do with the information after you extracted it from the report and depositions? (8)

W   I input it.

P   HOW did you do that? (8)

W   I used the computer keyboard.

P   HOW accurately did you input the data? (8)

W   It all was correct.

P   HOW do you know that? (8)

W   You put the data into a particular file on the computer. I called that file back on the screen and double-checked each entry against the original police report and depositions. Every entry was right.

P   WHAT did you do after you double-checked the data input to the computer? (9)

W   I entered a command, directing Autodynam to apply the programmed propositions of physics to that data to first determine where the truck and bicycle collided, and then to produce a computer animation showing the point of collision.

P   WHAT happened then? (10)

W   The computer generated the animation which I had requested.

P   HOW, if at all, was the animation recorded? (10)

W   It was downloaded and burned onto a DVD.

P   Your Honor, I request that this be marked Defense Exhibit C for identification.

J   It will be so marked.

P   Permission to approach the witness?

W   Granted.

P   Professor, I now hand you what has been marked Defense Exhibit C for identification. WHAT is it? (11)

W	It's the DVD I just mentioned.
P	HOW do you know that? (11)
W	A couple of ways.
P	Namely?
W	To begin with, I recognize the markings on the label affixed to the DVD. That's my handwriting. In my own handwriting, I noted the case name and the date on which I prepared the DVD. In addition, we viewed this DVD in its entirety in the judge's chambers about three hours ago, and I recognize the DVD as the one Autodynam produced after I input the data about this accident.
P	Your Honor, I now offer Defense Exhibit C for identification into evidence as Defense Exhibit C.
J	It will be so received.
P	Permission to play the DVD for the jury?
J	Granted.
P	Now, Professor Kamisar, in general terms, could you please tell the jury WHAT they are about to see?

Virtual Reality Technology

The substantive use of CGA is now well accepted. Virtual reality technology represents a step beyond CGA. In this type of technology, the user enters an immersive virtual environment (IVE).[36] The user can immerse himself or herself physically and mentally by means of a head-mounted display (HMD). The HMD

> can block out all views of the outside world in favor of the computer-generated environment depicted. By attaching a tracking sensor to the user's head, the HMD communicates to the computer system exactly where the user is looking and accordingly updates the visual image displayed to reflect the vantage point. Advanced virtual reality systems often track the movement of many of the major bodily joints, providing the user with an even greater level of sensory feedback. This technology increases the realistic nature of the IVE by allowing the user to explore and interact with the alternate environment.[37]

These features could make IVE especially persuasive to a juror utilizing the technology in court. Before permitting the use of an IVE system in court, the judge

---

[36] Note, *Employing Virtual Reality Technology at Trial: New Issues Posed by Rapid Technological Advances and Their Effect on Jurors' Search for "The Truth,"* 93 TEX L. REV. 257, 260 (2014).

[37] *Id.* at 273–274. There are several types of virtual reality technologies. Note, *From Presentation to Presence: Immersive Virtual Environments and Unfair Prejudice in the Courtroom*, 92 SO. CAL. L. REV. 411, 414–17 (2019). At one end of the spectrum, some techniques are non-immersive; in these systems, the users engage through a desktop display without a headset or glasses. At the polar extreme, true IVE "perceptually surrounds" the user "with a combination of three-dimensional computer graphics, high-resolution stereoscopic projections, and motion tracking technologies that continually render virtual scenes to match the movements and viewpoint of the user."

should demand a complete *Frye* or *Daubert* foundation validating the particular system the proponent proposes using.[38] In particular, the judge ought to carefully scrutinize any spherical photography used to create the virtual environment.[39] To date, there have been no published American opinions analyzing the permissibility of employing IVE in court.[40] However, the New Zealand Ministry of Justice is exploring the courtroom use of IVE.[41] Moreover, for use in prosecuting Nazi war criminals, the staff at the Bavarian State Criminal Investigation Office has prepared

> a digital recreation of the Auschwitz-Birkenau camp that allows users to virtually walk through a 15-mile perimeter. They can climb guard towers and visit barracks to figure out what someone walking at the camp may have avoided, and what was impossible to miss. The model can be used in trials to counter the objection of suspects who claim that they did not witness executions or marches to gas chambers from their vantage point . . . .[42]

[6]   ENHANCED PHOTOGRAPHS

The proponent may not be content to proffer the original photograph developed from the film. There are several possibilities. First, the proponent might offer a simple enlargement of the photograph. Enlargement is a multiplication process; an enlargement merely increases the size of the photograph. The foundation for an enlarged photograph can be relatively short, since the trial judge may judicially notice the validity of the technique for enlarging a photograph.

Second,[43] the proponent may attempt to introduce an enhanced photograph. Image enhancement is a subtractive process, which improves image contrast by removing "interfering colors and background patterns."[44] Testimony based on image enhance-

---

[38] *See* § 4.10, *infra.*

[39] Tung, Barr, Sheppard, Elliot, Tottey & Walsh, *Spherical Photography and Virtual Tours for Presenting Crime Scenes and Forensic Evidence in New Zealand Courtrooms,* 60 J. FORENSIC SCI. 753 (2015).

[40] However, VR technology was used in a California trial, Stephenson v. Honda Motors, Ltd. of America, No 81067 (Cal. Super., Placer County June 25, 1992). The purchaser of a Honda motorcycle sued the company. She alleged that her accident was due to the motorcycle's inherent instability. Honda countered that the accident was due to the unevenness of the terrain the plaintiff was riding on. Honda prepared a virtual reconstruction of the terrain. Using VR headsets, the jurors entered a virtual environment including the terrain. Schofield, *The Use of Computer Generated Imagery in Legal Proceedings,* 13 DIGITAL EVID. & ELEC. SIGNATURE L. REV. 13 (2016).

[41] 60 J. FORENSIC SCI. 753, 757–758 (2015).

[42] Jason Daley, *How Virtual Reality Is Helping Prosecute Nazi War Criminals,* http://www.smithsonian.com/smart-news (Oct. 12, 2016). The Nazi regime kept very detailed blueprints for its camps.

[43] There is a third possibility, namely, image restoration. State v. Hayden, 950 P.2d 1024, 1028 (Wash. App. 1998). That process is additive. The process adds details "based upon preconceived ideas about what the end result should look like." *Id.* The use of image restoration computer software presents a significant problem in the validation of the scientific process. To add details, the software predicts the missing details. The proponent must point to a body of solid empirical research validating the "preconceived idea[] about what the end result should look like." *Id.*

[44] *Id.*

ment technology is admissible provided that a sufficient foundation is laid validating the underlying scientific process.[45]

Image enhancement technology was developed during the late 1960s and early 1970s for the NASA space program.[46] The Jet Propulsion Laboratory of the California Institute of Technology was instrumental in pioneering image enhancement.[47] Due to the weight and power limitations of spacecraft, it was impractical for NASA to use state-of-the-art camera systems on unmanned craft.[48] The cameras used produced somewhat degraded photographs. Image enhancement reverses the degradation. Initially, researchers study the degradation properties of the use of a particular type of photographic equipment to capture a certain type of image: When this type of camera is used to photograph distant objects, what type of degradation can be anticipated? Then, the researchers design computer software to reverse the degradation and thereby improve the sharpness and image contrast of the photograph[49] by eliminating background patterns and colors.[50]

Digital cameras are now widely available. If the original image was digital, its format permits enhancement. However, suppose that the original image was a traditional film or analog photograph. Before the image on a normal film or analog photograph can be enhanced, the photographic image must be digitized.[51] "Digital images are composed of millions of tiny dots, referred to as 'pixels.' "[52] Digital photography "can capture approximately 16 million different colors and . . . differentiate between 256 shades of gray."[53] Then, based on degradation models developed in research,[54] computer software manipulates the pixels to filter out[55] graininess and improve brightness and contrast.[56]

Although image enhancement technology was developed for the space program to isolate distant galaxies,[57] the technology now has a wide variety of applications. The technology has been "applied in numerous areas, including medicine, physics, meteorology, resource exploration, factory automation, and robotics control."[58] For

---

[45] *See* Wagner v. State, 707 So. 2d 827 (Fla. Dist. Ct. App. 1998).

[46] State v. Hayden, 950 P.2d 1024, 1026 (Wash. App. 1998).

[47] Gregory P. Joseph, MODERN VISUAL EVIDENCE § 8.04[2] (rev. 2016).

[48] *Id.*

[49] State v. Hayden, 950 P.2d 1024, 1028 (Wash. App. 1998).

[50] *Id.* at 1025.

[51] Dolan v. State, 743 So. 2d 544, 545 (Fla. Dist. Ct. App. 1999).

[52] *Id.*

[53] State v. Hayden, 950 P.2d 1024, 1028 (Wash. App. 1998).

[54] Gregory P. Joseph, MODERN VISUAL EVIDENCE § 8.04[2] (rev. 2016).

[55] State v. Hayden, 950 P.2d 1024, 1026 (Wash. App. 1998).

[56] Nooner v. State, 907 S.W.2d 677, 686 (Ark. 1995).

[57] State v. Hayden, 950 P.2d 1024, 1026 (Wash. App. 1998).

[58] Gregory P. Joseph, MODERN VISUAL EVIDENCE § 8.04[2] (rev. 2016).

instance, forensic scientists utilize the technology to enhance photographs of finger and palm prints.[59] When the proponent has made a proper showing of the reliability of the technology, the courts have been receptive to enhanced photographs.[60] Indeed, in several cases trial judges have ordered that photographs be enhanced prior to trial.[61]

Assume that a prior witness has laid the foundation for the introduction of a normal analog[62] photograph. To justify the introduction of an enhanced version of that photograph, the proponent should lay the following foundation:

1. The witness is an expert in photography.

2. The witness describes image enhancement technology. The technology is a process including two steps: the creation of a digital photograph consisting of pixels and then the computer manipulation of the pixels.

3. In general, both steps of image enhancement technology are valid. In a *Frye* jurisdiction, the proponent should establish that the explanatory theory underlying the technology is generally accepted within the relevant specialty fields as producing an accurate result when properly applied. In a *Daubert* jurisdiction, the proponent must demonstrate that the underlying hypothesis has sufficient assurances of reliability in the sense that experts have empirically verified the hypothesis by sound scientific methodology, that is, controlled laboratory experimentation or systematic field observation.

4. There has been adequate research into the specific application of image enhancement technology involved in the case. Proof of such research is an essential part of the foundation in a *Daubert* jurisdiction. However, even in a *Frye* jurisdiction, the proponent should lay this element of the foundation in order to make the foundation as persuasive as possible to the trier of fact. The early cases evaluated the proponent's foundation rather laxly. However, several commentators criticized the cases for ignoring the technical limitations of digital photography.[63] Some more recent cases demand a more extensive showing of the research validating the particular application of the digital technology.[64]

---

[59] State v. Hayden, 950 P.2d 1024, 1025 (Wash. App. 1998).

[60] *Id.*; Dolan v. State, 743 So. 2d 544 (Fla. Dist. Ct. App. 1999); Wagner v. State, 707 So. 2d 827 (Fla. Dist. Ct. App. 1998); Nooner v. State, 322 Ark. 87, 907 S.W.2d 677 (1995); English v. State, 422 S.E.2d 924 (Ga. App. 1992).

[61] Gregory P. Joseph, MODERN VISUAL EVIDENCE § 8.04[4], at n. 33 (rev. 2016), citing Pyka v. Village of Orland Park, 906 F. Supp. 1196 (N.D. Ill. 1995) and State v. Newman, 1994 Minn. App. LEXIS 1246 (Dec. 13, 1994).

[62] State v. Hayden, 950 P.2d 1024, 1028 (Wash. App. 1998).

[63] Michael Cherry, Edward J. Imwinkelried & Larry Meyer, *Does the Use of Digital Techniques By Law Enforcement Authorities Create a Risk of Miscarriage of Justice?*, 28 THE CHAMPION 24, 26 (Nov. 2004) ("Digital images have less detail than the original impressions").

[64] People v. McWhorter, 47 Cal. 4th 318, 361–67, 97 Cal. Rptr. 3d 412, 212 P.3d 692 (2009) (the witness "could not identify the computer program he used to enhance or 'electronically emboss' the image in question, nor could he satisfactorily explain the full nature of the process he used."); State v. Swinton,

5.   The research resulted in the development of computer software for this application of image enhancement technology.

6.   At a given time and place, the witness received the analogue photograph previously introduced.

7.   The witness followed proper procedure in digitizing the analogue photograph.

8.   The witness also followed proper procedure in using the computer software to enhance the analogue photograph.

9.   The witness recognizes the exhibit proffered at trial as the photograph, which he or she produced when he or she used the software to enhance the analogue photograph.

The fact situation is a criminal prosecution for burglary. The prosecution alleges that on February 22, YR-3, the defendant broke into a residence in Coral Gables. Earlier in the trial, a crime laboratory technician, Officer O'Grady, testifies that she: visited the burglary scene, detected a fingerprint on a sheet in the master bedroom, and took an analogue photograph of the fingerprint. She added that she later took the film back to the crime laboratory, developed the film, produced a photograph of the print, and delivered that print to Mr. Julio Mendez on February 23, YR-3. Before the technician leaves the stand, the prosecution lays the foundation for and introduces People's Exhibit No. 3, the analogue photograph of the fingerprint found at the burglary scene. The prosecution calls Mr. Mendez as its next witness.

P   WHAT is your educational background? (1)

W   I obtained a B.A. in Fine Arts from the University of Miami in YR-13.

P   WHAT area, if any, did you specialize in while you were working on your degree? (1)

W   Photography. I had always loved that as a kid, and I thought that I might be able to turn my love for photography into a profession.

P   WHAT did you do after you obtained your B.A.? (1)

W   I took some additional college photography courses at the University of Florida.

P   WHY did you do that? (1)

W   Well, my parents lived near campus, and it was convenient to continue my course of studies there. More importantly, though, Florida had some advanced courses on new photographic technologies. I hadn't taken those courses while I was a student at Miami; I just couldn't fit them into my schedule while I was working on my degree at Miami. However, I

268 Conn. 781, 829–30, 847 A.2d 921 (2004) (the foundational witness "must be able to testify, adequately and truthfully, as to exactly what the jury is looking at, and the defendant has the right to cross-examine the witness concerning the evidence. Without a witness who can satisfactorily explain or analyze the data and the program, the effectiveness of cross-examination can be seriously undermined, particularly in light of the extent to which the evidence in the present case has been 'created' ").

decided that I really needed to master those technologies before I opened my own photographic business.

P   WHAT did you do after you completed those courses? (1)

W   I opened up a full-service photographic business here in town.

P   WHAT do you mean by a "full-service photographic business"? (2)

W   I mean that I offer virtually every type of photography—not just the conventional film photography which most people are familiar with but also digital photography and techniques such as image enhancement. If you need virtually any type of photographic service, I can provide it.

P   You just mentioned "image enhancement." WHAT do you mean by that term? (2)

W   It's a technology that was developed for the NASA space program. It was pioneered by the Jet Propulsion Laboratory at the California Institute of Technology. Unmanned space craft have severe power and weight limitations. For that reason, NASA couldn't put heavy, state-of-the-art film and photographic equipment on the craft. The practical limitations dictated that they use less than state-of-the-art equipment.

P   WHY was their use of that type of equipment important? (2)

W   In practical terms, what it meant is that they later needed to enhance the photographs produced by the equipment installed on the craft.

P   HOW do you "enhance" a normal photograph? (2)

W   It requires a couple of first steps. The first step is digitizing the images on the normal or analogue photograph. You convert each image into lots of dots called pixels. Sophisticated equipment can tell the difference between the pixels comprising thousands of different colors. In fact, the equipment can differentiate among over 250 shades of gray.

P   WHAT is the second step? WHAT do you do after you have digitized a normal photograph? (2)

W   After you've digitized the photograph, you're ready for the second step. Simply stated, you use computer software to reverse the degradation of the photograph. Especially when you use less than state-of-the-art cameras, you're not going to get ideal contrast and brightness—the term of art is "degradation." However, you can direct the computer to manipulate the pixels for certain shades of gray in a particular part of the normal photograph. Doing so eliminates some of the graininess and improves the contrast. You filter out the noise and background colors that make it difficult to see the details in the photograph.

P   HOW do you know that the computer software does that? (2)

W   You need scientific research. You have to engage in research and develop a degradation model. The empirical research tells you what type of degradation to expect if you use a certain type of camera on a particular type of subject. If you can predict the type of expected degradation, you can program a computer to eliminate some of that degradation and thereby improve the photograph. In a nutshell, that's how you produce an enhanced photograph.

P   WHAT, if any, details does enhancement add to the photograph? (2)

W   None. It subtracts graininess caused, for example, by the presence of certain shades of gray in the photograph. But it doesn't add any details. If you put the normal photo side by side with the enhanced photo, you'll be able to find every detail shown in the enhanced photo in the normal photo. It's just easier to see those details because enhancement improves the brightness in the other areas and therefore the contrast between those areas and the details you're interested in.

P   HOW valid is the first step in this process, digital photography? (3)

W   There's no question about the validity of the technology. It's universally accepted by experts in the field, and it's in worldwide use.

P   HOW valid is the second step of the process, using computer software to enhance photographs? (3)

W   The second step's also very reliable if the photographer applying the process has adequate training and knows what he or she is doing.

P   HOW do you get that training? (3)

W   You can get it on the job, or you could get it the way I did—by taking advanced courses at a college such as the University of Miami or Florida. One of my courses was in digital photography, and another dealt with advanced techniques such as image enhancement. I took special courses in both steps of the technology. Again, I went to Florida because I wanted to learn those advanced techniques.

P   HOW widely accepted is the first step in the process, the technology of digital photography? (3)

W   As I said, there's no question that it's accepted. Its use was formerly confined to professional photographers. Now the leading companies are making digital cameras commercially available even to amateur photographers. You can go down to your local camera store today and buy a digital camera off the shelf.

P   HOW widely accepted among photographers is the second step, the use of computer software for image enhancement? (3)

W   It's not only accepted among photographers. It's accepted in lots of professional fields. NASA has used it for years. It's also been applied in medicine, physics, meteorology, resource exploration, factory automation, and robotics control.

P   WHAT application, if any, does image enhancement have in fingerprint analysis? (4)

W   You can use it to enhance poor quality normal photographs of fingerprints.

P   HOW do you know that? (4)

W   Since photography is both my love and my line of work, I try to stay on top of developments in the field. In the last 25 years forensic experts—scientists interested in legal cases—have adapted photographic enhancement techniques to many of their tasks, including fingerprint analysis.

P   HOW do you know that? (4)

W   Several ways. First, I read the literature. The photographic and forensic journals contain tens of articles about photo enhancement in various forensic fields. Second, I've attended specialized short courses offered by both the photographic equipment companies and police agencies such as the Federal Bureau of Investigation. In fact, I've served as an instructor at some of those courses. Finally, in several civil and criminal cases, I've had occasion to use the technique myself.

P   HOW valid is the use of enhancement technology to improve photographs of fingerprints? (4)

W   I consider it to be a very reliable adaptation of the technology.

P   WHY do you say that? (4)

W   As I said before, the technology depends on developing a degradation model. There's been a lot of research—a lot of time and effort—invested in determining the type of degradation you can expect when you take a normal photograph of a fingerprint on various types of surfaces such as linen sheets. To be honest, you don't capture every minute detail and I can't quote you a specific percentage accuracy, but it's a high quality image.

P   HOW widely accepted is this adaptation of photographic enhancement technology? (4)

W   If you do sophisticated photographic work, as I do, you know the technique, and you accept the technique.

P   In your work, HOW do you use the technique? (5)

W   I employ computer software specifically developed for this adaptation of photographic enhancement.

P   WHO developed the software? (5)

W   It was perfected and then marketed by Phototek, one of the leading companies in the field.

P   HOW widely used is that software? (5)

W   It's commercially available, and it's employed at laboratories throughout the United States and overseas as well.

P   Mr. Mendez, I've asked you some questions about photographic enhancement technology. Now I'd like to shift topics. Do you remember WHERE you were on the afternoon of February 23, YR-3? (6)

W   Yes.

P   WHERE were you? (6)

W   At my office downtown here.

P   WHAT, if anything, happened that afternoon? (6)

W   Probably the only thing worth mentioning was that I had a visit from Officer O'Grady.

P   WHAT was the purpose of her visit? (6)

W   She gave me a normal analogue photograph of a fingerprint taken at a burglary scene and asked that I enhance it.

P   Mr. Mendez, I now hand you what has been marked as people's exhibit number three. Do you recognize it? (6)

W   Yes.

P   WHAT is it? (6)

W   It's the photograph which Officer O'Grady gave me.

P   HOW do you recognize it? (6)

W   To begin with, I recognize the contents. I've never seen a photograph quite like that before. In addition, I placed my initials and the date on the reverse side. That's my handwriting right there on the other side of the exhibit.

P   WHAT did you do with this photograph after Officer O'Grady gave it to you? (7)

W   I had agreed to enhance it for my regular fee. As I said before, the first step in enhancement is to convert it into a digital image. You digitize the normal photo into all those dots or pixels.

P   HOW did you do that? (7)

W   I used my specialized digital photography equipment.

P   HOW well was that equipment working that day? (7)

W   As far as I could tell, it was fine. I always check specialized equipment like that before I use it. I don't have occasion to use that sort of sophisticated instrumentation every day. I therefore inspected it, and it checked out just fine. I didn't encounter any problems preparing the digital photograph.

P   WHAT did you do after you prepared the digital photograph of the fingerprint? (8)

W	As I said before, the second step is using computer software to do the enhancement. It manipulates the pixels to eliminate certain dark shading and thereby improves brightness and contrast.
P	WHAT condition was that computer equipment in that day? (8)
W	It also seemed fine. I ran a diagnostic when I booted up, and the diagnostic indicated that everything was in working order. In addition, everything went smoothly during the process. For example, I didn't get any error messages on the screen.
P	WHAT was the result of your use of the software? (9)
W	It produced an enhanced photograph.
P	Your Honor, I request that this be marked people's exhibit number four for identification.
J	It will be so marked.
P	Please let the record reflect that I am showing the exhibit to opposing counsel.
J	The record will so reflect.
P	Permission to approach the witness?
J	Permission granted.
P	Mr. Mendez, I now hand you people's exhibit number four for identification. WHAT is it? (9)
W	It's the enhanced photo.
P	HOW can you recognize it? (9)
W	As in the case of the other exhibit, I recognize its contents and appearance. Moreover, as in the case of the film photo, I placed my initials and the date on the back. That's also my handwriting right there.
P	Mr. Mendez, HOW well does the enhanced photograph compare with the normal photograph? (9)
W	You can see for yourself. There are areas of brightness on the enhanced photo and therefore more contrast with the details of the fingerprint. However, if you compare the two photos carefully, you'll see that every detail reflected in the enhanced photo is also shown in the normal photo, the one which Officer O'Grady gave me.

§ 4.10   THE VALIDATION OF SCIENTIFIC EVIDENCE

[1]   THE DOCTRINE

At first glance, the validation of scientific evidence might appear to be a simple problem of authentication. The proponent could argue that Federal Rules of Evidence 901(b)(9) and 104(b) govern and that the proponent need only present sufficient evidence to support a rational jury finding that the underlying theory is valid and the instrument is reliable. However, the courts have long been suspicious of scientific evidence. In the first place, the courts have sometimes been skeptical of scientists' claims of the virtual infallibility of scientific techniques. Secondly, the courts fear that scientific evidence will overwhelm the jury; the jurors will be so impressed by the scientific evidence that the scientist witness will effectively usurp the jurors' fact-finding power. The concern is that the jurors will uncritically accept the scientist's testimony.

For these reasons, the overwhelming majority of courts require an extraordinary foundation for scientific evidence. *Frye v. United States*, 293 F. 1013 (D.C. Cir. 1923), holds that the proponent must show that the methodology (the theory or instrument) has been generally accepted within the relevant scientific circles. Absent that showing, the scientific evidence is inadmissible. Under *Frye*, the proponent must identify the pertinent scientific circles and then establish that the theory and instrument have gained a certain degree of popularity within those circles. The existence of the requisite degree of acceptance is a foundational fact to be resolved by the judge under Federal Rule of Evidence 104(a).

In 1993, the United States Supreme Court handed down its decision in *Daubert v. Merrell Dow Pharms.*, 509 U.S. 579, 113 S. Ct. 2786, 125 L. Ed. 2d 469 (1993). The *Daubert* Court held that the enactment of the Federal Rules of Evidence impliedly overturned the *Frye* standard. However, the Court emphasized that the abolition of the *Frye* test does not mean that purportedly scientific testimony is to be admitted willy-nilly. Rather, the trial judge has an important gatekeeping function to perform. The judge must ensure that the testimony qualifies as reliable "scientific knowledge" within the meaning of that expression in Federal Rule of Evidence 702. A proposition will qualify as "scientific knowledge" if the proponent can demonstrate that the theory is the product of sound scientific methodology. The Court defined scientific method-ology as the process of formulating hypotheses and then conducting controlled laboratory experiments or systematic field observations to prove or falsify the hypothesis. According to the majority opinion in *Daubert*, in deciding whether a proposition rests on sound scientific methodology, the trial judge should consider such factors as whether the proposition is testable, whether it has been tested, the validity rate attained in any tests, whether the research has been peer reviewed, whether there are standards for conducting the methodology, and whether the findings are generally accepted. Although the *Daubert* validation standard is now the law in federal court and approximately three quarters of the states, *Frye* remains the law in a significant minority of jurisdictions. Some of these *Frye* jurisdictions are among the most populous and litigious states, including California, Illinois, New York, Pennsylvania, and Washington. 1 P. GIANNELLI, E. IMWINKELRIED, A. ROTH, J. CAMPBELL MORIARTY & V. BEETY, SCIENTIFIC EVIDENCE §§ 1.08, 1.21 (Matthew Bender, 6th ed. 2020).[65]

A scientific evidence foundation will often require two witnesses. If the theory and instrument are very generally accepted, the judge will judicially notice those elements

---

[65] For that matter, even in some of the leading *Frye* jurisdictions, there has been significant, recent movement toward the *Daubert* standard. Sargon Enter., Inc. v. U.S.C., 55 Cal. 4th 747, 149 Cal. Rptr. 3d 614, 288 P.3d 1237 (2012); In re Amendments to the Fla. Evidence Code, 278 So. 3d 551 (Fla. 2019).

of the foundation upon a proper timely request by counsel. However, when judicial notice is inapplicable, the proponent will probably have to call an expert with heavy academic credentials to lay those elements of the foundation. The proponent will then call a technician as the second witness to lay the balance of the foundation.

[2] ELEMENTS OF THE FOUNDATION

1. Witness #1 is qualified to establish the theory's validity and the instrument's reliability. Since this witness is testifying to relatively theoretical issues, his or her qualifications often consist of knowledge gained through formal education.

2. The underlying theory is valid. Proof of the empirical data validating the theory is technically unnecessary under the *Frye* test, but in practice many trial judges in *Frye* jurisdictions tended to demand proof of empirical validation as well as general acceptance. Testimony about the empirical validation of the theory is usually essential under *Daubert*. Under *Daubert*, the question is not the global validity of the expert's discipline. Rather, the focus is on the validity of the methodology that the expert proposes relying on. The dispositive question is whether the proponent has presented enough empirical data and reasoning to convince the judge by a preponderance of the evidence that by using the specific methodology the expert contemplates relying on, the expert can accurately draw the particular type of inference the expert proposes testifying to. Edward Imwinkelried, *The Best Insurance Against Miscarriages of Justice Caused by Junk Science: An Admissibility Test that is Scientifically and Legally Sound*, 81 ALBANY L. REV. 851, 857 (2017/2018).

3. The underlying theory is generally accepted as valid. Proof of general acceptance is required under *Frye*. Although such proof is not invariably required under *Daubert*, the *Daubert* majority stated that the trial judge could consider general acceptance as a relevant factor. The fact that most specialists within a discipline subscribe to a theory is circumstantial evidence that the theory rests on sound scientific methodology; presumably they cannot find any substantial flaws in the research validating the theory. General acceptance is no longer dispositive, but many trial judges still attach a great deal of weight to this factor.

4. The reliability of the instrument or technique has been validated empirically. As previously stated, the bottom line is whether the available empirical data demonstrates that by using this technique, the expert can accurately draw the type of inference or opinion that she contemplates testifying to. The expert should describe the empirical validation studies in some detail. It is true that in the original *Daubert* decision, the Court described Article VII's standards as "liberal" and "permissive." *Daubert v. Merrell Dow Pharmaceuticals, Inc.*, 509 U.S. 579, 113 S. Ct. 2786, 125 L. Ed. 2d 469 (1993). However, in its last decision in the line of authority, the Court stated that Article VII prescribes "exacting standards of reliability." *Weisgram v. Marley Co.*, 528 U.S. 440, 120 S. Ct. 1011, 145 L. Ed. 2d 958 (2000). As in the case of element #2, proof of experiments establishing the reliability of the instrument is technically

unnecessary under *Frye*. However, in practice many trial judges in *Frye* jurisdictions insisted upon proof of empirical validation as well as a showing of general acceptance.

5.   The instrument is generally accepted as reliable. As in the case of element #3, proof of general acceptance is necessary under *Frye*. Again, general acceptance is a relevant factor in the *Daubert* analysis, and many trial judges continue to ascribe a good deal of weight to that factor.

6.   Witness #2 is qualified to conduct and interpret the test results.

7.   The instrument witness #2 used was in good working condition.

8.   The witness used the instrument in the test.

9.   The witness used the proper procedures. The courts are divided over the question of whether proof of proper test procedures is an essential element of the foundation. Some courts have held that questions about the use of correct test protocol affect the weight, but not the admissibility, of the evidence. The majority of courts still adhere to the traditional view demanding foundational proof of proper test procedures. As amended in 2000, Federal Rule of Evidence 702(d) requires that the proponent of expert testimony demonstrate that the expert "reliably applied the principles and methods to the facts of the case."

10.   The witness states the test results.

[3]   SAMPLE FOUNDATION

The following hypotheticals illustrate both *Frye* and *Daubert* foundations. Although the latter foundation goes into somewhat greater detail about the extent of the empirical verification of the underlying scientific principles, the foundations are similar. As previously stated, although *Daubert* no longer treats general acceptance as the test, the *Daubert* Court mentioned general acceptance as a pertinent factor in the judge's analysis. Moreover, again as previously stated, while proof of the extent of empirical validation is technically unnecessary under *Frye*, as a practical matter, many courts in *Frye* jurisdictions at the very least encouraged the proponent to present some minimal foundational testimony about the experiments conducted to validate the proponent's scientific hypothesis.

A *Frye* Foundation

The fact situation is a speeding prosecution. The government charges that the accused, Mr. Berton, was going 45 miles an hour on a street posted for 30 miles an hour. Officer Jones used a stationary radar speedmeter to clock the accused. Most jurisdictions would judicially notice the validity of the underlying theory and the reliability of speedmeters; but, for illustrative purposes, the prosecutor will call a witness to lay those elements of the foundation.

The prosecutor first calls Professor Jerold Harter. The professor has identified himself.

P   WHAT is your occupation? (1)

W   I teach at Ohio State University.

P	WHAT do you teach? (1)
W	I teach physics and electronics.
P	WHAT is your formal education? (1)
W	I have a B.S. from Ohio State and both a master's and a Doctorate from University of California, Davis.
P	WHAT was your major area of study? (1)
W	My specialty has been radar and electronics.
P	HOW long have you been teaching? (1)
W	For approximately 10 years.
P	WHAT, if anything, have you published? (1)
W	I've published roughly 20 articles, most of them dealing with radar and electronics.
P	Professor, WHAT is the Doppler Shift principle? (2)
W	It's a theory about beams of microwaves. If a beam bounces off an approaching object, the frequency of the beam changes; the change is an increase, and it is proportional to the speed of the approaching object.
P	WHAT would be a simple example of the operation of this principle? (2)
W	Well, suppose that you're standing at a train station. A train is coming, and it's blowing its whistle. When the train is approaching you, the pitch of the whistle sounds higher. As soon as the train passes you and begins receding, the pitch sounds lower. The whistle, of course, hasn't changed. It's the Doppler Shift principle which explains why it sounds as if the whistle is changing.
P	WHAT experiments, if any, have been conducted to verify this theory? (2)
W	You couldn't count the number. The theory is one of the most fundamental principles in the field.
P	HOW widely is the principle accepted? (3)
W	It's regarded as an axiom, a basic principle. Everyone in the field knows about and accepts the principle.
P	Now, professor, WHAT is a stationary radar speedmeter? (4)
W	It's a device for measuring the speed of cars.
P	WHAT are the components of a radar speedmeter? (4)
W	It has a component for transmitting a beam of microwaves and another component for receiving.
P	HOW does the speedmeter work? (4)
W	For example, the transmitter in a police car sends a beam toward an approaching vehicle. The beam strikes the vehicle, shifts, and then

bounces back to the receiver in the police car. The receiver measures the change in frequency, and the speedmeter then reads out the speed of the approaching vehicle.

P   WHAT experiments, if any, have been conducted to test the reliability of the speedmeter? (4)

W   There have been numerous experiments, particularly some at Northwestern and the University of North Carolina.

P   WHAT has been the outcome of these experiments? (4)

W   If the instrument is in good condition and the operator is qualified, the instrument will give you a very reliable speed estimate. The empirical data demonstrate that by using the instrument, an operator can get a very accurate speed estimate.

P   WHAT do you mean by "very accurate"? (4)

W   No technology is error free. But the experiments indicate that if the operator correctly uses the speedmeter, in the vast majority of cases—in the very high ninety percentages—the reading will be within a mile or two of the actual speed.

P   HOW widely is the radar speedmeter accepted? (5)

W   It's used extensively by law enforcement throughout the world, and its reliability is almost universally accepted by scientists familiar with the technology.

The second witness will be the officer who used a radar speedmeter to clock the accused. The officer has already testified that he arrived at the scene and set up his equipment.

P   WHAT equipment were you using? (8)

W   A General Electric stationary radar speedmeter.

P   WHAT training, if any, have you had in using a speedmeter? (6)

W   I spent two weeks studying the speedmeter in a course at the Police Academy.

P   HOW did you study the speedmeter? (6)

W   First, we had several lectures on the speedmeter and its operation. Then we saw demonstrations of its use. Finally, we participated in exercises where we used the speedmeter and more experienced officers double-checked us. After the exercises, we had to pass a graded test to graduate and be certified to operate the speedmeter.

P   Since graduating from that course, HOW many times have you used the speedmeter in the field? (6)

W   Hundreds of times.

P   HOW long have you used a speedmeter? (6)

W	I've been assigned to Traffic for three years, and you use the speedmeter almost daily in Traffic detail.
P	WHAT did you do after you arrived at the scene? (8)
W	I checked to ensure that the speedmeter was in working order.
P	WHAT condition was the speedmeter in? (7)
W	Good, operational condition.
P	HOW do you know that? (7)
W	I used a tuning fork test.
P	WHAT is the tuning fork test? (7)
W	The manufacturer supplies you with several tuning forks. I have 30-, 45-, and 60-mile-an-hour forks. You set them off, and the speedmeter is supposed to register those speeds.
P	HOW did you conduct the test on this occasion? (7)
W	I used all three forks, and the machine checked out all three times; it registered the right speed each time.
P	WHAT did you do then? (9)
W	I let the machine warm up and then aimed the transmitter down the road.
P	WHAT happened after you aimed the transmitter? (8)
W	I saw the accused's car approaching.
P	WHO is the accused? (8)
W	He's the fellow sitting at the table over there.
P	HOW is he dressed? (8)
W	He's wearing a blue suit and red tie.
P	HOW long did you have to observe the defendant at the scene? (8)
W	About ten minutes. I saw him as he passed by, and then later, after we stopped him, I talked to him for several minutes.
P	Your Honor, please let the record reflect that the witness has identified the accused. (8)
J	It will so reflect.
P	WHAT did you do when you saw the accused's car approaching? (8)
W	I checked to ensure that the speedmeter was on, and then I clocked his car.
P	WHAT does "clocked" mean? (10)
W	It means that I measured his speed.
P	WHAT was the clocking? (10)
W	The speedmeter flashed a signal that his car was going 45 miles an hour.

Daubert Foundation

In the following sample foundation, samples of blood from the accused and a crime scene stain have already been marked as prosecution exhibits number one and two for identification during the testimony of an earlier witness, Patrolman Gonzalez. At one time, the dominant DNA technology was single locus probe restriction fragment length polymorphism (RFLP). 2 P. GIANNELLI, E. IMWINKELRIED, A. ROTH, J. CAMPBELL MORIARTY & V. BEETY, SCIENTIFIC EVIDENCE § 18.03[b] (Matthew Bender, 6th ed. 2020). A variation of RFLP, short tandem repeat (STR) analysis, is now the most popular technique. *Id.* at § 18.03[d]. The FBI maintains a national Convicted Offender Database Information System (CODIS). For each offender, the database includes information for markers at 20 STR loci.

This foundation illustrates STR analysis producing an electropherogram or e-gram (EPG). Even today, though, in a case in which a litigant wanted to exhaust the possibilities, the litigant might use RFLP as well as STR. In this hypothetical, three witnesses are required to lay the foundation. Note also that the elements of the foundation are not necessarily developed in numerical sequence. Finally, these sample foundations do not go into detail about the chain of custody, which could be critical in a DNA case. Assume that a prior witness, Officer Gonzalez, traced the chain of custody until the delivery of the crime scene sample to the analyst at the laboratory. The first witness's testimony serves to educate the trier of fact about the general STR DNA typing methodology and the underlying scientific theory.

P   Please state your full name and spell your last name for the record.

W   My name is John Gilmore. The surname is spelled G-I-L-M-O-R-E.

P   WHAT is your address?

W   I reside at 1433 Macmillan Avenue in Houston, Texas.

P   WHAT is your occupation? (1)

W   I'm a professor at the University of Texas Health Science Center in Houston.

P   Please describe your educational background for the ladies and gentlemen of the jury.

O   Your Honor, this won't be necessary. We're perfectly willing to save the court some time by stipulating that Professor Gilmore is an expert.

    (Pause for discussion during which the proponent successfully argues that the jury is entitled to hear the qualifications of the expert witness in order to intelligently determine how much weight to give to the witness's testimony.)

P   Professor Gilmore, let me repeat the last question. Please describe your educational background. (1)

W   Well, I received my B.S. from the University of Texas Health Science Center in Houston. I then obtained my master's degree from the same institution.

P	When you studied for that degree, WHAT area of study, if any, did you concentrate in? (1)
W	Molecular biology.
P	WHAT did you do after you obtained your master's degree? (1)
W	I then worked for my Ph.D. I obtained that degree in YR-19 from the University of New Mexico.
P	During your study for the doctorate, did you concentrate on any particular area? (1)
W	Certainly.
P	And WHAT was that area? (1)
W	This time I narrowed my focus. I knew that DNA typing was a growing field, so I concentrated not only on molecular biology but more specifically on DNA typing. I wrote my dissertation on that topic.
P	WHAT did you do after you received your Ph.D. in YR-19? (1)
W	I joined the University of Texas Health Science Center faculty. I've taught in the College of Sciences since late YR-19.
P	WHAT is your current title? (1)
W	I'm a full professor in the College of Sciences.
P	HOW many times, if ever, have you testified in court as an expert witness? (1)
W	I have testified as an expert on 20 other occasions.
P	WHAT subjects did you testify on? (1)
W	On each occasion I testified as an expert on DNA.
P	Professor, earlier in your testimony, you used the expression, "on DNA typing." In general terms, could you tell us WHAT that is? (2)
W	Certainly. As we all learn in high school biology, DNA is the basic building block of life. Each person's DNA accounts for his or her individuality. Everyone has a certain number of chromosomes. Each chromosome is composed of a DNA molecule. If you think back to high school, you'll remember that the molecule is usually thought of as a double helix—a sort of twisted ladder or spiral staircase.
P	WHAT is this helix or ladder made of? (2)
W	The sides of the ladder are comprised of alternating molecules of sugar and phosphate. However, in DNA typing, what you're really interested in are the rungs of the ladder.
P	WHAT are they made of? (2)
W	What we call nucleotides. There are four: adenine (A), thymine (T), cytosine (C), and guanine (G). Each rung consists of two of these. There

are bonding rules: A always attaches to T, and C always attaches to G. A combination of two nucleotides forms each rung. The combination is called a base pair.

P   HOW many base pairs does each individual have? (2)

W   Each person has about three billion. Most base pair sequences—99.9% to be exact—are common to all human beings. It's what makes us all human beings rather than horses. However, there are others that vary from person to person—approximately three million of them. They're the so-called polymorphic sites or locations. A person's DNA at any given location on the nucleotide chain wouldn't be unique to that person. But when you consider all the possible locations, each person's overall sequence is peculiar to that individual. The odds against a random, complete match in nucleotides are astronomical. They run well beyond the trillions. That unique nucleotide sequence is the basis of DNA typing. In a nutshell, that's the underlying theory of DNA typing.

P   How WELL accepted is this theory? (2)

W   Universally by anyone who knows anything about molecular biology.

P   HOW can you use this theory in practice to identify people? (4)

W   There are a number of techniques which implement the theory, but by a wide margin the one that's most widely used today is STR analysis— short tandem repeat analysis. It's a multi-step procedure that enables you to identify some of the parts of the nucleotide sequence that vary from person to person. There have been tens of validation studies for STR analysis, and the empirical data clearly establish that by using the STR technique, an analyst can accurately identify segments of the nucleotide sequence.

P   In these validation studies for STR, HOW accurately do the analysts make the identifications? (4)

W   The error rate is consistently well below 1%—actually, only a small fraction of 1%.

P   Your Honor, I request that this be marked State's exhibit number three for identification.

          (*Counsel hands exhibit to court reporter, who marks it and hands it back.*)

P   Please let the record reflect that I am showing State's exhibit number three for identification to the defense counsel.

P   Permission to approach the witness?

J   Granted.

P   Professor, I now hand you what has been marked State's exhibit number three for identification. Do you recognize it? (4)

W	Yes.
P	WHAT is it? (4)
W	It's a chart showing the various steps in STR analysis. An oral description of the technique can be confusing if you don't visualize what's going on.
P	WHO prepared this chart? (4)
W	I did.
P	HOW accurate is the chart? (4)
W	It's a good basic depiction of all of the essential steps in STR.
P	Your Honor, I now offer State's exhibit number three for identification into evidence as State's exhibit number three.
J	Any objection?
O	No, Your Honor.
J	Very well. It will be received.
P	Your Honor, I would like your permission to distribute exact copies of the exhibit to each juror. They may find it helpful in following Professor Gilmore's testimony.
J	May I see the copies? And give one to opposing counsel.
	(*The judge and opposing counsel examine copies to ensure that they conform to the exhibit.*) O.K. You may proceed.
P	Now, Professor, using exhibit number three, please lead us through this process. (4)
W	O.K. Start on the left-hand margin. That shows the double helix or ladder in the cell. Any cell with a nucleus will contain DNA—for example, white blood cells, sperm, saliva, and those surrounding hair roots. The first thing we've got to do is extract the DNA from the nucleus. Take a look at the second column from the left. We use chemical techniques to extract or remove the DNA.
P	WHAT comes next? (4)
W	You target certain regions of the DNA and amplify or multiply them.
P	WHICH regions do you target? (4)
W	They're parts of the DNA which have some short nucleotide sequences that are repeated—the short tandem repeats. We know that there are a number of these regions which are: (1) flanked by certain nucleotide sequences; and (2) include a varying number of repetitions or STRs. The number of repetitions varies from person to person. This multiplication step involves several procedures.
P	WHAT is the first procedure? (4)

W	You create the reaction mixture.
P	HOW do you do that? (4)
W	You place the original DNA in a test tube. Then you add two primers of known nucleotide sequences. We know that those two sequences flank the specific STR.
P	WHAT do you do after you mix the original DNA and the primers? (4)
W	You heat the mixture. As you can see on exhibit number three, when the original DNA is heated, the double strand comes apart and yields two single strands. You then allow the mixture to cool.
P	WHY do you do that? (4)
W	When the mixture cools, the two primers attach to the two strands. As the exhibit shows, one primer attaches toward one end of one strand; according to the binding rules I discussed earlier, the primer will attach to a known complementary nucleotide sequence. Again, there are bonding rules. Thus, if part of the primer sequence is CA, it must attach to GT. The other primer attaches toward the opposite end of the other strand; again, that primer must attach at a binding site with a known complementary nucleotide sequence. The part of the original DNA nucleotide sequence between the two primers—in other words, flanked by the primers—is the target region containing the varying number of repeats.
P	WHAT happens after the two primers attach to the two strands? (4)
W	As you can see on the exhibit, after binding to the single strands, the primers extend or elongate. Again, the two primers attach toward opposite ends of the two single strands. The primers now extend toward each other. Essentially, the extension ends when it reaches the other primer. Together, the original DNA strand and the extension form an exact copy of the original region that we wanted to amplify. We repeat this cycle until we have a large number of exact copies of that DNA fragment, that target region. It's like a chemical Xerox machine.
P	After you have created all these copies of the target STR regions, WHAT is the next step? (4)
W	Separation. You need to separate or sort the fragments by size, as you can see in the column in the middle of exhibit number three. You insert the fragments into a long tube. You also insert dyed fragments of known length. The number of repeats in the fragment determines the length or size of the fragment, and in turn the size of the fragment determines how quickly the fragment moves through the tube. The longer fragments move more slowly than the shorter fragments going through the tube.
P	WHAT happens as the fragments pass through the tube? (4)
W	As I said earlier, they separate. The longer fragments take longer. At a

certain point in the tube, an instrument scans the material.

P   WHAT is the purpose of the scanning? (4)

W   The scanning determines when each fragment passes that point in the tube—in other words, how long it has taken that fragment to go through the tube. Again, the length of the fragment largely determines how much time it takes. The instrument scans both the fragments from the sample being analyzed and the dyed fragments of known length. Basically, instrument "sizes" the fragments—determines their length. By scanning both types of fragments and comparing the fragments being analyzed with the fragments of known length, the instrument determines the size. Ultimately, you get a printout which indicates when each fragment passes the scanner and, therefore, the size of the fragment. The printout is called an electropherogram, e-gram, or EPG.

P   After you've determined the size, WHAT do you do? (4)

W   The sizing instrument is hooked up to a computer.

P   WHAT does the computer do? (4)

W   The computer has a database of known genetic markers. The database contains the information as to the size or length of those markers. The computer compares the size of the analyzed samples to the information in the database to identify the genetic markers in the sample. That comparison confirms the accurate identification of each fragment.

P   WHY is this procedure called "DNA typing"? (4)

W   The analogy is to fingerprinting. Suppose you have a blood sample found at a crime scene and a sample taken from the accused who's suspected of committing the crime. You'd apply the procedure to both samples to see if the samples matched. In an STR test, if they match, you know that, at least at the sites tested, the two samples have the same nucleotide sequence.

P   WHAT, if anything, have you written about the procedure for conducting an STR test?

W   I published an article on the subject an issue of BIOTECHNIQUES magazine. I actually coauthored the article with a Dr. Munson.

P   WHO is Dr. Munson?

W   He is the director of the Cellmatch laboratory in Houston. One of their specialties is DNA testing.

P   Your Honor, I request that this be marked State's exhibit for identification next in order.

     (*Counsel hands to court reporter who marks it as State's exhibit four for identification and hands it back to counsel.*)

P   Please let the record reflect that I am showing what the court reporter has marked as State's exhibit number four for identification to the defense counsel.

P Permission to approach the witness?

J Yes.

P Professor, I hand you what has been marked as State's exhibit number four for identification. Do you recognize it?

W Yes, I most certainly do.

P WHAT is it?

W It's appendix A from my article.

P HOW do you recognize it?

W I ought to know the contents, since I coauthored it with Dr. Munson!

P Your Honor, I now offer State's exhibit number four for identification into evidence as State's exhibit number four.

J Any objection?

O Yes, Your Honor. This is incompetent hearsay.

P Your Honor, this isn't hearsay. I admit that it would be hearsay if we offered the body of the article, including assertions about molecular biology and the proper procedures for conducting an STR analysis. However, we're relying on the witness's in-court testimony for that. Instead, we're offering only Appendix A. Appendix is a checklist for technicians conducting STR tests. It's a series of imperative sentences: "Do this. Then do this." Imperative sentences aren't assertions under Federal Rule of Evidence 801(a).

J May I see the exhibit? (*Counsel hands to judge.*) Thank you.

J I agree that this appendix doesn't constitute hearsay. Objection overruled. State's exhibit number four for identification is admitted into evidence as State's exhibit number four.

P Professor Gilmore, would you please describe appendix A, which appears in your article?

W It's a comprehensive checklist for technicians who conduct STR DNA testing.

P And HOW well accepted is the reliability of the short tandem repeat analysis technique? (3)

W Almost universally. It's not only employed in universities and colleges. It's also used by hospitals for genetic testing and by crime laboratories throughout the world.

The proponent's second witness establishes the test result, that is, the outcome when the general methodology described by the first witness was applied to the specific samples in the instant case.

P	Please state your full name and spell your last name for the record.
W	My name is Ralph Harrison.
P	Would you please spell your last name for the court reporter?
W	Harrison is spelled H-A-R-R-I-S-O-N.
P	Thank you. WHERE do you live, Mr. Harrison?
W	I live in Houston, Texas.
P	Mr. Harrison, WHAT is your line of work? (6)
W	I'm a DNA genetic marker technician at Cellmatch Company in Houston, Texas.
P	WHAT is your educational background? (6)
W	I have a B.S. degree from the University of Texas Health Science Center.
P	WHEN did you receive your degree? (6)
W	YR-13.
P	WHAT did you do after receiving your degree? (6)
W	I went right to work for Cellmatch. Initially, I did bloodstain tests and electrophoretic analysis of enzymes and proteins. However, in YR-12 when we set up our DNA unit, I helped establish and later expand the unit.
P	WHAT, if any, special training did you receive when you joined the unit? (6)
W	I attended an intensive, three-week training program conducted by Dr. Munson in conjunction with his good friend, Professor John Gilmore. Dr. Gilmore flew down and spent two weeks with us going over every step of STR testing in great detail.
P	I hand you what has been marked as State's exhibit number four. Do you recognize it? (9)
W	You bet I do.
P	WHAT is it? (9)
W	It's an appendix from the BIOTECHNIQUES article about STR procedures which Professor Gilmore and Dr. Munson wrote.
P	HOW do you recognize it? (9)
W	Professor Gilmore distributed a draft of it on the first day of class, and we used it throughout his instruction. I know every period and footnote in that article backwards and forwards by now.
P	HOW, if at all, do you use the article in your work? (9)
W	I use it almost every day. Appendix A is a model protocol or test procedure for conducting STR tests. I use that protocol every time I conduct an STR test at Cellmatch.

P	When you use this protocol, HOW accurately can you be in identifying the DNA in the samples? (9)
W	Extremely accurate.
P	Could you please explain what you mean by "extremely accurate"? (9)
W	Before beginning using the protocol in case work at our laboratory, we did an internal validation study. We didn't have a single error in the validation study. Periodically, we administer proficiency tests to our analysts. In the vast majority of proficiency tests, using the protocol our analysts don't commit a solitary error.
P	WHAT do you mean by "in the vast majority" of these proficiency tests? (9)
W	Easily 95% of the time. It's an extremely rare occasion when, using this procedure, our analysts make even a single error on a proficiency test. Each analyst is subjected to regular, random testing. They don't have any advance notice of the test to make it as realistic as possible. We integrate the test samples into the flow of their regular casework; that way they handle the test sample exactly the same way they handle all the other samples submitted to our laboratory.
P	Now let's shift topics. WHERE were you on the afternoon of June 28, YR-3?
W	I was at work at Cellmatch.
P	WHAT, if anything, happened that afternoon?
W	Patrolman Gonzalez from the Houston Police Department stopped by. He delivered two blood samples and asked me to conduct a DNA test on them.
P	WHAT else, if anything, did Patrolman Gonzalez tell you about the case?
W	He basically just asked me to analyze the samples. The only other thing he mentioned was that there was an indication that the source of at least one of the samples was Caucasian. He didn't say anything else, and I didn't ask. You want your analysis to be as objective as possible. In our laboratory, we have a strict rule that the analyst should be shielded from any other information about the case. Although you get the samples, you don't get any unnecessary information about the case.
P	I now hand you what have previously been marked as State's exhibits number one and two for identification. Do you know WHAT these are?
W	Yes.
P	Could you please tell the jury what they are?
W	They are the two samples which Patrolman Gonzalez gave me.
P	HOW do you recognize them?

W   I know his initials, and my initials are on the plastic container where I placed them at the time I tested the samples.

P   WHAT did you do with the samples after Patrolman Gonzalez gave them to you?

W   I immediately tested them.

P   Between the time you received the samples from Patrolman Gonzalez and the time you tested the samples, WHO else handled the samples?

W   No one else. I was the only one.

P   During that same time, WHEN, if at all, were the samples out of your sight?

W   They never were. It had been a quiet day, and I was able to get right to the test. When Gonzalez arrived, I met him at the receptionist's desk. I went straight from here to my bench in the DNA unit. I conducted the test almost immediately.

P   Your Honor, I now offer State's exhibits number one and two for identification into evidence.

J   Any objection?

O   None, Your Honor.

J   All right. State's exhibits number one and two are admitted into evidence.

P   Thank you, Your Honor. Mr. Harrison, WHAT equipment did you use in the test of these samples? (7)

W   There's a variety of instruments. You need some chemicals and the equipment to scan and size the fragments.

P   WHAT condition were they in when used to test exhibits number one and two? (7)

W   They all were in good condition.

P   HOW do you know that? (7)

W   The chemicals were fresh.

P   WHAT do you mean by "fresh"? (7)

W   We get a fresh shipment from the manufacturer on Monday morning. I conducted this test on a Monday afternoon. The chemicals certainly had not lost any of their potency by then.

P   WHAT about the other apparatus and equipment? (7)

W   We have them serviced every Friday evening after work. Again, I conducted this test on a Monday afternoon. The equipment would have been checked shortly before that, and I know that I didn't encounter any problems in running the test.

P   HOW did you conduct the test? (9)

W   I did it "by the book"—or I should say "by the article." As I always do, I followed the appendix to the Gilmore BIOTECHNIQUES article step by step to ensure that I used the proper protocol.

P   Mr. Harrison, HOW well do you remember the specific occasion when you tested these two samples? (9)

W   I guess I generally do, but I have to admit that I've tested hundreds of these samples and the tests tend to run together in my mind.

P   Your Honor, I request that these be marked State's exhibit next in order for identification.

         (*Counsel hands exhibit to court reporter who marks it as State's exhibits number five and six for identification and returns it to counsel.*)

P   May the record reflect that I am showing what the court reporter has marked as State's exhibits number five and six for identification to opposing counsel.

         (*Counsel shows exhibits to opposing counsel who briefly examines them.*)

P   Your Honor, I request permission to approach the witness?

J   Granted.

P   Mr. Harrison, I now hand you what have been marked as State's exhibits number five and six for identification. WHAT are they? (10)

W   They're called electropherograms, e-grams, or EPGs—the STR printouts or charts of the two samples which Patrolman Gonzalez delivered to me. Five is the printout for one sample, exhibit number one, while six is the printout for the other sample, exhibit number two.

P   HOW do you recognize them?

W   You can see my initials and the date on the bottom of both printouts. These are the printouts that I got when I subjected both samples to STR analysis.

P   WHAT, if anything, did you do with the printouts? (10)

W   I compared them.

P   WHAT was the purpose of the comparison? (10)

W   I wanted to see if they matched.

P   WHAT do you mean when you say "match"? (10)

W   I mean that both samples contain fragments of the same size or length. In this case, they matched. Within expected length tolerances, the fragments were of identical size.

P   HOW do you know? (10)

W	The scanning instrument compared them to the dyed fragments of known length, and then the computer compared the measurements to its database.
P	WHAT did you do after declaring a match? (10)
W	I called in Dr. Munson. He's in charge of the next step in the DNA unit, that is, calculating the probability of a random match.

The proponent completes the DNA analysis with a third witness, Dr. Munson. The third witness's function is to explain the significance of the test result that the second witness attained when he applied the general methodology to the specific samples in the case.

P	Please state your full name and spell your last name for the record.
W	I'm Andrew J. Munson. You spell that, M-U-N-S-O-N.
P	WHERE do you live?
W	In Houston.
P	Dr. Munson, WHERE do you work? (6)
W	I work at the Houston laboratory of Cellmatch, Inc. I am the director of the DNA typing unit of the laboratory.
P	Please tell us your educational background. (6)
W	I attended undergraduate school at the University of California, Davis. I received a basic B.S. degree from U.C.D. Then I obtained my master's degree at Washington University in St. Louis. Finally, I obtained a doctorate.
P	WHERE did you obtain that degree? (6)
W	At Yale.
P	WHAT area, if any, did you specialize in during your doctoral program? (6)
W	Population genetics.
P	Could you please tell us WHAT that specialty involves?
W	In part, it involves the application of the laws of statistics and probability to genetics problems.
P	Please give us an example of such a problem.
W	For instance, as in a case like this one, you might be interested in trying to figure out what percentage of the population has a certain DNA marker or a particular set of DNA markers. Population genetics experts attempt to answer that type of problem.
P	Doctor, I hand you what has been admitted as State's exhibit number six. Do you recognize it?
W	Yes.

P	WHAT is it?
W	It's the electropherogram, the printout, which Mr. Harrison gave me to evaluate a few months ago.
P	HOW do you recognize it?
W	I recognize his initials and my initials on the comer of the printout. Also I recall the date that we ran the test.
P	WHAT did you do with this printout after Mr. Harrison gave it to you?
W	The printout indicated which genetic markers were present in the sample. I determined the percentage of the Caucasian population that would have the set of DNA markers indicated on the printout.
P	WHY did you attempt to determine that percentage in the Caucasian population rather than say, for example, the Hispanic population?
W	I was told by Mr. Harrison that there was an indication that the source of at least one sample was Caucasian.
O	Objection, Your Honor, that is hearsay.
P	Your Honor, we are not offering the statement for the truth of the matter. Instead, we are offering it for the nonhearsay purpose of showing why this witness conducted his analysis in this manner. It explains why he consulted the population frequency data for Caucasians. This is an example of a statement or information acted upon.
J	Objection overruled.
P	WHAT technique did you use to determine the percentage?
W	I used the multiplication or product rule.
P	WHAT is that?
W	Let me give you a simple example. Let's suppose that you want to know what percentage of the Caucasian population has blonde hair *and* a limp. You check the population frequencies, and you learn the following: Ten percent of the Caucasian population has blonde hair, and one percent has a limp. You multiply the two numbers, 10% by 1%. The multiplication yields the figure, one tenth of one percent. That is, the percentage of the Caucasian population that has both characteristics. That's the formula I used in this case.
P	WHY did you use it?
W	You use it when you're analyzing several "independent" factors.
P	HOW well accepted is the use of the formula in that situation?
W	Any mathematician would tell you that it's the appropriate formula to use when you have independent factors. There's unanimity on that point.
P	WHAT is an "independent" factor?

W   When factors are independent, they don't affect one another. In my example, a person with a limp might have blonde hair, black hair, brown hair, or no hair; the color of the hair doesn't have any effect on the probability whether they limp. In contrast, suppose you wanted to know how many Caucasian men not only have a mustache but also have a beard. Those obviously aren't independent factors, and you consequently couldn't use the multiplication or product rule to determine the percentage.

P   WHY did you apply the multiplication rule in this case to the various DNA markers shown on the printout?

W   I was confident that each band, representing a different DNA marker, was independent of the other bands.

P   WHY were you confident of that?

W   Because in STR testing we target sites on different chromosomes. In early days of DNA analysis, they often used multi-locus probes. When you do that, the probe hits several locations or sites on the same chromosome. If the sites are close together, they might not be independent; your DNA marker at one location might in fact affect the likelihood you have a particular DNA marker at the nearby site. However, it's generally accepted in biology that when you target sites on separate chromosomes, you have adequate assurance that the bands are independent. We did that in this case.

P   When you use this multiplication rule, exactly WHAT is it that you multiply?

W   You identify each DNA marker, and you insert into the formula the population frequency for that marker for that ethnic group.

P   WHERE did you get the numbers you used in this case?

W   We have an agreement with Lifecodes, one of the largest DNA laboratories in the world. By virtue of their agreement, we can use the population frequencies in their database. They've built up the database over the years, and it now includes the results of thousands of DNA tests of persons of virtually every conceivable ethnic group.

P   HOW many DNA markers did you identify?

W   I could definitely identify markers at 20 loci or sites.

P   WHAT did you do once you identified them?

W   I looked up the pertinent frequencies in the Lifecodes database and then inserted those frequencies as the variables in the multiplication rule.

P   When you multiplied those numbers, WHAT was the result?

W   The multiplication indicated that only one thousandth of one percent of the Caucasian population would possess this set of DNA markers.

It is especially important in *Daubert* jurisdictions to lay as complete a foundation as feasible in the trial court. In *GE v. Joiner*, 522 U.S. 136, 118 S. Ct. 512, 139 L. Ed. 2d 508 (1997), the Court announced that the standard for appellate review is abuse of discretion. The *Joiner* Court made it clear that it would apply that deferential standard to rulings excluding as well as admitting scientific testimony, even when the ruling is "outcome determinative" in the case. *Id.* at 142–43. As a practical matter, if the proponent does not prevail in the trial court, the odds of victory on appeal are slim. The proponent's only realistic hope of gaining an appellate reversal is to have laid an impressive foundation in the trial court.

CHAPTER 5

RULE 403 AND LEGAL IRRELEVANCE LIMITATIONS ON CREDIBILITY EVIDENCE

PART A.   Introduction

§ 5.01   OVERVIEW

The last chapter focuses on one aspect of the probative value of evidence, namely the authentication of the evidence. To be admissible, evidence must have probative value in two senses. First, on its face, the evidence must be material; the evidence must have some logical connection with a material fact of consequence in the case. In the words of restyled Federal Rule of Evidence 401(a), the evidence must have some "tendency to make the existence of a fact [that is of consequence in determining the action] more probable or less probable than it would be without the evidence." *If* the item is what its proponent claims it to be, does the item affect the balance of probabilities of the existence of any fact in issue? Second, as we have seen in Chapter 4, the evidence must have underlying probative value; the common law will not accept evidence at face value and stubbornly insists that the proponent authenticate his or her evidence. The proponent must prove that the exhibit *is* what he or she claims it to be. Rules 104(b) and 901–903 set out the authentication rules.

Even if the evidence is logically relevant in both senses, the trial judge may exclude the evidence on the ground that the evidence is "legally irrelevant." The expression, *"legal irrelevance,"* is a rubric for excluding evidence on the theory that the probative dangers attending the evidence outweigh the evidence's probative value. Restyled Federal Rule of Evidence 403 states the doctrine: "The court may exclude [logically] relevant evidence if its probative value is substantially outweighed by a danger of one or more of the following: unfair prejudice, confusing the issues, misleading the jury, undue delay, wasting time, or needlessly presenting cumulative evidence." Rule 403 is a one-way street. Although it does not authorize the admission of irrelevant evidence, it empowers trial judges to exclude logically relevant evidence in some circumstances.

Underlying Rule 403 is a model of optimal jury behavior. Ideally, we want the jury to: use admitted items of evidence as proof of only the factual propositions the judge admits them to prove, ascribe the proper probative weight to each item of evidence, and concentrate on the historical issues in dispute in the case. As a matter of institutional policy, we want the trier of fact to conform to this model. Rule 403 grants the judge discretionary power to exclude an item of technically relevant evidence that realistically

231

poses a danger to this model. This model not only explains the general discretionary power conferred on the judge under Rule 403; the model also helps explicate many of the more specific doctrines set out in Articles IV and VI of the Federal Rules of Evidence.

To begin with, if the judge admits an item of evidence to legitimately prove one factual proposition, we do not want the jury to misuse the item as proof of another factual proposition in the case. This probative danger helps to explain the doctrine stated in Rule 411. Rule 411 limits the admissibility of evidence of a defendant's liability insurance. Evidence of liability insurance creates a grave danger of jury misuse of the testimony; once the jury learns of the existence of the insurance, they may be tempted to find the defendant liable even though the evidence of fault is weak. Although the defendant may not be at fault, at a subconscious level the jurors may be inclined to allocate the loss to the "deep pocket" insurer. Evidence which realistically tempts the jury to decide the case on an improper basis is "prejudicial" within the technical meaning of that term in Rule 403. As the Advisory Committee Notes to both Rule 105 and Rule 403 explain, even when the judge administers a limiting instruction to the jury, the evidence may be objectionable under Rule 403 if it is unrealistic to assume that the jury will be willing and able to follow the limiting instruction.

Moreover, there might be a risk that the jury will overestimate the probative value of the evidence. Psychology studies tell us that on the one hand, laypersons tend to attach a great deal of weight to evidence of specific instances of a litigant's bad behavior. For instance, after learning of a defendant's criminal record, the jurors may form a simplistic notion of the defendant's character and reason that "if he did it once, he probably did it again." On the other hand, many studies indicate that a person's general character is a poor predictor of the person's conduct in a particular situation; situational factors tend to be more influential. In short, lay jurors could easily overvalue evidence of a party's bad character. That risk in part accounts for the restrictions on character evidence in Rule 404–405.

Finally, we want the jurors to concentrate on the historical facts and events in dispute under the pleadings. It is true that the jurors must also resolve incidental disputes over the witnesses' credibility. However, to the extent that the jurors become bogged down in resolving credibility contests, they may lose sight of their primary task, the resolution of the historical merits of the case. This risk accounts for many of the limitations on credibility evidence in Article VI.

As previously stated, these probative dangers both help to explain the specific rules in Articles IV and VI and factor into the general balancing test stated in Rule 403. Even when an item of evidence passes muster under the specific rules in Articles IV and VI, in most instances[1] the judge has discretion to exclude the item if the judge concludes that the probative dangers substantially outweigh the probative value of the item. Note

---

[1] The most important exception to this generalization is a conviction that qualifies for impeachment under Rule 609(a)(2). The Advisory Committee Note accompanying the 2000 amendment to Rule 609 states that such convictions "are to be automatically admitted . . . ." That is true in the sense that the judge cannot invoke Rule 403 to exclude such a conviction, but there is a strong statutory construction argument

two features of Rule 403. To begin with, the rule is cast in the passive voice, indicating that the opponent of the admission of the evidence has the burden of persuading the judge that the probative dangers outstrip the probative value. Moreover, the rule includes the adverb "substantially." The opponent must not only convince the judge that the dangers outweigh the probative value; the opponent must also persuade the judge that the dangers do so by a wide margin. Rule 403 thus reflects a marked bias in favor of the admission of logically relevant evidence.

§ 5.02   THE STAGES OF CREDIBILITY ANALYSIS

If the trial judge rules that the prospective witness is competent, the bailiff or court reporter administers the oath to the witness. The witness's proponent immediately begins direct examination. As soon as the witness answers one question on direct examination, his or her credibility becomes an issue in the case.

What is the significance of characterizing testimony as "credibility" evidence? Credibility evidence is not admitted as proof on the historical merits of the case. Consequently, on request the trial judge must give the jury a limiting instruction under Rule 105. Moreover, credibility evidence cannot be used to support a finding of fact. Thus, in the trial court the plaintiff cannot rely on such evidence to defeat a defense motion for a directed verdict. Similarly, if on appeal the defense attacks the legal sufficiency of the evidence to support a trial court judgment in the plaintiff's favor, the plaintiff cannot rely on credibility evidence to defeat the attack.

The proponent naturally wants to build up the witness's believability or credibility in the jury's eyes. Conversely, the opponent wants to tear down that credibility. The opponent's attacks on the witness's credibility are termed impeachment. If the proponent attempts to build up the witness's credibility before any attempted impeachment, the proponent is said to be bolstering the witness's credibility. For example, the proponent might attempt to increase the witness's credibility during the direct examination before the opponent has even had any opportunity to cross-examine the witness. If the proponent attempts to repair the witness's credibility after attempted impeachment, the proponent is said to be rehabilitating the witness's credibility. If the opponent attempted to impeach during cross-examination, the proponent could attempt to rehabilitate the witness during redirect.

Most of the Evidence law dealing with credibility focuses on impeachment. For that reason, most of the sections in this chapter deal with the various impeachment techniques. Some impeachment techniques may be used only during cross-examination of the witness to be impeached—intrinsic impeachment. In this form of impeachment, the opponent must accept the witness's answer, in the sense that the opponent may not present other evidence to contradict the witness's answer. § 5.05 of this chapter deals with such a technique, proof that the witness has committed bad acts which have not resulted in a conviction.

Other impeachment techniques necessarily entail extrinsic evidence and cannot be used during cross-examination. §§ 5.06, 5.07, and 5.08 of this chapter are illustrative.

---

that even such a conviction may be excluded as remote in time under Rule 609(b). Cretacci v. Hare, 533 F. Supp. 3d 605 (E.D. Tenn. 2021).

§ 5.06 deals with proof that witness #1 has a character trait of untruthfulness. Use of this technique requires that the opponent present witness #2, a character witness, to testify to the bad character of witness #1. § 5.07 deals with polygraph examination. Use of this impeachment technique requires that the opponent call a polygraph examiner to testify that a prior witness flunked an examination. § 5.08 discusses specific contradiction. In this technique, the opposing attorney calls witness #2 to contradict facts asserted in witness #1's testimony.

The remaining impeachment techniques permit both cross-examination and extrinsic evidence. §§ 5.09–5.12 analyze these techniques: convictions, prior inconsistent statements, bias, and attacks on the witness's mental capacity.

As you review the credibility doctrines in this chapter, remember that the doctrines are largely explicable in terms of the model of jury behavior underlying Rule 403. All of the evidence in question is logically relevant to the witness's credibility, but the doctrines discussed in this chapter restrict the admissibility of credibility evidence in the hope that the jury will focus primarily on the historical merits of the case.

PART B.   Bolstering Witnesses Before Impeachment

§ 5.03   PRIOR IDENTIFICATION

[1]   THE DOCTRINE

The general common-law rule is that the proponent may not bolster the witness's credibility before any attempted impeachment. It is true that some jurisdictions have abandoned this restriction. *E.g.*, *People v. Harris*, 47 Cal. 3d 1047, 1080–82, 255 Cal. Rptr. 352, 373–74, 767 P.2d 619, 640–41 (1989). However, the rule is still in effect in the vast majority of jurisdictions. The last sentence of Federal Rule 608(a) is a partial codification of the bolstering ban, and the Advisory Committee Note to the 2014 amendment to Rule 801 refers to "impermissible bolstering of a witness." The jurors' principal focus should be on the historical issues in the case rather than the witness's credibility. To ensure that the jurors maintain that focus, the common law ordinarily excludes evidence of the witness's believability until the opponent has attacked the witness. After all, there is always the possibility that the opposing party will not attack the witness; and if so, the trial time consumed by the presentation of the bolstering evidence will have been wasted.

There are special exceptions to the rule. One exception is the prior identification doctrine. In many jurisdictions, if the witness has already made an in-court identifica-tion of a person such as the criminal defendant, the witness's proponent may prove that the witness made a pretrial identification of the same person. At common law, the prior identification is not admitted as substantive evidence that the prior identification was correct; rather, the testimony is admitted for the limited purpose of increasing the witness's credibility. The fact that the witness identified the same person on a prior occasion tends to strengthen the inference of the witness's credibility; at least the witness is consistent. When the judge admits prior identification evidence on this theory, the opponent is entitled to a limiting instruction under Federal Rule of Evidence 105. Upon the opponent's request, the judge must instruct the jury that the proof is not admitted as substantive evidence but only on a bolstering theory. In the instruction, the judge would tell the jury that they could consider the prior identification testimony only for the limited purpose of deciding whether the witness was consistent and therefore somewhat more credible. In closing argument, the proponent may discuss the evidence only on that theory. The opponent could object if the proponent's statements suggested that the jury could treat the prior identification as proof of the accuracy of the in-court identification.

Some jurisdictions have taken a step beyond this view; they permit the proponent to use the prior identification as substantive evidence that the person identified was the perpetrator or actor. Federal Rule of Evidence 801(d)(1)(C) now exempts prior identification evidence from the definition of hearsay. The effect of the exemption is to enable the proponent to use the evidence as substantive proof. On this theory, the opponent has no right to a limiting instruction. Some courts have construed Rule 801(d)(1)(C) as applying even when the witness cannot make an in-court identification. The Supreme Court has held that a prior identification may be admitted as substantive evidence even when at trial the witness cannot explain the basis for the pretrial identification. *United States v. Owens*, 484 U.S. 554, 108 S. Ct. 838, 98 L. Ed. 2d 951 (1988).

[2] ELEMENTS OF THE FOUNDATION

The proponent must show that:

1. The witness has already made an in-court identification of the person.
2. The witness had a pretrial opportunity to observe the person.
3. The witness had an adequate opportunity to observe the person.
4. The pretrial encounter was conducted in a fair manner that was not unduly suggestive in violation of due process.
5. At the pretrial encounter, the witness identified the same person.

[3] SAMPLE FOUNDATION

The fact situation is a tort action arising from a hit-and-run accident. The plaintiff calls a witness, Jane Morris. The witness is prepared to testify that the defendant was the driver of the hit-and-run car. She is also ready to testify that she identified the defendant at a lineup at the local police station shortly after the accident. The witness has already described the accident which occurred at noontime. The proponent is the plaintiff.

P	WHAT did the car do after it struck the plaintiff?
W	It sped away from the scene.
P	WHO was driving that car? (1)
W	The defendant.
P	WHERE is he sitting? (1)
W	At the end of the table over there to the right.
P	HOW is he dressed? (1)

W	He's wearing a blue suit, white shirt, and striped tie.
P	Your Honor, may the record reflect that the witness has identified the defendant, John Ursin? (1)
J	It will so reflect.
P	Ms. Morris, HOW many times have you seen the defendant? (2)
W	Three times.
P	WHAT were those occasions? (2)
W	Well, I saw him at the scene of the accident, today in court, and one other time.
P	WHAT was that other time? (2)
W	It was at a lineup at the police station on Delaware Street.
P	WHEN did this lineup occur? (2)
W	It was about 5:00 p.m. the afternoon of the accident.
P	WHERE did the police hold this lineup? (2)
W	It was on a stage in the big room off the entrance.
P	HOW was the lighting in the room? (3)
W	It was fine.
P	HOW close were you to the stage? (3)
W	I was only 10 feet away.
P	HOW were you facing? (3)
W	I was facing straight ahead and looking at all the men in the lineup.
P	HOW long did the police permit you to observe the lineup? (3)
W	They gave me as much time as I wanted. I didn't need long.
P	HOW many men were in the lineup? (4)
W	There were six.
P	HOW were they dressed? (4)
W	They all were wearing dark clothes.
P	HOW tall were they? (4)
W	They were roughly the same height, five ten to six feet.
P	WHAT, if anything, did the police say about the men in the lineup? (4)
W	They didn't say anything. They just ushered me into the room and asked me if I recognized anyone.
P	WHAT did the men in the lineup do while they were on the stage? (4)
W	Nothing. They all just stood there.
P	WHAT happened after the lineup? (5)

W	The police asked me if I recognized the driver of the car in the lineup.
P	WHAT did you say? (5)
W	I told them that I did.
P	WHOM did you identify at that lineup? (5)
W	The defendant, the same person I just pointed out in court.
O	Your Honor, at this time, I would request a limiting instruction under Rule 105.
J	Very well. Ladies and gentlemen of the jury, you've just heard the witness testify about her identification of the defendant at a pretrial lineup. You may not consider her testimony as proof that the identification was correct. You may consider the testimony only for the light it sheds on this witness's credibility. The witness has identified the same person on a previous occasion, and you should decide for yourselves whether that consistency affects her credibility.

§ 5.04   FRESH COMPLAINT

[1]   THE DOCTRINE

Another exception to the norm against bolstering is the fresh complaint, "hue and cry," or "outcry" doctrine. Most jurisdictions restrict the doctrine to sex offense cases; a few jurisdictions also recognize the doctrine in burglary and robbery cases. The underlying assumption is that the victim of this type of offense is likely to make an immediate report or complaint about the offense. The fact of a fresh complaint tends to strengthen the inference of the truthfulness of the complainant. Moreover, especially in sex offense cases, there is a crying need for credibility evidence; there are rarely eyewitnesses, and the trial frequently becomes a swearing contest.

Under this theory, the courts usually restrict the evidence to proof that the victim made a complaint about a certain type of offense and identified a certain person as the perpetrator. The other details of the offense are inadmissible. As in the case of prior identification evidence, the opponent is entitled to a limiting instruction; and the proponent must treat the testimony solely as credibility evidence during closing argument. The judge is admitting the proof as credibility evidence rather than as substantive proof that a certain person committed the offense. Once again, the opponent could object to the proponent's closing argument if the proponent's statements suggested to the jury that the fresh complaint about the crime was itself evidence that the crime had occurred. On the other hand, the fresh complaint will sometimes qualify as an excited utterance. As Chapter 10 notes, excited utterances fall within an exception to the hearsay rule. If the fresh complaint qualifies as an excited utterance, all the details about the offense are admissible; and more importantly, the details are admissible as substantive evidence.

[2]   ELEMENTS OF THE FOUNDATION

The proponent must show that:

1.   The victim made a complaint.

2.   The victim made the complaint shortly after the offense.

3.   The victim made the complaint to the authorities or to the first person he or she encountered after the offense.

4.   The report stated that the complainant was the victim of an offense.

5.   The report identified the perpetrator of the offense.

[3]   SAMPLE FOUNDATION

The fact situation is a criminal prosecution for kidnapping and rape. The victim, Ms. McDonald, is on the stand on direct examination. She has already testified that the accused abducted her, drove her to a remote cabin, raped her, and then left her tied in the cabin. The proponent is the prosecutor.

P	WHAT did you do after the accused left?
W	I struggled to get free from the ropes. Fortunately, the knot was so loose that I got free.
P	WHAT did you do next?
W	I got out of the cabin and started running down the dirt road. I wanted to escape and get back to safety.
P	WHAT, if anything, happened while you were running down the road?
W	I ran into a fellow driving a jeep.
P	WHO was this person? (3)
W	He told me that his name was Jeff Seltzer.
P	Between the time you escaped from the cabin and the time you met Mr. Seltzer, HOW many people had you met? (3)
W	None. He was the very first person I met after escaping.
P	HOW much time elapsed between the rape and the time you met Mr. Seltzer? (2)
W	About an hour.
P	HOW much time elapsed between your escape from the cabin and the time you met Mr. Seltzer? (2)
W	Only about five minutes. I hadn't run very far before I met him.
P	WHAT, if anything, happened after you met Mr. Seltzer? (1)
W	I told him everything that had happened. Then he gave me a ride back to town and took me to the hospital.
P	Precisely WHAT did you tell him? (4)
W	I said I had just been raped at a cabin just up the road.
P	WHO did you say had raped you? (5)
W	I said it was the accused, Henry Miles.
O	Your Honor, at this time I request a limiting instruction under Rule 105.

J   Very well. Ladies and gentlemen of the jury, you have just heard Ms. McDonald testify that she made a complaint to Mr. Seltzer shortly after the alleged offense. In this complaint, she said she had been raped and that the accused was the rapist. You may not consider her testimony as proof that, in fact, a rape occurred or that the accused was the rapist. I'm admitting the testimony only for whatever light it sheds on Ms. McDonald's credibility. You must decide whether the fact that she made this complaint affects her credibility.

PART C.   Impeachment of Witnesses

§ 5.05   BAD ACTS THAT HAVE NOT RESULTED IN A CONVICTION

[1]   THE DOCTRINE

Modernly, most jurisdictions permit the opponent to impeach the witness with proof that the witness has committed untruthful acts. The opponent may do so even if the acts have not resulted in the witness's conviction. Federal Rule of Evidence 608(b)(1) states the prevailing view: "Except for a criminal conviction under Rule 609, extrinsic evidence is not admissible to prove specific instances of a witness's conduct in order to attack or support the witness's character for truthfulness. But the court may, on cross-examination, allow them to be inquired into if they are probative of the character for . . . untruthfulness of . . . the witness." The theory of logical relevance is simple: If the witness has been willing to commit untruthful and deceitful acts in the past, the witness may be willing to lie on the witness stand. Of course, the doctrine is limited to acts which reflect adversely on the witness's truthfulness. (Some courts tend to restrict the scope of Rule 608(b)(1) to the kinds of acts that qualify under Rule 609(a)(2) governing conviction impeachment. § 5.10 of this chapter discusses conviction impeachment.)

As the Federal Rule indicates and as is true at common law in many jurisdictions, the opponent using this technique is ordinarily restricted to cross-examination. On cross-examination, the opponent may inquire whether the witness committed the act. However, the opponent must "accept" or "take" the answer. It is true that the opponent can press the witness for a truthful answer, for example, by reminding the witness of the penalties for perjury. However, the opponent must take the answer in the sense that the opponent cannot use extrinsic evidence to contradict the answer. Thus, if witness #1, the witness to be impeached, denies committing the deceitful act, the opponent cannot call witness #2 to testify that he or she was an eyewitness to witness #1's act. The Advisory Committee Note to the 2003 amendments to Rule 608 states that "the extrinsic evidence prohibition of Rule 608(b) bars any reference to the consequences that a witness might have suffered as a result of an alleged bad act. For example, Rule 608(b) prohibits counsel from mentioning that a witness was suspended or disciplined for the conduct that is the subject of impeachment. '[C]ounsel should not be permitted to circumvent the no-extrinsic-evidence provision by tucking a third person's opinion about prior acts into a question asked of the witness who has denied the act.' " Despite this passage in the Note, some courts permit the cross-examiner to refer to judicial or jury findings rejecting the credibility of the witness's testimony in prior proceedings;

these courts regard such findings as especially trustworthy and probative. However, in most cases counsel should ask the witness directly and bluntly whether the witness committed the act.

This restriction is a remnant of the broader, common-law collateral fact rule. The collateral fact rule announced that the impeaching attorney is limited to intrinsic impeachment when the impeaching fact relates only to the witness's credibility. An untruthful act may reflect adversely on the witness's credibility; but the argument runs that when the act has no relevance to the historical merits of the case, it would be an undue expenditure of time to allow the impeaching attorney to present extrinsic evidence. By banning the use of "extrinsic evidence," the first sentence of Rule 608(b) codifies this aspect of the collateral fact rule.

[2] ELEMENTS OF THE FOUNDATION

The opponent must show:

1. When the witness committed the act.

2. Where the witness committed the act.

3. The nature of the act reflects adversely on the witness's character trait for truthfulness. An earlier version of Rule 608(b) referred to "credibility." However, the 2003 amendment to the statute deleted "credibility" and substituted "character for truthfulness or untruthfulness." The accompanying Advisory Committee Note described the term "credibility" as "overbroad."

[3] SAMPLE FOUNDATION

The fact situation is a contract action. The plaintiff alleges that the defendant corporation breached its contract to deliver a generator to the plaintiff. The plaintiff alleges that he entered into the contract with the defendant's president during a conversation in the president's office. The plaintiff calls Mr. Giles as a witness. Giles testifies that he is a friend of the plaintiff and accompanied the plaintiff to the defendant's president's office. Giles testifies that he overheard the conversation in which the parties formed the contract. Now the defendant has Giles on cross-examination. The defendant is the opponent.

O   Mr. Giles, ISN'T IT A FACT THAT on June 1st of this year, you applied for work with Acme Corporation downtown? (1)

W   Yes.

O   ISN'T IT TRUE THAT on that date, you had a job interview with Ms. Grant, the corporation's president, at her office? (2)

W   Yes.

O   ISN'T IT CORRECT THAT during that interview, you told her that you had a Master's degree from Harvard Business School? (3)

W   Yes.

O   ISN'T IT A FACT THAT you don't have a Master's degree from that school? (3)

W   Yes. I have only an undergraduate degree from that school.

Suppose that Giles denied making the false oral statement about his credentials. Under this impeachment technique, the cross-examiner could not call Ms. Grant to prove the misrepresentation. Such testimony would be a textbook illustration of the type of "extrinsic evidence" barred by Rule 608(b). (If Giles had admitted the lie in a writing, some courts would permit the cross-examiner to confront Giles with the writing. Giles is obviously competent to authenticate his own writing, and questioning Giles about the writing would consume little time.)

Note that in the above hypothetical, the cross-examiner directly and bluntly asked the witness whether the witness had lied to Ms. Grant. Even if Ms. Grant had subsequently discovered the lie and fired the witness, many judges would not allow the cross-examiner to elicit the fact of the firing. These judges believe that the additional fact of the witness's firing represents implied hearsay and improper opinion. Likewise, these judges might permit a cross-examiner to inquire whether a witness cheated on an examination at school; but they would not allow the cross-examiner to inquire whether the school disciplined or expelled the witness for cheating.

§ 5.06   PROOF OF THE CHARACTER TRAIT OF UNTRUTHFULNESS

[1]   THE DOCTRINE

To impeach the witness, the opponent may prove that the witness has a character trait of untruthfulness. The opponent uses the proof of the character trait as circumstantial proof of conduct. The opponent reasons that if the witness has that character trait, the character trait increases the probability that the witness is lying on the stand—acting "in character" in conformity with the character trait.

Unlike the last impeachment technique, the technique is not limited to the cross-examination of the witness to be impeached. Quite to the contrary, the opponent usually resorts to extrinsic evidence. To impeach witness #1, the opponent calls witness #2 who testifies that witness #1 has a character trait of untruthfulness. The courts usually term witness #2 a character witness. In some jurisdictions, the character witness must restrict his or her testimony to reputation evidence; the character witness describes the witness's reputation for untruthfulness in the community. Today, though, the majority view is that opinion evidence is also admissible; the character witness may express his or her opinion of witness #1's truthfulness. Federal Rule of Evidence 405(a) commits the federal courts to the latter view.

[2]   ELEMENTS OF THE FOUNDATION

The foundation varies, depending upon whether the evidence is reputation or opinion. The reputation foundation includes these elements:

1.   Witness #2 is a member of the same community (residential or social) as witness #1. Modernly, any large social group can qualify as a community. For instance, a church congregation or the student body of a school can constitute a community.

2.   Witness #2 has been a member of the community for a substantial period of

time.

3. Witness #1 has a reputation for untruthfulness in the community.

4. Witness #2 knows witness #1's reputation for untruthfulness.

5. Some jurisdictions permit witness #2 to add that given witness #1's reputation, witness #2 would not believe him or her under oath.

The opinion foundation includes the following elements:

1. Witness #2 is personally acquainted with witness #1.

2. Witness #2 knows witness #1 well enough to have formed a reliable opinion of witness #1's truthfulness. On the one hand, in general terms witness #2 may describe the extent of his or her familiarity with witness #1. Witness #2 could state the number of years he or she has known witness #1 or the number of times he or she sees witness #1 each week. On the other hand, even under the guise of stating the basis for his or her opinion, witness #2 may not describe specific untruthful acts committed by witness #1.

3. Witness #2 has an opinion of witness #1's untruthfulness.

4. Witness #2 has the opinion that witness #1 is an untruthful person.

5. Again, some courts permit witness #2 to opine whether, given that opinion, he or she would believe witness #1 under oath.

[3] SAMPLE FOUNDATIONS

The following is a reputation foundation. The witness to be impeached is Mr. Harding:

P	WHO is Mr. Harding?
W	He's an acquaintance of mine.
P	WHEN is the last time you saw him?
W	Here in the courtroom. He testified for the other side a couple of hours ago.
P	WHERE does he live? (1)
W	Here in Atlanta.
P	HOW long has Mr. Harding lived in Atlanta? (2)
W	All his life, I think. I can remember him twenty years back.
P	HOW long have you lived here in Atlanta? (2)
W	All my life.
P	HOW many years have you lived here? (2)
W	Thirty-seven years.
P	Does Mr. Harding have a reputation for truthfulness or untruthfulness in Atlanta? (3)
W	Yes.

P   WHAT is that reputation? (4)

W   It's bad. He's known as an untruthful person.

P   Given Mr. Harding's reputation, would you believe him under oath? (5)

W   No.

Even if Harding were the party to the litigation, this evidence would be admissible only for the limited purpose of aiding the jury in assessing his credibility. Thus, even if Harding were the civil defendant in a tort action for fraud, on request the trial judge would give the jurors a Rule 105 limiting instruction that they could not treat this testimony as proof that Harding is a bad person and therefore more likely to have committed the alleged tort. For the same reason, during closing argument it would be objectionable for the proponent to indicate to the jury that Harding's reputation for untruthfulness was evidence that he committed the fraudulent conduct alleged by the plaintiff.

The following is an opinion foundation:

P   WHO is Mr. Harding? (1)

W   He's an acquaintance of mine.

P   WHEN is the last time you saw him?

W   Here in the courtroom. He testified for the other side a few hours ago.

P   HOW did you come to know him? (2)

W   We've lived in the same neighborhood for a long time. I've had a lot of contact with him.

P   HOW many years have you known him? (2)

W   I'd say easily nine years.

P   In WHAT contexts have you known him? (2)

W   As I said, we've lived in the same neighborhood for a long time. I see him around the neighborhood a lot. In addition, we've worked at the same plant together for the last five years.

P   HOW often do you talk with him? (2)

W   Usually several times a week. We're always bumping into each other.

P   Do you have an opinion of his truthfulness? (3)

W   Yes.

P   WHAT is that opinion? (4)

W   In my opinion, he's an untruthful person.

P   Given that opinion, would you believe Mr. Harding under oath? (5)

W   No.

§ 5.07 PROOF THAT THE WITNESS HAS FAILED A POLYGRAPH EXAMINATION

[1] THE DOCTRINE

Like proof of the character trait of untruthfulness, this impeachment technique requires extrinsic evidence. The opponent calls a polygraph examiner, witness #2, to impeach witness #1. Numerous studies indicate that when used by an experienced, competent examiner, the polygraph can be an effective tool for detecting deception. The examiner's diagnosis of deception is logically relevant to show that when the witness gave a certain answer, the witness was lying.

The prevailing view today is still that polygraph evidence is inadmissible. Most jurisdictions jealously guard the jury's power to determine witness credibility, and they are reluctant to allow polygraph examiners to opine on the subject. However, in a minority of jurisdictions, the courts have gained a degree of faith in polygraphy. In these jurisdictions, polygraph evidence is admissible, at least when the parties stipulate to the admissibility of the evidence.

Even in the jurisdictions permitting polygraph evidence without a stipulation, the proponent must lay a good foundation. The traditional view is that scientific evidence is admissible only if the underlying principle and the instrument are generally accepted in the relevant scientific circles. The general acceptance requirement originated in the famous *Frye* case. The very first reported "polygraph" (systolic blood pressure) case, *Frye v. United States*, 293 F. 1013 (D.C. Cir. 1923), held that the proponent of scientific evidence must not only present expert testimony vouching for the principle and instrument; the proponent must also show that as a matter of historical fact, the principle and instrument have gained general acceptance in the pertinent scientific circles. § 4.10 discusses the *Frye* test. As § 4.10 points out, in 1993 the United States Supreme Court overturned *Frye*. In *Daubert*, the Court substituted a validation test, derived from Rule 702, for the old general acceptance standard. Some courts have ruled that under *Daubert*, there is no longer a rigid rule barring the admission of polygraph testimony; rather, the question is whether the proponent can lay a foundation satisfying the validation test. James R. McCall, *Misconceptions and Reevaluation—Polygraph Admissibility After Rock and Daubert*, 1996 U. ILL. L. REV. 363. Even under the new validation test, though, most lower federal trial courts continue to exclude polygraph evidence; and most appellate courts uphold such trial court rulings.

In *United States v. Scheffer*, 523 U.S. 303, 118 S. Ct. 1261, 140 L. Ed. 2d 413 (1998), the Supreme Court upheld the constitutionality of a military rule of evidence barring polygraph evidence. However, the Court did not rule that the Constitution forbids the receipt of polygraph evidence. The lead opinion holds only that polygraph is not so demonstrably reliable that a criminal defendant has a constitutional right to override common-law or statutory rules restricting its admissibility. Moreover, it is important to note the division of sentiment among the justices in *Scheffer*. Only four justices signed the lead opinion sustaining the constitutionality of the per se rule on its face. Other justices dissented and would have invalidated the rule. Still other justices concurred but stated that it was conceivable that in a future case—perhaps one in which the proponent had laid a better foundation—they would vote to strike down an application of the rule.

The upshot is that a majority of justices indicated that at the very least, they would entertain the argument that in a given case polygraph evidence was so reliable and critical that it would be unconstitutional to exclude the evidence. As a practical matter, *Scheffer* makes it more difficult to persuade a trial judge to admit testimony based on polygraphy. In 2002, the National Research Council released a report critical of polygraph. NATIONAL RESEARCH COUNCIL, THE POLYGRAPH AND LIE DETECTION (2002). The release of that report makes the introduction of polygraph evidence even more of an uphill battle. For that reason, the following foundation attempts to establish that the technique is generally accepted as well as empirically validated—satisfying both the traditional *Frye* standard and the modern *Daubert* reliability test.

[2] ELEMENTS OF THE FOUNDATION

1. The witness has the qualifications to establish the underlying principle's validity and the instrument's reliability.

2. The witness has the qualifications to administer a polygraph examination.

3. The witness has the qualifications to interpret a polygraph test result.

4. The underlying principle of polygraphy is valid.

5. The underlying principle is generally accepted as valid.

6. Empirical testing has established the reliability of the polygraph technique.

7. The instrument is generally accepted as reliable.

8. The examiner tested the subject.

9. When the examiner tested the subject, the witness to be impeached, the instrument was in working order.

10. At the time, the examiner used certain procedures to conduct the test.

11. The procedures used were proper.

12. The subject had a certain result on the test.

13. The results of the test indicate that the subject was lying when he or she made a certain statement.

[3] SAMPLE FOUNDATION

The fact situation is a paternity action. Ms. Gust sued Mr. Martin for child support. The witness is Mr. Bechtel, a polygraph examiner. Mr. Bechtel is prepared to testify that he examined Mr. Martin. Mr. Bechtel will testify that, in his opinion, Mr. Martin was telling the truth when he denied having intercourse with Ms. Gust. The proponent is the defendant.

P	WHAT is your name?
W	Cleve Bechtel.
P	WHAT is your address?
W	1554 Skinker Boulevard in St. Louis.
P	WHAT is your occupation? (1), (2), (3)

W	I am a polygraph examiner. I have my own business.
P	WHAT is your educational background? (1)
W	I have a bachelor's degree in Psychology from Stanford.
P	WHAT formal training, if any, have you had in polygraphy? (2), (3)
W	I attended the Keeler Polygraph Institute in Chicago.
P	WHAT is that Institute? (2), (3)
W	It's one of the best known and best established polygraph schools in the world.
P	WHAT sort of training did you receive there? (2), (3)
W	First we had classroom instruction on the underlying principles of polygraph and the instrument, the polygraph. Then we had training in conducting and interpreting polygraph tests. We were given an opportunity to conduct and evaluate tests during the course.
P	WHAT experience have you had in the polygraph field? (2), (3)
W	After completing my training at Keeler, I worked as an apprentice for a year. I worked for a very experienced examiner. Then I started my own business. I've owned that business for the past twelve years.
P	During your career, HOW many polygraph examinations have you conducted? (2), (3)
W	Several thousand. Too many to keep count of.
P	HOW many times, if any, have you qualified as a polygraph expert in court? (2), (3)
W	About fifty times.
P	HOW many times in this state? (2), (3)
W	Ten times.
P	WHEN was the last time? (2), (3)
W	About six months ago.
P	WHAT is the underlying principle of polygraphy? (4)
W	The theory is that conscious deception causes certain physiological changes that the subject has little or no control over—blood pressure, pulse rate, breath, and galvanic skin response.
P	WHAT experiments, if any, have been conducted to verify the theory? (5)
W	Actually, scientists have been working in this area for decades. Almost all the studies document the theory. Thousands of persons have been tested.
P	HOW widely accepted is the theory? (5)

W   Most people familiar with the area—examiners, psychologists and psychiatrists—accept the theory.

P   WHAT is the polygraph itself? (6)

W   It's the instrument the examiner uses. It measures the physiological responses I mentioned. It records them on a graph called the polygram.

P   WHAT experiments, if any, have been conducted to test the reliability of the instrument? (7)

W   Again, there have been a large number of reported tests involving thousands of subjects. Under typical laboratory conditions, the examiners employing the technique that I use reach accurate diagnoses in roughly 85% of the cases. In field conditions, the accuracy level often reaches the high ninety percents; in field conditions, there is a stronger motivation to deceive than in a laboratory setting, and diagnosing deception is consequently easier. It is one thing for an undergraduate in an experiment to know that he will win $10.00 if he "beats" the polygraph. It is quite another matter for a criminal to know that he will face felony charges if the polygraph accurately detects his deception.

P   HOW widely accepted is the instrument? (7)

W   There's been a lot of controversy over the years, but today I think that most experts in the field accept the polygraph. Most knowledgeable people would say that in the hands of a competent, experienced examiner, the polygraph is a reliable instrument for accurately diagnosing deception.

P   WHO is George Martin? (8)

W   He's the defendant in this case.

P   HOW do you know him? (8)

W   I had occasion to conduct a polygraph examination of Mr. Martin several weeks ago.

P   WHEN and WHERE did you do that? (8)

W   I did that at my office on February 13th. It was about 10 in the morning. I used my polygraph to test him.

P   WHAT condition was the polygraph in when you tested Mr. Martin? (9)

W   It was in proper working order.

P   HOW did you know that? (9)

W   I use a Lafayette polygraph, and the company provides purchasers with a checklist for ensuring the instrument's operational condition. I went through the checklist before the test, and the instrument checked out perfectly.

P   HOW did you conduct Mr. Martin's examination? (10)

W	I followed the standard operating procedure and took all the steps you're supposed to use.
P	HOW are you supposed to conduct an examination? (11)
W	First you conduct the pretest interview.
P	WHAT is that? (11)
W	Before you actually conduct a polygraph examination, you interview the subject. You show the subject the machine, explain its operation, and try to convince the subject that the instrument is effective. You also begin forming your relevant and control questions for the later test.
P	WHAT are relevant and control questions? (11)
W	Relevant questions are the questions about the incident being investigated.
P	WHAT would be an example? (11)
W	Here the most relevant question is "Mr. Martin, did you have intercourse with Ms. Gust?"
P	WHAT is a control question? (11)
W	It's a probable lie question. The subject will probably lie in response.
P	WHAT is an example? (11)
W	"In your first 25 years of life, did you ever steal anything?" The subject is likely to lie and deny stealing.
P	HOW do you use the relevant and control questions? (11)
W	You compare the responses on the chart to the relevant and control questions. Simply stated, if the subject reacts more to the relevant questions than to the control questions, the person's probably lying. On the other hand, if the subject reacts more to the control questions, the subject is probably telling the truth in his or her responses to the relevant questions.
P	HOW did you conduct the test of Mr. Martin? (11)
W	I followed the procedure I just described. I conducted a pretest interview and then formed my relevant and control questions, including the ones I've already mentioned. Next, I ran the test. I spaced the questions about 30 seconds apart to permit the reactions to register fully on the polygram. The test consisted of 10 questions, and I ran the test three times during the space of an hour.
P	Your Honor, I request that this be marked defense exhibit C for identification.
J	It will be so marked.
P	Your Honor, please let the record reflect that I am showing the exhibit to the opposing counsel.

J	It will so reflect.
P	Your Honor, may I have permission to approach the witness?
J	Yes.
P	Mr. Bechtel, I now hand you defense exhibit C for identification. WHAT is it? (12)
W	It's the chart of Mr. Martin's test.
P	HOW can you recognize it? (12)
W	I recognize my handwriting on it.
P	WHAT condition is it in? (12)
W	It's in roughly the same condition it was in when I ran the test.
P	WHERE has it been since that time? (12)
W	In my files. I personally removed it from my files before coming to court.
P	Your Honor, I now offer defense exhibit C for identification into evidence as defense exhibit C.
J	It will be received.
P	Mr. Bechtel, WHAT are the circled areas on exhibit C? (13)
W	They're the responses to the control questions, such as the one I mentioned about stealing.
P	WHAT are the areas in the squares? (13)
W	They're the responses to the relevant questions including the one about intercourse.
P	WHAT is your diagnosis of that response? (13)
W	In my opinion, Mr. Martin was telling the truth when he denied having intercourse with Ms. Gust.
P	WHAT is the basis for that opinion? (13)
W	The responses to the control questions were fairly marked. However, there were only mild reactions to the relevant questions. That indicates to me that Mr. Martin was not engaging in conscious deception when he denied intercourse.
P	Your Honor, I request permission to hand exhibit C to the jurors for their personal inspection.
J	Yes.

If the witness's opinion had been that Martin had been lying, the opinion would have been impeaching. If the opinion were admitted solely for the purpose of impeachment, on request the judge would give the jury a limiting instruction explaining to the jury that they could consider the testimony only for the purpose of evaluating Mr. Martin's credibility. For that reason, it would be objectionable if the proponent put the testimony to any other use during closing argument.

§ 5.08   PROOF THAT ANOTHER WITNESS SPECIFICALLY CONTRADICTS THE TESTIMONY OF THE WITNESS TO BE IMPEACHED

California Evidence Code § 780(i) states that the opposing attorney may impeach a witness by showing "[t]he . . . nonexistence of any fact testified to by him." This impeachment technique is usually termed contradiction or specific contradiction. Witness #1 testifies to *A*, and the opposing attorney calls witness #2 to testify to non-*A*. The impeaching effect of witness #2's testimony is indirect and inferential: If witness #2 is correct, witness #1 must be mistaken or lying. Just as Article VI of the Federal Rules is silent on bias impeachment, Article VI makes no mention of specific contradiction. Nevertheless, as in the case of bias impeachment, the courts continue to permit attorneys to employ specific contradiction impeachment. Federal Rule of Evidence 402 generally authorizes the admission of logically relevant evidence, and the courts recognize that specific contradiction testimony is logically relevant to witness #1's credibility. Moreover, Rule 408(a) mentions "impeach[ment] by . . . a contradiction."

Suppose, for example, that plaintiff's witness #1 testifies that the traffic light facing the defendant's car was red. The defense calls witness #2, who testifies that the light facing the defendant's car was green. Since witness #2's testimony is logically relevant to the historical merits, it is admissible both to prove that the light was green and to impeach witness #1 by contradiction.

The problem arises when witness #2's testimony is logically relevant only to witness #1's credibility. Suppose a traffic accident occurred in a rural area near Philadelphia. During his direct examination, witness #1 testified that he was walking near the intersection where the collision occurred. Witness #1 adds that in the adjacent field, there were "about 20 cows grazing." During the defense case-in-chief, the defense calls the farmer who owns the field. The farmer is prepared to testify that there were only 10 cows grazing at the time. The farmer's testimony would specifically contradict witness #1's testimony. The farmer's testimony is logically relevant to impeach witness #1; if the farmer is correct, witness #1 erred in perception or memory. However, the farmer's testimony has no logical relevance to the historical merits; the number of cows in the field has no impact on the facts relating to the traffic accident. Before the adoption of the Federal Rules, the common-law collateral fact rule would have mandated the exclusion of the farmer's testimony. *People v. Dice*, 120 Cal. 189, 52 P. 477 (1898). The rationale for the rule was that the evidence has meager probative value; the evidence shows that the witness being impeached is fallible, but the jurors should already know that.

However, the Federal Rules abolish a categorical collateral fact rule. The admission of extrinsic evidence to contradict witness #1 is now governed by Rule 403. To inform the exercise of his or her discretion under Rule 403, the judge weighs the importance of the witness and the strength of the inference that the witness is wrong about the historical merits if the witness is wrong about the detail in question. When the witness is the star witness for one side and the inference is strong, the judge can admit the extrinsic evidence. As the McCormick hornbook explains:

> Suppose a witness has told a story of a transaction crucial to the controversy. To prove him [or her] wrong in some trivial detail of time, place or circumstance is "collateral." But to prove untrue some fact recited by the witness that if he [or she] were really there and saw what he claims to have seen, he [or she] could not have been mistaken about, is a convincing kind of impeachment that the courts must make place for. . . . To disprove such a fact is to pull out the linchpin of the story. [W]e must recognize this . . . type of allowable contradiction . . . of any part of the witness' account of the background of a material transaction, which as a matter of human experience he [or her] would not have been mistaken about if his [or her] story were true.

C. MCCORMICK, EVIDENCE § 47, at 111–12 (3d ed. 1984). *See also* MCCORMICK ON EVIDENCE § 49 (8th ed. 2020). In many cases, the fact is a fundamental "linchpin" because if it was false, the witness could not have been in the right place at the right time to see what he or she testified to.

Suppose, for example, that in the hypothetical, witness #1 testified that there is a large, red cow barn at the intersection. The farmer will testify that the fields near the intersection are vacant, and that the nearest red barn is two miles away at another intersection. If witness #1 is mistaken about the barn, he may be testifying about another collision at another intersection. Under Rule 403, the trial judge would probably be justified in admitting the farmer's testimony to contradict witness #1.

If the extrinsic evidence in question passes muster under Rule 403, the proponent must simply ensure that he or she lays all the other foundations normally required for that type of evidence. In the case of the farmer's testimony, the only required foundation would be firsthand knowledge of the vicinity. Assume, for instance, that all the intersections in question are located within Meridian Township. The proponent might establish the farmer's personal familiarity:

P	WHERE do you live?
W	I live in Meridian Township.
P	HOW long have you lived there?
W	All my life. I was raised right here.
P	HOW many years have you lived here in Meridian?
W	Fifty-two years, give or take a couple of months.
P	HOW familiar are you with the roads in the township?
W	Real familiar. At one time or another, I've probably driven every one of them a time or two.
P	HOW well do you know the intersection of Rural Routes 31 and 98?
W	Real well. I live only about three miles from there. In fact, it's on the route I take to town almost every weekday.

P   HOW well do you know the intersection of Rural Routes 31 and 102?

W   Just about as well. That's right on the way we take to church on Sundays.

At this point, the proponent would elicit the farmer's testimony contradicting the testimony of the earlier witness. A common technique for highlighting the contradiction is to preface the questions to the farmer with references to the contradictory testimony by the earlier witness:

P   Earlier today a plaintiff's witness, Mr. Greenfield, testified that there's a large red barn at the intersection of Rural Routes 31 and 98. WHAT buildings, if any, are there at that intersection?

Some judges permit such references. However, the proponent certainly has no right to make such cross-references. The cross-references are declarative statements about witness #1's testimony, and the only thing the proponent has the right to do during the examination of witness #2 is to put questions to witness #2. Judges occasionally tolerate such references, though, to better enable the jury to appreciate the impeaching significance of witness #2's testimony. During closing argument, the proponent would tell the jury that the farmer's testimony establishes that Greenfield was mistaken about the existence of a large red barn at the intersection of Rural Routes 31 and 98. The proponent would argue that Greenfield's mistake calls into question the reliability of his testimony on the merits about the accident; the proponent would explain that if Greenfield was mistaken about as major a detail as the location of a large, bright red barn at the intersection, he might have been at another intersection and witnessed an accident other than the one involving the plaintiff and defendant.

§ 5.09 PROOF THAT THE WITNESS MADE A PRIOR INCONSISTENT STATEMENT

[1] IN GENERAL

Section 5.05 of this chapter discusses bad acts impeachment. As previously stated, that technique is ordinarily limited to intrinsic impeachment, that is, the cross-examination of the witness to be impeached. At the opposite extreme are the impeachment techniques discussed in §§ 5.06–5.08: proof of witness #1's character trait of untruthfulness, evidence that witness #1 failed a polygraph examination, and witness #2's testimony specifically contradicting witness #1's testimony. Those three techniques inherently require extrinsic evidence; and once the law has made the policy decision to permit those impeachment techniques, the law must allow the presentation of extrinsic evidence. This section begins our discussion of a series of impeachment techniques which can be developed by either cross-examination or extrinsic evidence. The first such technique is proof that the witness made a prior statement inconsistent with his or her trial testimony.

On the morning of January 15, YR-3, at the intersection of University and Felton Streets, Mr. Miller's car collided with Ms. Dolan's van. Mr. Miller's car is red, and Ms. Dolan's van is blue. Mr. Williams happened to be standing at a corner of the intersection when the collision occurred. Later that day, he had a conversation with his neighbor, Mr. Jensen. During the conversation, he told Mr. Jensen that he witnessed the collision and that the collision occurred because the red car (Mr. Miller's car) ran a red light. Mr. Miller files a personal injury action against Ms. Dolan. At the trial, Mr. Miller calls Mr. Williams as a witness. On direct examination, Mr. Williams testifies that he witnessed the collision and that Ms. Dolan's blue van caused the accident by running a red light. On cross-examination, may the defense attorney call Mr. Jensen as a defense witness to testify to Mr. Williams' earlier statement? In the last section, we saw that we may call witness #2 to specifically contradict witness #1's testimony. May we similarly prove that witness #1 has "contradicted" himself or herself by making an inconsistent statement?

[2] CROSS-EXAMINATION TO ELICIT A WITNESS'S CONCESSION THAT THE WITNESS EARLIER MADE AN INCONSISTENT STATEMENT

As soon as Mr. Williams testifies at the trial, his credibility becomes one of the facts in issue in the case. Common sense suggests that the jury is entitled to know that Mr. Williams made an earlier, inconsistent statement. The fact that he has made inconsistent statements about the same fact calls into question his memory and sincerity. In everyday life, if a person tells us differing stories about the same event, we pause before deciding to believe either story. For that reason, the Federal Rules permit the defense attorney to cross-examine Mr. Williams about his statement to Mr. Jensen. Rule 613(a) makes it clear that the cross-examination of Williams about the earlier statement is a proper method of impeachment.

At common law, if Ms. Dolan's attorney forced Williams to concede the earlier statement to Jensen, Mr. Miller's attorney would be entitled to a limiting instruction. In the instruction, the judge would tell the jurors that they could not use Mr. Williams' earlier statement to Jensen as evidence that, in fact, Mr. Miller ran a red light; the judge would instruct the jurors that they could consider the evidence only for the limited purpose of deciding whether they want to believe the testimony that it was green. So limited, the evidence would not be subject to a hearsay objection. Quite apart from its truth or falsity, the statement to Jensen is logically relevant; Mr. Williams' credibility is an issue, and the fact that he said one thing at one time and another thing another time about the same subject lowers his credibility. The jurors can infer from Williams' inconsistency that he is either uncertain or lying. Thus, the fact *of* the inconsistent statement is relevant to credibility even if the facts mentioned *in* the statement are false. On that reasoning, the common-law courts treated prior inconsistent statements as nonhearsay. The proponent may mention the statements during closing argument, but the proponent must make it clear that he or she is asking the jury to consider the statements for the purpose of evaluating the witness's consistency and credibility. It would be objectionable for the proponent to suggest to the jury that they could treat the statements as proof of the facts asserted in the statements.

However, in federal practice the impeaching attorney need not be content to offer the prior inconsistent statement for the limited purpose of attacking Williams' credibility. As we shall see in Chapter 10, Rule 801(d)(1)(A) provides that if a statement qualifies as a prior inconsistent statement of an in-court witness, in some circumstances the statement is admissible as substantive evidence. Under Rule 801, Williams' out-of-court statement could be used as evidence that the light was red if he had made the prior statement both under oath and in a formal proceeding. The person is available for questioning, and the cross-examiner can ask the witness about both the witness's direct testimony and the witness's earlier statements. Furthermore, the drafters of Rule 801 doubted that many jurors can follow a judge's limiting instruction admitting a prior inconsistent statement merely as credibility evidence.

The opponent seeking to cross-examine a witness about a prior inconsistent statement should lay the following foundation:

1.   The opponent should get the witness recommitted to the testimony he gave on direct examination. Unless the opponent does so, the witness may later attempt to explain away the inconsistency by testifying that he or she innocently misspoke. The opponent might attempt to lock the witness in by asking directly, "ISN'T IT TRUE THAT on direct examination you testified that . . . ?" Many experienced trial attorneys counsel against such direct questions because they alert the proponent and often the witness that the opponent is going to use a prior inconsistent statement. Moreover, on various theories, many trial judges believe that the question is objectionable. In the interests of completeness, we have included the question in the sample foundations, but be aware that this tactic can be dangerous.

1a. After recommitting the witness to the direct testimony, some attorneys immediately ask the witness whether the converse is true. Rick Collins, *Impeachment With a Prior Inconsistent Statement*, 27 CRIM. JUST. SECT. NEWSLETTER, Spr. 2019, at 4. However, doing so can be risky. A strong, well-prepared opposing witness may not only vehemently deny the converse proposition but also quickly volunteer an explanation why that proposition is false. Before you can even mention the prior inconsistent statement, you may have to try to control a very nonresponsive witness. Consequently, many, if not most, experienced cross-examiners proceed straight from element #1 to element #2. We omit this step in the following sample foundation.

2.   The witness made an earlier statement at a certain place. (For a written prior inconsistent statement, the place where the witness wrote the document is usually not essential.).

3.   The witness made a statement at a certain time.

4.   Certain persons were present.

5.   The statement was of a certain tenor.

6.   The statement is inconsistent with the witness's trial testimony. The statement need not contradict the trial testimony. For that matter, the statement might be inconsistent in effect rather than in express terms. The statement is inconsistent so long as it points in a different direction than the witness's direct testimony.

7.   The prior statement is more likely to be reliable than the present testimony. Evidence law does not mandate this element, but eliciting this testimony is a sound tactic. This is sometimes called "building up" or "accrediting" the prior

statement. In the sample foundations, the opponent attempts to force the witness to concede that the witness's memory was fresher at the time of the inconsistent statement, than the memory is at trial. Many experienced counsel prefer not to attempt to force that concession; these counsel elicit the facts about the statement's timing and then argue the relative reliability of the statements during closing argument. These attorneys forego attempting to force the concession in part because they realize that some judges regard such questions as objectionably argumentative. We have included the question in the sample foundations in the interests of completeness. But, as with element #1, be aware that this tactic can be dangerous.

If the witness made the prior statement at a deposition hearing, the opponent should elicit the following facts—the so-called "litany": The witness's attorney was present at the deposition; a court reporter was also there; the reporter administered an oath to the witness; the oath was similar to the oath the witness took before testifying today; at the beginning of the deposition, the opposing attorney told the witness that if any question was unclear, the witness should request clarification; the opposing attorney asked whether the witness was experiencing any mental or physical problem that would interfere with testifying at the deposition; the witness assured the attorney that there was none; the reporter later prepared a transcript of the questions and answers at the deposition; the reporter gave the witness a copy of the transcript to review; and the witness signed the transcript without making any changes.

If the statement is written, there is an additional element:

8. If the opponent proposes to hand the writing to the witness, the opponent should first show the writing to the other counsel. Under Federal Rule of Evidence 613(a), the opponent need not show the writing to the witness.

We shall now set out two sample foundations. The first foundation is based on the original version of our hypothetical involving Mr. Williams. In this version, the inconsistent statement is oral. In the second version, the inconsistent statement will be a writing. In both cases, the opponent is the defense counsel cross-examining Mr. Williams.

O	Mr. Williams, if I correctly understood your testimony on direct examination, my client's car was the car that ran a red light. IS THAT CORRECT? (1)
W	Yes.
O	ISN'T IT A FACT THAT on the afternoon of the accident, you had a conversation with a Mr. Walter Jensen at your house? (2), (3), (4)
W	Yes.
O	ISN'T IT CORRECT THAT during that conversation, you discussed the collision between my client's car and the plaintiff's car? (5)
W	Right.
O	ISN'T IT ALSO TRUE THAT during the conversation, you told Mr. Jensen that it was the plaintiff's car that had run a red light? (5), (6)

W	Yes.
O	ISN'T IT A FACT that, in point of time, that conversation was closer to the accident than your testimony today? (7)
W	Yes.
O	ISN'T IT CORRECT that your memory was fresher then? (7)
W	Yes.
P	Your Honor, may I please have a limiting instruction that the jurors may use this evidence only in evaluating Mr. Williams' credibility? Mr. Williams wasn't under oath at the time of the statement, and Rule 801(d)(1)(A) is therefore inapplicable.
J	Correct. For that reason, I am going to grant the request for a limiting instruction. Ladies and gentlemen of the jury, you've just heard Mr. Williams tell you that before trial, Mr. Williams told a Mr. Jensen that the defendant's car ran the red light. That testimony is not being admitted to prove that in fact the defendant's car ran the red light. The testimony is being admitted solely for the purpose of helping you evaluate Mr. Williams' credibility. If you decide that his prior statement is inconsistent with his testimony in court today, you may consider that inconsistency in deciding whether to believe Mr. Williams and how much weight, if any, to give to his trial testimony.

Now suppose that Williams made the inconsistent statement in a letter that he mailed to Jensen.

O	Mr. Williams, if I correctly understood your testimony on direct examination, my client's car was the car that ran a red light. IS THAT CORRECT? (1)
W	Yes.
O	Your Honor, may this be marked defense exhibit F for identification?
J	It will be so marked.
O	Please let the record reflect that I am showing the exhibit to the opposing counsel. (8)
J	It will so reflect.
O	Mr. Williams, I now hand you defense exhibit F for identification. WHAT is it?
	(If the exhibit were a deposition transcript, the opponent would show the witness the title page with the witness's name and the signature page with the notary's and the witness's signatures.)
W	It's a letter.
O	ISN'T IT TRUE THAT the letter is in your handwriting?
W	Yes.

O	ISN'T IT A FACT THAT you wrote that letter?
W	Yes.
O	ISN'T IT CORRECT THAT on the day of the collision between my client's car and the plaintiff's car, you wrote that letter at your house? (2), (3)
W	Right.
O	ISN'T IT A FACT THAT you then sent the letter to your friend, Mr. William Jensen? (4)
W	Yes.
O	Let me direct your attention to the third paragraph on page one of the exhibit.

(If the exhibit were a deposition transcript, the opponent would specify the page and line numbers: "Let me direct your attention to page 13, lines 11 through 20.")

	Please read that paragraph silently to yourself. ISN'T IT TRUE THAT in that paragraph, you wrote that it was the red car—the plaintiff's car—that ran a red light? (5), (6)
W	Yes.
O	Your Honor, I now offer paragraph three of the exhibit into evidence.
P	Your Honor, this is merely a prior inconsistent statement by a non-party witness. It can't be admitted as substantive evidence, and for that reason the exhibit shouldn't be formally received as evidence. Mr. Williams wasn't under oath at the time of the statement, and Rule 801(d)(1)(A) is therefore inapplicable.
J	I agree. The exhibit will not be received.
O	Mr. Williams, ISN'T IT CORRECT THAT, in point of time, the date of the letter was closer to the accident than your testimony today? (7)
W	Yes.
O	ISN'T IT ALSO A FACT THAT your memory was fresher then? (7)
W	Yes.

As in the case of the oral inconsistent statement, on request the judge would give the jury a limiting instruction about the evidentiary status of the statement. In closing argument, the proponent could invite the jury to consider the written inconsistent statement in evaluating Williams' credibility. However, it would be objectionable for the proponent to suggest to the jurors that Williams' written statement was itself evidence that the red car ran a red light.

[3] EXTRINSIC EVIDENCE OF A PRIOR INCONSISTENT STATEMENT

In both variations of the hypothetical in the last subsection, the witness obligingly admitted that he or she made the prior inconsistent statement. When the witness makes that concession, the impeachment is complete. However, if the witness denies the statement, the opponent has a choice. If the statement is in writing and the opponent has not yet shown the writing to the witness, the opponent can immediately confront the witness with the writing and attempt to refresh the witness's memory.[2] § 10.07 contains a sample foundation for present recollection refreshed. Alternatively, the opponent may attempt to introduce "extrinsic evidence" of the inconsistent statement after the witness leaves the stand. "Extrinsic evidence" refers to any other evidence of the inconsistent statement that Ms. Dolan's attorney might offer after Williams leaves the witness stand. For instance, if the defense attorney called Mr. Jensen to testify to Williams' oral inconsistent statement, Jensen's testimony would be extrinsic evidence. Or suppose that the defense attorney called another of Mr. Williams' acquaintances, Ms. Bigelow, to identify Williams' handwriting on a written inconsistent statement. Again, the writing would be extrinsic impeachment of Williams.

At common law, there were two restrictions on the admissibility of extrinsic evidence of a prior inconsistent statement.

One restriction was the rule that the opponent could present such evidence only if the opponent laid a foundation while cross-examining the witness to be impeached. The theory is that fairness dictates giving the witness an opportunity to explain or deny the impeaching evidence. The Federal Rules relax the common-law requirement. If the opponent is attacking an in-court witness's credibility, the Rules recognize alternatives to a traditional foundation on cross-examination. Rule 613(b) requires only that the witness be "given an opportunity to explain or deny" the statement. The opponent attacking the witness's credibility can "give[]" the witness that opportunity by having the witness excused subject to recall. The Advisory Committee Note to Rule 613 states that the Rule does not specify "any particular time of sequence." If the judge excuses the witness subject to recall, the witness's proponent can later recall the witness to deny the statement or explain away the apparent inconsistency.[3] In addition, even when there

---

[2] Some attorneys opt for immediate confrontation only when the facts suggest that the witness is lying. In contrast, they tend to opt for the subsequent introduction of the extrinsic evidence when the facts suggest only that the witness is innocently mistaken; these attorneys reason that when that is the thrust of the impeachment, there is no need to be confrontational with the witness.

[3] Despite the strong statutory construction argument that Rule 613(b) abolishes the traditional requirement to confront the witness on cross-examination, some courts continue to insist that the opponent generally comply with the traditional practice. United States v. Schnapp, 322 F.3d 564, 571 n. 6 (8th Cir. 2003) ("normally allowed only when"); United States v. Hudson, 970 F.2d 948, 959 (1st Cir. 1992) (Selya, J., concurring) ("most (though not all) of the circuits have rejected" the argument that Rule 613(b) eliminates the need for a foundation on cross). Moreover, there is a pending amendment to Rule 613 that will largely reinstate the common-law practice. As amended, Rule 613(b) would read:

 Unless the court orders otherwise, extrinsic evidence of a witness's prior inconsistent statement may not be admitted until after the witness is given an opportunity to explain or deny the statement and is no foundation on cross and the witness has been permanently excused, the judge retains discretion to admit extrinsic evidence in 'the interests of "justice' " under Rule 613(b). Despite the exercise of due diligence, the party seeking to introduce the statement may not have learned of its existence until after the witness has left the witness stand.

The common law imposed a further restriction on the admissibility of extrinsic evidence of a prior inconsistent statement. The collateral fact rule decreed that if the statement related to a purely collateral fact with no relevance to the historical merits, extrinsic evidence was automatically inadmissible. As previously stated, the Federal Rules do not codify the collateral fact rule. Only Rule 403 remains. If the trial judge believes that the issue is important enough to an assessment of the witness's credibility, the judge may permit the introduction of extrinsic evidence of the prior statement.

The following three foundations illustrate the presentation of extrinsic evidence of a prior inconsistent statement. For purposes of each foundation, assume that the defense attorney satisfied Rule 613(b). Initially, suppose that the defense calls Mr. Jensen to testify to Williams' oral prior inconsistent statement:

O   WHERE were you on the afternoon of January 15, YR-3? (2), (3)

W   At Mr. Williams' house.

O   WHO was there? (4)

W   Just Mr. Williams and myself.

O   WHAT happened while you were there?

W   We just talked.

O   WHAT did you talk about? (5), (6)

W   A lot of things, including the accident he evidently witnessed that morning.

O   WHAT did Mr. Williams say about the accident? (5), (6)

W   He said that the guy in the red car had clearly caused the accident by running a red light.

In the next variation of the hypothetical, Jensen will authenticate a letter, containing the inconsistent statement, that Williams sent to Jensen.

O   Your Honor, may this be marked defense exhibit F for identification?

J   It will be so marked.

O   Let the record reflect that I am showing the exhibit to the opposing counsel.

J   It will so reflect.

---

an adverse party is given an opportunity to examine the witness about it. This subdivision does not apply to an opposing party's statement under Rule 801(d)(2).

The amendment is tentatively scheduled to take effect in December 2024.

O	Mr. Jensen, I now hand you defense exhibit F for identification. WHAT is it? (4)
W	It's a letter I received.
O	WHEN did you receive it? (3)
W	It was in January of this year. It arrived in the mail at my apartment. (2)
O	WHOSE handwriting is the letter in?
W	Mr. Williams'.
O	HOW do you know that?
W	We've worked together for years in different offices of the same company.
O	HOW many times have you seen Mr. Williams' handwriting?
W	Hundreds of times. We exchange business memos. Sometimes we'll be at each other's office, and I'll be present when he signs documents.
O	HOW familiar are you with his handwriting style?
W	Very. Again, we've been co-workers for years. I can't tell you the specific number of times I've seen him sign a document, but there have been lots of times. When we worked on the same projects, some documents required both of us to sign off.
O	WHOSE handwriting appears on this letter?
W	Mr. Williams'. I'm certain of that.
O	Your Honor, I now offer the third paragraph of defense exhibit F for identification into evidence as defense exhibit F.
J	It will be received.
O	Mr. Jensen, permit me to direct your attention to the second sentence in paragraph three of the exhibit. WHAT does that sentence say? (5), (6)
W	It reads: "The guy in the red car ran right through a red light."
O	Your Honor, I now request permission to submit the exhibit to the jurors for their inspection.
J	Permission granted.

In the final version of the hypothetical, the written statement is in the form of a deposition transcript. The notary public's certificate at the end of the transcript makes the transcript self-authenticating under Rule 902. After the witness to be impeached leaves the stand, the opponent may request the judge's permission to read the inconsistent passage to the jurors. When the opponent makes the request, the opponent should specify the page and lines to be read. If the transcript has already been filed with the court, there is no need to mark the transcript even for identification. However, in some cases, the transcript has not been filed with the court. In that event, the opponent should have the transcript marked for identification:

O   Your Honor, I request that this be marked defense exhibit F for identification.

J   It will be so marked.

O   Please let the record reflect that I am showing the exhibit to the opposing counsel.

J   It will so reflect.

O   I now offer page 8, lines 17 through 23, into evidence and request permission to read those lines to the jurors.

J   The passage will be admitted, and you may read the passage to the jury.

Before reading the passage to the jury, the opponent might ask the judge to briefly describe deposition procedures to the jury. Many lay persons are unfamiliar with deposition hearings. The jury is likely to attach more significance to inconsistent deposition testimony after they learn that the deponent was under oath, was represented by counsel, and later had an opportunity to review and correct the transcript.

[4] EVIDENCE OF THE WITNESS'S FAILURE TO MENTION A FACT IN A PRIOR STATEMENT

Suppose that although he or she made a pretrial statement, for the first time a witness mentions a relevant fact at trial. By way of example, although he or she prepared a detailed report about a crime, for the first time on the witness stand a police officer purports to remember an incriminating fact that is not reflected in the report. Likewise, although he or she wrote a seemingly comprehensive report, for the first time at trial an expert purports to recall a highly relevant fact about his or her analysis. The witnesses did not refer to these facts in their statements, and the facts are the sort of information that a reasonable person would naturally have previously mentioned. The omission is impeaching because it amounts to prior inconsistent conduct.

The foundation for this type of impeachment is a variation of the foundation for proof of a prior inconsistent statement:

1. To maximize the impact of the impeachment, counsel should initially have the witness repeat the fact that the witness mentioned for the first time on direct examination. Counsel ought to "lock" the witness into his or her testimony.

2. The witness made an earlier oral or written statement at a certain place.

3. The witness made the statement at a certain time.

4. The witness made or addressed the statement to a certain person.

5. The statement dealt with the same topic as the witness's direct examination.

6. Given the nature and context of the pretrial statement, it would have been natural for the witness to have mentioned the fact in the statement.[4] In the case of a police officer, the cross-examiner's argument is often that at the police academy, the officer was trained to include information in his or her report.

---

[4] James W. McElhaney, *Impeachment by Omission*, 14 LITIGATION 45 (Fall 1987).

7. The fact stated on direct examination was not mentioned at all in the pretrial statement.

8. In many cases, the thrust of the impeachment is not that the witness is lying but rather that the witness is mistaken.[5] For instance, the cross-examiner may want to suggest that the witness has innocently confused the litigated event with other, similar events that the witness has been involved in. If so, at the end of the line of questioning, the cross-examiner may endeavor to elicit the witness's testimony that the witness has been involved in numerous, similar incidents. The suggestion is that the previously omitted detail actually relates to an incident other than the one involved in the instant trial. Rather than asking an unnecessary argumentative question about the suggestion, the cross-examiner can later make the suggestion explicit in closing argument.

The defendant has been charged with intentionally shooting the victim. The defense theory is that the shooting was accidental. The prosecution has presented the testimony of a police detective, Sergeant Norsted. On direct examination, he testified that when he arrived at the scene of the shooting, in addition to the body there were two people present—the defendant and his girlfriend, Amy Jones. During his direct testimony, the detective stated that the girlfriend was hysterical and attempting to get away from the defendant. However, the detective's report makes no mention of the girlfriend's hysteria or that she was trying to avoid the defendant. The proponent, the defense counsel, is cross-examining Sergeant Norsted.

P   Sergeant Norsted, on direct examination you testified that when you arrived at the scene, there were two people present. IS THAT COR-RECT? (1)

W   Yes.

P   And you testified, DID YOU NOT, that one of those people was the defendant's girlfriend, Amy Jones? (1)

W   Yes.

P   Then you testified that at the time, Ms. Jones was hysterical. RIGHT? (1)

W   That's true.

P   In fact, DIDN'T you also testify that she was trying to get away from the defendant? (1)

W   Yes, I did.

P   After visiting the scene, you prepared an official police report about this incident. DIDN'T YOU? (2)

---

[5] A cross-examiner's express or implied accusation that the witness is lying will usually backfire unless the cross-examiner has "the goods" on the witness. If the cross-examiner cannot prove the lie, the jurors may resent the accusation. In the words of the late Professor Irving Younger, a contention of a mistake usually "goes down more easily" than an accusation of a lie.

W   I certainly did.

P   You began preparing that report the very same day that you visited the scene of shooting. CORRECT? (3), (4), (5)

W   I did do that.

P   On direct examination, you testified that you've been a member of our police department for more than 15 years. RIGHT? (6)

W   Yes.

P   DIDN'T you begin your career as a police officer by attending the local police academy? (6)

W   That's also true.

P   At the academy, DIDN'T you take a course devoted to the preparation of police reports? (6)

W   Yes. I recall it well.

P   In that course, DIDN'T your instructors tell you that official police reports such as your report in this case often have to be used at trial? (6)

W   Of course.

P   DIDN'T they also tell you that for that reason, you have to make certain that your report is as complete as possible? (6)

W   Again, yes.

P   And your instructors said that your final report has to include all the important facts. RIGHT? (6)

W   Sure.

P   All right. Now let's talk about your report in this case. When you prepared the report, you realized that it was a report about a shooting. RIGHT? (6)

W   Obviously.

P   In fact, you knew that the alleged victim has died from a gunshot wound. CORRECT? (6)

W   Yes.

P   So when you were writing this report, you realized that it was a report about a very serious incident. RIGHT? (6)

W   I definitely realized that.

P   So you knew that it was especially important that this report be complete? CORRECT? (6)

W   Yes.

P   And in fact, you tried to carefully record all the important facts in your report. DIDN'T YOU? (6)

W	Absolutely.
P	Your Honor, please let the record reflect that I am showing the prosecutor what has been previously marked as Defense Exhibit B for identification.
J	The record will so reflect.
P	*(To the judge)* Permission to approach the witness?
J	Granted.
P	Sergeant, I am now showing you what has been marked as Defense Exhibit B for identification. Do you recognize it? (7)
W	Yes, I do.
P	Please tell the jury what this exhibit is? (7)
W	It's my report about this incident.
P	So this is your final, official report in this case. CORRECT? (7)
W	Yes. It is.
P	And, again, you started working on the report on the very day you visited the scene of the shooting. RIGHT? (6)
W	Yes.
P	And in this report, you did your very best to describe all the important facts that you had seen or heard at the crime. CORRECT? (6)
W	Yes. I tried my best.
P	Now, let's take a look at the contents of your report. The report states the position of the body. DOESN'T IT? (6)
W	Yes, it does.
P	The report says that the top of the decedent's head was 17 inches from the north wall. RIGHT? (5), (6)
W	Yes.
P	And the report also states that the gun was found 25 inches from the decedent's right hand? DOESN'T IT? (5), (6)
W	Yes.
P	So you went to the trouble to include some very precise measurements in your report. CORRECT? (5), (6)
W	Yes. As I testified, I knew that this was a fatal shooting. I was trying very hard to get everything down as exactly as I could.
P	Of course. Now, in addition to including those precise measurements, the report includes a description of the defendant's demeanor. RIGHT? (5), (6)
W	I'm not sure what you're getting at.

P	I'm sorry. Let me be more specific. For example, in the first paragraph on page three, DOESN'T your report state that when you first arrived at the scene, the defendant seemed "agitated"? (5), (6)
W	Yes. I guess so.
P	I don't want to rush you. Take your time and look at the first paragraph on page three. DIDN'T you use the word, "agitated," to describe the way the defendant was acting? (5), (6)
W	Yes. Thanks. I can see that now.
P	Now let's take a look at the second paragraph on the same page. In that paragraph, DOESN'T your report state that when the other detective questioned the defendant, the defendant was "still upset"? Again, it's the second paragraph on the same page. (5), (6)
W	Yes. I see that too.
P	Now, would you please show us where in your report, you stated that Ms. Jones was "hysterical"? Again, take your time. (7)
	(The cross-examiner should give the witness a reasonable period of time to read through the report.)
P	DID you find it? (7)
W	No.
P	Now the report does refer to Ms. Jones. DOESN'T IT? (6)
W	Yes.
P	In fact, the report refers to her several times. CORRECT? (6)
W	Yes.
P	But the report doesn't use the word "hysterical" to describe her? DOES IT? (7)
W	No.
P	And it doesn't say "upset" either. DOES IT? (7)
W	No.
P	It doesn't even say that she was "emotional." DOES IT? (7)
W	No, it doesn't.
P	All right. Now please show the jury where your report states that Ms. Jones was trying to get away from the defendant. As I said before, take your time.
P	Sergeant, did you find that statement in your report? (7)
W	I'm afraid that I can't.
P	Your report includes the detail that Ms. Jones asked for a drink of water. RIGHT? (6)

W	Yes.
P	And your report also says that she used her cellphone twice while you were on the scene. CORRECT? (6)
W	Yes.
P	But although the report specifically describes these things that she did, the report doesn't make any mention of her trying to get away from the defendant. DOES IT? (7)
W	I'm afraid that I can't find anything along those lines.
P	Now, Sergeant, in your 15 years on the force, I assume that you've investigated tens of shootings. CORRECT? (8)
W	Unfortunately, that's true. In fact, it might be in the hundreds, not the tens.
P	This incident occurred more than two years ago. RIGHT? (8)
W	Yes.
P	And in the two years since this incident, would it be fair to say that you've been involved in tens of other homicide investigations? (8)
W	Probably.
P	And at those scenes, you've often had to deal with hysterical people like family members. CORRECT? (8)
W	Yes.
P	People who were really upset? (8)
W	Certainly.
P	And all those shooting investigations—the ones in the last two years—occurred more recently than the investigation that this trial relates to? (8)
W	Yes.
P	And you had at least some memory of all those investigations in the back of your mind when you took the stand today. CORRECT? (8)
W	I guess you could say that.

§ 5.10   PROOF THAT THE WITNESS HAS SUFFERED A CONVICTION

[1]   THE DOCTRINE

If the witness has suffered a conviction, the conviction tends to impeach the witness's character trait for truthfulness. Proof of the conviction creates a general inference that the witness is sometimes willing to disobey social norms; the conviction thus strengthens the inference that the witness is violating another norm and lying now. Of course, the conviction has much more probative value if the underlying offense is a crime such as perjury or embezzlement involving an element of deceit or fraud. All jurisdictions recognize this method of impeachment, but they differ on the types of convictions usable to impeach. Most courts allow the opponent to use any felony conviction. Other courts restrict the technique to crimes involving an element of deceit or fraud. Federal Rule of Evidence 609(a) is a compromise reading:

> The following rules apply to attacking a witness's character for truthfulness by evidence of a criminal conviction:
>
> (1)   for a crime that, in the convicting jurisdiction, was punishable by death or by imprisonment for more than one year, the evidence:
>
> > (A)   must be admitted, subject to Rule 403, in a civil case or a criminal case in which the witness is not the defendant; and
> >
> > (B)   must be admitted in a criminal case in which the witness is the defendant, if the probative value of the evidence outweighs its prejudicial effect to that defendant; and
>
> (2)   for any crime regardless of punishment, the evidence must be admitted if the court can readily determine that establishing the elements of the crime required proving—or the witness's admitting—a dishonest act or false statement.

Convictions falling under Rule 609(a)(2) are automatically admissible; the judge cannot invoke Rule 403 to exclude them.[6] Convictions for offenses such as perjury and fraud certainly qualify as crimes of "false statement" under Rule 609(a)(2). However, the legislative history of the rule supports a strong argument that the expression " 'dishonesty' [in Rule 609(a)(2)] was devoid of significant meaning." Edward W. Cleary, *Preliminary Notes on Reading the Rules of Evidence*, 57 NEB. L. REV. 908, 919 (1978). The courts divide over the question of whether theft offenses such as larceny fall within Rule 609(a)(2). The Advisory Committee Note accompanying the 1990 amendment to Rule 609(a) criticizes the "decisions that take an unduly broad view of 'dishonesty,' admitting convictions such as for bank robbery and bank larceny." Since 1990, the clear trend in the case law has been to hold that theft offenses fall outside the ambit of Rule 609(a)(2). The 2006 amendment to 609(a)(2) added the language beginning "if it readily can be determined." In part, the accompanying Advisory Committee Note reads:

> Ordinarily, the statutory elements of the crime will indicate whether it is one of dishonesty or false statement. Where the deceitful nature of the crime is not apparent from the statute and the face of the judgment . . . a proponent may

---

[6] The Advisory Committee Note to the 2006 amendment to Rule 609 states that such convictions are to be "automatically admitted" and that Rule 609(a)(2) "mandates" their admission. However, the caveat is that even convictions falling under 609(a)(2) are arguably subject to discretionary exclusion under Rule 609(b). 609(b) does not contain any exclusion for 609(a)(2) convictions; rather, on its face 609(b) seems to apply to all convictions qualifying under 609(a). Cretacci v. Hare, 533 F. Supp. 3d 605 (E.D. Tenn. 2021). See also State v. Aranda, 319 Ore. App. 178, 509 P.3d 152 (2022) (due process requires that the trial judge have the power to exclude convictions in extreme cases), *rev. granted*, 370 Ore. 214, 516 P.3d 1175 (2022). It is true that 609(b) does not authorize the judge to conduct a full Rule 403 analysis. However, 609(b) permits the judge to exclude a conviction on the ground of remoteness in time, and remoteness in time is one of the factors courts routinely consider in assessing probative value in Rule 403 analysis.

offer information such as an indictment, a statement of admitted facts, or the jury instructions to show that the factfinder had to find, or the defendant had to admit, an act of dishonesty or false statement in order for the witness to have been convicted.

As in the case of prior inconsistent statement impeachment, this technique permits the opponent to both cross-examine the witness to be impeached and use extrinsic evidence. In most jurisdictions, the opponent may choose between cross-examination and extrinsic evidence. There is no requirement that the opponent lay a foundation on cross as a condition to introducing extrinsic evidence. However, if the opponent does cross-examine the witness and the witness admits all the facts about the conviction, under Rule 403 most courts then prohibit the introduction of extrinsic evidence. The rationale is simply that it would be cumulative and a waste of time to introduce the extrinsic evidence after the witness has conceded all the facts.

When the opponent resorts to extrinsic evidence, the evidence usually takes the form of an attested copy of the judgment of conviction. The properly attested copy is self-authenticating under Rule 902; the opponent does not need a live, sponsoring witness to authenticate the copy. In very rare cases, the opponent will present live testimony such as the testimony of someone who was present in the courtroom when the witness was convicted.

The courts differ on the number of details the opponent may prove about the conviction. Some courts limit the opponent's proof to evidence that in a certain jurisdiction in a certain year, the witness suffered "a felony conviction." These courts "sanitize" the evidence when the underlying crime is either heinous or so similar to the charged offense that the jurors might misuse the testimony as proof of the accused's bad character on the historical merits; the judge orders the direct examiner both to avoid referring to the specific nature of the underlying offense and to instruct his or her witness to refrain from mentioning that detail. However, most courts permit the opponent to identify the crime of which the witness was convicted. Some courts also allow the opponent to prove the sentence the witness suffered. The consensus is that the opponent may not inquire about other details, especially any aggravating facts about the particular manner in which the witness committed the crime, unless the details are admissible on another basis such as Rule 404(b).

[2] ELEMENTS OF THE FOUNDATION

The opponent must establish the following foundation:

1. The witness is the person who suffered the prior conviction. The lax standard set out in Federal Rule of Evidence 104(b) governs the sufficiency of the evidence that the witness is the convict. In some jurisdictions, if the witness's name is identical to that of the convict, the identity of names supports a permissive inference that the witness was the person convicted.

2. The conviction is for one of the crimes this jurisdiction holds to be impeaching.

3. The conviction was entered in a certain jurisdiction.

4. The conviction was entered in a certain year.

5.   The witness received a certain sentence.

> If the opponent is using a copy of the judgment of conviction, there is another element of the foundation:

6.   The copy of the judgment of conviction is authentic.

[3]   SAMPLE FOUNDATIONS

The first sample foundation illustrates cross-examination about a conviction. Assume that this jurisdiction limits conviction impeachment to felonies but permits the opponent to inquire about the sentence. The opponent is the attorney attempting to impeach the witness.

O   ISN'T IT TRUE THAT you are the same Steven Giles who once was convicted of a felony? (1), (2)

W   Yes.

O   ISN'T IT A FACT THAT the felony was a robbery? (2)

W   Yes.

O   ISN'T IT CORRECT THAT you were convicted of that crime in YR-8 in New York? (3), (4)

W   Yes.

O   ISN'T IT ALSO A FACT THAT you were sentenced to 15 years in state prison for that robbery? (5)

W   Yes.

The next foundation illustrates the use of an attested copy of a judgment of conviction to impeach. Assume that the witness, Mr. Giles, has already left the stand.

O   Your Honor, may this be marked defense exhibit D for identification?

J   It will be so marked.

O   Please let the record reflect that I am showing the exhibit to the opposing counsel.

J   It will so reflect.

O   I now offer defense exhibit D for identification into evidence as defense exhibit D.

P   Your Honor, I object on the grounds that there's insufficient authentication of this document.

O   Your Honor, the exhibit includes a properly executed attesting certificate. The certificate makes the exhibit self-authenticating under Rule 902(4). (6)

J   The objection will be overruled. The exhibit will be received.

O   Your Honor, may I read these two sentences to the jury?

J   Permission granted. Ladies and gentlemen of the jury, I have just accepted into evidence defense exhibit D. This exhibit is a properly authenticated copy of a judgment of a conviction of a crime. You will please bear in mind that the last prosecution witness was Mr. Steven Judson Giles, Jr. You may proceed.

O   Ladies and gentlemen, the exhibit reads: "On this day, July 13th, YR-8, the Supreme Court of the State of New York, Hudson County, the Honorable Paul Lederer presiding, duly found the defendant, Steven Judson Giles, Jr., guilty of the crime of robbery. (1), (2), (3), (4) For this crime, the defendant is hereby sentenced to 15 years' confinement in the prisons of the State of New York." (5)

Even if the witness were a party, the evidence of the conviction would be admissible solely on a credibility theory. Therefore, even if Giles were a criminal defendant, on request the judge would give the jury a limiting instruction that they could not use the evidence as a basis for concluding that Giles was a bad person and therefore more likely to have committed the charged offense. The judge would explain to the jurors that they could consider the evidence only for the purpose of deciding whether to believe Giles' testimony and how much weight to give to his testimony. During closing argument, the opponent could treat the conviction as credibility evidence; but it would be objectionable if he or she suggested to the jurors that the conviction showed that Giles was the sort of person likely to commit the type of crime he was charged with.

§ 5.11   PROOF THAT THE WITNESS IS BIASED

[1]   THE DOCTRINE

Like a conviction, the witness's bias is logically relevant to impeach the witness. Although Article VI of the Federal Rules does not expressly mention bias impeachment,[7] the Supreme Court has held that, as at common law, under the Federal Rules a witness may be impeached on the ground of bias. *United States v. Abel*, 469 U.S. 45, 105 S. Ct. 465, 83 L. Ed. 2d 450 (1984). Rule 402 generally authorizes the admission of logically relevant evidence; and the courts appreciate the relevance of bias to a witness's credibility. Bias might affect the witness consciously or subconsciously. The courts grant the opponent great latitude in proving bias. In fact, the courts often allow the opponent to use bias impeachment as a method of circumventing other evidentiary rules. For example, there is a general rule that in a civil action, the plaintiff may not prove that the defendant has settled any other claims arising from the same accident. The justification for the rule is that the admission of such evidence would discourage desirable, out-of-court settlements. Suppose, though, that the defendant calls a witness who has settled his or her claim with the defendant. The fact of the settlement is logically relevant and admissible to show the witness's bias in the defendant's favor. Another illustration is the rule that the plaintiff ordinarily may not prove that the defendant has liability insurance. The admission of such evidence would tempt the jury to decide the case on an improper basis; they might find in the plaintiff's favor because, in reality, the insurance company will pay the judgment. Assume, however, that the

---

[7] *But see* Fed. R. Evid. 411 ("such as proving a witness's bias"). The Court and parties overlooked the wording of Rule 411.

defendant calls one of the insurance company's investigators as a witness. In many jurisdictions, the plaintiff may now prove the defendant's liability insurance. The fact that the witness works for the defendant's liability carrier is logically relevant to show the witness's bias in favor of the defendant.

This impeachment technique is similar to conviction impeachment in another respect: The opponent may both cross-examine the witness to be impeached and use extrinsic evidence. On cross-examination, the courts grant the opponent a very wide scope of inquiry. Jurisdictions following the traditional view require that the opponent lay a foundation on cross-examination as a predicate for extrinsic evidence. These courts reason that as a matter of fairness, the opponent should give the witness an opportunity to explain or deny the impeaching facts. If the witness fully admits all the facts, under Rule 403, the judge may exercise discretion to limit or exclude extrinsic evidence. However, when the witness denies any of the relevant impeaching facts, the opponent may introduce extrinsic evidence. The Federal Rules do not require a foundation on cross-examination.

[2] ELEMENTS OF THE FOUNDATION

There are no special foundational requirements for bias evidence; the opponent may prove any fact or event logically relevant to show bias. If the impeaching evidence is an event, the foundation usually includes the following elements:

1. Where the event occurred.

2. When the event occurred.

3. Who was present.

4. What occurred.

Some counsel attempt to lay an additional element; namely, they seek the witness's concession that:

5. The fact or event will tend to bias the witness.

Most experienced counsel avoid such attempts. The witness will often not make that concession; and in the attempt to force the concession, the counsel might become objectionably argumentative. Experienced counsel prefer to invite the jury to draw the inference of bias during closing argument.

[3] SAMPLE FOUNDATIONS

The fact situation is a civil suit between a Mr. Martinez and a Mr. Saltzman. Mr. Martinez calls Mr. Fargo as a witness. After the direct examination, Mr. Saltzman's attorney begins cross-examination. Mr. Saltzman's attorney is the opponent.

O   ISN'T IT TRUE THAT on July 4, YR-3, you attended a party at Jane Fleming's house? (1), (2)

W   Yes.

O   ISN'T IT A FACT THAT Ms. Fleming and Mr. Saltzman, the defendant in this case, were also at the party? (3)

W   Yes.

O　　　　　ISN'T IT CORRECT THAT during the party, you punched Mr. Saltzman? (4)

W　　　　　Yes.

O　　　　　ISN'T IT ALSO TRUE THAT before you left the party, you told Ms. Fleming that you had a strong, personal dislike for Mr. Saltzman? (4)

W　　　　　Yes.

Assume that the witness had denied the impeaching facts. Then the opponent could present extrinsic evidence, such as Ms. Fleming's testimony.

O　　　　　WHERE were you on the evening of July 4, YR-3? (1), (2)

W　　　　　At my house. I was throwing a party for some friends.

O　　　　　WHO attended the party? (3)

W　　　　　There were a lot of people. Mr. Fargo, the last witness, was there. The defendant, Mr. Saltzman, was also in attendance.

O　　　　　WHAT, if anything, unusual happened during the evening? (4)

W　　　　　I couldn't believe it, but Mr. Fargo actually punched Mr. Saltzman. They were just standing talking, and all of a sudden Fargo slugged him.

O　　　　　WHAT happened then? (4)

W　　　　　I asked Fargo to get out.

O　　　　　WHAT, if anything, did Mr. Fargo say? (4)

W　　　　　He said he'd be glad to. He said that he had a strong, personal dislike for Mr. Saltzman and that he, Fargo, wouldn't stay under the same roof as Saltzman. Fargo said that if he'd known Saltzman was going to be at the party, he never would have accepted my invitation.

On request, the judge would have to give the jury a limiting instruction explaining that they could consider the bias evidence only for the purpose of evaluating Fargo's credibility. Likewise, in closing argument the opponent could treat the testimony solely as credibility evidence. Even if the witness were a party to the litigation, the opponent could not invite the jury to treat the evidence as proof of the party's bad character and therefore evidence that it is more likely that the party committed the criminal or tortious conduct alleged in the pleadings.

§ 5.12　PROOF THAT THE WITNESS IS DEFICIENT IN AN ELEMENT OF COMPETENCY

[1]　THE DOCTRINE

Section 3.01 listed the elements of competency. At common law, to be a competent witness, a person must possess the testimonial qualities of perception, memory, narration, and sincerity. If the opponent can negate one or more of those elements, the person is incompetent; the person cannot testify at all during the trial. However, even if the opponent's evidence does not completely negate one of the elements, the evidence may be logically relevant on an impeachment theory. For example, a color-blind person is a competent witness, but in a given case color blindness is a deficiency which might tend to reduce the believability of the witness's testimony.

The courts liberally admit evidence of deficiencies in elements of competency. The courts have admitted evidence that: The witness was intoxicated when he or she observed the event they testified about; the witness has a psychiatric disorder affecting his or her testimonial qualities; the witness has subnormal intelligence; and, in some jurisdictions, the witness is a drug addict or user.[8]

As a general proposition, the opponent may use either cross-examination or extrinsic evidence. For example, on cross-examination, the opponent may attempt to force a witness to concede that he or she was intoxicated at the time of event. Or the opponent may rely on extrinsic evidence and call a psychiatrist to testify that the psychiatrist examined the subject witness and discovered a disorder that calls into question the witness's credibility. Similarly, the opponent may cross-examine the witness to expose the witness's subnormal intelligence. The opponent may use the "hop, skip and jump" method of cross-examination to do so; the opponent cross-examines the witness about a number of events out of chronological sequence. The opponent's hope is that the witness will flounder and the jury will conclude that the witness has a deficient memory. However, in many jurisdictions, the courts feel that subnormal intelligence has relatively little probative value and bar extrinsic evidence.

[2] ELEMENTS OF THE FOUNDATION

This impeachment technique often requires proof of a particular historical event, such as an occasion when the witness was drunk. The normal foundation will include:

1. Where the event occurred.

2. When the event occurred.

3. Who was present.

4. What happened.

5. What happened may have affected the accuracy of the witness's testimony.

In addition, the technique often necessitates lay or expert opinion testimony. Chapter 9 illustrates the foundations for lay and expert testimony. When such testimony is necessary, the opponents will also have to establish:

6. The qualifications of the expert, if expert testimony is necessary.

7. The basis for the opinion.

8. The opinion itself.

---

[8] Some courts bar such evidence unless the opponent presents expert testimony that long-term abuse of the drug in question affects a person's cognitive ability. Without such evidence, these courts reason that the admission of testimony about addiction violates the character evidence prohibition. In their view, the evidence is relevant only if the person was under the influence of the drug at the time he or she observed the event; and in order to draw that inference the opponent must reason that if the person previously used drugs, they used them again at the time of the event.

[3] SAMPLE FOUNDATIONS

We shall first illustrate cross-examination to attack a deficiency in the witness's competency. The fact situation is a tort case arising from a traffic collision. The plaintiff, Ms. Schmitt, sues the defendant, Mr. Jackson. The plaintiff calls a witness, Mr. Oser. On direct examination, Mr. Oser testifies that he observed the accident from 150 feet away; he testifies that the defendant swerved into the plaintiff. The defendant is the opponent.

O ISN'T IT TRUE THAT on direct examination, you testified that on January 4th, you observed a collision between the plaintiff's and defendant's cars just outside the Sports Arena? (1), (2), (3)

W Yes.

O Mr. Oser, ISN'T IT CORRECT THAT you are nearsighted? (4)

W Yes.

O ISN'T IT A FACT THAT as a nearsighted person, you have difficulty seeing anything at a distance? (4)

W Yes.

O ISN'T IT CORRECT THAT your doctor has prescribed glasses for you to correct your nearsightedness? (4)

W Yes.

O ISN'T IT ALSO TRUE that when you supposedly saw the collision, you weren't wearing your glasses? (4)

W Yes.

O Finally, ISN'T IT A FACT THAT you were at least 150 feet away from the collision when you supposedly saw it? (5)

W Yes.

Next we turn to an example of extrinsic testimony impeaching a prior witness. Mr. Oser has left the witness stand. The defendant calls Mr. Thelan. The defendant is still designated the opponent. The defendant is conducting the direct examination of Mr. Thelan.

O WHERE were you on the evening of January 4th of this year? (1), (2)

W I was downtown with Mr. Oser.

O WHO is Mr. Oser? (3)

W He's Ed Oser, the last witness in this case.

O WHAT were you and Mr. Oser doing? (4)

W We had a bite and some drinks at a bar. Then we were going home to our respective wives.

O WHEN did you and Mr. Oser start drinking? (7)

W At about 5:30 in the early evening.

O   HOW many drinks did Mr. Oser have? (7)

W   He was really putting them away. I'd say he had five or six before we left.

O   WHAT was he drinking? (7)

W   He was having screwdrivers, orange juice and vodka.

O   WHEN did you leave the bar? (7)

W   At about 7. Maybe a little later.

O   WHO, if anyone, were you with when you left?

W   I stepped outside with Mr. Oser.

O   WHAT was Mr. Oser's appearance when you left?

W   His face was a little red.

O   HOW was he acting? (7)

W   Pretty silly. He was stumbling and acting giddy.

O   HOW did his breath smell? (7)

W   He had a strong odor of alcohol on his breath.

O   WHAT was his speech like? (7)

W   It was slurred. He was having trouble pronouncing words.

O   WHAT, if anything, happened after you and Mr. Oser left the bar?

W   Just down the street a collision occurred. It happened a short distance from us down the street.

O   WHAT collision? (7)

W   The collision Ed testified about, the one between the plaintiff and the defendant.

O   WHEN did you see this collision? (5)

W   Maybe five minutes after we left the bar.

O   In your opinion, WHAT was Mr. Oser's condition when the collision occurred? (5), (8)

W   I hate to say it, but I think he was drunk. He was pretty hammered.

The preceding foundation illustrates lay opinion testimony attacking the witness's credibility. The opponent may also use expert opinion testimony. § 3.04 contained a sample foundation for a psychiatrist's testimony. In Chapter 3, the opponent used the testimony to attack the prospective witness's competency. The opponent could use a very similar foundation to show a deficiency in the witness's competency.

The above evidence is admitted solely on a credibility theory. Thus, even if the witness being impeached were a party, on request the trial judge would give the jury a limiting instruction that they could consider the evidence only for the purpose of evaluating the credibility of the witness's testimony. Given that instruction, in closing argument the opponent could urge the jury to discount the witness's testimony for the reason that the witness was intoxicated at the time the witness supposedly observed the accident. However, even if the witness were a party, in closing argument it would be objectionable for the opponent to suggest to the jury that the evidence of drinking shows that the witness is a bad person and therefore more likely to have committed the criminal or tortious misconduct alleged in the pleadings.

PART D.   Rehabilitation of Witnesses After Impeachment

§ 5.13   PRIOR CONSISTENT STATEMENT

[1]   THE DOCTRINE

After the opponent attempts to impeach the witness's credibility, the witness's proponent may attempt to repair the damage. These attempts are called rehabilitation. One of the most common rehabilitation techniques is proof of a prior consistent statement. The proponent shows that the witness testified to the fact at the time of trial and that the witness made a pretrial statement to the same effect. Just as inconsistency has an impeaching effect, consistency has a rehabilitating effect.

However, the courts do not want trials to be bogged down with proof of all of the witness's pretrial statements. The courts fear that rehabilitation evidence can lead the jury far afield. To begin with, the testimony relates to credibility, not the historical merits; and to make matters worse, this evidence relates to a third stage in credibility analysis after bolstering and impeachment. For that reason, most jurisdictions impose timing requirements on prior consistent statements. For example, assume that the opponent impeached the witness with a prior inconsistent statement. Many jurisdictions follow the temporal priority doctrine and take the position that the proponent may rehabilitate with a prior consistent statement only if the consistent statement preceded the allegedly inconsistent statement. Or assume that the opponent charged that the witness recently fabricated his or her testimony. Many jurisdictions permit the proponent to rehabilitate by prior consistent statement only if the witness made the statement before he or she had any motive to lie. In *Tome v. United States*, 513 U.S. 150, 115 S. Ct. 696, 130 L. Ed. 2d 574 (1995), the Supreme Court held that Rule 801(d)(1)(B) codifies the common-law temporal priority requirement. Thus, at least when he or she wants to introduce the prior consistent statement as substantive evidence, the proponent must show that the statement satisfies the timing requirement. Admittedly, Rule 801(d)(1)(B) and *Tome* purports to govern only when the proponent offers the prior consistent statement for substantive purposes. Nevertheless, many jurisdictions believe that after *Tome* "the handwriting is on the wall"; they follow the temporal priority doctrine even when the proponent offers the statement on a credibility theory.

Originally, Rule 801(d)(1)(B) permitted the admission of prior consistent statements only in response to allegations of recent fabrication or improper motive. (B)(i) continues to authorize the receipt of testimony about the consistent statement in those situations. However, in 2014(B) was amended to add the following language, "(ii) to rehabilitate the declarant's credibility as a witness when attacked on another ground . . . ."

The 2013 Report of the Judicial Conference to the Chief Justice explained the expression, "another ground," by giving the examples of "explain[ing] an inconsistency or . . . rebut[ting] a charge of bad memory." It is true that Rule 801(d)(1)(B) deals only with the admission of the consistent statement as substantive evidence. However, the language recognizes that a consistent statement can be relevant on a credibility theory even absent an allegation of recent fabrication or improper motive.

[2] ELEMENTS OF THE FOUNDATION

The statement itself is an event. For that reason, the foundation includes the four normal foundational elements for proof of any event:

1.   Where the statement was made.

2.   When the statement was made.

3.   Who was present.

4.   The tenor of the statement.

In addition, if the proponent must comply with a timing requirement, the proponent must show that:

5.   The statement preceded (a) the prior inconsistent statement or (b) any motive on the part of the witness to fabricate.

[3] SAMPLE FOUNDATION

The fact situation is a tort action arising from a collision on December 14th. The plaintiff, Mr. Gillis, alleges that the defendant, Ms. Bollack, negligently caused the accident by crossing over into his lane. On direct examination, Mr. Gillis testifies to that effect. On cross-examination, the defense attorney charges that Mr. Gillis fabricated his story. Specifically, the defense attorney asked this question, "ISN'T IT TRUE THAT you never came up with that story until after you consulted your attorney, Mr. Clark?" The plaintiff now begins redirect examination. The plaintiff is the proponent.

P   Mr. Gillis, WHAT happened after the accident?

W   The police arrived, and I went down to the nearest station with them.

P   WHERE is the station located? (1)

W   I think it's at the intersection of Elm and Maryland.

P   WHEN did you arrive there? (2)

W   About two hours after the accident. It might have been three in the afternoon.

P   WHO was there? (3)

W   A lot of police officers, myself, and Ms. Bollack.

P   WHO were the officers? (3)

W   There was one named Jorgenson, and then there was Desk Sergeant Allen.

P   WHAT, if anything, did Desk Sergeant Allen do?

W   He questioned me about the accident.

P   Again, on WHAT day did you have this conversation with Desk Sergeant Allen? (2)

W   December 14th.

P   WHEN was the first time you ever consulted me about this case? (5)

W   I guess it was three weeks later.

P   So WHICH came first—your conversation with Desk Sergeant Allen or your conversation with me? (5)

(Many experienced trial attorneys omit this question. They feel that the timing is obvious and that the question will offend intelligent judges or jurors by insulting their intelligence.)

W   As I just said, my conversation with Allen.

P   WHAT, if anything, did you tell Allen? (4)

W   I told him about the accident. I said that the other driver caused it by coming into my lane. I was minding my own business, and then this car is coming across the lane right at me.

Now assume that in the same fact situation, the defendant attempted a different impeachment technique. On cross-examination, the defendant asked this question, "ISN'T IT TRUE THAT on Christmas Day that year, you told your brother that the accident occurred because your brakes failed?" This question amounts to attempted impeachment by prior inconsistent statement. The foundation would be exactly the same until the last three questions. Now the foundation on redirect would read:

P   WHEN did you have the conversation with your brother the defense attorney mentioned? (5)

W   I'm pretty sure it was on Christmas Day, December 25th.

P   So WHICH came first—your conversation with Desk Sergeant Allen or your conversation with your brother? (5)

W   My conversation with Allen—it was about a week and a half before I saw my brother over the holidays.

P   WHAT, if anything, did you tell Allen? (4)

W   I told him about the accident. I said that the other driver caused it by coming into my lane. I was minding my own business, and then this car is coming across the lane right at me.

Assume that under local law, in both of the above examples evidence of the prior consistent statement is admissible solely on a credibility theory. If so, on request the trial judge would give the jury a limiting instruction. The tenor of the instruction would be that although the jurors could consider the evidence in evaluating Gillis' credibility, they could not treat Gillis' prior statement as proof that the other car caused the accident by coming into Gillis' lane. Hence, during closing argument it would be objectionable for the proponent to suggest to the jurors that Gillis' statement was itself evidence that the other car had drifted into Gillis' lane.

§ 5.14 PROOF OF THE CHARACTER TRAIT OF TRUTHFULNESS

[1] THE DOCTRINE

Many of the impeachment techniques available to the opponent are express or implied attacks on the witness's character. The Advisory Committee Note to Rule 608(a) states: "Opinion or reputation that the witness is untruthful specifically qualifies as an attack, and evidence of misconduct, including conviction of crime, and of corruption also fall within this category. Evidence of bias or interest does not. Whether evidence in the form of a contradiction is an attack upon the character of the witness must depend upon the circumstances." Thus, if the opponent calls a character witness to testify to witness #1's character trait of untruthfulness, the testimony is an express attack. If the opponent proves specific bad acts or convictions, there is an implied attack on the witness's character. Even bias impeachment sometimes involves an attack on the witness's credibility; for instance, the proof of bias may be evidence of a corrupt financial motive. In all these cases, the judge will permit the proponent to rehabilitate by proving a character trait of truthfulness. The sequence would be the following. The proponent, perhaps the plaintiff, calls witness #1 to testify about the historical merits of the case. The opponent then calls witness #2, a character witness; witness #2 testifies that witness #1 has a reputation for untruthfulness. To rehabilitate witness #1, the proponent calls witness #3, another character witness. Witness #3 contradicts witness #2; witness #3 testifies that witness #1 has a good reputation for truthfulness.

In general, the rules governing the opponent's character evidence also apply to the proponent's character evidence. § 5.06 outlines those rules. There is only one additional rule the proponent should bear in mind: The trial judge is likely to limit the proponent's character evidence to the same type, time, and community as the opponent's evidence. If the opponent used reputation evidence, the judge may not permit the proponent to use opinion evidence. The judge may limit the proponent's character evidence to roughly the same time period and community as the opponent's evidence. If the opponent presented character evidence about the witness's reputation in Detroit within the past five years, the judge might exclude the proponent's character evidence relating to the witness's reputation in Las Vegas 10 years before. The courts do not want trials to bog down in collateral disputes over witnesses' credibility. After all, the third stage of credibility analysis—rehabilitation—is rather far removed from the historical merits. The proponent should respond directly in kind to the opponent's attacks on the witness's credibility.

[2] ELEMENTS OF THE FOUNDATION

The foundational elements are the same as in § 5.06.

[3] SAMPLE FOUNDATION

With one exception, the foundations are the same as in § 5.06. The exception is that the final answers will be favorable to witness #1 rather than unfavorable. Thus, the reputation foundation would end in this fashion:

P	WHAT is that reputation? (4)
W	It's good. He's known as a truthful person.
P	Given Mr. Harding's reputation, would you believe him under oath? (5)
W	Yes.

The opinion foundation would conclude in this fashion:

P	WHAT is that opinion? (4)
W	In my opinion, he's a truthful person.
P	Given that opinion, would you believe Mr. Harding under oath? (5)
W	Yes.

Like impeaching evidence of a witness's character trait of untruthfulness, rehabilitating evidence of a witness's character trait of truthfulness is admissible solely on a credibility theory. Hence, even if the witness were the civil or criminal defendant in the case, under Rule 105 on request the trial judge would instruct the jury that the jurors could not treat the evidence as proof that the defendant did not commit the criminal or tortious act alleged in the pleadings. The judge would direct the jury to consider the evidence only for the purpose of evaluating Harding's credibility. In closing argument, the proponent could put the evidence only to that limited use. It would be objectionable for the proponent to suggest to the jury that they should treat the evidence as substantive proof on the merits of the case.

CHAPTER 6

LEGAL IRRELEVANCE LIMITATIONS ON EVIDENCE THAT IS RELEVANT TO THE HISTORICAL MERITS OF THE CASE

§ 6.01 INTRODUCTION

In the last chapter, we saw that the dangers listed in Rule 403 can lead to the exclusion of evidence that is logically relevant to a witness's credibility. The "*legal irrelevance*" doctrine codified in Rule 403 is not limited to credibility evidence; the institutional policies supporting the doctrine can also apply to evidence that is logically relevant to the historical merits.

The premier danger noted in Rule 403 is "unfair prejudice." As the Advisory Committee Note to Rule 403 explains, in this context "unfair prejudice" means the evidence's tendency to tempt the jury to decide the case on an improper, usually emotional, basis. For instance, in a homicide prosecution, horrific photographs of the victim's body could be excluded if, after viewing them, the jurors could no longer dispassionately evaluate the evidence of guilt or innocence. Most of the types of evidence analyzed in this chapter present the danger of prejudice. Several sections discuss evidence of other misdeeds by a criminal accused. Such evidence creates a risk that the jurors will convict, not because they are convinced beyond a reasonable doubt of the accused's commission of the charged crime, but rather because they conclude that the accused is a bad person who should be behind bars. Evidence of a civil defendant's liability insurance raises similar danger. Although the evidence of liability may be weak, the jurors may return a plaintiff's verdict because they assume the insurer—the "deep pocket"—will absorb the economic loss.

Simply stated, Rule 403 embodies the doctrine that the trial judge has discretion to exclude logically relevant evidence if, in his or her judgment, the evidence's attendant dangers substantially outweigh its probative value. The evidence may be technically relevant, but realistically its admission will create a probative danger. The judge's application of the doctrine involves several steps. At the outset, the trial judge must assess the probative value of the evidence. How clear is the evidence? How strong is the logical link between the evidence and the fact it is offered to prove? Is the evidence remote in time? How positive is the witness? Is there alternative, less prejudicial evidence of the fact? The opponent's tender of a stipulation to the fact can be the functional equivalent of alternative evidence; the tendered stipulation can eliminate the proponent's need to resort to the more prejudicial evidence. *Old Chief v. United States*,

519 U.S. 172, 117 S. Ct. 644, 136 L. Ed. 2d 574 (1997). These are just some of the questions the judge asks in evaluating probative value. Then the judge identifies the countervailing dangers such as prejudice and undue time consumption. Finally the judge strikes the balance between the probative value and the countervailing dangers. For some types of evidence, such as inflammatory photographs, the application of the doctrine remains highly discretionary. Trial judges resolve the questions ad hoc case-by-case. As previously stated, Rule 403 is biased in favor of admitting logically relevant evidence. For other types of evidence, including most of those examined in this chapter, relatively firm guidelines or even rules have evolved.

§ 6.02   CHARACTER EVIDENCE

[1]   OVERVIEW

Section 4.06 discussed evidence of a witness's character trait of truthfulness. Under that theory of admissibility, the opponent of the witness uses the witness's character trait of untruthfulness as circumstantial proof of the witness's conduct. The opponent reasons that since the witness has a character trait of untruthfulness, the witness's present testimony is probably untruthful. We now turn to character evidence on the historical merits of the case. Much of what we said about character on a credibility theory applies here as well. Once again, we are using character as circumstantial evidence of conduct. For example, under the so-called "mercy rule" a criminal accused may elect to introduce testimony that he or she is a moral, law-abiding person. The accused attempts to establish that he or she has a good character and asks the jury to infer that he or she acted consistently with that character or "in character" on the alleged occasion. The jury is asked to conclude that an accused who is that type of person would probably not commit the charged crime. Or, in a prosecution for a violent crime, the accused may introduce evidence that the alleged victim is an aggressive person. The accused is inviting the jury to infer that the alleged victim was in reality the aggressor on the occasion in question.

The rules governing character evidence on the merits resemble the rules for character evidence of untruthfulness in another respect: the methods of proof. We previously noted that the opponent presenting evidence of the witness's character trait of untruthfulness is ordinarily restricted to reputation and opinion evidence. The same restriction generally applies to character evidence on the historical merits. Thus, the criminal accused is usually limited to reputation or opinion evidence of his or her moral, law-abiding character. Until 1994, the only major difference in methods of proof was that when the accused placed in issue the character of the alleged victim of a violent or sex offense, some jurisdictions permitted the accused to prove specific instances of the alleged victim's violent or promiscuous conduct. In 1995, Congress approved Federal Rules of Evidence 413–415, the so-called rape sword laws. Under the provisions of those statutes, in sexual assault (Rule 413) and child molestation (Rule 414) prosecutions and civil actions involving allegations of sexual assault or child molestation (Rule 415), the prosecution or plaintiff may offer evidence of other similar specific acts by an accused or civil party on a character theory of logical relevance. A few handfuls of states have adopted similar rules, and several states reach the same result by case law approving a "lustful disposition" doctrine.

There are several other differences between the credibility theory for character evidence and the use of character evidence on the historical merits. The following questions highlight those differences.

Whose character is "in issue"?[1] On a credibility theory, the character of any witness in any type of case is in issue. Once the person takes the witness stand and gives any testimony in the case, his or her credibility becomes one of the material facts of consequence. On a character theory on the merits, the rules are quite different. The following statements are over-simplifications, but it is generally true that: (1) the parties may not use character evidence as circumstantial proof of conduct on the merits in civil cases; and (2) in criminal cases, character evidence may be used as circumstantial proof of the conduct of only the accused and the alleged victim.

What part of the person's character is "in issue"? On a credibility theory, we focus squarely on the witness's character trait of truthfulness; that is the only part of the witness's character that is "in issue." In contrast, on a character theory on the merits, we are interested in a different part of the person's character. If the person is the criminal accused and the accused pleads entrapment, we may be interested in the accused's general, moral, law-abiding character. Or we may focus on a specific character trait relevant to the nature of the offense, such as peacefulness in an assault prosecution or honesty in a theft prosecution. Rule 404(a)(2)(A) permits the accused to offer testimony about a relevant "character trait."

Finally, when does the person's character come "into issue"? On a credibility theory, the witness's character trait of truthfulness becomes logically relevant as soon as the witness gives any testimony in the case. In most jurisdictions, the accused's character on the merits does not come "into issue" until the accused defendant elects to affirmatively present character evidence. It is not enough that the accused has taken the witness stand. The accused generally has the choice whether to place his or her character "in issue" on the merits. Aside from Rules 413–14, the prosecution ordinarily may present evidence of the accused's immoral, law-breaking character only in rebuttal to defense character evidence.

---

[1] A caveat is necessary. In character evidence opinions, the courts often state that a person's character is "in issue." For example, they frequently assert that a criminal accused may place his or her character "in issue." That expression is potentially misleading. The courts do not mean that the person's character comes directly into issue and becomes a fact of consequence or essential element under Federal Rule of Evidence 401. The vast majority of these cases are not situations in which the defendant has raised an entrapment defense making his or her subjective disposition an ultimate fact of consequence under Rule 401. Rather, the courts mean only that the person's character may be used as circumstantial proof of conduct. Thus, the essential element set out in the indictment might be that the accused committed a particular actus reus. Even if the trial judge allows the accused to place his or her character "in issue," the accused's character does not become an essential element of the charge. Under the substantive law and pleadings, the essential issue never becomes whether the accused is the kind or type of person who would commit the charged offense. The issue was and remains whether the accused committed the charged actus reus. In order to help the reader keep this caveat in mind, this subsection consistently places the expression "in issue" in quotation marks.

[2]   REPUTATION CHARACTER EVIDENCE

The foundation for reputation character evidence on the historical merits is strikingly similar to the foundation for reputation character evidence on credibility:

1. The witness is a member of the same community (residential, business, or social) as the accused.

2. The witness has been a member of the community for a substantial period of time.

3. The accused has a reputation for: (a) general, moral, law-abiding character; or (b) a specific, relevant character trait. Federal Rule of Evidence 404(a)(2)(A) seems to confine the defendant to a relevant specific trait. However, when the accused offers character evidence in support of an entrapment defense, many federal courts allow the accused to adduce evidence of his or her general, moral, law-abiding character.

4. The witness knows the reputation.

5. The witness states the reputation.

Our fact situation is an assault prosecution. The government has charged Mr. Lowe with a violent assault. During its case-in-chief, the defense calls Mr. Nieman as a character witness. Mr. Nieman has already identified himself. The defense is the proponent.

P	WHO is Mr. Lowe?
W	He's a neighbor of mine.
P	WHEN is the last time you saw him?
W	He's in the courtroom right now.
P	WHERE is he sitting?
W	He's sitting there at the table with you.
P	HOW is he dressed?
W	He's wearing a brown suit and yellow tie.
P	Your Honor, may the record reflect that the witness has identified my client, Mr. Lowe?
J	The record will so reflect.
P	Mr. Nieman, WHERE does Mr. Lowe live? (1)
W	Here in Scottsdale.
P	WHERE do you live? (1)
W	I also reside in Scottsdale.
P	HOW close do you live to Mr. Lowe? (1)
W	No more than half a mile away.
P	HOW long has Mr. Lowe lived in Scottsdale? (2)

W	I'd say easily seven years.
P	HOW long have you lived in Scottsdale? (2)
W	For the past 10 years.
P	Does Mr. Lowe have a reputation for violence or peacefulness in Scottsdale?
	(Or "Does Mr. Lowe have a reputation as a law-breaking or law-abiding person in Scottsdale?") (3)
W	Yes.
P	Do you know that reputation? (4)
W	Yes.
P	WHAT is that reputation? (5)
W	He's known as a peaceful person.
	(Or "He's known as a moral, law-abiding person.")

When this testimony is admitted, during the final jury charge, or on both occasions on request the trial judge might give the jury an instruction along these lines: "Evidence has been received for the purpose of showing the good character of the defendant for those traits involved in the commission of a crime of the kind charged here. Good character for the traits involved in the commission of the crime charged may be sufficient by itself to raise a reasonable doubt as to the defendant's guilt. It may be reasoned that a person of good character as to such traits would not be likely to commit the crime with which the defendant is charged."

During closing argument, the defense attorney could state:

Ladies and gentlemen, during the trial you heard the testimony of Mr. Nieman. As you'll recall, Mr. Nieman is one of Mr. Lowe's neighbors. They've been neighbors for the better part of a decade; as Mr. Nieman told you, they've both lived in Scottsdale for over seven years. Mr. Nieman took the stand and told you that Mr. Lowe has an excellent reputation for peacefulness. In Mr. Nieman's words, Mr. Lowe "is known as a peaceful person."

In a few moments her Honor will read you the legal instructions that you have to follow during your deliberations. She's going to tell you that in deciding Mr. Lowe's innocence or guilt, you can consider this evidence of Mr. Lowe's good character. In particular, her Honor will instruct you along these lines: "Good character for the traits involved in the commission of the crime charged may be sufficient by itself to raise a reasonable doubt as to the guilt of a defendant. It may be reasoned that a person of good character would not be likely to commit the violent crime with which the defendant is charged."[2]

---

[2] Although this instruction was once quite popular, many jurisdictions have abandoned the use of the instruction. In those jurisdictions, the judge no longer expressly tells the jury that standing alone, evidence of the defendant's good character is sufficient to raise a reasonable doubt.

Ladies and gentlemen, that instruction makes a lot of sense. Every day in the real world you make decisions about people based on their character. If they have a bad reputation, you think twice; but if they have a good reputation, you trust them because it would be "out of character" for them to violate the law. The uncontradicted evidence in this case—Mr. Nieman's testimony—shows you that Mr. Lowe has an unblemished reputation as a peaceful person. The prosecution has charged Mr. Lowe with an assault, a violent crime. Mr. Lowe simply isn't the kind of man who would commit that type of offense; he's a man with an excellent reputation as a peaceful person. Again, remember her Honor's words that good character "may be sufficient by itself to raise a reasonable doubt."

[3]　OPINION CHARACTER EVIDENCE

This foundation is very similar to the foundation for opinion character evidence on credibility:

1. The witness is personally acquainted with the accused.
2. The witness knows the accused well enough to have formed a reliable opinion of the accused's character. The trial judge has discretion to decide whether the extent of the witness's personal familiarity is sufficient.
3. The witness has an opinion of the accused's character.
4. The witness states his or her opinion.

Assume the same hypothetical assault prosecution:

P	WHO is Mr. Lowe? (1)
W	He's a neighbor of mine.
P	WHEN is the last time you saw him? (1)
W	He's in the courtroom right now.
P	WHERE is he sitting? (1)
W	He's sitting right there at the table with you.
P	HOW is he dressed? (1)
W	He's wearing a brown suit and yellow tie.
P	Your Honor, please let the record reflect that the witness has identified my client, Mr. Lowe.
J	It will so reflect.
P	Mr. Nieman, WHERE does Mr. Lowe live? (2)
W	Here in Scottsdale.
P	HOW long has he lived here? (2)
W	I'd say easily seven years.
P	WHERE do you live? (2)
W	I also reside in Scottsdale.

P	HOW close do you live to Mr. Lowe? (2)
W	No more than half a mile away.
P	HOW long have you lived in Scottsdale? (2)
W	Over 10 years.
P	HOW long have you known Mr. Lowe? (2)
W	I guess seven years—ever since he moved here.
P	HOW did you come to know Mr. Lowe? (2)
W	We have several mutual acquaintances, and we both are members of some local clubs, including the Optimists.
P	HOW often do you see Mr. Lowe? (2)
W	At least once or twice each week.
P	HOW well do you know him? (2)
W	I consider him a good, close friend.
P	Do you have an opinion whether he is a violent or peaceful person? *(Or "Do you have an opinion whether he is a law-breaking or law-abiding person?")* (3)
W	Yes.
P	WHAT is your opinion? (4)
W	In my opinion, he is a peaceful person.

(Or, "In my opinion, he is a moral, law-abiding person.")

At least a significant minority of jurisdictions permit the proponent to use expert opinion testimony as well as lay opinion. Federal Rule of Evidence 405(a) authorizes the receipt of "opinion" evidence, and neither the text of the rule nor the accompanying Advisory Committee Note indicates that the drafters intended to restrict the proponent to lay opinion testimony. Suppose, for example, that a psychiatrist diagnoses the accused as a passive personality with an aversion to violence. That expert opinion would certainly be relevant evidence to reduce the probability that the accused initiated a violent, unprovoked attack. If the proponent wanted to present such testimony, the proponent would have to comply with the foundational requirements for an expert opinion, described in Chapter 9.

Whether the evidence takes the form of lay or expert opinion, on request the judge would give the jury a limiting instruction similar to the one for reputation character evidence. In closing argument, the defense counsel could then state:

Mr. Nieman isn't just a passing acquaintance of Mr. Lowe. Mr. Nieman knows him well. The undisputed evidence is that Mr. Nieman has lived a few blocks from Mr. Lowe for over seven years. They have mutual friends, and they belong to some of the same organizations. In Mr. Nieman's words, they see each other "at least once or twice each week." Mr. Nieman knows Mr.

Lowe—he knows the type of man Mr. Lowe is. That's why you ought to believe Mr. Nieman when he tells you that Mr. Lowe simply isn't the kind of person who would commit this crime.

[4]   PROOF OF CHARACTER BY SPECIFIC INSTANCES OF CONDUCT

The Accused's Proffer of Evidence of the Alleged Victim's Character Trait for Violence or Promiscuity

In some jurisdictions, an accused charged with a violent crime may attempt to prove the violent character of the alleged victim. The logical relevance is that if the alleged victim has a violent personality, that personality increases the probability that the alleged victim threw the first punch and was the aggressor. The Federal Rules limit the accused to the use of reputation and opinion testimony as methods of proving the victim's violent character. However, many jurisdictions permit the accused to prove the alleged victim's violent character by specific instances of conduct.

The elements of the foundation are:

1.   Where the event occurred.

2.   When the event occurred.

3.   Who was involved.

4.   What happened—namely, a violent act by the alleged victim.

5.   The circumstances indicating that on the prior occasion, the alleged victim was the aggressor.

Assume that the government charges Mr. Lowe with assaulting Mr. Gilligan on December 1, YR-3. During the defense case-in-chief, the defense calls Mr. Nieman as a witness. Mr. Nieman has already identified himself. The defense is the proponent.

P	WHERE were you on the evening of November 1, YR-3? (1), (2)
W	I was at Tarantino's restaurant in downtown Topeka.
P	WHY were you there?
W	I was attending a party.
P	WHO else was there? (3)
W	A number of people, including Mr. Gilligan.
P	WHO is Mr. Gilligan? (3)
W	He's the complaining witness in this case.
P	WHEN did you last see him? (3)
W	About an hour ago.
P	WHERE was he? (3)
W	He was in this courtroom.
P	WHAT was he doing? (3)
W	He was testifying for the prosecution.

P	WHAT, if anything, happened at this party at the restaurant? (4)
W	Mostly we just had a good time. There was one unfortunate incident.
P	WHAT was that? (4)
W	There was a fight.
P	WHO was involved in the fight? (4)
W	Mr. Gilligan and a Mr. Jones.
P	WHERE were you when the fight started? (5)
W	I was standing only a few feet away.
P	HOW well could you see what happened? (5)
W	Very well. I was standing right next to both of them when the fight started.
P	HOW did the fight start? (5)
W	They were just talking, and then Mr. Gilligan started screaming at Mr. Jones.
P	HOW loudly was he screaming? (5)
W	At the top of his voice.
P	WHAT happened then? (5)
W	Mr. Gilligan punched Mr. Jones.
P	WHO threw the first punch? (5)
W	Mr. Gilligan.
P	HOW many punches did he throw? (5)
W	He threw five or six.
P	WHAT happened then? (5)
W	I grabbed Jones, someone else grabbed Gilligan, and we separated them.
P	WHAT happened when the other person grabbed Mr. Gilligan? (5)
W	He struggled to get free and started calling everyone names.

Notice that at the end of this line of questioning, the proponent does not attempt to elicit the witness's opinion that given Gilligan's violent character, it is more probable that Gilligan started the fight. It would be improper opinion for the witness to draw that inference. Moreover, it is unnecessary for the witness to draw that inference at this point; in the subsequent instructions the judge will tell the jury that they may decide whether to draw the inference, and in summation the proponent may expressly argue in favor of the inference.

Thus, when the testimony is admitted, during the final jury charge, or on both occasions the judge might tell the jury the following about the evidence: "In this case, the defendant claims that Mr. Gilligan was the aggressor. Evidence has been received for the purpose of showing that Mr. Gilligan has a violent character. You may consider that evidence in deciding whether the defendant or Mr. Gilligan was the real aggressor."

During final argument, the defense counsel could state:

Ladies and gentleman, as I told you in opening statement, this case boils down to a simple question: Who attacked whom? Did Mr. Lowe start the fight, or was Mr. Gilligan, the so-called victim, the real aggressor? When you discuss that question in the deliberation room, I ask you to remember the testimony of Mr. Nieman. Mr. Nieman testified about another incident involving Mr. Gilligan. It was a relatively recent incident; it happened on December 1st of last year. It started out as a pleasant evening, a party at Tarantino's. Most of us are familiar with that restaurant—it's a great place for a party, good food, nice surroundings, a peaceful atmosphere with a wonderful view of the Bay. But something shattered the peace that evening. A fight broke out. Remember how it broke out. For no good reason, someone just started screaming. Then that same person got violent. With no provocation, he threw one punch, then another, and another—and before it was over, he had thrown five or six punches. Who was that person? Mr. Nieman told you that it was none other than Mr. Gilligan. Ladies and gentlemen, that incident tells you something about Mr. Gilligan. It shows that he has a violent streak. In a few minutes her Honor will give you the legal instructions that you have to follow during deliberations. In particular, she is going to tell you that you may consider Mr. Nieman's testimony "in deciding whether the defendant or Mr. Gilligan was the real aggressor." I want you to do exactly what her Honor tells you. If you do that, if you consider the evidence of Mr. Gilligan's violent temper, you'll reach the only reasonable conclusion in this case, namely, that Mr. Lowe was the real victim and that the so-called victim, Mr. Gilligan, actually started the fight.

A very few jurisdictions also permit a criminal accused to attack the chaste character of the alleged victim in a sex offense prosecution. Today, though, the vast majority of courts and legislatures restrict this type of evidence. However, in some jurisdictions, the defendant may still prove specific instances of promiscuous conduct by the alleged victim. The line of reasoning is that if the alleged victim consented to intercourse on prior occasions, her prior consent increases the probability that she consented to intercourse with the accused.

Roughly the same foundation would apply if the accused were trying to prove the promiscuous character of the alleged victim of a sex offense:

1. Where the act occurred.

2. When the act occurred.

3. Who was present.

4. What happened.

5. The circumstances indicating that the alleged victim was acting promiscuously on the prior occasion.

Assume that the government charges Mr. Lowe with raping Ms. Younger on December 1, YR-3. During the defense case-in-chief, the defense calls Mr. Norton as a witness. Mr. Norton has already identified himself. The defense is the proponent.

P	WHERE were you on the evening of November 1, YR-3? (1), (2)
W	I was at Gino's bar in downtown Peoria.
P	WHAT were you doing there?
W	I was hanging out and looking for some women to pick up.
P	WHAT do you mean by "pick up"?
W	I was trying to find someone to have some fun with that night.
P	WHAT happened after you arrived at the bar? (3)
W	I bumped into a woman.
P	WHO was the woman? (3)
W	Ms. Nancy Younger.
P	WHEN did you last see her? (3)
W	Today.
P	WHERE was she? (3)
W	She was testifying for the prosecution a couple of hours ago in this courtroom.
P	WHAT happened after you met Ms. Younger? (4)
W	We spent a couple of hours at the bar and had some drinks.
P	WHAT happened next? (4)
W	We went to my apartment.
P	WHAT happened then? (4)
W	We had a couple of more drinks there, and she spent the night.
P	WHAT, if anything, happened that night? (5)
W	We had sex.
P	WHAT do you mean by "we had sex"? (5)
W	We had intercourse.
P	WHAT was your legal relation to Ms. Younger at that time? (5)
W	We didn't have any legal relation. We weren't married or engaged or anything like that.
P	HOW long had you known her before she had intercourse with you? (5)
W	A couple of hours.
P	WHAT force did you use to get her to consent to intercourse? (5)
W	None.

P	WHAT threats did you make against her? (5)
W	None. She did it of her own free will.
P	WHAT happened the next morning? (5)
W	She just left. I didn't see her again until today when I walked into the courtroom.

Notice that at the end of this line of questioning, the proponent does not ask the witness to opine whether Ms. Younger has a propensity for extra-marital intercourse or whether her propensity increases the probability that she consented to intercourse with the defendant. It would be improper opinion for the witness to attempt to draw those inferences. Moreover, it is unnecessary for the proponent to invite the witness to draw the inferences; in the subsequent instructions the judge will tell the jury that they are to decide whether to draw the inferences, and in summation the proponent may expressly argue in favor of those inferences.

When the testimony is admitted, during the final jury charge, or on both occasions, the judge might tell the jury the following about the evidence:

> One of the questions in this case is whether Ms. Younger consented to sexual intercourse with the defendant. Evidence has been presented that on another occasion, the alleged victim consented to intercourse with Mr. Norton, another man she was not married to. You may consider that evidence in deciding whether Ms. Younger gave her consent to intercourse with the defendant.

During closing argument, the defense counsel could state:

> Ladies and gentlemen, as I told you in opening statement, Mr. Lowe admits having had sex with Ms. Younger. It's not a crime to have sex with someone. It's a crime only if you force them to have sex with you. And, again as I said during opening, the only real question in this case is whether Ms. Younger agreed to have sex with Mr. Lowe. In a few minutes her Honor will give you the legal instructions that you must follow during your deliberations in this case. One of those instructions relates to the testimony given by Mr. Norton earlier today. As you'll recall, Mr. Norton told you that in November of last year, he met Ms. Younger at a bar and that later that night they had consensual sex. In her instructions, her Honor will tell you that you may consider Mr. Norton's testimony in deciding whether Ms. Younger consented to having sex with Mr. Lowe. Let's talk about Mr. Norton's testimony. Consider all the striking similarities between Ms. Younger's contact with Mr. Norton and her contact with Mr. Lowe. The incidents occur very close in time. She ran into Mr. Norton in early November of last year. She met Mr. Lowe in the middle of the following month, December. In both cases, the men were complete strangers to her. Mr. Norton testified that he'd never met Ms. Younger before that night, just as Mr. Lowe testified and freely admitted that he'd never seen Ms. Younger before. Both men meet her at a local bar and have a couple of drinks with her. On both occasions, she freely agrees to accompany them to their apartments. And both times she has sex with them at the apartment. Mr. Norton testified in no uncertain terms that Ms. Younger consented to sex that night. Mr. Lowe took

the stand, looked you in the eye, and told you that she also consented that night. There are so many parallels between the two incidents that Mr. Norton's testimony confirms Mr. Lowe's testimony. The evidence shows that she consented in November, and the only reasonable conclusion is that a few weeks later in strikingly similar circumstances she consented again.

In federal practice, Rule 412, the rape shield law, governs defense attacks on the character of the alleged victim in sex offense prosecutions. Rule 412(b)(1)(B) states that evidence of "specific instances of a victim's sexual behavior with respect to the person accused of the sexual conduct" is admissible "to prove consent." In contrast, evidence of the alleged victim's sexual conduct with third parties is generally inadmissible. Most courts have construed "sexual behavior" with third parties broadly as encompassing: activities involving actual physical contact such as intercourse, activities such as the use of contraceptives which imply sexual intercourse, and even some mental activities such as sexual fantasies and viewing pornography. However, Rule 412(b) lists a number of exceptions permitting the proponent to introduce evidence of the alleged victim's other sexual behavior. Suppose, for example, that in order to corroborate the victim's testimony that the defendant forced her to have intercourse, the prosecution introduced a physician's testimony that a vaginal swab revealed the presence of semen. Under Rule 412(b)(1)(A), to provide an alternative, innocent explanation for the physician's testimony, the defense could establish that the alleged victim had intercourse with a third party such a short time before the scientific test that the semen resulting from that intercourse could still have been present at the time of the test.

Evidence Proffered by the Prosecution or a Civil Litigant

In 1995, Congress approved three amendments to the Federal Rules of Evidence. The amendments added three new rules, Rules 413–415, the rape sword laws. Rule 413(a) reads:

> In a criminal case in which the defendant is accused of an offense of sexual assault, the court may admit evidence that the defendant committed any other sexual assault. The evidence may be considered on any matter to which it is relevant.

Rule 414(a) sets out a similar provision for child molestation prosecutions, and Rule 415(a) comes into play in any "civil case involving a claim for relief based on a party's alleged sexual assault or child molestation." Under this legislation, a prosecutor or civil litigant may introduce testimony about a specific act of misconduct on a character theory even if the other side did not open up the issue of character. As proponent, the prosecutor or civil litigant would lay a foundation with the following elements:

1. Where the event occurred.

2. When the event occurred.

3. Who was involved. The proponent would have to show that the perpetrator of the sexual assault or molestation was the accused or the opposing civil litigant. Given *Huddleston v. United States*, 485 U.S. 681, 108 S. Ct. 1496, 99 L. Ed. 2d 771 (1988), the court would probably hold that Federal Rule of Evidence

104(b) governs this foundational fact.

4. What happened—a sexual assault under Rule 413 or 415 or a child molestation under Rule 414 or 415. Rule 413(d) sets out a broad definition of an offense of "sexual assault," and Rule 414(d) is a corresponding statutory definition of an offense of "child molestation." Those definitions apply under Rule 415.

5. The similarities between the pleaded sexual assault or molestation and the unpleaded assault or molestation. On their face, the text of the amendments does not require any showing of similarity other than proof that both acts are sexual assaults or molestations. However, even after the 2011 restyling the title of each statute includes the adjective, "[s]imilar." Moreover, as a practical matter, the proponent would almost always want to emphasize the similarities. To begin with, a showing of extensive similarities would make the evidence less vulnerable to an objection under Federal Rule of Evidence 403. To date, most courts have assumed that Rule 403 applies to evidence otherwise admissible under Rules 413–415. Moreover, in closing argument, on a character theory the proponent will urge the jury to treat the unpleaded act as circumstantial proof of the conduct of the accused or civil party; and the jury will ordinarily find the act more probative on that theory if there are numerous similarities between the pleaded and unpleaded acts.

Assume that the plaintiff, Ms. Chang, brings a tort action against the defendant Mr. Keeton. The complaint alleges that the defendant committed a sexual assault against Ms. Chang on December 10, YR-3. The complaint alleges that the assault occurred in the defendant's car in the parking lot of the Castle Restaurant on Hoffman Avenue. Ms. Chang has already testified that she knew the defendant because they both were members of a skiing club. Ms. Chang testified that the defendant invited her to dinner and a movie and that he assaulted her in his car after they left the restaurant to leave for the movie. Ms. Chang testified that after they both entered the car, he reached over and without permission began kissing her on the mouth and fondling her breasts. Ms. Chang testified that when she resisted, he called her a "prude" and insisted that she exit the car. The defendant then drove away. The next witness is Ms. Leslie. Ms. Leslie has already identified herself. The plaintiff is the proponent.

P   Ms. Leslie, WHERE were you on December 1, YR-3?

W   I was at home that evening.

P   WHAT phone calls, if any, did you receive that night?

W   The defendant called me.

P   HOW do you know the defendant? (3), (5)

W   We both belong to the Active 20–30 Club here in Peoria.

P   Prior to December 1, YR-3, HOW long had you known him? (3)

W   About six months.

P   HOW many times had you spoken with him? (3)

W	Maybe 10 or 12 times. We had met and chatted at some of the activities sponsored by the club.
P	HOW do you know that it was the defendant who called that night? (3)
W	I recognized his voice. We'd met and spoken several times before.
P	When the defendant called that night, WHAT did he say? (5)
W	He invited me to dinner and a movie the next evening.
P	HOW did you respond to the invitation?
W	I said that I'd be delighted to. He seemed like a nice enough guy.
P	WHAT happened the next evening? (2), (5)
W	He picked me up at my condo and initially took me to a local restaurant.
P	WHICH restaurant was that? (1), (5)
W	The Castle Restaurant.
P	WHERE is the restaurant located? (1), (5)
W	It's at the corner of Hoffman and 17th.
P	WHAT happened after you arrived at the restaurant? (5)
W	We had a nice time in the restaurant. We both had a good meal, and he was the perfect gentleman while we were there.
P	WHAT happened after you finished eating? (4), (5)
W	We left the restaurant to go to the movie. We stepped outside the restaurant and walked to where we were parked. When we got to the car, he opened my door first. Then he walked over to the driver's side and got into the car.
P	WHAT, if anything, happened then? (4), (5)
W	As soon he got into the car, with no warning at all he reaches over, grabs me, and starts kissing me.
P	WHERE did he grab you? (4), (5)
W	He had one arm around my waist, and he put his other hand on my left breast. I was shocked that he was groping me.
P	WHERE did he kiss you? (4), (5)
W	Right on the mouth.
P	WHAT did you do then? (4), (5)
W	I shoved him back as hard as I could, and I told him in no uncertain terms to just knock it off. I was more than angry; I was outraged. I've never had an experience like that.
P	WHAT, if anything, did he say then? (4), (5)
W	To begin with, he acted as if he was upset. He had the nerve to call me a "prude." Then, to top it all off, he basically kicks me out of his car and

	drives off. I ended up taking an Uber home that night.
P	Ms. Leslie, please think carefully before you answer this question. WHO was the person who did that to you on the evening of December 2, YR-3? (3)
W	It was the defendant right over there.
P	WHERE is he sitting? (3)
W	He's at the table over there near the large window.
P	HOW is he dressed? (3)
W	He's wearing a brown suit, white shirt, and red tie.
P	Your Honor, please let the record reflect that the witness has identified the defendant.
J	It will so reflect.
P	Your Honor, I have no further questions of the witness at this time.

Notice that at the end of this line of questioning, the proponent does not attempt to elicit the witness's testimony that the defendant has a propensity to engage in sexual misconduct or that given that propensity, it is more probable that the defendant committed the charged offense. It would be improper opinion testimony for the witness to draw those inferences. It is the jury's province to decide whether to draw those inferences. Moreover, it is unnecessary for the proponent to invite the witness to draw those inferences; in the subsequent instructions the judge will tell the jury that they are to decide whether to draw the inferences, and during summation the proponent may expressly argue in favor of the inferences.

When this testimony is admitted, during the final jury charge, or on both occasions, the judge could tell the jury the following about the evidence:

> Evidence has been introduced for the purpose of showing that the defendant engaged in a sexual offense on another occasion than that charged in this case. If you find that the defendant committed a prior sexual offense, you may, but are not required, to infer that the defendant has a disposition to commit the same type of sexual offense. If you find that the defendant has this disposition, you may treat it as some evidence that the defendant was likely to commit and did commit the crime he is charged with.

During closing argument, the prosecutor might state:

> Ladies and gentlemen, during the trial you heard the testimony of Ms. Leslie. You heard her describe a sexual assault—an assault made on Ms. Leslie by the defendant in December of last year. In a few minutes his Honor will read you the legal instructions that you have to follow during your deliberations in the case. He is going to tell you that in deciding the defendant's guilt or innocence of the sexual attack on Ms. Chang, you can consider Ms. Leslie's testimony. In particular, his Honor is going to tell you the following: "If you find that the defendant committed a prior sexual offense, you may, but are not required, to infer that the defendant had a disposition to commit the same type of criminal

offense. If you find that the defendant had this disposition, you may treat it as some evidence that he was likely to commit and did commit the crime" against Ms. Chang.

Ladies and gentlemen, with that instruction in mind, let's consider Ms. Leslie's testimony. Take a look at this chart. Think of all the striking similarities between the attack on Ms. Chang and the assault on Ms. Leslie: The attack on Ms. Chang occurred on December 2nd of last year. The attack on Ms. Leslie happened one day earlier—the very day before the attack on Ms. Chang. The attack on Ms. Chang occurred at the Castle Restaurant here in town on Huffman Avenue. That's the identical location of the assault on Ms. Leslie. Before the attack, the defendant got to know Ms. Chang because he joined the same ski club she was in. Prior to the assault on Ms. Leslie, she got to know her by joining the same Active 20–30 Club that she was a member of. The defendant invited Ms. Chang to dinner and a movie—the very same invitation he extended to Ms. Leslie. After dinner on the way to the movie, the defendant reaches over and begins trying to kiss Ms. Chang without her permission. That's also exactly what he did to Ms. Leslie. Next, he attempted to fondle Ms. Chang's breasts. He tried the same stunt with Ms. Leslie. When Ms. Chang told him to stop, he had the audacity to call her a "prude." That's the identical expression he used when Ms. Leslie told him to knock it off. When it was all over, the defendant dumped Ms. Chang and forced her to find her own way home. Again, that's the very same thing he did with Ms. Leslie. Ask yourselves, ladies and gentlemen: In the words of his Honor's instruction, did the defendant have "a disposition to commit the same type of sexual offense"? You bet he did. A leopard doesn't change its spots. The defendant did exactly the same thing just days before the attack on Ms. Chang. Ms. Leslie's testimony shows you the type of man the defendant is. He is exactly the kind of sexual predator who would commit the assault on Ms. Chang.

[5] CROSS-EXAMINATION OF A CHARACTER WITNESS

After the defense conducts the direct examination of a character witness, the prosecution has a right to cross-examine the witness.

Suppose that on direct examination, the witness testified that the accused had a reputation for peacefulness. Further assume that the prosecutor knows that the accused was arrested for a violent battery only two months before the alleged battery. The traditional view is that during the cross-examination, the prosecutor may ask; "Have you heard a report that the accused was arrested for battery in October YR-3?" If the witness denies hearing the report, the denial impeaches the witness; the denial indicates that the witness really is not familiar with the accused's reputation. If the witness admits hearing the report, the admission impeaches the witness; the admission indicates that the witness is biased or has a rather strange standard for evaluating good reputation. The prosecutor may inquire about reports that the accused committed or was arrested for, indicted for, or convicted of a crime. Of course, the crime must be logically relevant to the character trait the witness testified to on direct examination. The criminal act must be disreputable; its nature must be such that it calls into question the good reputation which the witness has testified to. Thus, if on direct examination the witness testified to the defendant's character trait of peacefulness, the prosecutor may not inquire about an arrest for mere drunkenness.

If the jurisdiction permits opinion character evidence and on direct examination the witness expresses his or her opinion, the traditional wording of the question on cross-examination is slightly different. The prosecutor no longer uses the "Have you heard . . . ?" formula. Rather, the prosecutor may ask; "Do you know that the accused was arrested for battery in October YR-3?" If the witness denies knowing about the arrest, the denial indicates that the witness may not know the accused well. If the witness admits knowing about the arrest, the admission indicates that the witness is biased or has a strange personal standard for evaluating good character. Again, the crime inquired about must be logically relevant to the character trait the witness testified to on direct examination.

Federal Rule of Evidence 405 governs character evidence in federal trials, and the Advisory Committee's Note to the Rule states that the Committee intended to abolish the old, formal distinctions in the phrasing of the questions on cross-examination. The Note asserts that the Committee intended to "eliminate them [the distinctions] as a factor in formulating questions." However, Rule 405 does not forbid the use of the older phrasing, and many attorneys continue to use the traditional wording. Thus, under the Federal Rules, it would still be permissible to use normal, cross-examination phrasing: "HAVEN'T YOU HEARD A REPORT THAT the accused was arrested for battery in October YR-3?"

Of course, in any jurisdiction, the prosecutor must have a good faith basis in fact for inquiring about the incident. The prosecutor cannot smear the accused's character by inventing derogatory reports about the accused. Hence, the prosecutor must have a basis in fact for believing that the accused committed, was arrested for, was indicted for, or was convicted of the crime. The basis in fact need not be independently admissible evidence. For example, the prosecutor could use an eyewitness's written statement or a police report as the basis in fact. The statement and report would normally be inadmissible hearsay, but they are sufficient to give the prosecutor a good faith belief that the incident occurred. When the defense attorney challenges the prosecutor to show the basis in fact for the belief that the incident occurred, the prosecutor usually makes a statement for the record outside the jurors' hearing—either at sidebar or during a period when the judge excuses the jury from the courtroom. In some jurisdictions, it is customary for the prosecutor to insert any documentary material into the record. The material is not admitted as a formal exhibit to be submitted to the jury, but it is sometimes marked for identification or marked as an appellate exhibit.

Assume that during cross-examination of a character witness, the prosecutor inquired about an arrest of the accused for battery. The prosecutor might have used the classic language: "Have you heard a report that the accused was arrested for battery in October YR-3?" As opponent, the defense counsel objects:

O   Your Honor, may we approach the bench?

J   Yes.

O   Your Honor, I want to object to the last question on the ground that the prosecutor hasn't shown a good faith basis in fact for believing that this arrest occurred.

P   Your Honor, I would like to mark this document as prosecution appellate exhibit number one.

O   What is that document?

P   It is an arrest report from the Salt Lake City Police Department. The report names the accused, George Larson, as the arrestee and states that he was arrested for battery on a Mr. Frank Statsky.

O   That report is inadmissible hearsay.

P   That would normally be true, but the material creating the basis in fact for believing the incident occurred need not qualify as admissible evidence.

J   I agree with the prosecutor. I will receive the appellate exhibit, and the objection to the question will be overruled.

P   Mr. Stacey, let me repeat the question. Have you heard a report that the accused was arrested for battery in October YR-3?

W   No.

Notice that at the end of this line of questioning, the proponent does not take a further step and ask: "Well, how then can you say that you know the defendant's reputation well?" It would be objectionably argumentative for the proponent to pose that question. Moreover, it is unnecessary for the proponent to put that question to the witness; in the subsequent instructions the judge will tell the jury that they can decide whether to draw the inference, and during summation the proponent may argue in favor of that inference.

When the cross-examiner asks a character witness about an incident, during the final jury charge, or on both occasions, the judge might tell the jury the following:

> When on cross-examination a witness is asked if he has heard reports of certain conduct of a defendant inconsistent with the traits of good character to which the witness has testified, these questions and the witness's answers to them may be considered only for the purpose of determining the weight to be given to the witness's testimony about the defendant's good reputation. These questions and answers are not evidence that the reports are true, and you must not assume from them that the defendant in fact committed the act inconsistent with those traits of character.

During closing argument, the prosecutor could state:

> Ladies and gentlemen, as you'll recall, the defense called a Mr. Stacey in an attempt to convince you that Mr. Larson is a peaceful person, not the type of man who would commit the violent battery that Mr. Larson is on trial for. In a few minutes, her Honor will read you the legal instructions that you must follow during your deliberations in this case. One of those instructions deals

with Mr. Stacey's character testimony. Her Honor is going to tell you that you don't have to accept Mr. Stacey's testimony; it's up to you to decide how much weight, if any, to give it. She's also going to instruct you that in making that decision, you can consider the way Mr. Stacey answered my questions on cross-examination. On cross-examination, I asked Mr. Stacey whether he'd heard a report that the defendant had been arrested for battery a mere two years ago. (Mr. Stacey said that he'd never heard any such report. Think about that answer. Mr. Stacey expects you to believe that he knows the defendant's reputation for peacefulness well, but he's never heard a report about a battery only two years ago. A battery is a violent crime, and word gets around— especially in a town as small as ours. Yet Mr. Stacey claims he never heard of the report. That answer tells you that Stacey really doesn't know the defendant's reputation well. If he knew the defendant's reputation well, he certainly would have heard about that report. And that's why you should reject Stacey's testimony.) *Or* (Stacey admitted that he had heard that report. Think about that answer. On the one hand, he testifies that the defendant had a good reputation for peacefulness, and he expects you to believe that he's a good judge of character. On the other hand, he admits that he's heard that the defendant was arrested for a battery a mere two years ago. Ladies and gentlemen, Mr. Stacey must have a pretty strange standard for deciding whether someone has a good reputation for peacefulness. When someone is reported to have committed a battery, most reasonable people would say that that person had a terrible reputation for peacefulness. But not Mr. Stacey. Either he has a crazy standard for judging character, or he's simply a biased witness. After all, he conceded on cross-examination that he and the defendant have been good friends for almost ten years. In either case, you just can't trust Stacey's testimony.)

§ 6.03   HABIT OR ROUTINE PRACTICE EVIDENCE

[1]   THE DOCTRINE

The proponent may use personal habit or routine practice evidence as well as character evidence as circumstantial proof of conduct. Federal Rule of Evidence 406 states the doctrine: "Evidence of a person's habit or an organization's routine practice may be admitted to prove that on a particular occasion the person or organization acted in accordance with the habit or routine practice. The court may admit the evidence regardless of whether it is corroborated or whether there was an eyewitness."

Although both character and habit/routine evidence serve as circumstantial proof of conduct, there are major differences between the two theories of admissibility.

The first difference is that although character evidence is usually admissible only after the criminal accused opens the issue, under the modern view either party in a civil or criminal case may introduce habit or routine practice evidence. It is true that some jurisdictions admit habit or routine evidence only if there are no eyewitnesses to the conduct in question or only when there is corroboration of the conduct. However, Rule

406 embodies the emerging view that habit or routine evidence is admissible to prove the conduct of a person or business organization.

The second difference is that while character evidence permits the proponent to prove general character or character traits, habit or routine evidence requires proof of a very specific, consistent, frequently repeated behavioral pattern. For instance, under the so-called probability theory of habit evidence, the proponent may prove the precise manner in which a decedent routinely executed right-hand turns or the specific mailing procedure a business customarily used. Some jurisdictions rely on a psychological theory of habit evidence and employ an even more restrictive definition of habit. In these jurisdictions, the courts limit the scope of habit to relatively automatic behavior such as the way a person ties his shoelaces. Some jurisdictions compromise by applying the automaticity requirement to evidence of personal habit but not to evidence of business routine.

Finally, the habit/routine and character evidence theories differ in the method of proof. The proponent of character evidence ordinarily presents reputation or opinion evidence. In contrast, the proponent of habit or routine evidence may not use reputation evidence. However, most jurisdictions sanction opinion character evidence, and opinion is the most common method of proving habit. To be qualified to express an opinion on the existence of a habit, the witness must have been familiar with the person or business for a substantial time and observed numerous instances of the person's or business' conduct. Opinion habit or routine practice evidence is typically presented by a single witness who is familiar with a large number of instances of the conduct of the person or business in question. Other jurisdictions permit habit to be proven by the testimony of several witnesses. Each witness testifies to the instances of conduct he or she knows of; if the behavioral pattern is specific enough and in aggregate the instances are sufficiently numerous, the judge allows the jury to infer the existence of the habit or routine. When the proponent opts for this method of proving the existence of a habit or routine, each witness's testimony must comply with the foundational requirements set out in § 6.02[4] of this chapter.

[2] ELEMENTS OF THE FOUNDATION

The foundation for opinion habit or routine practice evidence includes these elements:

1. The witness is familiar with the person or business.

2. The witness has been familiar with the person or business for a substantial period of time.

3. In the witness's opinion, the person or business has a personal habit or routine, a specific behavioral pattern.

4. The witness has observed the person or business act in conformity with the habit or routine on numerous occasions. It is ideal if the occasions are numerous in both an absolute and a relative sense. Absolutely, the proponent is on shaky ground if there are only a handful of instances on which the person acted in conformity with the alleged habit or routine. Relatively, the person

should have followed the behavioral pattern in a very high percentage of the occasions when he or she had an opportunity to do so. In the words of the Advisory Committee Note to Rule 406, habit is "one's regular response to a repeated specific situation."

In some jurisdictions, in addition to establishing these elements of the foundation, the proponent must show that:

5. The record indicates that there were no eyewitnesses to the person's or business' conduct on the occasion involved in the case; or

6. The record contains corroboration that the person or business acted in conformity with the habit or routine on the occasion involved in the case, *e.g.*, an eyewitness who described the person's conduct as consistent with the habit or routine.

[3] SAMPLE FOUNDATION

The fact situation is a tort action. The plaintiff sues the decedent's estate on the theory that the decedent negligently caused the traffic accident. The decedent is Mr. Myles. The collision occurred as the decedent was making a right-hand turn at a stop sign. The estate's personal representative contends that the decedent drove carefully. To support that contention, the representative desires to offer evidence of the decedent's driving habits. To do so, the representative calls Ms. Vincent, an acquaintance of the decedent. The decedent's personal representative is the proponent. Ms. Vincent has already identified herself.

P	WHO was Joshua Myles? (1)
W	He was a friend of mine. I know that he died in an accident about a year and a half ago.
P	HOW long did you know him? (2)
W	For about seven years.
P	HOW did you come to know him? (2)
W	We worked at the same bank. In fact, for a long time we were in the same car pool.
P	HOW many people were in this car pool? (2)
W	Three of us, Joshua, Kathy Jacobs, an assistant manager, and I.
P	HOW often did you see the decedent drive a car? (2)
W	Hundreds of times. I couldn't give you a precise number.
P	WHEN did you see him drive a car? (2)
W	He did a lot of the driving in our car pool; he regularly took me to and from work.
P	HOW many times a week did the decedent drive you to work? (2)
W	Usually twice.
P	HOW many weeks during the year did he drive you? (2)

W	About 50 per year. Of course, you have to exclude our vacation times.
P	HOW many years were you in this car pool? (2)
W	Roughly five years.
P	HOW many years was the decedent in this car pool? (2)
W	The same—five years.
P	WHAT did the decedent do when he came to a stop sign? (3)
W	He came to a complete stop.
P	HOW consistently did he do that? (4)
W	Always.
P	HOW often did you see him do that? (4)
W	Hundreds of times.
P	HOW did the decedent make right-hand turns after coming to a stop? (3)
W	He'd look both ways and start up only after he could see that it was safe.
P	HOW fast did he go immediately after starting up? (3)
W	Usually quite slowly and cautiously.
P	HOW often did you see him make a right-hand turn in that manner? (4)
W	All sorts of times.

At the end of this line of questioning, the proponent does not attempt to elicit the witness's opinion that given Myles' driving habit, it is more probable that he drove in the manner alleged in the pleadings. That testimony would amount to an improper opinion. It is unnecessary for the proponent to invite the witness to draw the inference; during the subsequent instructions the judge will instruct the jury that they can decide whether to draw that inference, and during summation the proponent may expressly argue in favor of the inference.

When the testimony is admitted, during the final jury charge, or on both occasions the trial judge might tell the jury the following about the evidence:

> Evidence has been presented of the decedent's driving habits. You can infer that a person acts consistently with their personal habits. Therefore, you may consider evidence of the decedent's driving habits in deciding how the decedent made his right-hand turn on the occasion when his car collided with the plaintiffs' car.

During closing argument, the defense attorney could state:

> Ladies and gentleman, as I told you in opening statement, this case boils down to the question of whether Mr. Myles used due care in making his right-hand turn at 1st and Martin Streets just before the collision with the plaintiff's car. When you discuss that question in the deliberation room, I want you to consider the testimony of Ms. Vincent. She was the witness who testified about Mr. Myles' driving habits. In a few minutes her Honor will give you the legal instructions that you must follow during your deliberations in this case. One of

those instructions concerns Ms. Vincent's testimony about Mr. Myles' driving habits. In the instructions, her Honor will tell you that you can consider Ms. Vincent's testimony in deciding how Mr. Myles made his right-hand turn that day. How much importance should you attach to her testimony? Think back to the undisputed testimony she gave you. She knew Mr. Myles well—for about seven years. They were in the same carpool to work together. Their carpool's route included the intersection of 1st and Martin, the very intersection where this collision occurred. They both were in the carpool for five years. Each year Mr. Myles drove for the carpool roughly 50 times. It's simple arithmetic: five years, 50 times, over 250 drives. And on each occasion, Mr. Myles always came to a complete stop at the stop sign. And on every occasion, he looked both ways before entering the intersection and started up only after it was clearly safe. In her words, he "didn't take chances. It was a busy intersection, and he didn't have any close calls there." Not just sometimes, not just most of the time, but "always"—that was the exact word she used. Common sense tells you that you ought to give Ms. Vincent's testimony a lot of weight. If Mr. Myles followed that practice so religiously so many times, it's ridiculous to think that he'd abandon it for no reason at all on the day of the collision.

§ 6.04   OTHER CRIMES OR UNCHARGED MISCONDUCT EVIDENCE

[1]   THE DOCTRINE

Unless Rules 413–14 apply, even in rebuttal to defense character evidence, the prosecution may not prove other crimes by the accused simply to prove that the accused is a law-breaking, immoral person. However, the prosecution may introduce such evidence for other purposes. As Federal Rule of Evidence 404(b) announces:

(1)   Prohibited Uses. Evidence of a crime, wrong, or other act is not admissible to prove a person's character in order to show that on a particular occasion the person in accordance with the character.[3]

(2)   Permitted Uses: . . . . This evidence may be admissible for another purpose, such as proving motive, opportunity, intent, preparation, plan, knowledge, identity, absence of mistake, or absence of accident.

Thus, if the evidence is logically relevant on a theory that does not require an assumption about the defendant's character, and the prosecution's need for the evidence outweighs its prejudicial character, the prosecution may introduce the proof of the uncharged act. The federal courts follow the inclusionary approach to the uncharged misconduct doctrine: The prosecution may offer the evidence on *any* theory of logical relevance other than the theory explicitly forbidden by Rule 404(b).

---

[3] A December 1, 2020 amendment to Rule 404(b) reworded subsection (b)(1) to read: "Evidence of any other crime, wrong, or act is not admissible to prove a person's character in order to show that on a particular occasion the person acted in accordance with the character." The amendment inserted "any other" before "crime." According to the Advisory Committee, the purpose of the amendment is to make it clear that the requirement for a showing of a non-character theory of logical relevance applies only when the conduct is not intrinsic to or part of the "crime, wrong, or act."

The prosecutor offering uncharged misconduct evidence faces two primary problems. First, the prosecutor must demonstrate that the evidence is logically relevant to a material fact in issue without positing an assumption about the accused's personal, subjective bad character. For instance, suppose that the accused is charged with a February 1st bank robbery. While fleeing from the crime scene, the robber dropped his pistol that bore a serial number. Without violating the character evidence prohibition, the prosecution could introduce evidence that on January 1st, the accused stole that very pistol from a local gun store. The evidence of the earlier larceny puts the accused in possession of the same, one-of-a-kind instrumentality used to perpetrate the charged crime.

Today one particular noncharacter theory, the doctrine of objective chances, is growing in importance. Suppose that a defendant charged with infanticide claims that the child's death was an accident. Invoking the doctrine, the prosecution may introduce evidence that several other children in the defendant's custody suffered the same fate under similar circumstances. The prosecution can argue that it is not relying on a forbidden inference as to the defendant's personal, subjective bad character; rather, the inference of actus reus arises from the objective improbability of so many accidents befalling the same innocent person. *United States v. Woods*, 484 F.2d 127 (4th Cir. 1973), *cert. denied*, 415 U.S. 979, 94 S. Ct. 1566, 39 L. Ed. 2d 875 (1974). The courts also apply the doctrine to allow the admission of similar acts to prove the defendant's mens rea. Admittedly, innocent persons sometimes find themselves enmeshed in suspicious circumstances. However, the more frequently the defendant is found in possession of contraband drugs, the stronger is the inference that on one or some of the occasions the defendant knowingly possessed the drugs. Finally, prosecutors are starting to resort to the theory to justify the admission of uncharged misconduct to prove identity. Here their contention is that it is objectively implausible that numerous persons would independently accuse the defendant of similar misconduct; it is objectively unlikely that all the accusers are fabricating. Imwinkelried, *The Evidentiary Issue Crystalized by the Cosby and Weinstein Scandals: The Propriety of Admitting Testimony About an Accused's Uncharged Misconduct Under the Doctrine of Objective Chances to Prove Identity*, 48 Sw. U. L. Rev. 1 (2019).

Second, the prosecutor should argue that the prosecution's legitimate need for the evidence outweighs its prejudicial character. To be sure, such evidence is highly prejudicial, and there is a grave danger that the jurors will misuse it as evidence of the accused's bad, law-breaking disposition. The defense can attempt to reduce the prosecution's need to resort to uncharged misconduct evidence by tendering a stipulation to the fact which the prosecution claims the evidence is relevant to. *Old Chief v. United States*, 519 U.S. 172, 117 S. Ct. 644, 136 L. Ed. 2d 574 (1997). However, if the element of the crime which the prosecution wants to offer the uncharged misconduct evidence to prove is disputed, the judge will likely admit the evidence. Hence, if the prosecution wants to offer the evidence to prove identity and the accused denied committing the crime, the judge would probably rule in the prosecution's favor.

[2]   ELEMENTS OF THE FOUNDATION

The foundation includes these elements:

1.   Where the other act occurred.

2.   When the act occurred.

3.   What the nature of the act was.

4.   The defendant committed the other act. In *Huddleston v. United States*, 485 U.S. 681, 108 S. Ct. 1496, 99 L. Ed. 2d 771 (1988), the Court held that Rule 104(b) governs this foundational fact. The judge accepts the prosecution's foundational evidence at face value and asks only whether the evidence is sufficient to create a permissive inference that the accused committed the act. However, a significant minority of states take a different view because they deem this type of evidence to be so highly prejudicial. These states treat the issue as a Rule 104(a) question, and some even insist that the judge find that the accused committed the act by clear and convincing evidence.

5.   The surrounding circumstances making the uncharged act relevant to the charged crime. More specifically, the prosecutor must convince the trial judge that the act is logically relevant to a material fact without positing an assumption about the defendant's criminal disposition or propensity.

Even after the prosecutor lays a proper foundation, the defense counsel will have a right to a limiting instruction. Under Rule 105, the judge must inform the jury that they may not use the evidence as general character evidence; rather, the jury must use the evidence only in deciding the existence of the fact the judge admitted the evidence to prove, *e.g.*, motive, intent, or identity. During closing argument, the prosecution may mention the evidence only in connection with the noncharacter theory of logical relevance.

[3]   SAMPLE FOUNDATION

Suppose that the government has charged the accused, Mr. Standish, with armed robbery in June of this year. During the prosecution case-in-chief, a single eyewitness identified the accused as the robber. A police officer also testified on behalf of the prosecution. He testified that he searched the crime scene and found a .32 caliber pistol with the serial number, 789444. During the defense case-in-chief, the accused testified and denied committing the robbery. During the prosecution rebuttal, the prosecution calls Mr. Usher. Mr. Usher has already identified himself. The prosecution is the proponent.

P   WHAT is your occupation?

W   I own a gun store.

P   WHERE were you on March 15th of this year? (1), (2)

W   I was at work at my store.

P   WHAT, if anything, happened that day? (3)

W   I was the victim of a theft that day.

P	WHAT was stolen? (5)
W	A pistol.
P	WHAT pistol? (5)
W	It was a .32 caliber pistol, serial number 789444.
P	HOW do you know that? (5)
W	I handle all my inventory personally, and I refreshed my memory by reviewing my records before trial.
P	HOW was the pistol stolen? (4)
W	A guy came in, in broad daylight, pretended he was looking to buy, and then grabbed the pistol and ran out the door.
P	HOW well did you see the thief? (4)
W	Very well.
P	HOW close were you to the thief? (4)
W	When he was at the counter, he was only about five feet away.
P	HOW much time did you have to observe the thief? (4)
W	He was in the store for at least a couple of minutes.
P	WHO was the thief? (4)
W	I'm not sure of his name, but I see him in the courtroom right now.
P	WHERE is he sitting? (4)
W	At that table over there.
P	HOW is he dressed? (4)
W	He's wearing a blue suit and green tie.
P	Your Honor, may the record reflect that the witness has identified the accused?
J	It will so reflect.
P	Your Honor, at this point, I would request a limiting instruction.
J	I will grant the request. Ladies and gentlemen of the jury, you have just heard testimony that the accused stole a pistol, serial number 789444. You may not infer from that evidence that the accused is generally a bad person and, for that reason, more likely to have committed the robbery. However, there is evidence that a pistol with that serial number was found at the robbery scene. You may use Mr. Usher's testimony in deciding whether the accused had possession of that pistol before the robbery.

At the end of this line of questioning, the proponent does not attempt to elicit the witness's testimony that it is therefore more likely that the defendant committed the charged offense. That testimony would amount to improper opinion. It is unnecessary for the proponent to invite the witness to draw that inference; during the subsequent instructions the judge will instruct the jury that they can decide whether to draw the inference, and during summation the proponent may expressly argue in favor of the inference.

When the testimony is admitted, during the final jury charge, or on both occasions the judge might tell the jury the following about the evidence:

> Evidence has been introduced for the purpose of showing that the defendant committed a crime other than the one he is presently on trial for. This evidence, if believed, may not be considered by you to show that the defendant is a person of bad character or that he has a disposition to commit crimes. It may be considered by you only for the limited purpose of determining if it tends to show the identity of the person who committed the crime of which the defendant is presently accused.

During closing argument, the prosecutor could state:

> Ladies and gentlemen, the key issue in this case is identity. This case boils down to the question of whether the defendant is the person who committed the armed robbery at the liquor store. In deciding that question, I want you to especially consider the testimony of three witnesses. One witness was Officer Salcido. He testified that he arrived at the crime scene a few minutes after the robber made his getaway. Right there on the floor of the liquor store he found People's Exhibit #2—the .32 caliber pistol, serial number 789444, which I'm holding right now. The second witness, the liquor store owner, Mr. Vermont, told you that he doesn't even own a gun, much less keep one in the store. And liquor store customers don't go around tossing guns on the floor of the store. Mr. Vermont told you that when the alarm went off, the robber panicked; Mr. Vincent saw the robber drop this pistol and run out of the store. Ladies and gentlemen, it's undisputed—this is the pistol the armed robber used. Now think back to the testimony by the third witness, Mr. Usher. He took the stand and told you that he owns a gun store downtown. He testified that in March of this year, a man came to his store—a man he recognizes as the defendant. More importantly, he testified that the defendant grabbed a pistol and ran out of the store. Mr. Usher immediately checked his records. And guess what? There was only one missing gun, a .32 caliber pistol, serial number 789444. This is People's Exhibit #3, Mr. Usher's inventory sheet. It lists all weapons in Mr. Usher's inventory that day. You're going to have this exhibit in the deliberation room. Check it against exhibit #2. You'll see that the number matches perfectly. There's only one pistol out there that perfectly fits that description. It's this one. This is the pistol the defendant stole from Mr. Usher, and it's the same one he used to rob Mr. Vermont. Put the testimony of Officer Salcido, Mr. Vermont, and Mr. Usher together, and what do you get? You get the only reasonable conclusion, namely, that the defendant is the man who robbed the liquor store. In a few minutes, her Honor will give you the legal instructions you have to follow during your deliberations. One of those instructions relates to Mr. Usher's testimony. In her Honor's words, you can consider that testimony "if

it tends to show the identity of the person who committed the crime of which the defendant is presently accused." I want you to do exactly what her Honor is going to tell you to do. Think about Mr. Usher's testimony when you deliberate on the question of the identity of the robber. If you do that, I'm confident you'll find that the defendant was the robber and that the defendant is guilty as charged.

§ 6.05   UNCHARGED MISCONDUCT EVIDENCE IN CIVIL ACTIONS

[1]   THE DOCTRINE

Rule 404(b) refers not only to evidence of other "crime[s]" but also to evidence of other "wrong[s] . . . or other act[s]."[4] Moreover, while some statutes such as Rule 404(a)(2) are expressly limited to criminal actions, there is no such limitation in Rule 404(b). Therefore, Rule 404(b) should apply to civil actions as well as prosecutions. In a prosecution, the government may not use evidence of an accused's other crimes as circumstantial proof of conduct; the prosecution may not argue that the accused has a bad character and that his bad character increases the probability that he committed the charged crime. Similarly, in a tort action, the plaintiff may not use evidence of a defendant's other torts as circumstantial proof of conduct; the plaintiff may not argue that the defendant is a careless driver and that his character trait of careless driving increases the likelihood that he ran the red light. To this extent, the criminal and civil cases are parallel.

However, in another respect, the civil cases differ from the criminal cases. As stated in the last section, in contemporary criminal cases most courts follow the inclusionary approach; they permit the prosecutor to rely on any noncharacter theory of logical relevance. They do so because Rule 404(b) prefaces the list of acceptable theories of logical relevance with the words, "such as." In practice, though, in civil cases many jurisdictions still follow an exclusionary approach that was popular at common law; they insist that the proponent of other misconduct in a civil case bring the evidence within a previously recognized pigeonhole exception such as proof of a defendant's earlier notice of the existence of a dangerous condition. However, the use of an exclusionary approach violates Rule 404(b). As the preceding paragraph pointed out, the text of Rule 404(b) is not restricted to prosecutions; and Rule 404(b) codifies an inclusionary approach. In the past, the courts have in effect looked to Rule 403 as a source of authority to continue to enforce the rigid, common-law restrictions on the admission of a defendant's other torts. It is a mistake to treat Rule 403 in that fashion; to reconcile Rules 402 and 403, Rule 403 must be construed as contemplating ad hoc, case-specific balancing rather than as a source of power to promulgate general exclusionary rules. Rather than enforcing a general exclusionary rule under Rule 403, the courts should test the admissibility of the evidence under Rule 404(b). As the more specific statute, Rule 404(b) controls. Hence, like a criminal prosecutor, the proponent of uncharged misconduct in a civil case should be permitted to introduce the evidence on any noncharacter theory. Rule 404(b) prescribes the inclusionary approach for civil

---

[4] For discussion of an amendment to 404(b)(1) that took effect on December 1, 2020, *see* § 6.04.

actions as well as criminal prosecutions. Hence, a civil proponent should be able to rely on any theory of logical relevance other than the general inference that the person's other negligent or wrongful acts increase the likelihood of fault on the pleaded occasion. The federal cases increasingly apply Rule 404(b) in civil cases.[5] Modernly, civil plaintiffs frequently offer evidence of a defendant's other misdeeds to establish the tortious intent necessary for a recovery of punitive damages.[6]

[2] ELEMENTS OF THE FOUNDATION

The list of foundational elements is the same as the list for uncharged misconduct evidence in criminal cases:

1. Where the other act occurred.

2. When the act occurred.

3. What the nature of the act was.

4. The defendant committed the other act.

5. The surrounding circumstances make the unpleaded act relevant to the pleaded act.

Again, the proponent must convince the trial judge that the act is logically relevant to a material fact without positing an assumption about the defendant's disposition or propensity.

[3] SAMPLE FOUNDATION

The fact situation is a wrongful discharge action. The plaintiff, Morrison, contends that the defendant, Ziegler, fired him because the plaintiff is Afro-American. The complaint alleges that the defendant employed the plaintiff as a Shop Supervisor and that the defendant fired the plaintiff on May 12, YR-3. The defendant purchased the company in YR-4. As his next witness, the plaintiff calls Mr. Foote. Mr. Foote has already identified himself.

P	WHERE do you work?
W	At the moment, I'm unemployed.
P	WHAT was your last job? (4), (5)
W	I worked for the defendant, Ron Ziegler.
P	WHERE is he now? (4)
W	In the courtroom. He's sitting at the table to my right. He's got on a brown suit.
P	Your Honor, please let the record reflect that the witness has identified the defendant.
J	It will so reflect.

---

[5] Annot., 64 A.L.R. Fed. 648 (1983); 2 IMWINKELRIED, UNCHARGED MISCONDUCT EVIDENCE 2022 EDITION Ch. 7 (2021).

[6] State Farm Mut. Auto. Ins. Co. v. Campbell, 538 U.S. 408, 123 S. Ct. 1513, 155 L. Ed. 2d 585 (2003).

P	WHAT type of work did you do for the defendant? (5)
W	I was a Shop Supervisor from YR-8 to YR-3. I worked on the assembly line from YR-17 to YR-8.
P	WHY did you stop working for him? (3)
W	He fired me.
P	WHEN did he do that? (2)
W	It was in late April YR-3.
P	WHERE did it happen? (1)
W	One day over the public address system he just called me into his office. I reported there as soon as I heard the call.
P	WHAT happened after you reported to his office? (3)
W	He said he was firing me.
P	WHAT did you do then? (5)
W	I demanded an explanation. I was pretty angry. I'd put in a lot of good years at that company, and I wanted to know why he was letting me go.
P	WHAT, if anything, did the defendant say when you demanded an explanation? (5)
W	It was just the two of us in the room. He said he was letting me go because I was Afro-American and had been "stirring up" the other Afro-American employees. He said he didn't like me; and since there were no witnesses to our conversation, he didn't mind telling me to my face the real reason he was giving me my walking papers.
O	Your Honor, may we approach the bench?
J	Certainly.
O	Your Honor, I move to strike this entire line of questioning on the ground that it's irrelevant and that it amounts to bad character evidence.
P	May I be heard?
J	Yes.
P	Your Honor, I'm not going to offer this evidence to support a general inference that the defendant is a bad person. I know that it would violate Rule 404(b). Rather, I'm offering this evidence on a noncharacter theory of logical relevance. The defendant fired Mr. Foote a few days before he fired the plaintiff. Like the plaintiff, Mr. Foote is an Afro-American. Given the surrounding circumstances, including the defendant's statements to Mr. Foote, the firing of Mr. Foote shows that the defendant had a racial prejudice that motivated him to fire Afro-American employees. In this case, we have to show that the defendant fired the plaintiff because he was Afro-American, and this April incident tends to show the defendant's later intent. Rule 404(b)(2) expressly mentions "motive" as

a permissible purpose for introducing 404(b) evidence.

J   I agree. Motion to strike denied.

O   If you're going to overrule my motion, will you at least give the jury a limiting instruction?

J   Of course. I'll tell them that they can't use it as proof that your client is a bad person. I'll direct them to consider the evidence only in deciding why your client discharged the plaintiff.

At the end of this line of questioning, the proponent did not attempt to elicit the witness's testimony that given the prior incident, it is more probable that the defendant's termination of the plaintiff was motivated by racial discrimination. That testimony would amount to improper opinion. It is unnecessary for the proponent to invite the witness to draw that inference; during the subsequent instructions the trial judge will tell the jurors that they can decide whether to draw the inference, and during summation the proponent may expressly argue in favor of the inference.

When the testimony is admitted, during the final jury charge, or on both occasions the judge might tell the jury the following about the evidence:

Evidence has been introduced to show that the defendant discriminated against an employee other than the defendant. This evidence, if believed, may not be considered by you to prove that the defendant is a bad person or that he has a disposition to perform illegal acts. It may be considered by you only for the limited purpose of determining whether it shows that the defendant has a bias against a class of persons that includes the plaintiff. Does the evidence tend to show the defendant's motive for firing the plaintiff?

During closing argument, the plaintiff's attorney could state:

Ladies and gentlemen, as I told you in opening statement, there wouldn't be any denying that Mr. Morrison worked for the defendant or that the defendant fired him this May. As I said then, this case was going to boil down to one question: Why did the defendant fire Mr. Morrison? What was the defendant's motive? Did the defendant fire Mr. Morrison because Mr. Morrison is an Afro-American? In a few minutes her Honor will read you the legal instructions that you must follow during your deliberations. One of those instructions relates to some of the key testimony in this case, the testimony given by Mr. Foote. As you'll recall, Mr. Foote told you what happened when the defendant fired him. That firing also occurred in May of this year. In her instructions her Honor will tell you that you may consider Mr. Foote's testimony in deciding why the defendant let Mr. Morrison go. Mr. Foote told you that, like Mr. Morrison, he had worked for the defendant for years. Like Mr. Morrison, Mr. Foote was called into the defendant's private office. There the defendant flabbergasted Mr. Foote. With absolutely no advance warning, the defendant gives Mr. Foote his walking papers; and to add insult to injury, the defendant told him point blank that he was firing Mr. Foote because he's Afro-American! Now think about it, ladies and gentlemen. This all happened a few weeks before the defendant fired Mr. Morrison. And remember that we're talking about racial bias. Racial bias runs deep. It takes years for those attitudes to build up, and they last and last and last. You're not a bigot one day and a completely tolerant person the next day. If the defendant acted out of racial bias when he fired Mr. Foote, it stands to reason that he did the same thing when he fired Mr. Morrison a mere six days later. Following her Honor's instruction. Consider Mr. Foote's testimony; and when you do, you'll come to the only reasonable conclusion, namely, that the defendant fired Mr. Morrison out of pure, bigoted racism.

§ 6.06   SIMILAR HAPPENINGS EVIDENCE

[1]   THE DOCTRINE

In the last section, we saw that Rule 404(b) applies in a civil case when a party offers evidence of a person's misdeeds that are not mentioned in the pleadings. The first sentence of Rule 404(b) bars the party from using the misdeeds as circumstantial proof of the person's conduct, but the second sentence permits the party to use noncharacter theories of logical relevance to introduce evidence of the misdeeds. Whether the case is a prosecution or a civil action, under Rule 404(b) the focus is on the conduct of some person.

In other cases, the focus is on the qualities or properties of a physical object. Was a sidewalk cracked at the time the plaintiff slipped and fell? Was a steering wheel's design dangerously defective? To prove the quality of the object, the plaintiff may attempt to introduce evidence of other accidents involving the same or similar objects.[7] For example, the plaintiff may offer evidence that the day before her mishap, another passerby slipped and fell at the same location on the sidewalk.

On the one hand, Rule 404(b) arguably does not apply directly when a plaintiff offers evidence of such a similar happening. Rule 404(b) comes into play when the party offers evidence of another incident to prove a person's conduct. The focus is now on the property of an object rather than any conduct by a person. On the other hand, like evidence of a person's misdeeds used as circumstantial proof of the person's conduct, evidence of the other slip and fall poses probative dangers. The presentation of the testimony about the other accident may confuse the trier of fact, consume an undue amount of time, and sidetrack the trial. For that reason, although the evidence of the other slip and fall is relevant to prove the existence of the crack in the sidewalk, the judge might exclude the evidence under Rule 403.

In the past, many, if not most, courts adopted an exclusionary approach to the admission of evidence of other accidents in civil cases. The courts announced a general rule that such evidence is inadmissible. The courts recognized only a limited number of exceptions to the general rule; they permitted plaintiffs to introduce evidence of other torts to show that: (1) a particular physical condition existed at the time of plaintiff's accident; (2) the condition was dangerous or defective; (3) the defendant had noticed

---

[7] Article, *Similar Facts Evidence: Balancing Probative Value Against the Probable Dangers of Admission*, 9 U.C. DAVIS L. REV. 395 (1976).

that the condition existed; or (4) the condition caused the accident. Further, even if the evidence otherwise fell within an exception to the general exclusionary rule, the plaintiff had to demonstrate that the conditions obtaining at the time of the pleaded accident were substantially similar to the circumstances surrounding the unpleaded tort, especially when the plaintiff offered the evidence for purpose (4).

The courts have begun to liberalize the standards for admitting evidence of other torts and accidents. In *Ault v. International Harvester Co.*, 13 Cal. 3d 113, 117 Cal. Rptr. 812, 528 P.2d 1148 (1974), the plaintiff claimed that he was injured when the gear box of the vehicle manufactured by the defendant failed. The plaintiff offered evidence of several other accidents involving the defendant's motor vehicle and seemingly caused by metal fatigue of the aluminum gear box. However, the plaintiff did not introduce any other evidence of the circumstances surrounding the other accidents. On appeal, the California Supreme Court held that the evidence of the other accidents was admissible. One commentator writes:[8]

> *Ault* . . . creates an exception to the general rule. . . . This exception permits evidence of a prior or subsequent accident in a defective-product-strict-liability case without a showing of similarity of circumstances . . . if the defect claimed is that of the physical and mechanical characteristics of a product, and the evidence of the prior or subsequent accident establishes that the product involved in such accident and the product involved in the accident in question possessed inherent similarities in their physical and mechanical characteristics, and that the two products possessed similar defects because of the product's physical and mechanical characteristics that caused the two accidents. If these conditions are satisfied, it is of no moment that the two accidents may have occurred under substantially different circumstances or conditions.

[2] ELEMENTS OF THE FOUNDATION

The foundation is similar to the foundation for evidence of an uncharged crime in a prosecution or tort offered under Rule 404(b):

1. Where the other accident occurred.

2. When the accident occurred.

3. What the nature of the accident was.

4. The defendant's responsibility for the accident.

5. The surrounding circumstances making the unpleaded happening relevant to show the property or quality of the object mentioned in the pleading.

[3] SAMPLE FOUNDATION[9]

The plaintiff has already testified. During her testimony the plaintiff testified that she was driving north on a freeway and entered an off-ramp leading to the eastbound lane

---

[8] 1 B. JEFFERSON, CALIFORNIA EVIDENCE BENCHBOOK § 21.65, at 324–25 (3d ed. 1997). *See also* 1 B. JEFFERSON, CALIFORNIA EVIDENCE BENCHBOOK § 21.74, at 21-54–21-55 (4th ed. rev. 2014).

[9] Adapted from 2 IMWINKELRIED, UNCHARGED MISCONDUCT EVIDENCE 2022 EDITION § 9:31 (2021). Reprinted with permission.

of a street near the freeway. She described the off-ramp as turning to the right, sloping slightly uphill, and being approximately 2,000 feet in length. The plaintiff stated that the steering wheel froze when her car was halfway through the off-ramp. The plaintiff used a chart to illustrate her testimony.

The plaintiff's attorney calls Mr. Dorsey to testify about another accident involving Dorsey's YR-3 Polecat Centuria with a stick shift. The purpose of Dorsey's testimony is to show the existence of a defect in the Centuria's steering mechanism.

Assume that the witness has already identified himself. As in the criminal case, the next part of the direct examination establishes the witness's personal knowledge of the uncharged accident.

P	WHERE were you on the morning of September 19th?
W	I drove from my home in San Lorenzo to downtown Livermore. (1), (2)
P	WHO was driving the car?
W	I was.

(The next part of the direct examination is devoted to showing the similarity of circumstances between the uncharged accident and the accident alleged in the pleading. The plaintiff wants to demonstrate that the physical layout of the site of the uncharged accident is comparable to that of the pleaded accident.)

P	WHAT route did you take?
W	I drove Highway 580 most of the way. (1)
P	In WHAT direction were you driving on Highway 580? (1)
W	I was traveling east.
P	WHEN did you get off Highway 580? (2)
W	I tried to get off at the exit for traffic going south on Hanley Avenue.
P	HOW can you remember that exit?
W	I use it all the time when I go into Livermore.
P	Your Honor, I request that this be marked plaintiff's exhibit number four for identification.
J	It will be so marked.
P	Please let the record reflect that I am showing the exhibit to the opposing counsel.
J	The record will so reflect.
P	I request permission to approach the witness.
J	Permission granted.
P	Mr. Dorsey, I now hand you what has been marked plaintiff's exhibit number four for identification. WHAT is it? (1)

W	It's a map showing Highway 580 and the off-ramp for Hanley going south.
P	HOW can you recognize it? (1)
W	As I said, I've used that off-ramp lots of times.
P	When you enter this off-ramp, in WHAT direction are you traveling?
W	At first, you're still going east.
P	Please use this blue marker and write "east" at the mouth of the off-ramp.
W	Yes.
P	Your Honor, please let the record reflect that the witness has complied with my request.
J	It will so reflect.
P	When you finally reached Hanley, in WHAT direction were you traveling? (1)
W	South.
P	Please write "south" at the off-ramp's exit.
W	Done.
P	In WHAT direction were you turning on the off-ramp? (1)
W	I was turning to the right.
P	HOW long is the off-ramp? (5)
W	It's pretty long. It's a gradual thing. It's maybe 2,000 feet.
P	HOW does the off-ramp slope? Does it go up to Hanley or down to Hanley? (5)
W	It slopes up. You're going up maybe 10 feet in all.
P	Please draw an arrow from the mouth of the off-ramp to the exit and write "up" next to the arrow.
W	O.K.
P	HOW steep is the slope? (5)
W	I'm no engineer, but it's pretty gradual.
P	In general, HOW accurate is this exhibit? (1)
W	I don't know if it's to scale, but on the whole it seems correct.
P	Your Honor, I now offer plaintiff's exhibit number four for identification into evidence as plaintiff's exhibit number four.
J	It will be received.

(The plaintiff now begins to invoke process-of-elimination reasoning. To single out the defect in the vehicle's steering as the cause of the accident,

the plaintiff questions the witness to negate other possible causes of the accident such as lack of maintenance, speeding, intoxication, poor visibility, and the witness' inattention.)

P   Now, Mr. Dorsey, I'd like to ask you a few questions about the car you were driving toward this off-ramp. WHERE did you purchase this car? (4)

W   From a Polecat dealer in Hayward.

P   Was the car new or used?

W   New. I believe I was the first owner. The dealership sold it to me as new, not used.

P   HOW long had you owned the car before the accident on September 19th? (4)

W   I'd had it for only two months before this occurred.

P   HOW often, if at all, had you had the car serviced before the accident? (4)

W   I took it in twice. The first time I took it in about two weeks after buying it, and then I took it in about a week before the accident for the 2,500-mile maintenance under the warranty.

P   WHERE did you take the car for service? (4)

W   I took it back to the same Polecat dealer that I initially bought it from.

P   Mr. Dorsey, to the best of your knowledge, WHAT was the condition of your car on the day of the accident?

W   As far as I knew, it was in good working order.

P   All right, now let's get back to the exhibit. Could you show us approximately WHERE your car was on the map when you were 1,000 feet from the entrance to the off-ramp? (1)

W   I'd say right here.

P   Please place a dot and "D-1" at that point.

W   Here it is.

P   At that point, HOW fast were you doing? (5)

W   I was doing about 55, but this is the point where I began to slow down.

P   WHAT is the posted speed limit along this portion of Highway 580? (5)

W   55.

P   Now please indicate with a dot and "D-2" WHERE you would be when you were 100 feet from the entrance to the off-ramp. (1)

W   Right.

P   HOW fast were you going then? (5)

W	I had slowed to 30.
P	WHAT is the posted speed limit at the entrance to the off-ramp? (5)
W	I'm pretty sure it's 30.
P	WHAT was the condition of the pavement? (5)
W	It was dry.
P	WHEN was the last rain? (5)
W	Not in weeks. We'd been in a drought.
P	HOW well could you see when you reached the mouth of the off-ramp? (5)
W	Perfectly.
P	WHAT were the lighting conditions at that time? (5)
W	It was mid-morning, and it was a beautiful, clear day.
P	WHAT, if anything, obstructed your view of the off-ramp? (5)
W	Nothing. The only shrubbery in the area is grass. There are no big trees or anything.
P	HOW closely were you paying attention to your driving? (5)
W	I was watching it close.
P	WHY? (5)
W	Hanley is a pretty busy street, and I wanted to have good control of my car before I got on a busy thoroughfare like Hanley.
P	HOW good was your vision that morning? (5)
W	Fine. I have 20-20 vision, and I've never worn glasses.
P	WHAT was your physical condition? (5)
W	Excellent.
P	HOW many drinks, if any, had you had that morning? (5)
W	None. None at all.
	(At this point, the plaintiff elicits the description of the accident itself. The plaintiff wants to make the uncharged accident sound as similar as possible to the pleaded accident.)
P	WHAT happened after you entered the off-ramp? (3)
W	At first, everything was going smoothly.
P	WHAT happened next?
W	About halfway into the turn, the steering wheel just plain froze.
P	WHAT do you mean by "froze"? (5)
W	I couldn't move it at all.

P	Please indicate by placing "D-3" WHERE you were when the steering first froze. (1)
W	Right there.
P	HOW fast were you going then? (5)
W	Probably only 20 or 25.
P	WHAT did you do then? (5)
W	I hit the brakes and tried to move the wheel.
P	HOW quickly did you hit the brakes? (5)
W	As soon as I realized I was in trouble—immediately.
P	HOW did the wheel respond? (5)
W	Not at all.
P	WHAT happened after you hit the brakes? (5)
W	I slowed a bit, but it was just too late.
P	WHERE did the car go? (5)
W	It plowed through the railing, flew off the off-ramp, and finally stopped over here.
P	Please mark the resting point of your car with "D-4."
W	Right here.

(*At this point, the plaintiff elicits the witness's testimony that his automobile contained the same design feature as the plaintiff's.*)

P	Now the car that you were driving that morning, the car that eventually came to rest at D-4, WHAT was the make of that car? (4), (5)
W	It was a Polecat.
P	WHAT was the model of Polecat? (5)
W	It was the Centuria.
P	WHAT was the year of that model? (5)
W	YR-3.
P	Was the car automatic or stick shift? (5)
W	Stick shift.
P	WHAT, if any, accessories did you have on the car? (5)
W	Other than air-conditioning and radio, there were none. It was a basic YR-3 Polecat Centuria right off the showroom floor.
P	Thank you, Mr. Dorsey. (*To the defense counsel.*) Your witness.

§ 6.07 IN-COURT EXHIBITIONS

The proponent will sometimes want to display something other than a normal, inanimate physical exhibit to the jurors. For example, in a personal injury case, the plaintiff's attorney may want the plaintiff to display the injured part of the body to the jurors. Such an exhibition can be helpful to the jury in determining the damages in the case. The probative danger is that the exhibition will inflame the jurors; after viewing a badly mangled limb, the jurors may not be able to dispassionately weigh the evidence on liability or damages.

Under Rule 403, the trial judge has wide discretion in deciding whether to permit an exhibition. The judge ordinarily considers three factors: (1) whether the object to be exhibited is relevant to the case; (2) whether the jurors need to see the object to understand the oral testimony about the object; and (3) the magnitude of the risk that viewing the object will inflame the jurors' emotions.

The fact situation is a products liability action. The plaintiff, Mr. Jansen, brought the action against Kenway, Inc., which manufactures electrical saws. The plaintiff alleges that the defendant defectively designed the saw and that the design defect caused the blade to come loose and slice the plaintiff's arms. The plaintiff takes the witness stand; when he does so, the plaintiff is wearing a jacket. The plaintiff has testified about his injuries in general terms. The proponent, the plaintiff's attorney, now wants to exhibit the injuries to the jurors.

P	WHAT were your injuries?
W	The blade sliced both of my arms very badly.
P	Mr. Jansen, would you please take off your jacket and show your arms to the jurors?
O	Your Honor, may we approach the bench?
J	Certainly.
O	Your Honor, I strenuously object to this exhibition.
P	Your Honor, the plaintiff's arms were injured in this accident, and it's certainly logically relevant to show the jurors what the arms look like now.
O	I admit that the exhibition would be relevant, but I object on the ground that the sight of the plaintiff's badly cut arms will arouse the jurors' emotions and prejudice my client.
P	The jurors simply won't understand the extent of the plaintiff's injuries unless they actually see the arms.
J	I tend to agree. The objection is overruled. You may proceed with the exhibition.

§ 6.08   IN-COURT DEMONSTRATIONS

A demonstration is a step beyond an exhibition. In an exhibition, the proponent merely displays something for the jurors' view. In a demonstration, the proponent illustrates some physical or mechanical process in action. The proponent may want to demonstrate how poorly the plaintiff can move his limbs or how a particular machine operates. Once again, under Rule 403, the trial judge has wide discretion in deciding whether to permit the demonstration. In exercising their discretion, judges look to the factors relevant to exhibitions plus an additional factor. The fourth factor is the risk that the party demonstrating a physical process may be feigning. A plaintiff can easily feign the extent of his or her disability, and it will be very difficult to expose the feigning plaintiff during cross-examination.

We shall continue the hypothetical in § 6.07. Suppose that the plaintiff claims that as a result of the saw accident, he can no longer straighten his arms.

P	Mr. Jansen, let me repeat my request. Please show your arms to the jurors.
W	*(The witness does so.)*
P	HOW has the accident affected your arms?
W	I have a good deal of pain, and I can't straighten them all the way any more.
P	Please show us how far you can straighten your arms.
O	Your Honor, may we approach the bench again?
J	Yes.
O	I hate to object again, Your Honor, but I feel compelled to register my objection to this demonstration.
P	Your Honor, this demonstration is indisputably logically relevant. To show the plaintiff's disability, we have to show the extent to which he's lost the use of his arms.
O	Your Honor, how can I cross-examine a demonstration? There's too great a risk that the plaintiff will be able to feign the extent of his disability.
P	We need this demonstration to help the jury understand our medical testimony about the extent of disability, and the defendant can cross-examine the experts about whether the plaintiff is faking.
J	This is a close question in my mind. Frankly, this is a much closer call than the propriety of the earlier exhibition, but the objection will be overruled. The demonstration may proceed.

§ 6.09   LIABILITY INSURANCE

By virtue of Federal Rule 411, a tort plaintiff ordinarily may not prove that the defendant has liability insurance. There is a weak argument that the defendant's liability coverage is logically relevant to show the defendant's negligence; knowing that he or she has liability insurance, the defendant might be less careful. However, there is the counterargument that carrying insurance is itself an indication that the person is responsible and careful. Moreover, there is a prominent probative danger that the evidence will tempt the jury to decide the case on an improper basis; the jurors may find for the plaintiff—not because they are convinced of the defendant's fault, but rather because they feel the insurance company can better afford to absorb the economic loss. Federal Rule of Evidence 411 states the norm: "Evidence that a person was or was not insured against liability is not admissible to prove whether the person acted negligently or otherwise wrongfully. But the court may admit this evidence for another purpose, such as proving a witness's bias or prejudice or proving agency, ownership, or control."

On the one hand, the evidence of the defendant's liability insurance may not be used to support a generalized inference of the defendant's negligence. On the other hand, as Rule 411 makes clear, the plaintiff may use the evidence for other purposes. The following foundations illustrate both the rule and two of the more important exceptions to the rule.

The first fact situation is a tort case. The plaintiff, Ms. Greenwich, sues the defendant, Mr. Fenton. The plaintiff alleges that the defendant's negligent driving caused the collision in which she was injured. The defendant takes the stand and denies driving carelessly. The plaintiff then begins cross-examination. The plaintiff is the opponent.

O   Mr. Fenton, ISN'T IT TRUE THAT you carry liability insurance?

P   Your Honor, I object to that question on the ground that it calls for evidence of liability insurance.

J   Objection sustained.

P   Your Honor, I request a curative instruction.

J   Yes. Ladies and gentlemen of the jury, you have just heard a reference to possible liability insurance in this case. You are to disregard that reference. You may not speculate whether the defendant has insurance, and you may not consider the possible existence of insurance in your deliberations. You are to decide whether the defendant is liable solely on the basis of the evidence admitted in this case.

P   Now, Your Honor, I must move for a mistrial.

J   Well, I don't think that the reference is serious enough to warrant that. The motion will be denied.

The hypothetical continues. Assume that the defendant called Mr. Graham as a witness. Mr. Graham inspected the accident scene and measured the plaintiff's skidmarks. The skidmarks supported the defendant's theory that the plaintiff caused the accident by speeding. The plaintiff now takes Mr. Graham on cross-examination.

P   Mr. Graham, ISN'T IT TRUE THAT you work for Allied Insurance Company?

W   Yes.

P   AND ISN'T IT ALSO A FACT THAT your company insures the defendant, Mr. Fenton?

O   Your Honor, I object to that question on the ground that it calls for evidence of liability insurance.

P   Your Honor, may we approach the bench?

J   Yes.

P   Your Honor, we are not offering the evidence to support a general

	inference of negligence on Mr. Fenton's part. Rather, we would offer the evidence to impeach Mr. Graham; the evidence is logically relevant to show Mr. Graham's bias in the defendant's favor.
J	The objection is overruled.
P	Mr. Graham, let me repeat the question. ISN'T IT CORRECT THAT your company insures the defendant?
W	Yes.
O	Your Honor, I request a limiting instruction under Rule 105.
J	Very well. Ladies and gentlemen of the jury, you have just heard evidence that the defendant has liability insurance. You may not consider that evidence in deciding whether the defendant was at fault in the accident. You also should not consider whether the insurance company is in a better economic position to absorb any loss than the plaintiff. I am admitting the evidence for one limited purpose—to shed light on Mr. Graham's credibility. You may consider the fact that Mr. Graham works for Mr. Fenton's insurance company in deciding how believable you find Mr. Graham and how much weight to attach to his testimony.

The hypothetical continues. Now assume that Jennings Trucking Company is the codefendant. The codefendant denies that Fenton is its employee. The codefendant calls Mr. Munster as a witness. Mr. Munster testifies that he is the codefendant's general manager. On direct examination, he testifies that, although Fenton once worked for Jennings Trucking Company, he was not an employee at the time of the accident. Suppose that the plaintiff gave Jennings notice to produce its insurance policy and thereby satisfied the best evidence rule. The plaintiff now takes Mr. Munster on cross-examination.

P	Mr. Munster, ISN'T IT TRUE THAT your company carries liability insurance?
O	Your Honor, I object to that question on the ground that it calls for evidence of liability insurance.
P	Your Honor, may we approach the bench?
J	Yes.
P	I offer to prove that if the witness is permitted to answer, the witness will testify that the codefendant's insurance policy listed Mr. Fenton as an employee at the time of the accident. The codefendant denies that Mr. Fenton was its employee at that time, and I am offering the evidence for the limited purpose of showing Mr. Fenton's agency.
J	The objection will be overruled.
P	Mr. Munster, let me repeat the question. ISN'T IT TRUE THAT your company carries liability insurance?

W   Yes.

P   ISN'T IT CORRECT THAT you are the custodian of the insurance policy?

W   Yes.

P   AND ISN'T IT A FACT THAT Appendix II to the policy lists the employees covered by the policy?

W   That's correct.

P   ISN'T IT TRUE THAT at the time of the accident, Appendix II to your policy listed Mr. Fenton as one of your employees?

W   That's right.

O   Your Honor, I would like a limiting instruction.

J   Yes. Ladies and gentlemen of the jury, you have just heard a reference to the codefendant's liability insurance. You are not to consider that evidence in deciding whether either defendant acted negligently. You are also not to speculate as to whether the insurance company could absorb the loss resulting from the accident. You are to consider the evidence only for the purpose of deciding whether, at the time of the accident, Mr. Fenton was an employee of Jennings Trucking Company.

CHAPTER 7

PRIVILEGES AND SIMILAR DOCTRINES

§ 7.01 INTRODUCTION

In the past two chapters, we examined rules based on the concerns listed in Federal Rule of Evidence 403. The concerns are that the jury will misuse the item of evidence, overestimate the probative value of the evidence, or lose sight of the historical merits of the case. The concerns reflect institutional policies governing the way in which we want jurors to behave. Ideally, we want the jury to use items of evidence properly, ascribe the proper weight to each item, and concentrate on the historical merits of the case. When we exclude evidence under Rule 403 or any of the more specific rules in Articles IV and VI, we are excluding logically relevant evidence for a policy reason—a policy related to the way in which trials should be conducted.

This chapter is devoted to another type of evidentiary doctrine which results in the exclusion of logically relevant evidence for policy reasons. This type of doctrine bars the evidence to promote an extrinsic social policy, that is, a policy related to conduct outside the courtroom. The privileges for confidential relations epitomize this type of rule. Suppose that a party makes damaging admissions in a letter to his or her attorney. The party had firsthand, personal knowledge of the facts admitted. These admissions are not only logically relevant; they are also highly reliable, since the party had personal knowledge of the facts. Moreover, the admissions or statements of a party-opponent fall within an exemption from the hearsay rule. However, the judge will routinely exclude the letter on the ground that the letter is a privileged communication. The courts want to give clients the assurance that they can disclose all the facts to their attorneys without fear that the facts will be divulged to strangers. With fuller disclosure from their clients, attorneys can render more effective service. The courts believe that the policy is important enough to warrant excluding even relevant, reliable evidence. That belief has led the jurisdictions to recognize the communications privileges discussed in §§ 7.02–7.06 of this chapter.

Similar reasoning underlies the topical government privileges. Modern government needs a vast amount of information to perform its tasks, especially its regulatory functions, and sometimes the government cannot obtain information from particular sources without assuring confidentiality. The government's interest is even more compelling if the government information qualifies as a military or state secret. The balance of interests favors creating a doctrine which the government may invoke to suppress the information. The information may be highly relevant and thoroughly trustworthy, but the paramount public interest in maintaining the information's secrecy outweighs the parties' interest in disclosure.

§ 7.02 PRIVILEGES FOR CONFIDENTIAL RELATIONS—IN GENERAL

When the Supreme Court submitted the draft of the Federal Rules of Evidence to Congress, the Court's draft included a detailed Article V devoted to privileges. The draft article contained 13 provisions, including specific provisions for the lawyer-client, psychotherapist-patient, husband-wife, penitent-clergy communications privileges and the topical privileges for political votes, trade secrets, military and state secrets, and an informer's identity. The draft seemed to contract some personal privileges while expanding government privileges. The negative public reaction to the draft prompted Congress to intervene. However, revising the specific provisions proved to be a political "hot potato" for Congress, since the provisions affected so many special interest groups. Ultimately, the Congress rejected the Court's draft and substituted a single provision, Rule 501, which now reads:

> The common law—as interpreted by United States courts in the light of reason and experience—governs a claim of privilege unless any of the following provides otherwise:
>
> - the United States Constitution;
> - a federal statute; or
> - rules prescribed by the Supreme Court.
>
> But in a civil case, state law governs privilege regarding a claim or defense for which state law supplies the rule of decision.

We can summarize the current law of privileges for confidential relations in this fashion: *In certain types of proceedings, the holder has certain privileges with respect to privileged information unless (1) the holder has waived the privilege, or (2) there is an applicable exception to the privilege's scope*. This summational sentence raises six issues.

The first issue is in what types of proceedings privileges apply. The general rule is that privileges apply in any proceeding in which testimony can be compelled. A few privileges have a peculiar, limited scope. For instance, in many states, the statutory physician-patient privilege does not apply in criminal prosecutions and workers' compensation proceedings. Moreover, in a large number of states and in federal practice, the privileges recognized by the courts do not apply to hearings conducted by legislative committees. However, with such rare exceptions, privileges apply in all legal proceedings. The holder of the privilege need not be a joined party in the proceeding. A holder may move to intervene in a legal proceeding in which there is a risk that the court will compel the revelation of the holder's confidential communications.

The second question is who is the holder of the privilege. The original holder is the intended beneficiary of the privacy. Thus, the client is the holder of the attorney-client privilege, the patient the holder of the physician-patient privilege, and the penitent the holder of the penitent-clergy privilege. Most jurisdictions consider both spouses holders of the spousal privilege. If the original holder of the privilege becomes mentally incompetent, that person's guardian or conservator becomes the successor holder of the privilege. In some jurisdictions, if the original holder dies, the personal representative such as the executor or heir automatically becomes a successor holder of the privilege. Finally, the holder's agent may sometimes assert the privilege on the holder's behalf. The client may authorize the attorney to claim the attorney-client privilege for the client at a particular hearing. In some jurisdictions, certain types of representatives such as attorneys have implied-in-law authority or even a duty to do so.

The third question is what is the nature of the privilege. The privilege encompasses three primary rights. The first right is the personal right to refuse to disclose the privileged information. A judge may neither hold the privilege holder in contempt nor impose discovery sanctions on the holder if the holder is properly invoking a privilege. In most jurisdictions, the privilege is a two-way street, allowing the holder to refuse to disclose both his or her disclosures to the confidant such as an attorney and the confidant's response communicating advice to the holder. The second right is the right to prevent third parties from making disclosure. The intended addressee of the communication, the attorney, physician, or clergyman, is clearly bound by the privilege. The troublesome question is whether eavesdroppers and interceptors are bound. The traditional view has been that they are not bound and may testify to the privileged communications unless the intended addressee colluded with them to enable them to overhear or intercept. However, in recent years the courts have attached more weight to the interest in privacy, and the trend in both the cases and statutes is to silence eavesdroppers and interceptors such as hackers. The third and final right is the right to preclude the opposing counsel and the judge from commenting on the invocation of the privilege. In roughly half the jurisdictions, the opposing counsel may argue that since the holder invoked a privilege to suppress the information, the information probably would have been unfavorable. In contrast, approximately half the jurisdictions prohibit such comment; they reason that it is inconsistent, on the one hand, to grant the privilege and, on the other hand, to permit adverse inferences from the privilege's invocation.

However, there is one right which a common-law or statutory privilege does not encompass in many jurisdictions: the right to exclude evidence derived from a violation of the privilege. In this respect, common-law and statutory privileges differ from constitutional privileges like the Fourth Amendment exclusionary rule. Assume that the police conduct an illegal warrantless search of the accused's apartment and discover a diary showing the location of evidence of the crime. The police immediately go to the location and dig up the evidence. The police deliver the evidence to the prosecutor. The accused can move to suppress not only the diary but also the derived evidence; the derived evidence is also suppressible as the fruit of the poisonous tree. In contrast, suppose that one spouse reveals a confidential communication from the other spouse to the police. The police then use that revelation as an investigative lead and uncover other evidence that incriminates the other spouse. In this setting, the prevailing view is that the derivative evidence is admissible. The accused spouse could preclude the other spouse from repeating the revelation of the confidential communication on the witness stand, but the accused cannot suppress the evidence the police derived from the violation of the accused's confidence.

The fourth question is the most difficult: What is privileged information? Simply stated, privileged information is a confidential communication between properly related parties and incident to the relation. This question presents several sub-issues.

What is a "communication"? Oral and written statements fall within the definition of "communication." However, in the case of some privileges, many jurisdictions use extraordinarily broad definitions of "communication." In the case of the statutory physician-patient privilege, many states extend the privilege to any information the physician gains by examining the patient. The physician could not testify about the patient's physical condition even though the observation of the patient's physical condition is not a "communication" in the conventional sense of the term. Moreover, several jurisdictions use a broad definition of communication in the spousal privilege. These jurisdictions sometimes privilege any information one spouse gains from the other spouse by virtue of the marital relation. In some cases, the courts have applied the spousal privilege when one spouse witnessed the other spouse bury incriminating evidence in the backyard. The second spouse is relying upon marital privacy when he or she performs the act in the other spouse's presence, and the courts reason that the marital privacy deserves legal protection.

The privilege protects only the communication, not the underlying facts. By way of example, suppose that after a car strikes a pedestrian, the pedestrian sues the driver. The driver consults with a defense attorney. During the consultation with the attorney, the driver makes statements describing his recollection of the accident. After the consultation, the pedestrian's attorney deposes the driver. At the deposition, the driver may invoke the attorney-client privilege as a justification for refusing to reveal his statements to his attorney about the facts of the accident. However, the driver cannot refuse to answer questions about the facts of the accident.

When is a communication "confidential"? Confidentiality entails two elements: (1) physical privacy at the time of the communication; and (2) an intent on the holder's part to maintain secrecy in the future. If third parties are present to the holder's knowledge, the courts usually hold that the communication is not confidential. For practical business reasons, however, the courts have allowed clerks and secretaries to be present without destroying confidentiality; the courts realize that attorneys and physicians use assistants to conduct their professional work. In a minority of jurisdictions, the presence of family members and friends will not negate confidentiality so long as they are present to support the person consulting the attorney or physician.[1] Even if there was physical privacy at the time of the communication, the communication is unprivileged if the holder intended subsequent disclosure outside the circle of confidence. Suppose that the client gave the attorney information for the specific purpose of including the information in a press release about the case. The normal inference would be that the client never intended confidentiality.

---

[1] Many jurisdictions recognize the common interest, pooled information, or joint defense privilege. They apply the attorney-client privilege to confidential communications between attorneys who represent separate clients but are pursuing a legal strategy shared by their clients. Distinguish this fact situation from a "joint client" case in which several clients consult the same attorney. § 7.05[3] addresses the later situation.

Next, what are the protected relations? Did the confidential communication occur between parties to a protected relationship? The answer varies from jurisdiction to jurisdiction. There are now statutes and decisions recognizing privileges for the following relations, among others: attorney-client, physician-patient, psychotherapist-patient, accountant-client, social worker-client, penitent-clergy, parent-child, and between spouses. *See generally* 1 E. IMWINKELRIED, THE NEW WIGMORE: EVIDENTIARY PRIVILEGES, Ch. 6 (4th ed. 2021). In *Jaffee v. Redmond*, 518 U.S. 1, 116 S. Ct. 1923, 135 L. Ed. 2d 337 (1996), the Supreme Court recognized a psychotherapist-patient privilege, extending to licensed clinical social workers. Significantly, the *Jaffee* Court refused to construe Rule 501 as confining privileged relationships to the relations that enjoyed a common-law privilege prior to the enactment of the Federal Rules of Evidence. The courts and legislatures believe that these are useful social relationships and that the nature of the relationship requires an element of confidentiality. This belief is the policy judgment underlying the very existence of the privileges.

In applying the relationship requirement, the courts have found two fact situations troublesome. One situation is the case in which a corporate employee communicates with corporate counsel. When is the communication deemed a communication between the corporate client and the corporate counsel? Which employees personify the corporation for purposes of the privilege? Some jurisdictions limit the corporate attorney-client privilege to communications between corporate counsel and the members of the corporate "control group," the narrow circle of directors, officers, and high-ranking employees needing direct access to corporate counsel. However, in *Upjohn Co. v. United States*, 449 U.S. 383, 101 S. Ct. 677, 66 L. Ed. 2d 584 (1981), the Court made it clear that it favors a broader test. Under the *Upjohn* or subject-matter test, a communication between any employee and the corporate counsel constitutes a corporate attorney-client communication if the employee is divulging information that he or she gained in the course of performing employment duties. Today many courts extend the privilege beyond technical employees and apply it to "functional" employees, persons who are technically independent contractors who serve as depositories for the corporation's business information. In part, due to rising employee health care costs, many corporations have outsourced essential business functions that were previously handled inhouse.

The second situation is the case in which the client communicates with an expert hired by the attorney. Suppose, for example, that the defense attorney sends the defendant to a psychiatrist for an evaluation. The client possesses private information, namely, his or her mental condition. The attorney needs an evaluation of the information to prepare for trial. However, neither the client nor the attorney possesses the expertise to perform the evaluation. In this situation, the majority view in state court is that the attorney-client privilege attaches. The privilege protects not only the client's revelations to the expert but also the expert's report to the attorney.

Fourth and finally, when does a communication occur "incident to the relationship"? It is not enough that the communication occur between an attorney and his or her client. The client must be consulting the attorney in his or her professional capacity, *qua* attorney. The incidence requirement necessitates that the court examine the purpose of the communication. Why did the client consult the attorney? If the client was seeking legal information or advice, the communication satisfies the incidence requirement; the communication need not occur incident to pending or threatened litigation.

If all of the above requirements are satisfied, there is a prima facie case for recognizing an "absolute" communications privilege. The privilege is not absolute in the sense that it can never be overcome. As we shall see in the ensuing paragraphs, the party opposing the privilege claim can defeat the privilege claim by establishing a waiver by the holder or the applicability of a previously recognized special exception. The privilege is absolute in the sense that it cannot be defeated by an ad hoc, case-specific showing of need for the privileged information.

The fifth issue is waiver. If a holder invokes the right type of privilege in the right type of proceeding to suppress privileged information, there is a prima facie case for privilege. However, the opposing counsel can defeat the privilege by showing that the holder has waived the privilege.[2] The waiver can occur inside or outside court. On direct examination by his or her attorney, the holder may have referred to the privileged communication. The in-court reference waives the privilege. The court may also find a waiver if the holder voluntarily discloses the privileged information to a third party outside the courtroom. However, not every out-of-court disclosure effects a waiver, because the disclosure itself might be a privileged communication; a husband might tell his wife what he previously told his attorney.

In 2008, Congress enacted Federal Rule of Evidence 502. The scope of Rule 502 is limited to waivers effected by disclosure; the Rule does not address other types of waivers such as waivers under the "at issue" doctrine that is triggered by references to privileged communications in pleadings. Despite its limited scope, Rule 502 is quite important. Rule 502(b) announces a general rule that when made in a federal proceeding or to a federal office or agency, the disclosure does not operate as a waiver in a federal or state proceeding if:

(1)   the disclosure is inadvertent;

(2)   the holder of the privilege . . . took reasonable steps to prevent disclosure; and

(3)   the holder promptly took reasonable steps to rectify the error, including (if applicable) following Federal Rule of Civil Procedure 26(b)(5)(B).

While 502(b) addresses the question of whether there has been a waiver, 502(a) relates to the scope of the waiver:

When the disclosure is made in a federal proceeding or to a federal officer or agency and waives the attorney-client privilege . . . , the waiver extends to an undisclosed communication or information in a federal or state proceeding only if:

---

[2] There is a split of authority over the allocation of the burden on this issue. Many jurisdictions take the position that the alleged holder must show both that there was confidentiality at the time of the communication and that the holder has since maintained the confidentiality of the communication.

    (1)   the waiver is intentional;

    (2)   the disclosed and undisclosed communication or information concern the same subject matter; and

    (3)   they ought in fairness to be considered together.

Other provisions in Rule 502 concern the effect of disclosure in a state proceeding (502(c)), a federal court order that certain disclosure does not effect a waiver (502(d)), and a party agreement to that effect (502(e)).

The sixth and final question is whether there is any special exception to the privilege's scope. The opponent can defeat a privilege by showing either waiver or a special exception. It may not serve the purpose of the privilege to apply it in a particular situation, or there may be a countervailing interest that overrides the privilege. In § 7.05 of this chapter, we shall illustrate several special exceptions to the privilege's scope. The special exceptions are announced beforehand; as previously stated, the party resisting the privilege claim cannot surmount the privilege on the basis of the argument that his or her ad hoc, compelling need for the information creates an exception to the scope of the privilege. If the courts permitted the privilege to be trumped in that manner, at the time of deciding whether to consult and confide it would be far more difficult for the holder to predict whether a court will later shield the communication. The traditional rationale for recognizing privileges is that without the firm assurance of future confidentiality provided by the privilege, the average client or patient would supposedly be unwilling to consult and confide.

§ 7.03   PRIVILEGES FOR CONFIDENTIAL INFORMATION—INVOKING A PRIVILEGE

[1]   ELEMENTS OF THE FOUNDATION

The claimant has the burden of proving the existence of the elements of the prima facie case for privilege. The prima facie case for privilege includes these elements:

    1.   The privilege applies to this type of proceeding. The judge makes this determination by examining the pleadings in the case.

    2.   The claimant of the privilege is asserting the correct type of right. The judge makes this determination by insisting that the claimant specify the right he or she is claiming, that is, the right to personally refuse to disclose, the right to prevent a third party from disclosing, or the right to preclude comment on the invocation of the privilege.

    3.   The claimant is a proper holder of the privilege or a person authorized to assert the privilege on the holder's behalf.

    4.   The information the claimant seeks to suppress is privileged information.

        a.   It was a communication.

        b.   It was confidential. Some jurisdictions presume that a communication between properly related parties is confidential. Again, in most cases, there must have been physical privacy at the time of the communication;

and the holder must have intended to maintain the confidentiality of the communication in the future.

    c.   It occurred between properly related parties.

    d.   It was incident to the relationship.

Federal Rule of Evidence 104(a) governs the judge's determination of these preliminary facts.

[2] SAMPLE FOUNDATION

Our fact situation is a tort action arising from a collision. The plaintiff, Ms. Campbell, alleges that the defendant, Mr. Harris, caused the accident by speeding. Mr. Harris takes the stand during the defense case-in-chief. On direct examination, he testifies that he was going only 20 miles an hour, five miles under the speed limit. On cross-examination, the following occurs. The plaintiff's attorney is the proponent:

P	Mr. Harris, ISN'T IT A FACT THAT you testified on direct examination that you were going only 20 miles an hour before the collision?
W	Yes.
P	ISN'T IT TRUE, Mr. Harris, THAT when you spoke with Mr. Riley, you told him that you were going 35 miles an hour?
O	Your Honor, I object to that question on the ground that it calls for information protected by the attorney-client privilege. (2) I request permission to take the witness on voir dire examination outside the jury's hearing.
J	Permission granted.
O	Mr. Harris, WHO is this Mr. Riley? (4c)
W	He's a long-time friend of mine.
O	WHAT is his occupation? (4c)
W	He's an attorney.
O	HOW do you know he is an attorney? (4c)
W	His office door says attorney, he has degrees on his wall, and he's represented my family in court before.
O	WHERE and WHEN did you talk to Mr. Riley about his case?
W	I think the first time was January 12th or 13th of YR-4, just after the accident occurred. We met in his office.
O	WHAT happened during that meeting? (4a)
W	I told him about the accident.
O	Precisely, HOW did you give him information about the accident? (4a)
W	I told him about it. I didn't put it in writing or anything like that.
O	HOW many people were present when you had this meeting with Mr. Riley? (4b)

W	Just the two of us.
O	HOW many doors are there to his office? (4b)
W	Just one.
O	WHAT position was the door in while you talked with him? (4b)
W	It was closed.
O	After you told him about the accident, to WHOM did you authorize him to give the information? (4b)
W	No one.
O	WHAT did you want him to do with the information? (4b)
W	Keep it secret, of course. He was my attorney.
O	WHY did you talk to him that day? (4d)
W	I thought I might need legal help. Even at the accident scene, the plaintiff said something about suing.
O	In WHAT capacity did you consult Mr. Riley? (4d), (2)
W	I was talking to him as an attorney, not just a family friend. We were meeting in his office, not at his house.
O	Your Honor, I have no further questions on voir dire. I renew my objection and assert my client's privilege to refuse to disclose his communications with his attorney. (2)
J	Objection sustained.

§ 7.04 PRIVILEGES FOR CONFIDENTIAL RELATIONS—DEFEATING A PRIVILEGE BY PROVING WAIVER

[1] IN GENERAL

The party opposing a privilege claim can defeat the claim by showing that the holder waived the privilege. Although some courts assign the claimant the burden of proof on the non-waiver issue, other courts allocate the burden to the party opposing the claim. The former courts reason that just as the claimant must show that the communication was confidential when made, the claimant should be required to demonstrate that the holder maintained its confidentiality—the antithesis of waiver.

[2] IN-COURT WAIVER

If the party opposing the privilege claim is going to argue an in-court waiver, that party must be prepared to identify the witness's testimony that effected the waiver. The following is a continuation of the immediately preceding tort hypothetical. The plaintiff is the proponent.

P	Mr. Harris, ISN'T IT A FACT THAT when you first spoke with your family attorney, Mr. Riley, you told him that you were going 35 miles an hour?
O	Your Honor, I object to that question on the ground that it calls for

information protected by the attorney-client privilege.

P   Your Honor, may we approach the bench?

J   Yes.

P   Your Honor, I concede that this communication would ordinarily be privileged. However, I contend that the defendant has already waived the privilege. I would request that the court reporter read back the last question and answer on direct examination.

J   Very well.

CR   It'll take me just a second to find the passage. Yes, here it is. My notes show that the last question on direct was: "What was your speed just before the collision?" The last answer was: "I was going at a safe rate of speed. That's what I told my attorney when I first discussed the accident with him, and it's the same story I'm telling today. That's the truth."

P   This shows that on direct examination, the defendant expressly referred to his previous conversation with his attorney about the collision. That reference waives the privilege.

J   I agree. The objection is overruled.

P   Mr. Harris, let me repeat the question. ISN'T IT TRUE THAT you told your attorney that you were going 35 miles an hour?

W   Yes.

A few jurisdictions take the position that only a disclosure on direct examination can effect a waiver. These jurisdictions believe that cross-examination is so inherently compulsive that any disclosure on cross-examination should be deemed involuntary. However, a witness may invoke a privilege on either direct or cross. For that reason, the prevailing view is that like a revelation on direct, a disclosure on cross can result in a waiver.

[3] OUT-OF-COURT WAIVER

If the party opposing the privilege relies on the theory of out-of-court waiver, the party must lay the following foundation:

1. Where the out-of-court statement was made.
2. When the statement was made.
3. To whom the statement was made.
4. The holder knew that the addressee was outside the circle of confidence.
5. The holder disclosed information to the addressee.
6. The disclosure was voluntary.

We continue the hypothetical. Now the proponent will attempt to show that the holder waived the privilege by an out-of-court disclosure.

P   Mr. Harris, ISN'T IT A FACT THAT when you first spoke with your family attorney, Mr. Riley, you told him that you were going 35 miles an hour?

O	Your Honor, I object to that question on the ground that it calls for privileged information protected by the attorney-client privilege.
P	Your Honor, I request permission to take the witness on voir dire examination before you rule on the objection.
J	Granted.
P	Mr. Harris, ISN'T IT TRUE THAT on January 19th of this year, you had dinner with your cousin, James Carol? (1), (2), (3)
W	Yes.
P	ISN'T IT CORRECT THAT during this dinner, you discussed the accident with your cousin? (3)
W	Yes.
P	ISN'T IT A FACT THAT at the time, you knew your cousin wasn't working for your attorney in this case? (5)
W	Right.
P	ISN'T IT TRUE THAT you told your cousin what you told your attorney about the accident? (5)
W	Yes.
P	And no one forced you to tell that to your cousin. DID THEY? (6)
W	No.
P	And no one made any threats to compel you to tell your cousin. ISN'T THAT TRUE? (6)
W	Yes.
P	Your Honor, I have no further questions on voir dire.
J	I see. The objection will be overruled.
P	Mr. Harris, let me repeat the question. ISN'T IT CORRECT THAT you told your attorney that you were going 35 miles an hour?
W	Yes.

The courts are split over whether inadvertent production of a privileged document waives a privilege that otherwise attaches to the document. 2 E. IMWINKELRIED, THE NEW WIGMORE: EVIDENTIARY PRIVILEGES § 16.12.4.b(4) (4th ed. 2021). This issue frequently arises during pretrial discovery. One view is that only a knowing revelation of privileged material effects a waiver. At the polar extreme, another view is that any production of a privileged document—even an unintentional one—results in a waiver. The third view is that the occurrence of a waiver turns on whether the producing party acted reasonably. If the pretrial discovery schedule in the case requires the litigant to screen millions of documents for production in a short time frame, the judge might well find that the inadvertent production of a privileged document was excusable and that there was no waiver. In evaluating the reasonableness of the party's conduct, the judge considers both the precautions the party took to prevent the disclosure of privileged information and any steps the party took after he or she discovered the inadvertent production. This last view is the trend in the case law and has achieved the status of a majority rule. As previously stated, in 2008 Congress approved new Federal Rule of Evidence 502. Rule 502(b) codifies a version of the last view.

The courts also differ over the scope of the waiver effected by out-of-court statements. Some courts tend to limit the extent of the waiver to the very communications previously disclosed. However, at common law other courts are inclined to apply a broad subject-matter test to define the scope of the waiver. Under this view, the waiver is not limited to the communications previously disclosed; instead, these courts sometimes hold that the waiver extends to other privileged communications relevant to the same subject-matter. Rule 502(a) now governs the issue in federal practice. As previously stated, Rule 502(a) provides that when a disclosure "in a federal proceeding or to a federal office or agency" resulted in a waiver, the waiver extends to undisclosed communications only if three conditions concur: The waiver was intentional, the disclosed and undisclosed communications relate to the same subject matter, and "they ought in fairness to be considered together."

§ 7.05 PRIVILEGES FOR CONFIDENTIAL RELATIONS—DEFEATING A PRIVILEGE BY PROVING A SPECIAL EXCEPTION

[1] IN GENERAL

As previously stated, there are numerous special exceptions to the various privileges. Some privileges are virtually riddled with exceptions. The party opposing the claim of privilege usually relies on voir dire examination to show the factual predicate for the exception. Most courts assign the burden of proof on the applicability of an exception to the party opposing the privilege claim.

The exceptions do not include a rule allowing the party opposing the claim to defeat the privilege by demonstrating a substantial, ad hoc need for the privileged information. Most jurisdictions treat communications privileges as "absolute" in this sense. As previously stated, the courts reason that the typical holder is so concerned about the prospect of subsequent compelled judicial disclosure of his or her communication that they would not confide without the assurance of a formal evidentiary privilege. The holder could not have that assurance if a court could later surmount the privilege on the ground that the party opposing the privilege has an acute, case-specific need for the information.

The following subsections illustrate some of the more important, commonly recognized exceptions.

[2] AT THE TIME OF THE COMMUNICATION, THE HOLDER SOUGHT THE INFORMATION TO FACILITATE A FUTURE CRIME OR FRAUD

The courts will not permit holders to abuse and pervert the privileges. For that reason, the courts usually reject a privilege claim if the party opposing the claim shows that at the time of the communication, the holder sought the information or advice to facilitate the commission of a future or ongoing crime or fraud. The United States

Supreme Court recognized this exception in *United States v. Zolin*, 491 U.S. 554, 109 S. Ct. 2619, 105 L. Ed. 2d 469 (1989). The foundation for the exception usually requires proof that:

1. At the time of the communication, the holder knew that the contemplated course of conduct was illegal or fraudulent.

2. The purpose of the communication was to obtain information or advice to facilitate the commission of a future or ongoing crime or fraud. Because of the difficulty of proving the holder's state of mind, many courts recognize the exception so long as there is a prima facie case or permissive inference of the existence of the improper intent in the holder's mind. The holder's state of mind—not the attorney's—is dispositive. Judges often find it necessary to review the allegedly privileged communication in camera to decide whether the particular communication had that purpose.

Our fact situation is a prosecution for willful tax evasion. Suppose that El Dorado law requires that the purchaser of goods pay a four percent sales tax unless the goods are intended for interstate shipment. If the goods are intended for interstate shipment, the purchaser obtains a tax exemption form from the seller and submits the completed form to the Franchise Tax Board. The People allege that in early August YR-3, the accused, Mr. Lloyd Marx, purchased goods for intrastate shipment and willfully evaded the tax. The People allege that later in August, the accused entered into a contract to sell 230 air conditioners to an in-state firm. The accused took the stand during his case-in-chief. On direct examination, the accused admits that he purchased the air conditioners and neither paid the tax nor filed the exemption form. However, he also testifies that he did not understand the procedures for filing the form and claiming the exemption. The following occurs on cross-examination. The proponent is the prosecutor. The prosecutor is attempting to prove willfulness.

P   Mr. Marx, ISN'T IT TRUE THAT in June YR-3, you spoke with Mr. Fenton of the local office of the Franchise Tax Board? (1)

W   Yes. He had come by my office to inspect some records.

P   ISN'T IT A FACT THAT during this conversation, you asked him whether you had to pay a sales tax on purchases for intrastate shipments? (1)

W   Right.

P   AND DIDN'T HE tell you that you had to do so? (1)

W   Yes.

P   ISN'T IT CORRECT THAT after your conversation with Mr. Fenton, in late August, YR-3 you entered into a contract for the sale of air conditioners to Johnson Construction Company? (2)

W   Yes.

P   ISN'T IT TRUE THAT Johnson has its office in this city and state—Morena, El Dorado? (2)

W	Yes.
P	ISN'T IT A FACT THAT you promised to deliver the air conditioners in September to their office in this state? (2)
W	Yes.
P	ISN'T IT CORRECT THAT the number of air conditioners you promised to sell them was 230? (2)
W	Yes.
P	AND ISN'T TRUE THAT that was the exact number of air conditioners you bought in early August, YR-3? (2)
W	Yes.

Later, during the prosecution rebuttal, the prosecutor calls Ms. Celia Waylan as a witness. The prosecutor is still the proponent. Ms. Waylan has already identified herself and stated that she is an attorney.

P	Ms. Waylan, WHERE were you on the morning of July 20, YR-3?
W	I was in my office.
P	WHERE is your office?
W	Downtown on High Street.
P	WHAT happened that morning?
W	I had a visit from a client.
P	WHO was that client?
W	It was the accused, Mr. Marx.
P	WHERE is Mr. Marx now?
W	In this courtroom.
P	Specifically, WHERE in the courtroom?
W	He's sitting right there.
P	HOW is he dressed?
W	In plaid slacks and a blue shirt.
P	Your Honor, please let the record reflect that the witness has identified the accused.
J	It will so reflect.
P	WHAT happened when the accused came to your office that morning?
W	He asked for some advice.
P	WHAT advice?
O	Your Honor, I object to that question on the ground that it calls for information protected by the attorney-client privilege.
P	Your Honor, may we approach the bench?

J   Yes.

P   Your Honor, I concede that Ms. Waylan is an attorney and that the accused consulted her as such. However, I offer to prove that the attorney will testify that the defendant asked how he could evade paying a tax or filing a form on this particular intrastate shipment. She will further testify that she advised him that there was no way to avoid paying or filing. This conversation occurred in July, well before the sale of the air conditioners in August. She will finally testify that he said that she obviously misunderstood his question and that he wanted her advice as to the best way to evade the law without getting caught. Since the defendant had already talked with Mr. Fenton, the inference is that the defendant sought Ms. Waylan's advice to facilitate a future crime and get around the requirement Mr. Fenton had informed him of.

J   I think there's a sufficient showing to invoke the exception. I shall overrule the objection.

P   Ms. Waylan, WHAT advice did the accused ask for?

W   He asked how he could get around paying a tax or filing a form.

P   WHAT did you tell him?

W   I said that there wasn't; he had to do one or the other. If the goods were destined for intrastate sale, he had to pay the tax. If the goods were destined for interstate shipment, he had to file an exemption form with the state. It was one or the other.

P   WHAT did the accused say then?

W   He told me that I'd obviously misunderstood his question. He said that he was definitely going to enter into a contract for an intrastate shipment and that he wanted my advice as to how to evade the law without getting caught.

In *United States v. Zolin*, 491 U.S. 554, 109 S. Ct. 2619, 105 L. Ed. 2d 469 (1989), the Supreme Court discussed the procedures for applying the crime/fraud exception. Most lower courts read *Zolin* as holding that:

— The judge may conduct an in camera examination of the allegedly privileged material so long as the party seeking discovery presents sufficient facts to support a good faith belief that an examination "may" reveal facts establishing the applicability of the exception. An examination is often necessary to determine whether the particular communication was in furtherance of an illicit purpose.

— However, the judge may subsequently order the material disclosed to the party seeking discovery only if the examination establishes a prima facie case that the client sought the attorney's advice for the purpose of facilitating a future or ongoing crime or fraud. The courts differ over the meaning of "prima facie case" in this setting.

[3] THE JOINT CONSULTATION SITUATION

If two parties consult an attorney about a common problem, there is an attorney-client privilege. Either party may assert that privilege against a third party outside the circle of confidence. What happens, though, if the parties have a falling-out and sue each other? May one party claim the privilege against the other party? In this situation, the courts have generally denied the privilege. The courts reason that there was no confidentiality as between the two parties; they freely communicated with each other and the attorney. To establish the joint consultation exception to the privilege, the party opposing the claim must show that:

1. They both met with the attorney.

2. They met with the attorney at a certain time.

3. They met with the attorney at a certain place.

4. The party claiming the privilege knew that the other party was present.

5. The party claiming the privilege voluntarily participated in the joint consultation.

6. The purpose of the consultation was to seek legal advice.

7. The advice related to a common problem.

Our fact situation is a contract action. The plaintiff, Zikes, sues the defendant, Adams, on a contract. The contract provides that the defendant was to pay the plaintiff a percentage of the receipts of the defendant's business in exchange for the plaintiff's investment in the business. The central dispute in the case is over the meaning of the term, "receipts." The plaintiff contends that the term means gross receipts while the defendant asserts that the term means net receipts after deducting certain expenses. The plaintiff takes the stand during his case-in-chief. The following occurs on cross-examination. The proponent is the defendant.

P	Mr. Zikes, ISN'T IT TRUE THAT you entered this contract on February 14, YR-3?
W	Yes.
P	ISN'T IT A FACT THAT before you entered this contract, you consulted an attorney?
W	Yes.
P	ISN'T IT TRUE THAT that attorney was Marcia Harris?
W	Yes.
P	ISN'T IT CORRECT THAT you met with Ms. Harris at her office on February 12, YR-3? (1), (2), (3)
W	Yes.
P	ISN'T IT TRUE THAT the defendant, Mr. Adams, was also present? (1)
W	Yes.
P	And no one forced you to attend the meeting with Mr. Adams. DID THEY? (5)

W	No.
P	And no one threatened you if you didn't attend the meeting. DID THEY? (5)
W	No.
P	ISN'T IT TRUE THAT at this meeting, you both spoke with Ms. Harris about the same contract? (6), (7)
W	Yes.
P	AND ISN'T IT A FACT THAT you both asked for her advice about drafting the contract? (6), (7)
W	Yes.
P	ISN'T IT CORRECT THAT during this meeting, you told her that the receipts should be computed by deducting salary expenses?
O	Your Honor, I object to that question on the ground that it calls for information protected by the attorney-client privilege.
P	Your Honor, may we approach the bench?
J	Yes.
P	Your Honor, the record shows that this meeting was a joint consultation with the attorney. The plaintiff and defendant jointly consulted Ms. Harris about a common problem and the plaintiff cannot assert the privilege against the defendant after a falling out.
J	I concur. The objection will be overruled.
P	Mr. Zikes, let me repeat the question. ISN'T IT A FACT that during your meeting with the attorney, you told her that the receipts should be computed by deducting salary expenses?
W	Yes.

[4] THE PATIENT-LITIGANT EXCEPTION

One of the most important exceptions to the physician-patient privilege and the psychotherapy privilege is the patient-litigant doctrine. If the patient sues and tenders the issue of his or her condition, the patient loses the privilege for communications relevant to that condition. The theory is that it would be unfair to permit the patient-litigant to suppress such highly relevant information. In effect, by suing, the patient makes a limited waiver of the privilege. To decide whether this exception applies in a particular case, the judge must examine the complaint and determine whether the complaint tenders an issue of physical condition to which the communication is logically relevant. (A defendant can trigger the exception by including an allegation about his or her condition in their answer, but in most cases it is the plaintiff who tenders the issue in their complaint.)

Our fact situation is a tort action in which the plaintiff claims extensive personal injuries. In particular, the complaint prays for $200,000 for a phobia of automobiles, allegedly caused by the defendant's conduct. The defendant calls Dr. Metal as a witness.

Dr. Metal identifies himself and states that he formerly treated the plaintiff. He testifies that he examined the plaintiff two months after the accident. The defendant is the proponent.

P   Dr. Metal, during this examination, WHAT, if anything, did the plaintiff say about his fear or phobia of automobiles?

O   Your Honor, I object to that question on the ground that it calls for privileged information protected by the physician-patient privilege.

P   Your Honor, may we approach the bench?

J   Yes.

P   Your Honor, I offer to prove that the witness will testify that the plaintiff said that although the accident initially made him fearful of driving or riding in a car, he was quickly overcoming the fear. On page nine of his complaint, the plaintiff prays for $200,000 in damages for a phobia of automobiles. As a litigant, the plaintiff tendered the issue of the extent of his phobia. The statement he made to his physician is logically relevant to his condition and alleged phobia.

J   The objection is overruled.

P   Dr. Metal, let me repeat the question. WHAT, if anything, did the plaintiff say about his phobia?

W   He said it had been a problem at first. However, he then added that he was quickly overcoming the fear.

The courts are currently badly divided over the scope of the patient-litigant exception to the psychotherapy privilege. Some courts apply the exception whenever the patient plaintiff seeks any emotional distress damages, others only when the patient seeks more than "garden variety" damages, and still others only if the patient goes to the length of calling the therapist as a witness.

Think back to § 7.02. That section pointed out that in situations in which a litigant consults an expert such as a psychiatrist for purposes of trial preparation, many courts invoke the attorney-client privilege to cloak both the litigant's disclosures to the expert and the expert's report. Although the medical privileges are subject to a patient-litigant exception, many jurisdictions do not recognize a comparable exception to the attorney-client privilege. In these jurisdictions, even if the exception rendered the medical privileges inapplicable, the litigant could still assert the attorney-client privilege.

§ 7.06   THE WORK PRODUCT PROTECTION

[1]   THE CONDITIONAL WORK PRODUCT PROTECTION

In the three previous sections, we examined the absolute privileges for confidential relations. At this point we should remember the limitations of the attorney-client privilege. Because of the requirements discussed in the last three sections, the attorney-client privilege may not protect such material as a witness's statement, an expert's report, or a model prepared for trial.

However, ours is an adversary system of litigation; and given their adversary training, most attorneys find it highly distasteful to disclose their pretrial preparation materials to opposing counsel. In addition, many judges believe that pretrial preparation materials deserve some protection; it strikes them as unfair to permit the opposing counsel to reap the benefit of the other attorney's factual investigation and legal research. Since the attorney-client privilege does not protect these materials, attorneys and courts looked elsewhere for a rationale to protect trial preparation materials.

In the leading case of *Hickman v. Taylor*, 329 U.S. 495, 67 S. Ct. 385, 91 L. Ed. 451 (1947), the Supreme Court purported to construe the Federal Rules of Civil Procedure, but the Court in effect created a new doctrine, work product, to protect pretrial preparation materials. The Court commented: "Proper preparation of a client's case demands that he (the lawyer) assemble information, sift what he considers to be the relevant from the irrelevant facts, prepare his legal theories and plan his strategy without undue and needless interference." The Court emphasized that it was not creating an absolute privilege: "We do not mean to say that all written materials obtained or prepared by an adversary's counsel with an eye toward litigation are necessarily free from discovery in all cases. Where relevant and non-privileged facts remain hidden in an attorney's file and where production of those facts is essential to the preparation of one's case, discovery may properly be had." At first, the doctrine was viewed simply as a limitation on pretrial discovery. However, the doctrine has evolved into an evidentiary immunity or protection sometimes assertable at trial.[3]

Ultimately, the Supreme Court promulgated Federal Rule of Civil Procedure 26(b), stating and refining the *Hickman* doctrine. Civil Rule 26(b)(3) generally protects "documents and tangible things that are prepared in anticipation of litigation or for trial by or for another party or its representative (including the other party's attorney, consultant, surety, indemnitor, insurer, or agent)" from discovery unless "the party shows that it has substantial need for the materials to prepare its case and cannot, without undue hardship, obtain their substantial equivalent by other means."

The party invoking the work product protection must establish the following foundational elements:

1.   The party is invoking the protection in the right type of proceeding. Although the protection originated in civil actions, the majority of jurisdictions now recognize the doctrine in criminal cases.[4] Most of these jurisdictions have

---

[3] United States v. Nobles, 422 U.S. 225, 239, 95 S. Ct. 2160, 45 L. Ed. 2d 141 (1975); Steven W. Feldman, *The Work Product Rule in Criminal Practice and Procedure*, 50 U. CIN.. L. REV. 495, 547 (1981). Although courts and commentators sometimes refer to the work product "privilege," it is best to conceive of the doctrine as a procedural immunity. Edward Imwinkelried, *The Validity of the 2010 Federal Rule of Civil Procedure 26 Amendment Governing the Waiver of Work Product Protection: Is the Work Product Doctrine an Evidentiary Privilege?*, 37 U. DAYTON L. REV. 279 (2012). Although the doctrine benefits individual client and attorneys, the primary rationale for recognizing the doctrine is that the doctrine promotes a public interest, that is, the functioning of the adversary system.

[4] Steven W. Feldman, *The Work Product Rule in Criminal Practice and Procedure,* 50 U. CIN. L. REV. 495 (1981).

codified the doctrine in statute or court rule.[5] The trial judge examines the pleadings to determine whether the instant case is the right type of proceeding. The trend is to allow the party to assert the privilege not only in the case for which the material was created but also in other, subsequent litigation.

2. The party is asserting the right type of protection. The work product protection is the personal right to refuse to disclose the material during pretrial discovery or at trial.

3. The party claiming the protection is a proper holder. In most of the decided cases, the attorney has asserted the protection. However, some cases grant the client standing to assert the protection.

4. The information the party seeks to suppress is work product material. To qualify as work product material, the information must satisfy three requirements:

   a. The information is derivative rather than primary material. Primary material is material historically connected to the case such as the actual brake from the car involved in an accident. An example of derivative material would be a model of the brake. Primary material would be the witness's knowledge of the accident; a party cannot invoke the work product protection to prevent the opposing counsel from deposing a witness. However, in some jurisdictions, the witness's written statement would be considered derivative material. In short, the attorney's effort and imagination play a role in the very creation of derivative material.

   b. The information is the work product of an attorney. A few jurisdictions still insist that the attorney personally prepare the material. However, that requirement interferes with the manner in which attorneys customarily conduct their business. They often use clerks, investigators, and the client to gather information and prepare reports. For that reason, the overwhelming majority of jurisdictions now extends the protection to information collected by the attorney's agent.

   c. The material must be prepared in anticipation of litigation. Suit need not be filed, but the client and attorney must anticipate litigation when the material is prepared. In this respect, the work product protection is narrower than the attorney-client privilege.

Some of the statutes and court rules codifying the work product protection in criminal cases purport to create an absolute protection.[6] However, absent such a statute or court rule, in civil cases the prevailing view is that the protection is conditional and that the opposing party can override the protection by a compelling showing of need.

---

[5] *Id.*

[6] Steven W. Feldman, *The Work Product Rule in Criminal Practice and Procedure,* 50 U. CIN L. REV. 495, 506 (1981).

Even under this view, it is far more difficult to overcome a work product claim for material reflecting the attorney's opinions; but it is possible to do so.[7] The opposing party can do so by showing that:

5.   The information is logically relevant to the material facts of consequence in the case.

6.   The information is highly relevant to the outcome of the case. The opponent should argue that the information relates to the central or one of the pivotal issues in the case. More precisely, the attorney should show that the information on that issue is needed to effectively prepare for trial.

7.   There is no reasonably available, alternative source for the information. Either there is no alternative source at all, or resort to the alternative source would involve prohibitive expense or inconvenience.

The work product protection issue ordinarily arises during pretrial discovery; one party seeks discovery of a document, and the opposing party resists discovery by claiming the protection. Given the pretrial context, attorneys usually present their supporting facts in affidavits rather than eliciting live testimony. To illustrate the doctrine, we shall present first a claimant's affidavit, then a sample foundation for the claimant in the unlikely eventuality that the claimant uses live testimony, and finally the opponent's affidavit. In our hypothetical, the party seeking discovery is a civil defendant. The defendant desires an accident reconstruction report. The party resisting discovery is the plaintiff, Ms. Leonard. The expert was Professor Suarez. When the plaintiff submitted the affidavit, the attorney would simultaneously submit a memorandum of points and authorities. The memorandum would cite the statutes, rules, and cases granting the material work product protection.

---

[7] As we shall see in [2], *infra,* the courts sometimes distinguish between absolutely protected "core" or "opinion" work product and conditionally protected "fact" or "ordinary" work product. The courts confer absolute or at least more extensive protection on the former because it reflects the attorney's theories and analysis of the case.

Form 7-1

STATE OF EL DORADO	
COUNTY OF MORENA	AFFIDAVIT

I, the undersigned, being duly sworn, depose and say that:

1. My name is Stephen Metzger. I reside at 452 Madison Street, Morena, El Dorado. I am an attorney with the firm of Luce, Gray, Forward, and Ames, 433 B Street, Morena, El Dorado.

2. I represent Ms. Adrienne Leonard, the plaintiff in Leonard v. Morton, civil action number 1778 now pending in Morena Superior Court (1).

3. The defendant has moved for the production of a report submitted to me by Professor Paul Suarez. My client and I hereby claim the work product protection, (3) and on that ground we refuse to surrender Professor Suarez' report to the defendant. (2)

4. On February 14, YR-4, I decided that I needed an expert evaluation of the physical evidence left at the scene of the collision between the defendant's van and my client's car on February 11, YR-4. (4c) In her complaint, my client alleges that the defendant's car drifted into her lane and that the point of impact was in her lane. The defendant's answer denies these allegations, and I lack the expertise in physics and the laws of motion to evaluate the physical evidence left at the accident scene. Consequently, on February 15, YR-4, I telephoned Professor Paul Suarez who teaches in the Physics Department at the University of El Dorado, Morena. I have used him in several prior cases as an accident reconstruction expert. I told Professor Suarez that I needed an expert evaluation of the accident scene as part of my pretrial preparation; I asked him for a confidential report on that subject. He agreed to prepare the report and submit it to me. (4b) On February 16, YR-4, Professor Suarez and I visited the accident scene, and on February 20, YR-4, he submitted his personal written report to me. (4a) The report recites his findings and conclusions as to the manner in which the collision occurred. I have maintained the report's confidentiality; the only persons who have viewed the report are Professor Suarez, my client, and myself. At the present time, I have not decided whether to call Professor Suarez as a witness at trial.

_____

/s/ Stephen Metzger

On April 2, YR-3, before the undersigned, a Notary Public for the State of El Dorado, personally appeared Stephen Metzger, known to me to be the person whose name is subscribed to the within instrument, and acknowledged that he executed the same.

/s/ Linda Draper
Notary Public
My license expires May 1, YR+4

In some instances, the party asserting the work product protection might present live testimony in opposition to the motion for the production of the protected report. Or the party could offer live testimony if the other side subpoenas the report's author and the party moves pretrial to quash the subpoena or objects at trial. In the following example, the witness is Professor Suarez. He has already identified himself and stated his occupation. The plaintiff, the party resisting discovery, is the proponent.

P	Professor, WHERE were you on the morning of February 15, YR-4?
W	I was in my office at the U.E.D. Campus in Morena.
P	WHAT happened that morning?
W	I received a telephone call from you.
P	WHAT was said during this telephone call? (4a)
W	You told me that you wanted an expert evaluation of the scene of the accident between your client and the defendant.
P	WHAT was the purpose of this evaluation? (4c)
W	At least your stated purpose was that you needed it as part of your pretrial preparation.
P	WHAT was your response when I asked you to conduct the evaluation? (4b)
W	I agreed to do so.
P	WHAT happened then?
W	I met you and visited the accident scene on February 16.
P	Please be specific. WHERE did you go?
W	I went to the intersection of C and 5th Streets where this accident supposedly occurred.
P	WHAT did you do after you visited the accident scene? (4a)
W	I prepared a report.
P	WHAT form was the report in? (4a)
W	It was a typed, four-page document.
P	WHAT did you do with the report?
W	I gave the original and two copies to you.
P	HOW many copies were there?
W	Three.
P	WHAT did you do with the other copy?

W	I have it in my files.
P	WHO has access to your files?
W	Only myself.
P	WHOM have you shown the report to?
W	Only you.
P	WHY haven't you shown the report to other people?
W	You instructed me to keep it confidential, and I've carried out your instructions.
P	WHAT role will you have at the trial in this case?
W	I do not intend to testify in this case. You have not asked me to. For my part, I have not agreed to or indicated any willingness to do so.

Finally, the following is the format for an affidavit by the party seeking discovery:

Form 7-2

| STATE OF EL DORADO | AFFIDAVIT |
| COUNTY OF MORENA | |

I, the undersigned, being duly sworn, depose and say that:

1. My name is James Gamer. I reside at 7076 Vista Way, Del Mar, El Dorado. I am the attorney with the firm of Sullivan and Archer, 1234 1st Street, Morena, El Dorado.

2. I represent Mr. Philip Morton, the defendant in Leonard v. Morton, civil action number 1778 now pending in Morena Superior Court.

3. We have moved for the production of a report submitted by Professor Paul Suarez to the plaintiff's attorney, Mr. Stephen Metzger. The subject of the report is an expert evaluation of the physical evidence left at the scene of the collision between the plaintiff's car and my client's van at the intersection of C and 5th Streets in downtown Morena. The report is logically relevant to the material facts in this case. On page 12 of the plaintiff's complaint, she alleges that my client's van drifted into her traffic lane and the point of impact was in her lane. Page 4 of the defendant's answer denies those allegations. Thus, the point of impact is a material fact of consequence in this case, and Professor Suarez' accident reconstruction report undoubtedly discusses point of impact. (5)

4. The information contained in Professor Suarez' report is essential to the effective pretrial preparation of this case. If the jury finds as a matter of fact that my client's van drifted into the plaintiff's lane, that fact alone may persuade the jurors to conclude that my client was negligent. However, if the jury finds as a matter of fact that the point of impact was in my client's lane, again that fact alone may convince the jurors that the plaintiff's own carelessness caused the accident. (6)

5. There is no reasonably available, alternative source for this information. In the first place, Professor Suarez is widely regarded as the leading accident reconstruction expert in Morena County. During the past five years, our own law firm has used him more often than any other accident reconstruction witness in our cases. His report would be more authoritative than any other local expert's report. Secondly, Professor Suarez' report may contain a more detailed description of the physical evidence at the accident than any other report. Page 4 of the February 12, YR-4, Morena Police Department Accident Report filed in this case states that there was "a good deal of debris," but neither the accident report's narrative section nor the attached diagram indicates the nature or specific location of the debris. The report does not include any photographs of the accident scene. Mr. Morton did not employ this law firm until March 13, YR-4. We immediately hired an accident reconstruc-

tion expert, but she was unable to visit the accident scene until March 16, YR-4—weeks after the accident. I accompanied her to the scene; but when we did so, we could not locate any skidmarks, gouge marks, or debris clearly attributable to the accident. In contrast, Professor Suarez visited the scene only a few days after the collision. Hence, Professor Suarez' report may be the only source for critical information about the accident scene.

/s/ James Gamer

On May 13, YR-3, before the undersigned, a Notary Public for the State of El Dorado, personally appeared James Gamer, known to me to be the person whose name is subscribed to the within instrument, and acknowledged that he executed the same.

/s/ Stanley Crosby
Notary Public
My license expires June 13, YR+4.

[2] THE ABSOLUTE WORK PRODUCT PROTECTION

In most cases, work product protection is conditional; the party seeking discovery can overcome the protection by showing a compelling, case-specific need for the information. However, by statute, some jurisdictions recognize an absolute work product protection for certain types of very sensitive trial preparation materials. Some courts construe the language of Federal Rule of Civil Procedure 26(b) as conferring absolute protection on certain types of information—sometimes described as "core" or "opinion" work product rather than "fact" or "ordinary" work product.[8] After stating the conditional work product protection, the Rule continues: "If the court orders discovery of those materials, it must protect against disclosure of the mental impressions, conclusions, opinions, or legal theories of a party's attorney or other representative concerning the litigation." Under this construction of Rule 26, those materials are absolutely privileged; even if the party seeking discovery shows a compelling need for the material, the material cannot be discovered. The problem is definitional; if the material falls within one of the categories listed in the statute, the discovery motion must be denied. If a party seeks discovery of such material, the party claiming the absolute work product protection usually responds by affidavit.

With one exception, the foundation for absolute work product protection is roughly the same as the foundation for conditional work product protection:

1.   The party is invoking the protection in the right type of proceeding. The judge

---

[8] However, in *United States v. Nobles*, 422 U.S. 225, 239, 95 S. Ct. 2160, 45 L. Ed. 2d 141 (1975), the Court remarked that "[t]he privilege derived from the work-product doctrine is not absolute." The Court stated that *Hickman* afforded only "qualified" protection. *Id.* at 237–39. *See* Note, *Baker v. General Motors: The Work Product Doctrine in the Eighth Circuit*, 34 CREIGHTON L. REV. 475, 476, 514–15 (2001) (the protection for opinion work product is "nearly absolute").

examines the pleadings on file to determine whether the case is the right type of action. As previously stated, some jurisdictions recognize absolute protection in criminal cases.[9]

2.   The party is asserting the right type of protection. The protection is the personal right to refuse to disclose the material during pretrial discovery or at trial.

3.   The party claiming the protection is a proper holder. The courts treat the attorney as holder but sometimes grant clients standing to invoke the work product doctrine.[10]

4.   The information the party seeks to suppress is absolutely protected. In a civil action, to qualify for absolute protection, the material would ordinarily have to satisfy these requirements:

   a.   The material reflects the attorney's creative thought process. A memorandum summarizing the attorney's impressions of a witness or outlining the attorney's legal theories would be absolutely protected.

   b.   The material is the work product of an attorney. In the case of absolutely protected material, most courts require that the attorney personally prepare the material.

   c.   The material was prepared in anticipation of litigation.

The following is an affidavit an attorney might file to assert absolute work product protection:

---

[9] Steven W. Feldman, *The Work Product Rule in Criminal Practice and Procedure,* 50 U. CIN. L. REV. 506 (1981).

[10] In most cases, the holder asserts the protection against a stranger to the attorney-client relation. However, in some cases the attorney asserts the protection against the former client. For instance, the attorney might claim the protection in the client's malpractice suit against the attorney or the attorney's suit against the client for fees. There is a split of authority over the question of whether the absolute protection applies in these settings.

Form 7-3

STATE OF EL DORADO

COUNTY OF MORENA   AFFIDAVIT

I, the undersigned, being duly sworn, depose and say that:

1. My name is Peter Mehalick. I reside at 1333 Cape May Street, Morena, El Dorado. I am an attorney with the firm of Seltzer, Muns, and Mason, 2444 4th Street, Morena, El Dorado.

2. I represent Ms. Michelle Lucerne, the plaintiff in Lucerne v. Rodriguez, civil action number 1999 now pending in Morena Superior Court. (1)

3. The defendant has moved for the production of the witness statement of Mr. Giles Folsom, an eyewitness to the collision that gave rise to this suit. The defendant's motion specifically stated that the defendant desired Mr. Folsom's statement "and all attachments." My client and I hereby claim the absolute work product protection, (3) and on that ground we refuse to surrender one attachment, a memorandum that I personally prepared and that is dated February 17, YR-4. (2)

4. On February 16, YR-4, I interviewed Mr. Folsom at my office in downtown Morena. I interviewed Mr. Folsom because I realized that we might call him as a witness at trial. (4c) We had filed suit before I interviewed Mr. Folsom. (4c) After the interview, I had my secretary type a copy of his statement and submit it to him for his signature. My secretary did so before he left my office, and I have his signed statement dated February 16, YR-4. We do not oppose the discovery of that witness statement. However, the next day, February 17, YR-4, I dictated a memorandum for file. (4b) The memorandum outlines my impressions of Mr. Folsom as a potential witness. (4a) The memorandum also contains my conclusion as to how his potential testimony can impact my theory of the case as well as how to conduct his direct examination and prepare him for cross-examination. (4a) Given the memorandum's contents, the memorandum is entitled to absolute work product protection. Although the memorandum is presently physically attached to Mr. Folsom's witness statement, the memorandum is not discoverable.

_____

/s/ Peter Mehalick

On May 13, YR-3, before the undersigned, a Notary Public for the State of El Dorado, personally appeared Peter Mehalick, known to me to be the person whose name is subscribed to the within instrument, and acknowledged that he executed the same.

/s/ Stanley Crosby
Notary Public
My license expires June 13, YR+4

As in the previous hypothetical, when the attorney submitted this affidavit, the attorney would also submit a memorandum of law. The memorandum should mention the statutes, rules, and cases conferring absolute work product protection. At oral argument on the discovery motion, the attorney would use the memorandum as the source of law and the affidavit as the source of facts.

Like the attorney-client privilege, the work product immunity is subject to a crime-fraud exception. Douglas R. Richmond, *Understanding the Crime-Fraud Exception to the Attorney-Client Privilege and Work Product Immunity*, 70 S. C. L. REV. 1 (2018). However, in some jurisdictions the scope of the exception to the immunity differs from the scope of the exception to the privilege. In a number of jurisdictions both the attorney and the client are considered holders of the immunity; and some of these jurisdictions take the position that the attorney's wrongful state of mind vitiates the immunity even if the client has an innocent state of mind. Moreover, again like the attorney-client privilege, the work product immunity can be waived. However, the scope of the waiver doctrine for the immunity differs from the scope of the doctrine for the privilege. The privilege is ordinarily waived whenever the holder discloses the communication to anyone outside the circle of confidence. In contrast, the immunity is intended to protect the adversary system; and the holder waives the immunity only if he or she discloses the information in a manner that "substantially increase[s] the opportunity for potential adversaries to obtain the information." *Brown v. NCL (Bahamas), Ltd.*, 155 F. Supp. 3d 1335, 1339–40 (S.D. Fla. 2015).

§ 7.07   GOVERNMENT PRIVILEGES—MILITARY AND STATE SECRETS

[1]   THE DOCTRINE

Military and state secrets affect the vital interest of the country. The magnitude of the interest justifies creating an evidentiary privilege to cloak these secrets. Following the English precedents, the United States Supreme Court recognized a topical privilege for military and state secrets in *United States v. Reynolds*, 345 U.S. 1, 73 S. Ct. 528, 97 L. Ed 727 (1953). The Court created an absolute privilege; if the material falls within the definition of military or state secret, the material is not discoverable even if the party seeking discovery can demonstrate a compelling need for the information. The extent of the showing of need determines how deeply the court probes to determine whether the information is privileged; but if the court ultimately finds that the absolute privilege applies, a case-specific, ad hoc showing of need does not trump the privilege. Since the 9/11 terrorist attack on New York, the federal government has asserted this privilege more frequently. The government can move to intervene to assert the privilege in cases in which it is not a named party. The government often does so in order to claim the privilege in lawsuits between private parties, especially government contractors.

The most troublesome problem has been defining military and state secret. Although no court has developed a simple definition of these terms, one commentator—now a federal judge—has offered a relatively comprehensive list of the types of materials falling within the definition of military secret: "The specific areas of sensitive information appear to be: (a) The plans and capabilities of specific combat operations; (b) the official estimates of the military plans and capabilities of potential enemy nations; (c) the existence, design, and production of new weapons or equipment or the existence and results of research programs specifically directed toward producing new weapons and equipment; (d) the existence and nature of special ways and means of organizing combat operations; (e) the identity and location of vulnerable areas such as production facilities, critical supply depots, or weapons installations; (f) the existence and nature of clandestine intelligence operations; (g) the keys to communication codes; and (h) the existence and nature of international agreements relative to military plans and capabilities and the exchange of intelligence."[11]

It is more difficult to define "state secrets." To date, no court has furnished as specific or useful a definition of that term as the above explanation of "military secrets." The privilege for state secrets should be upheld only when the likely effect of disclosing the information would be to so anger officials of a foreign government or international organization that the disclosure would imperil relations between the United States and that government or organization. For instance, the privilege might protect information about our government's bargaining position in sensitive, ongoing negotiations with a foreign government. In *United States v. Husayn aka Zubaydah*, 142 S. Ct. 959, 212 L. Ed. 2d 65 (2022), the Supreme Court upheld the government's state secret claim to refuse to confirm the existence of a CIA detection center in Poland. The CIA Director had filed a declaration that confirmation would imperil "clandestine relationships with foreign intelligence services." The declaration stated that such relationships are "based on mutual trust that the classified existence and nature of the relationship will not be disclosed." Although there was information in the public domain about the site, neither the American nor the Polish government had officially acknowledged its existence.

[2] ELEMENTS OF THE FOUNDATION

The government can assert this privilege in any type of proceeding. As previously stated, the government need not be a party to the litigation. Hence, the type of proceeding is not a required element of the foundation. The foundation includes these elements:

1. The government is asserting the right type of privilege. The government may refuse to disclose the information and prevent a third party from making unauthorized disclosure.

2. The party asserting the privilege is a holder. The holder is ordinarily the official in charge of the government department with jurisdiction over the information. The head of the department should make a formal, written claim of privilege. The claim should reflect that the department head gave personal consideration to the question of whether the public interest required the assertion of the privilege.

---

[11] James Zagel, *The State Secrets Privilege*, 50 MINN. L. REV. 875, 884–85 (1966).

3.   The information the holder seeks to suppress is a military or state secret. The written claim should indicate the general nature of the privileged information and assert that the government department has maintained the confidentiality of the information.

[3] SAMPLE FOUNDATION

The fact situation is a suit arising from a plane crash. Advanced Aircraft Company was testing a plane with a new guidance system for air-to-air missiles. The plane crashed during the test, and the test pilot was killed. The pilot's widow brings a wrongful death action against the company and the United States Government. If the government attorney anticipated claiming the military secret privilege, the attorney should contact the appropriate government official before trial and have that official prepare a formal, written claim of privilege.

Form 7-4

CITY OF WASHINGTON

DISTRICT OF COLUMBIA

AFFIDAVIT

I, the undersigned, being duly sworn, depose and say that:

1. My name is John R. Overholt. I reside at 230 Fellmeth Drive, Arlington, Virginia. I am the Secretary of Defense of the United States. (2) My offices are in the White House at the nation's capital.

2. The United States is a party defendant to Jennings v. Advanced Aircraft Co. and the United States, civil action C1477 now pending in Federal District Court in Washington, D.C.

3. It is my understanding that the plaintiff may seek to discover information about the guidance system for air-to-air missiles installed in the airplane involved in the crash which gave rise to this suit. That information is within the jurisdiction of my government department, and I hereby claim the military secret privilege for such information. (2) On that ground, I refuse to disclose the information and request that the court preclude any third party from disclosing the information. (1)

4. I have personally reviewed the requested materials about the guidance system. This new guidance system has been in development for the past seven years. The system incorporates new features which, to the best of my knowledge, foreign countries neither use nor have knowledge of. (3) If perfected, the system would give our planes a decided advantage in aerial combat. (3) The disclosure of this information would significantly harm our national defense interests. (3) To date, our department has maintained the secrecy of this information. (3) The information has been classified COSMIC TOP SECRET, and only persons with both a proper security clearance and a proven need to know have had access to this information. (3)

_____

/s/ John R. Overholt

On September 19, YR-3, before the undersigned, a Notary Public for the District of Columbia, personally appeared John R. Overholt, known to me to be the person whose name is subscribed to the within instrument, and acknowledged that he executed the same.

_____

/s/ Marcia Gallagher

Notary Public

My license expires October 19, YR+4

At trial, the plaintiff's attorney calls Mr. Garrett Winslow as a witness. Winslow identifies himself and states that he is Advanced Aircraft's chief engineer in charge of the development of the new guidance system. The plaintiff is the proponent. The plaintiff is examining Mr. Winslow as a hostile witness. Since the written claim of privilege will not be tendered to the jury, it will be inserted in the record of trial,[12] but it will not be offered as a formal exhibit.

P	Mr. Winslow, ISN'T IT TRUE THAT before this crash, the model of plane involved had a perfect safety record?
W	Yes.
P	ISN'T IT ALSO TRUE THAT you installed a new guidance system for missiles on this plane just before the test?
W	Yes.
P	IN FACT, WASN'T the very purpose of the flight to test the new guidance system?
W	Yes.
P	Please describe this guidance system for us.
O	Your Honor, I object to that question on the ground that it calls for privileged information. May we approach the bench?
J	Yes.
O	Your Honor, I request that this be marked defense exhibit C for identification.
J	It will be so marked.
O	Your Honor, please let the record reflect that I am showing the exhibit to the opposing counsel.
J	It will so reflect.
O	Your Honor, since this document is properly notarized and bears the purported signature of a public official, it is self-authenticating under Rule 902. The exhibit is a formal claim of the military secret privilege for the information about the guidance system.
J	Give me a minute to read the exhibit. *(Pause.)* The claim seems to be in proper order.
P	Your Honor, my client has a compelling need for that information. We contend that that guidance system caused this accident.
O	The military secret privilege is absolute. So long as the information falls within the definition of military secret, the information is undiscoverable. Secretary Overholt's affidavit clearly shows that this information falls within the definition.
J	I think you're right. The objection will be sustained.

---

[12] It might be designated as an appellate exhibit.

When the court sustains the privilege claim, the immediate effect is that the privileged information becomes unavailable as evidence. However, there may be other important consequences. If the federal government successfully asserts the privilege in a federal prosecution and as a result the accused is denied information relevant to the issue of guilt or innocence, the government may have to dismiss the charges. If the government asserts the privilege in a lawsuit between private parties and as a result the plaintiff has insufficient evidence to sustain the initial burden of production, the defendant can obtain summary judgment. There is also authority that dismissal is mandatory when the government's successful privilege assertion deprives a private defendant of information needed to maintain a defense on the merits.

§ 7.08 GOVERNMENT PRIVILEGES—MINOR GOVERNMENT SECRETS

[1] THE DOCTRINE

Military and state secrets are such major government secrets that the courts have granted them an absolute evidentiary privilege. There are other, lesser government secrets that also warrant a measure of protection. Like major secrets, these subjects are protected by a topical privilege. However, minor government secrets are usually subject to a merely conditional privilege; the secret is ordinarily privileged, but the party seeking discovery can defeat the ad hoc privilege by demonstrating a compelling need for the information.

Confidential Communications Within Government. The definition of a minor government secret varies from jurisdiction to jurisdiction. The federal courts have adopted a relatively narrow definition. In *Ackerly v. Ley*, 420 F.2d 1336, 1340 (D.C. Cir. 1969), the court referred to "the familiar doctrine that the Executive branch is privileged not to disclose intragovernmental documents reflecting advisory opinions, recommendations, and deliberations comprising part of a process by which governmental decisions are formulated." The federal courts have attempted to protect the secrecy of the decision-making process. The courts reason that the ultimate government decision will be of higher quality if public officials are candid in their policy discussions and they are more likely to be candid if they know that the decision-making process is confidential. The doctrine is sometimes called the predecisional, deliberative process privilege; to be protected, the document must both reflect the deliberative process and be predecisional. To begin with, federal courts limit their minor government secret privilege to documents which are an integral part of a government decision-making process such as subordinates' recommendations and drafts. In most cases, this privilege does not protect raw factual data submitted to or gathered by the government if that data is reasonably segregable from the deliberative portions of the writing. Moreover, the document must be predecisional; thus, documents embodying the final government decision are discoverable—unless they amount to state or military secrets. Although the deliberative process privilege is the newest federal governmental privilege, it is now the governmental privilege asserted most frequently in federal practice, especially in Freedom of Information Act litigation.

Confidential Communications to Government. Many states use a much broader definition. Although the federal deliberative process privilege is designed to promote candor within government, as we shall see in § 7.09 the federal courts also recognize a privilege for an informer's identity to encourage informers to come forward and provide information about criminal activity to law enforcement authorities. Many states have created a broad privilege to facilitate the flow of information to government. In these states, a minor government secret privilege attaches if the government shows that: (1) It has a legitimate need for a certain type of information; and (2) it cannot be assured of a free flow of that type of information unless it assures confidentiality to the sources of information. A good example is a parole board. A parole board needs background information about prisoners applying for parole. The board cannot expect candid evaluation from citizens unless it assures those citizens that their letters and interviews will remain confidential.

Even if the government makes out a *prima facie* case for the application of the minor government secret privilege, the party seeking discovery can often defeat the privilege. The party can ordinarily overcome the privilege by showing an overriding need for the information. Unlike the communications privileges for relationships such as attorney-client, the deliberative process privilege[13] and other privileges are minor government secrets are not absolute. Rather, the party can show an ad hoc need in the same fashion as a party seeking to defeat a conditional work product privilege. The courts often override the privilege when the party seeking the information makes a plausible allegation that the government has engaged in misconduct.

[2]   ELEMENTS OF THE FOUNDATION

To establish a *prima facie* case for invoking the minor government secret privilege, the party opposing discovery must show these foundational elements:

1. The party asserting the privilege is a holder. The government agency receiving the information is the holder. The judge will usually permit any government agent, including the prosecutor, to invoke the privilege.

2. The party is asserting the right type of privilege. The government may refuse to disclose the information and prevent a third party from making disclosure.

3. The information is privileged. In federal court, to invoke the deliberative process privilege the party must show that:

    a. The document is deliberative in nature in the sense that it reflects the give-and-take of the decision-making process. All courts agree that the deliberations are protected when they relate to the discretionary formu-

---

[13] Although the courts normally treat the deliberative process privilege as qualified, in one context, Freedom of Information Act (FOIA) litigation, the privilege is absolute and cannot be defeated by a showing of need. In *EPA v. Mink*, 410 U.S. 73, 93 S. Ct. 827, 35 L. Ed. 2d 119 (1973), the Supreme Court held that in an FOIA suit, the question is not whether the information would be privileged in normal federal litigation. Rather, the Court construed the Act as limiting the judge's inquiry to whether the type of information in question would fall within the general scope of the privilege. If the information falls within that scope, the judge does not engage in balancing to determine whether the individual filing the FOIA request has demonstrated a need for the information that overrides the government's interest in confidentiality.

lation of general government policy. Most courts concur that the deliberations are also protected when they concern the exercise of discretion in applying government policy in specific cases, such as in deciding whether to grant a permit. Many courts have extended the privilege to deliberations over how to respond to inquiries from Congress, the media, and the public. The document states the author's personal, subjective opinions such as proposals rather than the agency's final policy;

b.   The document was predecisional. The document does not embody the final decision; and

c.   The government has maintained the confidentiality of the document.

  To invoke the state privilege encouraging the flow of information to the government, the party must show that:

d.   The government has a legitimate need for this type of information; and

e.   The government cannot obtain a free flow of this type of information unless it assures its sources confidentiality.

f.   The government has maintained the confidentiality of the information.

  In general to defeat the privilege, the party seeking discovery must show that:

4.   The information is logically relevant to the material facts of consequence in the case.

5.   The information is highly relevant to the outcome of the case. The party should argue that the information relates to the central or one of the pivotal issues in the case.

6.   There is no reasonably available, alternative source for the information.

In addition, some courts recognize an exception to the scope of the privilege when misconduct such as a coverup conspiracy occurs during the government deliberations. Moreover, the privilege is waivable.

[3]   SAMPLE FOUNDATIONS

This issue can arise during pretrial discovery or at trial. For that reason, we shall illustrate both an affidavit and a foundation at trial.

The first illustration is an affidavit claiming the deliberative process privilege in federal court. The fact situation is a product liability suit. The suit is in federal court because of diversity of citizenship. The plaintiff, Mr. Michael Lindsey, sues Maitland Company. The plaintiff alleges that the defendant negligently manufactured a bottle of medicine and that when he consumed some of the medicine, he sustained serious internal injuries. The plaintiff has served a subpoena duces tecum on the Federal Trade Commission (F.T.C.). Three years ago, the F.T.C. conducted a national survey of drug stores to determine the number of complaints about certain medicines. One of the medicines was the product the plaintiff purchased. The plaintiff seeks the F.T.C.'s preliminary report evaluating the survey results. The F.T.C. moves to quash the subpoena. The following is the affidavit supporting the F.T.C.'s motion.

Form 7-5

CITY OF WASHINGTON

DISTRICT OF COLUMBIA   AFFIDAVIT

I, the undersigned, being duly sworn, depose and say that:

1. My name is Mrs. Jane Garson. I reside at 1440 Gilder Drive, Silver Springs, Maryland. I am the Chairperson of the Federal Trade Commission. (1) My offices are on Pennsylvania Avenue in the nation's capitol.

2. The plaintiff in Lindsey v. Maitland Company, civil action C2001, now pending in Federal District Court in Washington, D.C., has served a subpoena duces tecum upon me. The subpoena directs me to produce for inspection and copying our preliminary YR-4 report entitled "Complaints to Druggists About Medicines." That information is within the jurisdiction of my Commission. (1) I hereby claim the government information, deliberative process privilege for this report. (2) On that ground, I refuse to surrender the report and respectfully request that the court quash the subpoena served upon me. (2)

3. We began this survey in YR-6 to decide whether we should remove any of the studied drugs and medicines from the market. (3a) The preliminary report itself was drafted in early YR-4. The report summarizes the survey and discusses medical problems possibly caused by the various medicines. The report states conclusions and recommendations with respect to each medicine studied. (3a) In my judgment, it would be contrary to the public interest to release this report for public inspection. We assured the druggists responding to the survey that we would maintain the confidentiality of their responses; many expressed a strong fear of reprisal from the manufacturers which they depend on as their suppliers.

4. In addition, this sort of decision-making process requires candor among public officials, and we can achieve that candor only if the decision-making process is confidential. It is true that later in YR-4 we formally published our order, removing certain medicines from the market, in the Federal Register. (3b) However, this particular report was completed well before the issuance of the order and was part of the deliberative process which culminated in the issuance of that order. The report reflects the personal policy views and analyses of the report authors, not the commission's final policy. (3b) The report itself has never been released to any private person. (3c) Indeed, the report has been shared with only government agencies directly concerned with medicine and health care; and we instructed them to maintain the confidentiality of the report. (3c)

_____

/s/ Jane Garson

On December 22, YR-3, before the undersigned, a Notary Public for the District of Columbia, personally appeared Jane S. Garson, known to me to be the person whose name is subscribed to the within instrument, and acknowledged that she executed the same.

———————————————
/s/ Thomas Barton
Notary Public
My license expires January 22, YR+4

Even if the judge was inclined to sustain this privilege claim, the plaintiff might request that the judge examine the report in camera to determine whether the survey responses referenced in the report constitute factual data that are reasonably segregable from the deliberative parts of the report.

We shall now illustrate a foundation at trial for a state minor government secret privilege.

The fact situation is a wrongful death action. The plaintiffs are the surviving relatives of the decedent, Andrew Kaye. The defendant is Gary Shelton. The complaint alleges that the defendant and a Mr. Michaels fatally shot Andrew Kaye during a civil rights rally in early YR-4. The defendant's answer denied all involvement in the shooting. Michaels was tried, convicted, and sentenced in late YR-4. The plaintiff's civil action against Shelton comes to trial today. During their case-in-chief, the plaintiffs called Ms. Martha McGill. She testified that she witnessed the shooting. She identified the defendant as one of the assailants. During the defense case-in-chief, the defendant calls Mr. Daniel Riley as a witness. Earlier in the testimony Mr. Riley identified himself and stated that he is an employee of the El Dorado Board of Prison Terms. Riley testifies that he prepared a parole report on Michaels when the Board was considering Michaels' parole application. The defendant hopes to prove that Riley interviewed Ms. McGill and that during the interview, Ms. McGill said that although she could recognize Michaels as one killer, she could not identify the other assailant. The defendant is the proponent. The opponent is a Deputy Attorney General. When Riley was subpoenaed, he notified the Office of the Attorney General; and the State entered an appearance for the purpose of asserting the minor government secret privilege.

P	When you prepared this report, WHOM did you interview?
W	Several people.
P	Specifically WHOM?
W	A Genevieve Morton, Brian Michaels, and a Ms. McGill, who witnessed the shooting itself.
P	WHAT is Ms. McGill's full name?
W	Martha McGill.
P	WHAT was her occupation?
W	She was the cashier at a store near the killing.

P	WHAT did she say during her interview?
O	Your Honor, I object to that question on the ground that it calls for privileged government information. I request permission to take the witness on voir dire.
J	Permission granted.
O	Mr. Riley, WHY did you interview Ms. McGill? (3d)
W	I wanted to get some information about the robbery.
O	WHY did you need that information? (3d)
W	Actually, it's the Board who needs it. The Board wants to know as much as they can about the gravity of the crime to determine an appropriate release date.
O	HOW do you get the information? (3d)
W	I interview the witnesses to the crime.
O	WHERE and WHEN did you interview Ms. McGill? (3e)
W	In my office three months ago.
O	WHO else was there? (3e)
W	Only the two of us.
O	HOW many doors does your office have? (3e)
W	Two.
O	WHAT position were the doors in at the time of the interview? (3e)
W	They both were closed.
O	WHAT, if anything, did you tell Ms. McGill at the beginning of the interview? (3e)
W	I thanked her for taking the time to stop by. I told her that her information would be very helpful to the Board, and I assured her that we would keep the interview confidential to the extent possible.
O	WHY did you give her that assurance? (3e)
W	People are often reluctant to talk to the parole officials.
O	WHY? (3e)
W	The most obvious reason is that they're afraid of reprisals from the criminal and his or her associates. That's a huge concern in gang cases. We always tell interviewees that we'll keep the information confidential as far as possible.
O	WHAT did you do after you interviewed Ms. McGill? (3e)
W	I summarized her statements and included them in the report.
O	WHOM did you give the report to? (3e)
W	The Board.

O	HOW did you deliver it to them? (3e)
W	I hand-delivered it to them in a sealed envelope.
O	WHOM else have you shown the report to? (3e)
W	No one.
O	WHY haven't you shown it to anyone? (3e)
W	I want to keep my promise to the interviewees that the information will be confidential. Once word gets out that you don't keep that promise, the sources of information dry up.
O	Your Honor, I have no further questions of this witness on voir dire. May we approach the bench?
J	Yes.
O	Your Honor, it's clear at this point that the witness was gathering information that the government has a legitimate need for. It's also the type of information that the government can't gather unless it assures its sources confidentiality. For that reason, the privilege applies here.
J	I agree. The objection will be sustained.

If the party seeking discovery wants to overcome the conditional privilege, the party should file an affidavit. The affidavit ought to detail the logical relevance of the information, the party's need for the information, and the unavailability of reasonably equivalent, alternative proof. The party should use the same format as James Gamer's affidavit in § 7.06 of this chapter. Paragraph 3 of that affidavit explains the logical relevance of the information sought. Paragraph 4 demonstrates that the information relates to a pivotal issue in the case. Finally, paragraph 5 shows that it would be difficult or impossible for the party to obtain substitute evidence.

§ 7.09 GOVERNMENT PRIVILEGES—AN INFORMANT'S IDENTITY

[1] THE DOCTRINE

The last section discussed the rules for the qualified privilege for minor government secrets. This section deals with a particular application of those rules: the government privilege for an informer's identity. In many cases, an informant would not report a law violation unless the government assured him or her confidentiality; the informant sometimes fears reprisals from the criminal, and in other cases the informant does not want to expose his or her own involvement in the crime to public scrutiny. To encourage informants to report violations of the law, the courts have created a conditional privilege for the informant's identity. The privilege ordinarily does not protect the informant's report; given its narrow purpose, the privilege protects only the identity of a person who confidentially reports a law violation to law enforcement authorities.

Like other conditional privileges, this privilege can be defeated if the accused shows a compelling need for the informant's testimony. In most cases, the court will find a compelling need when the accused demonstrates that the informant has personal knowledge of the facts determining the accused's guilt or innocence. If the informer merely supplied an investigative lead and pointed a finger of suspicion at the defendant but did not observe the crime, the informer is only a "tipster"; and the court will not order the disclosure of the informer's identity. However, when the informer personally observed the facts relevant to the crime's elements or an affirmative defense, the informer is a "percipient witness"; and the court will usually order disclosure. In *Roviaro v. United States*, 353 U.S. 53, 77 S. Ct. 623, 1 L. Ed. 2d 639 (1957), the Supreme Court stated that the defendant has a due process right to override the privilege when the informant is a percipient witness. The defense does not have to make a preliminary showing that the percipient witness's testimony will be favorable. The defense need show only that the witness has personal knowledge of facts material to the theory of the defense. In many cases, if the defense makes that showing, the judge then interviews the alleged informant in chambers. If the interview convinces the judge that the informant can give testimony that would strengthen the accused's defense on the merits, the judge then orders the prosecution to disclose the informant's identity to the defense.

[2] ELEMENTS OF THE FOUNDATION

The foundation for the privilege itself includes these elements:

1. The privilege applies in this type of proceeding. Most of the cases recognizing the privilege are criminal prosecutions. However, the issue can arise in civil actions such as civil rights cases and actions for libel or malicious prosecution.

2. The party claiming the privilege is a proper holder. The government is the formal holder. The courts usually permit the government's agents, including prosecutors, to invoke the privilege on the government's behalf.

3. The holder is asserting the right type of privilege. The government can refuse to disclose the informer's identity; this privilege does not entitle the government to suppress the informant's report unless its contents will tend to give away the informant's identity. Further, the government can prevent another person from disclosing the informer's identity. However, the government cannot silence the informer himself or herself; if the informer is brave or foolhardy enough to admit his or her identity, the government loses the privilege.

4. The information is privileged.

    a. A person made a confidential report.

    b. The subject of the report was a violation of law.

    c. The person made the report to a law enforcement agency such as the police, a prosecutor's office, an administrative agency charged with enforcing the law, or a legislative committee investigating law enforcement.

The foundation for the percipient witness exception is quite simple. The defendant shows that the informer was in a physical position—the proper time and place—to observe the facts determining guilt or innocence. As previously stated, in some jurisdictions the practice now is to have the informer testify in chambers after the defendant makes the preliminary showing. If, in the judge's mind, the informer's testimony is favorable to the defense, the judge then orders disclosure of the informer's identity to the defense. When the judge concludes that the informer's testimony would not be helpful to the defense, the judge denies the discovery motion. The record of the testimony in chambers is sealed and filed with the regular record of trial; if there is an appeal, the appellate court opens the sealed transcript to review the trial judge's determination.

[3] SAMPLE FOUNDATION

Our fact situation is a drug prosecution. The government alleges that the accused, Ms. Jane Moreland, unlawfully sold heroin to a Mr. Vincent Styles. The prosecution calls Officer Bernard Lopardo as a witness. Officer Lopardo testifies that he was hiding in the house where the alleged sale occurred and observed the sale. Then cross-examination begins. The defense attorney is the proponent.

P	Officer Lopardo, ISN'T IT TRUE THAT someone else was with you when you observed the alleged heroin sale?
W	Yes.
P	WHO was that other person?
O	Your Honor, I object to that question on the ground that it calls for privileged information. May we approach the bench?
J	Yes.
O	Your Honor, on behalf of the government, I claim the privilege for the identity of an informer. (2), (3) I request permission to take the witness on voir dire examination.
J	Permission granted.
O	WHEN did you first meet the person who was with you in the house?
W	About two months before.
O	WHAT happened when you met this person? (4b)
W	He told me that he thought a drug sale was going to occur in the neighborhood within the next few months.
O	WHERE did he make this report? (4c)
W	At the local police station.
O	WHOM did he report it to? (4c)
W	To me.
O	HOW were you dressed at the time? (4c)
W	I was wearing my regular police uniform.
O	WHO else was present when he made this report? (4a)
W	No one else. Just the two of us.
O	WHERE did this conversation occur? (4a)

W	In a room at the station.
O	HOW many doors did the room have? (4a)
W	Only one.
O	WHAT position was the door in when you met this person? (4a)
W	It was closed.
O	WHAT, if any, assurances did you give the informant when he made this report to you? (4a)
W	I told him that I wouldn't disclose his identity to anyone.
O	To WHOM have you revealed his identity? (4a)
W	No one. I've worked with him directly. I haven't even revealed his identity to the desk sergeant. I'm the informer's only contact.
O	Your Honor, I have no further questions on voir dire. I renew my claim of the privilege for an informer's identity.
	(Now the defense counsel will attempt to lay the foundation for the percipient witness exception.)
P	Your Honor, may I also voir dire the witness?
J	Very well.
P	Officer Lopardo, ISN'T IT TRUE THAT this person actually accompanied you to the house where the alleged sale occurred?
W	Yes.
P	ISN'T IT A FACT THAT the informer was standing next to you when you observed the alleged sale?
W	Yes.
P	ISN'T IT CORRECT THAT most of the time the informer was facing in the same direction as you?
W	Yes.
P	Your Honor, I have no further questions on voir dire examination. Although the privilege for the informer's identity applies in this case, the percipient witness viewed the very transaction that the accused's guilt or innocence depends on.
J	I concur. I am going to order the prosecutor to produce the informer in my chambers tomorrow morning. At that time, I shall question the informer and determine whether his testimony would be helpful to the defense. If his testimony would be favorable, I'll order that the prosecution disclose his identity to the defense. Court will be recessed. The prosecutor, the informer, and I will meet in my chambers at 9:00 a.m. tomorrow morning. Open court will convene promptly at 10:30 a.m.

§ 7.10 SUBSEQUENT REPAIRS

[1] THE DOCTRINE

The next two sections analyze evidentiary doctrines similar to the privileges for confidential relations; they are doctrines excluding logically relevant evidence to promote extrinsic social policies. The subsequent repair doctrine bans evidence of subsequent precautionary measures by tort defendants; the primary rationale for the doctrine is that admitting the evidence would discourage desirable safety improvements. The second doctrine, excluding statements made during civil settlement and criminal plea negotiations, has a similar justification; the doctrine's underlying theory is that the admission of such statements would discourage negotiated settlements and pleas. The adherents of the doctrine argue that settlements and pleas serve the critical function of easing the trial courts' burden. Litigants would be less candid during negotiations if they feared that their statement might come back to haunt them at trial. Since, like privileges, these doctrines exclude logically relevant evidence to promote extrinsic policies, some commentators refer to these doctrines as quasi-privileges.

Federal Rule of Evidence 407 states the exclusionary rule for subsequent repairs:

When measures are taken that would have made the earlier injury or harm less likely to occur, evidence of the subsequent measure is not admissible to prove:

- negligence;
- culpable conduct;
- a defect in a product or its design; or
- a need for a warning or instruction.

The courts have stated two justifications for this doctrine. One is that the evidence is logically irrelevant; the defendant's subsequent conduct has no bearing on the question whether the defendant was guilty of antecedent negligence. This justification is flawed. The subsequent repair has some, slight probative value on the question of negligence; at the very least, the evidence suggests that the defendant could have taken steps to eliminate or reduce the danger. Increasingly, however, the courts are relying on a second justification for the doctrine: Admitting the evidence would create a disincentive for repairs, and the public interest in safety will not tolerate such a disincentive. Thus, like communications privileges, this doctrine rests to an extent on extrinsic social policy.

This doctrine is not an absolute communications privilege; rather, it is a rule of limited admissibility. D. LEONARD, THE NEW WIGMORE: SELECTED RULES OF LIMITED ADMISSIBILITY (3d ed. 2019). In this respect the doctrine is similar to Rule 404(b) governing uncharged misconduct evidence, discussed in § 6.04. The subsequent repair doctrine bans the evidence only when the evidence is offered for a particular, forbidden purpose; in the words of the Federal Rule, the evidence is inadmissible when the proponent offers the evidence "to prove negligence, culpable conduct, a defect in a product or its design, or a need for a warning or instruction." The exclusionary rule bans the evidence when the only theory of logical relevance the proponent articulates is the general inference that the defendant was negligent or culpable. If the proponent can articulate a different theory of logical relevance, the rule is inapplicable. Federal Rule of Evidence 407 declares: "But the court may admit this evidence for another purpose, such as impeachment or—if disputed—proving ownership, control, or the feasibility of precautionary measures." When the proponent identifies a theory of logical relevance other than a general inference of negligence or fault, the opponent is entitled to a limiting instruction; the trial judge informs the jury of the permissible and impermissible uses of the evidence. The proponent may use the evidence only for the permissible purpose during closing argument.

[2] ELEMENTS OF THE FOUNDATION

The party attempting to exclude the repair evidence should lay the following foundation:

1. The defendant took certain action. The strongest case for invoking the exclusionary rule is a fact situation in which the person who made the repair is formally joined as the defendant at trial. However, some jurisdictions apply the rule even when the person who made the repair is not a party to the litigation. D. LEONARD, THE NEW WIGMORE: SELECTED RULES OF LIMITED ADMISSIBILITY, at § 2.6.3 (3d ed. 2019).

2. The defendant took the action as a safety measure.

3. The defendant took the action after the accident that gave rise to the suit. (Some jurisdictions have extended Rule 407 in product liability cases in which the defendant made the design change after the sale to the plaintiff, but before the accident. These courts argue that this extension is a legitimate, purposive construction of Rule 407; even before an accident has occurred, a manufacturer might be deterred from making a desirable safety improvement by the fear that the improvement would be used as evidence against the manufacturer at a subsequent trial involving the product. In those jurisdictions, the earlier version of Rule 407 is still in effect; that version begins, "When, after an event, measures are taken." Effective December 1, 1997, though, Rule 407 was amended to begin; "When after an injury or harm allegedly caused by an event, measures are taken." The accompanying Advisory Committee Note states that the purpose of the amendment was "to clarify that the rule applies only to changes made after the occurrence that produced the damages giving rise to the action.")

The party can assert this doctrine pretrial by a motion *in limine*. If the issue arises at trial, the party can conduct voir dire examination to lay the foundation.

If the party seeking to introduce the evidence is going to invoke an alternative theory of logical relevance, the party must make a proper offer of proof. The offer of proof should include these elements:

4. What the witness will testify to if the judge permits the proponent to pursue the line of inquiry.

5. The evidence is logically relevant to some issue other than the general question

of negligence or fault. In *Ault v. International Harvester Co.*, 13 Cal. 3d 113, 117 Cal. Rptr. 812, 528 P.2d 1148 (1974), the California Supreme Court held that its statutory version of the subsequent repair doctrine does not apply to strict product liability actions. The Court reasoned that strict product liability is not "culpable conduct" within the meaning of the statute. Most jurisdictions, however, have rejected the *Ault* view. Effective December 1, 1997, Rule 407 was amended to add "a defect in a product, a defect in a product's design, or a need for a warning or instruction" after "culpable conduct." The Advisory Committee Note explains that the purpose of this amendment was to codify the position taken by "a majority of the circuits," rejecting *Ault*.

6. The issue the evidence relates to is disputed in the case. Many judges insist on this showing as a separate element of the foundation. The Federal Rules explicitly impose this requirement; the restyled rule uses the language, "if disputed." The evidence will always be technically relevant to show the feasibility of repairs; if the courts did not require that the issue be genuinely disputed, the feasibility theory of logical relevance would swallow the exclusionary rule. The proponent of the evidence should point to specific testimony by the opposing witnesses which disputes the issue.

As previously stated, if the proponent of the evidence successfully invokes an alternative theory of logical relevance, the opponent has the right to insist that the judge give the jurors a limiting instruction under Rule 105.

[3] SAMPLE FOUNDATIONS

Our first fact situation illustrates the general rule. The fact situation is a tort action arising from a slip and fall on the entrance to a department store. The plaintiff, Mr. Jarvis, alleges that the defendant, Merrill Department Store, had a dangerous and unsafe slope at its entrance. During the defense case-in-chief, the defense calls Ms. Fenton as a witness. Ms. Fenton identifies herself and states that she was the store manager the day of the accident. She describes the day, including her conversation with the plaintiff after the slip and fall. On cross-examination, the following occurs. The proponent is the plaintiff.

P   Ms. Fenton, ISN'T IT TRUE THAT one week after the plaintiff's accident, you hired a contractor to reduce the slope at the entrance?

O   Your Honor, I object to that question on the ground that it calls for evidence of a subsequent repair.

J   Objection sustained.

O   Your Honor, will you please give the jury a curative instruction?

J   Yes. Ladies and gentlemen of the jury, the plaintiff's attorney just referred to a change made in the entrance to the defendant's store. I am instructing you to disregard that reference. You may not even speculate whether there were any subsequent changes. The only issue before you is whether the defendant was negligent at the time the alleged accident occurred.

(If the defendant thought that the reference would taint the rest of the case, the defendant would next move for a mistrial. Many trial judges feel very strongly about this matter. They will rebuke the questioner— often even before an objection. These same judges frequently grant the mistrial motion.)

O   Your Honor, I now move for a mistrial.

If there is any doubt about the soundness of the objection, the opponent should request permission to take the witness on voir dire outside the jury's hearing to lay a complete foundation for the objection.

P   Ms. Fenton, ISN'T IT TRUE THAT one week after the plaintiff's accident, you hired a contractor to reduce the slope at the entrance?

O   Your Honor, I object to that question. May we approach the bench?

J   Yes.

O   Your Honor, I object to that question on the ground that it calls for evidence of a subsequent repair. I request that you excuse the jurors and permit me to voir dire the witness before you rule on my objection.

J   Very well. Ladies and gentlemen of the jury, I am going to excuse you from the courtroom for a few moments. The bailiff will escort you to the jury room.

         (The jurors leave.)

O   Ms. Fenton, WHAT did you hire this contractor to do? (1)

W   I hired a Mr. Darby to reduce the angle of the slope leading to the entrance.

O   WHY did you do that? (2)

W   We did it as a safety measure. We wanted to ensure that there wouldn't be a recurrence of the accident. We're concerned about the safety of our customers.

O   WHEN did you hire Mr. Darby? (3)

W   In late February of YR-3.

O   WHEN did the plaintiff's accident occur? (3)

W   In early February. I think it was February 2.

O   Your Honor, I have no further voir dire questions of this witness. I renew my objection.

J   The objection will be sustained.

The second fact situation is a suit against a railroad company. The plaintiff, Hughes Corporation, sues West Central Railroad. The plaintiff alleges that the defendant's train derailed near the plaintiff's plant and caused extensive property damage. The defendant's answer alleges that the cause of the derailment was the defective condition of the track and that under the railroad's contract with the adjacent landowner, the landowner was responsible for maintaining the track. The plaintiff calls Mr. Karl as a witness. Mr. Karl identifies himself and states that he is one of the plaintiff's employees. He is prepared to testify that on December 3, YR-4, the day after the accident, one of the defendant's work crews repaired the track. The proponent is the plaintiff.

P	Mr. Karl, WHERE were you on December 3, YR-4?
W	I was at work at our main plant in Cheyenne.
P	WHAT happened that day?
W	I was working outside, trying to repair some of the damage caused by the derailment the day before.
P	WHAT, if anything, did you see while you were outside?
W	I saw some of the defendant's employees arrive.
P	HOW do you know that they were the defendant's employees?
W	They all had coveralls on, and the coveralls had the defendant's name on them. They drove to the site in a truck with the defendant's name on the side.[14]
P	WHAT were the defendant's employees doing?
O	Your Honor, I object to that question. May we approach the bench?
J	Yes.
O	Your Honor, it appears that the plaintiff is attempting to elicit inadmissible evidence of subsequent repairs to the track.
J	(*To the plaintiff's attorney*) Is that your intention?
P	Your Honor, I do intend to try to prove a subsequent repair. However, I contend that the evidence is admissible. I offer to prove that the witness will testify that he saw the defendant's employees repair the track. (4) The evidence is logically relevant to prove that the defendant had control of the track and thus a duty to keep the track in a state of good repair. (5) The defendant's answer specifically denied that it had control of the track or a duty to repair. (6) The defendant's general manager testified to that effect yesterday afternoon. (6) The evidence should be admitted for the limited purpose of proving the defendant's control of the track.
J	I agree. The objection is overruled.
P	Mr. Karl, let me repeat the question. WHAT were the defendant's employees doing?
W	They were repairing the track.
O	Your Honor, I request a limiting instruction.
J	Granted. Ladies and gentlemen of the jury, you have just heard evidence

---

[14] The inscriptions on the coverall and truck are arguably self-authenticating under Federal Rule of Evidence 902(7).

that the day after the accident, the defendant's employees were repairing the track. You are not to use that evidence as proof that the defendant was careless at the time of the accident. You may use the evidence only in deciding whether the defendant had control of the track and a duty to repair it.

Given the judge's instruction, during summation the plaintiff could discuss the testimony when arguing the question of whether the defendant had control of the defective track which caused the damage to the plaintiff's property. However, it would be objectionable if during summation the plaintiff suggested to the jury that the defendant was somehow admitting fault in the accident by sending its work crew to the site.

The third fact situation is a product liability suit. The plaintiff, Mr. James Barry, sues the defendant, Enright Corporation. The plaintiff alleges that in January YR-3, the defendant sold plaintiff a defectively designed microwave oven and that in February YR-3, the oven exploded, injuring the plaintiff. During the defense case-in-chief, the defendant calls Dr. Verna Gunther. Dr. Gunther identifies herself and states that she is the defendant's chief safety engineer. On direct examination, she testifies that in her opinion, the oven was properly designed. She adds that the oven was the safest oven on the market and represented the state of the art; it was as safely designed as the state of the art permitted. The following occurs on cross-examination. The plaintiff is the proponent.

P   Dr. Gunther, ISN'T IT TRUE THAT in March YR-3 you redesigned the oven?

O   Your Honor, may we approach the bench?

J   Yes.

O   Your Honor, I object to that question on the ground that it calls for evidence of a subsequent repair.

J   (*To the plaintiff*) Is that what you're attempting to prove?

P   Yes, Your Honor. However, I think the evidence is admissible. I offer to prove that the witness will testify that the oven's safety features were redesigned only a month after the plaintiff's accident. (4) Since there is such a short time lapse between the accident and the redesign, the evidence is logically relevant to show that the defendant could have marketed a safer product. (5) On direct examination, this witness expressly claimed that the oven was as safe as possible; she said that the state of the art wouldn't have permitted a safer design. Your Honor, I think that I heard that testimony on direct very clearly; but if you have any question, you could have the court reporter read back that portion of the testimony. (6) The evidence should be admitted for the limited purpose of rebutting the state of the art defense.

J   I concur. The objection will be overruled.

P	Dr. Gunther, ISN'T IT A FACT THAT in March YR-3, you redesigned the oven?
W	Yes.
P	AND ISN'T IT CORRECT THAT the part of the oven you redesigned was the heating coil?
W	Yes.
P	AND DIDN'T the redesign make an accidental explosion less likely?
W	Yes.
O	Your Honor, I request a limiting instruction.
J	Certainly. Ladies and gentlemen, you've just heard the doctor's testimony that she redesigned the oven shortly after the plaintiff's accident. You may not use this evidence as general proof of the defendant's negligence. You are to use the evidence for only one specific purpose, namely, deciding whether the state of the art would have permitted the defendant to market a safer product.

Once again, the tenor of the limiting instruction would restrict the manner in which the plaintiff used the evidence during closing argument. On the one hand, during closing the plaintiff could point to Dr. Gunther's direct testimony and argue that the evidence contradicts Gunther's claim that the state of the art would not have permitted a safer design. The contradiction would be proof that in a relative sense, the design could have been better. On the other hand, it would be objectionable if the plaintiff suggested that by redesigning the oven, the defendant was admitting that the earlier design was negligent or defective.

§ 7.11 COMPROMISE STATEMENTS

[1] STATEMENTS DURING CIVIL SETTLEMENT NEGOTIATIONS

The courts have long favored the out-of-court settlement of legal claims. That attitude has become even more pronounced in recent years; in many areas, the trial courts are so badly backlogged that it is imperative that we encourage out-of-court settlements. The attitude expresses itself in a doctrine excluding statements made during civil settlement negotiations. The courts reason that if negotiators know that their statements are privileged, their discussions will be more candid and, hopefully, more successful.

Federal Rule of Evidence 408(a) states the norm:

(a) Prohibited Uses. Evidence of the following is not admissible—on behalf of any party—either to prove or disprove the validity or amount of a disputed claim or to impeach by a prior inconsistent statement or a contradiction:

(1) furnishing, promising, or offering—or accepting, promising to accept, or offering to accept—a valuable consideration in compromising or attempting to compromise the claim; and

(2) conduct or a statement made during compromise negotiations about the

claim—except when offered in a criminal case and when the negotiations related to a claim by a public office in the exercise of its
regulatory, investigative, or enforcement authority.

Like the subsequent repair doctrine, this doctrine is not an absolute exclusionary rule;
it too is a rule of limited admissibility. In the words of Federal Rule of Evidence 408(a),
the proponent may not offer the evidence "to prove or disprove the validity or amount
of a disputed claim or to impeach by a prior inconsistent statement or a contradiction."
Again, however, the proponent may offer the evidence on other theories of logical
relevance. Rule 408(b) adds: "The court may admit this evidence for another purpose,
such as proving a witness's bias or prejudice, negating a contention of undue delay, or
proving an effort to obstruct a criminal investigation or prosecution."

The party attempting to exclude the evidence should lay this foundation:

1. At the time of the statement, a dispute had already arisen between the parties
    over the existence or extent of civil liability. Although a dispute must have
    risen, suit need not have been filed yet. If on his or her own motion a person
    freely and unilaterally admits liability immediately after an incident occurs, the
    rule is inapplicable.

2. The party made the statement for the purpose of settling the dispute.

3. The subject-matter of the statement is proper. All jurisdictions protect an offer
    to settle. However, some jurisdictions protect accompanying statements of fact
    only if the speaker expressly states that the statements of fact are "hypotheti-
    cal" or "without prejudice."

The party attempting to introduce the evidence must be ready to make an offer of
proof. In the offer of proof, the party should state:

4. What the witness will testify to if the judge permits the party to pursue the line
    of questioning.

5. The evidence is logically relevant to some issue other than the general question
    of the claim's validity. Prior to 2006, the federal courts were split over the
    question of whether Rule 408 permits the use of compromise statements as
    prior inconsistent statements under Rule 613. However, effective December 1,
    2006, Rule 408 was amended to read: "Evidence of the following is not
    admissible on behalf of any party, when offered to prove liability for, invalidity
    of, or amount of a claim that was disputed as to validity or amount, or to
    impeach through a prior inconsistent statement or contradiction."

6. The issue the evidence relates to is a genuinely disputed question in the case.

The first fact situation is a tort action for personal injuries. The plaintiff, Mr. James
Stone, sues the defendant, Ms. Rachel Damer. The plaintiff alleges that the defendant
caused a collision and that in the collision, the plaintiff suffered injuries in the amount
of $100,000. The plaintiff takes the witness stand to testify in his own behalf. On
cross-examination, the following occurs. The proponent is the defendant.

P　　　　　Mr. Stone, ISN'T IT TRUE THAT in your complaint in this case, you claim that you've suffered $100,000 in damages?

W   Yes.

P   ISN'T IT A FACT THAT on February 17, YR-3, you were at my office?

W   Right.

P   ISN'T IT CORRECT THAT while you were there, you offered to settle your whole claim for only $20,000?

O   Your Honor, I object to that question. May we approach the bench?

J   Yes.

O   Your Honor, I object to that question on the ground that it calls for an inadmissible compromise statement. I request permission to voir dire the witness before you rule on my objection. I request that you excuse the jurors.

J   Yes. Ladies and gentlemen of the jury, I am going to ask you to leave the courtroom for a few minutes. The bailiff will accompany you to the deliberation room.

O   Mr. Stone, WHY did you go to the opposing attorney's office on February 17th? (2)

W   I went there to discuss my claim against his client.

O   WHAT was your claim? (1)

W   I took the position that Ms. Damer was at fault in the accident and caused my injuries.

O   WHAT was your belief about the validity of your claim? (1)

W   I thought I was in the right. I thought the claim was valid. As I remember the accident, I had the green light.

O   WHAT did the defendant say about your claim? (1)

W   She denied that she was at fault.

O   WHAT was the purpose of the meeting on February 17th? (2)

W   We wanted to see if we could settle without going to trial.

O   WHY did you want to settle if you thought that your claim was valid? (2)

W   You told me that juries are unpredictable and that sometimes it's better to be conservative and accept less money than you ask for in your complaint. I still thought that I had a good claim, but that's why I was willing to talk about settling.

O   Your Honor, I have no further voir dire questions. The witness's testimony shows that there was a dispute over his claim's validity and that he made his offer in a bona fide effort to compromise. The question I'm objecting to calls for the settlement offer itself. (3) The question is

	objectionable.
J	The objection is sustained.
	(As in the case of subsequent repair evidence, the opponent should consider moving for a mistrial.)

The second fact situation is a contract action. The plaintiff, Mr. John Peterson, sues the defendant, Aramco Construction Company. In its answer, the defendant alleges that the plaintiff did not reasonably mitigate damages; the answer alleges that after the defendant's breach, the plaintiff delayed three months before looking for another contractor. The plaintiff takes the witness stand in his own behalf. The plaintiff has already testified to the contract's formation and the defendant's breach. The plaintiff is the proponent.

P	WHAT happened after the defendant's work crew walked off the site?
W	The next day I contacted Mr. Garner, the defendant's president.
P	WHAT happened when you contacted him?
W	He and I discussed how we might settle my claim against his company.
O	Your Honor, I move to strike the last answer. May we approach the bench?
J	By all means.
O	Your Honor, the answer refers to inadmissible compromise negotiations.
P	Your Honor, may I be heard?
J	Yes.
P	I offer to prove that the witness will testify that the parties began settlement negotiations that day and that the negotiations continued for over two months. (4) The testimony is logically relevant to explain the plaintiff's delay in hiring another contractor. (5) In its answer, the defendant alleged that the plaintiff did not properly mitigate damages. (6) The evidence is admissible for the limited purpose of rebutting the defendant's allegation.
J	In that light, motion denied.
P	Mr. Peterson, permit me to repeat the question. WHAT happened when you contacted Mr. Garner?
W	We discussed settling my claim against his company.
P	HOW long did these discussions last?
W	On and off for over two months. I kept trying to get them back on the project; I wanted a warehouse, not a lawsuit.
O	Your Honor, I request a limiting instruction.
J	Granted. Ladies and gentlemen of the jury, you've just heard testimony about settlement negotiations between the plaintiff and defendant. You

are not to use the evidence of the defendant's willingness to negotiate as an admission of liability. The fact that the defendant was willing to talk settlement is no evidence that he was at fault. There are many reasons why a potential defendant might be willing to discuss settlement. You are to use this evidence only for the limited purpose of deciding whether the plaintiff acted with reasonable speed in finding a new contractor to finish the project. The defendant claims that the plaintiff did not. The plaintiff offers these pending settlement negotiations as an explanation for his delay in hiring a new contractor.[15]

Criminal Cases

At one time, the courts were badly divided over the question of the extent, if any, to which Rule 408 applied in criminal cases. In 2006, the rule was amended to clarify that issue. As amended, Rule 408(a)(2) generally prohibits the introduction of evidence of conduct or statements made in compromise negotiations regarding the claim, except when offered in a criminal case and the negotiations related to a claim by a public office or agency in the exercise of regulatory, investigative, or enforcement authority.

The accompanying Advisory Committee Note explains the 2006 amendment.

- First, the Note points out that in contrast to "conduct or statements" covered by Rule 408(a)(2), "[a]n offer or acceptance of a compromise of any civil claim is excluded" under (a)(1) "if offered against the [criminal] defendant as an admission of fault." "[U]nlike a direct statement of fault, an offer or acceptance of a compromise is not very probative of the defendant's guilt. Moreover, admitting such an offer or acceptance could deter a defendant from settling a civil regulatory action."

- Even the amended Rule 408(a)(2) does not allow the introduction of all direct statements of fault in criminal cases. As the Note explains, the amendment distinguishes between statements made in negotiations with different types of opponents. On the one hand, the amendment permits the admission "in a criminal case of statements or conduct during compromise negotiations regarding a civil dispute by a government regulatory, investigative, or enforcement agency. Where an individual makes a statement in the presence of government agents, its subsequent admission in a criminal case should not be unexpected. The individual can seek to protect against subsequent disclosure

---

[15] The above hypothetical is based on the prevailing view. However, Stockman v. Oakcrest Dental Center, 480 F.3d 791 (6th Cir. 2007) departs from that view. There the court noted that Rule 408(a) prohibits the proponent from using the evidence "to prove or disprove the validity or *amount* of a disputed claim . . . ." The court reasoned that Rule 408 applies to disputes over a plaintiff's failure to mitigate because the failure can reduce the amount of damages the plaintiff recovers. However, *Stockman* is wrongly decided. The court is correct in thinking that by raising the failure to mitigate argument, the defense is contesting the "amount" of the claim. However, that means only that the argument triggers the general exclusionary rule stated in Rule 408(a). Rule 408(b) lists various exceptions (such as "negating a contention of undue delay") that come into play even when the general exclusionary rule would ordinarily apply.

through negotiation and agreement with the civil regulator or an attorney for the government." In this situation, the individual should negotiate with the government representative to obtain protection against or in a later criminal case. On the other hand, "[w]hen private parties enter into compromise negotiations, they cannot protect against the subsequent use of statements in criminal cases by way of private ordering. The inability to guarantee protection against subsequent [criminal] use could lead to parties refusing to admit fault, even if by doing so they could favorably settle the private matter. Such a chill on [private] settlement negotiation would be contrary to the policy of Rule 408."

Although Rule 408 is in the nature of a rule of limited admissibility, several states have gone beyond Rule 408 and recognized a true privilege for settlement negotiations. In such a jurisdiction, the proponent's intended use of the statement at trial is immaterial; the statement is inadmissible. The doctrine is a true privilege rather than a rule of limited admissibility. However, most federal courts have refused to recognize this privilege.[16] They reason that Congress' enactment of Rule 408 manifests a legislative intention that 408 should be the only protection for compromise statements.

[2]   STATEMENTS DURING PLEA BARGAINING NEGOTIATIONS

The last subsection examined the doctrine excluding statements made during civil settlement negotiations. The reason for that doctrine is that the courts want to encourage out-of-court settlements and save court time. For a similar reason, many jurisdictions recognize a parallel doctrine excluding statements made during criminal plea bargaining negotiations. Federal Rule of Evidence 410 places the federal courts among the ranks of the jurisdictions following the doctrine. The latest version of Rule 410(a) generally excludes "(1) a guilty plea that was later withdrawn; (2) a nolo contendere plea; (3) a statement made during a proceeding on either of those pleas under Federal Criminal Procedure 11 or a comparable state procedure; or (4) a statement made during plea discussions with an attorney for the prosecuting authority if the discussions did not result in a guilty plea or they resulted in a later-withdrawn guilty plea."

The jurisdictions following this doctrine usually recognize a few exceptions to the general norm. Some permit the prosecutor to use plea bargaining statements to impeach the accused's testimony. The federal courts take a more restrictive view. The latest version of Rule 410(b) recognizes only two narrow exceptions, providing that the evidence is admissible

(1)   in any proceeding in which another statement made during the same plea or plea discussions has been introduced, if in fairness the statements ought to be considered together; or

(2)   in a criminal proceeding for perjury or false statement, if the defendant made the statement under oath, on the record, and with counsel present.

The second exception is limited to statements the accused makes formally while a judge is questioning the accused under oath, on the record, about a proposed plea.

---

[16] *But see* Goodyear Tire & Rubber Co. v. Chiles Power Supply, Inc., 332 F.3d 976 (6th Cir. 2003).

The accused attempting to invoke this doctrine must lay this foundation:

1. At a certain time and place, the accused met with the authorities, that is, the prosecutor, or the police acting with the prosecutor's consent.

2. The accused subjectively believed that the purpose of the meeting was to negotiate a plea in exchange for charge or sentence concessions. Although in the past, most courts have required proof of this element to invoke Rule 410, some courts have construed the latest amendment to Rule 410 as dispensing with proof of the defendant's subjective belief. *State v. Fox*, 760 P.2d 670 (Haw. 1988).

3. The accused's belief was objectively reasonable. The authorities' statements and conduct reasonably led the accused to that belief.

4. The accused made the statement during the plea bargaining session.

5. The subject matter of the statement was proper. The jurisdictions recognizing this doctrine tend to protect both offers and accompanying statements of fact. ·

Our fact situation is a medical aid fraud prosecution. The government alleges that the accused, Mr. George Aston, is a pharmacist and knowingly filled fraudulent prescriptions for doctors receiving medical aid payments from the state. The indictment alleges that the accused filled excessive prescriptions and prescriptions for fictitious patients. Since this is a white collar crime prosecution, the accused was not in custody. The government's primary interest was convicting the doctors with whom the accused conspired. Prior to trial, the accused makes a motion *in limine* to suppress certain statements he made to the prosecutor during a meeting at the prosecutor's office. Since the accused was not in custody and there is no evidence of force or threats, the defense counsel cannot invoke *Miranda* or the voluntariness doctrine. Rather, the defense counsel rests the motion squarely on the doctrine excluding statements made during plea bargaining negotiations. The defense counsel calls the accused as a witness in support of the motion. The accused has already identified himself. The accused is the proponent.

P	Mr. Aston, WHERE were you on the afternoon of April 3, YR-3? (1)
W	I went to the D.A.'s office in downtown Gainesville.
P	WHO else was there? (1)
W	My attorney was there, and the other person present was a Deputy D.A.
P	WHO was that? (1)
W	I think her name was Hester Martin.
P	WHAT was the purpose of this meeting? (2)
W	Plea bargaining. I hoped to get some concessions, maybe even immunity.
P	WHY did you think that was the purpose of the meeting? (2)
W	My attorney told me that before we got there.
P	WHAT, if anything, did Ms. Martin say about the purpose of the meeting? (3)

W	When we got there, she said that she wanted to be honest with me. She said that I was just a small fish and that they were really interested in nailing all the fat cat doctors I had filled false prescriptions for. She said that if I came clean, they might give me a break. She even mentioned some sort of possible immunity.
P	WHAT did you say then to Ms. Martin? (4), (5)
W	With my attorney's permission, I told her about my involvement with the doctors. I said that I'd be willing to repeat those statements in court in exchange for full immunity.
P	HOW did Ms. Martin respond to your offer?
W	She said that she'd have to talk it over with her boss, Mr. Ching, before giving us a final answer.
P	WHAT was the final answer?
W	Ms. Martin phoned me at work about three days later. She said that her boss would O.K. some sentence concessions, but wouldn't buy immunity.
P	WHAT, if anything, did you say then?
W	I told her that it was too bad because my attorney and I had agreed that I'd talk only if I got immunity.
P	WHAT happened to your plea bargaining with the District Attorney's office?
W	That conversation ended the negotiations.
P	Your Honor, I have no further questions of the accused. I renew my motion to preclude any reference to my client's statements during the plea bargaining session at the District Attorney's office.
J	I shall grant the motion.

On its face, Rule 410 does not purport to bar the defense's use of the prosecution's statements during plea negotiations. However, in *United States v. Verdoorn*, 528 F.2d 103 (8th Cir. 1976), the court permitted the prosecution to invoke the exclusionary rule. In its Note to an amended version of Rule 410, the Advisory Committee stated: "[N]o disapproval is intended of such decisions as *United States v. Verdoorn*." Some commentators have suggested that *Verdoorn* reached the right result but for the wrong reason; they have argued that the prosecution is entitled to exclude plea negotiation statements under Rule 408. Some courts have adopted that argument. However, other courts are contra. The latter courts reasoned that the reference to "claims" in the original version of Rule 408 manifested a legislative intent to limit that rule to civil actions. However, the amended version of Rule 408(a)(2), expressly referring to "a criminal case," undermines that reasoning.

CHAPTER 8

THE BEST EVIDENCE RULE

§ 8.01 INTRODUCTION

The last three chapters analyzed rules which exclude logically relevant evidence for policy reasons—either institutional policies relating to jury behavior or extrinsic social policies. The next three chapters also discuss rules that have the effect of barring the admission of logically relevant evidence. However, the doctrines discussed in these chapters exclude relevant evidence for a very different reason, namely, doubts about the reliability of the evidence.

The common law prefers that evidence take the form of a witness walking into court, subjecting himself or herself to cross-examination, and either reciting observed facts or quoting a document produced in the courtroom. In the mind of the common-law courts, that type of testimony is the most trustworthy. Whenever the proponent of evidence attempts to deviate from the norm, the proponent is likely to encounter an exclusionary or preferential rule. If the proponent offers testimony about an out-of-court statement rather than calling the declarant as a witness at trial, the proponent may have to surmount the hurdle of the hearsay rule. When the proponent attempts to elicit opinions from the witness rather than statements of observed fact, the proponent may encounter the opinion prohibition. Finally, if the proponent invites the witness to quote or paraphrase a document rather than producing the document in court, the proponent may face a best evidence objection. The proponent may be able to introduce the hearsay, opinion, or paraphrase; but in order to do so, the proponent must establish an exceptional reason for deviating from the preference.

The best evidence rule is illustrative. The best evidence rule excludes secondary evidence of a writing's contents; the rule expresses a preference for the more reliable evidence, the writing itself. Federal Rules of Evidence 1001-1008 set out the rule. Briefly, the Rule is that *when a writing's terms are in issue, the proponent must either (1) produce an original or duplicate or (2) both excuse the non-production of the originals and present an admissible type of secondary evidence.* The Rule presents five issues: What is a "writing" for purposes of the rule? When are a writing's terms "in issue"? What is an "original" or a "duplicate"? What are the admissible types of secondary evidence? And what are adequate excuses for non-production?

The proponent can usually defeat a best evidence objection. The proponent can do so because the five issues convert into several different bases for overriding the objection. The judge can overrule the objection on the grounds that the article involved is not a "document"; the document's terms are not "in issue"; the document's terms are only collaterally "in issue"; the evidence offered is an "original"; the evidence offered is a "duplicate"; and there is an adequate excuse for the non-production of the originals, and the proponent is offering an admissible type of secondary evidence. The following sections illustrate the various bases for defeating best evidence objections.

§ 8.02 THE OBJECT INVOLVED IS NOT A "WRITING"

The title of the doctrine, "the best evidence rule," is a misnomer. There is no general requirement that the proponent produce or account for the best evidence. To be sure, during summation the opponent can invite the trier of fact to draw an adverse inference whenever the proponent neglects to proffer the best evidence; on that basis, the opponent can question the weight of the inferior evidence that was introduced. However, the doctrine under consideration is a full-fledged exclusionary rule which renders some types of evidence inadmissible. The exclusionary rule's scope is limited to writings; the rationale is that detail is often more important in the analysis of writings. Thus, a more accurate title for the doctrine would be the "original writing rule."

Yet, Federal Rule of Evidence 1002 contains a broad definition of the rule's scope. Rule 1002 applies the rule to writings, recordings, and photographs. Rule 1001(a) defines writings and records as "letters, words, or numbers, or their equivalent, set down in any form." Rule 1001(c) defines a photograph as "[a] photographic image or its equivalent stored in any form."

However, in some jurisdictions, "writing" has a relatively narrow meaning. For instance, a few jurisdictions do not apply the rule to photographs. Other jurisdictions hold that the rule does not apply to inscribed chattels, articles, or personal property such as tires bearing inscriptions.

The fact situation is a products liability action. The plaintiff, Mr. Konert, brings a tort action against Goodyear Tire Company. He alleges that the defendant negligently manufactured his tire, and that the negligent manufacture caused the tire to blow out and thereby cause an accident. The defendant has generally denied liability. The plaintiff calls Mr. Langdale, the police officer who investigated the accident. The witness has already identified himself and generally described the investigation at the accident scene. The officer has stated that he carefully examined the condition of the plaintiff's car. The plaintiff is the proponent.

P   WHICH parts of the car did you inspect?

W   Any part that might have contributed to the accident—the steering wheel, the engine, and the tires.

P   WHAT condition were the tires in?

W   Three were O.K.

P   WHAT was the condition of the fourth tire?

W   It had blown out. There was no air in it, and there was a large hole in it.

P   HOW large was the hole?

W   I'd say that it was easily two inches in diameter.

P   WHERE was the hole located?

W	On the tread part of the tire.
P	WHAT was written on the tire?
W	There were size specifications and a trade name.
P	WHAT was the trade name on the tire?
O	Your Honor, I object to that question on the ground that it calls for secondary evidence.
P	Your Honor, may I be heard?
J	Yes.
P	In this jurisdiction, the best evidence rule does not apply to inscribed chattels such as tires.
J	I agree. Objection overruled.
P	Let me repeat the question. WHAT was the trade name on the tire?
W	It was Goodyear.

§ 8.03   THE WRITING'S TERMS ARE NOT "IN ISSUE"

In the words of Federal Rule of Evidence 1002, the rule applies only when the proponent attempts "to prove [the] content" of a writing. The Advisory Committee Note accompanying Rule 1002 expressly states that the rule does not "apply to testimony that books or records have been examined and found not to contain any reference to a designated matter." There are three situations, though, in which a document's terms are "in issue" for purposes of triggering the best evidence rule.

The first situation is the case in which the material facts of consequence themselves under Federal Rule of Evidence 401 automatically place the document's terms in issue. For example, in a forgery prosecution, the terms of the allegedly forged document are automatically in issue; and the same analysis applies in a contract action if the complaint alleges that the agreement was a written contract. In both instances, the pleadings—the indictment in the criminal case and the complaint in the contract action—will include express references to the contents of a document.

Distinguish the above situation from the situation in which a fact exists independently of the writing, but the writing is convenient evidence of the fact. Thus, a witness who observed payment of a debt may testify to that fact without producing the receipt; the receipt is merely convenient evidence of payment. Similarly, in most jurisdictions, a witness who attended a wedding ceremony may testify to the marriage without producing the marriage certificate. Again, the certificate is convenient evidence, but the wedding is an historical event that occurred independently of the writing.

The second situation is a case in which the witness expressly or impliedly refers to the writing in his or her testimony. Suppose that the proponent attempting to prove the marriage cannot find an eyewitness to the ceremony. The proponent instead calls a deputy county clerk to testify to the contents of the marriage certificate on file. The clerk will expressly or impliedly rely upon the document's contents; the express or implied reference to the document's contents triggers the best evidence rule.

Finally, in some jurisdictions, there are statutes declaring that certain types of documents are "legal proof" of particular facts. For instance, some statutes announce that the marriage certificate is "legal proof" of the marriage. The question of statutory construction is whether the legislature intended the statute to extend the best evidence rule's scope. Some courts have answered that question in the affirmative; they have held that the statute manifests a legislative intent to make the certificate the best evidence even when there is an available eyewitness to the ceremony.

Our hypothetical fact situation is a probate contest. The contestants are challenging the will and claiming by intestate succession. To prove their right to take by intestate succession, they have to show that on March 1, YR-9, Joan Merchant married Thomas Kleven. The contestants call Ms. Trudy Guinn, an eyewitness to the marriage. The contestants are the proponents.

P   Ms. Guinn, WHERE were you on March 1, YR-9?

W   I was in Chicago, Illinois.

P   WHAT were you doing there?

W   I was attending a wedding.

P   WHOSE wedding?

O   Your Honor, I object to that question on the ground that it calls for secondary evidence; the marriage certificate is the best evidence.

P   Your Honor, may I be heard?

J   Yes.

P   The event of the wedding occurred independently of the certificate; a witness could observe the wedding ceremony without ever seeing the certificate. This eyewitness is prepared to testify without relying on the certificate. Thus, the certificate's terms are not in issue.

J   Objection overruled.

P   Ms. Guinn, let me repeat the question. WHOSE wedding?

W   The marriage of Joan Merchant and Thomas Kleven.

P   HOW can you remember a wedding that occurred over 20 years ago?

W   It sticks in my mind because I was Joan's maid of honor. I knew Joan and Thomas well, and Joan asked me to stand up with her.

§ 8.04 THE WRITING'S TERMS ARE ONLY COLLATERALLY "IN ISSUE"

Even if the writing's terms are technically in issue, on occasion, the judge may dispense with compliance with the best evidence rule. Sometimes the writing's terms relate to a minor issue in the case, and the judge concludes that it is not worth the time and inconvenience to require the proponent to comply with the best evidence rule. Suppose, for instance, that the opponent wants to impeach the witness with a written prior inconsistent statement. If the opponent is going to use the document solely to impeach the witness, the judge is likely to hold that the document is only collaterally relevant. The opponent could dispense with compliance with the best evidence rule and use a Xerox copy of the written prior inconsistent statement.

Federal Evidence Rule 1004(d) recognizes this limitation on the scope of the best evidence rule. That subsection states that the proponent need not comply with the best evidence rule if "the writing, recording, or photograph is not closely related to a controlling issue." The judge considers the importance of the issue the document relates to and makes a pragmatic judgment. When the judge concludes in his or her discretion that the writing relates to a minor question in the case, the proponent need not comply with the best evidence rule.

The fact situation is a tort action arising from a hit-and-run accident. The plaintiff, Ms. Difiglia, alleges that the defendant, Mr. Walker, negligently struck her in a crosswalk. The defendant denies that he was the driver. The plaintiff calls Mr. Meese, an eyewitness to the accident. Mr. Meese has just testified that he saw the accident and observed the car's license plate number. The plaintiff is the proponent.

P	WHAT was that license plate number?
W	I'm sorry, but I can't remember offhand.
P	WHAT, if anything, might help you remember?
W	Well, I made a note of the license number right after the accident. If I could see that note, I could probably remember.
P	Your Honor, I request that this be marked plaintiff's exhibit number two for identification.
J	It will be so marked.
P	Please let the record reflect that I am showing the exhibit to the opposing counsel.
J	It will so reflect.
O	Your Honor, I am going to have to object to the use of this document to refresh the witness's recollection. It's obvious that this is a Xerox copy and not the original best evidence.
P	Your Honor, may I be heard?
J	Yes.
P	I intend to use the exhibit solely to refresh the witness's recollection; I am not going to use the exhibit as substantive evidence of its contents. The exhibit is being used only collaterally. I'm not going to try to introduce the exhibit into evidence or have the witness quote it to the jury.
J	Objection overruled.
P	I request permission to approach the witness.
J	Granted.
P	Mr. Meese, I now hand you plaintiff's exhibit number two for identification.

	WHAT is it?
W	It's a copy of the note I just mentioned.
P	HOW can you recognize it?
W	I recognize my handwriting style.
P	WHO prepared the original note?
W	I did.
P	WHEN did you prepare it?
W	Right after the accident.
P	HOW soon after the accident?
W	It was a matter of minutes at most.
P	WHEN was the copy made?
W	When the lawsuit was filed, I became worried that the original might get lost. I made the copy just to be on the safe side. I thought that having a copy would be a good idea.
P	Please read the exhibit to yourself silently. *(The witness does so.)* Now please hand the exhibit back to me. *(To the judge.)* Your Honor, please let the record reflect that I am holding the exhibit away from the witness and out of the witness's sight.
J	The record will reflect that.
P	Mr. Meese, you've had an opportunity to read the exhibit to refresh your memory. Now, without relying on the exhibit, HOW well can you remember the license number?
W	Now it's clear in my mind.
P	WHAT was the license number?
W	It was a South Carolina license, FIA 986.

§ 8.05 THE EVIDENCE OFFERED IS AN "ORIGINAL"

[1] THE DOCTRINE

If the object involved is a writing *and* its terms are in issue, the proponent must comply with the best evidence rule. The simplest method of complying is by offering an original or duplicate. At common law, the "original" is usually the first document prepared, the first writing signed, the first audio recording prepared, or the negative of the photograph.

However, the common-law test for originality is legal rather than chronological. Suppose that the case is a threat prosecution. The government alleges that the accused sent a bomb threat through the mail. The accused first prepared the threat by typing it. However, the accused realized that it would be more difficult for a questioned document examiner to identify the paper or typewriter if he mailed a copy rather than the original. Consequently, the accused Xeroxed a copy of the typed threat and mailed the Xerox copy to the bank. For purposes of the best evidence rule, the Xerox copy is the original. It is a copy in a chronological sense. However, since it is the very threatening writing the accused mailed to the bank, the copy is the legal original.

As the preceding paragraph indicates, at common law there was usually an original writing—in the singular. The Federal Rules broaden the definition of "original." Rule 1001(d) states that "[a]n 'original' of a writing or record means the writing or record itself or any counterpart intended to have the same effect by the person who executed or issued it. For electronically stored information, 'original' means any printout—or other output readable by sight—if it accurately reflects the information. An 'original' of a photograph includes the negative or a print from it." Assume, for example, that the purchaser of a car signs a single copy of the contract of purchase and leaves the writing with the seller. The next day the seller decides that the buyer should have her own copy of the writing. For that reason, the seller Xeroxes a copy and mails it to the buyer. Since the Xerox is an exact copy made by reliable, mechanical means and it is intended to have essentially the same effect as the copy earlier signed in ink, both writings would be "originals" in federal practice.

[2]   ELEMENTS OF THE FOUNDATION

The foundation includes these elements:

1.   The witness recognizes the document.

2.   The witness specifies how he or she recognizes the document.

3.   The witness states the facts bringing the document within the jurisdiction's definition of an original. At common law, it will often suffice for the witness to testify that the exhibit was the first document in a chronological sense. In federal practice, the witness could testify that even if the exhibit was not the first in time, the exhibit was intended to have the same effect.

[3]   SAMPLE FOUNDATION

The fact situation is a contract action. The plaintiff, Mr. Levine, alleges that the defendant, Mr. Bratton, breached a written employment contract by discharging Levine without cause. The plaintiff's attorney calls the plaintiff to the stand. The plaintiff has already identified himself and described the parties' oral agreement. The plaintiff is the proponent.

P	WHAT did you do after you reached the oral agreement?
W	Mr. Bratton's secretary reduced the agreement to writing.
P	WHEN did she do that?
W	The very afternoon we reached the agreement. Mr. Bratton had standard forms with blanks, so it didn't take the secretary long to get the contract ready for signature.
P	Your Honor, I request that this be marked plaintiff's exhibit number one for identification.
J	It will be so marked.

P	Please let the record reflect that I am showing the exhibit to the opposing counsel.
J	The record will reflect that.
P	I request permission to approach the witness.
J	Granted.
P	Mr. Levine, I now hand you plaintiff's exhibit number one for identification. WHAT is it? (1)
W	It's the contract I was describing.
P	HOW can you recognize it? (2)
W	I can tell by its general appearance and especially by the signatures on page five. I certainly know my own handwriting.
P	HOW many copies of this did you make? (3)
W	Three. We signed one in ink, and two were carbon copies.
P	WHICH one is this exhibit—the one in ink or one of the carbon copies? (3)
W	This is the one in ink.
P	WHEN did you sign this one? (3)
W	We signed it first.
P	HOW did you sign the carbon copies? (3)
W	The signature just pressed through to them and marked them as we signed the one in ink.
P	Your Honor, I now offer plaintiff's exhibit number one for identification into evidence as plaintiff's exhibit number one.
O	Your Honor, I object to the introduction of the exhibit on the ground that the plaintiff has not accounted for the other documents.
P	Your Honor, may I be heard?
J	Yes.
P	The testimony shows that this exhibit is the original, the very first writing the parties signed. Thus, we've complied with the best evidence rule.
J	Objection overruled. The exhibit will be received.
P	I request permission to hand the exhibit to the jurors for their inspection.
J	Permission granted.

Again, under Rule 1001(d) there can be multiple "originals" so long as they are prepared by reliable mechanical or electronic means and they all were "intended to have the same effect."

§ 8.06   THE EVIDENCE OFFERED IS A "DUPLICATE"

[1]   THE DOCTRINE

In many cases, the proponent can comply with the best evidence rule by offering a duplicate rather than an original. At common law, a duplicate original is as admissible as the original; the proponent may offer a duplicate original without proving any excuse for the non-production of the original. The common law developed a fairly narrow definition of duplicate. The common law insisted that the duplicate be prepared for the same purpose at the same time as the original and executed with roughly the same formalities. Carbon copies signed by the same stroke of the pen as the original are acceptable duplicate originals at common law.

However, the common law balked at accepting subsequently prepared documents as duplicates. The common law refused to accept subsequently prepared documents even if they were prepared by reliable, mechanical means of reproduction. The trend, however, is to include such documents within the definition of duplicate. Federal Rule of Evidence 1001(e) follows that trend. That subsection broadly defines "duplicate" as "a counterpart produced by a mechanical, photographic, chemical, electronic, or other equivalent process or technique that accurately reproduces the original." So long as the writing is prepared by reliable, mechanical means, it qualifies as a duplicate even if it was prepared much later and for a different reason. The Advisory Committee Note to Rule 1001 adds, though, that "[c]opies subsequently produced manually, whether handwritten or typed," do not qualify as duplicates.

[2]   ELEMENTS OF THE FOUNDATION

To qualify a document as a duplicate at common law, the proponent must establish the following foundational elements:

1.   The witness recognizes the writing.

2.   The witness specifies the basis on which he or she recognizes the writing.

3.   The writing is a copy of the original.

4.   The parties made the copy at the same time as the original.

5.   The parties intended the copy to have the same legal effect as the original.[

6.   The parties executed the copy with roughly the same formalities as the original.

If the proponent is invoking the broader, modern definition of duplicate original, the proponent must lay the following foundational elements:

1.   The witness recognizes the writing.

2.   The witness specifies the basis on which he or she recognizes the writing.

3.   The writing is a copy of the original.

4.   The witness states the time when the copy was made.

5.   The witness specifies the reason why the copy was made. In federal practice, this element is unnecessary. However, in some jurisdictions, the writing does

not qualify if it was prepared specially for purposes of trial.

6. The copy was made by a reliable, mechanical means of reproduction. Given the language "[or] photographic" in Federal Rule of Evidence 1001(e), the federal courts treat photographs of objects qualifying as writings as duplicates of the original writings. Thus, a photograph of a check or money wrapper constitutes a duplicate of the check or money wrapper.

[3] SAMPLE FOUNDATIONS

We shall assume that we are continuing the hypothetical involving the employment contract in the last section. The first foundation qualifies a document as a duplicate under the common-law definition. The plaintiff has already stated that the parties reached an oral agreement and had the agreement reduced to writing. The plaintiff is still the proponent.

P	HOW many documents did you prepare?
W	Three.
P	HOW did the documents differ, if at all?
W	We signed the one on top in ink, and the other two were carbon copies.
P	WHERE was the carbon paper? (6)
W	It was between the sheets of white paper.
P	WHEN did you prepare the copies? (4)
W	At the same time as we signed the originals.
P	HOW did you prepare the copies? (5)
W	The secretary typed them by carbon, and then we signed them by carbon at the same time we signed the one on top in ink.
P	WHY did you prepare the copies? (5)
W	So that everyone would have his own copy of the agreement—the original for Mr. Bratton's files, one copy for his general personnel files, and another copy for me.
P	WHAT legal effect did you want the original to have? (5)
W	It was supposed to be our agreement.
P	WHAT legal effect did you want the copies to have? (5)
W	The same effect as the original. As I said, everyone was to have his or her own copy of the contract.
P	Your Honor, I request that this be marked plaintiff's exhibit number one for identification.
J	It will be so marked.
P	Please let the record reflect that I am showing the exhibit to the opposing counsel.
J	The record will so reflect.

P	I request permission to approach the witness.
J	Granted.
P	Mr. Levine, I now hand you plaintiff's exhibit number one for identification. WHAT is it? (1)
W	It's the contract.
P	HOW can you recognize it? (2)
W	I know it by its general appearance and the signatures at the end of page five. I certainly ought to know my own handwriting style.
P	Again, HOW many documents did you prepare? (3)
W	As I said, an original and two copies.
P	WHICH one is this? (3)
W	It's one of the copies.
P	HOW can you tell? (3)
W	The signature is obviously a carbon impression rather than ink.
P	Your Honor, I now offer plaintiff's exhibit number one for identification into evidence as plaintiff's exhibit number one.
O	Your Honor, I object to the introduction of this exhibit on the ground that it is not the best evidence. The plaintiff has not produced or accounted for the original.
P	Your Honor, may I be heard?
J	Certainly.
P	The testimony shows that this exhibit is a duplicate—an accurate copy made at the same time for the same purpose with roughly the same formalities. As a duplicate, it is just as admissible as the original.
J	The objection will be overruled, and the exhibit will be received into evidence.
P	I request permission to hand the exhibit to the jurors for their inspection.
J	Permission granted.

Now we shall work through the same hypothetical with the expanded, modern definition of "duplicate."

P	HOW many documents did you prepare when you signed the contract?
W	Three.
P	HOW did the documents differ, if at all?
W	We signed one in ink, there was a carbon copy, and we made one other copy.
P	WHEN did you prepare the carbon copy?
W	When we signed the original.

P	WHEN did you prepare the other copy? (4)
W	About a week after the signing of the contract.
P	HOW did you prepare this other copy? (5)
W	I ran it off on my Xerox machine at work.
P	WHAT condition was the Xerox machine in when you made the copy? (6)
W	It seemed to be in good, working condition. I didn't have any mechanical difficulties with the machine.
P	WHY did you make this other copy? (5)
W	I just wanted to be on the safe side. I wanted one copy, the carbon, at home and the other, the Xerox, at my office. I was going to use both copies for essentially the same purposes.
P	Your Honor, I request that this be marked plaintiff's exhibit number one for identification.
J	It will be so marked.
P	Please let the record reflect that I am showing the exhibit to the opposing counsel.
J	It will so reflect.
P	I request permission to approach the witness.
J	Permission granted.
P	Mr. Levine, I now hand you plaintiff's exhibit number one for identification. WHAT is it? (1)
W	It's the contract.
P	HOW can you recognize it? (2)
W	I know it by its general appearance and the signatures at the end of page three. I certainly ought to know my own handwriting style.
P	Again, HOW many documents did you prepare? (3)
W	Three—the ink original, one carbon copy, and one Xerox copy.
P	WHICH one is this? (3)
W	It's the Xerox copy.
P	HOW can you tell? (3)
W	It's obviously a Xerox copy rather than an ink or carbon. You can tell by its appearance and the feel of the paper.
P	Your Honor, I now offer plaintiff's exhibit number one for identification into evidence as plaintiff's exhibit number one.
O	I object to the introduction of this exhibit on the ground that it is not the best evidence.

P   Your Honor, may I be heard?

J   Yes.

P   The testimony shows that this exhibit is a duplicate. It is true that it was prepared subsequently; but under the law in this jurisdiction, it can still qualify as a duplicate so long as it was made by a trustworthy mechanical means of reproduction.

J   The objection will be overruled, and the exhibit will be received into evidence.

P   I request permission to hand the exhibit to the jurors for their inspection.

J   Permission granted.

On the one hand, the Federal Rules expand the definition of "duplicate." On the other hand, in federal practice, a duplicate is not necessarily as admissible as an original. Federal Rule of Evidence 1003 reads: "A duplicate is admissible to the same extent as the original unless a genuine question is raised about the original's authenticity or the circumstances make it unfair to admit the duplicate." The opposing counsel cannot create "a genuine question" simply by asserting that there are doubts about the original's authenticity. However, the opposing attorney might invoke Rule 1003 by presenting evidence that the original document was a forgery; the purported author might deny ever signing such a writing. A denial that there ever was such an original obviously sharpens the need to examine the claimed original. Similarly, the opposing attorney could resort to the proviso in Rule 1003 if he or she established that the copy was incomplete and omitted a potentially important part of the original. In either event, the proponent would have to establish excuses for the non-production of all originals before introducing a duplicate.

§ 8.07   ADMISSIBLE TYPES OF SECONDARY EVIDENCE

[1]   IN GENERAL

If the object involved is a writing and the writing's terms are in issue, there are two methods of satisfying the rule. The last two sections dealt with the first, preferred method: proving that the evidence offered qualifies as an original or duplicate. However, sometimes the preference yields. There is a second method of complying with the rule. The second method involves two steps: (1) proving an adequate excuse for the non-production; and (2) offering an admissible type of secondary evidence. There are two admissible types of secondary evidence. The first is an authenticated copy; the witness testifies that the document is an accurate copy of the original. The second is oral recollection testimony; the proponent does not have even a written copy of the original, but the witness can recall the substance of the contents of the original.

[2]   AN AUTHENTICATED COPY

One acceptable type of secondary evidence is an authenticated copy. The witness need not have personally prepared the copy. However, the witness must remember the tenor or contents of the original, read the copy, and finally testify that the exhibit is a true and accurate copy of the original. The elements of the foundation are:

1.　On a previous occasion, the witness read the original.

2.　The witness still remembers the original.

3.　As best he or she can tell, the exhibit is a true and accurate copy of the original.

Our fact situation is a civil tort action. The plaintiff, Mr. Smythe, alleges that the defendant, Mr. Wiggins, is guilty of libel. The complaint alleges that the defendant committed the libel in a letter to Mr. Jackson. The plaintiff calls Mr. Jackson as a witness. Mr. Jackson first testifies that he received the letter in the defendant's handwriting. The plaintiff then establishes an excuse for the non-production of the original letter, such as the loss of the letter; the next section describes the foundation for that excuse. Now the proponent, the plaintiff, will attempt to authenticate a Xerox copy of the letter.

P	WHAT did you do when you first received the letter? (1)
W	I read it.
P	HOW carefully did you read it? (1), (2)
W	Very carefully.
P	WHY did you read it carefully? (1), (2)
W	It shocked me. I had to read it several times before I could believe what I saw.
P	HOW many times did you read it? (1), (2)
W	At least three.
P	WHY did you read it three times? (1), (2)
W	Again, it was hard to believe what I read in that letter.
P	HOW well do you remember the contents of the letter? (2)
W	Very well. I can't quote it word for word, but I have a distinct recollection of the body of the letter.
P	HOW can you remember it so well? (2)
W	Well, it was fairly short; and I read it both carefully and several times.
P	Your Honor, I request that this be marked plaintiff's exhibit number two for identification.
J	It will be so marked.
P	Please let the record reflect that I am showing the exhibit to the opposing counsel.
J	It will so reflect.
P	I request permission to approach the witness.
J	Permission granted.
P	Mr. Jackson, I now hand you plaintiff's exhibit number two for identification. WHAT is it? (3)

W	It's a Xerox copy of the letter I just described.
P	HOW can you recognize it? (3)
W	I recognize the handwriting, the general contents, and some phrases that stick in my mind.
P	HOW accurate is this copy? (3)
W	As far as I can tell, it's verbatim.
P	Your Honor, I now offer plaintiff's exhibit number two for identification into evidence as plaintiff's exhibit two.
O	I object to the introduction of this exhibit on the ground that it is not the best evidence; it's only a secondary copy.
P	Your Honor, may I be heard?
J	Yes.
P	It's true that this is secondary evidence. However, we've established the loss of the original which is an adequate excuse for non-production. In addition, the witness has authenticated the copy.
J	The objection will be overruled, and the exhibit will be received into evidence.
P	Mr. Jackson, would you please read the last paragraph of the letter to the jurors?
W	The paragraph reads: "I heard this juicy rumor about our mutual friend, James Smythe. He evidently slipped $10,000 to Councilman Wild to get a favorable ruling on a zoning application. Old Smythe is a lot slicker—and a lot less honest—than I thought."
P	WHOSE handwriting is that letter in?
W	The defendant's, Marvin Wiggins.
P	I request permission to hand the exhibit to the jurors for their inspection.
J	Granted.

[3] ORAL RECOLLECTION TESTIMONY

Even if the proponent does not have a copy, the witness can testify to his or her recollection of the original's contents. Again, the proponent must establish an excuse for non-production. The foundation is quite simple:

1. On a previous occasion, the witness read the original.

2. The witness still remembers the substance of the original's contents.

3. The witness states the substance of the original's contents.

We shall use the same hypothetical to illustrate this type of secondary evidence. Again, assume that the proponent has already established an excuse for non-production of the original letter.

P	WHAT did you do when you first received the letter? (1)

W	I read it.
P	HOW carefully did you read it? (1), (2)
W	Very carefully.
P	WHY did you read it carefully? (1), (2)
W	It shocked me. I had to read it several times before I could believe what I saw there.
P	HOW many times did you read it? (1), (2)
W	At least three times.
P	WHY did you read it three times? (1), (2)
W	Again, it was so hard to believe what I read there.
P	HOW was the letter prepared? Was it printed, written, or typed? (2)
W	It was handwritten.
P	HOW well do you remember the contents of the letter? (2)
W	Very well. I can't quote it word for word, but I have a distinct recollection of the body of the letter.
P	HOW can you remember it so well? (2)
W	It was relatively short, and I read it carefully several times.
P	WHAT were the contents of the letter? (3)
W	It talked about a lot of things.
P	WHAT, if anything, did the letter say about Mr. Smythe? (3)
O	Your Honor, I object to that question on the ground that it calls for secondary evidence.
P	Your Honor, may I be heard?
J	Yes.
P	It's true that the witness's recollection is secondary evidence. However, we've established the loss of the original which is an adequate excuse for the non-production of the original. In addition, the witness has testified to recalling the substance of the letter.
J	Objection overruled.
P	Mr. Jackson, let me repeat the question. WHAT, if anything, did the letter say about Mr. Smythe? (3)
W	It said that he had bribed Councilman Wild in connection with a zoning application.
P	WHOSE handwriting was the letter in?
W	The defendant's, Marvin Wiggins.

§ 8.08   EXCUSES FOR NON-PRODUCTION

[1]   IN GENERAL

As we have seen, if the proponent's evidence does not qualify as an original or duplicate, the proponent must both authenticate the evidence and establish an excuse for non-production. At common law, there was authority that the proponent must excuse the non-production of all originals and duplicates before resorting to secondary evidence. The Federal Rules make it easier to introduce secondary evidence; they typically require an excuse for the non-production of only the originals. The following are the most common excuses for non-production.

[2]   THE PROPONENT LOST THE ORIGINAL

Federal Rule of Evidence 1004(a) states that there is an adequate excuse for non-production if "all the originals are lost." Sometimes the witness can testify directly to the original's loss; for example, perhaps the witness saw the original fall into a sewer. In most cases, however, the proponent will have to rely on circumstantial proof of loss. Although the witness conducted a diligent search for the original, the witness could not locate it. Some jurisdictions impose hard-and-fast rules to determine the search's diligence; by way of example, the proponent must always search the last known place of custody or contact the last known custodian. However, in most jurisdictions, there are no hard-and-fast rules; the trial judge makes a discretionary determination whether the proponent exercised sufficient diligence to locate the original.

The foundational elements include the following:

1.   The witness discovered that the original was lost.

2.   The witness then searched for the original.

3.   The search was reasonably diligent.

4.   Despite the search, the witness could not locate the original.

Our fact situation is the previous hypothetical. The plaintiff will use Mr. Jackson's testimony to establish the excuse for non-production. Mr. Jackson has already testified about receiving a handwritten letter from the defendant.

P   WHAT did you do with the letter after you received it? (1)

W   I put it in my dresser in our bedroom.

P   WHERE is the letter now? (1)

W   I don't know.

P   WHEN did you discover that the letter was missing? (1)

W   I looked for it three weeks ago when you told me we would be going to trial.

P   HOW did you discover that the letter was missing? (1)

W   I went to the dresser, looked through it, and couldn't find the letter.

P   WHAT did you do then? (2)

W   I searched for the letter.

P	HOW did you conduct this search? (3)
W	I went through each drawer in the dresser very carefully.
P	HOW carefully? (3)
W	I went through it item by item and still couldn't find the letter.
P	WHERE else did you search? (3)
W	I looked all around the room.
P	WHERE else did you look? (3)
W	I checked my desk to see if I might have put it there.
P	WHAT else did you do? (3)
W	I asked my wife if she had seen it.
P	WHAT did she say? (3)
W	She said she hadn't seen it.

(Note that her response is being offered for a nonhearsay purpose under Federal Rule of Evidence 801(c)(2); the purpose is to prove the effect on the hearer's state of mind. Given the wife's response, it was reasonable for the witness not to search further.)

P	WHAT did you do then? (3)
W	I stopped searching.
P	Before you stopped, HOW much time had you spent searching? (3)
W	At least four hours. You made it clear to me that the letter was awfully important, so I basically tore the place apart to look for it.
P	WHY did you stop the search? (3)
W	I just couldn't think of anywhere else to look. I had looked high and low with no success.
P	WHAT was the outcome of your search? (4)
W	I couldn't find it. I just don't know where it got to.

Authentication of the Secondary Evidence

At this point, the proponent authenticates the secondary evidence. See § 8.07[3], *supra*. Assume that the proponent authenticates the witness's recollection of the letter's contents.

P	WHAT, if anything, did the letter say about Mr. Smythe?
O	Your Honor, I object to that question on the ground that it calls for secondary evidence.
P	Your Honor, may I be heard?
J	Yes.
P	It's true that the witness's recollection is secondary evidence. However,

we've established the loss of the original which is an adequate excuse for non-production. In addition, the witness says he can remember the substance of the letter.

J   The objection will be overruled.

P   Mr. Jackson, let me repeat the question. WHAT, if anything, did the letter say about Mr. Smythe?

W   It said that he had bribed Councilman Wild in connection with a zoning application.

P   WHOSE handwriting was the letter in?

W   The defendant's.

[3] THE PROPONENT INNOCENTLY DESTROYED THE ORIGINAL

The early, common-law view was that if the proponent intentionally destroyed the original, the proponent could not introduce secondary evidence of the original's contents. However, modern courts realize that an intentional destruction might have been in perfect good faith. For example, businesses routinely destroy their original records after a number of years; they retain only electronic or microfilm copies because they do not want warehouses jammed with voluminous, outdated records. (Of course, today many businesses and government agencies store copies of their records "in the cloud." Chapter 4 discusses cloud storage.) The current test is whether the proponent destroyed the original in bad faith. If the proponent destroyed the original intentionally but in good faith, the secondary evidence is admissible. Federal Rule of Evidence 1004(a) adopts this doctrine. The subsection provides that secondary evidence is admissible if "all the originals [have been] destroyed, and not by the proponent acting in bad faith."

The foundation includes these elements:

1. The witness had the original.

2. The witness destroyed the original.

3. The destruction was accidental, or the witness's intentional destruction of the original was in good faith.

The fact situation is an anti-trust action. Belmar Corporation sues Dutton Corporation for various violations of the federal anti-trust statutes. Belmar alleges that over a 10-year period, it lost $5,000,000 in sales because of Dutton's anti-competitive practices. To show its damages, the plaintiff calls its chief records custodian, Ms. Gerst. Ms. Gerst has already identified herself and testified to her familiarity with Belmar's records policies. The proponent is the plaintiff.

P   WHAT, if any, procedures does Belmar use to record its sales? (1)

W   We first prepare sales memoranda.

P   WHAT is a sales memorandum? (1)

W   It is a permanent record of all the data concerning the sale—customer, product, date, amount, and the like.

P	WHO prepares the memorandum? (1)
W	One of the people in bookkeeping.
P	WHAT do they do with the memorandum? (1)
W	They place it in their files.
P	WHAT happens to the memoranda after they are inserted in the files? (2)
W	They're kept there for two years.
P	WHAT happens after two years pass? (2)
W	They're transferred to a records holding area in our warehouse.
P	WHAT happens to the memoranda after they are stored in the warehouse? (2)
W	They're kept there for another two years.
P	WHAT happens after that two-year period passes? (2)
W	We're sort of old school. We make microfilm copies of the records and destroy the originals. We don't store much "in the cloud."
P	WHY do you do that? (3)
W	We just don't have enough room to keep the originals. We don't want warehouses stuffed with nothing but records; we need the warehouse space for equipment and merchandise.
P	Ms. Gerst, WHAT were your company's sales in YR-8?
W	I don't know offhand.
P	WHERE could you find that data?
W	Either in the sales memoranda or the microfilm entries.
P	WHERE are the sales memoranda for that year? (2)
W	They're gone.
P	HOW do you know that? (2)
W	I searched for them in the warehouse and couldn't find them.
P	WHAT happened to them? (3)
W	In all probability, they were destroyed after sitting in the warehouse for the two-year period. As I said, that is our customary practice.
P	WHEN would they have been destroyed? (3)
W	By my estimates, probably in YR-4.
P	WHEN did you first learn of this lawsuit? (3)
W	About a year ago.
P	WHAT year was that? (3)
W	YR-3.

P	WHAT did you know about this suit in YR-4 when you destroyed the sales memoranda? (3)
W	Nothing. I had no notice of the suit at all.

In 2006, Federal Rule of Civil Procedure 37 was amended to include a "safe harbor" provision, based on a similar good faith standard. As amended, Rule 37(e) formerly read: "Absent exceptional circumstances, a court may not impose [discovery] sanctions under these rules on a party for failing to produce electronically stored information lost as a result of the routine, good-faith operation of an electronic information system." Rule 37(e) currently provides that the judge may impose sanctions only if the information "should have been preserved in the anticipation or conduct of litigation" and the party "failed to take reasonable steps to preserve it." The rule adds that the judge may impose the most serious sanctions such as adverse jury instructions and dismissal only if the judge finds that the party destroyed the information with "intent to deprive another party of the information's use in the litigation."

Authentication of the Secondary Evidence

At this point, the proponent authenticates the secondary evidence, the microfilm entries. The proponent marks the microfilm entries as plaintiff's exhibit number three for identification. The witness then describes the reliable equipment and procedures the corporation uses to produce its microfilm copies. Finally, the witness states that she took the copies from the right file cabinet.

P	Your Honor, I now offer plaintiff's exhibit number three for identification into evidence as plaintiff's exhibit number three.
O	Your Honor, I object to the introduction of that exhibit on the ground that the microfilm copies are not the best evidence. The plaintiff intentionally destroyed the originals.
P	May I be heard?
J	Yes.
P	It's true that the microfilm entries are secondary evidence and that the plaintiff intentionally destroyed the original sales memoranda. However, the witness's testimony shows that the destruction was in good faith; the plaintiff did not destroy the originals for the fraudulent purpose of making them unavailable to the defendant.
J	The objection will be overruled, and the exhibit will be received into evidence.

[4] THE ORIGINAL IS IN OFFICIAL CUSTODY

If the original is in official custody, the original's non-production is automatically excused. As Federal Rule of Evidence 1005 declares, "[t]he proponent may use a copy to prove the content of an official record—or of a document that was recorded or filed in a public office as authorized by law—if these conditions are met: the record or document is otherwise admissible, and the copy is certified as correct in accordance with Rule 902(4) or is testified to be correct by a witness who has compared it with the original." There are several reasons for this doctrine. First, the removal of the original from official custody might inconvenience other persons who wanted to use the original. Second, the removal would create the risk of the loss of the original. Some jurisdictions restrict the excuse to documents that cannot lawfully be removed from official custody; there must be a statute or regulation prohibiting or restricting the removal of the original from official custody. However, many jurisdictions broadly apply the excuse to any document in official custody.

There is one peculiar aspect of this excuse. This excuse does not generally authorize the admission of any secondary evidence. Rather, most courts insist that the proponent produce a specific type of secondary evidence, that is, a properly attested copy of the original. Federal Evidence Rule 1005 states this preference for attested or compared copies; the Rule ordinarily requires a copy "certified as correct in accordance with Rule 902 or testified to be correct by a witness who has compared it with the original." The Rule states that the proponent may introduce oral recollection testimony only if "no such copy can be obtained by reasonable diligence."

The foundation includes the following elements:

1. The original is in official custody.

2. (*In some jurisdictions*) It would be unlawful to remove the original from official custody.

Our fact situation is a probate contest. The contestants claim by intestate succession. To establish their claim, they must prove the marriage between Joan Merchant and Thomas Kleven. The contestants want to offer the marriage certificate to prove the marriage. We shall work the hypothetical first with live testimony and then with an attesting certificate. In the first variation of the hypothetical, the witness is Mr. John Stern, the deputy county clerk. Mr. Stern has already identified himself and described his duties as deputy county clerk.

P	Your Honor, I request that this be marked contestants' exhibit B for identification.
J	It will be so marked.
P	Please let the record reflect that I am showing the exhibit to the opposing counsel.
J	The record will so reflect.
P	I request permission to approach the witness.
J	Permission granted.
P	Mr. Stern, I now hand you contestants' exhibit B for identification. WHAT is it?
W	It's a copy of a marriage certificate.
P	HOW can you tell that it is a copy?
W	It's obviously a Xerox rather than an ink original.

P	WHERE are the ink originals of marriage certificates kept in this county? (1)
W	In our office.
P	WHERE is the ink original of this certificate kept? (1)
W	In our office.
P	HOW do you know that? (1)
W	I saw it there only a few days ago when I ran off this copy at your request.
P	WHEN may you lawfully remove the original certificate from the official files? (2)
W	You can't.
P	WHY not? (2)
W	There's a state statute that generally prohibits us from permitting the originals to leave our custody.[1] We can remove the originals only in very extraordinary circumstances.
P	WHAT did you do when I requested that you copy the original marriage certificate in this case?
W	I made this copy.
P	HOW did you make it?
W	I did it by mechanical means, our Xerox machine.
P	WHAT condition was the Xerox machine in?
W	Fine, as far as I could tell. I didn't experience any mechanical difficulties when I used it.
P	WHAT did you do with the copy after you made it?
W	I compared it with the original to make sure I had a good copy.
P	HOW did it compare with the original?
W	It was a clear, verbatim copy.
P	Your Honor, I now offer contestants' exhibit B for identification into evidence as contestants' exhibit B.
O	Your Honor, I object to the introduction of this exhibit on the ground that the copy is not the best evidence.
P	May I be heard?
J	Yes.

---

[1] As Chapter 11 points out, in some jurisdictions the formal judicial notice doctrine applies to legal "facts" such as the existence of a state statute. In such a jurisdiction, the proponent could request judicial notice of the statute in question. Federal Rule of Evidence 201(a) limits the scope of the federal judicial notice doctrine to factual material.

P   We've shown that the original is in official custody and cannot be removed from that custody; that is an adequate excuse for non-production. We've also authenticated the copy.

J   The objection will be overruled, and the exhibit will be received into evidence.

P   Mr. Stern, would you please read exhibit B to the jurors?

W   Yes. It states, "On this day, March 1, YR-9, in Chicago, Illinois, I, the Honorable Judge Louis Welsh, married Miss Joan Merchant and Mr. Thomas Kleven in accordance with the laws of the State of Illinois."

P   I request permission to hand the exhibit to the jurors for their inspection.

J   Permission granted.

In the second variation of the hypothetical, the proponent does not use live testimony. Rather, the proponent merely offers a properly attested copy of the original marriage certificate.

P   Your Honor, I request that this be marked contestants' exhibit B for identification.

J   It will so reflect.

P   I now offer contestants' exhibit B for identification into evidence as contestants' exhibit B.

O   Your Honor, I object to the introduction of this exhibit on the ground that it is not the best evidence. On its face, it shows that it is a Xerox copy rather than an original.

P   Your Honor, may I be heard?

J   Yes.

P   It's true that this is a purported copy of the original. However, there is an attached attesting certificate. The certificate is self-authenticating under Rule 902 because it is in proper form, and the certificate states that the original is in official custody of the county clerk.

O   Your Honor, in this jurisdiction, that excuse applies only to documents which cannot be removed from official custody.

P   In that respect, I would ask that Your Honor judicially notice Civil Code § 76. That section describes the duties of the county clerks. It states that county clerks must accept marriage certificates for filing and that they may not release the original certificate to any private party.

J   I will grant the request for judicial notice and overrule the objection. The exhibit will be received into evidence.

P   I request permission to hand the exhibit to the jurors for their inspection.

J   Permission granted.

[5]   THE ORIGINAL IS IN THE POSSESSION OF A THIRD PARTY BEYOND THE REACH OF THE COURT'S COMPULSORY PROCESS

Federal Rule of Evidence 1004(b) reads that there is an excuse for non-production if "an original cannot be obtained by any available judicial process." The proponent usually relies on this excuse when the original is in the possession of a third party beyond the reach of compulsory process. Some states impose an additional requirement; they insist that the proponent show that he or she could not induce the third party to voluntarily send the document to the place of trial. In federal practice, the proponent must exhaust all compulsory process. According to the Advisory Committee Note to Rule 1004, that requirement "includes subpoena duces tecum as an incident to the taking of a deposition in another jurisdiction." However, the Federal Rules do not require resort to any extra-legal means such as requests that the custodian voluntarily produce the writing.

The foundation includes these elements:

1. A third party has the original.

2. The third party resides in a certain place.

3. That place is beyond the reach of the court's compulsory process.

4. (*In some jurisdictions*) The proponent unsuccessfully attempted to persuade the third party to voluntarily send the document to the place of trial, or the circumstances indicate that it would be futile for the proponent to attempt to persuade the third party to do so.

Our fact situation is a civil libel action. The plaintiff, Mr. Smythe, alleges that the defendant, Mr. Wiggins, is guilty of libel. The complaint alleges that the defendant committed the libel in a letter to a Mr. Jackson. The witness is the plaintiff, Mr. Smythe. Mr. Smythe has already identified himself. The plaintiff is the proponent. The place of the trial is Topeka, Kansas.

P	WHERE were you on the afternoon of January 15, YR-3?
W	I was visiting Bill Jackson in Morena.
P	WHERE is Morena located? (2)
W	It's in El Dorado.
P	WHAT did you do while you visited Mr. Jackson?
W	We were just talking about some mutual acquaintances.
P	WHICH acquaintances?
W	Several, including the defendant, Mr. Wiggins.
P	WHAT, if anything, did Mr. Jackson say about Mr. Wiggins? (1)
W	He said that Wiggins had just sent him a handwritten letter about me.
P	WHAT did Mr. Jackson do after he told you about the letter? (1)
W	He showed it to me.

P	WHOSE handwriting was the letter in?
W	Clearly the defendant's.
P	HOW do you know that?
W	I've known the defendant for years, and I've seen him sign his name on innumerable occasions.
P	WHAT did you do after Mr. Jackson showed you the letter? (4)
W	I asked him if I could have it. I told him it made me real angry and that I wanted to use the letter to sue the defendant.
P	HOW did Mr. Jackson respond to your request for the letter? (4)
W	He refused to let me have it.
	(Mr. Jackson's statement is being used for a nonhearsay purpose. The statement is a verbal act or operative fact under Federal Rule of Evidence 801(c)(2); it is the refusal that satisfies the fourth element of the foundation.)
P	WHY did he refuse to let you have it? (4)
W	He said he didn't want to become involved.
P	WHAT other efforts did you make to persuade Mr. Jackson to give you the letter? (4)
W	I phoned him several times since returning to Kansas. Each time I asked him to send it to me.
P	WHAT was his answer? (4)
W	He still insists that he won't send it to me.

Authentication of the Secondary Evidence

At this point, the proponent authenticates the witness's oral recollection. See § 8.07[3], *supra*.

P	WHAT, if anything, did the letter say about you?
O	Your Honor, I object to that question on the ground that the witness's testimony is not the best evidence.
P	Your Honor, may I be heard?
J	Certainly.
P	The testimony shows that a third party, Mr. Jackson, has the original. Mr. Jackson lives in El Dorado, and Your Honor may judicially notice the fact that under our Code of Civil Procedure, Mr. Jackson is beyond the reach of Kansas' compulsory process. You can further notice that, unfortunately, El Dorado procedure won't allow us to obtain any process to compel him to turn the document over. I have copies of the pertinent provisions of the El Dorado Civil Procedure Code for insertion in the record. Finally, the testimony shows that Mr. Jackson refused to send the

original here. The testimony hence establishes an excuse for the original's non-production.

J   I will judicially notice those matters and overrule the objection.

P   Mr. Smythe, let me repeat the question. WHAT, if anything, did the letter say about you?

W   It said that I had bribed Councilman Wild in connection with a zoning application.

P   WHOSE handwriting was the letter in?

W   The defendant's.

[6] THE PARTY-OPPONENT HAS POSSESSION OF THE ORIGINAL AND FAILS TO PRODUCE IT AFTER NOTICE TO PRODUCE

Federal Rule of Evidence 1004(c) recognizes an excuse for non-production if "the party against whom the original would be offered had control of the original; was at that time put on notice, by pleadings or otherwise, that the original would be a subject of proof at the trial or hearing; and fails to produce it at the trial or hearing." Sometimes the proponent has direct evidence of the party-opponent's possession of the original. More often, the proponent must rely on circumstantial evidence, tracing the original to the party-opponent.

The other problem facing the proponent is proving that the party-opponent had fair notice the original would be needed at trial. The proponent can sometimes argue that the terms of the pleadings gave the party-opponent implied notice; the implication would be very strong in a contract action based on breach of a written contract. However, to be safe, the proponent should give the party-opponent express notice that the original will be needed at trial.

The foundation includes these elements:

1. The party-opponent has the original.

2. The party-opponent knew that the original would be needed at trial. The proponent need not serve the party-opponent with compulsory process such as a subpoena duces tecum to produce the original. As the Advisory Committee Note to Rule 1004 states, a simple notice to produce suffices.

3. The party-opponent nevertheless failed to produce the original at trial.

The fact situation is a civil contract action. The plaintiff, Mr. Renfield, alleges that the defendant, Mr. Payntor, warranted that the car the defendant sold plaintiff would get at least 30 miles per gallon on the open highway. The complaint alleges that the defendant breached the warranty because, on the open highway, the car gets only 20 miles to a gallon. The plaintiff takes the stand. The proponent is the plaintiff. The plaintiff wants to testify that before agreeing to buy the car, he wrote to the defendant and made it clear that he did not want the car unless it got at least 30 miles per gallon. The plaintiff has identified himself and described his preliminary oral negotiations with the defendant.

P   WHAT did you do after your oral discussion with the defendant? (1)

W	I thought about the deal and then decided to write to the defendant and outline the parts of the deal I was really insistent on.
P	WHEN did you write this letter? (1)
W	I wrote it on February 14, YR-3.
P	WHAT did you do with the letter? (1)
W	I mailed it to the defendant.
P	HOW did you mail it to him? (1)
W	I stuck it in an envelope and addressed it to the defendant.
P	WHERE did you get the defendant's address? (1)
W	From the telephone book.
P	WHAT did you do with the letter after you addressed it? (1)
W	I stamped it and deposited it in a mailbox.
P	WHAT response, if any, did you receive from the defendant? (1)
W	I didn't get any written response.
P	WHEN, if ever, did you see the letter again? (1)
W	Well, when we sat down to sign the final contract, the defendant pulled it out and showed it to me.
P	WHEN was the last time you saw the letter? (1)
W	The day I signed the contract for the car.
P	WHO had the letter? (1)
W	The defendant.
P	WHERE were you on the morning of November 17th of this year? (2)
W	I was here at the Courthouse.
P	WHY were you here? (2)
W	We were having a conference in this case.
P	WHO attended the conference? (2)
W	You and I were there. The defendant and his attorney were also there.
P	WHAT happened during the conference? (2)
W	We discussed some aspects of the case.
P	WHAT, if anything, did you tell the defendant during the conference about the letter? (2)
W	I told him that you and I wanted him to bring the letter to trial. We asked him to bring it to trial.

(This request is an imperative sentence rather than a declarative one. Hence, the request is not a hearsay statement under Rule 801(a).)

P	WHAT was the defendant's response? (3)
W	He refused to cooperate. He said to forget about the letter. *(This statement is being offered for a nonhearsay purpose under Rule 801(c)(2). The answer is the party-opponent's refusal, the last foundational element.)*
P	WHAT, if anything, did you tell the defendant today about the letter? (3)
W	I again asked the defendant for the letter.
P	WHAT was his response then? (3)
W	He said he didn't have it.
P	WHAT did you tell the defendant in your letter to him?
O	Your Honor, I object to that question on the ground that it calls for secondary evidence. The letter is the best evidence.
P	Your Honor, may I be heard?
J	Yes.
P	The testimony shows that the defendant was the last known custodian of the letter. The testimony also indicates that the defendant knew we wanted the original letter at trial today. That amounts to an excuse for the letter's non-production.
J	The objection will be overruled.
P	Mr. Renfield, let me repeat the question. WHAT did you tell the defendant in your letter to him?
W	I wrote that unless the car got at least 30 miles a gallon, I didn't want the car at all.

[7] VOLUMINOUS OR BULKY RECORDS

Federal Rule of Evidence 1006 declares: "The proponent may use a summary, chart, or calculation to prove the content of voluminous writings, recordings, or photographs that cannot conveniently be examined in court. The proponent must make the originals or duplicates available for examination or copying, or both, by other parties at a reasonable time and place. And the court may order the proponent to produce them in court." Federal Rule of Evidence 1006 generally codifies the common law.

The foundational elements are:

1. The original entries would be admissible in evidence.

2. The original entries are so voluminous or bulky that it would be inconvenient for the trier of fact to examine them. The operative verb is "examine[]." It is immaterial that the entries have already been formally admitted.

3. The witness was qualified to review the records.

4. The witness reviewed the records. According to some courts, it is sufficient if the witness was a member of a team such as a group of accountants who reviewed the records to prepare the summary.

5.   The witness's testimony is a summary of the records. If the proponent offers a written summary, it is not merely demonstrative evidence. In federal practice, the summary is substantive evidence. Hence, the summary can be formally admitted and sent to the jury room during deliberation.

Rule 1006 does not preclude the proponent from using demonstrative charts for pedagogic purposes at trial. Under Rule 611(a), a trial judge has discretion to permit the use of such charts. Such charts have some advantages over Rule 1006 summaries; for instance, while a summary must be confined to an accurate summary of the underlying records, in the judge's discretion a pedagogic chart can state inferences or conclusions from the underlying data. Moreover, although a Rule 1006 chart must summarize records, a Rule 611(a) chart may summarize oral testimony. However, according to the prevailing view, unlike a Rule 1006 summary, a Rule 611(a) chart does not amount to substantive evidence and cannot be sent to the deliberating jury.

The fact situation is a civil action to rescind a corporate merger. The Gemini Corporation was to merge into Rohr Corporation. Gemini sues to rescind the merger agreement; the complaint alleges that the contract is voidable because of Rohr's fraud. Specifically, the complaint alleges that the defendant overstated the amount of its yearly sales. The defendant denies that its representations were false. The defendant is attempting to prove the amount of its annual sales. To prove its annual sales, the defendant would probably call two witnesses. The first witness would be the defendant's bookkeeper or records custodian. The first witness would describe the original records and show that they fall within the business entry exception to the hearsay rule. This testimony would lay the first element of the foundation. The witness would conclude her testimony by stating that she gave the second witness access to the relevant records.

The second witness is Mr. Beer. Mr. Beer has already identified himself. The defendant is the proponent.

P	WHAT is your occupation? (3)
W	I am a certified public accountant.
P	WHERE do you work? (3)
W	I am self-employed. I own my own C.P.A. firm downtown.
P	HOW long have you been a C.P.A.? (3)
W	Roughly 10 years.
P	WHAT is your formal education? (3)
W	I have a Bachelor's, a Master's, and a doctorate.
P	WHAT was your field of study? (3)
W	Accounting.
P	WHAT school awarded you your degrees? (3)
W	Cornell.
P	WHERE were you on April 15th of this year? (4)

W	I went to the offices of Rohr Corporation.
P	WHY did you go there? (4)
W	You asked me to review the corporation's sales records from YR-8 to the present.
P	WHAT did you do when you arrived at the corporation's offices? (4)
W	First I met Mr. Gaynor, the head bookkeeper.
P	WHAT did he do?
W	He led me to the office where all the records are kept.
P	WHAT did you do when you arrived at the office? (4)
W	I immediately started reviewing the records to compute the annual sales for each year since YR-8.
P	HOW did you do that? (4)
W	I used generally accepted accounting techniques, a computer, and a calculator to double check my computations.
P	HOW many pages of records did you review? (2)
W	I couldn't give you a precise number. The number would run into the thousands.
P	HOW long did it take you to compute the yearly totals? (2)
W	Five workdays.
P	HOW long is your workday? (2)
W	A solid eight hours a day.
P	Mr. Beer, WHAT was the total amount of Rohr Corporation's sales in YR-8? (5)
O	Your Honor, I object to that question on the ground that it calls for secondary evidence. The best evidence would be the records themselves.
P	Your Honor, may I be heard?
J	Yes.
P	Mr. Gaynor's testimony established that the original records would be admissible. Mr. Beer's testimony shows that the original records are too voluminous to be used in the courtroom. Moreover, last week we offered to let the plaintiff's accountants review the records. I have a copy of the email that I sent to the plaintiff's attorney.
J	*(To the opposing attorney)* Is that true?
O	Yes, your Honor.
J	I think there's an adequate excuse for non-production. The objection will be overruled.
P	Mr. Beer, let me repeat the question. WHAT was the total amount of

Rohr Corporation's sales in YR-8? (5)

W   It was $5,312,400.

CHAPTER 9

OPINION EVIDENCE

§ 9.01 INTRODUCTION

Like the best evidence rule, the opinion prohibition is based on doubts about the reliability of a certain type of evidence. The common law has doubts about the trustworthiness of opinions. For that reason, the common law prefers that witnesses restrict their testimony to statements of observed fact. Step #1 is that the witness states the primary, sensory data, and at step #2 the jurors then decide which the inferences or conclusions to draw from the underlying data.

The opinion prohibition is a general preferential norm rather than an absolute, categorical rule. There are two situations in which the law allows opinion testimony. In the first situation, the common-law model breaks down at the initial step; a lay witness may express an opinion on a subject if the lay witness cannot verbalize all the underlying data and communicate the data to the jury. For example, a witness cannot articulate all the primary sensory impressions which led the witness to the conclusion that a car was going 45 miles an hour rather than 60. The lay witness's inability to verbalize the underlying data necessitates permitting the lay witness to voice an opinion. Federal Rule of Evidence 701 allows this type of lay opinion testimony.

In the second situation, the model breaks down at the second step; the lay trier of fact lacks the knowledge or skill to draw the proper inferences from the underlying data. If the subject matter is scientific or technical, the lay jurors may lack the expertise necessary to evaluate the hard data; lacking the expert knowledge and skill, they cannot draw reliable inferences or opinions from the facts. In this situation as well, the law sanctions opinion testimony: expert opinion testimony. Federal Rule of Evidence 702 authorizes such testimony.

§ 9.02 LAY OPINION TESTIMONY

[1] IN GENERAL

As previously stated, Federal Rule of Evidence 701 governs the admissibility of lay opinion testimony. The Rule reads: "If a witness is not testifying as an expert, testimony in the form of an opinion is limited to one that is: (a) rationally based on the witness's perception; (b) helpful to clearly understanding the witness's testimony or to determining a fact in issue; and (c) not based on scientific, technical, or other specialized knowledge within the scope of Rule 702." In practice, the courts have construed the Rule as authorizing two types of lay opinion testimony: (1) collective fact or shorthand rendition opinions; and (2) skilled lay observer opinions. Some courts also admit a third type of lay opinion, namely, owners' opinions about the value of their property, which are admissible at common law.

[2] COLLECTIVE FACT OPINIONS

The commentators have coined various titles for this doctrine; they sometimes call it the collective fact doctrine, and on other occasions they refer to it as the shorthand rendition doctrine. The requirements of the doctrine are these: The witness's opinion is based on perceived facts; the opinion is a type of inference that lay persons commonly and reliably draw; and—the key to the doctrine—the lay witness cannot verbalize all the underlying sensory data supporting the opinion. This doctrine sanctions opinions on such subjects as height, weight, distance, speed, color, age, and identity. Under the doctrine, some judges even allow a layperson to opine about a third party's "apparent" or "seeming" state of mind so long as the witness makes it clear that he or she is basing the opinion on the third party's demeanor. The trial judge passes on the second and third requirements as questions of law. The judge asks himself or herself whether lay persons commonly draw this type of inference[1] and whether it would be practical for the lay witness to articulate all the underlying factual data.

The foundation for the doctrine's first element includes proof that:

1. The witness was in a position to observe.

2. The witness in fact observed.

3. The witness observed enough data to form a reliable opinion.

4. The witness states the opinion.

Our fact situation is a tort action arising from a collision. The plaintiff, Ms. Cook, alleges that the defendant, Mr. Armato, caused the accident by speeding. The accident occurred on November 17, YR-3, at the intersection of Haight and Ashbury Streets. The plaintiff calls Mr. Carona as a witness. Mr. Carona has already identified himself. The plaintiff is the proponent. Mr. Carona will testify to lay opinions about an automobile's speed and a person's identity.

P	WHERE were you on the morning of November 17, YR-3, at approximately 10 o'clock? (1)
W	I was standing at the intersection of Haight and Ashbury Streets in San Francisco.
P	HOW were you facing? (1)
W	I was ready to enter the crosswalk, so I was facing the intersection itself.
P	WHAT, if anything, did you see while you were standing there? (2)
W	I saw a red car on Haight Street approaching the intersection.
P	WHAT else did you see? (2)

---

[1] In determining whether laypersons can reliably draw this kind of inference, the judge often introspects and asks himself or herself whether it is the type of inference he or she often draws and finds the inference to be accurate. For example, in driving to work, the judge relies on judgments about the speed of other cars and the distance between cars. If the judge can make such speed and distance judgments accurately, the judge projects that other laypersons can do so as well.

W	There was a blue car approaching the intersection on Ashbury Street.
P	HOW far was the red car from the intersection when you first saw it? (3)
W	A couple of 100 feet away.
P	HOW long did you have to observe the red car before it reached the intersection? (3)
W	Several seconds. I had a pretty good chance to eyeball it.
P	Do you have an opinion of the red car's speed? (4)
W	Yes.
P	In your opinion, WHAT was the speed of the red car? (4)
W	I'd say 40 miles an hour. It was moving at a pretty good clip.
P	WHAT happened when the red car reached the intersection?
W	It hit the blue car.
P	WHO was the driver of the red car? (4)
W	The fellow sitting at the table over there.
P	WHAT is he wearing?
W	He's wearing a blue suit and a striped tie.
P	Your Honor, may the record reflect that the witness has identified the defendant, Mr. Armato?
J	It will so reflect.
P	HOW can you recognize him? (2), (3)
W	After the two cars hit, he got out of the car, and I walked over to see what had happened.
P	HOW long did you stay at the accident scene? (3)
W	About an hour. I talked to the parties and then to the police.
P	HOW close were you standing to the defendant? (3)
W	At one time, I was talking to him. He was no more than a foot or two away from me.
P	WHAT were the lighting conditions? (3)
W	It was broad daylight.
P	HOW well could you see him? (3)
W	Very well.
P	WHO was the driver of the blue car? (4)
W	That lady over there.
P	HOW is she dressed?
W	She's wearing a green dress and white shoes.

P	Your Honor, please let the record reflect that the witness has identified the plaintiff, Ms. Cook.
J	The record will reflect that.
P	HOW can you recognize her? (2), (3)
W	She was also at the accident scene. I had a chance to look at and talk with her.

[3] SKILLED LAY OBSERVER TESTIMONY

The judge will assume that the witness has enough common, human experience to be able to estimate distance, time, or height. The judge's assumption explains why the foundation for collective fact opinions is so minimal. However, there is a second type of lay opinion testimony that requires a more extensive foundation. The courts sometimes use the expression, "skilled lay observer testimony," to describe this second type of lay opinion. This category includes lay opinions about a person's voice, handwriting style, or sanity. A lay witness cannot express an opinion identifying someone's voice unless the witness has had repeated opportunities to hear that voice. Similarly, a lay witness cannot identify a person's handwriting style unless the witness had numerous occasions to observe that person's writing. Finally, a lay witness cannot express an opinion about a person's sanity unless the witness is intimately familiar with the person and knows the person's normal, baseline behavior. In each of these situations, if the witness has had repeated, prior opportunities for observation, the witness qualifies as a skilled lay observer.

The foundation for skilled lay observer testimony includes these elements:

1. The witness is familiar with the person or his or her voice, handwriting style, or normal, rational behavior. The witness is relying on a generalization derived exclusively or primarily through personal experience.

2. The witness explains how he or she became familiar.

3. The witness states his or her opinion.

To illustrate this doctrine, we can use the foundation set out in § 4.02[3] of Chapter 4 on Authentication. As you will recall, the witness is Mr. Bucher. Mr. Bucher did not observe the check's execution, but he is familiar with the author's handwriting style.

P	Your Honor, I request that this be marked plaintiff's exhibit number seven for identification.
J	It will be so marked.
P	Please let the record reflect that I am showing the exhibit to the opposing counsel.
J	It will so reflect.
P	I request permission to approach the witness.
J	Permission granted.
P	Mr. Bucher, I now hand you plaintiff's exhibit number seven for identification. WHAT is it?

W	It seems to be a check.
P	Do you have an opinion as to who signed the check? (3)
W	Yes.
P	In your opinion, WHO signed the check? (3)
W	I'd say that the defendant signed it.
P	WHY do you say that? (1)
W	I recognize his handwriting style on the check.
P	HOW well do you know the defendant's handwriting style? (1)
W	Very well.
P	HOW did you become familiar with his handwriting style? (2)
W	We've been friends for years.
P	HOW many years? (2)
W	About 13.
P	HOW often have you seen the defendant sign his name? (2)
W	Tens, maybe hundreds, of times.
P	Your Honor, I now offer plaintiff's exhibit number seven for identification into evidence as plaintiff's exhibit number seven.
J	It will be received.
P	I request permission to hand the exhibit to the jurors for their inspection.
J	Permission granted.

[4]   OWNERS' OPINIONS ABOUT THE VALUE OF THEIR PROPERTY

At common law, most courts received a third type of lay opinion testimony, the opinion of an owner about the value of his or her real or personal property. The only required foundation included proof that (a) the witness was the owner and (b) he or she had owned the property for a substantial period of time. Many courts continue to accept this testimony under the Federal Rules. The Advisory Committee Note accompanying the 2000 amendment to Rule 701 states: "[M]ost courts have permitted the owner or officer of a business to testify to the value or projected profits of the business, without the necessity of qualifying the witness as an accountant, appraiser, or similar expert." Indeed, some courts now permit the managers of business entities to express similar opinions about the value of the entity's real property.

§ 9.03   EXPERT OPINION TESTIMONY

[1]   IN GENERAL

There are several illustrative scientific evidence foundations in Chapter 4 of this text. However, this section dissects the foundation for expert opinion in greater detail.

The Federal Rules of Evidence admit expert opinion testimony in addition to lay opinion testimony. The Rule in point is 702:

A witness who is qualified as an expert by knowledge, skill, experience, training, or education may testify in the form of an opinion or otherwise if:

(a)   the expert's scientific, technical, or other specialized knowledge will help the trier of fact to understand the evidence or to determine a fact in issue;

(b)   the testimony is based on sufficient facts or data;

(c)   the testimony is the product of reliable principles and methods; and

(d)   the expert has reliably applied the principles and methods to the facts of the case.

In reality, the proponent may use an expert witness in four different ways. First, under Rule 602 the proponent may use an expert purely as a fact witness. Suppose that the accused is being prosecuted for rape. The complaining witness testifies that during the rape, she scratched the rapist's face and drew blood. It just so happened that the accused visited his doctor the day after the alleged rape. The accused could call his doctor and elicit the doctor's testimony that there were no scratches on the accused's face. The witness certainly did not have to be an expert to observe the defendant's face, but it is equally clear that the witness is not incompetent to testify to facts solely because he or she is an expert.

Secondly, as the expression "or otherwise" in Rule 702 suggests, the proponent may use the expert to teach the jurors scientific or technical principles they need to evaluate the facts in the case. The Advisory Committee Note to Rule 702 states that the drafters included those two words in the rule to allow the expert to "give a dissertation or exposition . . . ." The expert witness explains the principles without applying them to the specific facts of the case; the jurors themselves apply the principles to the facts. This use of expert testimony is quite common. As previously noted in Chapter 4, there is a sharp controversy over the reliability of sound spectrography (voiceprint) evidence. A prosecutor offering sound spectrography evidence must not only have the evidence admitted; more importantly, the prosecutor must persuade the jurors to believe the evidence. The prosecutor might call several speech scientists to testify only about the validity of the underlying theories of interspeaker variability and invariant speech; the witnesses might not even refer to the voiceprint examination in that particular prosecution. The witnesses' sole function would be to educate the jurors on the general theories and convince the jurors that the theories and techniques are valid.

The third possibility is to have the expert witness testify to a lay opinion about the significance of the facts in the case. As previously stated, under Rule 701, lay witnesses may opine on the subject of the speed of a motor vehicle. Suppose that a police officer, who is a certified radar speedmeter operator, observes a passing car. The officer could not only testify to the speedmeter reading if the proponent laid a proper foundation for that evidence; since the officer personally saw the car, the officer could also testify to his or her lay opinion of the car's speed. Just as a witness who happens to be an expert may relate facts any layperson could observe, the witness may express any opinions which a layperson could testify to.

Finally, the proponent may have the witness express an expert opinion evaluating the facts in the case. This is probably the most common use of expert testimony. When the proponent uses an expert in this manner, the expert usually employs a general methodology (a theory or technique) to evaluate the facts of the case. After stating his or her qualifications, the expert's testimony follows a syllogistic structure. The expert describes a general explanatory methodology (a theory or technique) as a major premise, states the case-specific facts to be evaluated (the minor premise), and derives an opinion (the conclusion) by applying the major premise to the minor premise. Experienced litigators often conclude the examination by eliciting the expert's testimony explaining the opinion and tying the opinion to the key case-specific facts. The testimony therefore covers six topics: the witness's qualification as an expert, the general methodology, the facts of the case, the application of the methodology to the case-specific facts, the opinion itself, and the explanation of the opinion. Each topic requires a foundation. The following subsections analyze the six topics and their respective foundations.

[2] THE EXPERT'S QUALIFICATIONS TO FORM THE OPINION

The law permits expert opinion testimony because the expert can either form inferences entirely beyond the capability of lay jurors or draw the inferences far more reliably. The expert can do so because the expert has knowledge or skill the jurors lack. Under Rule 702, the expert can acquire the knowledge or skill by education, experience, or a combination of education and experience. The expert's background often includes both theoretical education and practical experience.

In the past, the courts have been fairly liberal in assessing the qualifications of proposed experts. That liberality is understandable, since the test stated in Rule 702 is whether the witness possesses more knowledge or skill than the trier of fact, not whether the witness is a full-fledged specialist on the issue before the court or the best qualified expert in the field. However, in *Daubert v. Merrell Dow Pharmaceuticals, Inc.*, 509 U.S. 579, 597, 113 S. Ct. 2786, 125 L. Ed. 2d 469 (1993), the Supreme Court indicated that the trial judge must find that the witness is competent to perform the specific "task at hand." That language has led many lower courts to raise the bar for qualification as an expert.

The foundation for the expert's qualifications can include the following elements:

1. The witness has acquired degrees from educational institutions.

2. The witness has had other specialized training in this field of expertise.

3. The witness is licensed to practice in the field.

4. The witness has practiced in the field for a substantial period of time.

5. The witness has taught in the field.

6. The witness has published in the field.

7. The witness belongs to professional organizations in the field.

8. The witness has previously testified as an expert on this subject.

Our fact situation is a civil personal injury action. The plaintiff, Mr. Nowick, alleges that the defendant, Mr. Johnson, negligently caused the collision in which Mr. Nowick was injured. The complaint alleges that the plaintiff has suffered severe brain injury as a result of the accident. The plaintiff calls Dr. Worth. The plaintiff is the proponent. Dr. Worth has already identified himself.

P	WHAT is your formal education? (1)
W	I have a Bachelor's degree and a medical degree.
P	WHICH undergraduate school did you attend? (1)
W	Arizona State University.
P	WHAT degree did you obtain there? (1)
W	I earned a Bachelor of Science degree.
P	WHAT was your major field of study? (1)
W	Biology.
P	WHICH medical school did you attend? (1)
W	The Johns Hopkins University Medical School in Baltimore.
P	WHAT degree did you obtain there? (1)
W	My M.D.
P	WHAT did you do after you graduated from medical school? (2)
W	I interned at the University of Southern California Medical Center.
P	HOW long was your internship? (2)
W	A year.
P	WHAT did you do after your internship? (2)
W	I became a resident at Gross Hospital in Lexington, Kentucky.
P	WHAT is a residency? (2)
W	You specialize in a certain field and get practical experience.
P	WHAT was your specialty? (2)
W	Neurology, brain problems.
P	HOW long was your residency? (2)
W	Three years.
P	WHEN did your residency end? (2)
W	In YR-18.
P	WHAT did you do when your residency ended? (3)
W	I moved here to Denver and began practicing.
P	WHAT did you have to do to practice in Denver? (3)
W	I had to become licensed in Colorado.
P	WHEN did you obtain your license in this state? (3)
W	In YR-17.

P	WHAT did you do after you obtained your license? (4)
W	I began my practice, specializing in neurology.
P	HOW long have you practiced in this state? (4)
W	Nine years now.
P	HOW many clients with neurological problems have you treated? (4)
W	I can't name a number. By this time, I've probably treated thousands.
P	HOW much of your time do you devote to the practice of medicine? (5)
W	About 80% of my working time.
P	WHAT else do you spend your time on? (5)
W	For one thing, I teach at the University of Colorado Medical School in Boulder.
P	HOW long have you taught there? (5)
W	For four years now.
P	WHAT courses do you teach? (5)
W	I teach three upper division courses in the field of neurology.
P	WHAT else do you spend your professional time on? (6)
W	I try to publish with some frequency.
P	WHAT journals have published your articles? (6)
W	Some of the leading medical and neurological journals, including the A.M.A. Journal.
P	What is the "A.M.A."?
W	I'm sorry. It's the American Medical Association.
P	HOW many articles have you published? (6)
W	Nine.
P	WHAT topics did you discuss in these articles? (6)
W	All the articles relate to neurology. *(Although Rule 702 does not require that the witness be a specialist to qualify as an expert, as a matter of trial advocacy the proponent should attempt to establish the witness's stature as a specialist on the specific, narrow issue before the court.)*
P	WHAT professional organizations do you belong to? (7)
W	Several, including the American College of Neurological Specialists and the American Board of Neurology.
P	HOW do you become a member of the American College? (7)
W	You have to have specialized in the neurological field for at least five years.
P	HOW do you become a member of the Board? (7)

W	There are strict requirements. You not only have to have practiced for several years, you also have to pass oral and written examinations.
P	HOW often have you testified in court? (8)
W	I'd say at least 100 cases.
P	HOW many times were you permitted to give expert opinion testimony? (8)
W	Every time.
P	WHAT subjects did you testify on? (8)
W	Most of the time I testified on neurology.

In the above foundation, the expert had formal academic degrees as well as practical experience. In some cases, formal degrees are unnecessary; standing alone, practical experience is sufficient to qualify the witness as an expert. For example, a farmer can qualify as an expert on agricultural practices; and a police officer may testify as an expert on the modus operandi for various crimes. In other cases, practical experience is mandatory. In many jurisdictions, there are statutes which prescribe the qualifications for expert witnesses in medical malpractice cases. These statutes typically provide that to qualify as an expert in such cases, the witness must have a certain number of years' experience practicing the field of medicine involved in the case.

[3]   THE GENERAL METHODOLOGY (THE THEORY OR TECHNIQUE) THE EXPERT RELIES ON

After describing his or her credentials, the expert often states the major premise: The general scientific methodology, the theory or technique the expert proposes to rely on. For example, if the witness is a psychiatrist, the witness may testify that there is a recognized symptomatology for a particular mental disease or disorder. While skilled lay observer witnesses rely on generalizations derived from their personal experience, the expert's testimony about the methodology will rest on sources such as lectures that he or she has heard and texts and articles they have read.

To be a permissible premise for expert testimony, the methodology must pass two tests. One test is stated in Rule 702(a); the theory or principle must "help the trier of fact." If the subject is a matter of common knowledge, there is no need for expert testimony. Relying on his or her personal experience, the judge decides whether there is a sufficient need for expert testimony on the subject. The judge typically finds a sufficient need when he or she concludes either that the subject is altogether beyond a layperson's ken or that an expert can draw a substantially more reliable conclusion on this subject than a layperson. Although the early common-law cases purported to enforce a strict "necessity" test, modernly the courts apply a liberal helpfulness standard.[2]

---

[2] In its May 15, 2021 draft Note to a proposed amendment to Rule 702, the Advisory Committee points out that a few courts use the expression, "appreciably help." However, the Committee asserts that that expression represents an "[u]nfortunate[]" misreading of Rule 702.

The methodology must also satisfy a second test: either the traditional *Frye* test (still followed in a significant minority of states) or the *Daubert* test (governing in federal court and approximately three quarters of the states). Under *Frye*, the proponent of scientific testimony must show that the principle or theory in question is generally accepted within the relevant scientific field. Although most of the cases enforcing *Frye* are criminal, *Frye* has also been applied to scientific testimony in civil cases.[3] Similarly, while most cases applying *Frye* involve instrumental techniques such as polygraphy, other cases extend *Frye* to non-instrumental techniques employed in psychology.[4] However, other *Frye* jurisdictions exempt "soft" science from the general acceptance test. When *Frye* applies, the proponent of the witness's testimony must present foundational evidence that the theory or technique has gained widespread popularity within the pertinent scientific circles.

As Chapter 4 also noted, in 1993 in the *Daubert* case, 509 U.S. 579, 113 S. Ct. 2786, 125 L. Ed. 2d 469 (1993), the United States Supreme Court ruled that the general acceptance standard is no longer the controlling test in federal court. Instead, *Daubert* requires the proponent to demonstrate that the methodology qualifies as reliable "scientific knowledge" within the meaning of that expression in Federal Rule of Evidence 702. The proponent does so by showing that there has been adequate empirical verification of the validity of the theory or technique.

Under *Daubert*, the question is not the global validity of the expert's discipline. Rather, the focus is on the reliability of the particular theory or technique that the expert proposes relying on. In *Kumho Tire Co. v. Carmichael*, 526 U.S. 137, 119 S. Ct. 1167, 143 L. Ed. 2d 238 (1999), the Court announced that the proponent of any type of expert testimony must establish the reliability of the expert's underlying methodology. The Court acknowledged that non-scientific expertise often cannot be validated in the same manner as a scientific theory; but the Court stressed that whether or not the expertise is purportedly scientific, the trial judge may not accept the *ipse dixit* assertion of the expert.

Whatever type of expertise the witness claims, the nature of the required validation foundation varies with the kind of knowledge claim that the expert is making.

Suppose, for example, that in a contract case, the question is whether the expression "50% protein" in the agreement includes deliveries containing 49.6% protein. The expert is an experienced member of the industry, who proposes testifying that there is an industry custom or convention that anything in excess of 49.5% counts as 50%. The expert is merely describing or

---

[3] *In re* "Agent Orange" Prod. Liab. Litig., 611 F. Supp. 1223, 1242 (E.D.N.Y. 1985); Cameron v. Knapp, 520 N.Y.S.2d 917 (N.Y. Sup. Ct. 1987).

[4] People v. Shirley, 31 Cal. 3d 18, 34, 181 Cal. Rptr. 243, 252, 723 P.2d 1354, 1374–1375, *cert. denied*, 459 U.S. 860 (1982). However, in Sargon Enterprises, Inc. v. University of Southern California, 55 Cal. 4th 747, 149 Cal. Rptr. 3d 614, 288 P.3d 1237 (2012), the same court adopted a *Daubert*-style reliability test which seems to apply to all types of expert testimony. The court directed trial judges to "determine whether, as a matter of logic, the studies and other information cited by experts adequately support the conclusion that the expert's general theory or technique is valid."

summarizing her industry experience, including industry literature and conversations with other industry members. The only necessary foundation would be a showing that the witness has been involved in or learned of a large number of similar transactions (involving agreements specifying "50% protein") and that in those transactions the parties treated anything in excess of 49.5% as 50%.

In contrast, assume that in a criminal case, the expert is a dog handler who proposes testifying that her dog's alert to the accused's luggage indicates that the luggage contained explosive material. In this situation, the expert is drawing an inference from the dog's behavior. To justify that inference, the expert would have to establish that the results of the prior use of the dog indicate that that inference may accurately be drawn from the dog's conduct—in other words, testimony about the dog's track record. On how many occasions when the dog "alerted" was there a subsequent search? What percentage of those searches yielded explosive material?

In essence, under *Daubert* the bottom line is that the proponent must lay a foundation marshaling enough empirical data and reasoning to demonstrate that by using the particular theory or technique the expert contemplates relying on, the expert can accurately draw the specific type of inference he or she proposes testifying to.[5]

To lay this element of the foundation for an expert opinion, ideally the proponent should establish that:

1. The expert used a particular methodology to evaluate the facts in the case;

2. The expert's claim about the methodology has been validated in an appropriate manner; and

3. The methodology is generally accepted by the majority of experts in the pertinent scientific specialty. As Chapter 4 pointed out, although *Daubert* ruled that general acceptance is no longer dispositive as it was under *Frye,* the extent of acceptance of a methodology is a factor in the trial judge's reliability analysis.

The fact situation is a rape prosecution. The People allege that on October 15, YR-3, the accused, Marx, raped the complainant, Ms. Jane Whitlow. During her direct testimony, Ms. Whitlow described the rape and identified the accused as the rapist. On cross-examination, she admitted that although on the day in question she reported the alleged rape to the police, the next day in a conversation with her mother, Ms. Whitlow refused to confirm or deny that there had been a rape. As their next witness, the People call Dr. Herbert Dubowski, a licensed psychiatrist. The People propose to elicit Dr. Dubowski's testimony about rape trauma syndrome (RTS) to rehabilitate Ms. Whitlow's credibility. In *People v. Bledsoe*, 36 Cal. 3d 236, 251, 203 Cal. Rptr. 450, 460, 681

---

[5] The Advisory Committee Note accompanying the 2000 amendment to Rule 702 makes it clear that it is not the judge's province to determine whether the specific opinion the expert proposes testifying to is correct. That issue is for the trier of fact.

P.2d 291, 301 (1984), the California Supreme Court held that the prosecution may not use the fact that the complainant displays RTS symptoms as substantive evidence that there has been a rape. However, the court indicated that RTS evidence could be used for other purposes, such as rehabilitating the credibility of an impeached complainant. *People v. Roscoe*, 168 Cal. App. 3d 1093, 1099, 215 Cal. Rptr. 45, 49 (1985), applied *Bledsoe* and held RTS evidence admissible "to support the victim's credibility." After stating his credentials, Dr. Dubowski testifies to establish the empirical validity as well as the general acceptance this use of RTS:

P	Doctor, WHAT is your specialty? (1)
W	For the past few years, I've concentrated my practice and research in the area of rape trauma syndrome.
P	WHAT is rape trauma syndrome? (1)
W	The theory holds that in most cases, after a rape women cope with that traumatic event in a predictable manner.
P	WHAT manner is that? (1)
W	Their reaction usually progresses through two phases. The initial stage is the acute phase. They try to come to terms with the physical trauma and the immediate psychological impact. They experience disorganization in their lives. They become confused.
P	WHAT do you mean by "confused"? (1)
W	They're indecisive. Even if someone asks them point blank about the rape, out of shame or a sense of morality, they are often reluctant to discuss it. Again, that's the acute phase. That's followed by the long-term phase.
P	WHAT happens during that phase? (1)
W	They begin reorganizing their lives. They may move, change their telephone number, and visit friends and family much more frequently to gain moral support. They often develop phobias. They may have a fear of being alone.
P	WHAT empirical research, if any, have you done on rape trauma syndrome? (2)
W	I was fortunate enough to participate in the original research done on the subject. Before I moved to Dallas, I lived in Boston. That's where Burgess and Holmstrom did the first intensive study of this subject.
P	WHEN and WHERE did they conduct that study? (2)
W	Between July 1972 and July 1973, they interviewed all the rape victims admitted to the emergency ward of Boston City Hospital.
P	HOW many persons did they study? (2)
W	About 150 women were included in the data base.

P	WHAT types of women were included in the study? (2)
W	All sorts—they were all races. About 70% were adult, and the rest were minors. In fact, there were three male children included in the study.
P	HOW did the researchers conduct the study? (2)
W	They initially interviewed these people, and they then followed up by studying the changes in the life patterns after the traumatic incident.
P	WHAT findings did the researchers make? (2)
W	In the overwhelming majority of cases, there was a clear pattern.
P	WHAT do you mean by "overwhelming majority"? (2)
W	I mean about 85 to 90% of the cases.
P	WHAT was the pattern? (2)
W	It was the two stages, the acute and long-term phases, that I described a few moments ago.
P	WHAT other research, if any, has been done on rape trauma syndrome? (2)
W	There have been several other studies, including Sutherland and Scherl.
P	WHAT were the findings in those studies? (2)
W	About the same. As a generalization, the subsequent empirical studies confirm the findings in the Burgess-Holmstrom study. You can quibble with percentages, but the virtually uniform finding is that in most cases, there is a definite pattern of coping behavior after a rape. Moreover, this body of research demonstrates that these symptoms appear much more frequently among rape victims than they do among the baseline or general population.
P	Doctor, HOW well accepted is rape trauma syndrome? (3)
W	It's very well accepted in my field.
P	WHAT evidence is there that the syndrome is well accepted? (3)
W	The latest editions of the leading, authoritative treatises on psychiatry all mention the syndrome.
P	WHAT professional organizations are there in your field? (3)
W	One is the A.P.A., the American Psychiatric Association.
P	To WHAT extent has the American Psychiatric Association recognized the existence of rape trauma syndrome? (3)
W	The A.P.A. has an official manual, the Diagnostic and Statistical Manual of Mental Disorders. It's now in the fifth, 2013 edition—DSM V. The previous 1987 edition, DSM III-R, and the 2004 fourth edition both listed post-traumatic stress disorder as a recognized syndrome. The fifth edition, DSM V, also recognizes post-traumatic stress disorder.

P   WHAT, if anything, does DSM V say about rape trauma syndrome? (3)

W   One of the examples of post-traumatic stress disorder in DSM V is its application after the stressor of a rape.

P   HOW do you use the diagnostic criteria in the DSM? Do you use them to determine whether the patient was in fact raped? (2)

W   No. I would be the first to admit that I can't tell you that. They've yet to conduct empirical studies proving that.

P   Well then, HOW do you use the criteria? (2)

W   You utilize them to determine only whether the patient sincerely believes that he or she has suffered that type of stressor. The available studies establish the general proposition that by using these criteria, you can accurately infer the patient's state of mind. For the most part for treatment purposes, it's their belief that really matters. If the patient exhibits the criteria, in all probability they have that belief; and if so, we can treat them effectively for PTSD.

[4] THE CASE-SPECIFIC FACTUAL BASES OF THE EXPERT'S OPINION

[a] OVERVIEW

The expert should now state the minor premise, the case-specific factual data to which the theory will be applied. Federal Rule 702(b) requires that the opinion be based on "sufficient facts or data." For its part, Federal Rule of Evidence 703 governs the types or kinds of information that an expert may base an opinion on: "An expert may base an opinion on facts or data in the case that the expert has been made aware of or personally observed. If experts in the particular field would reasonably rely on those kinds of facts or data in forming an opinion on the subject, they need not be admissible for the opinion to be admitted. But if the facts or data would otherwise be inadmissible, the proponent of the opinion may disclose them to the jury only if their probative value in helping the jury evaluate the opinion substantially outweighs their prejudicial effect." Hence, there are three potential sources for the data and three types of case-specific bases for an expert's opinion.

[b] FACTS THE EXPERT PERSONALLY KNOWS OR THAT ARE OTHERWISE INDEPENDENTLY ADMISSIBLE

All jurisdictions allow an expert to base an opinion on facts the expert has personal or firsthand knowledge of. For instance, doctors usually base their opinions in part on conditions and symptoms they personally observed during an examination of the patient. The foundation for this basis ordinarily includes these elements:

1. Where the witness observed the fact.

2. When the witness observed the fact.

3. Who was present.

4. How the witness observed the fact.

5.   A description of the fact(s) observed.

We shall continue our hypothetical with the neurologist.

P	WHERE were you on the afternoon of July 11, YR-3? (1), (2)
W	In my office.
P	WHAT, if anything, happened that afternoon? (3)
W	I conducted an examination of the plaintiff, Mr. Nowick.
P	WHO is Mr. Nowick? (3)
W	He's the gentleman sitting over there at the end of the table.
P	HOW is he dressed? (3)
W	He's wearing the white suit with the gray tie.
P	Your Honor, please let the record reflect that the witness has identified the plaintiff, Mr. Nowick.
J	The record will reflect that.
P	WHO was present during this examination? (3)
W	Just Mr. Nowick, myself, and my nurse, Ms. Cartwright.
P	WHAT happened during the examination? (4)
W	I personally examined the plaintiff for any symptoms of brain damage.
P	HOW did you conduct the examination? (4)
W	I conducted a manual inspection of his cranium and then administered a battery of standard eye and coordination tests.
P	HOW long did this examination take? (4)
W	A good three hours. I conducted a very thorough examination.
P	WHAT, if anything, did you observe during the examination? (5)
W	I saw some symptoms and signs of brain damage.
P	WHAT were the symptoms? (5)
W	For one thing, there was a deep scar on the front, right side of Mr. Nowick's head.
P	HOW deep? (5)
W	Almost 1/8 of an inch into the surface—easily deep enough to cause some damage.
P	WHAT else did you observe? (5)
W	There was a sort of vacancy in the plaintiff's eyes, again possibly indicating brain problems. Finally, the plaintiff exhibited real difficulty in the eye-to-hand coordination tests.

Just as the expert can rely on his or her personal knowledge, the expert may base an opinion on independently admissible hearsay evidence. As [c] explains, sometimes the expert may rest an opinion on out-of-court statements that do not pass muster under the hearsay rule.

[c]   SECONDHAND REPORTS FROM THIRD PARTIES

There is a of authority whether the expert may rely on out-of-court reports from third parties such as other experts if the reports do not fall within any hearsay exception. The traditional view has been that the expert may not do so. However, the Federal Rules follow the trend in the case law that the expert may do so in certain circumstances. Rule 703 allows an expert to rely on a "hearsay"[6] report "[i]f experts in the particular field would reasonably rely on those kinds of facts or data in forming an opinion on the subject." A few courts equate "reasonably" with "customarily"; if the judge finds under Rule 104(a) that it is the specialty's practice to consider a particular type of data, the judge must allow the witness to use that type of information as part of the basis for the opinion. However, most courts interpret "reasonably" as giving the trial judge the power to second-guess the specialty's use of that type of data; although the judge should ordinarily defer to the specialty's customary practice, in an extreme case the judge may rule that the specialty's practice is objectively unreasonable. The conventional wisdom is that under either construction of Rule 703, the evidence of the report is not admitted as substantive proof of the report's truth; rather, the report is admitted for the limited purpose of showing the basis of the expert's opinion. The fact that the expert has heard and considered the report is some evidence that the opinion is well grounded. Consequently, upon request, under Rule 105 the opponent is entitled to a limiting instruction by the trial judge.

The foundation for this basis includes these elements:

1.   The source of the third-party report.

2.   The content or tenor of the report.

3.   It is customary within the specialty to consider that type of report.

---

[6] The courts often use the term "hearsay" to refer to this type of information that the expert may rely on under Rule 703. However, that terminology is misleading. In principle, Rule 703 legitimates this practice as a nonhearsay use of the out-of-court statement under Rule 801(c). As the Note to Rule 703 indicates, the statement is not being admitted as substantive proof of the truth of the assertions in the statement. Rather, the theory of admissibility is a variation of the "mental input" nonhearsay theory discussed in § 10.02[3][d]. We are interested in the effect of the report on the expert's state of mind: The expert's receipt of the report makes it more reasonable for the expert to reach the conclusion he or she is testifying to.

Although the above paragraph describes the conventional wisdom, that view has been challenged. In Williams v. Illinois, 567 U.S. 50, 132 S. Ct. 2221, 183 L. Ed. 2d 89 (2012), five justices—Justice Thomas in concurrence and four dissenters led by Justice Kagan—forcefully expressed the view that as a matter of logic, "basis" reports are necessarily admitted for the truth of the assertions in the report. If the truth of the opinion is conditioned on the truth of the reports, the jurors cannot accept the truth of the opinion unless they posit the truth of the reports. The justices' statements were technically dicta, but the statements were so emphatic that the statements may prompt some lower court judges to reconsider the conventional approach. Some lower courts have already done so. *E.g.*, People v. Sanchez, 63 Cal. 4th 665, 204 Cal. Rptr. 3d 102, 374 P.3d 320 (2016).

Our hypothetical continues:

P   Dr. Worth, in addition to the symptoms you personally observed during your examination of Mr. Nowick, WHAT else have you considered? (1)

W   For one thing, I talked to Mr. Nowick's family physician, Dr. Stiles.

P   WHO is Dr. Stiles? (1)

W   Maynard Stiles is a general practitioner here in town.

P   HOW long has he been in practice here? (1)

W   Maybe 15 years. He's a well-respected member of our local medical community.

P   WHEN did you talk with him? (1)

W   The day after I examined the plaintiff.

P   WHY did you talk to him? (3)

W   I had to get Mr. Nowick's medical history. Specifically, I wanted to know whether he had that scar or displayed the vacant stare or lack of coordination before his car accident.

P   WHAT is the importance of the medical history? (3)

W   You just can't make an intelligent diagnosis without that.

P   WHAT is the customary medical practice concerning the use of medical history? (3)

W   I followed the custom here. It would be malpractice not to gather the history and consider it in evaluating your diagnosis. Use of the history is good, accepted practice.

P   WHAT did Dr. Stiles tell you about the plaintiff's medical history? (2)

W   He said that prior to the accident, there was no scar on the plaintiff's cranium. Further, prior to the collision, the plaintiff had not exhibited the symptoms of either vacancy of stare or lack of coordination.

O   Your Honor, I request a limiting instruction.

J   Yes. Ladies and gentlemen of the jury, Dr. Worth has just referred to a statement made by a Dr. Stiles. You may not consider Dr. Stiles' statement as proof that before the accident, the plaintiff had no scar or vacant stare or lack of coordination. You may consider Dr. Stiles' statement only for the limited purpose of showing one factor or element Dr. Worth considered in arriving at his opinion.

When the information considered by the expert is otherwise inadmissible under the hearsay rule, the courts differ over the extent to which the expert's proponent may expose the jury to the information. Some courts would not permit Dr. Worth to describe Dr. Stiles' statement in detail; in these courts, Dr. Worth could testify only in very general terms that he relied upon Dr. Stiles' description of the plaintiff's medical history. Other courts follow the practice illustrated in the above foundation; they permit the expert to elaborate on the content of the hearsay statement. When the hearsay statement is in written form, some courts go to the length of allowing the proponent to formally introduce the writing and submit the writing to the jury for their inspection. The December 1, 2000 amendment to Rule 703 settled the question in federal practice by adding the third sentence to the statute. That sentence announces a general rule that the expert ordinarily may not give the jury a detailed description of the otherwise inadmissible information. Most trial judges still permit the expert to describe the general type of information that he or she is relying on (*e.g.,* "reports from bystanders"). However, the drafters of the amendment feared that a detailed recitation of the content of the inadmissible reports would create too great a risk that the jurors would disregard any Rule 105 limiting instruction and misuse the information as substantive evidence. The amendment permits the expert to go into detail only when the probative value of the detail substantially outweighs any incidental probative dangers. The exception might come into play when the factual detail is essential to understanding the expert's reasoning process but the opinion itself does not coincide with a pivotal disputed fact on the merits of the case.

[d] HYPOTHETICALLY ASSUMED FACTS

Sometimes the testifying expert has neither examined the party nor even talked with an expert who has personally examined the party. The testifying expert may still express an opinion in response to a hypothetical question. In the hypothesis, the proponent specifies the facts he or she wants the expert to assume. The expert then relies on his or her expert knowledge and skill to draw a proper inference from the facts in the hypothesis.

There are two major limitations on hypothetical questions. The first limitation is that in most jurisdictions, the proponent must have already introduced evidence to support a finding that the assumed facts exist. The trial judge may permit the proponent to vary the order of proof and introduce proof of the assumed facts later, but judges are often reluctant to permit the proponent to do so. The second limitation is that in many jurisdictions, the hypothesis must include all the undisputed, material facts. The reason for this limitation is obvious; if the hypothesis is incomplete and omits critical facts, the ultimate opinion will be misleading rather than helpful.

Hypothetical questions can take two forms. In the first "long" form, the proponent specifies the historical facts he or she wants the expert to assume. For example, the proponent could say:

P   Dr. Worth, please assume the following facts as true:

One, in the accident, the plaintiff sustained a cut three inches in length and 1/8 inch in depth on the right, front part of his head.

Two, the plaintiff bled profusely from that cut.

Three, immediately after the accident, the plaintiff began experiencing sharp, painful headaches in the right, front part of his head.

In the second "short" form, the proponent asks the witness to assume the truth of the testimony of another witness or witnesses. Assume, for instance, that the ambulance attendant, Mr. Phelan, has already testified. During his testimony, Phelan stated that he observed the cut on plaintiff's head, noted the bleeding, and heard plaintiff complain about a headache. The plaintiff now calls Dr. Worth. Dr. Worth was exempted from the Rule 615 sequestration order in the case and was, therefore, present in court to hear the testimony by the previous witnesses.

P   Dr. Worth, WHERE were you this morning?

W   Here in the courtroom.

P   WHAT were you doing?

W   Listening to the testimony.

P   WHOSE testimony did you listen to?

W   Mr. Phelan, the ambulance attendant, was on the stand most of the morning.

P   HOW well could you hear his testimony?

W   Very well. I had no problems hearing what he was saying.

P   Specifically, WHERE were you sitting?

W   In the first row reserved for spectators.

P   HOW often did you leave the room during Mr. Phelan's testimony?

W   I didn't leave; I stayed in the courtroom the whole time.

P   Dr. Worth, please assume the truth of Mr. Phelan's testimony about Mr. Nowick's condition immediately after the accident.

Many trial attorneys prefer the "long form" because it gives them greater control over the witness. For their part, many jurisdictions prohibit the second "short form" of hypothetical question. These jurisdictions reason that at the very least, this form is ambiguous; it can be difficult for the jurors to determine the specific facts the expert witness is assuming. Moreover, if the proponent invites the expert to assume the truth of several witnesses' testimony and there are any conflicts between those witnesses' testimony, the proponent is really asking the expert to resolve those conflicts. In effect, the proponent is asking the expert to usurp the jury's function. However, other jurisdictions sanction this form of hypothetical question if the assumed testimony is simple and internally consistent.

[e]   THE SUFFICIENCY OF THE FACTS OR DATA TO SUPPORT THE OPINION

As previously stated, Rule 703 governs the quality or type of facts or data that the expert may rely on. However, there are also quantitative concerns, since Rule 702(b) declares that the opinion must rest on "sufficient facts or data." For example, an accident reconstruction expert may not base an opinion as to colliding cars' point of impact solely on the cars' final resting places. To make it clear to the judge and jury that the expert has sufficient information, after eliciting the testimony identifying the case-specific information, the expert's proponent might ask:

P   Professor, you've described several types of information about the

	accident scene. WHAT additional information, if any, would you need to draw a conclusion about the point of impact of the two cars?
W	None. The information that I've listed is more than enough to allow me to draw a reliable conclusion as to where the point of impact occurred.

[5] THE PROPER APPLICATION OF THE GENERAL METHODOLOGY TO THE CASE-SPECIFIC INFORMATION

The prior subsection pointed out that Rule 702(b) requires the exclusion of the expert's opinion if the expert has not identified enough case-specific information to support a reliable opinion. Such situations are one example of the expert's failure to properly apply the methodology. Rule 702(d) expressly states that the proponent must show that "the expert has reliably applied the principles and methods to the facts of the case." In its May 15, 2021 report accompanying a proposed amendment to Rule 702, the Advisory Committee stated that "a fair number of cases" have stated that issues as to reliable application are "questions of weight and not admissibility," but the Committee asserts that those statements misread Rule 702(d). To satisfy this element of the foundation, the expert must do two things: (a) describe the essential steps in properly applying the methodology; and (b) testify that he or she followed those steps.

In order to identify the proper steps, the expert might refer to a standard promulgated by an organization such as the American Society for Testing and Materials International (ASTM) or a subcommittee of NIST's Organization of Scientific Area Committees (OSAC). The hearsay rule would not preclude the expert from referring to the requirements set out in such a standard, since those requirements are imperative sentences rather than assertions under Federal Rule 801(a). If the proponent wanted to introduce the standard itself during the expert's direct examination, the proponent might be able to rely on Rule 902(5) or (7) as the basis for authenticating the standard.

After the expert's description of the required procedures, the proponent has several options for showing that the expert complied with the procedure in the instant case. It is ideal if under Rule 602 the expert could testify from present memory that he or she had personally done so. If initially the expert cannot do so, under Rule 612 the proponent could use a writing such as the expert's report to refresh his or her recollection. Failing that, the proponent might be able to introduce the report itself as past recollection recorded (Rule 803(5)), a business entry (Rule 803(6)), or perhaps an official record (Rule 803(8)).

[6] THE STATEMENT OF THE OPINION ITSELF

In the next part of the expert's testimony, the proponent should elicit the ultimate opinion. Some jurisdictions insist that the expert vouch that his or her opinion is "reasonably certain" or formed "to a reasonable degree of certainty." Other jurisdictions demand a "reasonably probable" opinion or an opinion formed "to a reasonable degree of probability." The witness must be willing to testify that he or she has formed the opinion to a reasonable medical or scientific certainty or probability. Still other jurisdictions have abandoned these formal limitations; so long as the opinion is likely to be helpful to the jurors, these jurisdictions allow an expert to state a possibility, probability, or certainty. If the opinion is couched as a mere possibility, the opinion is more vulnerable to an objection under Federal Rule of Evidence 403; but the text of Rule 704 does not codify a categorical rule precluding the admission of opinions phrased in that fashion. The trend to abandon the requirement for such formulaic language is sound. Experts do not use this language when they communicate with each other; the prior practice is an artificial requirement that the courts have imposed on expert witnesses.

The complete foundation for the opinion includes these elements:

1. The witness has formed an opinion.

2. The witness believes that the opinion is a reasonable medical or scientific certainty or probability. Again, the trend is to abandon this formulaic language. Following this trend, many courts now simply allow the expert to express his or her actual level of confidence in the opinion. However, there is a pending amendment to Rule 702(d). As amended, Rule 702(d) would read: "the expert's opinion reflects a reliable application of the principles and methods to the facts of the case." The accompanying Advisory Committee Note explains that the purpose of the amendment is to bar overstated opinions such as "assertions or absolute or one hundred percent certainty . . . ."

3. The witness states the opinion.

The hypothetical fact situation continues:

P	Dr. Worth, do you have an opinion whether Mr. Nowick suffered brain damage as a result of the accident? (1)
W	Yes.
P	HOW positive are you of your opinion? (2)
W	I'm fairly confident in it. I think that any competent neurologist would reach the same conclusion.
P	WHAT is the degree of your certainty? (2)
W	You can't treat this sort of question as an absolute, but I'm reasonably confident of my conclusion.
P	WHAT is that conclusion? (3)
W	In my opinion, Mr. Nowick has suffered permanent brain damage, located in the right, front part of his cranium, as a direct result of the accident.

When the expert states his or her final conclusion, two common-law restrictions can come into play: one prohibiting opinions on ultimate issues in the case and a second forbidding opinions on matters of law. In the above foundation, the expert opines on the question of causation. That question falls squarely within the witness's medical expertise. Federal Rule of Evidence 704(a) abolishes the common-law rule forbidding an expert from opining on "an ultimate issue" to be decided by the trier of fact. Under

704(a), the witness's conclusion is not objectionable merely because the conclusion directly addresses the ultimate issue of causation.[7]

Given 704(a)'s broad reference to "ultimate issue" rather than "ultimate fact," some jurisdictions now permit experts to opine directly on mixed questions of law and fact. For instance, a few courts have permitted accident reconstruction experts to testify that a particular driver failed to yield the right-of-way. However, while most jurisdictions allow such experts to opine on such factual issues as velocity and point of impact, they refuse to admit opinions about failure to yield, since right-of-way is a legal concept. *Jackson v. E-Z Go Div. of Textron, Inc.*, 326 F. Supp. 3d 375, 401 (W.D. Ky. 2018) ("an expert's testimony can 'embrace[] an ultimate issue.' [H]owever, 'the issue embraced must be a factual one' "). The 1977 Committee Comment to Minnesota Rule 703 states the traditional view:

> A distinction should be made between opinions as to factual matters, and opinions involving a legal analysis or mixed questions of law and fact. Opinions of the latter nature are not deemed to be of any use to the trier of fact.

Many of these jurisdictions conceive of the issue as a Rule 702 problem rather than a 704 issue. These courts reason that when the witness opines on a legal matter, the witness is violating Rule 702; the witness is exceeding the limits of his or her expertise as a physicist or chemist. In a jurisdiction following the traditional view, the proponent should check the wording of the question calling for the expert's opinion to ensure that the wording does not solicit an opinion on a mixed question of law and fact.

[7]   THE EXPLANATION OF THE OPINION

Evidence law does not require that the expert explain the opinion. However, common sense tells the proponent that unless the expert explains the opinion, the jurors may not be persuaded. The proponent cannot expect the jurors to make a blind act of faith in the expert and accept the expert's opinion as *ipse dixit*. As a practical matter, the jury is unlikely to attach much weight to the opinion unless the expert explains his or her reasoning process in plausible, common sense terms. Consequently, it is a common practice for the proponent to invite the expert to explain the opinion. The expert should explain the opinion in general terms and then specifically relate the opinion to the factual bases the expert previously recited. The opinion will be most persuasive if the expert can show the jurors that the opinion is firmly grounded in the facts that are the bases of the opinion.

In short, the foundation for this last part of the expert's testimony consists of two elements:

1.   In general terms, the expert explains the opinion.

2.   The expert explains the significance of each factual basis of the opinion. The

---

[7] To an extent, Rule 704(b) preserves the ultimate fact prohibition. That provision reads:

In a criminal case, an expert witness must not state an opinion whether the defendant did or did not have a mental state or condition that constitutes an element of the crime charged or of a defense. Those matters are for the trier of fact alone.

expert demonstrates how each basis contributes to and supports the opinion.

The hypothetical finally concludes:

P   Dr. Worth, WHY did you reach that conclusion? (1)

W   The symptoms evidence the existence of brain damage, and the medical history discloses only one possible cause.

P   WHAT symptoms are you referring to? (2)

W   Well, the scar, the vacancy of gaze, and the lack of eye-to-hand coordination.

P   WHAT is the significance of those symptoms? (2)

W   The scar is deep enough to indicate a wound that probably would have applied damaging pressure to the brain. The part of the brain located directly under the scar is the part that controls vision and eye-to-hand coordination. The other symptoms of vacant stare and lack of manual coordination confirm that pressure in fact was applied with resulting damage.

P   WHAT medical history are you relying on? (2)

W   My consultation with Dr. Stiles and the plaintiff's hospital records.

P   WHAT is the significance of the medical history? (2)

W   It establishes the causation. The scar was apparently inflicted in the accident. The other symptoms not only didn't exist before the accident, they arose immediately after the accident. The timing is almost conclusive in my mind.

§ 9.04　EVIDENCE OF AN OUT-OF-COURT EXPERIMENT

[1]　THE DOCTRINE

Suppose that in a particular case, the central issue is whether a traffic accident occurred in a certain manner. The plaintiff and defendant advance conflicting theories as to how the accident occurred. To corroborate her theory, the plaintiff might offer testimony about an out-of-court experiment.[8] The plaintiff would hire an expert to design and conduct an experiment duplicating the conditions obtained at the time of the accident in question. Suppose that the result of the experiment indicated that the accident occurred in the manner claimed by the plaintiff. The experiment might be important corroboration for the plaintiff's theory of the case. At trial, the plaintiff could present an expert witness or witnesses to provide an oral description of the experiment. In addition, the plaintiff could offer a photograph or videotape[9] depicting part or all of the experiment.

---

[8] C. Phillip Colver, *The Persuasive Impact of Simulation Experimentation*, 17 TRIAL 64 (1981).

[9] Silverman v. General Motors Corp., 99 Ill. App. 3d 593, 54 Ill. Dec. 882, 425 N.E.2d 1099 (1981).

[2] ELEMENTS OF THE FOUNDATION

To lay a proper predicate for evidence of an out-of-court experiment, the proponent must lay the following foundation:

1. The witness must possess the expertise to design and conduct the experiment. The witness must qualify as an expert. In the accident reconstruction context, the witness might have prior experience as a traffic police officer and a background in engineering,[10] notably physics.

2. The proponent asked the witness to design and conduct an experiment. The request itself, a weak imperative sentence, is not an assertive statement under Rule 801(a). Hence, the witness may testify to the request without violating the hearsay rule. Further, the witness may testify that he or she agreed to comply with the request without violating the hearsay rule. The promise to comply is a verbal act which is nonhearsay under Rule 801(c)(2).

3. The witness studied the accident which the proponent asked the witness to duplicate. At this point, Federal Rule of Evidence 703 comes into play. As § 9.03[4] indicates, under Rule 703, the expert may gain his or her information about the accident from three sources.

   To begin with, the expert can rely on personal knowledge. For instance, the expert might personally visit the accident scene or go to the mechanic's shop to inspect the vehicles involved in the accident.

   Next, the expert could rely on facts posited to the expert in the form of a hypothetical question. When the proponent opts to rely on this source, the proponent must introduce independent admissible evidence of all the facts. As previously stated, the trial judge will ordinarily require that the proponent present such evidence before calling the expert. In wording the hypothesis in many, if not most, cases, the proponent specifies the facts which he or she wants the expert to assume. In other cases, the judge exempts the expert from any sequestration order; and the proponent then invites the expert to assume the truth of particular testimony that the expert has heard in court.

   Lastly, the expert may sometimes rely on secondhand sources of information. The expert certainly can do so when the out-of-court statement is independently admissible pursuant to a hearsay exception. Moreover, by the terms of Rule 703, the expert may even rely on secondhand reports that would not be independently admissible so long as that type of information is reasonably relied upon by experts in that particular field. Thus, an accident reconstruction expert might testify that she read the police report containing the officer's description of the accident scene.

4. After studying the accident, the witness identified the variables which would have to be duplicated to replicate the accident. In laying this element of the

---

[10] *See* Spraker v. Lankin, 218 Kan. 609, 545 P.2d 352 (1976).

foundation, the witness is testifying as an expert. In an accident reconstruction case, the proponent might be attempting to introduce the expert's testimony about an experiment involving braking distance. The witness would testify that the following factors, *inter alia*, determine braking distance: the type of road surface, the wet or dry condition of the surface, the condition of the tire tread, the tire pressure, and the amount of pressure which the driver applied to the brake.

The witness might explicitly or implicitly rely on a scientific hypothesis about the factors necessary to determine the outcome of the experiment. Depending on the jurisdiction, when the expert relies on a purportedly scientific hypothesis, the expert must be prepared to testify to the general acceptance of the hypothesis pursuant to the traditional *Frye* test or the empirical validation of the hypothesis under *Daubert*.

5. In designing the experiment, the witness ensured that the experimental conditions were similar to those obtained at the time of the accident.[11] The two sets of conditions need not be perfectly identical. The judge has considerable discretion in assessing the degree of similarity between the two sets of conditions, but the judge should ensure similarity in the essential or salient respects. In most published opinions, the appellate court asserts that when the experiment is offered to recreate how the specific incident occurred, the trial judge must find substantial similarity.[12] However, the courts tend to accept a lesser degree of similarity when the experiment is for the limited purpose of generally demonstrating the operation of a relevant scientific law.[13] If the proponent offered the experimental evidence for that purpose, the opponent is entitled to a limiting instruction. In the instruction, the judge would inform the jury that although the experiment illustrates the operation of a physical law relevant to the accident, the experiment is not intended to duplicate the accident.

6. The witness later conducted the experiment or supervised the experiment. Any instructions the witness issued or received for conducting the experiment would be nonhearsay under Rule 801(a), since the out-of-court statements constitute imperative sentences. Furthermore, even if the witness did not personally conduct every facet of the experiment, under Rule 703, she could rely on secondhand reports from the other participants in the experiment.

7. The experiment yielded a particular result. The proponent could present the experiment's outcome to the trier in several different ways. The simplest way would be eliciting a description of the outcome from a witness with personal

---

[11] People v. Wills, 153 Ill. App. 3d 328, 106 Ill. Dec. 207, 505 N.E.2d 754 (1987).

[12] Barth v. International Harvester Co., 160 Ill. App. 3d 1072, 112 Ill. Dec. 479, 513 N.E.2d 1088 (1987).

[13] Van Steemburg v. General Aviation, Inc., 243 Ill. App. 3d 299, 183 Ill. Dec. 496, 611 N.E.2d 1144 (1993).

knowledge. In addition, the same witness could lay the foundation to authenticate a photograph or videotape of the experiment under Rule 901. The proponent usually prefers incorporating the last method of presentation. A photograph or videotape helps the trier visualize the expert's testimony, and in turn that usually enhances the trier's immediate understanding of the testimony as well as the trier's long-term memory.

[3] SAMPLE FOUNDATION

The fact situation is a civil tort action. The plaintiff alleges that the defendant was driving inattentively and negligently rear-ended the plaintiff's auto. In particular, the complaint alleges that but for the defendant's inattention, the defendant could have stopped his car in time to avoid striking the rear of the plaintiff's car. The proponent is the plaintiff. The plaintiff calls Professor Ernest Kamisar as its next witness. Professor Kamisar will lay the foundation for an experiment about braking distance.

P	Please state your full name and spell your last name for the record.
W	My name is Ernest Kamisar. My last name is spelled K-A-M-I-S-A-R.
P	WHERE do you live?
W	I live and work in Champaign, Illinois.
P	WHERE do you work? (1)
W	I teach in the Engineering Department of the University of Illinois.
P	WHAT is your educational background? (1)
W	I obtained my Bachelor of Science degree in engineering from Iowa State University in YR-12.
P	In general terms, WHAT is engineering? (1)
W	Engineering is applied science. Engineers are specialists in using the laws of physics to create machines and other technology for human use.
P	WHAT did you do after you obtained your bachelor's degree? (1)
W	We moved to Ann Arbor, Michigan, so I could begin my graduate studies at the University of Michigan. I got the Master's in YR-10 and my doctorate in YR-8.
P	WHAT subjects did you study in the course of obtaining those degrees? (1)
W	I pretty much specialized in vehicle dynamics.
P	WHAT do you mean by the expression, "vehicle dynamics"? (1)
W	That's the study of how automobiles like cars behave as they move and travel down a highway.
P	WHAT licenses do you hold in this state? (1)
W	I'm registered as an engineer.
P	How many professional papers, if any, have you had published? (1)

W	Approximately 40.
P	WHAT topics did those papers relate to? (1)
W	They all deal with aspects of vehicle dynamics. The vast majority of them relate to braking.
P	WHAT professional engineering organizations, if any, do you belong to? (1)
W	For years I've been a member of the Society of Automotive Engineers and the American Society of Mechanical Engineers. I've served as the president of the state chapter of the SAE, the Society of Automotive Engineers.
P	WHAT practical experience, if any, do you have in vehicle dynamics? (1)
W	I've consulted with major manufacturers such as General Motors and Ford on a number of brake system design projects.
P	HOW many times, if ever, have you qualified as an expert witness in a court of law? (1)
W	On over 50 occasions.
P	WHAT topics did you testify about as an expert witness? (1)
W	On every occasion I've testified about braking vehicles, including both passenger cars and trucks.
P	Professor, WHERE were you on January 19, YR-3? (2)
W	I was at my office at the University in Champaign.
P	WHAT happened that day? (2)
W	That was the day your associate phoned me about this case.
P	WHO phoned you? (2)
W	Your associate, Ms. Clark.
P	WHAT, if anything, did she ask you to do? (2)
W	She requested that I study the material about a braking problem in this case with a view to possibly testifying at this trial.
P	Specifically, WHAT type of analysis did she ask you to perform? (2)
W	Ms. Clark explained that it had been raining that day of the accident and that the defense might contend that the real cause of the accident was the design of the road. She said that the road curves just before the stop sign where the plaintiff's car had stopped. She said that she expected the defense to contend that on a rainy day, given that curve, even an attentive driver wouldn't be able to stop in time to avoid hitting a car sitting at the stop sign.
P	WHAT, if anything, did you say to Ms. Clark? (2)

W	I agreed to review the problem, conduct the analysis, and testify at trial if necessary.
P	WHERE were you earlier today? (3)
W	Right here in court.
P	WHICH witnesses, if any, did you hear testify? (3)
W	I heard the testimony by the witness to the accident, the mechanic, and the police officer.
P	HOW well do you remember their testimony about the physical layout of this stretch of road, the type of vehicle, and the condition of both the tire tread and the brake lining? (3)
W	I recall it well. I was paying special attention to that testimony.
P	WHAT exhibits, if any, did you hear read? (3)
W	I heard the weather report read into evidence.
P	HOW well do you remember the contents of the report? (3)
W	Again, I remember it quite well. I was trying to be especially attentive.
P	Professor Kamisar, WHEN did you first learn this information about stretch of road and the vehicle? (3)
W	Actually, I got a lot of the information a couple of days after I spoke with Ms. Clark.
P	HOW did you obtain the information? (3)
W	A few days later, Ms. Clark sent me a Federal Express package containing the material in the case.
P	Specifically, WHAT material did that package contain? (3)
W	Let's see. As I recall, it included the police reports, an auto mechanic's report on the post-accident inspection of both vehicles, a U.S. Weather Service report about the rain the day of the accident, and the depositions of both the plaintiff and the defendant.
P	When you analyze braking problems, WHAT type of material do you ordinarily review? (3)
W	Exactly the sort of material which Ms. Clark had sent me. I specifically asked her to send that material.
P	HOW many experts in your field make it a practice to consider that type of material? (3)
W	Virtually everyone. It would be irresponsible not to gather that type of material.
P	WHAT other information, if any, did you gather? (3)
W	In March, I flew out to Seattle and inspected the stretch of road before I prepared my final design for the experiment.

P	WHY did you do that? (3)
W	I wanted to measure the coefficient of friction of that stretch of road.
P	WHAT is a "coefficient of friction"? (3)
W	It's sometimes loosely called the drag factor. In general terms, the type of road surface determines how much horizontal force you need to move an object across the road surface.
P	HOW did you determine the coefficient of friction? (3)
W	There's an instrument known as a drag sled or box that measures the coefficient. I brought mine with me from Michigan, and I used the sled to personally measure the coefficient on the road surface where the accident occurred.
P	Professor, for the balance of your testimony, I want you to take into consideration: (1) the coefficient of friction you personally measured; (2) the truth of the prior testimony about the section of road, the model of car, and the condition of the car's tire tread and brake lining; and (3) the truth of the weather report. (3)
W	Very well.
P	WHAT, if anything, did you do after studying all this written material and measuring the coefficient of friction? (5)
W	At that point, I designed an experiment to duplicate the defendant's attempt to brake just before impact.
P	HOW did you do that? (5)
W	Whenever you design an experiment like this, you're trying to duplicate the conditions that were obtained at the time of the event. You identify the key conditions and try your best to recreate or replicate them.
P	WHAT are the key conditions? (4)
W	In a braking experiment like this, excluding the human factor, they're the following: the type of road and its coefficient of friction, the wet or dry condition of the surface, the condition of the tire tread, the tire pressure, the condition of the brake lining, and the type of vehicle. The literature indicates that those are the most important variables.
P	You said "excluding the human factor." WHY do you exclude the factor? (4)
W	That's what you're trying to determine by this experiment. You're trying to figure out whether an attentive human could have braked in time. You duplicate the physical conditions in order to draw a conclusion about the other condition, namely, the attentiveness of the human being behind the wheel.
P	After you identified these key conditions, WHAT did you do? (5)

W	I went about trying to duplicate them.
P	In particular, HOW did you do that? (5)
W	Well, to begin with, we ran our experiment over the very same stretch of road. Then we got hold of another car of exactly the same year, make, and model as the defendant's. We had the tire tread and brake lining modified by a mechanic to ensure that they were essentially identical to the tread and lining on the defendant's car at the time of this accident. Next, after reading the Weather Service report, we waited to conduct the experiment until there had been the same amount of rain on a given day as there had been the day of the accident. As I said, the wet or dry condition of the road surface will affect braking. I hired six test drivers from local auto manufacturing companies to actually drive the car during the experiment.
P	WHEN did you conduct the experiment? (6)
W	We had our act together to be ready for the right weather, and the weather condition was almost ideal on June 1st. That's when we conducted the experiment.
P	HOW did you conduct the experiment? (6)
W	We initially coordinated with the Highway Patrol to briefly block off that section of highway. The patrol was very cooperative. I gave a detailed set of instructions to the test drivers. For example, I instructed the drivers to follow a particular route to the stop sign. It was the same route the defendant took that day. I also instructed them to drive at the same speed that the defendant claimed in his deposition. We had an unoccupied car parked at the stop sign in the same position in which the plaintiff had stopped. We didn't tell the test drivers that a car would be stopped there; we didn't want them to anticipate that and give them an unfair advantage in braking—a forewarning that the defendant did not have on the day of the accident.
P	WHAT happened next? (6)
W	We actually ran the experiment. Each driver drove the designated route and turned the curve at the speed indicated by the defendant.
P	HOW do you know that they had the right speed? (6)
W	Each time we ran the test, there was a researcher in the passenger seat. That person's sole responsibility was ensuring that the test driver hit the curve at the right speed. They did every time.
P	Professor, at the time of the accident the defendant was the only occupant of his car. You've just said that during the test, there were both a driver and a researcher in the car. HOW might the presence of the second person have affected the outcome of your case? (6)
W	It really wouldn't.

P   WHY not? (6)

W   To begin with, the researcher's weight wouldn't have affected the braking distance. Moreover, we instructed the researcher to remain both silent and stationary during the test. Their only function was to passively note the speed of the test car when the driver reached the curve.

P   WHAT was the result of your experiment? (7)

W   On each occasion, the driver stopped well before hitting the rear of the parked car.

P   WHAT do you mean by "well before" hitting the car? (7)

W   The closest any test vehicle came to striking a car was 30 feet away. In the six tests, the average distance was 46 feet.

P   WHAT do you mean by "the average distance"—from where to where? (7)

W   From the rear of the vehicle parked at the stop sign to the front of the test vehicle.

P   WHO measured the distance? (7)

W   I did so myself.

P   HOW did you measure the distance? (7)

W   I used a type of tape measure officially approved by the Society of Automotive Engineers. It's the most accurate one currently available on the market.

CHAPTER 10

THE HEARSAY RULE, ITS EXEMPTIONS, AND ITS EXCEPTIONS

PART A. Introduction

§ 10.01   OVERVIEW

The hearsay doctrine is the last major preferential exclusionary doctrine based on doubt about the reliability of a type of evidence. The best evidence rule's underlying rationale is a fear of untrustworthy secondary evidence. The opinion rule expresses the courts' doubts about the reliability of opinions. Underlying the hearsay rule is a skepticism about the reliability of in-court testimony about out-of-court statements when the proponent is attempting to use the statements as substantive evidence in the case. The common law prefers that the third party (the declarant) appear in court and subject himself or herself to cross-examination. The common law assumes that evidence will be more trustworthy if the declarant testifies under oath, in the jury's view, and subject to cross-examination. The opponent may use cross-examination to expose any latent errors of perception, memory, narration, or sincerity.

Lay persons commonly think that the hearsay rule applies to any out-of-court statement. In truth, the rule has a relatively narrow scope. Evidence constitutes hearsay only if it is: (1) an assertive statement (2) by a human being (3) still considered an out-of-court declarant at the time of trial and (4) offered at trial to prove the truth of the assertion. Federal Rule of Evidence 801 follows this view. The rationale for the rule explains the rule's limited scope. We are interested in the declarant's credibility only when his or her out-of-court statement is being used to prove the truth of the assertion. In that circumstance, the evidence's value depends on the credibility of the out-of-court declarant. For example, suppose that an in-court witness testifies that an out-of-court declarant said that the defendant's car ran a red light. The plaintiff wants to offer the testimony for the purpose of showing that in fact, the defendant's car ran the red light. For that purpose, the testimony's value depends upon the perception and memory of the out-of-court declarant. The declarant is functionally a trial witness, and the opponent thus needs to cross-examine the out-of-court declarant to test the evidence.

However, if the proponent does not offer the out-of-court declaration for its truth, the opponent does not need to cross-examine the declarant. If the declaration is logically relevant on some other theory, the evidence's value usually depends on the credibility of the in-court witness. Suppose that the plaintiff has sued a defendant for slander. The plaintiff alleges that the defendant repeated the slanderous statement to X. The plaintiff calls X, the in-court witness, to testify that the defendant made an out-of-court statement

447

that the plaintiff bribed a public official. The plaintiff does not want to offer the statement for its truth; quite to the contrary, if the defendant can show that the statement is true, the defendant has a complete defense to tort liability. The plaintiff wants to show only that at a particular time and place the defendant made the slanderous statement. The value of X's testimony depends on X's credibility. Did X hear the statement correctly? Does X remember the statement correctly? If X testifies in court, the defendant can test the value of the evidence. Hence, the limitation on the hearsay rule's scope is a corollary of the rule's rationale; the rule is limited to statements offered to prove their truth because then and only then does the opponent have an acute need to cross-examine the out-of-court declarant.

Even if a statement falls within the definition of hearsay, the statement may be admissible. There are numerous exemptions from and exceptions to the hearsay rule. Federal Rule 801(d) sets out the exemptions for some prior statements and admissions or statements of a party-opponent, Federal Rules 803 and 804 contain a lengthy list of exceptions, and Rule 807 adds a final, residual exception. Part C of this chapter discusses the admission exemption. As that part explains, to bring a statement within the admission exemption, the proponent need not show that the statement was reliable or that there is any necessity for resorting to the statement; all the proponent has to do is to show that the statement should be imputed to the party-opponent. Part D describes a series of hearsay exceptions based primarily on an inference of the reliability of the statement. In contrast, Part E addresses a number of exceptions resting in large part on a showing of necessity; all of these exceptions require proof that the out-of-court declarant is unavailable at the time of trial. Finally, Part F of this chapter describes the residual hearsay exception. To invoke this exception, the proponent must demonstrate both reliability and an element of necessity.

PART B.   Hearsay

§ 10.02   THE DEFINITION OF HEARSAY

[1]   IN GENERAL

As previously stated, the definition of hearsay is narrow. Federal Rule of Evidence 801(c) states that " '[h]earsay' means a statement that: (1) the declarant does not make while testifying at the current trial or hearing; and (2) a party offers in evidence to prove the truth of the matter asserted in the statement." Rule 801(a) adds that a " '[s]tatement' means a person's oral assertion, written assertion, or nonverbal conduct, if the person intended it as an assertion." Under the Federal Rules, evidence constitutes hearsay only if four conditions are present: (1) the evidence is an assertive statement or act; (2) the assertion was made out of court by a human being; (3) at trial, that person is still considered an out-of-court declarant; and (4) the evidence is being used at trial to prove the truth of the assertion. Evidence falls within the hearsay definition only when all four elements are present; if any element is missing, the evidence is not hearsay, and there is no need to search for a hearsay exemption or exception. We shall now examine each of the four elements of the hearsay definition.

[2]   THE EVIDENCE IS AN ASSERTIVE STATEMENT OR ACT

[a]   ASSERTIVE STATEMENTS

All courts agree that assertive statements fall within the hearsay definition. If the person makes an oral out-of-court statement or records the statement out of court by reducing it to writing, the statement could be hearsay. However, it must be remembered that not all statements are assertive. Grammar tells us that there are four types of sentences: declarative, imperative, exclamatory, and interrogatory. As a practical matter, only declarative sentences ordinarily fall within the hearsay definition; they declare or assert facts, including states of mind. Imperative sentences giving orders or making requests, exclamatory sentences, and interrogatory sentences posing questions usually fall outside the hearsay definition; if these sentences are relevant at all, they are ordinarily relevant simply because the sentences were uttered, and for that purpose the attorneys can question the in-court witness, the person who heard the declarant utter the sentence. There is little or no need to cross-examine the declarant of an imperative, exclamatory, or interrogatory sentence about perception or memory.

If the proponent is going to offer evidence on the theory that it is a non-assertive statement, the foundation usually includes these elements:

1.   Where the statement was made.

2.   When the statement was made.

3.   Who was present.

4.   The tenor of the statement.

5.   In an offer of proof outside the jury's hearing, the proponent states that the tenor of the statement is nonassertive.

6.   In the same offer of proof, the proponent shows that the nonassertive statement is logically relevant to a fact of consequence in the case.

Our fact situation is a criminal prosecution. The government charges that Messrs. Cetina and Britton conspired to sell and actually sold heroin. The witness is Ms. Grace. Ms. Grace identifies herself. She then testifies that she is a government informant and infiltrated the meeting of a drug ring. The prosecutor is the proponent.

P	Ms. Grace, WHERE were you on the evening of January 17, YR-3? (1), (2)
W	I was at 70 Aberdeen Court in downtown Indianapolis.
P	WHO else was there? (3)
W	The two defendants, Cetina and Britton.
P	WHERE are they now? (3)
W	In the courtroom.
P	Specifically, WHERE in the courtroom? (3)
W	At that table over there.
P	HOW are they dressed? (3)

W	Cetina is wearing a blue suit with red tie. Britton has a brown suit and yellow tie.
P	Your Honor, please let the record reflect that the witness has identified the two accused.
J	It will so reflect.
P	Ms. Grace, WHAT happened during this meeting? (4)
W	The accused made some plans.
P	WHAT plans did they discuss? (4)
O	Your Honor, I object to that question on the ground that it calls for incompetent hearsay.
P	Your Honor, may we approach the bench and be heard?
J	Yes.
P	(*Out of the jury's hearing*) Your Honor, I offer to prove that the witness will testify that the accused Cetina ordered the accused Britton to get some bags of heroin out of Britton's car and that Britton did so. (4) Cetina's statement is not hearsay because it is not assertive; the statement is not a declarative sentence but rather an imperative one, ordering Britton to do something. (5) The only thing we're interested in is whether he gave the order. You might say that Ms. Grace is an "earwitness" to the fact that he gave the order. The statement is logically relevant to prove the existence of a conspiracy between them. (6)
J	The objection will be overruled.
P	Ms. Grace, let me repeat the question. WHAT plans did they discuss? (4)
W	The plans for a drug sale. Cetina ordered Britton to get some bags of heroin out of Britton's car to get them ready for sale.
P	WHAT happened then?
W	Britton left for a couple of minutes and then came back with some bags.
P	WHAT was the appearance of the bags?
W	The bags themselves were transparent.
P	WHAT, if anything, could you see in the bags?
W	There was a white, powdery substance in each bag.

In the final analysis, it is always a question of interpretation whether the statement is being used as an assertion. Sometimes an exclamatory, imperative, or interrogatory sentence contains an assertion, and the proponent may be interested only in the assertion. Assume, for instance, that in the above hypothetical, the accused were charged with substantive drug offenses rather than conspiracy and that the only question was whether the bags contained heroin. It is true that overall Cetina's utterance is an imperative sentence: "Go out to your car and get the bags of heroin." However, in this context, the prosecutor would be interested only in the part of the sentence in which

Cetina referred to "the bags of heroin." In fact, at trial, rather than questioning Grace about the entire sentence, the prosecutor might ask only: "How did Mr. Cetina describe the bags?" or "What did Mr. Cetina say about the contents of the bags?" Although the overall formal classification of the sentence is imperative, the prosecutor is attempting to elicit an assertion embedded in the sentence; and for that reason, functionally the question calls for hearsay.

[b]   ASSERTIVE ACTS

Sometimes a person intends an act to be a true substitute for speech. For instance, persons sometimes nod or shake their heads in response to questions. In principle, these acts should be treated in the same fashion as verbal hearsay statements; these acts present the same probative dangers of perception, memory, narration, and sincerity. For this reason, all courts agree that like assertive statements, assertive acts fall within the hearsay definition. Federal Rule of Evidence 801(a)(2) is illustrative; that rule includes within the hearsay definition "nonverbal conduct of a person, if the person intended it as an assertion." The prevailing view is that the opponent objecting to the admission of the testimony as hearsay has the burden of convincing the judge that the conduct was assertive in nature. The Advisory Committee Note to Rule 801(a) states that "[t]he rule is worded as to place the burden upon the [objecting] party claiming that the intention [to assert] existed . . . ." If the opponent fails to satisfy that burden, the judge will overrule the hearsay objection.

The following hypothetical illustrates the scope of the hearsay definition. The fact situation is a robbery prosecution. The witness is a police officer. The officer, Patrolman Glancy, has already identified himself. He testifies that he investigated the crime, interviewed the victim, and brought the victim to the police station. Assume that in this jurisdiction, a witness's prior identification of a person is not admissible to bolster the witness's credibility. The proponent is the prosecutor.

P	WHAT happened after you took the victim, Mr. Clayton, to the police station?
W	I talked to him, and then I took him to the lineup room.
P	WHAT is the lineup room?
W	It's the room in the station where we permit victims and eyewitnesses to view suspects. We hope that they can pick the criminal out of the lineup parade. We take eyewitnesses into the room one at a time.
P	WHAT happened after you took Mr. Clayton into the interview room?
O	Your Honor, I object to that question on the ground that it calls for incompetent hearsay.
P	Your Honor, may we approach the bench and be heard?
J	Yes.
P	Your Honor, the witness is prepared to testify that at the lineup, Mr. Clayton pointed to the accused. The evidence can't be hearsay because Mr. Clayton didn't say anything. He just pointed.

O   Mr. Clayton's act of pointing is an assertive act; he subjectively intended it to be a substitute for the verbal statement that the defendant was the robber. Assertive acts fall within the hearsay definition.

J   I agree with the defense counsel. Under Rule 104(a), I find that the act was subjectively intended to be the functional equivalent of an assertive statement. The objection will be sustained.

Again, the prevailing view is that the objecting party has the burden of proving that the statement was subjectively intended as a true substitute for speech and, therefore, constituted hearsay.

[c]   NONASSERTIVE ACTS

Although the courts agree that assertive statements and acts are within the hearsay definition, they disagree over a third category of evidence: nonassertive acts. A classic English case, *Wright v. Tatham*, contained this fact situation. The issue was a testator's mental capacity. The proponent of the will was attempting to prove that the testator was mentally competent. To prove that, the proponent offered to show that several persons had written serious business letters to the testator. Although the act of writing the letter incidentally involved assertions in the letters, the act itself was nonassertive; the persons did not subjectively intend their act to substitute for the verbal statement that the testator was competent. However, the authors of the letters obviously assumed that the testator was competent to understand the contents of the letters they sent the testator, and the proponent of the will offered the evidence to show the truth of their assumption and belief. The proponent of the will reasoned that they would not have mailed the testator serious letters unless they believed he was competent; and if they, his close acquaintances, believed him to be competent, he probably was competent. The English court held that the evidence fell within the hearsay definition; the court argued that even though the act was nonassertive, it presented probative dangers of perception and memory. *Wright* was the landmark case for the traditional common-law view that evidence of a nonassertive act is hearsay if (1) the act is apparently actuated or prompted by a certain belief and (2) the proponent offers the evidence to prove the truth of the belief. In 1992, the English House of Lords reaffirmed that *Wright* is still good common law in that jurisdiction.[1]

The trend in the American statutes and case law has been to the contrary. If the person is willing to act on his or her belief, the person's willingness removes most doubts about the person's sincerity; and there is much less justification for including the evidence within the hearsay rule. Federal Rule of Evidence 801 excludes this evidence, sometimes called Morgan hearsay, from its hearsay definition. The Advisory Committee took the position that the dangers of this type of evidence are "minimal in the absence of an intent to assert and do not justify the loss of the evidence on hearsay grounds."

---

[1] However, the Lords have construed the 2003 Criminal Justice Act as overturning the common-law rule.

The following hypothetical illustrates the third category of evidence. We can adapt the basic fact situation in *Wright*. The testator is the decedent, Mr. Marsden. The decedent owned a large car dealership. The proponent of the will is Mr. Wright. Mr. Wright calls Mr. Toscher as a witness. Mr. Toscher owns a janitorial services company. Mr. Wright wants to show that Toscher sent Mr. Marsden a serious business proposal for janitorial services on the decedent's car lot. During closing argument, Mr. Wright's attorney wants to use Toscher's conduct as evidence of Mr. Marsden's competency: Toscher would not have sent Marsden the letter unless he, Toscher, believed that Marsden was mentally competent. Mr. Toscher has already identified himself and stated his line of business.

P	WHERE were you on the morning of April 16, YR-3?
W	In my office in downtown Kansas City.
P	WHAT were you doing there?
W	I was getting some bids ready on some new contracts for janitorial services.
P	WHAT is a bid?
W	We offer services to a company at a certain monthly rate. Then they decide whether they want to award the work to us or another company.
P	WHAT did you do after you finished the bids?
W	I mailed them.
P	WHOM did you mail them to?
W	Several people, including the decedent, Mr. Marsden.
O	Your Honor, I move to strike the last question and answer on the ground that they are irrelevant.
P	Your Honor, may we approach the bench?
J	Yes.
P	Your Honor, the evidence shows that Mr. Toscher mailed a serious business proposal to Mr. Marsden. That conduct shows Mr. Toscher's belief in Mr. Marsden's mental competency; he wouldn't have mailed him that sort of letter unless he thought Mr. Marsden was competent.
O	Now I object on the ground that the evidence is hearsay.
P	How can it be hearsay if it's evidence of a nonassertive act?
O	Your Honor, as you know, this jurisdiction subscribes to the traditional view that even a nonassertive act is hearsay if (1) it's actuated by a belief and (2) it's used to prove the truth of the belief. The opposing counsel has shown he's really interested in Mr. Toscher's belief in Mr. Marsden's competency, and the counsel wants to use the belief as evidence of Marsden's competency.
J	The objection will be sustained.

Assume that this case arose in a jurisdiction following the modern view that nonassertive acts fall outside the hearsay definition. The proper objection would be that the proponent has not laid a proper foundation for skilled lay observer opinion testimony under Rule 701. On the witness stand, a lay person may not express an opinion of another person's sanity unless he or she is intimately familiar with that person. Change the judge's hearsay ruling and continue the hypothetical.

J	Counsel, you overlook the fact that this jurisdiction recently adopted the Federal Rules, excluding nonassertive acts from the hearsay definition.
O	Very well, Your Honor. My other objection is that the proponent hasn't shown that the witness knew Mr. Marsden well enough to express an opinion about Marsden's competency. Your Honor, if you admit this evidence, you are in effect permitting Toscher to give skilled lay observer opinion testimony about Marsden's competency or sanity. I request permission to take the witness on voir dire.
J	Permission granted.
O	Mr. Toscher, ISN'T IT TRUE THAT you never personally met the decedent, Mr. Marsden?
W	Yes.
O	ISN'T IT A FACT THAT the only letters you ever received from his company were signed by other persons?
W	Yes.
O	ISN'T IT CORRECT THAT you never had a telephone conversation with Mr. Marsden?
W	Yes.
O	ISN'T IT TRUE THAT your only information about Mr. Marsden is what other people told you about him?
W	Yes.
O	Your Honor, I have no further voir dire questions of this witness. I renew my objection that the question calls for improper lay opinion testimony.
J	That objection will be sustained. The foundation doesn't satisfy Rule 701.

[3]   THE STATEMENT IS OFFERED FOR A HEARSAY PURPOSE

[a]   OVERVIEW

Even if the statement is assertive, the statement is not hearsay under Rule 801(c)(2) unless the proponent offers the statement to prove the truth of the assertion. Offering the statement for that purpose creates the need to cross-examine the declarant about perception or memory. This step in hearsay analysis parallels the second step in best evidence analysis: Just as the best evidence rule does not come into play unless the writing's terms are in issue, a statement is not hearsay unless the proponent offers the statement to prove the truth of an assertion contained in the statement. The statement is deemed hearsay only when the immediate inference the proponent wants to draw is the truth of the assertion on the statement's face. If the proponent can demonstrate that the statement is logically relevant on any other theory, the statement is nonhearsay. When the proponent offers the statement for a nonhearsay purpose, we are primarily interested simply in the fact that the statement was made. The fact *of* the statement is relevant; the truth of the facts *in* the statement is irrelevant. The only need to cross-examine is the need to question on the stand the witness who heard the statement made.

When the proponent is going to argue a nonhearsay theory for admitting a statement, the foundation includes these elements:

1. Where the statement was made.

2. When the statement was made.

3. Who was present.

4. The tenor of the statement.

5. In an offer of proof, the proponent states that he or she intends to use the statement for a specified nonhearsay purpose.

6. In the same offer of proof, the proponent shows that on that nonhearsay theory, the statement is logically relevant.

There are three common nonhearsay uses of evidence. First, the proponent may argue that the statement is circumstantial evidence of the declarant's state of mind. If the declarant's state of mind is logically relevant in the case, the proponent may use the declarant's statements as circumstantial proof of such states of mind as malice, hatred, premeditation, and love. Sometimes the mere fact that a person makes a certain statement gives us valuable insight into that person's frame of mind. Second, the statement may be an operative fact or verbal act in the case. In some situations, legal consequences flow directly from the use of certain words such as the offer in a contract suit or the slander in a tort action. Written contracts typically contain many assertive sentences, but given the objective theory of mutual assent the contracts are admissible as nonhearsay. This theory is applicable to commercial instruments such as promissory notes and mortgages. Again the mere fact that the declarant uttered the words is logically relevant; under substantive law, the words themselves have legal consequences. Finally, the proponent can prove the statement to show its effect on the state of mind of the hearer or reader. For example, if it is disputed whether the defendant knew of a certain dangerous condition, it is logically relevant to prove that someone told him of the condition. Quite apart from the truth of the third party's statement, the statement puts the defendant on notice. The following hypotheticals illustrate these various nonhearsay uses.

In all these cases, on request under Rule 105 the judge would give the jurors a limiting instruction forbidding them from treating the testimony as substantive evidence of any assertion in the statement and explaining the nonhearsay use of the evidence. In most, but not all, cases the courts assume that the jury will be able and willing to follow the limiting instruction. However, the Advisory Committee Notes to

Rules 105 and 403 state that the judge should realistically assess the likely effectiveness of the instruction. If the judge thought that there was an intolerable risk that the jury would disregard the 105 instruction, the judge could exclude the testimony under Rule 403 unless the statement also fell within a hearsay exemption or exception.

[b]   THE STATEMENT IS CIRCUMSTANTIAL PROOF OF THE DECLARANT'S STATE OF MIND—MENTAL OUTPUT

Our fact situation is a dispute over title to real property. The decedent, Joan Furlow, formerly owned the land. Before she died, she gave her nephew, Garrett Furlow, a deed to the property; she gave him the deed on April 14, YR-3. The executor claims that although Ms. Furlow gave Garrett the deed, she did not intend the deed to be immediately effective; and since she did not have the intent required by Real Property law, the deed was ineffective. The nephew calls Ms. Barbara Peterson as a witness. Ms. Peterson identifies herself and states that she knew the decedent for several years. The nephew is the proponent.

P	WHERE were you on April 13, YR-3? (1), (2)
W	I was visiting Joan at her house on Dwight Street.
P	WHO else was there? (3)
W	Only the two of us.
P	WHAT happened while you were there? (4)
W	We just had a nice chat.
P	WHAT did you chat about? (4)
W	A lot of things, including Joan's nephew, Garrett.
P	WHAT did Ms. Furlow say about her nephew, Garrett? (4)
O	Your Honor, I object to that question on the ground that it calls for hearsay.
P	Your Honor, may we approach the bench?
J	Yes.
P	Your Honor, I offer to prove that Ms. Peterson will testify that Ms. Furlow said that her nephew was a man in a million. (4) Ms. Furlow may have been mistaken in thinking that her nephew was a man in a million, but that is beside the point. I want to offer that testimony for a nonhearsay purpose, as circumstantial proof of Ms. Furlow's affection for Garrett. (5) The testimony is logically relevant to show that she had donative intent when she gave him the deed the next day. (6)
J	The objection will be overruled. I will admit the evidence for that nonhearsay purpose.
P	Ms. Peterson, let me repeat the question. WHAT did Ms. Furlow say about her nephew, Garrett? (4)
W	She said that he was a man in a million.

O   Your Honor, I request a limiting instruction under Rule 105.

J   Yes. Ladies and gentlemen of the jury, you have just heard Ms. Peterson's testimony about Ms. Furlow's statement. I am admitting the evidence of Ms. Furlow's statement only for the purpose of showing Ms. Furlow's state of mind, her feeling or affection for her nephew.

Given the trial judge's limiting instruction, during closing argument the proponent's attorney could legitimately use the testimony about the decedent's statement to prove her donative intent: "Ladies and gentlemen, in her instructions your Honor is going to tell you that we need to prove that on April 14, YR-3, when Ms. Furlow handed Garrett the deed to the house on Dwight Street, she actually intended to make a gift to Garrett. Think back to Ms. Peterson's testimony. She told you that on April 13th—one day before—Ms. Furlow told her that Garrett was a man in a million. Obviously, you don't have to decide whether Garrett is one man in a million. However, the fact that Ms. Furlow said that the day before tells you a lot about how much affection she had for her nephew Garrett—such strong affection and love that she wanted him to have the property on Dwight Street."

[c]   THE STATEMENT IS AN OPERATIVE FACT OR VERBAL ACT

To illustrate this foundation, we shall use a variation of the fact situation in *Hanson v. Johnson*, 161 Minn. 229, 201 N.W. 322 (1924). In that case, the plaintiff Hanson owned a farm that he leased to Schrik. There were a number of large cribs on the farm for storing corn, and Schrik intended to use the farm to raise corn. In our variation of the fact situation, Schrik falls behind in his rent. He then enters into an agreement with Hanson. Under the agreement, Hanson will accept the corn stored in two cribs, five and seven, in lieu of rent due for June and July. When they enter into the agreement at the farm, Schrik says: "It's a deal. The corn in cribs five and seven is yours." Later Schrik obtains a loan from Cattlemen's Bank. He pledges "my corn" as security for the loan. He defaults on the loan. The bank forecloses and sells all the corn on the premises, including the corn in cribs five and seven. Hanson then sues the bank for conversion. Hanson is the witness. He has already identified himself, explained that he was Schrik's landlord, and testifies that Schrik was delinquent on his rent. The plaintiff is the proponent.

P   Mr. Hanson, WHERE were you on the afternoon of July 6, YR-3? (1), (2)

W   I was at the farm, the one I rented to Schrik.

P   WHO else was there? (3)

W   Schrik was the only one around. I didn't see his wife or kids.

P   WHY were you there? (4)

W   As I said, he'd fallen behind in his rent. He was supposed to pay at the beginning of the month, and he'd missed the June and July payments. I asked him what he intended to do about the delinquent rent.

P   WHAT happened when you asked him that? (4)

W	He offered me a deal.
O	Your Honor, I move to strike that last answer on the ground that it is hearsay.
P	Your Honor, may we approach the bench?
J	Yes.
P	Your Honor, I offer to prove that Mr. Hanson will testify that Mr. Schrik offered to give my client the corn in two cribs, cribs five and seven, in exchange for the delinquent rent. (4) I want to use the statement for a nonhearsay purpose, namely, to show the offer itself. (5) The words constituting the offer for the contract are an operative fact or verbal act; in Contract law, legal consequences flow directly from the fact that Schrik uttered those words. (6)
J	The motion will be denied.
P	Mr. Hanson, let me repeat the question. WHAT happened when you asked him about the delinquent rent? (4)
W	He offered to give me the corn in two cribs in exchange for the late rent.
P	WHAT were his words? (4)
W	As best I recall, he said, "It's a deal. The corn in cribs five and seven is yours."
P	WHAT did you say then? (4)
W	I just said that I accepted the offer, and we shook on it.

[d]   THE EFFECT OF THE STATEMENT ON THE MIND OF THE HEARER OR READER—MENTAL INPUT

Suppose that the plaintiff, Zillman, alleged that the defendant has been negligent in two respects. First, the defendant was speeding. Second, the defendant carelessly drove the car although he knew that the car had bad brakes. Under the second theory, one issue would be whether the defendant knew that the brakes were defective. The plaintiff calls Mr. John Horne. Horne testifies that he manages the auto repair shop near the defendant's house. Horne adds that on January 14, YR-4, the defendant dropped off his car for regular maintenance. The plaintiff is the proponent.

P	Mr. Horne, WHERE were you on January 16, YR-4? (1), (2)
W	I was at my repair shop.
P	WHO else was there? (3)
W	We had several customers, including the defendant.
P	WHAT happened when the defendant came into the shop? (4)
W	He was there to pick up his car.
P	WHAT happened while he was there? (4)
W	He got the car, and we talked for a while.

P	WHAT did you talk about? (4)
W	Mostly his car.
P	WHAT did you tell him about the car? (4)
O	Your Honor, I object to that question on the ground that it calls for hearsay.
P	Your Honor, may we approach the bench?
J	Yes.
P	Your Honor, I offer to prove that the witness will testify that he told the defendant that one of his employees, a mechanic, had discovered that the defendant's brakes were bad. (4) I want to use the witness's prior statement for a nonhearsay purpose, namely, to show its effect on the defendant's state of mind; it gave him knowledge and put him on notice that his brakes were bad. (5) Under our second cause of action, this evidence is logically relevant even if it is not used to prove that the brakes were defective; our second cause is that the defendant negligently drove the car when he knew it had defective brakes. (6) I intend to offer other evidence to show that in fact the brakes were bad. For example, my next witness will be the mechanic who inspected the defendant's car.
J	The objection will be overruled.
P	Mr. Horne, let me repeat the question. WHAT did you tell the defendant about his car? (4)
W	I told him that my mechanic had discovered that the brakes were bad and could go out any time.
P	HOW close were you standing to the defendant when you told him that?
W	Only a foot or two away.
P	HOW noisy was the repair shop at the time?
W	It was very quiet.
P	HOW were you facing when you told him about his brakes?
W	I was talking right at him.
P	WHO else was talking to him at the time?
W	No one else. We were the only two talking.
P	HOW did he react when you told him about the bad brakes?
W	He nodded his head, shrugged his shoulders, and got into his car.
O	Your Honor, I request a limiting instruction under Rule 105.
J	Yes. Ladies and gentlemen of the jury, you have just heard the witness's testimony that he told the defendant that the defendant's brakes were bad. You may not consider the witness's testimony as evidence that in fact, the brakes were bad. You may consider the witness's testimony

only in deciding whether the next day, the defendant knew the car was defective and acted negligently in driving the car. If other evidence in this case establishes that the brakes were bad, then and only then may you consider the witness's testimony—and then only in deciding whether the next day, the defendant knew the brakes were bad and acted negligently in driving the car despite that knowledge.

Of course, to sustain the burden of going forward and defeat a directed verdict motion, the proponent will have to introduce other, substantive evidence that the brakes were defective. The plaintiff could call the mechanic who actually worked on the brakes to describe the condition of the brakes. However, the plaintiff could use Mr. Horne's testimony for the limited, nonhearsay purpose of proving that the defendant knew of the brakes' hazardous condition. Thus, in closing argument, the plaintiff's attorney might state: "In his instructions to you, his Honor will tell you that we have the burden of proving that before the collision, the defendant knew that his brakes were bad. Ladies and gentlemen, we've proven that. Remember the testimony by Mr. Horne, the owner of the repair shop that the defendant took his car to. Mr. Horne told you that on January 16th—several days before the accident—he had a conversation with the defendant. Mr. Horne added that in that conversation, he told the defendant point blank that his mechanic had found that the defendant's brakes were bad and could go out at any time. When the defendant drove away from Mr. Horne's shop, the defendant knew good and well that his brakes were defective."

[4]   THE STATEMENT WAS NOT MADE BY A HUMAN DECLARANT

Federal Rule of Evidence 801(a) defines a statement as an assertion by "a person[]." In turn, Rule 801(b) states that a declarant is "the person who made the statement." Those definitions explain why the hearsay rule applies to computer-stored statements but not to computer-generated statements.

Suppose that a business employee inputs data about a sale into a company computer. The input amounts to a statement by a human declarant, the employee. It is true that the statement is stored on the computer hard drive in electronic form. Yet, in the final analysis, the accuracy of the statement depends on the testimonial qualities of the human declarant who was the source of the input. If the company later prints out that data and at trial a litigant offers the printout as proof of the truth of the data, the printout constitutes hearsay; and the proponent will need to lay a foundation for a hearsay exception such as the business entry provision codified in Rule 803(6).

Distinguish a statement generated by an instrument. For instance, assume that the defendant is standing trial on a charge of driving while intoxicated. The prosecutor calls a police officer who administered an intoxilyzer test to the defendant. The officer is prepared to testify that when she administered a test to the defendant, the instrument displayed "0.17." That display is elliptical; it amounts to the assertive statement that the breath alcohol concentration of the person who just blew into the instrument is 0.17. That statement is assertive. Moreover, the prosecution certainly wants to offer the evidence to prove the truth of the assertion. However, the statement was not made by a person under Rule 801(b). The statement was generated by a mechanical instrument. As § 10.01 pointed out, the primary rationale for the hearsay rule is that it safeguards the right to cross-examination. Although it makes sense to give the opposing attorney an opportunity to cross-examine a human declarant, the attorney cannot cross-examine an intoxilyzer. Consequently, the defense could not successfully object on hearsay grounds to the introduction of the testimony about the readout.

Although the hearsay rule is inapplicable to computer-generated statements, there is a validation problem under *Daubert v. Merrell Dow Pharms.*, 509 U.S. 579, 113 S. Ct. 2786, 125 L. Ed. 2d 469 (1993). To generate "0.17," the instrument relied on formulae and scientific propositions embedded in the source code of its software. Those formulae and propositions determine the accuracy of the assertion that the defendant's breath alcohol concentration was 0.17. The proponent of the testimony must establish either that those propositions are judicially noticeable under Federal Rule of Evidence 201(b)(2) or that they qualify as reliable "scientific . . . knowledge" within the meaning of that expression in Rule 702.

Suppose that in a drunk driving prosecution, the government has called a state trooper to testify that when she administered an intoxilyzer test to the defendant, the instrument displayed "0.17." The defense objected on both scientific evidence and hearsay grounds. The trial judge has already overruled the former objection. The prosecutor is the proponent.

J	The first objection will be overruled. As I recall, though, you objected on alternative grounds. Correct?
O	Yes, Your Honor. I also objected on hearsay grounds. "0.17" is shorthand for an assertion—the assertion that my client's breath alcohol concentration was 0.17%. That's clearly a statement under Rule 801(a).
J	Ms. Prosecutor, do you have any response? That statement certainly strikes me as being assertive.
P	Your Honor, I agree it's assertive, but it's still not hearsay. To be hearsay, it not only has to be an assertive statement, it has to come from a hearsay declarant. You have to interpret Rule 801(a) in the light and context of Rule 801(b). Rule 801(b) expressly states that a declarant must be a "person."
O	But, Your Honor, someone programmed the formulae that generated "0.17" into the intoxilyzer. We should be entitled to cross-examine that person before you admit this testimony.
P	Your Honor, you've already ruled that all those formulae are either judicially noticeable or satisfy *Daubert*. This isn't computer-stored information. This isn't a case in which a human being prepared a report and stored the report in a computer. In contrast, this is computer-generated data. The accuracy of "0.17" doesn't depend on the credibility of any human being; rather, it depends on the validity of the formulae, and you've already overruled the defense's first objection. It's well-settled that computer-generated data is not hearsay.
J	I agree. The second objection will also be overruled. You may proceed.

[5] THE STATEMENT WAS MADE OR THE ACT PERFORMED BY A PERSON STILL CONSIDERED AN OUT-OF-COURT DECLARANT

Assume that the proponent is offering testimony about a human declarant's out-of-court statement for the truth of the assertion. Offering the evidence for that purpose creates an acute need to cross-examine the declarant about his or her perception, memory, and other testimonial qualities. However, suppose that the declarant becomes a witness at trial. If so, the opposing attorney can cross-examine the person both about the person's in-court testimony and about the earlier statements. The person's current availability seemingly satisfies the need for cross-examination. Does the person's current availability for cross-examination remove the earlier statements from the definition of hearsay?

The traditional view is "once an out-of-court declarant, always an out-of-court declarant." If the person was not on the stand when he or she made the statement, it is immaterial that the person later becomes a witness and subjects himself or herself to cross-examination. Consider this example. On Monday, the person tells a friend that the person saw the defendant's car run the red light. On Tuesday, that same person becomes a witness in the suit between plaintiff and defendant. The person testifies that he or she saw the defendant's car run the red light. To increase the impact of the testimony, the plaintiff's attorney attempts to elicit the person's testimony that Monday the person told the friend the same story. If the proponent attempts to use the statement on Monday as substantive proof of the defendant's fault, the statement is hearsay; although the person is now the witness, the person was not on the witness stand when the person made the statement. Under the traditional view—"once a hearsay declarant, always a hearsay declarant"—the hearsay rule would apply even if the person made the statement on the courthouse steps ten minutes before taking the witness stand.

Several commentators, including Morgan, argued that the definition of hearsay should not include prior statements made by witnesses now on the stand and subject to cross-examination. These commentators begin with the premise that the primary purpose of the hearsay rule is to protect the opponent's right to cross-examine. They then argue that the opportunity to cross-examine is adequate even if the opportunity is delayed until trial; on Tuesday, the opponent can cross-examine the witness about Monday's statement. These commentators conclude that if the person is now a witness available for examination in court, the person should no longer be considered an out-of-court declarant; and the hearsay rule should not apply to the witness's prior statements. To date, only one jurisdiction, Kansas, has formally adopted this view, although several older Georgia opinions also contain broad language seemingly endorsing this view.

There is a compromise view that has gained a large number of adherents. The compromise view is that if the witness's prior statement is otherwise admissible for a nonhearsay purpose (as a prior identification to bolster, as a prior inconsistent statement to impeach, or as a prior consistent statement to rehabilitate), the statement should be admitted as substantive evidence. Federal Rules of Evidence partially embrace the compromise view. Rule 801(d)(1) exempts certain prior statements of the witness from the hearsay definition and permits their use as substantive evidence: "A statement that meets the following conditions is not hearsay: (1) A Declarant-Witness's Prior Statement. The declarant testifies and is subject to cross-examination about a prior statement, and the statement: (A) is inconsistent with the declarant's testimony and was given under penalty of perjury at a trial, hearing, or other proceeding or in a deposition; (B) is consistent with the declarant's testimony and is offered: (i) to rebut an express or implied charge that the declarant recently fabricated it or acted from a recent improper influence or motive in so testifying or (ii) to rehabilitate the declarant's credibility as a witness when attacked on another ground; or (C) identifies a person as someone the declarant perceived earlier." This compromise view reflects two beliefs. First, its supporters believe that there is substantial merit in Morgan's position. Second, they frankly suspect that limiting instructions are often ineffective; although the judge tells the jurors to use the prior statement for the limited purpose of bolstering, impeaching, or rehabilitating, many jurors will misuse the statement and treat it as substantive evidence of the assertion. These two beliefs lead the supporters of the compromise view to favor admitting prior statements as substantive evidence when the statements are otherwise admissible, usually on one of the credibility theories discussed in Chapter 5.

In a jurisdiction wholeheartedly embracing Morgan's view, the foundation for the prior statement is simple. The foundation includes these elements:

1.   Where the prior statement was made.

2.   When the statement was made.

3.   Who was present.

4.   The present witness made the prior statement.

5.   The tenor of the statement.

The fact situation is a tort action arising from a collision. The plaintiff, Mr. Kionka, contends that on January 17, YR-3, the defendant caused the accident by speeding. Mr. Kionka calls Ms. Gerst as a witness. She identifies herself, states that she observed the two cars, and expresses her opinion that defendant's car was going 60 miles an hour. Her direct examination continues. The proponent is the plaintiff.

P	WHERE were you on January 18, YR-3? (1), (2)
W	I went down to the police station on Mission Boulevard.
P	WHY did you go there?
W	The officer at the accident scene told me to stop by and give a statement the next day.
P	WHAT happened when you arrived at the police station? (3)
W	I met Officer Grouton, the traffic sergeant.
P	WHAT, if anything, did you tell him about the accident? (4), (5)
O	Your Honor, I object to that question on the ground that it calls for hearsay.
P	Your Honor, may we approach the bench?
J	Yes.

P	Your Honor, the witness is present in court and available for cross-examination. In this jurisdiction, in that situation, the witness's prior statements are no longer considered hearsay.
J	Correct. The objection will be overruled.
P	Ms. Gerst, let me repeat the question. WHAT, if anything, did you tell Officer Grouton about the accident? (4), (5)
W	I said I thought the defendant caused the accident because he was speeding about 60 miles an hour.

In a jurisdiction following the compromise view, the proponent would have to show that the prior statement is admissible on a nonhearsay theory. The proponent would have to lay a complete foundation for prior identification, prior inconsistent statement, or prior consistent statement. Chapter 5 outlines those foundations. Suppose that on February 14, YR-3, Ms. Gerst told a friend that she thought the defendant was going only 40 miles an hour. In a compromise jurisdiction, the defendant could use Ms. Gerst's prior inconsistent statement as substantive evidence; no limiting instruction would be given. The hypothetical continues, and the defendant now attempts to prove the prior inconsistent statement during Ms. Gerst's cross-examination. The defendant is the proponent.

P	ISN'T IT A FACT THAT on February 14, YR-3, you had a conversation with your friend, Charles Gill, at your house?
W	Yes.
P	ISN'T IT CORRECT THAT during the conversation, you told him that the defendant was going only 40 miles an hour?
W	Yes.
O	Your Honor, I request a limiting instruction.
J	What type of limiting instruction?
O	An instruction that the jurors may consider Ms. Gerst's statement only in so far as it reflects on her credibility.
P	Your Honor, may we approach the bench?
J	Yes.
P	Your Honor, a limiting instruction would be inappropriate.
O	The defendant is obviously introducing this statement as a prior inconsistent statement to impeach; it can't be used as substantive evidence of the defendant's speed.
P	Your Honor, in our jurisdiction, if a witness's prior statement is admissible for a nonhearsay purpose such as impeachment and the witness is available for cross-examination, the hearsay rule no longer applies. Since Ms. Gerst is available for cross-examination, I can use her prior inconsistent statement both to impeach and as substantive evidence.
J	I agree. I shall not give the jurors a limiting instruction.

Note that Federal Rule of Evidence 801(d)(1)(A) stops short of wholeheartedly embracing the compromise view. Under that subsection, it is not enough that the statement be otherwise admissible as a prior inconsistent statement. To ensure that the statute would not violate the confrontation clause, Congress wrote into the statute the additional requirement that the statement had been made both under oath and at a prior formal proceeding such as a grand jury hearing. In short, even if a statement qualifies as a prior inconsistent statement under Rule 613, the statement might not be admissible as substantive evidence under Rule 801(d)(1)(A).

Moreover, in its 1995 decision in *Tome v. United States*, 513 U.S. 150, 115 S. Ct. 696, 130 L. Ed. 2d 574 (1995), the United States Supreme Court ruled that, at least when a prior consistent statement is offered as substantive evidence, the statement must antedate any improper motive. In effect, the Court held that Rule 801(d)(1)(B) incorporates the common-law temporal priority doctrine. At the time of the writing of the prior edition, 801(d)(1)(B) required that the consistent statement be offered "to rebut an express or implied charge that the declarant recently fabricated [his or her testimony] or acted from a recent improper influence or motive in so testifying." However, the Supreme Court approved an amendment to (d)(1)(B) extending the provision to consistent statements offered "to rehabilitate the declarant's credibility as a witness when attacked on another ground." The amendment took effect on December 1, 2014. The accompanying Advisory Committee Note states that "[t]he intent of the amendment is to extend substantive effect to consistent statements that rebut other attacks on a witness—such as charges of inconsistency or faulty memory."

PART C. The Admissions Exemption Requiring a Showing of Neither Reliability Nor Necessity

§ 10.03 THE EXEMPTION FOR STATEMENTS OR ADMISSIONS OF A PARTY-OPPONENT

[1] IN GENERAL

If the statement falls within the definition of hearsay, the proponent of the statement must find an applicable hearsay exemption or exception. One of the most frequently used exemptions is that for the statements or admissions of a party-opponent. For example, in a tort action the plaintiff can prove the defendant's out-of-court statements acknowledging fault. From the plaintiff's perspective, the defendant's statements are admissions of the party-opponent. The same hearsay exemption permits prosecutors to introduce accused's confessions acknowledging guilt.

Although the common law treats the admission doctrine as a hearsay exception, the admission doctrine differs from most hearsay exceptions. Commentators have had some difficulty rationalizing the admission doctrine. Unlike most hearsay exceptions, admissions do not have to have a circumstantial guarantee of trustworthiness; although the admission is obviously disserving at the time of trial, the admission is admissible even if it was self-serving when made. Nor is there any need to show a necessity for resorting to the hearsay; the opposing party may be available at trial and perfectly willing to testify about the subject-matter of the earlier statement. The truth of the matter is that like the work product doctrine discussed in § 7.06, the admission doctrine is a product of the adversary litigation system; the opponent can hardly complain that he or she does not have an opportunity to cross-examine himself or herself. The opponent can always take the stand to deny or explain the statement. Because of the unique rationale for this exception, some commentators do not even classify admissions as hearsay. Thus, Federal Rule of Evidence 801(d)(2) exempts admissions from the hearsay definition and admits admissions as "not hearsay." The restyled Rules effect a second change from the common law; the new Rules use the expression, "an opposing party's statement," rather than the traditional terminology "admission."

Although the commentators and courts disagree over the question whether admissions should be classified as hearsay, there is general consensus on the foundational elements of the various types of admissions. There are three basic kinds of admissions: personal, adoptive, and vicarious. The basis of the classification is the reason for which we attribute the statement to the party-opponent. In the case of personal admissions, we attribute the statement to the party-opponent because we find the statement in the party's own words or acts. In the case of adoptive admissions, a third party makes the statement, but we impute the statement to the party-opponent because the opponent manifests agreement with the assertion in the statement. The opponent thereby "adopts" the statement. Finally, in the case of vicarious admissions, again a third party makes the statement, but the party-opponent does not manifest agreement. Instead, we attribute the statement to the party-opponent because of a close legal relationship, such as agency, between the third party and the party-opponent. We shall now examine the foundations for these various types of admissions in detail.

[2] PERSONAL ADMISSIONS

[a] OVERVIEW

All jurisdictions admit the party-opponent's own personal admissions in civil and criminal cases. Federal Rule of Evidence 801(d)(2)(A) sanctions the receipt of personal admissions. It permits the proponent to introduce a statement when "(t)he statement is offered against an opposing party and . . . was made by the party in an individual or representative capacity." Personal admissions are liberally admissible; the phrasing of the admission can be highly opinionated, and the admission need not even be based on personal knowledge.

[b] IN CIVIL CASES

In civil cases, the foundation for personal admissions is very simple. The foundation includes these elements:

1. The witness heard a declarant make a statement.

2. The witness identifies the declarant as the present party-opponent.

3. The statement is inconsistent with the position the party-opponent is taking at trial. (Although the appellate courts often phrase this requirement in this negative manner and seem to insist upon inconsistency, in practice trial judges apply the requirement affirmatively; trial judges ask only whether the statement is logically relevant under Rule 401 to an issue the proponent has a

right to prove in the case. The phrasing of the question eliciting the statement usually ensures the statement's logical relevance; the question inquires "about" a specific topic relevant under Rule 401.)

Our fact situation is a civil tort action. The case arose from a collision on May 19, YR-3. The plaintiff, Ms. Langdale, alleges that the defendant, Mr. Maire, caused the collision by speeding. The speed limit in this section of town is 25 miles an hour. The plaintiff calls the investigating officer, Patrolman Hightower. The witness has already identified himself and testified that he went to the accident scene. The proponent is the plaintiff.

P	WHAT did you do when you arrived at the scene of the collision?
W	I investigated the accident.
P	HOW did you investigate the accident? (1)
W	I viewed the debris and interviewed the persons involved.
P	WHOM did you interview? (2)
W	Ms. Langdale and Mr. Maire.
P	WHERE is Mr. Maire now? (2)
W	In the courtroom.
P	Specifically, WHERE in the courtroom? (2)
W	He's sitting at the table.
P	HOW is he dressed? (2)
W	In a green suit and blue tie.
P	Your Honor, please let the record reflect that the witness has identified the defendant.
J	It will so reflect.
P	Officer Hightower, WHAT did the defendant say about the accident? (3)
O	Your Honor, I object on the ground that the question calls for hearsay.
P	Your Honor, may I be heard?
J	Yes.
P	The statement is hearsay, but it falls within the exception for admissions of a party-opponent.
	(In federal court, the proponent would say, "The statement is exempt from the hearsay rule because it is the statement or admission of a party-opponent" or "The statement is not hearsay because it is the statement or admission of a party-opponent.")
J	The objection will be overruled.
P	Let me repeat the question. WHAT did the defendant say about the accident? (3)

W	He said he was really sorry about it because he thought he caused it by going too fast.
P	HOW fast did he say he was going? (3)
W	He said maybe 40 miles an hour.

[c] IN CRIMINAL CASES

The foundation for a criminal accused's confession is more complex than the foundation for admissions in civil cases. The foundation is more complex because in a criminal case, the prosecutor must comply with constitutional requirements as well as non-constitutional hearsay requirements. The prosecutor must first demonstrate that the confession was voluntary; the Fifth and Fourteenth amendment due process clauses bar the admission of involuntary confessions. Furthermore, if the accused was in custody, the prosecutor must demonstrate that the police administered proper *Miranda* warnings; *Miranda* imposes requirements in addition to traditional voluntariness. Finally, the prosecutor must prove that the accused properly waived his or her *Miranda* rights. In 2000, in *Dickerson v. United States*, 530 U.S. 428, 120 S. Ct. 2326, 147 L. Ed. 2d 405 (2000), the Supreme Court affirmed that *Miranda* is still good law. Thus, the complete foundation includes these elements:

1. The witness heard a declarant make a statement.

2. The witness identifies the declarant as the present accused.

3. Any confession was voluntary.

4. The police administered proper *Miranda* warnings to the accused.

5. The accused waived his or her rights.

6. The statement is inconsistent with the position the accused takes at trial; the statement is logically relevant to some issue the prosecution has a right to prove at trial. If the accused pleads not guilty, the accused defendant requires the prosecution to prove all the elements of the crime. By pleading not guilty, the defendant takes the general position that all the facts alleged are false.

Our fact situation is a prosecution for robbery. The accused is Mr. Walters. The prosecution calls Officer Gannon as a witness. Officer Gannon identifies himself and then testifies that he is assigned to the robbery detail of the Lincoln, Nebraska Police Department. The proponent is the prosecutor.

P	Officer Gannon, WHERE were you on the afternoon of January 20, YR-3?
W	I was at our downtown station on duty in the robbery detail office.
P	WHAT happened that afternoon?
W	Some other officers brought in someone for questioning.
P	WHO was that person? (2)
W	James Walters.
P	WHERE is James Walters now? (2)

W	Here in the courtroom.
P	Specifically WHERE in the courtroom? (2)
W	He's sitting right there.
P	HOW is he dressed? (2)
W	He's attired in a brown shirt and green pants.
P	Your Honor, please let the record reflect that the witness identified the accused.
J	It will so reflect.
P	WHAT happened after the officers brought Mr. Walters in? (3)
W	I took him to the interrogation room.
P	WHAT happened then? (3)
W	I began questioning him.
P	WHAT promises, if any, did you make to him during the questioning? (3)
W	None.
P	WHAT force, if any, did you use during the interrogation? (3)
W	None. I never touched him.
P	WHAT threats, if any, did you make? (3)
W	I didn't make any. I didn't threaten him or his family in any way.
P	WHAT requests, if any, did he make during the questioning? (3)
W	He asked for a cigarette, for coffee, and to go to the bathroom—that sort of thing.
P	HOW did you respond to his requests? (3)
W	I granted them. I gave him cigarettes and coffee. I let him go to the bathroom. I tried to make him as comfortable as possible.
P	WHAT, if anything, did you say to Mr. Walters? (4)
W	I read him his rights.
P	HOW did you read him his rights? (4)
W	I read them verbatim from a warning card.
P	Your Honor, I request that this be marked prosecution exhibit number three for identification.
J	It will be so marked.
P	Please let the record reflect that I am showing the exhibit to the opposing counsel.
J	It will so reflect.
P	I request permission to approach the witness.

J	Permission granted.
P	Officer Gannon, I now hand you prosecution exhibit number three for identification. WHAT is it? (4)
W	It's the warning card I just referred to.
P	HOW can you recognize it? (4)
W	I initialed it, and I had the defendant initial it as well. I see the initials and the date we wrote in pencil on the card.
P	HOW did you use the card during the questioning? (3)
W	I read from it verbatim to make certain I gave the suspect the correct warnings.
P	Your Honor, I now offer prosecution exhibit number three for identification into evidence as prosecution exhibit three.
J	It will be received.
P	Officer Gannon, please read prosecution exhibit three.
W	It says: "You have a right to remain silent. Anything you say can and will be used against you in a court of law. You also have a right to an attorney. You have a right to consult an attorney before any questioning. You have a right to have an attorney present during any questioning. If you cannot afford an attorney, one will be appointed to represent you."
P	WHAT happened after you read Mr. Walters these rights? (5)
W	I asked him whether he understood his rights.
P	WHAT was his answer? (5)
W	He said he did.
P	WHAT happened then? (5)
W	I asked him whether he wanted an attorney.
P	WHAT was his response?
W	He said no.
P	WHAT happened then? (5)
W	I asked him whether he was willing to talk about the robbery.
P	WHAT was his response? (5)
W	He told me about the robbery.
P	WHAT did he say about the robbery? (6)
W	He said he had held up the McDonald's on 4th Street, and he was very sorry he had done it. He said he desperately needed money for food and rent, and he couldn't figure out any other way to get it.

Many jurisdictions impose an additional requirement for the admission of confessions; these jurisdictions follow the corpus delicti rule and require corroboration. In these jurisdictions, apart from the defendant's confession, there must be independent evidence that a crime was committed. For example, in a robbery case, the store owner would have to testify that he found his locks broken and discovered money or merchandise missing. The corroboration need not show the identity of the perpetrator of the crime; it need show only that a crime was committed. The prosecutor ordinarily presents the corroborating evidence first and then calls the witness who will testify about the accused's confession to the crime.

[3] ADOPTIVE ADMISSIONS

[a] OVERVIEW

In personal admissions, the party-opponent himself or herself says or writes the statement constituting the admission. In adoptive admissions, a third party says or writes the statement. The party-opponent then manifests assent to the substantive content of the statement in some fashion. In the words of Federal Rule of Evidence 801(d)(2)(B), the party "manifested that [the party] adopted or believed [the assertion] to be true." When a criminal-accused signs a confession typed by a secretary at the police station, the accused is manifesting assent to the contents of the writing. A party-opponent can manifest assent expressly or impliedly, even by silence.

[b] EXPRESS ADOPTION

The foundation includes these elements:

1. A declarant made a statement.

2. The declarant made the statement in the party's presence.

3. The party heard and understood the statement. The declarant's statement is thus offered for a nonhearsay purpose—to show its effect on the state of mind of the party.

4. The party made a statement which expressed agreement with the declarant's statement. It is not enough that the party referred to or repeated the declarant's statement; the party must manifest agreement with the substantive content of the declarant's assertion.

Most jurisdictions treat these foundational facts as Rule 104(b) issues. Hence, for example, the proponent need present only sufficient evidence to create a permissive inference that the party-opponent heard the declarant's statement. The jury ultimately decides whether the party-opponent heard the statement.

To illustrate this doctrine, we shall use a tort action involving a hit-and-run accident. On July 1, YR-3, the plaintiff, Ms. Waylen, was crossing a street in downtown Iowa City when a car struck her and fled the scene. The plaintiff's complaint alleges that the driver of the car was the defendant, Brad Benton. Benton works as a salesperson at an electronics store in Iowa City. The defendant denies any involvement in the accident. In his pretrial deposition, he claimed that he was on vacation in Mexico on the date of the accident. The plaintiff is the proponent. The plaintiff calls Mr. George Nickmeyer as her next witness. Mr. Nickmeyer testifies that he is the manager of the store where Benton works.

P	Mr. Nickmeyer, WHAT are your duties as manager?
W	I'm generally in charge of everything—purchasing, finance, personnel, you name it, and I do it at the store. It's a pretty small operation.
P	Please tell us more about your personnel responsibilities.
W	Being manager carries with it a lot of responsibilities. I make sure that everyone is signed up for fringe benefits, medical plans, and the like. I also keep track of work days and vacations. We don't have an old-fashioned time clock.
P	HOW do you keep track of vacation days? (1)
W	I keep a personnel log of when people work and when they're off. Then at the end of each month I prepare a summary for each employee and have them verify its accuracy.
P	HOW do you do that? (2), (3)
W	I hand them the statement. At the end of each month, everyone checks by my office to inspect their work and vacation statement. They read it, and then they sign it.
P	Your Honor, I request that this be marked plaintiff's exhibit number one for identification.
J	It will be so marked.
P	Please let the record reflect that I am showing the exhibit to the opposing counsel.
J	The record will so reflect.
P	Permission to approach the witness?
J	Granted.
P	Mr. Nickmeyer, I now hand you plaintiff's exhibit number one for identification. WHAT is it? (1), (4)
W	It's Brad Benton's statement for the month of July YR-3.
P	HOW do you recognize it? (1)
W	I was the one who prepared it; I recognize the contents and the form. In addition, I see Brad's signature at the bottom. He's worked for me for over three years.
P	HOW many times have you seen the defendant sign his name? (4)
W	I can't give you a precise number, but I've probably seen him do it dozens of times during that period. Like I said, the employees come by at the end of every month to sign these statements right in my presence.
P	HOW was this form prepared? (2), (3), (4)
W	I always do it the same way. I don't want any hassles with them over their vacation time. I call them into the office; or they stop by on their

own, read the statement while I'm present, and then put their John Hancock on it.

P   Your Honor, I now offer plaintiff's exhibit number one for identification into evidence as plaintiff's exhibit number one.

O   Your Honor, I must object on the ground that this is inadmissible hearsay. There's obviously an inadequate foundation for a business entry.

P   Your Honor, may I be heard?

J   Yes.

P   I'm not offering this exhibit as a business entry. I'm offering it as an adoptive admission. Mr. Nickmeyer prepared the form, but his testimony shows that the defendant had an opportunity to read and check it before signing it. By signing it, the defendant manifested his assent to the accuracy of the form. The form lists July 1, YR-3, as a workday for the defendant—not a vacation day. (4)

J   Objection overruled. The exhibit will be received.

P   Mr. Nickmeyer, let me direct your attention to the extreme, left-hand margin of the exhibit. WHAT is listed on that margin?

W   That margin lists each day of the month.

P   Now let me direct your attention to the middle column of the form and the column on the extreme right-hand margin. WHAT do those columns represent?

W   The middle column is for checkmarks indicating workdays. The column on the right is for vacation days. If someone works a particular day, I place a checkmark in the middle of the form. If they're on vacation, I place the check in the right-hand column.

P   Please look at the columns for July 1st, YR-3.

W   O.K.

P   WHERE is the checkmark for July 1st—in the middle or on the right-hand margin?

W   It's in the middle.

P   Again, WHAT does the middle column represent?

W   Workdays.

P   Your Honor, I now request permission to circulate the exhibit to the jurors for their inspection.

J   Certainly.

[c]   IMPLIED ADOPTION BY SILENCE—"TACIT ADMISSION"

Sometimes, if a person stands silent in the face of an accusation, we may infer the person's assent to the accusation from his or her silence. Thus, there can be an implied adoption by silence; the courts sometimes refer to this doctrine as "tacit admission." The foundation includes these elements:

1. The declarant made a statement.

2. The statement was an accusation against the party-opponent.

3. The declarant made the statement in the party's presence.

4. The party heard and understood the statement.

5. The party had the opportunity to deny the statement.

6. The party either remained silent or made an evasive or equivocal reply.

7. Under similar circumstances, a reasonable innocent person would have immediately denied the accusation. While the preceding six elements are foundational facts falling under Rule 104(b), this element presents a mixed question of law and fact. For that reason, the judge resolves this element. (Of course, even if the judge admits the evidence under this doctrine, during their deliberations the jurors can decide not to draw that inference.)

Our fact situation is another tort case arising from a collision. The plaintiff, Mr. Girard, alleges that the defendant, Ms. Ratner, caused the accident by disregarding a stop sign. The investigating officer was Highway Patrolman Kuns. The plaintiff calls Patrolman Kuns. He has already identified himself and testified that he responded to the accident scene. The plaintiff is the proponent.

P	WHAT did you do when you responded to the scene?
W	I immediately sought out the two drivers.
P	WHO were the drivers?
W	Your client, Mr. Girard, and Ms. Ratner.
P	WHERE is Mr. Girard now?
W	At the table over there.
P	HOW is he dressed?
W	He's wearing a gray business suit and blue tie.
P	Your Honor, please let the record reflect that the witness has identified the plaintiff.
J	It will so reflect.
P	WHERE is Ms. Ratner now?
W	At the other table there.
P	HOW is she dressed?
W	She has on a pink dress and red shoes.
P	Your Honor, please let the record reflect that the witness has also identified the defendant.
J	It will so reflect.

P	WHERE did you find the plaintiff and defendant at the accident scene?
W	They were standing on the northeast corner of the intersection.
P	HOW close were they to each other?
W	Right next to each other.
P	WHAT were they doing?
W	They were talking.
P	WHAT were they talking about?
W	The accident.
P	WHAT, if anything, did Mr. Girard tell the defendant about the accident? (1), (2)
O	Your Honor, I object to that question on the ground that it calls for hearsay.
P	Your Honor, may we approach the bench?
J	Yes.
P	I offer to prove that Mr. Girard told the defendant she had run a stop sign and that she adopted the statement by remaining silent. I am using Mr. Girard's statement for a nonhearsay purpose; I am not offering the statement itself for its truth. I simply want to prove that the plaintiff made the statement, the defendant heard it, and the defendant then adopted it.
O	There's been no foundation for an adoptive admission yet.
J	I will admit the statement subject to a motion to strike.
P	Officer Kuns, let me repeat the question. WHAT, if anything, did Mr. Girard tell the defendant about the accident? (1), (2)
W	He told her that she had caused the accident by running a stop sign. He said she was as blind as a bat.
P	WHAT language was Mr. Girard speaking in? (4)
W	English.
P	HOW close was Mr. Girard to the defendant when he made that statement? (3)
W	Two feet away at most. As I said, they were standing talking.
P	HOW much noise was there when Mr. Girard made the statement? (4), (5)
W	It was pretty quiet. The traffic congestion had died down.
P	HOW many other people were talking to the defendant at the time? (4), (5)
W	No one else.

P	WHOM was Mr. Girard facing when he made the statement? (4), (5)
W	He was looking right at Ms. Ratner.
P	HOW was she facing? (4), (5)
W	She was facing him.
P	WHAT was Mr. Girard's tone of voice when he made the statement? (5), (7)
W	He was obviously excited, but he wasn't screaming at her.
P	WHAT threats, if any, did Mr. Girard make against the defendant at the time? (5), (7)
W	None. He was upset, but he wasn't menacing or anything like that.
P	WHAT gestures did Mr. Girard make? (5), (7)
W	He was animated, but he wasn't making a fist or pointing a finger in Ms. Ratner's face. He was just exasperated.
P	WHAT was the defendant's facial expression immediately after Mr. Girard made the statement? (7)
W	She looked worried.
P	WHERE did she look? (4), (5), (7)
W	Right after he made the statement, she looked down and away from the plaintiff.
P	WHAT was her physical condition at the time? (4), (5), (7)
W	She didn't appear to be hurt. I didn't see any injuries, and she wasn't expressing any pain.
P	HOW would you characterize her mental condition? (4), (5), (7)
W	She understandably seemed a bit upset, but otherwise she appeared to be OK. Before that, she'd been talking just fine.
P	HOW well did the defendant appear to understand the statement? (4), (5), (7)[2]
W	She didn't seem confused or distracted.
P	WHAT, if anything, did the defendant say then? (6)
W	Nothing.
P	WHAT was her response to Mr. Girard's statement that she had run the stop sign? (6)
W	None. She didn't say anything in response to his remark.

---

[2] As Chapter 9 pointed out, under Rule 701 many courts now permit a layperson to opine about a third party's "apparent" or "seeming" state of mind so long as the witness makes it clear that he or she is basing their opinion on the third party's conduct and demeanor.

[4] VICARIOUS ADMISSIONS

[a] IN CIVIL CASES

In vicarious admissions, the basis for imputing the statement to the party-opponent is the party's close relationship with the declarant. A principal debtor's statement may be admitted against a surety, the statements of a predecessor in title against the present titleholder, and the statements of an agent against the principal. The foundation consists of demonstrating the relation between the declarant and the party-opponent. Once the relation has been demonstrated, the declarant's statements are vicariously admissible against the party-opponent. There is currently a division of authority over the question of whether vicarious admissions must be based on the declarant's personal knowledge.

Most vicarious admissions in civil cases are statements made by agents and admitted against the agent's principal. The traditional view is that the declarant must have been an authorized spokesperson for the principal. Under this view, it is not sufficient that the declarant was an agent or employee of the party-opponent. The declarant must have been a special type of agent, namely, a spokesperson authorized to make statements on the principal's behalf. In the words of Federal Rule of Evidence 801(d)(2)(C), "the statement" was made "by a person whom the party authorized to make a statement on the subject." In these jurisdictions, the foundation includes the following elements:

1. The declarant was an agent of the party-opponent.

2. The party-opponent authorized the declarant to make the particular statements. In *Bourjaily v. United States*, 483 U.S. 171, 107 S. Ct. 2775, 97 L. Ed. 2d 144 (1987), the Court held that Rule 104(a) governs the foundational facts for the coconspirator exemption codified in Rule 801(d)(2)(E). Rule 801(d)(2) was amended effective December 1, 1997, by adding a sentence at the end of the subdivision. The accompanying Advisory Committee Note explained that the purpose of the amendment was to extend the same treatment to the "preliminary questions relating to the declarant's authority under subdivision (C)."

3. The statement is inconsistent with a position the party-opponent is taking at trial. More precisely, the statement must be logically relevant to an issue the proponent has a right to prove at trial.

The fact situation is a suit against an insurance company. Delta Corporation sues Grant Insurance Company. The complaint alleges that the defendant insured the plaintiff against fire; a fire occurred on the plaintiff's premises and caused $200,000 in damages; and the defendant has wrongfully refused to compensate the plaintiff. The policy excluded any fire that the plaintiff's employees negligently started. In discovery, the defendant obtained a copy of a report the plaintiff's safety investigator, Mr. Grant Richards, prepared. The report includes the finding that one contributing cause of the fire was some careless welding by plaintiff's employees; the welder negligently cut into a furnace and permitted flames to escape. During its case-in-chief, the defendant calls Mr. Richards. In many jurisdictions, the defendant could treat him as an adverse witness under Rule 611(c)(2) and conduct the direct examination as cross-examination and use leading questions. For our purposes, we shall restrict the defense attorney to non-leading questions. The defendant is the proponent. Mr. Richards has already identified himself.

P	WHERE do you work? (1)
W	I work for Delta Corporation in Albuquerque.
P	HOW long have you worked for them? (1)
W	Seven years, give or take a few months.
P	WHAT is your job with Delta Corporation? (2)
W	I am the chief safety and accident investigator.
P	HOW long have you held that position? (2)
W	The last five years.
P	WHERE were you on November 13, YR-3? (2)
W	At our plant in Santa Fe.
P	WHAT were you doing there? (2)
W	I was investigating the fire that had occurred the day before.
P	HOW long did you spend investigating the fire? (2)
W	The whole day.
P	WHAT did you do when you finished the investigation? (2)
W	As is my normal practice, I prepared a report of the investigation.
P	Your Honor, I request that this be marked defense exhibit F for identification.
J	It will be so marked.
P	Please let the record reflect that I am showing the exhibit to the opposing counsel.
J	It will so reflect.
P	I request permission to approach the witness.
J	Permission granted.
P	Mr. Richards, I now hand you defense exhibit F for identification. WHAT is it? (2)
W	It's my report on the fire.
P	HOW can you recognize it? (2)
W	I recognize my handwriting on the last page. I also generally recall the report's contents.
P	Again, WHAT are your duties for Delta Corporation? (2)
W	As I said before, I'm the lead safety and accident investigator.
P	In general terms, WHAT is the subject of this particular report?

W	It relates to the fire I investigated as part of my duties.
P	WHY did you prepare this particular report? (2)
W	It's part of my job. In fact, the vice-president for operations ordered me to get that report finished and submitted as soon as possible.
P	Your Honor, I now offer defense exhibit F for identification into evidence as defense exhibit F.
J	It will be received.
P	Mr. Richards, please turn to page 18 of exhibit F and read finding #4 to the jury. (3)
W	The report reads, "Another contributing factor may have been our own employees' carelessness. Some of our welders were evidently working next to furnace #3 on the second floor. Some eyewitness reports indicated that the welders accidentally cut into the furnace, releasing the flames that started the fire."

A few jurisdictions limit this doctrine to statements made to third parties outside the business organization. In this hypothetical, the document was an internal report; Richards submitted the report to his superiors in the corporation. Those jurisdictions would exclude the report. Even in those jurisdictions, the report would be admissible if Richards prepared the report for a third party outsider such as a government safety agency. The trend is to abandon this limitation. Federal Rule of Evidence 801(d)(2)(C) follows the trend and would permit the admission of Richards' report as a vicarious admission.

The emerging view is that the party-opponent need not have authorized the particular statement; the declarant does not have to have been a spokesperson. Under the modern view, it is sufficient that the declarant was an agent of the party-opponent at the time of the statement and the statement related to the agent's employment duties. Federal Rule of Evidence 801(d)(2)(D) opts for this view. That Rule authorizes the admission of "a statement . . . made by the party's agent or employee on a matter within the scope of that relationship and while it existed." Under this view, the only foundational elements are:

1. The declarant was an agent of the party-opponent.

2. The declarant made the statement while he or she was an agent.

3. The statement related to the agent's employment duties. The proponent first elicits testimony about the agent's employment duties. The proponent then asks the agent "about" a topic related to the duties. As previously stated, *Bourjaily v. United States*, 483 U.S. 171, 107 S. Ct. 2775, 97 L. Ed. 2d 144 (1987) announces that Rule 104(a) governs the foundational facts for the coconspirator exemption codified in subdivision 801(d)(2)(E). According to the accompanying Advisory Committee Note, the December 1, 1997 amendment to Rule 801(d)(2) was intended to extend the same treatment to "preliminary questions relating to . . . the agency or employment relationship and scope thereof under subdivision (D)."

4. The statement is inconsistent with a position the party-opponent is taking at trial; the statement is logically relevant to an issue the proponent has a right to prove at trial.

Our fact situation is a tort action arising from a collision. Ms. Henning, the plaintiff, alleges that Carrington Company's driver, Mr. Julius, negligently caused the accident. The only named defendant is the company, Carrington. During the plaintiff's case-in-chief, she calls Mr. Julius as a witness. As in the previous hypothetical, many courts would permit the proponent to treat the witness as an adverse witness and conduct the direct examination with leading questions as if it were cross-examination. However, for teaching purposes, our proponent will use non-leading questions. Mr. Julius has already identified himself.

P   WHERE do you work? (1)

W   I work for the Carrington warehouse here in Billings.

P   HOW long have you worked there? (1)

W   Eight years.

P   WHAT are your duties? (1)

W   I'm a driver. I haul our deliveries all over the United States. I do mostly intrastate moves, but I occasionally do cross-country moves.

P   Mr. Julius, WHERE were you on the afternoon of October 13, YR-3? (2)

W   I was driving along Highway 84 headed for Colorado.

P   WHO were you working for that day? (2)

W   My regular employer, Carrington.

P   WHAT happened that afternoon? (2)

W   I was involved in an accident with a Ms. Henning. (*Here the proponent would elicit facts about the collision itself.*)

P   WHAT happened immediately after the accident? (3)

W   I talked to the police officer who investigated the accident.

P   WHAT was his name? (3)

W   I think his name was Patrolman Blue.

P   WHAT, if anything, did you tell him about your speed just before the collision? (3), (4)

O   Your Honor, I object to that question on the ground that it calls for hearsay.

P   Your Honor, may we approach the bench?

J   Yes.

P   Your Honor, I offer to prove that the witness will admit he said he was going 70 miles an hour. My theory of admissibility is that Mr. Julius' statement about his speed is a vicarious admission against his employer.

O	Carrington hires drivers to drive rather than to act as spokespersons or hold press conferences.
P	As you know, Your Honor, this jurisdiction has adopted the Federal Rules of Evidence. Rule 801 authorizes the admission of agents' statements so long as they relate to the agent's employment duties. This statement relates to the speed at which Mr. Julius was driving.
J	The objection will be overruled.
P	Mr. Julius, let me repeat the question. WHAT, if anything, did you tell Patrolman Blue about your speed just before the collision? (3), (4)
W	I told him I thought I was going about 70 miles an hour. I was a little behind schedule, and I was trying to make up time.
P	WHAT is the posted speed limit on the stretch of highway where the collision occurred?
W	55 miles an hour.

At common law, many courts applied the vicarious admission notion in other civil settings. For example, in cases involving real and personal property interests, they admitted the statement of a prior holder of the right against a successor in interest.[3] However, none of the provisions in Rule 801(d)(2) contained wording broad enough to extend to such fact situations. To admit such statements, the courts either had to ignore Rule 802 and apply common-law doctrine or stretch the residual exception. To eliminate that problem, the Advisory Committee has proposed inserting the following language at the end of 801(d)(2):

> If a party's claim or potential liability is directly derived from a declarant or the declarant's principal, a statement that would be admissible against the declarant or the principal under this rule is also admissible against the party.

The accompanying Note explains that this provision would also apply when "an estate is bringing a claim for damages suffered by the decedent . . . ." The amendment is tentatively scheduled to take effect in December 2024.

[b] IN CRIMINAL CASES

The criminal counterpart of the exception for agents' statements is the co-conspirator doctrine. Federal Rule of Evidence 801(d)(2)(E) states the doctrine. That Rule exempts a "statement . . . made by the party's coconspirator during and in furtherance of the conspiracy." The foundation includes these elements:

1. There was a conspiracy.

2. The conspiracy was in progress when the declarant made the statement. The conspiracy continues at least until the conspirators attempt to commit the crime. If the crime is a theft offense, the conspiracy also continues until the conspirators divide the proceeds of the theft. However, in most jurisdictions,

---

[3] 2 MCCORMICK ON EVIDENCE § 260 (8th ed. 2020).

absent an actual (express or implied-in-fact) agreement, the conspiracy does not continue while the individual conspirators later try to evade arrest and prosecution.

3. The declarant was a co-conspirator.

4. The declarant made the statement in furtherance of the conspiracy. For instance, the declarant furthers the conspiracy by attempting to recruit new conspirators or updating current conspirators on the state of their plans. If the declarant has already been arrested, his or her confession is usually not deemed to promote the conspiracy.

5. The accused was a member of the conspiracy. The accused need not be a member of the conspiracy when the declarant makes the statement; if the accused later joins the conspiracy, the accused is deemed to ratify the earlier statements.

In *Bourjaily v. United States*, 483 U.S. 171, 107 S. Ct. 2775, 97 L. Ed. 2d 144 (1987), the Supreme Court announced that in deciding whether the prosecution has established all the foundational elements, under Rule 104(a) the trial judge may consider the content of the proffered statement itself. After *Bourjaily*, the uniform view among the lower federal courts was that although the prosecution may use the content of the proffered statement to help establish the foundation, standing alone the statement itself is insufficient to lay the foundation. The December 1, 1997 amendment to Rule 801 codified that view at the very end of 801(d)(2).

To lay the foundation, the prosecutor often calls an informer or a conspirator who has turned state's evidence. Our fact situation is a prosecution for conspiracy to sell cocaine. The accused is Mr. George Sherr. The indictment alleges that the accused conspired with Mr. James Blanton. The prosecution calls Mr. Donald Peterson as a witness. The prosecutor hopes to use Mr. Peterson's testimony to prove the intent to sell. The witness has already identified himself. The prosecution is the proponent.

P   WHAT is your occupation?

W   I am a police officer, a member of the Tucson Police Department.

P   WHAT are your duties?

W   I specialize in undercover work for the Narcotics Division.

P   HOW long have you done that type of work?

W   For the last three years.

P   WHERE were you on the evening of September 3, YR-4? (1)

W   I was at James Blanton's house near the City Hall in Tucson.

P   WHO else was there? (1), (3), (5)

W   It was just me, Blanton, and the accused.

P   WHAT happened while you were there? (1)

W   Blanton showed me some bags containing a drug. Both Blanton and the accused referred to it as cocaine.

P	WHAT happened after Blanton showed you the bags? (1)
W	I pretended to get high on some marijuana; and while I was doing that, Blanton and the defendant discussed their plans for getting more cocaine.
P	WHAT plans did they discuss? (1)
W	Blanton said he had a contact in Mexico for some really good, cheap cocaine; and the accused said he could fly down in a small plane, pick up the cocaine, and smuggle it back across the border.
P	WHEN did they say they would carry out these plans? (2)
W	Over the next couple of months.
P	WHAT happened after they discussed their plans?
W	The accused took me home.
P	WHAT happened the next day? (2)
W	I met Blanton for lunch.
P	WHAT happened during the lunch? (4)
W	Blanton invited me to help the accused and him carry out their plans.
P	HOW did he want you to help him? (4)
W	He said he wanted me to hide some bags of cocaine in my apartment. He said he thought it would be a good idea to divide up his cache rather than storing it in only one place.
P	HOW did you respond? (4)
W	I said that I wanted to make certain there was something in it for me.
P	WHAT, if anything, did Blanton say then? (4)
O	Your Honor, I object to that question on the ground that it calls for hearsay.
P	Your Honor, may we approach the bench?
J	Yes.
P	Your Honor, I offer to prove that the witness will testify that Blanton said he and the accused were going to sell the cocaine and make enough money to pay the witness $10,000. The testimony is directly relevant to prove the intent to sell. Since Blanton was the accused's co-conspirator, Blanton's statement is vicariously admissible against the accused.
J	The objection will be overruled.
P	Mr. Peterson, let me repeat the question. WHAT did Mr. Blanton say when you said you wanted to make certain there was something in the proposal for you? (4)
W	He said that he and the accused weren't simply stockpiling the cocaine supply for their personal use. He told me that they intended to sell the

cocaine. He was certain that they would make enough money to pay me $10,000 for the use of my apartment for a few days.

PART D. Hearsay Exceptions Based Primarily on a Showing of Reliability

§ 10.04 IN GENERAL

As we saw in the last section, a proponent offering a statement as the admission of a party-opponent need not establish the reliability of the statement or any necessity to resort to the statement. In contrast, many hearsay exceptions require a showing of reliability. These exceptions fall into two categories. In one category, the exception is usually a spinoff of the old *res gestae* doctrine; and there is an inference of sincerity on the part of the declaration. Sections 10.08 through 10.11 of this chapter focus on the exceptions falling into this category. The second category includes primarily documentary statements. There is something about the process of generating these types of writings which creates an inference of the reliability of the written statement. Sections 10.05 through 10.07 of this chapter discuss those hearsay exceptions.

§ 10.05 BUSINESS ENTRIES

[1] THE DOCTRINE

At common law, business entries are exceptionally admissible. Federal Rule of Evidence 803(6) restates the modern doctrine:

The following [is] not excluded by the rule against hearsay . . . : A record of an act, event, condition, opinion, or diagnosis if:

(A) the record was made at or near the time by—or from information transmitted by—someone with knowledge;

(B) the record was kept in the course of a regularly conducted activity of a business, organization, occupation, or calling, whether or not for profit;

(C) making the record was a regular practice of that activity;

(D) all these conditions are shown by the testimony of the custodian or another qualified person, or by a certification that complies with Rule 902(11) or (12) or with a statute permitting certification; and

(E) the opponent does not show that the source of information or the method or circumstances of preparation indicate a lack of trustworthiness.

In the case of business entries, the circumstantial guarantee of trustworthiness is that since the entry is routine, the business' employees have developed habits of precision in gathering and reporting the data. If they do not and the business is a for-profit company in the private sector, it is highly likely that the business' customers will complain loudly, for example, about the amount due stated on their bills. The employees' habits help to ensure the reliability of the report. There is also necessity for resorting to the hearsay report. If a business conducts hundreds or thousands of similar transactions during a year, it is doubtful whether any employee will remember the particular transaction recorded in the entry. Even when an employee remembers, the employee's memory is likely to be incomplete or hazy. Thus, the business entry is probably the most reliable evidence available.

[2] ELEMENTS OF THE FOUNDATION

Some commentators have suggested that the Federal Rules of Evidence "collapse" the traditional, common-law elements of the business entry foundation into a single requirement for a general showing of reliability. However, most commentators and courts still assume that the proponent must establish the following foundational elements:

1. The report was prepared by a person with a business relationship with the company. It is ideal if the person is an employee of the company. However, the person might also work for a parent, subsidiary, or affiliated company.

2. The informant (the ultimate source of the report) had a business duty to report the information. This requirement is traceable to the leading case of *Johnson v. Lutz*, 253 N.Y. 124, 170 N.E. 517 (1930). There the court held that a report is not prepared in the course of business unless all the persons contributing to the report have a business duty to do so. In that case, the business entity was the police department. The parts of the police report reflecting bystanders' statements did not qualify as business entries, since the civilian bystanders were not employees of the police department.[4] The informant's business duty is one of the guarantees of the report's trustworthiness. The test is the existence of the business duty, not the informant's status as an employee of the business. Thus, the employee of a subsidiary corporation would qualify, since he or she would have a business duty to the parent entity. The Advisory Committee Note to Rule 803(6) approvingly refers to *Johnson*. (Some courts apply the business entry exception to hotel registration records when the foundation includes proof that the hotel routinely demands proof of identity before allowing someone to register as a guest.)

3. The informant had personal knowledge of the facts or events reported.

4. The written report was prepared contemporaneously with the facts or events.

5. It was a routine practice of the business to prepare such reports.

6. The report was recorded such as by being reduced to written form.

7. The report was made in the regular course of business. The expression, "regular course of business," at least requires that the entry be related to the nature of the business. For instance, a sales slip is obviously related to the nature of a retail merchandise business. *Palmer v. Hoffman*, 318 U.S. 109, 64 S. Ct. 477, 87 L. Ed. 645 (1943) adds another level of meaning to "regular course of business." The lower courts and commentators have construed

---

[4] The passage represents double hearsay under Rule 805: The author of the report asserts that the bystander made an assertion. Since the bystander has no business duty, the proponent cannot apply Rule 803(6) to both levels of hearsay. However, suppose that the bystander's statement qualified as an excited utterance. The proponent could then tack Rule 803(6) together with Rule 803(2).

> *Palmer* as meaning that reports specially prepared for litigation are not made "in the regular course of business." If the trial judge finds that the business entry is in reality a special litigation report, the judge has discretion to exclude the entry as being suspect and unreliable. The Advisory Committee Note to Rule 803(6) approvingly cites *Palmer*.

> 8. The entry is factual in nature. Rule 803(6) relaxes this requirement by expressly allowing the admission of an "opinion . . . or diagnosis." However, some courts do not apply this language literally. For instance, these courts balk at admitting highly evaluative opinions such as psychiatric diagnoses. The standards for some psychiatric diagnoses are "soft" and subjective, and there is an acute need to cross-examine the expert who arrived at the diagnosis.

The witness need not have personal knowledge of the entry's preparation. In fact, the witness rarely possesses such knowledge. The witness is ordinarily the business' records custodian or librarian. Rule 803(6)(D) permits foundational testimony by "the custodian or another qualified witness." The witness testifies to his or her connection with the business and then describes the routine method with which the business prepares and maintains its reports. The proponent lays the foundation for such routine by following the procedure outlined in § 6.03 of Chapter 6. The habit or routine evidence has sufficient probative value to support a finding that the business followed that procedure on the occasion in question.

[3] SAMPLE FOUNDATION

The fact situation is a contract suit. The plaintiff is Armor Corporation. Its complaint alleges that it delivered 500 stereophonic speakers to Hyatt Corporation and that the defendant wrongfully failed to pay for the speakers. The defendant filed an answer, generally denying the complaint's allegations. The plaintiff wants to introduce a Delivery Sheet, stating that its employees delivered the 500 speakers to the defendant. The plaintiff calls Mr. James Merton as a witness. Mr. Merton has already identified himself. The plaintiff is the proponent.

P	WHERE do you work?
W	I am the records librarian for Armor Corporation.
P	HOW long have you held that position?
W	About six years.
P	WHAT are your duties as records librarian?
W	I establish company-wide procedures for preparing records. I ensure that the records that are prepared are properly filed, and I'm finally in charge of records retirement and destruction.
P	Your Honor, I request that this be marked plaintiff's exhibit number three for identification.
J	It will be so marked.
P	Please let the record reflect that I am showing the exhibit to the opposing counsel.

J	It will so reflect.
P	I request permission to approach the witness.
J	Permission granted.
P	Mr. Merton, I now hand you plaintiff's exhibit number three for identification. WHAT is it?

Authentication

The complete foundation would include proof of the document's authenticity. See §§ 4.02 and 4.03 of Chapter 4.

Best Evidence

The complete foundation will also include proof of compliance with the best evidence rule. See Chapter 8.

Hearsay

P	WHO prepared this document? (1)
W	Well, it seems to have been prepared by Bob Grant.
P	HOW do you know that? (1)
W	I recognize his handwriting style. I've seen his writing on hundreds of occasions.
P	WHO is Bob Grant? (1)
W	He's one of our delivery personnel.
P	As a delivery man, WHAT are Mr. Grant's duties? (2)
W	He picks up merchandise in our warehouse in Scranton, makes sure that it gets to the customer, and prepares the paperwork on the delivery.
P	WHICH of your employees are authorized to prepare the paperwork? (3)
W	Only the delivery person in charge of that particular delivery. That's the employee who fills out the delivery report or sheet.
P	WHEN does the delivery person make out the report? (4)
W	He's supposed to make it out as soon as they make the delivery. At the very latest, they make it out when they get back to our office.
P	HOW often do your employees prepare these reports? (5)
W	Every time they make a delivery. I'd say that they send us 50 to 80 of those delivery sheets each week.
P	WHAT form does the report take? (6)
W	It's a standard, written report we call a Delivery Sheet. Like the one we have here, exhibit number three or whatever the number is.
P	WHY do you require that the delivery personnel prepare these reports? (7)
W	There are all sorts of business reasons for the reports—accounting,

	inventory, taxes. You just can't run an efficient, profitable business establishment unless you keep very, very close tabs on your deliveries.
P	WHAT does the delivery person do with the report after he or she prepares it? (7)
W	He or she hands it to someone in our front office.
P	WHAT does your office do with it? (7)
W	We store it in a separate file, including the Delivery Sheets for that week. Eventually a lot of our forms are converted into electronic form, but at first we store the actual paper Delivery Sheets.
P	WHERE did you find plaintiff's exhibit number three for identification?
W	In the file for that week's Delivery Sheets.
P	WHEN did you remove it from that file?
W	Just this morning before trial.
P	Your Honor, I now offer plaintiff's exhibit number three for identification into evidence as plaintiff's exhibit number three.
O	Your Honor, I object to the exhibit's introduction on the ground that the exhibit is incompetent hearsay.
J	The objection will be overruled, and the exhibit will be received.
P	Mr. Merton, please read the circled part of the exhibit to the jury.
W	That part reads, "January 18—delivered 500 stereo speakers to Hyatt Corp."
P	Your Honor, I request permission to submit the exhibit to the jurors for their personal inspection.
J	Permission granted.

In 2000, Rule 902 was amended to provide that a proper attesting certificate renders a domestic business record self-authenticating. Construed together, Rules 803(6) and 902(11) permit the proponent to dispense with live, sponsoring testimony.

§ 10.06 OFFICIAL RECORDS

[1] THE DOCTRINE

The second major documentary exception to the hearsay rule is the official records doctrine. Just as business employees presumably are careful in gathering and recording information for their employers, public employees presumably are diligent in gathering and recording information for their employer, the government. For this reason, the common law and the Federal Rules admit official records as well as business entries. Federal Rule of Evidence 803(8) states the basic doctrine:

The following [is] not excluded by the rule against hearsay . . . : A record or statement of a public office if:

(A) it sets out:

(i)   the office's activities;

(ii)   a matter observed while under a legal duty to report, but not including, in a criminal case, a matter observed by law-enforcement personnel; or

(iii)   in a civil case or against the government in a criminal case, factual findings from a legally authorized investigation; and

(B)   the opponent does not show that the source of information or other circumstances indicate a lack of trustworthiness.

Section 4.04 of Chapter 4 discusses the authentication of official records. As that section noted, the proponent of an official record rarely presents live, sponsoring testimony to authenticate the record. In most instances, live testimony is similarly unnecessary to lay the foundation for the official records exception to the hearsay rule. Two doctrines make the live testimony unnecessary. The first doctrine is judicial notice. The judge will ordinarily judicially notice the statute,[5] regulation, or custom requiring that the public official prepare the record. Next, if the attested copy is fair on its face (complete with no erasures), the document's face creates a permissive inference that the officials followed the proper procedures in preparing the particular record.

[2]   ELEMENTS OF THE FOUNDATION

At common law, a complete foundation for the official records hearsay exception includes these elements:

1.   The record was prepared at or near the time of the fact or event recorded. Some cases and statutes no longer explicitly require this element. Federal Rule of Evidence 803(8) is illustrative; its language does not impose this requirement. In jurisdictions dispensing with this element, the only requirement is that the entry be properly prepared. If, long after the original event, the official discovers an error in the record and follows prescribed procedures for making a corrected entry, the corrected entry will qualify as an official record.

2.   The record is in official custody.

3.   The record is open to public inspection. The early, English cases impose this requirement. Most jurisdictions have dispensed with this element; in these jurisdictions, it is sufficient that the record is in official custody. Rule 803(8) adopts the latter view.

4.   The record was properly prepared. The official must substantially comply with the procedures prescribed for the report's preparation.

5.   The preparer was a public official.

6.   The official had a duty to record the fact.

7.   The official had personal knowledge of the fact. Rule 803(8)(A)(iii) relaxes

---

[5] Strictly speaking, the judicial notice provision, Rule 201(a), is limited to notice of factual matters. However, in practice judges sometimes loosely use the expression "judicial notice" when they take informal notice of the existence of legal material such as statutes.

this requirement "in a civil case or against the government in a criminal case." That subsection allows the admission of "factual findings from a legally authorized investigation." Some lower courts construed this language as permitting the admission of findings about events even when the investigating officer lacked firsthand knowledge of the event. The Supreme Court adopted that construction in *Beech Aircraft Corp. v. Rainey*, 488 U.S. 153, 109 S. Ct. 439, 102 L. Ed. 2d 445 (1988).

8.   The entry is factual in nature. In footnote 13 in *Beech Aircraft*, the Court stated that it was "express[ing] no opinion as to whether legal conclusions contained in an official report are admissible as 'findings of fact' under Rule 803(8)(C)." Most lower courts have ruled that legal conclusions are inadmissible.

[3]   SAMPLE FOUNDATIONS

We shall first illustrate the admission of an official record without live testimony. The fact situation is a quiet title action. The plaintiff, Mr. Thelan, and the defendant, Mr. Garrett, both claim title to the same parcel of land in Miami, Florida. Both claim from the same grantor, but Mr. Thelan contends that he recorded his deed first. Mr. Thelan proposes to offer a properly attested copy of the recordation of the deed in the County Clerk's office. The copy shows the date of recording. The plaintiff is the proponent.

P   Your Honor, I request that this be marked plaintiff's exhibit number four for identification.

J   It will be so marked.

P   Please let the record reflect that I am showing the exhibit to the opposing counsel.

J   It will so reflect.

P   I now offer plaintiff's exhibit number four for identification into evidence as plaintiff's exhibit number four.

O   Your Honor, I object to the introduction of the exhibit on the ground that the exhibit is hearsay.

P   Your Honor, may we approach the bench?

J   Yes.

O   Your Honor, this record is an assertive out-of-court statement, and the plaintiff is obviously going to use it for its truth, namely, the date of the recordation of his deed. The exhibit is undeniably hearsay.

P   That's true, but the record falls within the official record exception to the hearsay rule.

O   There's been no foundation for that exception. No sponsoring witness has come forward to lay the foundation.

P   Live testimony is unnecessary. Your Honor, you can judicially notice Civil Code section 1477 which requires the County Clerk to record deeds relating to land in the county. Moreover, the attached copy is fair on its face; it's complete, and there are no erasures or unexplained marks. The face of the document creates an inference that the public official properly carried out his duties. The attesting certificate renders this exhibit self-authenticating under Rule 902(4).

J   I agree. The objection will be overruled, and the exhibit will be received.

P   Your Honor, I request permission to read the exhibit to the jury.

J   Permission granted.

P   Ladies and gentlemen, I am about to read this exhibit to you. The exhibit purports to be a Xerox copy of a page from the records of the Dade County Clerk. The exhibit reads, "Date of recordation—January 13, YR-4, grantor—Paul A. Peterson, grantee—John D. Thelan, parcel number—17,886." Your Honor, I now request permission to hand the exhibit to the jurors for their inspection.

J   Permission granted.

In the next hypothetical, we shall use live testimony. The plaintiff, Mr. Schmitt, has sued the defendant, the State of Missouri. Mr. Schmitt sustained personal injuries when his car left a Missouri highway and crashed. Mr. Schmitt alleges that the degree of slope in the curve where he lost control of his car was too sharp. His expert will testify that for that type of road, any slope greater than 17 degrees would represent negligent design and engineering. Mr. Schmitt wants to introduce a Missouri Department of Transportation report, listing the degree of slope on the curve as 19 degrees. Mr. Schmitt calls Mr. Justin as a witness. Mr. Justin has already identified himself. The plaintiff is the proponent.

P   WHAT is your educational background?

W   I have bachelor's and master's degrees in civil engineering from the University of Missouri.

P   WHERE do you work? (5)

W   I am a civil engineer for the Missouri Department of Transportation.

P   WHAT is the Department of Transportation? (5)

W   It's an official department of our state government.

P   HOW long have you worked there? (5)

W   The past seven years.

P   Your Honor, I request that this be marked plaintiff's exhibit number six for identification.

J   It will be so marked.

P   Please let the record reflect that I am showing the exhibit to the opposing counsel.

J   It will so reflect.

P   I request permission to approach the witness.

J	Permission granted.
P	Mr. Justin, I now hand you plaintiff's exhibit number six for identification. WHAT is it?
W	It's a report I prepared on the curve on Missouri Highway 10 seven-tenths of a mile south of the Columbia turnoff.
P	WHERE have you been this morning?
W	Right here in the courtroom.
P	WHAT stretch of road have the witnesses this morning been talking about?
W	The same curve I surveyed in this report.
P	WHEN did you make this survey? (1)
W	In early YR-3.
P	WHY did you make the survey? (6)
W	The regional office decided to conduct a safety inspection of the area, and the local supervisor ordered me to do the field work.
P	WHO actually inspected the curve? (7)
W	I did personally.
P	WHO actually prepared the report? (7)
W	I did. Well, to be exact, I dictated it. A secretary typed it, and then I reviewed and signed it.
P	HOW long after the survey did you prepare the report? (1)
W	The very next day. I always follow that practice with surveys. I don't want my memory to go stale.
P	WHAT procedures are you supposed to follow in conducting this type of survey and preparing the report? (4)
W	The practice is that you both drive the road and walk it with appropriate surveying equipment. You take detailed notes and then have them immediately transcribed.
P	WHAT procedure did you actually follow? (4)
W	I did it by the book. As far as I know, I complied with all the required steps.
P	WHERE is this report ordinarily kept? (2)
W	In my office files at the Department's local office.
P	WHO can inspect the report? (3)
W	It's generally open to the public.
P	Your Honor, I now offer plaintiff's exhibit number six for identification into evidence as plaintiff's exhibit number six.

O   Your Honor, I object to the introduction of the exhibit on the ground that the exhibit is hearsay.

P   Your Honor, may we approach the bench?

J   Yes.

P   Your Honor, I concede that the exhibit is hearsay, but I submit that I've laid a complete foundation for the official record exception to the hearsay rule.

O   In general, that's true. However, an additional requirement is that the entry offered be factual. Page 10 of the report has a lot of conclusory opinions. I want to know whether the plaintiff's counsel intends to read that page to the jury.

J   (*To the proponent*) What is your intention?

P   I only want the witness to read one of the measurements listed on page seven.

O   Very well, I have no objection to that.

J   Then the exhibit will be received, and you have permission to have the witness read that portion of page seven to the jury. I won't let the exhibit itself go to the jury because it contains inadmissible opinion.

P   Mr. Justin, please read the first measurement on page seven to the jurors.

W   The report reads, "While at the scene, I measured the slope of the curve. I determined the angle to be 19 degrees."

§ 10.07 PAST RECOLLECTION RECORDED AND PRESENT RECOLLECTION REFRESHED OR REVIVED

[1] PAST RECOLLECTION RECORDED

The next documentary hearsay exception is the past recollection recorded doctrine. Suppose that the witness on the stand cannot recall a particular fact or event. The witness's inability to recall supplies necessity for resorting to hearsay evidence. If at the time of the event, the witness had made a record of the fact or event, the record would be a reliable substitute for the witness's present recall. The recognition of this necessity and reliability led to the development of the past recollection recorded doctrine.

Federal Rule of Evidence 803(5) states the doctrine succinctly:

The following [is] not excluded by the rule against hearsay . . . : A record that:

(A)   is on a matter the witness once knew about but now cannot recall well enough to testify fully and accurately;

(B)   was made or adopted by the witness when the matter was fresh in the witness's memory; and

(C)   accurately reflects the witness's knowledge.

If the proponent can show that the exhibit satisfies the doctrine, the real evidence is the document. In many jurisdictions, since the real evidence is the document, the judge formally admits the document and permits it to be submitted to the jury. Other courts take a different position. They reason that the document is the functional equivalent of oral testimony and that it would place undue emphasis on that evidence to permit the jury to examine the document. This reasoning partially persuaded the drafters of the Federal Rules of Evidence. Federal Rule of Evidence 803(5) provides that "[i]f admitted, the record may be read into evidence but may be received as an exhibit only if offered by an adverse party." "Admitted" authorizes formal admission by the judge while the reference to "received" prohibits the physical submission of the exhibit to the jury.

The foundation for this hearsay exception includes these elements:

1. The witness previously gained personal knowledge of the fact or event recorded. There is authority that if the declarant disavows personal knowledge, the proponent may rely on other testimony to establish this element of the foundation. *State v. Nava*, 177 Wn. App. 272, 311 P.3d 83 (2013).

2. The witness subsequently prepared a record of the facts. All courts accept the foundation if the witness personally prepared the record. *Most* courts accept the record if a third party prepared it but the witness verified the record while the events were still fresh in the witness's memory. Some courts also accept cooperative past recollection recorded; witness #1 gives an accurate oral report to witness #2, and witness #2 testifies that he or she accurately transcribed the oral report. The cooperative theory necessitates that both witnesses appear at trial and testify. (Most jurisdictions now recognize the present sense impression exception codified in Federal Rule 803(1). If the judge is willing to apply that exception to witness #1's statement, witness #2's live testimony should suffice to justify the admission of the record.)

3. The witness prepared the record while the events were still fresh in his or her memory. The courts have interpreted Rule 803(5) as liberalizing this timing requirement. In *United States v. Patterson*, 678 F.2d 774 (9th Cir. 1982), the court found a declarant's memory sufficiently fresh despite a 10-month time lapse. *See also United States v. Senak*, 527 F.2d 129 (7th Cir. 1975), *cert. denied*, 425 U.S. 907 (1976) (a three-year delay).

4. The witness vouches that when he or she prepared the record, the record was accurate. Ideally, the witness will recall the very occasion on which he or she prepared the document. Alternatively, the witness may testify that he or she habitually records that type of information and that their habit is to record the information carefully. A police officer assigned to the traffic detail could give that type of testimony about measurements at accident scenes. Finally, in some jurisdictions, it is acceptable if the witness at least recognizes his or her handwriting on the document. In this last situation, in reality the witness is vouching for his or her own honesty; they are really testifying that they are an honest person and would not knowingly record false data.

5. At trial, the witness cannot completely and accurately recall the facts even after reviewing the document. The early view was that the witness had to

completely forget the event. In other words, the witness had to "draw a complete blank." Most modern courts are of the view that it is sufficient if the witness's memory is partial or hazy. In the words of Federal Rule of Evidence 803(5), the witness cannot remember "fully and accurately."

As previously stated, on the one hand, Rule 803(5) can be interpreted as permitting the formal admission of the exhibit. On the other hand, the Rule forbids physically submitting the exhibit to the jurors for their inspection. *Maggipinto v. Reichman*, 607 F.2d 621 (3d Cir. 1979) (construing similar language in Rule 803(18)).

Our fact situation is a bank robbery prosecution. The government charges that Mr. Gary Vincent robbed the First National Bank in downtown Phoenix. The witness is Ms. Jane Millot. Ms. Millot has already identified herself. She has testified that she works as a teller at the First National Bank. The prosecution is the proponent.

P	Ms. Millot, WHERE were you on the morning of February 14, YR-3? (1)
W	I was at work at the bank.
P	WHAT happened that morning? (1)
W	The bank was robbed.
P	HOW were the robbers dressed? (1)
W	They all had masks on. That's why I can't identify any faces.
P	WHAT happened immediately after the robbers took the money? (1)
W	They made their getaway.
P	HOW did they make their getaway? (1)
W	In a white car parked in front of the bank.
P	WHAT was the car's license number? (1), (5)
W	I can't remember. I saw it, but I can't remember it now.
P	WHAT, if anything, might help you remember? (2)
W	I made a note on a slip of paper I had at the time.
P	WHAT did you note on this slip of paper? (2)
W	The license number of the getaway car.
P	WHO prepared this slip? (3)
W	I did it myself.
P	WHEN did you prepare this slip? (3)
W	Right after the car got away.
P	HOW many minutes passed between the time the car left and the time you wrote on the slip? (3)
W	One or two. Not any more than that. I had the slip of paper at my teller window and a pen in the pocket of my dress.

P	HOW clear was your memory of the license number when you wrote the number down? (3), (4)
W	I don't remember making any mistakes. I looked at it carefully, and it seemed O.K. at the time.
P	Your Honor, I request that this be marked prosecution exhibit number five for identification.
J	It will be so marked.
P	Please let the record reflect that I am showing the exhibit to the opposing counsel.
J	It will so reflect.
P	Ms. Millot, I now hand you prosecution exhibit number five for identification. WHAT is it?
W	It's the slip of paper I mentioned.
P	HOW can you recognize it?
W	I recognize my handwriting.
P	Please read the exhibit silently to yourself. (*Pause.*) Have you done so?
W	Yes.
P	Now please hand it back to me. (*The witness does so.*) Your Honor, please let the record reflect that I am holding the exhibit away from the witness and out of her view.
J	It will so reflect.
P	Ms. Millot, you've had a chance to read the exhibit and refresh your memory. Now, without relying on the exhibit, WHAT was the car's license number? (5)
W	I still can't remember apart from the exhibit.
P	WHY can't you remember? (5)
W	I have a bad memory for numbers. I can't honestly say that I now remember the license number.

In jurisdictions prohibiting the introduction of the exhibit:

Please read the slip of paper to the jury.

W	It reads, "USC 247."
P	WHAT does that stand for?
W	That's the license number of the getaway car.

In jurisdictions permitting the introduction of the exhibit:

P	Your Honor, I now offer prosecution exhibit number five for identification into evidence as prosecution exhibit number five.
J	It will be received.

P	Ms. Millot, please read the exhibit to the jurors.
W	It reads, "USC 247."
P	WHAT does that stand for?
W	It's the license number of the getaway car.

[2] PRESENT RECOLLECTION REFRESHED OR REVIVED

In past recollection recorded, even after viewing the document, the witness cannot recall the relevant fact or event. Suppose that viewing the document refreshed the witness's recollection. Then the witness may testify from his or her revived recollection. The courts use the expressions, "present recollection refreshed" or "present recollection revived" to describe the use of exhibits to refresh present memory. Under this theory, the real evidence is the witness's oral testimony, and the exhibit serves only as a memory aid or jogger. A few courts apply the foundational requirements for past recollection recorded to documents used to refresh recollection. However, most courts draw a clear distinction between the two doctrines and permit the proponent to use any document to refresh recollection. Some courts even broadly permit the proponent to use photographs or songs to revive a witness's memory.

Federal Rule of Evidence 612 governs this practice in federal courts:

(a) Scope. This rule gives an adverse party certain options when a witness uses a writing to refresh memory:

(1) while testifying; or

(2) before testifying, if the court decides that justice requires the party to have those options.

(b) Adverse Party's Options; Deleting Unrelated Matter. Unless 18 U.S.C. § 3500 provides otherwise in a criminal case, an adverse party is entitled to have the writing produced at the hearing, to inspect it, to cross-examine the witness about it, and to introduce in evidence any portion that relates to the witness's testimony. If the producing party claims that the writing includes unrelated matter, the court must examine the writing in camera, delete any unrelated portion, and order that the rest be delivered to the adverse party. Any portion deleted over objection must be preserved for the record.

If the jurisdiction does not apply the past recollection recorded requirements to present recollection revived, the foundation for present recollection refreshed or revived is quite simple:

1. The witness states that he or she cannot recall a fact or event.

2. The witness states that a certain writing or object could help refresh his or her memory. Most jurisdictions do not require this showing as a formal element of the foundation, but many trial attorneys think that it is good practice to have the witness first mention the writing or object.

3. The proponent tenders the writing or object to the witness.

4. The proponent asks the witness to silently read the writing or study the object.

5.　The proponent then removes the exhibit from the witness's view.

6.　The witness states that viewing the document or object refreshes his or her memory.

7.　The witness then testifies from revived memory.

On this theory, the evidence is the witness's oral testimony, and the proponent does not formally offer the writing or object into evidence. For purposes of making a good record, many trial judges prefer that the proponent at least mark the writing or object as an exhibit for identification.

We can use the same robbery hypothetical to illustrate present recollection refreshed. In this variation of the hypothetical, Ms. Millot has a better memory for numbers.

P	WHAT was the getaway car's license number? (1)
W	I can't honestly remember right now.
P	WHAT, if anything, might help you remember? (2)
W	I wrote the number down on a slip of paper.
P	Your Honor, I request that this be marked prosecution exhibit number five for identification.
J	It will be so marked.
P	Please let the record reflect that I am showing the exhibit to the opposing counsel.
J	It will so reflect.
P	I request permission to approach the witness.
J	Granted.
P	Ms. Millot, I now hand you prosecution exhibit number five for identification. (3) WHAT is it? (2)
W	It's the slip of paper I mentioned.
P	HOW can you recognize it? (2)
W	I ought to know my own handwriting style.
P	Please read the exhibit silently to yourself. (4) (*Pause.*) Have you done so?
W	Yes.
P	Now hand it back to me. (*The witness does so.*) Your Honor, please let the record reflect that I am holding the exhibit away from the witness and out of her view. (5)
J	It will so reflect.
P	Ms. Millot, you've had a chance to read the exhibit to refresh your memory. Now without relying on the exhibit, can you remember the license number? (6)
W	Yes.

P   WHAT was the license number? (7)

W   USC 247.

Many experienced trial attorneys use the following combination of past recollection recorded and present recollection refreshed. As soon as a witness states that he or she cannot recall a fact or event, if possible the proponent lays elements one through four of the past recollection recorded foundation. The proponent then tenders the writing to the witness in an attempt to revive present recollection. If the attempt is successful, the witness testifies from present, refreshed memory. If the attempt is unsuccessful, the witness's inability to recall lays the last element of the past recollection recorded foundation. Questioning the witness in this sequence puts the proponent in a "no loss" situation; whichever response the witness gives, the proponent can elicit the desired testimony.

§ 10.08   LEARNED TREATISES

[1]   THE DOCTRINE

At common law, most jurisdictions permitted the opponent to use a learned text or article to cross-examine an expert witness to impeach the expert. The cross-examiner could confront the expert with a passage that contradicted something that the expert said on direct examination. However, the overwhelming majority of jurisdictions refused to allow an attorney to introduce a passage in a text or article as substantive evidence. For that matter, although a minority of jurisdictions allowed the substantive use of a text or article, even they narrowly limited the scope of the hearsay exception to publications dealing with "exact" sciences such as mathematics and "static" fields such as geography. Yet, there is a strong case for recognizing the exception, since the author is likely to be more impartial than any partisan expert called as a witness at trial.

The drafters of the Federal Rules both embraced and expanded the scope of the exception. Rule 803(18) currently codifies a hearsay exception for
[a] statement contained in a treatise, periodical, or pamphlet, if:

    (A)   the statement is called to the attention of an expert witness on cross-examination or relied on by the expert on direct examination; and

    (B)   the publication is established as a reliable authority by the expert's admission or testimony, by another expert's testimony, or by judicial notice.

If admitted, the statement may be read into evidence but not received as an exhibit.

The original version of Rule 803(18) made it clear that the exception is not confined to texts and articles dealing with "exact" sciences or "static" disciplines; that version of the statute referred to publications "on a subject of history, medicine, or other science or art." The Advisory Committee Note accompanying the 2011 restyling of Rule 803 states that the changed wording was not intended "to change any result in any ruling on evidence admissibility."

While the drafters decided to broaden the scope of the common-law exception, they appreciated the dangers that could arise if texts and articles are used too freely. One danger is that the jury might misinterpret the passage being quoted. After all, the jurors are not experts. For that reason, the rule provides that the passage may be admitted only while an expert is on the stand. The expert's presence as a witness on the stand enables the opponent to question the expert about the meaning of the passage. Another danger is that if the judge sent the text or article into the deliberation room, the jurors could focus on—and misinterpret—other passages. To eliminate that danger, the rule forbids physically submitting the text or article to the jury. The proponent may have the expert quote the passage or, in the judge's discretion, display the passage on, for example, a PowerPoint slide. However, the proponent may not hand the text or article to the jurors for their inspection, and the judge will not send the text or article into the deliberation room.

[2] ELEMENTS OF THE FOUNDATION

To invoke Rule 803(18), the proponent must lay the following foundation:

1. A witness, qualified as an expert under Rule 702, is on the witness stand.

2. A treatise, periodical, or pamphlet contains a passage dealing with the subject-matter of the expert's testimony.

3. The proponent brings the treatise, periodical, or pamphlet to the expert's attention.

4. The treatise, periodical, or pamphlet has been published.

5. The treatise, periodical, or pamphlet is "a reliable authority" on the subject. This element is fairly liberal. To begin with, the rule recognizes several different methods by which the proponent can establish the publication's reliable status. In a rare case, the text may be so well known that the judge may judicially notice the status under Rule 201(b)(2). Alternatively, based on a prior expert witness's testimony, the proponent may have persuaded the judge to find that the publication is a reliable authority. Finally and more commonly when the text is being used on direct examination, the proponent elicits the witness's testimony to that effect. Moreover, although the proponent must show that in general the publication is reliable, the proponent need not show that the particular passage being quoted has attained authoritative status.

[3] SAMPLE FOUNDATION

The fact situation is a medical malpractice action. The plaintiff alleges that she suffered permanent brain injuries as a result of surgery to remove what the surgeon suspected was a cancerous tumor. It turned out that the tumor was benign. Because of the peculiar location of the tumor in the plaintiff's brain, the surgeon had to use a rare procedure. The plaintiff alleges that the procedure in question has a very high risk of causing brain damage and that to obtain her informed consent, the defendant surgeon should have expressly told her that the procedure posed such a significant danger. The plaintiff contends that if the surgeon had properly warned her, she would not have consented to the surgical procedure that caused her brain injuries. The plaintiff has called Dr. Akhil Seaman. Dr. Seaman initially described his credentials as an expert on brain surgery. Dr. Seaman then expressed his personal opinion that the defendant surgeon violated the standard of care by not specifically telling the plaintiff that the procedure the surgeon contemplated using posed a very significant risk of causing permanent brain damage. The direct examination continues.

P	Dr. Seaman, you've just expressed your personal opinion about the need to warn patients that this procedure poses a substantial risk of causing permanent brain damage. WHAT texts, if any, in your field, discuss this topic? (2)
W	The leading text is Welby on *Modern Brain Surgery*, sixth edition, YR-4.
P	WHO publishes the text? (4)
W	As I recall, the publisher is Medical Books in Chicago.
P	HOW long has this text been in publication? (4), (5)
W	I've had the text in my personal library since the first edition came out in YR-18. It's now in a sixth, YR-4 edition.
P	WHO is the author of the text? (5)
W	Dr. Susan Welby.
P	WHO is Dr. Welby? (5)
W	She's one of the leading brain surgeons in the world. She's currently the head of the brain surgery department at the medical school of The Johns Hopkins University, one of the most respected medical schools in the world. She's been a president of both national and international organizations of neurosurgeons.
P	HOW well regarded in her text, *Modern Brain Surgery*? (5)
W	It's one of the standard, pre-eminent texts in the field. I teach at our local medical school, and I have always assigned the text as a required reading in my course. I believe it's the most widely used text on brain surgery at American medical schools. Moreover, it's frequently widely cited as authority in articles by other surgeons. In my last article, I included several citations to the text.
P	Does Dr. Welby's text discuss the procedure that the defendant doctor used in this case? (2)
W	It most certainly does. There's a very detailed discussion of the topic in Chapter 13 of the sixth edition.
P	In particular, does the text discuss the warnings needed to obtain truly informed consent to the procedure? (2)
W	Yes.
P	Your Honor, I request that this be marked plaintiff's exhibit number seven for identification.
W	It will be so marked.
P	Your Honor, please let the record reflect that I am showing the exhibit

	to the defense counsel.
W	The record will so reflect.
P	Permission to approach the witness?
W	Granted.
P	Dr. Seaman, I now hand you what has been marked as plaintiff's exhibit number seven for identification. Do you recognize it? (2)
W	Of course.
P	WHAT is it? (2)
W	It's the latest, sixth edition of Dr. Welby's book.
P	HOW do you recognize it? (2)
W	I recognize both the cover and, quickly browsing through the book, the contents as well. As I said, I have this edition in my personal library. In fact, it sits on my desk. It's one of my "go to" texts. I regularly consult it.
P	Your Honor, I now request the admission of the first full paragraph on page 367 of the exhibit?
J	Any objection?
O	Yes. Your Honor, he can't introduce the text.
	Do you wish to be heard before I rule?
P	Yes, Your Honor, the statute expressly says "[i]f admitted." The statute obviously authorizes me to admit the text and read a relevant passage to the jury. It simply forbids me from handing the text to the jury; the statute says it cannot be physically "received." I'm not asking for permission to hand the text to the jury. All I want Dr. Seaman to do is read that passage to the jurors.
J	Objection overruled. Permission granted.
P	Thank you, Your Honor. Dr. Seaman, please read the first full paragraph on page 367 to the ladies and gentlemen of the jury.

§ 10.09   EXCITED OR STARTLED UTTERANCES

[1]   THE DOCTRINE

In the last three sections, we analyzed documentary hearsay exceptions resting primarily on a showing of reliability. In each case, the showing is based on testimony describing the trustworthy manner in which the document was generated. The next four sections address other hearsay exceptions recognized principally because of an inference of reliability. In these exceptions, however, the inference of reliability has a different basis; each exception in this category is a variation of the ancient *res gestae* doctrine and rests on an inference of the declarant's sincerity. This category includes excited utterances, present sense impressions, declarations of bodily condition, and statements of mental condition.

The exception for excited utterances illustrates the common rationale of the exceptions in this category. A startling event occurs, an observer becomes excited, and the observer then makes a spontaneous statement about the event. The statement's spontaneity is the circumstantial guarantee of the declarant's sincerity. Federal Rule of Evidence 803(2) describes the doctrine in this fashion: "The following [is] not excluded by the rule against hearsay . . . . : A statement relating to a startling event or condition, made while the declarant was under the stress of excitement that it caused."

[2]   ELEMENTS OF THE FOUNDATION

The foundation for an excited utterance includes the following elements:

1. An event occurred. Many jurisdictions, including the federal courts, do not require any independent, corroborating evidence that the event occurred; these courts accept the declarant's assertion of the event's occurrence at face value. The Advisory Committee Note to Rule 803(2) describes that view as the "prevailing practice." A minority of jurisdictions requires independent evidence as part of the foundation. However, even in these jurisdictions, the quantum of required corroboration is usually slight. For example, if the declaration refers to an assault on the declarant and, at the time, the declarant's clothing was dirty and disheveled, the declarant's appearance might be sufficient corroboration that the assault occurred.

2. The event was startling, or at least stressful. This element is the objective guarantee of the statement's sincerity. The nature of the event was likely to inspire stress or nervous excitement.

3. The declarant had personal knowledge of the event. The declarant must have been a participant in or observer of the event. Again, the courts apply this element laxly. In some cases, the declarants have been unidentified bystanders. The courts have admitted the bystanders' excited statements so long as the time and place of the statement indicate that the bystander actually observed the event. Thus, if a person made a statement a few minutes after an accident and at the same intersection where the accident occurred, the court might well assume that the declarant observed the accident.

4. The declarant made a statement about the event. At the end of the foundational questioning, the proponent usually asks the witness whether the out-of-court declarant made a statement "about" the event. Some courts have relaxed this requirement. In *United States v. Napier*, 518 F.2d 316 (9th Cir. 1975), a kidnapping victim was injured and became unconscious. Weeks later she saw a newspaper article containing a photograph of the defendant. She immediately stated, "He killed me, he killed me." The court admitted the statement as evidence of the defendant's identity as the kidnapper. Some state courts are following suit and accepting so-called "re-excited" utterances.[6] This trend is

---

[6] Comment, *The Crying Game: How* Hunt v. State *Unnecessarily Expands the Definition of an Excited Utterance in Texas*, 56 BAYLOR L. REV. 723, 724–725 (2004) (under the state version of Rule 803(2), some

dubious, since the assertions relate to the earlier event and the time lapse can be so significant that there are grave doubts about the quality of the declarant's memory. Nevertheless, this trend is emerging.

5.   The declarant made the statement while he or she was in a state of nervous excitement. This element is the subjective guarantee of the statement's sincerity.

[3]   SAMPLE FOUNDATION

Our fact situation is a tort action arising from a collision at an intersection. The plaintiff was driving a blue car. The defendant was driving a red car. The issue is which car was facing and ran a red light. The plaintiff calls Ms. Reynolds as a witness. Ms. Reynolds has already identified herself. The plaintiff is the proponent.

P	WHERE were you on the afternoon of March 13, YR-3? (1)
W	I was in downtown Jefferson City at the intersection of Cedar Street and Sixth Avenue.
P	WHY were you there? (1)
W	I just happened to be walking my dog.
P	WHAT, if anything, happened at the intersection while you were there? (1), (2)
W	There was a collision.
P	HOW noisy was the collision? (1), (2)
W	It was an awful, shattering sound.
P	HOW many bystanders were there? (1)
W	I'd say that there were about 20 people in the immediate vicinity.
P	WHAT was their reaction to the collision? (2)
W	We were all shocked. It happened so fast, and the noise was so loud. And as soon as we looked, we could see that some people were injured and bleeding. It was just an awful sight.
P	WHO else besides yourself was in the crowd of bystanders? (3)
W	There were a number of people mingling around, but there was one guy in particular who stuck in my mind.
P	WHAT was his name? (3)
W	I never got his name.
P	WHAT did he look like?
W	He was a male Caucasian, maybe 30 or 35.
P	WHERE was he at the time of the collision? (3)

---

courts admit statements about crimes even when the statement was prompted by a later exciting event such as a movie depicting a similar crime).

W	Standing right next to me.
P	HOW was he facing? (3)
W	He was looking right into the intersection. He was evidently waiting for the light to change to walk across.
P	WHAT was his condition right after the collision? (5)
W	He was just like the rest of us—shocked and frightened.
P	WHAT was his facial expression? (5)
W	He had his mouth open—I guess he was dumbfounded at first.
P	WHAT was his tone of voice? (5)
W	He was shouting in a loud voice.
W	WHAT were his gestures? (5)
W	He was pointing at the wreck and gesturing wildly. He was very animated.
P	WHAT, if anything, did he say about the accident? (6)
O	Your Honor, I object to that question on the ground that it calls for hearsay.
P	Your Honor, may I be heard?
J	Yes.
P	Although the statement is hearsay, it pretty clearly falls within the excited utterance exception.
J	I agree. The objection will be overruled.
P	Ms. Reynolds, let me repeat the question. WHAT, if anything, did this man say about the accident? (4)
W	He said that the fellow in the red car had gone right through the red light and caused the collision.

§ 10.10 PRESENT SENSE IMPRESSIONS OR CONTEMPORANEOUS STATEMENTS

[1] THE DOCTRINE

The spontaneity of the statement is the basic rationale for the excited utterance exception. The statement's contemporaneity can also serve as proof of the statement's trustworthiness. Misrecollection is one of the most common causes of testimonial error, and the fact that the declarant makes the statement at roughly the same time the event occurs is some evidence of the statement's reliability. A growing number of courts accept the contemporaneous statement or present sense impression doctrine as a separate hearsay exception. The federal courts joined ranks with those courts when Congress enacted Federal Rule of Evidence 803(1): "The following [is] not excluded by the rule against hearsay . . . : A statement describing or explaining an event or condition, made while or immediately after the declarant perceived it."

The present sense impression doctrine differs from the excited utterance doctrine in three important respects. First, the timing requirement is more rigorous under the present sense impression doctrine. To qualify as a contemporaneous statement, the declaration must usually be made within minutes after the event. If the declarant is still excited or in pain, an excited utterance can be made hours after the event. Second, the event need not be startling to prompt a present sense impression statement. The guarantee of trustworthiness is contemporaneity rather than nervous spontaneity. Finally, in some jurisdictions such as California, contemporaneous statements are limited to statements describing or explaining the declarant's own conduct. A declarant may make an excited utterance about any startling, external event; but in a minority of jurisdictions, a present sense impression must relate to the declarant's own conduct. In these jurisdictions, the statement must describe, explain, or qualify the declarant's acts.

[2] ELEMENTS OF THE FOUNDATION

The foundation for present sense impression includes these elements:

1. An event occurred. As in the case of excited utterances, there is a split of authority whether the proponent must present independent, corroborating evidence that the event occurred.

2. The declarant had personal knowledge of the event.

3. The declarant made the statement during or very shortly after the event. While an acceptable delay under Rule 803(2) is often measured in terms of hours, under Rule 803(1) the delay is usually measured in terms of seconds or minutes.

4. The statement describes or explains the event. As previously stated, a minority of jurisdictions follows a more restrictive approach. These jurisdictions insist that the declaration relate to the declarant's own conduct. Even the jurisdictions that do not limit the scope of the exception in that respect construe the "describing or explaining" language in Rule 803(1) more narrowly than the "relating to" wording in Rule 803(2).

5. In some jurisdictions, the witness on the stand must have observed the same event—the percipient witness limitation. This element ensures that a witness is available to verify or contradict the declaration. The modern statutes codifying the present sense impression doctrine usually omit this requirement. For example, the text of Federal Rule of Evidence 803(1) makes no mention of this requirement. Moreover, Rule 804(b)(3) serves as part of the context for Rule 803(1); and unlike Rule 803(1), 804(b)(3)(B) includes an express requirement for corroboration. However, some commentators have pointed out that the Advisory Committee Note to Rule 803 cites many of the older writings about the present sense impression doctrine advocating the percipient witness limitation. Moreover, the Note contains a passage which seemingly assumes compliance with the limitation: "If the witness is not the declarant, he may be examined as to the circumstances as an aid in evaluating the statement." Given that Note, several courts enforce the percipient witness limitation; and while they stop short of embracing the limitation, other courts require corroboration.

See the discussion of element #1, *supra*.

[3] SAMPLE FOUNDATION

To illustrate this doctrine, we can use the same hypothetical as in § 10.08. In this variation of the hypothetical, the proponent deletes the questions designed to show the declarant's nervous excitement.

P   WHERE were you on the afternoon of March 13, YR-3? (1), (5)

W   I was in downtown Jefferson City at the intersection of Cedar Street and Sixth Avenue.

P   WHY were you there? (1), (5)

W   I just happened to be walking my dog there.

P   WHAT, if anything, happened at the intersection while you were there? (1), (5)

W   There was a collision.

P   HOW far were you from the collision when it occurred? (1), (5)

W   I was about 30 feet from the point of impact. That's just a rough estimate.

P   HOW were you facing? (1), (5)

W   I was waiting for the light to change, so I was looking right into the intersection.

P   HOW clear was your line of sight to the collision? (1), (5)

W   It was clear. I don't think there were any cars obstructing my view.

          HOW much of the collision did you see? (1), (5)

W   Just about the whole thing. I saw the cars approaching the intersection and actually collide.

P   HOW many other bystanders were there? (2)

W   I'd say that there were about 20 people in the immediate vicinity.

P   WHO were the bystanders? (2)

W   I didn't know any by name, but one guy in particular stuck in my mind.

P   WHAT did he look like? (2)

W   He was a male African-American gentleman, maybe 30 or 35.

P   WHERE was he at the time of the collision? (2)

W   He was standing right next to me.

P   HOW was he facing? (2)

W   He was looking right into the intersection. He was evidently waiting for the light to change to walk across.

P   WHAT did he do after the collision? (3)

W	He was pointing to the wreck, and we talked about the collision.
P	WHEN did you and this bystander talk about the collision? (3)
W	Right after it.
P	HOW many minutes elapsed between the collision and your discussion of the collision with this bystander? (3)
W	It may have taken us a minute or two to get over the shock of what we had witnessed, but it was no longer than that.
P	WHAT, if anything, did this bystander say about the accident? (4)
O	Your Honor, I object to that question on the ground that it calls for hearsay.
P	Your Honor, may I be heard?
J	Yes.
P	I concede that the question calls for hearsay, but the record shows that any statement by the bystander qualifies as a present sense impression or contemporaneous statement.

In most jurisdictions:

J	The objection will be overruled.
P	Ms. Reynolds, let me repeat the question. WHAT, if anything, did this bystander say about the accident? (4)
W	He said that the fellow in the red car had gone right through the red light and caused the collision.

In the minority of jurisdictions restricting present sense impressions to statements describing the declarant's own conduct:

O	It's true that the statement was roughly contemporaneous with the event. However, as Your Honor knows, this jurisdiction limits present sense impressions to statements describing the declarant's own conduct. The bystander was describing an external event, the collision, rather than his own conduct.
J	Objection sustained.

§ 10.11 DECLARATIONS OF STATE OF MIND OR EMOTION

[1] OFFERED TO PROVE STATE OF MIND OR EMOTION

One of the most difficult things for a trial attorney to prove is a person's state of mind. The attorney must usually rely on circumstantial proof such as conduct that evidences a certain state of mind. However, sometimes a person openly asserts his or her state of mind. Because of the difficulty of proving state of mind, the courts have been especially eager to admit any evidently sincere declarations of state of mind or emotion. These declarations often give us the best insight into the declarant's state of mind or emotion. Thus, the courts have developed a general rule that these declarations are admissible; if a person declares his or her then existing state of mind or emotion, the declaration is admissible to prove the existence of that state of mind or emotion. Federal Rule of Evidence 803(3) provides: "The following [is] not excluded by the rule against hearsay . . . : A statement of the declarant's then existing state of mind (such as motive, intent, or plan) or emotional . . . condition (such as mental feeling)."

Ideally, the declarant will make the statement at the pivotal time under the substantive law. For example, under Real Property law, the grantor must have the intent to pass title when handing the deed to the grantee. If at the very instant of handing the deed to the grantee, the grantor announces the intent to pass title, the statement is certainly admissible. What if the grantor makes such a statement shortly before or shortly after the manual delivery of the deed? The courts still admit the statement on the theory of continuity of state of mind; there are no intervening events that would plausibly change the person's frame of mind, and the time lapse between the statement and the critical event is so short that we may reasonably assume that the declarant's state of mind was the same at both times.

The foundation for this doctrine is simple. The making of the statement by the declarant is an event. The proponent need establish only the normal foundation for an event:

1. Where the statement was made.

2. When the statement was made. The declarant must make the statement at or near the pivotal time under the substantive law.

3. Who was present.

4. Who made the statement.

5. The substantive content of the statement.

Our fact situation is a quiet title action. The plaintiff, Ms. Sheila Morris, has brought suit against the defendant, Ms. Marilyn Winters. Ms. Morris claims title from the original titleholder, Mr. Forest Morris, her grandfather. She claims that on December 25, YR-4, her grandfather gave her a deed to the property as a Christmas present. The plaintiff calls Mr. Thomas Morris, her brother, as a witness. The plaintiff is the proponent.

P	WHERE were you on December 25, YR-4? (1), (2)
W	I was at our family Christmas party at Camden.
P	WHO else was there? (3)
W	All the close relatives, including Grandfather and my sister, Sheila.
P	WHAT, if anything, unusual happened during the party?
W	As an unexpected Christmas gift, Grandfather handed Sheila a deed to our land in Vermont.
P	WHAT, if anything, did he do when he handed her the deed? (4)
W	Well, he did say something.
P	WHAT did he say? (5)
W	He said that he wanted her to have the land because, ever since she was

a little girl, she had loved to vacation there.

In the next variation of the hypothetical, the grantor makes the statement shortly before delivery of the deed.

P	WHERE were you on December 25th, YR-4? (1), (2)
W	I was at our family Christmas party at Camden.
P	WHO else was there? (3)
W	All the close relatives, including Grandfather and my sister, Sheila.
P	WHAT, if anything, unusual happened during the party?
W	As an unexpected Christmas gift, Grandfather handed Sheila a deed to our land in Vermont.
P	WHAT, if anything, did he say about the deed during the party? (5)
O	Objection, Your Honor. That question calls for hearsay.
P	Your Honor, may we approach the bench?
J	Yes.
P	Your Honor, I offer to prove that the witness will say the Grandfather said he wanted Sheila to have the land. The witness will also testify the Grandfather made this statement only an hour before handing the deed to Sheila. The time lapse is so short that we may assume that the Grandfather's state of mind was the same at both times. At the party there were no intervening events that could have changed his state of mind.
J	The objection will be overruled.
P	Mr. Morris, let me repeat the question. WHAT, if anything, did your Grandfather say about the deed during the party? (5)
W	He said he wanted Sheila to have the land because, ever since she was a little girl, she had loved to vacation there.
P	WHEN did your Grandfather say that? (4)
W	A little while before he handed the deed to her.
P	Specifically, HOW many minutes or hours before he handed her the deed? (4)
W	About an hour—maybe a little less.

[2] OFFERED TO PROVE SUBSEQUENT CONDUCT

In § 10.10[1], we use declarations of state of mind when state of mind itself is in issue. There is another use for state of mind declarations. Suppose that the declaration is a statement of present plan, intention, or design: "I plan to," "I intend to," or "I am going to." These declarations indicate that the declarant currently plans to engage in subsequent conduct. Moreover, the fact that the declarant expressed that intent increases the probability that the declarant subsequently performed the planned act.

Federal Rule of Evidence 803(3) also sanctions this use of state of mind declarations; it expressly authorizes the admission of statements of "intent, . . . or plan."

The foundation is the same as in § 10.10[1]:

1. Where the statement was made.

2. When the statement was made.

3. Who was present.

4. Who made the statement.

5. The substantive content of the statement.

The fact situation is a burglary prosecution. The government alleges that the accused, Mr. Michael Waylen, burglarized a drug store in Tulsa on August 17, YR-3. The defendant has raised an alibi defense. The defendant testified that he was with his girlfriend in Oklahoma City on the day of the burglary. His girlfriend testified to the same effect. Now the defendant calls Mr. John Farmer as a witness. Mr. Farmer has already identified himself. The defendant is the proponent:

P	Mr. Farmer, WHERE were you on the evening of August 15, YR-3? (1), (2)
W	I was at a party at a friend's here in Tulsa.
P	WHO else was at the party?
W	A lot of people, including the accused, Michael Waylen.
P	WHERE is the accused now? (3)
W	He's in the courtroom.
P	Specifically, WHERE in the courtroom? (3)
W	He's sitting at that table.
P	HOW is he dressed? (3)
W	He's wearing a gray sweater and black pants.
P	Your Honor, please let the record reflect that the witness has identified the accused.
J	It will so reflect.
P	Mr. Farmer, WHAT happened during the party? (4)
W	It was just a quiet party. I drank a little and talked with some friends.
P	WHOM did you talk with? (4)
W	I had a nice long talk with Michael, the accused. We sat together near a coffee table.
P	WHAT did you talk about? (5)
W	A lot of things, especially his plans for the future.
P	WHAT, if anything, did the accused say about his immediate plans? (5)

O   Your Honor, I object to that last question on the ground that it calls for self-serving hearsay.

P   Your Honor, may we approach the bench to be heard?

J   Yes.

P   Your Honor, I offer to prove that the witness will testify that the accused said he intended to visit his girlfriend in Oklahoma City the weekend of the alleged crime. The accused's statement falls within the hearsay exception for declarations of present state of mind.

J   The objection will be overruled. You may proceed.

P   WHAT, if anything, did the accused say about his immediate plans? (5)

W   He said that that weekend he was going to visit his girlfriend, Norma, in Oklahoma City.

P   WHICH weekend was he referring to? (5)

W   He mentioned the weekend of August 17 and 18.

Assume that a murder victim made a statement that she presently intended to meet the accused at a particular location. Later the victim's body is found at that location. Under this exception, the victim's statement is certainly admissible to prove that she carried out her plan and went to that location. Is the statement also admissible as evidence that the accused met her at that location? The courts have long divided over that question. There is a strong argument that the evidence is inadmissible for that purpose. The courts ordinarily do not allow one witness to directly speculate as to another person's state of mind;[7] without more facts, the judge would have barred the declarant from testifying on the witness stand that the accused shared her plan and intention,[8] If the jurisdiction holds that the statement is inadmissible for that purpose, the judge must either redact the reference to the accused or give the jury a limiting instruction about the proper use of the statement. In the limiting instruction, the judge would tell the jury that although they could treat the statement as the basis for an inference as to the declarant's own later conduct, they could not use the statement as evidence of the accused's conduct. Thus, in closing argument the prosecutor could employ the statement as evidence that the declarant went to the location she mentioned, but the prosecutor could not utilize the statement as evidence that the accused went to that location.

---

[7] However, as § 9.02[2] points out, Rule 701 permits a lay witness to opine about a third party's "apparent" or "seeming" state of mind if the opinion is based on the witness's observation of the third party's demeanor.

[8] If the accused stated their plan to the declarant, the accused's statement would fall within 803(3). However, at trial it may be extremely difficult for the proponent to prove that the accused made such a statement.

§ 10.12 DECLARATIONS OF BODILY CONDITION

[1] PRESENT BODILY CONDITION

The courts are almost as willing to admit evidently sincere statements of bodily condition as they are to admit statements of mental condition. Federal Rule of Evidence 803(3) specifically authorizes the admission of statements of "sensory . . . or physical condition (such as . . . pain . . . or bodily health)." Ordinarily, if a declarant proclaims his or her present bodily sensation or condition, the declaration is admissible. However, many courts exclude statements made to a physician who was consulted solely to qualify the physician to testify at trial.

The foundation includes these elements:

1. Where the statement was made.

2. When the statement was made.

3. Who was present.

4. Who made the statement.

5. Whom the statement was made to. The statement can be made to a lay person or a physician. The traditional, common-law view is that the statement may not be made to a physician consulted solely for purposes of trial testimony. However, the Federal Rules abandon that view.

6. The substantive content of the statement. The statement must refer to the person's present bodily condition.

This fact situation will illustrate the doctrine. The plaintiff, Ms. Joan Gillette, brings a product liability action against Miller Pharmaceuticals. The plaintiff alleges that the defendant sold her defective medication and that the medication caused her serious internal injuries. Her complaint prayed for $60,000 for pain and suffering. At the trial, she called Mr. Leonard Wright as a witness. Mr. Wright identifies himself and states that he is a physician. The plaintiff is the proponent.

P	Doctor Wright, WHERE were you on the afternoon of January 28, YR-3? (1), (2)
W	In my office.
P	WHO else was there? (3)
W	The plaintiff, Ms. Gillette.
P	WHERE is the plaintiff now? (3)
W	In this courtroom.
P	Specifically, WHERE in the courtroom? (3)
W	She's sitting at that table to your right.
P	HOW is she dressed? (3)
W	She's wearing a white blouse and a green skirt.
P	Your Honor, please let the record reflect that the witness identified the plaintiff.

J	It will so reflect.
P	WHAT happened while the plaintiff was at your office? (3)
W	I examined her.
P	WHAT, if anything, did she say to you about her physical condition during the examination? (4), (5), (6)
O	Your Honor, I object to that question on the ground that it calls for hearsay.
P	Your Honor, may we approach the bench?
J	Yes.
P	I concede that the question calls for hearsay. However, I offer to prove that the witness will testify that the plaintiff said she was then in terrible pain. That statement qualifies as a declaration of present bodily condition.
O	Your Honor, I request permission to take the witness on voir dire before you rule on my objection.
J	Permission granted.
O	Doctor Wright, ISN'T IT TRUE THAT you didn't give the plaintiff any medicine during this examination?
W	Yes.
O	ISN'T IT A FACT THAT the plaintiff never asked you for medication? (5)
W	Yes.
O	ISN'T IT TRUE THAT you never prescribed any treatment for her? (5)
W	Yes.
O	AND ISN'T IT CORRECT THAT the plaintiff told you that she was consulting you so that you could testify at this trial? (5)
W	Yes.
O	Your Honor, I renew my objection. It's clear that Dr. Wright is a physician consulted solely for purposes of testimony. The hearsay exception is inapplicable.
J	The objection will be sustained.

The above ruling would be proper under the traditional, common-law rule forbidding the receipt of statements to physicians consulted solely for purposes of trial preparation. However, as previously stated, that ruling would be erroneous under the Federal Rules.

[2] PAST BODILY CONDITION

A majority of jurisdictions now admit statements of past bodily condition as substantive proof in limited circumstances. The Federal Rules commit the federal courts to this view. Federal Rule of Evidence 803(4) states: "The following [is] not excluded by the rule against hearsay . . . : A statement that: (A) is made for—and is reasonably pertinent to—medical diagnosis or treatment; and (B) describes medical history; past or present symptoms or sensations; their inception; or their general cause." Thus, the rule requires a showing of both the declarant's subjective medical motivation and the objective pertinence of the declaration to medical diagnosis or treatment.

In the common-law jurisdictions admitting declarations of past bodily condition, the foundation usually includes these elements:

1. The declarant made the statement to a proper addressee. Many jurisdictions limit this exception to statements made to physicians. The Federal Rules do not contain that limitation. The Advisory Committee's Note to Rule 803 states that the exception encompasses statements made to "hospital attendants, ambulance drivers, or even members of the family." Such statements are admissible so long as the other foundational elements are satisfied—for instance, when the declarant makes a statement to a hospital attendant to be relayed to a treating physician.

2. The declarant made the statement for a medical motive. This element relates to the declarant's subjective motivation for making the statement. At common law, most jurisdictions subscribing to this exception require that the declarant have a significant treatment motive; it is insufficient if the declarant is consulting a physician to testify at trial. The Federal Rules opt for a more liberal view. The Rules permit the statement's admission if the declarant sought "medical diagnosis *or* treatment."[9] Given the alternative wording of the rule, a diagnosis for purpose of trial is sufficient. The Advisory Committee Note expressly repudiates the "[c]onventional doctrine . . . exclud(ing) from the hearsay exception, as not within its guarantee of truthfulness, statements to a physician consulted only for the purpose of enabling him to testify." In most cases, the declarant entertaining the medical motive is the potential patient. However, in a number of cases in which the potential patient was unconscious or very seriously injured, the courts have treated family members or even bystanders as proper declarants so long as their evident motive was to provide information relevant to the treatment of the potential patient.

3. The subject-matter of the statement was proper. Most jurisdictions recognizing the exception limit its scope to statements of past bodily condition. Once again, the Federal Rules adopt a broader view. Rule 803(4) also authorizes the admission of statements of the "inception . . . or general cause" of a physical condition. The Advisory Committee's Note contains this explanatory language: "Statements as to fault would not ordinarily qualify under this latter language. Thus a patient's statement that he was struck by an automobile would qualify but not his statement that the car was driven through a red light." Hence, a general reference to an external cause is admissible, but a statement specifically attributing fault to a person will probably be excluded.

---

[9] Emphasis added.

4. The content of the statement was objectively pertinent to medical diagnosis or
    treatment. Rule 803(4) uses the language, "reasonably pertinent." As previ-
    ously stated, the declarant's subjective motivation is not only relevant but also
    a requirement. See element #2. However, the rule demands a further circum-
    stantial guarantee of reliability. From a hypothetical reasonable doctor's
    perspective, the information disclosed in the statement must be pertinent to
    diagnosis or treatment.

Our fact situation is a personal injury action. The plaintiff, Ms. Norton, alleges that
she sustained severe internal injuries after drinking some of the defendant's medicine.
The defendant is Shavers Drug Company. The plaintiff wants to introduce a hospital
record. The record contains the following entry in section #15 Medical History: "The
patient stated she experienced intense pain after drinking from a bottle of cough
medicine." The plaintiff calls Mr. Florence as a witness. Mr. Florence identifies himself,
states that he is University Hospital's records librarian, and lays a proper business entry
foundation for the hospital record itself. The exhibit has already been marked for
identification as plaintiff's exhibit number four. The plaintiff is the proponent.

P	Now, doctor, permit me to direct your attention to this section on exhibit #4 for identification, the section labeled #15. WHAT is that section?
W	That's the case history part of the patient's record.
P	WHAT is case history?
W	The patient's past medical history.
P	WHO took this medical history? (1)
W	Dr. Morrell, one of our internists.
P	HOW do you know he took it? (1)
W	I recognize his signature and handwriting style.
P	WHO normally takes the history? (1)
W	The physician who's the intern.
P	WHEN does the intern ordinarily take the history from the patient? (2)
W	As soon as the patient arrives at the first processing station.
P	WHY does the intern take the history? (2), (4)
W	It's often critical to diagnosis and treatment. The case history helps you make a much more informed evaluation of the patient's condition.
P	WHAT, if anything, does the intern usually tell the patient about the purpose of taking the case history? (2)
W	Some patients are very resentful of prying, and we always tell them that we are taking the history to give them better treatment. We tell them we need to know everything about their medical past.
P	Now, doctor, without disclosing to the jury the precise entry on the

exhibit, WHY would this particular entry have been included in the patient's case history? (2), (4)

W   Well, it describes how the patient suffered the injuries. The treating doctor has to have that sort of data to do a professional, competent job.

P   Your Honor, I now offer plaintiff's exhibit number four for identification into evidence as plaintiff's exhibit number four.

O   Your Honor, I object to the introduction of the exhibit on the ground that it is hearsay. In fact, it is double hearsay.

P   Your Honor, may we approach the bench?

J   Yes.

P   Your Honor, even double hearsay is admissible if each statement falls within a hearsay exception. The first statement, the hospital record itself, qualifies as a business entry.

J   Are we in agreement on that point?

O   Yes, Your Honor. So far so good.

P   The second statement, of course, is my client's statement reflected in section #15 of the report. I feel that it qualifies as a statement of past bodily condition. My client had a subjective motivation to be truthful; my client made the statement to a physician for a treatment motive. Moreover, as Mr. Florence's testimony indicates, this information was objectively pertinent to diagnosis or treatment. In this jurisdiction, in such circumstances statements of past condition and external cause are admissible.

J   The objection will be overruled, and the exhibit will be received.

P   Doctor Florence, would you please read section #15 to the jury?

W   It reads: "The patient stated she experienced intense pain after drinking from a bottle of cough medicine." (3)

[3]   EXTERNAL CAUSE OR SOURCE

As the preceding subsection pointed out, Federal Rule of Evidence 803(4) permits the admission of statements describing the "inception . . . or general cause" of the physical condition. The drafters undoubtedly contemplated that this exception would be used primarily in civil cases. However, numerous jurisdictions have utilized the exception in criminal cases as well. In particular, many courts have extended the exception in child abuse prosecutions to justify admitting the child's pretrial statement identifying the abuser. In *White v. Illinois*, 502 U.S. 346, 112 S. Ct. 736, 116 L. Ed. 2d 848 (1992), the Supreme Court rejected a confrontation clause challenge to the extension.

Although there is a large body of case law approving this application of the exception, several courts have stated that the exception must be used with "great caution." For that reason, the proponent must ensure that he or she lays a satisfactory foundation. A complete foundation would include these elements:

1. The person who made the statement was a proper declarant. In the typical case, the declarant is the patient. However, if the patient is unconscious or unavailable, a relative, friend, or even a Good Samaritan bystander may be the declarant who provides the information to the medical personnel.

2. The declarant made the statement to a proper addressee. All courts agree that physicians (including psychiatrists) and clinical psychologists are proper addressees. Some courts also admit statements made to social workers. However, most courts would likely balk at invoking this exception to uphold the admission of a statement made to a high school guidance counselor.

3. The declarant knew that the person they were speaking with was a proper addressee. In one case, the court excluded the statement for the stated reason that there was no foundational showing that the declarant child knew that the addressee was a physician. The addressee's statements to the child, identifying the addressee's occupation, would be admissible for the nonhearsay purpose under Rule 801(c)(2); the statements are relevant as mental input to show their effect on the child's state of mind, namely, placing the child on notice of the addressee's occupation.

4. The declarant consulted the physician for a medical motive, either treatment or diagnosis. This subjective motivation indicates that the declarant was being truthful. As in the case of element #2, the addressee's statements to the child, identifying the purpose of the meeting, are admissible for a nonhearsay purpose under Rule 801(c)(2). Moreover, the child's statements, declaring his or her purpose in seeking assistance, qualify for admission under Rule 803(3).

5. The particular statement offered was medically relevant in an objective sense. The language of Rule 803(4) confines the scope of the exception to statements "reasonably pertinent to . . . medical diagnosis or treatment." The addressee should explain why the particular detail in question could affect either the diagnosis or treatment. In a child abuse prosecution, the detail of the perpetrator's identity arguably possesses both diagnostic and therapeutic relevance. If the child has been victimized by a family member rather than a complete stranger, the symptomatology will be somewhat different. Moreover, when the abuser is a family member, the therapy can differ radically; effective treatment may necessitate the child's removal from the home environment.

6. The declarant, for example a child, realized that the particular statement was medically relevant. In his lead opinion in *White*, Chief Justice Rehnquist focused on the inference of sincerity which arises from the fact that "the declarant knows that a false statement can cause misdiagnosis or mistreatment." One of the leading treatises took the position that the statement should be admissible under Rule 803(4) so long as this foundational element is present even if "the . . . physician viewed the matter as irrelevant." 4 DAVID W. LOUISELL & CHRISTOPHER B. MUELLER, FEDERAL EVIDENCE § 444, at 598

(1980). The authors of the successor text also argue that the subjective understanding of the speaker should be determinative. CHRISTOPHER B. MUELLER, LAIRD C. KIRKPATRICK & LIESA RICHTER, EVIDENCE § 8:42, at 911 (6th ed. 2018). However, some courts take a contrary view and contend that the language of restyled Rule 803(4)(A) appears to resolve the issue; according to the revised wording, the statement must both be "made for . . . medical diagnosis or treatment" "and" be "reasonably pertinent to . . . medical diagnosis or treatment." As in the case of elements #2 and #3, the addressee's statements to the child are admissible nonhearsay under Rule 801(c)(2); and the child's statements reflecting the realization can qualify for admission under Rule 803(3).

The fact situation is a child abuse prosecution. The accused is Paul Leslie. The indictment alleges that the accused sexually abused his minor son Walter. The prosecution calls Dr. Kevin Amar as its next witness.

P	Please state your full name and spell your last name for the record.
W	My name is Kevin Amar. My surname is spelled A-M-A-R.
P	Mr. Amar, WHERE do you live?
W	I live right here in Colorado Springs.
P	WHAT is your occupation? (2)
W	I am a licensed physician and psychiatrist in this state.
P	WHAT is your educational background? (2)
W	I received my M.D. degree from the University of Texas. I then did my internship at U.S.C. Medical Center. I next spent three years as a resident in psychiatry in New York. I have specialized in pediatric psychiatry.
P	WHERE were you on the afternoon of November 12th of last year?
W	I was in my office in Colorado Springs.
P	WHAT happened that afternoon at your office? (1)
W	That was the afternoon when the social worker, Ms. Lucey, brought Walter Leslie by my office.
P	WHERE is Walter right now? (1)
W	He's in the courtroom. He's sitting in the first row of the spectators' area of the courtroom.
P	HOW is he dressed? (1)
W	He's wearing a blue suit, white shirt, and green tie.
P	Your Honor, please let the record reflect that the witness has identified Walter Leslie, the alleged victim in this case. (1)
J	The record will so reflect.
P	Doctor Amar, when Walter arrived, HOW did you identify yourself to him? (3)

W	I told him that I was Doctor Amar and that I was going to talk to him to see if I could help him.
P	During the balance of this meeting, HOW did he refer to you? (3)
W	He called me either "Doctor Amar" or "Doctor."
P	After you identified yourself, WHAT did you tell him about the purpose of your interview with him? (4)
W	I told him that I wanted to talk to him to see if I could help him. I told him that I heard that he was having some emotional problems, and I wanted to see if I could help him overcome those problems.
P	WHAT, if anything, did he say about his reason for coming to see you? (4)
W	He said that Ms. Lucey had told him that I was a doctor and he had agreed to visit me to obtain some medical advice about his problems.

(*During this part of the direct examination, the prosecutor would elicit Walter's statements generally describing both his emotional problems and the abuse which caused the problems. The direct examination continues.*)

P	WHAT, if anything, did you ask Walter about the identity of the person who abused him? (5)
W	I asked him point-blank who did it.
P	WHY did you do that? (5)
W	I needed to know that for both diagnostic and therapeutic purposes.
P	Please be more specific. HOW could the identity of the abuser affect your diagnosis in Walter's case? (5)
W	Well, to confirm a diagnosis, you need to review the case history to see if it contains an indication of symptoms appropriate for that diagnosis. When the abuser is a family member—someone the child has trusted and then betrayed the child—you expect somewhat different symptoms than those you encounter when the child is abused by a stranger. In the latter case, abuse by a stranger, you may find a phobia about leaving the house and going out into public. In the former case, abuse by a family member, you'll often have a very different phobia about remaining in the home.
P	And HOW might the identity of the abuser affect the treatment prescribed in Walter's case? (5)
W	If the abuser is a family member likely to remain in the household, you have to consider the drastic step of having the child removed from the home environment and at least temporarily placed in foster care. That's a big step, since it's so disruptive of the family unit; and you ordinarily wouldn't recommend that as part of the treatment except in cases of intrafamily abuse.

P	When you asked Walter about the identity of the abuser, WHAT did you tell him about your reason for wanting to know that? (6)
W	That's such a delicate subject that you want to try to put the patient at ease as much as possible. Before I put the question to Walter, I explained that my medical advice could depend on who had abused him. I said that I needed that particular information. In very general terms, I told him that I'd make one type of recommendation if the person were a stranger and a different recommendation if the person were a friend or family member.
P	WHAT, if anything, did Walter say after you explained that? (6)
W	He said that he understood and that he'd tell me the truth about that just as he'd told me the truth about everything else.
P	Doctor Amar, WHO did Walter name as the person who had been abusing him?
W	His father, Paul Leslie.
P	To the best of your recollection, WHAT were Walter's exact words?
W	He began to sob, but he clearly said, "My daddy, Paul."

PART E.   Hearsay Exceptions Based on a Showing of Unavailability

§ 10.13   IN GENERAL

The preceding seven sections analyze hearsay exceptions recognized primarily because of an inference of the reliability of the hearsay statement. Other exceptions, though, depend to a greater degree for their recognition on a showing of necessity for resorting to the hearsay. These exceptions require proof of the declarant's unavailability at the time of trial. The following section discusses the test for unavailability in federal practice. §§ 10.14 through 10.16 then describe three hearsay exceptions requiring proof of unavailability as part of their foundation.

§ 10.14   THE UNAVAILABILITY OF THE DECLARANT AT TRIAL

[1]   AT COMMON LAW AND BY STATUTE

At common law, the exceptions requiring proof of unavailability emerged at different times and developed varying tests for unavailability. Some exceptions demanded proof of the declarant's death, while others were satisfied by proof that the declarant was beyond the reach of compulsory process. The drafters of the Federal Rules elected to prescribe a single, uniform definition of unavailability. Federal Rule of Evidence 804(a) sets out that definition:

A declarant is considered to be unavailable as a witness if the declarant:

(1)   is exempted from testifying about the subject matter of the declarant's statement because the court rules that a privilege applies;

(2)   refuses to testify about the subject matter despite a court order to do so;

(3)   testifies to not remembering the subject matter;

    (4)   cannot be present or testify at the trial or hearing because of death or a then-existing infirmity, physical illness, or mental illness; or

    (5)   is absent from the trial or hearing and the statement's proponent has not been able, by process or other reasonable means, to procure:

        (A)   the declarant's attendance, in the case of a hearsay exception under Rule 804(b)(1) or (6); or

        (B)   the declarant's attendance or testimony, in the case of a hearsay exception under Rule 804(b)(2), (3), or (4).

But this subdivision (a) does not apply if the statement's proponent procured or wrongfully caused the declarant's unavailability as a witness in order to prevent the declarant from attending or testifying.

Under Rule 804(a), there are numerous methods of demonstrating the prior witness's unavailability. In the first three subsections of Rule 804(a), the witness is technically unavailable but actually present at trial (hearing #2). For example, under Rule 804(a)(1), the witness is deemed unavailable if the witness "is exempted from testifying about the subject matter of the declarant's statement because the court rules that a privilege applies." The prior witness from hearing #1 actually takes the stand in hearing #2, but the witness properly refuses to testify on the ground of privilege. Under Rule 804(a)(2), the witness is considered unavailable if he or she "refuses to testify about the subject matter despite a court order to do so." Here the witness does not have a legitimate ground for refusing to answer; but if the witness refuses to answer notwithstanding a court order to answer, as a practical matter the witness is unavailable. Under Rule 804(a)(3), the witness is unavailable if the witness "testifies to not remembering the subject matter."[10] Here too the witness is physically present, but as a practical matter the witness's testimony is unavailable. When the proponent is relying on one of these three grounds to show unavailability, the proponent need ensure only that the witness's refusal or failure to recall is reflected on the record. The proponent should ask point blank about the topic of the prior testimony: "WHAT was the color of the defendant's car?" If the witness responds "I refuse to answer" or "I cannot remember," there is a sufficient showing of unavailability.

Rule 804(a)(4) declares that the prior witness is unavailable when the witness "cannot be present to testify at the trial or hearing because of death or a then-existing infirmity, physical illness, or mental illness." If the witness is now dead, the proponent may introduce a properly attested death certificate. The death certificate qualifies as an official record. If the witness is ill, under Rule 104(a), the jurisdiction may permit the proponent to prove the illness by a physician's affidavit, declaration, or letter. (Remember that in determining the existence of preliminary facts under Rule 104(a), the trial judge need not follow the technical exclusionary rules such as hearsay.) Otherwise the proponent may have to call the physician at hearing #2 to prove the illness of the prior witness. The proponent would have to lay the expert opinion

---

[10] Note that the judge need not find that the witness in fact cannot remember. According to the plain wording of the rule, it is sufficient the witness "testifies" to an inability to recall.

testimony foundation outlined in § 9.03 of Chapter 9: the physician's qualifications, the physician's methodology or major premise, the case-specific basis of the expert's opinion or minor premise, the ultimate opinion that the former witness is now too ill to appear and testify, and the expert's explanation of the opinion.

Finally, Rule 804(a)(5) announces that the former witness is considered unavailable if the witness "is absent from the trial or hearing and the statement's proponent has not been able, by process or other reasonable means, to procure" the witness's attendance or, under Rules 804(b)(2)–(4), the witness's attendance or testimony. In the case of the latter exceptions, the proponent must explore the possibility of deposing the declarant before the trial or hearing; even if the proponent cannot secure the witness's physical "attendance," a deposition hearing would enable to obtain the witness's "testimony" under oath." This subsection usually comes into play in two situations.

The first situation is the case in which the proponent simply cannot locate the former witness. The proponent could use a process server's testimony to establish the former witness's unavailability.

P	WHAT is your name?
W	Michelle Senet.
P	WHERE do you live?
W	At 1440 Alsworth Street here in Alexandria.
P	HOW long have you lived there?
W	For the past five years.
P	WHAT is your occupation?
W	I am a process server.
P	WHERE do you work?
W	I work for the Speedy Process Service Company downtown.
P	HOW long have you worked there?
W	Three years.
P	HOW long have you been a process server?
W	Three years.
P	Ms. Senet, WHERE were you on the morning of January 17th of this year?
W	I stopped by your office.
P	WHY did you visit my office?
W	You had phoned and asked me to pick up a subpoena.
P	WHO was the subpoena for?
W	John Milton.
P	WHAT was his address?

W	Both the subpoena and the telephone directory listed his address as 40 Oxford Street, Apartment 201.
P	WHAT did you do after you picked up the subpoena?
W	I went directly to the address given.
P	WHAT happened when you arrived there?
W	I inquired whether he still lived there.
P	WHAT was the result of your inquiry?
O	Your Honor, I object to that question on the ground that it calls for hearsay.
P	Your Honor, may we approach the bench?
J	Yes.
P	Your Honor, I offer to prove that this witness will testify that the manager said Mr. Milton had moved. I want to use the testimony for a nonhearsay purpose under Rule 801(c)(2), its effect on the process server's state of mind. The issue is whether the process server acted reasonably and diligently. We have to judge her diligence in light of the information about Mr. Milton she was given by other persons such as the apartment manager.
J	The objection will be overruled.
P	Ms. Senet, let me repeat the question. WHAT was the result of your inquiry at Mr. Milton's apartment?
W	The manager said he had moved.
P	WHAT was Mr. Milton's new address?
W	Unfortunately, he did not leave a forwarding address.
P	WHAT did you do then?
W	Over the next few days I contacted other companies and agencies that might have Milton's new address.
P	WHICH companies and agencies did you contact?
W	To list just some, I talked to people at the telephone company, the gas company, the electricity company, and the welfare department.
P	WHAT was the result of your contact with these companies and agencies?
W	It was negative. None of them knew where I could locate Mr. Milton.
P	HOW many hours did you spend talking to people at these companies and agencies?
W	Over the period of days, I'd estimate I spent at least 10 full hours trying to hunt him down.
P	Ms. Senet, WHERE is Mr. Milton now?

W   I'm afraid that I have no idea.

The second situation is the case in which the former witness is in another jurisdiction. In some states, it is sufficient to show that the former witness is now beyond the reach of compulsory process. In the case of dying declarations and declarations against interest, the proponent must not only show that there was no compulsory process to compel the declarant's attendance at trial, the proponent must also show that he or she could not depose the deponent before trial. At hearing #2, the judge can, of course, take notice of the constitutional and statutory provisions setting out the territorial limits of the court's compulsory process.[11] In other states, the proponent must show not only that the former witness is now beyond the reach of compulsory process, the proponent must also show that the proponent unsuccessfully attempted to persuade the former witness to voluntarily attend hearing #2 or that any attempt would probably be futile. Federal Rule 804(a)(5) expressly requires the proponent to attempt to use "other reasonable means."[12]

Suppose that Mr. Watson has sued Ms. Belson for personal injuries resulting from a traffic accident. At the first trial of the case, Mr. Green testified on behalf of the plaintiff. Mr. Green was a passing acquaintance of the plaintiff and happened to be in the plaintiff's car at the time of the accident. The trial resulted in a judgment for plaintiff, but the defendant appealed. After the trial, Mr. Green moved from California to Minnesota. On appeal, the court reversed the judgment and remanded for a second trial. At trial #2, the plaintiff wants to use Mr. Green's former testimony. The plaintiff himself takes the stand to establish Mr. Green's unavailability.

P   WHO were your witnesses at the first trial in this case?

W   Myself, Officer Halston, and a Mr. Ted Green.

P   WHERE does Mr. Green live now?

W   In St. Paul, Minnesota.

P   HOW do you know that?

W   For one thing, I've received letters from him postmarked St. Paul, Minnesota.

P   HOW do you know the letters came from Mr. Green?

W   I recognized his handwriting.

P   HOW did you recognize his handwriting?

W   I'm familiar with it. We worked together for several years, and I saw his handwriting on numerous occasions.

---

[11] As previously pointed out, strictly speaking the judicial notice provision, Rule 201(a), applies only to factual matters. However, courts sometimes loosely use the expression "judicial notice" when they informally notice legal matters such as statutes and administrative regulations.

[12] Contrast the unavailability standard prescribed by Rule 1004(b) for the best evidence rule. Under that provision, it is sufficient that "an original cannot be obtained by any available judicial process." Unlike Rule 804(a)(5), 1004(b) does not require the proponent to also resort to "other reasonable means."

P	WHY else do you think he now lives in Minnesota?
W	I tried to contact him by telephone. I went through the operator in St. Paul and eventually reached him.
P	HOW do you know you were speaking with Mr. Green?
W	I recognized his voice just as I recognized his handwriting.
P	WHERE is Mr. Green today?
W	I don't know for sure.
P	WHERE was he when you last spoke with him?
W	In St. Paul.
P	WHY isn't he here?
W	He refused to come.
P	HOW do you know that?
W	I asked him to come during our last telephone conversation. He flat out refused and said he was too tied up with his own business and affairs to come.
P	WHAT efforts have you made to persuade him to attend this trial?
W	I phoned him several times. I even volunteered to pick up the tab for his airline ticket. He just won't cooperate. He said that he doesn't want any more to do with trials and lawyers.

[2]   AS A MATTER OF CONSTITUTIONAL LAW

The Necessity for a Showing of the Unavailability of a Declarant of "Testimonial"
Hearsay

The preceding paragraphs analyze the issue of unavailability from the perspective of the common law and modern statutes such as Federal Rule of Evidence 804(a). However, the Supreme Court has announced that in some cases, the Sixth Amendment confrontation guarantee imposes a separate requirement for a showing of the declarant's unavailability at trial.

Prior to 2004, the Court had generally restricted the scope of the constitutional unavailability requirement to hearsay exceptions that traditionally required such a showing at common law. The Court recognized that restriction in decisions such as *United States v. Inadi*, 475 U.S. 387, 106 S. Ct. 1121, 89 L. Ed. 2d 390 (1986) and *White v. Illinois*, 502 U.S. 346, 112 S. Ct. 736, 116 L. Ed. 2d 848 (1992).

However, the Court significantly altered the requirement in 2004 in its decision in *Crawford v. Washington*, 541 U.S. 36, 124 S. Ct. 1354, 158 L. Ed. 2d 177 (2004). There the majority declared that the confrontation clause imposes special restrictions on the prosecution's ability to introduce "testimonial statements." Writing for the majority, Justice Scalia stated that the Court was not providing a definitive, comprehensive definition of the expression. However, in his lead opinion the Justice gave several examples of statements that should be classified as "testimonial." To begin with, prior in-court testimony such as statements at prior trials, preliminary hearings, and grand jury hearings falls within the definition. Furthermore, the expression includes formalized out-of-court statements such as affidavits. Finally, Justice Scalia mentioned a third category. To give the reader a sense of the scope of this category, the Justice cited two formulations proposed in the briefs in *Crawford*. One was included in the amicus brief of the National Association of Criminal Defense Lawyers: "statements that were made under circumstances that would lead an objective witness reasonably to believe that the statement would be available for use in a later trial." The other was proposed by the Petitioner's Brief: "pretrial statements that declarants would reasonably expect to be used prosecutorially." The admissibility of a statement is no longer assured simply because the statement falls within a categorical hearsay exception recognized by common law or statute; the Sixth Amendment may bar the admission of the statement. The judge must make an ad hoc, case-specific determination whether the statement was testimonial in character.

Although some points of consensus among the commentators and courts have already emerged, there are still unsettled issues under *Crawford*. At one extreme, as Justice Scalia's opinion indicates, a statement by one coconspirator to another is not testimonial. If the police have lawfully intercepted and taped the statement, the confrontation clause does not bar its admission. At the other extreme, if a government attorney meets with an alleged victim at the prosecutor's office and, after "structured questioning," asks the victim to make a videotaped statement, the statement is testimonial. Likewise, the Supreme Court has ruled that formal certificates stating the results of forensic tests are testimonial. *Bullcoming v. New Mexico*, 564 U.S. 647, 131 S. Ct. 2705, 180 L. Ed. 2d 610 (2011) (a report certifying the results of a gas chromatograph test of a blood sample in a DWI case); *Melendez-Diaz v. Massachusetts*, 557 U.S. 305, 129 S. Ct. 2527, 174 L. Ed. 2d 314 (2009) (a certificate of a gas chromatography/mass spectrometry analysis of a suspected contraband drug). Decisions such as *Bullcoming* and *Melendez-Diaz* have brought some clarity to the law. However, the doctrine continues to evolve.

Statements made in the course of an "ongoing emergency." One of the battlegrounds in the cases has been statements by victims such as calls to 911 dispatchers and on-the-scene statements to police. In many cases, the prosecutor can make a prima facie showing that the statement would otherwise fall within Federal Rule of Evidence 803(1) or (2). However, if the declarant had calmed down and realized that he or she was speaking to a law enforcement agent, some courts characterize these statements as testimonial. In *Davis v. Washington*, 547 U.S. 813, 126 S. Ct. 2266, 165 L. Ed. 2d 224 (2006), the Court issued rulings in two related cases. One case involved a 911 call. The alleged victim made certain statements in a telephone conversation with the 911 dispatcher. Using primarily sentences with present tense verbs, the victim described what was then happening and called for help. The other case involved crime scene statements. Here the alleged victim made statements to an investigating police officer at the scene. After the police separated the victim from the suspected assailant, the victim used primarily sentences with past tense verbs to explain what the suspect had done to her. The Court held that the statements in the 911 call were nontestimonial but that the crime scene statements were testimonial. Justice Scalia elaborated:

Statements are nontestimonial when made in the course of police interrogation under circumstances objectively indicating that the primary purpose of the interrogation is to enable police assistance to meet an ongoing emergency. They are testimonial when the circumstances objectively indicate that there is no such ongoing emergency, and that the primary purpose of the interrogation is to establish or prove past events potentially relevant to later criminal prosecution.

In *Michigan v. Bryant*, 562 U.S. 344, 131 S. Ct. 1143, 179 L. Ed. 2d 93 (2011), the Court expanded the concept of an ongoing emergency. In *Davis*, the Court had found an emergency still imperiling a domestic violence victim. In *Bryant*, the police discovered a shooting victim several blocks from the crime scene. The shooter was at large and perhaps still in possession of the firearm. Medical personnel attended to the victim during part of the police questioning. The Court found that the victim's statements to the police were nontestimonial. Writing for the majority, Justice Sotomayor stated that as in *Davis*, there was an ongoing emergency, in the instant case "extend[ing] beyond an initial victim to a potential threat to the responding police and the public at large." She insisted that it would be a mistake to "narrowly focus on whether the threat solely to the first victim had been neutralized because the threat to the first responders and public may continue." The police conversation with the victim included "the exact type of questions necessary" to assess the threat to their own safety and that of the public.

In *Ohio v. Clark*, 576 U.S. 237, 135 S. Ct. 2173, 192 L. Ed. 2d 306 (2015), the Court revisited the topic and further broadened the emergency concept. In *Clark*, a child made a statement to a teacher who was a mandatory child abuse reporter. The teacher noticed that the child had some injuries although the child was not complaining about them. The child answered the teacher's questions about the cause of the injuries. Although the state supreme court characterized the child's statements as testimonial, the Court reversed. Justice Alito delivered the opinion of the Court. While he stopped short of announcing that all statements to private parties are nontestimonial, the justice concluded that the child's answers to the teacher's questions were nontestimonial. In explaining his conclusion, Justice Alito pointed to several factors: The statements occurred "in the context of an ongoing emergency involving suspected child abuse," since at the end of the day the teacher had to decide whether to release the child back to a household that might include the child's abuser; during their "informal" conversation, the teacher did not suggest that the child's answers would be used to arrest or punish the abuser; and "[s]tatements by very young children will rarely, if ever, implicate the Confrontation Clause. Few preschool children understand the details of our criminal justice system."

Forensic reports. Despite *Bullcoming* and *Melendez-Diaz*, the admissibility of forensic reports remains problematic. The Court's subsequent decision in *Williams v. Illinois*, 567 U.S. 50, 132 S. Ct. 2221, 183 L. Ed. 2d 89 (2012) muddied the waters. In this rape case, the police sent a vaginal swab to Cellmark, a private laboratory conducting DNA testing. Cellmark extracted a male DNA profile from the sample and sent its report to the Illinois State Laboratory (ISP). At trial, relying on the Cellmark report, an ISP specialist testified. The question was whether the specialist's reference to the Cellmark report violated the Confrontation Clause. The prosecution argued that there was no violation because at trial, the report was used for the limited, nonhearsay purpose of showing the basis for the specialist's opinion. The fact situation sharply divided the Court.

— Four dissenters, led by Justice Kagan, argued that Cellmark's report was a testimonial statement that was clearly offered for its truth.

— Justice Thomas filed a concurrence. He agreed with the dissent that as a matter of logic, the report had been treated as substantive evidence admitted for its truth. However, he voted to affirm the conviction on the ground that Cellmark's report was too informal to qualify as a testimonial statement.

— Like Justice Thomas, a four-justice plurality, led by Justice Alito, voted to uphold the conviction. However, the plurality relied on a different rationale than Justice Thomas. The plurality reasoned that Cellmark's report was nontestimonial because the police had not identified a particular suspect at the time of Cellmark's test. That reasoning appeared to narrow the test and make it far more difficult to classify a statement as testimonial. Given the fragmented nature of the decision in *Williams*, the lower courts are understandably struggling with the application of *Crawford* to forensic reports.

The Sufficiency of the Showing of Unavailability

While *Crawford* changes the scope of the unavailability requirement, it does not purport to modify the standard for determining the sufficiency of a showing of unavailability. That standard is governed by *Barber v. Page*, 390 U.S. 719, 88 S. Ct. 1318, 20 L. Ed. 2d 255 (1968). Under *Barber*, the prosecution must establish that it made a good faith, diligent effort to bring the witness to the site of trial. A showing complying with Federal Rule of Evidence 804(a) will ordinarily satisfy *Barber* as well.

§ 10.15 DECLARATIONS AGAINST INTEREST

[1] THE DOCTRINE

Statements or admissions of a party-opponent are disserving to the declarant's interest at the time of trial; the admission is inconsistent with some position the party-opponent is defending at trial. So long as the statement is disserving at that time, it is admissible even if it was highly self-serving when made. Declarations against interest contrast with admissions in several respects. Declarations against interest are admissible only if at the time of the statement, the declarant believed the statement was contrary to his or her interest. The declarant's belief is the guarantee of the reliability of declarations against interest. Moreover, declarations against interest are admissible only if the declarant is unavailable at the time of trial. The declarant's unavailability supplies the necessity for resorting to the hearsay. In the case of admissions, the party-opponent is usually available and present at trial. Finally, the declarant of an admission must be the party-opponent while any person can make a declaration against interest.

Federal Rule of Evidence 804(b)(3) states the doctrine: "The following [is] not excluded by the rule against hearsay if the declarant is unavailable as a witness: A statement that: (A) a reasonable person in the declarant's position would have made only if the person believed it to be true because, when made, it was so contrary to the declarant's proprietary or pecuniary interest or had so great a tendency to invalidate the declarant's claim against someone else or to expose the declarant to civil or criminal liability; and (B) is supported by corroborating circumstances that clearly indicate its trustworthiness, if it is offered in a criminal case as one that tends to expose the declarant to criminal liability."

[2] ELEMENTS OF THE FOUNDATION

The foundation for this hearsay exception includes the following elements:

1. The declarant subjectively believed that the statement was contrary to his or her interest. Even at common law, the belief of the hypothetical, reasonable person could be used as circumstantial evidence of the subjective belief of the declarant. On its face, Federal Rule of Evidence 804(b)(3) refers only to the objective reasonableness test; and some federal courts have read the statute literally.[13]

    In applying this element, the courts focus on the specific statement proffered rather than the overall narrative including the statement. In *Williamson v. United States*, 512 U.S. 594, 114 S. Ct. 2431, 129 L. Ed. 2d 476 (1994), the Supreme Court announced that Rule 804(b)(3) permits the admission only of statements which are individually self-inculpatory; the rule does not authorize the introduction of collateral, non-self-inculpatory statements in the same narrative. For purposes of this exception, the unit of analysis is the individual hearsay assertion. The judge should separately test each assertion to determine whether it was disserving. For that reason, the proponent's question must be narrowly phrased to target the admissible statement. In *Lilly v. Virginia*, 527 U.S. 116, 119 S. Ct. 1887, 144 L. Ed. 2d 117 (1999), to a degree the Court essentially elevated the *Williamson* doctrine to constitutional status under the confrontation clause. Although *Lilly* does not mandate the use of *Williamson*'s assertion-by-assertion mode of analysis under the Sixth Amendment, *Lilly* does evince the same skepticism about the reliability of custodial statements that is manifest in *Williamson*. If a person made a statement in police custody and the content of the statement suggests that the person was endeavoring to shift blame to the defendant, the Sixth Amendment may bar the introduction of the statement.

2. The interest was a recognized type of interest. All jurisdictions recognize pecuniary and proprietary interest, and most jurisdictions have expanded those categories to admit any statement that would subject the declarant to civil liability. Most jurisdictions now recognize penal interest, and roughly a fourth of the states admit statements contrary to social interest. However, the Federal

---

[13] *But see* United States v. Lozado, 776 F.3d 1119 (10th Cir. 2013) ("the actual knowledge of the declarant, when the evidence establishes it, is part of the 'reasonable person in the declarant's position' calculus. The reasonable person standard applies when proof of the declarant's state of mind is lacking").

Rules do not treat mere social interest as adequate.

3.   The declarant is unavailable at the time of trial.

4.   In some jurisdictions, if the defense offers a third party's confession to the crime the accused is charged with on the theory that the confession is a declaration against interest, there must be corroboration that the third party committed the crime. As Federal Rule of Evidence 804(b)(3) originally declared: "A statement tending to expose the declarant to criminal liability and offered to exculpate the accused is not admissible unless corroborating circumstances clearly indicate the trustworthiness of the statement." To eliminate a potential equal protection challenge to the statute, several courts read in the same corroboration requirement when the prosecution offers a declaration against interest against a defendant. The statute was later amended to prescribe the corroboration requirement for prosecution as well as defense evidence in Rule 804(b)(3)(B).[14]

[3]   SAMPLE FOUNDATION

Our fact situation is a robbery prosecution. The government alleges that the accused, Mr. Charles Bosley, robbed the Midland Stereo Store in New Orleans on February 17, YR-3. The eyewitness testimony about the crime indicates that there was only one robber. The defense theory is that Mr. Gregory Bennett actually committed the robbery. During the defense case-in-chief, the defense called Bennett to the stand. Bennett refused to answer any questions about the robbery. His refusal would render him "unavailable" in most jurisdictions. As his next witness, the accused calls Mr. William Store. Mr. Store has already identified himself. The accused is the proponent.

P   WHAT is your occupation?

W   I am a member of the New Orleans Police Department.

P   HOW long have you held that position?

W   For about eight years.

P   WHERE were you on the morning of February 19, YR-3?

W   I was on duty at the Dupont Street station.

P   WHAT happened while you were on duty that morning?

W   Some patrolmen brought in a suspect for questioning.

P   WHO was the suspect?

W   A Gregory Bennett.

---

[14]   There is a pending amendment to the Rule. As amended, 804(b)(3)(B) would read:

If offered in a criminal case as one that tends to expose the declarant to criminal liability, [the statement] is supported by corroborating circumstances that clearly indicate its trustworthiness after considering the totality of the circumstances under which it was made and evidence, if any, corroborating it.

The new reference to corroboration brings the standard into close alignment with the reliability standard under Rule 807. The amendment is tentatively scheduled to take effect in December 2024.

P	WHEN was the last time you saw Mr. Bennett?
W	A few moments ago.
P	WHERE was he then?
W	He was on the witness stand. He's the witness who just left the stand.
P	WHAT happened after the patrolmen brought in Mr. Bennett?
W	As is my custom, I first informed him of his rights.
P	WHAT rights did you tell him about? (1), (2)
W	I told him he had a privilege against self-incrimination and a right to counsel.
P	WHAT was his condition when you informed him of his rights? (1)
W	He seemed O.K. He was alert, and there didn't seem to be anything physically wrong with him.
P	HOW did he react when you informed him of his rights? (1)
W	He seemed concerned.
P	WHAT did you do after you informed Mr. Bennett of his rights? (1)
W	I asked him if he understood his rights.
P	HOW did he respond? (1)
W	He said he understood and waived them, and then he gave me some factual information I wanted.
P	WHAT did you do after you spoke with Mr. Bennett? (4)
W	I attempted to verify some of the facts Mr. Bennett had told me.
P	WHAT facts? (4)
W	He told me about the location of some of the stolen property, some receivers and speakers.
P	WHAT did Mr. Bennett say about the location of the stolen property? (4)
W	He said that several of the stolen receivers and speakers were in his apartment.
P	WHAT steps did you take to verify his statement? (4)
W	With his consent, I visited and searched his apartment.
P	WHAT did you find in his apartment? (4)
W	I found his personal effects. In addition, I found several receivers and speakers. I checked the serial numbers against the list supplied by Midland Stereo. The numbers matched.
P	Mr. Store, during your questioning of Mr. Bennett, WHO did he say robbed the Midland Stereo Store on February 17, YR-3? (1)
O	Your Honor, I object to that question on the ground that it calls for

hearsay.

P Your Honor, may we approach the bench?

J Yes.

P Your Honor, I offer to prove that the witness will testify that Mr. Bennett confessed to the robbery my client is charged with. In light of the warnings Officer Store gave Bennett, Bennett must have realized his confession was contrary to his penal interest. There is corroboration that Bennett was involved in the robbery; some of the stolen property was found in his apartment. Finally, Bennett's refusal to answer makes him unavailable.

J The objection will be overruled.

P Officer Store, let me repeat the question. WHO did Mr. Bennett say robbed the Midland Stereo Store?

W He said that he did. He said that he felt terrible about what he had done.

§ 10.16 DYING DECLARATIONS

[1] THE DOCTRINE

Another type of evidently sincere statement that is exceptionally admissible is a dying declaration. At early common law, the courts admitted the decedent's dying declarations in homicide prosecutions. The courts reasoned that there was a peculiar need for dying declarations in homicide prosecutions; the courts feared that if they excluded the victim's dying declaration, the murderer might go free. The circumstantial guarantee of the trustworthiness of dying declarations is the declarant's sense of impending death; at the point of death, the declarant should not have any reason to lie, and there is the theistic belief that the decedent will not want to face the Creator with a last lie on his or her lips. At common law, the necessity for admitting the hearsay is that at the time of trial, the declarant was dead.

The most arbitrary limitation on the common-law doctrine was its restriction to homicide prosecutions. Some jurisdictions now admit dying declarations in any type of criminal prosecution. Other jurisdictions admit such declarations in any type of case, civil or criminal. Congress decided to adopt a compromise view. Restyled Federal Rule of Evidence 804(b)(2) declares that "[t]he following [is] not excluded by the rule against hearsay if the declarant is unavailable as a witness: In a prosecution for homicide or in a civil case, a statement that the declarant, while believing the declarant's death to be imminent, made about its cause or circumstances." The most radical aspect of the Federal Rule is its abandonment of the requirement that the declarant be dead at the time of trial. The Federal Rule requires that at the time of trial, the declarant be "unavailable," as that term is defined in Rule 804(a). However, it is no longer necessary to prove the declarant's subsequent death.

[2] ELEMENTS OF THE FOUNDATION

The common-law doctrine included the following foundational elements:

1. The case is a prosecution for homicide or a crime including homicide as an

element. As we previously noted, many jurisdictions now admit dying declarations in other criminal prosecutions and civil actions. To determine whether this element is present, the trial judge looks to the indictment, information, or complaint; the charging pleading specifies the offense the defendant is on trial for.

2. The declarant is the victim named in the charging pleading. The witness must identify the declarant. The trial judge then examines the charging pleading to determine whether the declarant is the named victim. The consequence of this rule was that a declaration by decedent #2 was inadmissible in a prosecution for killing decedent #1 even if the defendant killed them at the same time and by the same blow. Many jurisdictions, including the federal courts, have abandoned this requirement.

3. At the time of the statement, the declarant had a sense of impending death. The declarant had abandoned all hope and concluded that certain death was imminent. The declarant sometimes voices his or her belief. The proponent may also rely on such circumstances as the nature of wound, the administration of last rites, and statements made by third parties to the declarant. Since the question is the declarant's state of mind and third party statements can affect his or her state of mind, the statements are admissible as nonhearsay under Rule 801(c)(2).

4. At the time of trial, the declarant is dead. Under the Federal Rules, it is sufficient if the declarant is unavailable within the meaning of that expression in Rule 804(a).

5. The statement relates to the event inducing the declarant's dying condition. The proponent usually asks "about" the cause of death. The statement may not describe previous quarrels or fights between the declarant and the defendant.

6. The statement is factual in nature. The early common law limited dying declarations to statements of observed fact. Modernly, the courts have relaxed the application of the opinion prohibition to dying declarations. The courts now admit conclusory statements such as the defendant killed the declarant "intentionally" or "without provocation."

At common law and under the Federal Rules, if the proponent can lay the above foundation, the dying declaration is admissible even though a criminal defendant did not have a prior opportunity to question the declarant. However, as previously stated, in *Crawford v. Washington*, 541 U.S. 36, 124 S. Ct. 1354, 158 L. Ed. 2d 177 (2004), the Supreme Court significantly altered confrontation clause analysis. There the majority announced that if a statement is "testimonial" in character, the prosecution must demonstrate both that the declarant is unavailable at trial and that the defendant had a prior opportunity to question the declarant. § 10.13[2] discusses the concept of "testimonial statements." It is true that in footnote 6, the *Crawford* majority acknowledged that in *Mattox v. United States*, 156 U.S. 237, 15 S. Ct. 337, 39 L. Ed. 409 (1895), the Court had upheld the admission of a dying declaration without imposing a requirement for a prior opportunity to question the declarant. However, at the end of the footnote, Justice Scalia added: "We need not decide in this case whether the Sixth Amendment incorporates an exception for testimonial dying declarations. If this exception must be accepted on historical grounds, it is sui generis." Some lower courts have held that *Crawford* applies to dying declarations made under circumstances in which a reasonable declarant would have realized that the police would likely put the statement to prosecutorial use. However, the prevailing view is to the contrary.

[3] SAMPLE FOUNDATION

The fact situation is a homicide prosecution. The indictment alleges that the accused, Mr. James Ireland, murdered Ms. Grace Shafer. The indictment thus supplies the first element of the foundation. The prosecution calls Mr. William Turner as a witness. Mr. Turner has already identified himself. The prosecutor is the proponent.

P	Mr. Turner, WHAT is your occupation?
W	I am a physician.
P	WHERE are you licensed to practice medicine?
W	In three states, including here in New Hampshire.
P	WHERE were you on the morning of February 22, YR-3?
W	I was in my office.
P	WHAT happened that morning?
W	I received an emergency call.
P	WHAT was the nature of the call?
W	Someone was hurt very badly, and they needed immediate medical attention.
P	WHAT did you do after you received this call?
W	I jumped in my car and drove to 1444 Garnet Street.
P	WHAT did you find there?
W	I found several police surrounding a very badly injured person.
P	WHO was that person? (2)
W	A Ms. Grace Shafer.
P	HOW do you know that? (2)
W	She identified herself, and I also checked the ID that she had in her purse.
P	WHAT condition was she in? (3)
W	Very bad. She had several stab wounds.
P	HOW many stab wounds? (3)
W	Five in her chest.
P	HOW deep were the wounds? (3)
W	Some were several inches deep.

P	HOW much blood was she losing? (3)
W	She was bleeding profusely.
P	WHERE was she bleeding? (3)
W	All over the chest area.
P	WHAT did you do after you discovered these wounds? (3)
W	I helped her as best I could; and when I realized that she was dying, I tried to make her as comfortable as possible.
P	WHAT, if anything, did you tell her about her condition? (3)
O	Your Honor, I object to that question on the ground that it calls for hearsay.
P	Your Honor, may we approach the bench?
J	Yes.
P	Your Honor, I offer to prove that the witness will testify he told Ms. Shafer that she was dying. I want to use that statement for a nonhearsay purpose as mental input under Rule 801(c)(2), namely, to show its effect on her state of mind. His statement helped produce a sense of imminent death in her mind. That is part of the foundation for the dying declaration I ultimately want to offer.
J	The objection will be overruled.
P	Doctor Turner, let me repeat the question. WHAT, if anything, did you tell Ms. Shafer about her condition? (3)
P	I felt terrible, but I was honest with her. She asked, and I told her she was dying.
P	HOW did she respond? (3)
W	She looked frightened. Then she sighed very deeply.
P	WHAT happened then? (3)
W	She asked that I contact a Catholic priest. She said that she wanted to receive the last rites of her church before she died.
P	WHAT happened then? (3)
W	The priest arrived and administered the sacrament. Then the priest and I accompanied her to the hospital.
P	Doctor, WHERE is Ms. Shafer now? (4)
W	She's dead.
P	HOW do you know that? (4)
W	She died in the ambulance on the way to the hospital.
P	WHAT, if anything, did she say about the cause of her death before she died? (5), (6)

W	She said someone had stabbed her with an ice pick.
P	WHO did she say stabbed her? (5), (6)
W	She said it was Jim Ireland.

§ 10.17   FORMER OR PRIOR TESTIMONY

[1]   THE DOCTRINE

The next exception we shall consider is former testimony. As we noted in § 10.01 of this chapter, the primary rationale for the hearsay rule is that opponent has not had an opportunity to test the hearsay by cross-examination. What if the opponent had an opportunity to test the hearsay by cross-examination in a prior trial? Does that opportunity satisfy the hearsay rule and justify admitting the prior testimony in the present proceeding? Most courts have answered that question in the affirmative.

Federal Rule of Evidence 804(b)(1) states the doctrine:

> The following [is] not excluded by the rule against hearsay if the declarant is unavailable a witness: Testimony that:
>
> > (A)   was given as a witness at a trial, hearing, or lawful deposition, whether given during the current proceeding or in a different one; and
> >
> > (B)   is now offered against a party who had—or, in a civil case, whose predecessor in interest had—an opportunity and similar motive to develop it by direct, cross-, or redirect examination.

The most controversial aspect of the doctrine has proven to be the requirement that the parties to the two hearings be identical. Early common law insisted upon complete identity of parties; the parties to hearing #2 were parties to hearing #1, and there were no additional parties at either hearing.

The common law quickly realized that the complete identity requirement was unnecessarily strict. So long as the present parties were parties to hearing #1, the courts concluded it was immaterial that there were additional parties to either hearing.

The courts then developed the modern "same party" view: The prior testimony is admissible *against* a party to hearing #2 if that party was a party to hearing #1. The courts focus on the party the testimony is now being offered against, and they inquire whether that party had a fair opportunity to develop the facts at hearing #1 by direct or cross-examination. If the opponent had a fair opportunity to do so, it should not make any difference that the present proponent of the former testimony was not a party to hearing #1. The opponent had a prior opportunity to test the evidence, and that opportunity satisfies the purpose of the hearsay rule. Suppose that several passengers are injured when an airplane crashes during landing. In hearing #1, passenger A sues the airline and introduces the testimony of a safety engineer. During hearing #1, the airline can test and attack the engineer's testimony. Subsequently passenger B sues the airline. If the engineer dies prior to hearing #2, passenger B may use the record of the engineer's prior testimony against the airline. The "same party" view is the prevailing view in contemporary criminal cases.

In civil cases, most jurisdictions also recognize the "privity" view. Once again, the court begins its analysis by focusing on the party the testimony is now offered against.

However, in the next step of analysis the court poses this question: Was the party the evidence is now offered against a party to hearing #1 *or* in technical privity with a party to hearing #1? The testimony is admissible against the party in hearing #2 if that party was a party to hearing #1 or in technical privity with a party to hearing #1, as in the case of successor owners of the same parcel of real estate. Since Federal Rule of Evidence 804(b)(1) uses the expression "predecessor in interest," some courts have construed the rule as codifying the "privity" view for civil cases. The statute uses the expression "motive" as well as "interest"; and these courts reason that if the drafters employed both terms, they must have intended that "interest" would mean something other than a mere similar motive.

Some courts and legislatures have taken a step beyond the "same party" and "privity" views; they recognize the "similar party" view. They still begin their analysis by focusing on the party to hearing #2 that the former testimony is offered against. However, they then pose a different question. Under the prevailing view discussed in the preceding paragraph, the pivotal question is whether that party had an opportunity in hearing #1 to probe the testimony. Under this new view, the question is whether there was *a* party to hearing #1 who had a similar motive to probe the testimony. The present opponent need not have had that opportunity; it is sufficient if there was a similarly situated party, a party with a motive and interest similar to that of the present opponent. To illustrate this view, we can revisit the last hypothetical. Suppose that in hearing #1, the airline had offered the testimony of a safety engineer against passenger *A*. The engineer dies before passenger *B* sues. Under this new view, at hearing #2 between passenger *B* and the same airline, the airline could use the engineer's testimony against passenger *B*. It is true that passenger *B* was not a party to hearing #1. However, passenger *A* was a party, and the two plaintiffs' motive and interest are sufficiently similar. We can assume with fair assurance that passenger *A* attacked the engineer's testimony as vigorously as passenger *B* would have. This view is the trend, but it is applied in only civil cases.

[2] ELEMENTS OF THE FOUNDATION

1. Hearing #1 was a fair, adversary hearing.

    a. The witness testified under oath.

    b. The opponent had an opportunity to cross-examine the witness.

    c. If the hearing was a critical stage in a criminal prosecution, the defendant was afforded the right to counsel.

2. There is substantial identity of issues between the two hearings. Although the courts often refer to issues in the plural, the best approach is to compare *the* issue the evidence was offered on in hearing #1 and *the* issue the evidence is now being offered on in hearing #2. The comparison of those issues largely determines whether there was a sufficiently similar motivation to develop the testimony in the two cases. In *United States v. Salerno*, 505 U.S. 317, 112 S. Ct. 2503, 120 L. Ed. 2d 255 (1992), the defense argued that the accused need not show substantial identity of issues when the accused invokes the exception against the prosecution and the prosecution could obtain the witness's live trial

testimony by immunizing the witness. However, the Supreme Court rejected the argument. The Court noted that the text of Rule 804(b)(1) does not recognize any special exception for the criminal accused.

3. There is substantial identity of parties between the two hearings. Subsection 1, *supra*, describes the split of authority on the test for substantial identity of parties.

4. At hearing #2, the witness is unavailable within the meaning of that term in Rule 804(a).

In many cases, the proponent will need two witnesses. One witness will establish the unavailability of the prior witness. The second witness will then describe the prior witness's testimony. The second witness may have been a spectator at hearing #1 who simply remembers the substance of the prior testimony; the witness need not be able to recite the testimony verbatim. It suffices if the witness can recall the substance of the witness's cross-examination as well as the direct testimony. Or the second witness may be the court reporter who describes the testimony with or without relying on notes. Finally, the proponent may entirely dispense with live testimony if the jurisdiction permits the authentication of the documentary record of hearing #1 by the court reporter's attesting certificate. In such a jurisdiction, the transcript is self-authenticating. The judge examines the transcript to determine whether the foundational elements are present.

[3] SAMPLE FOUNDATION

Assume that the proponent has already established the declarant's unavailability. In the following hypotheticals, the proponent is laying the other elements of the foundation.

We shall first illustrate the testimony of a spectator who happens to remember the substance of the witness's testimony at hearing #1. Our fact situation is a homicide prosecution. The government charges that Mr. John Gentile murdered his wife. An eyewitness to the killing, Mr. John Walton, testified at the preliminary hearing. Walton died after the hearing and before the trial. The prosecution has already proven Walton's unavailability by introducing a properly attested death certificate. Now the prosecutor calls Ms. Pamela Martin to lay the other elements of the foundation. The prosecutor is the proponent. Ms. Martin has already identified herself.

P	Ms. Martin, WHERE were you on the afternoon of March 12, YR-4?
W	I was in another courtroom in this building.
P	WHAT were you doing there?
W	I was a spectator at a court proceeding.
P	WHY were you there?
W	I had read a lot about the case in the papers, and I was interested in watching it.
P	WHAT proceeding did you see the afternoon of March 12, YR-4? (2), (3)

W	It was the preliminary hearing in this case.
P	WHO was there attending the hearing? (3)
W	For one, the accused himself, Mr. Gentile.
P	WHERE is Mr. Gentile now? (3)
W	He's in the courtroom right now.
P	Specifically, WHERE in the courtroom? (3)
W	Over there at the end of that table.
P	HOW is he dressed? (3)
W	He's wearing a blue suit, white shirt, and red tie.
P	Your Honor, please let the record reflect that the witness has identified the accused.
J	It will so reflect.
P	WHAT happened at this hearing you attended on March 12th? (1)
W	They called witnesses to testify.
P	WHAT did they do when they first called the witnesses to the stand? (1a)
W	They would swear them.
P	WHO questioned the witnesses? (1b)
W	Usually the prosecutor would start, and then the defense counsel would ask questions.
P	WHO asked questions on behalf of the defendant? (1c)
W	Some attorney. I honestly can't remember her name.
P	WHO were the witnesses that day?
W	There were three who stand out in my mind.
P	WHO were they?
W	A police officer named Strait, a doctor, and an eyewitness. The eyewitness was on the stand most of the day.
P	WHO was the eyewitness?
W	His name was John Walton.
P	HOW long was he on the stand?
W	About three hours.
P	HOW much of his testimony did you hear?
W	All of it.
P	HOW often did you leave the room while he was on the stand?
W	I didn't. I wanted to hear all of it. It was really exciting. The trial had received a lot of media attention.

P	HOW well could you hear Mr. Walton while he testified?
W	Very well. I didn't have any problem hearing him.
P	HOW loudly was he speaking?
W	In a normal voice, but his voice carried well.
P	HOW close were you sitting to him while he was on the stand?
W	About 15 feet away. I was in the very first row for the spectators.
P	HOW well do you remember his testimony?
W	Very well. I was really enthralled. As I said, it was very exciting.
P	WHAT did he say during his testimony?
O	Your Honor, I object to that question on the ground that it calls for hearsay.
P	Your Honor, may we approach the bench?
J	Yes.
P	Your Honor, I concede that the testimony will be hearsay. However, it falls within the former testimony exception. The witness's testimony shows that there was oath, cross-examination, and counsel at the preliminary hearing. Since it was the preliminary hearing in this case, there's obviously identity of issues and parties. Finally, the death certificate shows that the former witness is now unavailable.
J	The objection will be overruled.
P	Ms. Martin, let me repeat the question. WHAT did Mr. Walton say during his testimony?

The proponent should now elicit all the important facts Walton previously testified to.

We shall now illustrate the use of a properly attested or certified transcript of the former testimony. To do so, we shall continue the same hypothetical. In this variation of the hypothetical, there is a documentary transcript of the preliminary hearing. We shall assume that the rule in this jurisdiction is that if the court reporter attaches a proper certificate to the transcript, the transcript is self-authenticating. Again, please assume that the prosecutor has already introduced Mr. Walton's death certificate.

P	Your Honor, I request that this be marked prosecution exhibit number seven for identification.
J	It will be so marked.
P	Please let the record reflect that I am showing the exhibit to the opposing counsel.
J	It will so reflect.
P	I now offer prosecution exhibit number seven for identification into evidence as prosecution exhibit number seven.

O	Your Honor, I object to the introduction of the exhibit on the ground that the exhibit is hearsay.
P	Your Honor, may we approach the bench?
J	Yes.
P	Your Honor, I concede that the exhibit is hearsay; but it is a properly certified transcript, and it falls within the former testimony exception.
P	Where is the foundation for the former testimony exception?
P	The transcript purports to be the record of the preliminary hearing in this case; there is obviously identity of issues and parties. I've already introduced Mr. Walton's death certificate, showing his unavailability. Page 2 of the transcript shows that the defendant had counsel at the hearing, page 16 shows that Mr. Walton was sworn before he testified, and page 142 shows that the defense had an opportunity to cross-examine Mr. Walton.
J	I agree. The objection will be overruled, and the exhibit will be received.
P	Your Honor, I request permission to read pages 22–43 to the jurors. I shall read the questions, and my clerk will take the witness stand and read the answers.
J	Permission granted.

§ 10.18　FORFEITURE BY WRONGDOING

[1]　THE DOCTRINE

After its enactment, Rule 804 was amended to include a new subdivision (b)(6), now reading: "The following [is] not excluded by the rule against hearsay if the declarant is unavailable as a witness: A statement offered against a party that wrongfully caused—or acquiesced in wrongfully causing—the declarant's unavailability as a witness, and did so intending that result."

In the 1980s and early 1990s, the federal courts began developing a line of authority recognizing the proposition that an accused waives his or her rights under the confrontation clause by killing an adverse witness or otherwise rendering the witness unavailable to testify at trial. The drafters of the amendment reasoned that if such wrongdoing could forfeit constitutional rights, *a fortiori* it should result in a forfeiture of a litigant's rights under the statutory hearsay rule. Moreover, although the federal decisions in question were criminal cases, the amendment applies in civil cases as well as prosecutions.

[2]　ELEMENTS OF THE FOUNDATION

1. A certain person was a potential witness in a particular proceeding. If a witness list had been filed in the case, the court could judicially notice the witness list.
2. Someone contacted the potential witness.
3. The purpose of the contact was to procure the person's unavailability as a witness in the proceeding. If the third party announced his or her intent, the

statement would be exceptionally admissible as an assertion of state of mind under Rule 803(3). Moreover, if the third party is the party-opponent in the litigation, any relevant statement would be admissible nonhearsay under Rule 801(d)(2)(A). Initially, some commentators distinguished the confrontation clause standard from the test under Rule 804(b)(6). Richard D. Friedman, *Adjusting to* Crawford: *High Court Decision Restores Confrontation Clause Protection*, 19 CRIM. JUST. 4, 12 (Summer 2004). On the one hand, it is arguable that the defendant should be held to have forfeited his or her Sixth Amendment rights whenever he or she causes the witness's unavailability. Thus, if the defendant killed a victim in the heat of passion, the confrontation clause would not bar the admission of the victim's statements even though in the fit of anger the defendant gave no thought at all to rendering the victim unavailable as a witness. On the other hand, the wording of the statute, "intended to," appears to prescribe an intent requirement. In *Giles v. California*, 554 U.S. 353, 128 S. Ct. 2678, 171 L. Ed. 2d 488 (2008), the Supreme Court held that a defendant forfeits his or her confrontation clause rights only if the defendant's conduct is designed to prevent the potential witness from testifying.

4. The contact rendered the potential witness unavailable. Unavailability would be clear if the third party killed the person. However, unavailability can take other forms. For example, if, immediately after a threat, the potential witness stated that he or she intended to leave the jurisdiction and avoid appearing at trial, under Rule 803(3) the statement would be admissible both to prove the witness's then existing intent and the fact that they later carried out that intention. Moreover, the natural tendency of a threat would be to cause the potential witness to absent himself or herself from trial; and if the witness made the statement immediately after the threat, there would be a common-sense inference that the threat caused the potential witness to become unavailable.

5. The third party's conduct was imputable to the party the declarant's statement is offered against. The conduct would be imputable if:

   a. The third party was the party to the proceeding; or

   b. The party authorized the third party to contact the potential witness and cause the witness's unavailability; or

   c. After the third party's contact with the potential witness, the party learned of the third party's conduct and acquiesced in it.

[3] SAMPLE FOUNDATION

Assume that the proponent has already established that Grant Couch was a potential witness in a trial and that Couch was unavailable at the time of trial. In the following hypothetical, the proponent is laying the other elements of the foundation. The witness has already made an in-court identification of the defendant.

P   WHERE were you on the afternoon of April 13, YR-3?

W	I was at the defendant's house.
P	WHO else was there? (2), (5)
W	Grant Couch.
P	HOW do you know that the other person was Grant Couch?
W	I've known him for years. We went to high school together. Grant, the defendant, and I have known each other since high school.
P	WHAT, if anything, did the defendant say to Mr. Couch? (3)
W	He threatened him.
P	Please be more specific. To the best of your recollection, WHAT did the defendant say? (3)
W	He told Grant that he'd heard that Grant was going to testify against him in his pending drug case. He added that if Grant took the stand, he, the defendant, would "blow him away."
P	HOW did Grant react when the defendant said that? (4)
W	He turned pale as a ghost and started shaking.
P	WHAT, if anything, did Grant say to the defendant? (4)
W	He told the defendant that he, Grant, would "get out of town right away" and that the defendant would "never have to lay eyes on" him again.
P	WHAT did Grant do then? (4)
W	He immediately stood up and virtually ran out the door. He jumped in his car and sped away.

PART F.   The Residual Hearsay Exception Based on Showings of Reliability and Necessity

§ 10.19   THE RESIDUAL HEARSAY EXCEPTION

[1]   THE DOCTRINE

The list of hearsay exemptions and exceptions in §§ 10.03–10.17 of this chapter is incomplete. In the first place, the Federal Rules enumerate other hearsay exceptions. For example, Rules 803(13) and 804(b)(4) create exceptions for certain statements about family history. Rules 803(14)–(15) set out exceptions relating to documents affecting property interests. Rule 803(16) recognizes an exception for ancient documents, 803(17) another exception for market reports, and 803(22) still another exception for judgments.

However, the list is incomplete in a second, more fundamental sense. The Rules explicitly confer residual discretion on the trial judge to admit hearsay that falls outside the enumerated exceptions. Prior to December 1, 1997, the discretion was set out in Rules 803(24) and 804(b)(5). Effective December 1, 1997, the two statutes were merged into Rule 807. By virtue of that amendment, the Rule read:

(a)   In General. Under the following circumstances, a hearsay statement is not excluded by the rule against hearsay even if the statement is not specifically covered by a hearsay exception in Rule 803 or 804:

   (1)   the statement has equivalent circumstantial guarantees of trustworthiness;

   (2)   it is offered as evidence of a material fact;

   (3)   it is more probative on the point for which it is offered than any other evidence that the proponent can obtain through reasonable efforts; and

   (4)   admitting it will serve the purposes of these rules and the interests of justice.

(b)   Notice. The statement is admissible only if, before the trial or hearing, the proponent gives an adverse party reasonable notice of the intent to offer the statement and its particulars, including the declarant's name and address, so that the party has a fair opportunity to meet it.

In 2019, Rule 807 was amended again. The Rule now reads:

(a) General Rule. Under the following circumstances, a hearsay statement is not excluded by the rule against hearsay even if the statement is not specifically covered by a hearsay exception in Rule 803 or 804:

(1) the statement is supported by sufficient guarantees of trustworthiness— after considering the totality of circumstances under which it was made and evidence, if any, corroborating the statement; and

(2) it is more probative on the point for which it is offered than any other evidence that the proponent can obtain through reasonable efforts.

(b) Notice. The statement is admissible only if the proponent gives an adverse party reasonable notice of the intent to offer the statement—including its substance and the declarant's name—so that the party has a fair opportunity to meet it. The notice must be provided in writing before the trial or hearing—or in any form during the trial or hearing if the court, for good cause, excuses a lack of earlier notice.

The amendment effects several changes to Rule 807. To begin with, the amendment eliminates the prior reference to "equivalent circumstantial guarantees." Under the prior language, several courts had adopted a "near miss" doctrine, namely, that a statement proffered under Rule 807 was automatically inadmissible if the statement came close to but fell just short of satisfying the requirements of a Rule 803 or 804 exception. However, the May 24, 2018 report of the Evidence Advisory Committee interprets the "sufficient guarantees" language in the amendment as meaning that "a statement that nearly misses a standard exception can be admissible under Rule 807 so long as the court finds that there are sufficient guarantees of trustworthiness." Moreover, the amendment resolves the previous split of authority over the question of whether the judge could consider corroborating evidence in deciding whether the statement was reliable enough to be admissible. In addition, the pretrial notice must now be "in writing." However, the Committee on Rules of Practice and Procedure report on the amendment states that the writing requirement "is satisfied by notice in electronic form." Finally, the amendment eliminates the need for the notice to state the declarant's address.

During the mid-1970s and early 1980s, most courts applied the residual exceptions conservatively. However, in the mid-1980s, some courts became more receptive to invocations of the residual exceptions. One of the battlegrounds was the admissibility of transcripts of the grand jury testimony of deceased witnesses. Since even the target of the grand jury investigation does not have a right to cross-examine at the hearing, the grand jury testimony cannot be admitted as former testimony under Rule 804(b)(1). If the testimony is going to be admitted, it must be introduced, if at all, under the residual exception. Prior to 2004, there were numerous decisions admitting grand jury testimony on that theory under Rule 807's predecessor, 804(b)(5). However, grand jury testimony is undeniably a "testimonial statement" as the majority used that expression in *Crawford v. Washington*, 541 U.S. 36, 124 S. Ct. 1354, 158 L. Ed. 2d 177 (2004). Indeed, Justice Scalia expressly used grand jury testimony as one of his examples. Thus, *Crawford* curtailed the judicial trend to admit grand jury testimony under the residual exception in criminal cases.

[2] ELEMENTS OF THE FOUNDATION

Under the residual exception, the proponent must lay the following foundation:

1. The proponent gave the opposition adequate, advance notice of the tenor of the hearsay statement and the proponent's intention to offer the statement at trial.

2. The statement was reliable. Again, by virtue of the 2019 amendment, the proponent need not show that the statement possesses circumstantial guarantees of trustworthiness "equivalent" to those of a Rule 803 or 804 exception. The standard is now whether the statement has "sufficient guarantees of trustworthiness." It is ideal if the proponent shows that there was little possibility of insincerity or of flaws in the declarant's perception, memory, or narrative ability. The courts tend to place the greatest stress on the factor of the declarant's sincerity; if there is a common-sense reason to believe that the declarant was speaking sincerely, that factor cuts strongly in favor of admitting the statement. The proponent can show that there was a factor present giving the declarant a positive motivation for sincerity, as in the case of the nervous excitement making startled declarations admissible. Alternatively, the proponent can show that there was a factor present creating a disincentive for lying, as in the case of the disserving quality of declarations against interest. Although the 2019 amendment substitutes "sufficient" for "equivalent," the proponent can still analogize to an enumerated exception and argue that that exception treats a similar inference of reliability as "sufficient."

3. There is some necessity for resorting to the hearsay. At the very least there should be the relative necessity required by Rule 803: the out-of-court statement is more likely to be reliable than any testimony now available from the same source. The case is stronger when the necessity is absolute, that is, unavailability satisfying Rule 804(a).

[3]   SAMPLE FOUNDATION

The hypothetical fact situation is a civil wrongful death action. The plaintiff alleges that the accused Nelson was speeding, ran a red light, and struck a pedestrian named Garner, the plaintiff's husband. Garner died as a result of the injuries he sustained. A month after the accident, the grand jury conducted an investigation into the accident and indicted Nelson. An eyewitness, Mr. West, testified at the hearing. At the hearing, West identified the defendant's car and testified positively that the defendant ran the red light. West died unexpectedly after the hearing and before trial. The plaintiff has made a motion *in limine* in the nature of a motion to admit the transcript of West's grand jury testimony. Under the rules of court in this jurisdiction, at these hearings the judge receives affidavits rather than hearing live testimony. The following is the oral argument on the motion:

J   I'm prepared to hear argument on the motion. Ms. Plaintiff, are you ready to proceed?

P   Certainly, Your Honor. Your Honor, let me say at the outset that we realize that we cannot offer Mr. West's testimony under Rule 804(b)(1); the defendant didn't have an opportunity to cross at the grand jury hearing, and we therefore can't offer the transcript as former testimony.

However, we believe very strongly that this is an appropriate case for admitting the testimony under the residual exception, Rule 807. To begin with, we've complied with the advance notice requirement. (1) We served notice of this motion on the defense more than two weeks ago. There is a copy of the service in the court file. To make sure that the defense understood exactly what we intended to offer, we attached a Xerox copy of the relevant pages of the transcript to the notice of motion.

J   Mr. Defense Attorney, would you like to be heard?

O   I certainly would, Your Honor. I'll be brief.

First, we don't believe that this is a proper use of Rule 807. On pages two and three of our memorandum of law, we've noted the many cases stating that Congress intended the residual exceptions to be used sparingly. Even more to the point, page four of the memo lists the cases specifically holding that the exception does not apply to grand jury transcripts. We urge you to follow those cases.

J   Ms. Plaintiff, do you have any response?

P   Yes, Your Honor. I'll also try to be brief.

We acknowledge that there are cases urging a narrow interpretation of the residual exception and even cases specifically rejecting grand jury transcripts offered under the exceptions. However, we'd ask you to note that all the cases cited in the defense memorandum were decided in the late 1970s. On page three of our memorandum, we conceded that until the early 1980s, the trend in the case law was toward a narrow interpretation of the residual exception. However, pages four through seven of our memorandum cite more recent decisions. After carefully considering the legislative history of the residual exception, those decisions adopt a more expansive interpretation of the residual exception, and many cases now admit grand jury transcripts. This is a civil case, and consequently confrontation clause concerns are inapplicable.

J   I agree. The motion to admit will be granted.

CHAPTER 11

SUBSTITUTES FOR EVIDENCE

§ 11.01 INTRODUCTION

The previous 10 chapters analyze the legal restrictions on the process of admitting evidence during a trial. However, there are substitutes for conventional evidence: The parties may stipulate to certain propositions, the judge may judicially notice a proposition, or the jurors themselves may be taken outside the courtroom to view a scene or object that is relevant to the case. This chapter discusses the limitations on those substitutes.

§ 11.02 STIPULATIONS

[1] THE DOCTRINE

It is very common for the parties to stipulate before or during a trial. A stipulation can save both parties time, and by stipulating in the jury's presence, a party can attempt to create the impression in the jurors' minds that he or she is a reasonable, fair person.

There are several types of stipulations. For example, the parties may stipulate to continuances or to the admission of a particular exhibit.[1] However, we are concerned primarily with two types of evidentiary stipulations. The first is a stipulation of fact; the parties agree that a certain fact existed or that a certain event occurred. If the parties enter a stipulation of fact, neither party can ordinarily introduce evidence to contradict the stipulated fact. As the Court recognized in *Old Chief v. United States*, 519 U.S. 172, 117 S. Ct. 644, 136 L. Ed. 2d 574 (1997), the mere tender of a stipulation to a fact can reduce or eliminate the proponent's need to resort to an item of evidence to prove the fact; the tender makes the evidence more vulnerable to an objection based on Rule 403. The second type of stipulation is a stipulation of expected testimony; the parties agree that if a particular person were present in court as a witness, the person would give certain testimony. The parties are not stipulating that the testimony is admissible, truthful, or correct; the parties may introduce evidence to contradict what the person would testify to, and they may object if particular sentences in the stipulation are objectionable under evidence law. The parties are agreeing on only what the person's testimony would be if the person appeared and testified in court.

---

[1] When the parties enter into such a stipulation, both parties waive any potential objections to the exhibit. At trial, either party may then introduce the exhibit without any live, sponsoring testimony. However, as a matter of trial advocacy, if the party has a witness familiar with the exhibit, the party might ask the witness some foundation-type questions about the authenticity of the exhibit. Although given the stipulation such testimony is technically unnecessary, the testimony may increase the persuasiveness of the exhibit.

The procedure for introducing stipulations varies. Some judges commonly permit the attorneys to recite oral stipulations. Other judges prefer that the parties reduce their stipulation to writing. Written pretrial stipulations obviously reduce the possibility for disagreement at trial over the content of the stipulation.

The final procedural question is whether the judge accepting the stipulation must personally question the parties. May the judge accept the attorneys' assurances that the parties assent? In civil actions, the judges routinely do so.

The answer is more complex in criminal cases. In *Boykin v. Alabama*, 395 U.S. 238, 89 S. Ct. 1709, 23 L. Ed. 2d 274 (1969), the Supreme Court held that since an accused waives certain constitutional rights by pleading guilty, the trial record must reflect that the accused knowingly waived the rights. In many cases, the accused stipulates to a trial on the basis of the preliminary hearing transcript. This practice is sometimes called a "slow (guilty) plea." Even if the accused does not stipulate to the truth of all the facts recited by the prosecution witnesses at the preliminary hearing, the accused is entering into a stipulation of expected testimony; the defense is agreeing that if the same witnesses appeared at trial, they would give the testimony they gave at the earlier hearing. The accused is implicitly waiving the Sixth Amendment rights to confront these witnesses and to have the jurors determine the witnesses' credibility. The argument was made that since this practice is practically a guilty plea, the courts should apply *Boykin* by analogy. A minority of state and federal courts have accepted the analogy. For example, in *United States v. Brown*, 428 F.2d 1100 (D.C. Cir. 1970), in which the accused raised an insanity defense, the court commented: "[W]here a defendant in a criminal case seeks to waive trial on all issues except insanity, the trial judge should address the defendant personally in determining whether the waiver is made voluntarily with understanding of the consequences of the act." The California Supreme Court imposed similar requirements in *Bunnell v. Superior Court*, 13 Cal. 3d 592, 119 Cal. Rptr. 302, 531 P.2d 1086 (1975).

[2] ELEMENTS OF THE FOUNDATION

The procedure for entering a stipulation includes these steps:

1. One attorney announces to the judge that there has been a stipulation.

2. The judge then inquires of the other attorney whether there has been a stipulation.

3. The second attorney answers in the affirmative.

4. The proponent of the stipulation establishes the tenor or content of the agreement. If the stipulation is oral, the proponent simply states the nature of the agreement on the record. If the stipulation is in writing, the proponent introduces the writing.

5. When required, the judge personally questions the party or parties before accepting the stipulation. The judge ensures that the party understands the nature and consequences of the stipulation.

After the judge accepts the stipulation, the judge informs the jury of the stipulation and instructs the jury on the legal effect of the stipulation. The parties often present the stipulation to the judge at a pretrial hearing. After the judge accepts the stipulation at the pretrial hearing, the parties may use the stipulation during the trial.

[3] SAMPLE FOUNDATIONS

The first fact situation is a suit for breach of contract. The plaintiff, Marshall Industries, alleges that on January 10, YR-3, it entered into a contract with the defendant, Rowl Company. The complaint alleges that under the terms of the contract, Rowl Company promised to excavate a site, lay a foundation, and build a two-story shopping center for the plaintiff. In its answer the defendant raises the affirmative defenses of impossibility and financial impracticability. The answer alleges that a week after beginning excavation, the defendant discovered a subsoil condition that made it prohibitively expensive for it to do the promised construction work. The proponent is the plaintiff.

P	Your Honor, I would like to announce that the parties in this case have reached a stipulation as to their actual knowledge of the existence of the subsoil condition that the defendant discovered in March YR-3. (1)
J	(*To the defense attorney*) Is that true? (2)
O	Yes, Your Honor. (3)
J	What is the nature of this stipulation? (4)
P	We have stipulated that before the defendant's discovery of the layer of granite in March YR-3, none of the employees of either the plaintiff or the defendant had actual, subjective knowledge that the layer of granite existed.
J	(*To the defense attorney*) Is that the tenor of the stipulation?
O	Yes.
J	And both of your clients consent to this stipulation?
P	Yes.
O	Yes, Your Honor.
J	Has this agreement been reduced to writing?
P	No, Your Honor.
O	No—it's an oral stipulation.
J	Very well. If that is the case, I shall accept the stipulation of fact. Ladies and gentlemen of the jury, the plaintiff and the defendant have just entered into an agreement or stipulation. All parties agree that before the defendant discovered the layer of granite at the construction site in March YR-3, none of the employees of the plaintiff or defendant had actual, subjective knowledge that the granite was there. Will both parties state for the record that I have correctly described the stipulation for the jury?
O	Certainly, Your Honor.

P   I concur.

J   And ladies and gentlemen of the jury, because of the stipulation, you will not hear any evidence on that issue. However, I am instructing you that you are simply to assume the truth of the stipulated fact. All right, let's proceed with the evidence.

The second fact situation is a criminal prosecution for theft. The People allege that the accused, Mr. David Miles, stole $1,700 from a local Vons Department Store. An acquaintance of the accused saw him leave the department store in a furtive, hurried fashion immediately after the alleged theft. Unfortunately for the prosecution, that person is now vacationing in Florida. Rather than forcing the witness to return or seeking a continuance, the parties enter into a stipulation of expected testimony. On this occasion, the parties decided to reduce the stipulation to writing before trial.

Form 11-1

STIPULATION OF EXPECTED TESTIMONY

It is hereby stipulated between the People and the defense, with the accused's express consent, that if Robert Prothero, 766 Somerset Street, Daly City, California, were present in court and sworn as a witness, he would give the following testimony:

I know the accused, David Miles. We have been members of the same labor union for the past three years. I can recognize him by sight. On the afternoon of July 28, YR-3, as I was walking by the entrance to the Vons Department Store on H Street in downtown Millbrae, I saw the accused exit the store. As soon as he stepped outside, he looked both ways—up and down the street. He seemed to be nervous. Then he stuck his hand in his right pants pocket; there was a big bulge in the pocket. As soon as he removed his hand from his pocket, he began running away from the store.

/s/ Deputy District Attorney
_____

/s/ Defense Counsel
_____

/s/ Defendant

Dated: November 1, YR-3

The parties now offer the stipulation at trial. The prosecutor is the proponent. Since the parties are not stipulating to a trial on the preliminary hearing transcript, *Brown* does not apply directly. However, the judge decides to conduct an abbreviated *Brown* inquiry.

P	Your Honor, I want to announce that the parties in this case have reached a stipulation as to the expected testimony of an unavailable witness. (1)
J	(*To the defense counsel*) Is that true? (2)
O	Yes, Your Honor. (3)
J	What is the stipulation? (4)
P	Your Honor, I request that this be marked People's exhibit number four for identification.
J	It will be so marked.
P	Please let the record reflect that I am showing the exhibit to the opposing counsel.
J	It will so reflect.
P	I now offer People's exhibit number four for identification into evidence as People's exhibit four.
J	(*To the defense counsel*.) Is this the stipulation?
O	Yes, Your Honor.

J	Mr. Miles, please hold the exhibit in your hands while I ask you a few questions. (5)
D	Yes, sir.
J	Have you ever seen this document before? (5)
D	Yes.
J	When? (5)
D	My attorney showed it to me when he asked me to sign it.
J	Are you familiar with the contents? (5)
D	Yes.
J	Is that your signature on the bottom of the page? (5)
D	Yes.
J	Has your lawyer advised you that you do not have to enter into this stipulation? (5)
D	Yes. He told me that.
J	Has your lawyer informed you that you have a right to insist that the prosecution produce Mr. Prothero at this trial? (5)
D	Yes.
J	Do you realize that if Mr. Prothero appeared at this trial, he would have to testify under oath? (5)
D	Yes.
J	Do you understand that if he testified at trial, he would have to testify in view of the jury? (5)
D	Yes.
J	Do you realize that if he testified under oath, the jury would determine whether or not to believe his testimony? (5)
D	Yes.
J	Do you realize that if he testified at trial, you would have an opportunity to cross-examine him? (5)
D	Yes.
J	Do you understand that you are surrendering and losing these rights by agreeing to this stipulation? (5)
D	Yes, sir.
J	Has your counsel advised you that even if you stipulate to Mr. Prothero's testimony, you can introduce evidence to rebut or contradict what Mr. Prothero says? (5)
D	Yes.
J	Has your counsel told you that even if you stipulate to Mr. Prothero's

	testimony, your counsel can make objections on evidentiary grounds to the testimony? (5)
	(*As a practical matter, there will rarely be evidentiary objections after the entry of the stipulation; the parties usually eliminate any objectionable material during the bargaining over the content of the stipulation.*)
D	Yes.
J	Do you consent to this stipulation? (5)
D	Yes.
J	Well, I find that the accused is knowingly and voluntarily entering into this stipulation. Therefore, the stipulation will be accepted. The exhibit will be received.
P	Your Honor, I request permission to read the exhibit to the jurors.
J	Permission granted.
P	Both parties, the People and defense, have agreed and stipulated that if Mr. Robert Prothero, 766 Somerset Street, Daly City, California, were present in court, he would give the following testimony: "I know the accused, David Miles. We have been members of the same labor union for the past three years. I can recognize him on sight. On the afternoon of July 28, YR-3, I was walking by the entrance to the Vons Department Store on H Street in downtown Millbrae. I saw the accused exit the store. As soon as he stepped outside, he looked both ways—up and down the street. He seemed to be nervous. Then he stuck his hand in his right pants pocket; there was a big bulge in the pocket. As soon as he removed his hand from his pocket, he began running away from the store."
O	Your Honor, will you please instruct the jury about the stipulation?
J	Yes. Ladies and gentlemen of the jury, the prosecutor has just read a stipulation of expected testimony. The parties have agreed as to what the testimony of Mr. Prothero would be if he appeared here and testified under oath. The stipulation does not admit the truth of the testimony, and it does not add anything to the weight of Mr. Prothero's testimony. The defense may attack, contradict, or explain Mr. Prothero's testimony. In deciding how much weight to attach to Mr. Prothero's testimony, you may consider the fact that you have not had an opportunity to personally observe his demeanor.

§ 11.03 JUDICIAL NOTICE

[1] THE DOCTRINE

By entering into a stipulation, the opposing parties can eliminate the need for live testimony. However, absent a stipulation, acting alone the judge can eliminate the need for such testimony. Like the stipulation technique, judicial notice is an alternative to the presentation of formal evidence. Federal Rule of Evidence 201(a) "governs judicial notice of an adjudicative fact only, not a legislative fact."[2] The judge relieves the parties of the duty to present evidence by noting a fact and informing the jury of the fact's existence. What types of facts may be judicially noticed? Federal Rule 201(b) answers that to be judicially noticeable, a fact must be one that is either "(1) generally known within the trial court's territorial jurisdiction; or (2) can be accurately and readily determined from sources whose accuracy cannot reasonably be questioned." The Rule typifies the modern common law of judicial notice; the Rule recognizes two separate, independent bases for judicial notice: (1) the fact is a matter of common knowledge within the court's territorial jurisdiction; and (2) the fact is a so-called readily verifiable certainty. (Although the courts and commentators often use the expression "verifiable certainty" to describe the types of facts qualifying under the second basis, it is best to remember, as Justice Blackmun commented in *Daubert v. Merrell Dow Pharms.*, 509 U.S. 579, 113 S. Ct. 2786, 125 L. Ed. 2d 469 (1993), "arguably, there are no certainties in science." "Verifiable certainty" would be an unrealistically high standard.) Moreover, the statute, Rule 201(b)(2), uses the expression, "cannot reasonably be questioned," rather than referring to "certainty." The courts are increasingly applying (b)(2) to information posted on government websites and even private sources such as Google Maps. Bellin & Ferguson, *Trial by Google: Judicial Notice in the Information Age*, 108 Nw. U. L. Rev. 1137 (2014).

The procedure for judicial notice varies from jurisdiction to jurisdiction. Many courts permit attorneys to orally request judicial notice during trial. Other courts prefer that the attorneys submit judicial notice requests in writing before trial. Perhaps the emerging view is that the procedure depends on the basis for judicial notice the party is invoking. When the party claims that the fact is a matter of common knowledge, the request can be informal. If the knowledge of the fact is widespread in the territorial area, the judge and attorneys ought to know the fact; and a formal hearing would be a waste of time. On the other hand, if the party claims that the fact is a readily verifiable certainty, the request should be written and supported by documentary material. For example, when the party requests judicial notice of a scientific principle, the party should submit at least documentary proof of the principle's validity. Courts usually relax the hearsay rule when the parties are litigating the propriety of judicial notice; the judge often permits the parties to use affidavits, declarations, and letters that would usually be considered inadmissible hearsay. In federal practice, the parties may do so by virtue of the last sentence in Rule 104(a).

[2] SAMPLE FOUNDATIONS

Matter of Common Knowledge

The first fact situation illustrates the first basis for judicial notice, matters of common knowledge. The fact situation is a tort action arising from a traffic accident. The

---

[2] Although some jurisdictions such as California extend the concept of judicial notice to legal matters, again Federal Rule of Evidence 201(a) "governs judicial notice of an adjudicative fact only . . . ." Federal courts sometimes use the expression "judicial notice" loosely when they informally note legal matters such as ordinances or legislative history, but the procedures prescribed by Rules 201(c)–(f) do not apply in those situations.

plaintiff, Ms. Garnet, alleges that the defendant, Mr. Simmons, was speeding and carelessly struck her as she was crossing the street. The plaintiff has already called Mr. James Farnsworth as a witness. Mr. Farnsworth testifies that he observed the accident. He testified that the defendant's car struck the plaintiff at the intersection of F and Girard Streets in downtown Bismarck. Mr. Farnsworth also expresses his opinion that the defendant was driving 35 miles an hour just before the accident. Mr. Farnsworth leaves the witness stand, and the following occurs. The plaintiff is the proponent.

P   Your Honor, I now request that you judicially notice two facts.

J   What are the facts?

P   The first is that in this state, the speed limit in any business district is 25 miles an hour.[3] The second is that the intersection of F and Girard Streets in downtown Bismarck is part of our business district. Both facts are matters of common knowledge in this area.

J   I agree.

P   Would you please instruct the jury about the judicially noticed facts?

J   Yes. Ladies and gentlemen of the jury, I am now judicially noticing two facts. The first fact is that in the State of North Dakota, the speed limit in any business district is 25 miles an hour. The second fact is that the intersection where this accident occurred—F and Girard Streets—is in Bismarck's business district. Since these facts are matters of common knowledge, I am authorized to note these facts without requiring formal evidence from the parties. You are to accept these facts and assume them to be true even though you will not hear any evidence on these facts.

Verifiable "Certainty"

The second fact situation illustrates the second basis for judicial notice, verifiable certainty. The second situation is a continuation of the first. The plaintiff ultimately wants to offer the testimony of Officer Newton Ripley. Officer Ripley had his police car parked near the intersection when the accident occurred. His police car was equipped with a radar speedmeter. The speedmeter clocked the defendant's car at 36 miles an hour just before the accident. As § 4.10 points out, part of the foundation for an offer of scientific evidence is proof of the underlying theory's validity and the instrument's reliability. Since the radarspeed meter is a scientific instrument, the plaintiff must lay those two elements of the foundation in our hypothetical. However, since those facts are readily verifiable certainties, the plaintiff need not present live testimony; the plaintiff

---

[3] As [1] pointed out, Federal Rule 201(a) states that it governs "judicial notice of an adjudicative fact only." In this hypothetical, the plaintiff is requesting judicial notice of law rather than fact. Despite Rule 201(a)'s express limitation of the scope of the doctrine to factual matters, some federal courts use the expression "judicial notice" when they take note of legal matters. In some jurisdictions such as California, the formal judicial notice doctrine applies to legal propositions as well as factual matters. However, by its terms, Rule 201(a) is inapplicable to legal propositions. The only significance of the limitation in Rule 201(a) is that the procedural safeguards prescribed by Rules 201(e)–(f) are inapplicable when the judge is informally noting legal propositions.

can use judicial notice to supply the first two elements of the scientific evidence foundation. Before trial, the plaintiff could submit this affidavit.

Form 11-2

STATE OF NORTH DAKOTA	
CITY OF BISMARCK	AFFIDAVIT

I, the undersigned, being duly sworn, depose and say that:

1. My name is Glenda Schneider. I reside at 7144 Frontier Boulevard, Bismarck, North Dakota.

2. I teach Electronics at the University of North Dakota. I have taught that subject there for the past seven years. I have a B.S., a Master's, and a Doctorate in that field from Michigan State University.

3. The underlying theory of the radar speedmeter is the Doppler shift principle. The principle is that if a beam of microwaves of known frequency strikes an approaching or receding object, the beam changes frequency. The change in frequency is proportional to the speed of the object. This theory has been experimentally verified by hundreds of empirical experiments throughout the world. It is accepted as a valid theory by all experts in the field.

4. The radar speedmeter is a device that applies the Doppler shift principle. The speedmeter consists of a transmitter and a receiver. The transmitter generates and sends out the beam of microwaves. The receiver measures the frequency change after the beam strikes an object and bounces back to the car containing the radar speedmeter. Like the underlying theory, the radar speedmeter instrument has been subjected to numerous well-designed, empirical validation experiments. The conclusion of the experiments is that if the speedmeter is in proper, working order and operated properly, the instrument will accurately measure speed to within a few hundredths of a mile per hour. At one time or another speedmeters have been used by law enforcement agencies in every state in the United States. Experts in my field almost universally accept the reliability of radar speedmeters.

/s/ Glenda Schneider

On September 17, YR-3, before the undersigned, a Notary Public for the State of North Dakota, personally appeared Glenda Schneider, known to me to be the person whose name is subscribed to the within instrument, and acknowledged that she executed the same.

/s/ Mildred Adams
Notary Public
My license expires October 17, YR+4

In addition to using affidavits from experts, the party can sometimes use an affidavit from a professional school librarian. The librarian's affidavit is attached to Xerox copies of the title page and the pertinent pages from a learned treatise in the scientific field. The librarian's affidavit states the librarian's position, lists the credentials of the author of the treatise, and finally asserts that the treatise is a standard, authoritative text in its field. The party then uses the excerpts from the treatise to establish that the principle's validity or the instrument's reliability is a verifiable certainty.

The plaintiff would use the affidavit at trial in this fashion. As soon as the judge granted the first request for judicial notice, the plaintiff could make this request before calling Officer Ripley as a witness. The plaintiff is still the proponent.

P	Your Honor, I have one last request for judicial notice.
J	What is that?
P	May we approach the bench?
J	Yes.
P	Your Honor, I request that you judicially notice the validity of the theory underlying radar speedmeters and the general reliability of speedmeters. Both facts are verifiable certainties.
J	(*To the opposing attorney*) Did you have advance notice that the plaintiff was going to make this request?
O	Yes, Your Honor. He gave me notice a week ago.
P	Your Honor, I request that this be marked plaintiff's exhibit number nine for identification.[4]
J	It will be so marked.
P	Please let the record reflect that I am showing the exhibit to the opposing counsel.
J	It will so reflect.
P	I now offer plaintiff's exhibit number nine for identification into evidence as plaintiff's exhibit number nine.
J	(*To the opposing attorney*) Have you seen this exhibit before?
O	Yes. The plaintiff's attorney gave me a copy about a week ago.
J	Do you have any objection?
O	Yes, Your Honor. This affidavit is gross hearsay.
P	Your Honor, at this point we're litigating the propriety of judicial notice. In this jurisdiction, under Rule 104(a), the hearsay rule doesn't apply to your determination whether these facts are verifiable certainties.

---

[4] In some jurisdictions, this type of exhibit receives a special designation as an appellate exhibit. On the one hand, it is given a formal designation, since it is inserted in the record of trial. In the event of an appeal, the court can review the exhibit. On the other hand, it is not designated as a normal trial exhibit, since the exhibit would never be submitted to the jury.

J You're right. The objection will be overruled, and the exhibit will be received.

P The exhibit establishes that the validity of the underlying principle and the reliability of the instrument are verifiable, scientific certainties. For that reason, judicial notice is appropriate.

J I will grant your request.

P I request that you inform the jury of these facts.

J Yes. Ladies and gentlemen of the jury, I am now going to judicially notice two more facts. One fact is the validity of the theory underlying radar speedmeters. As you may know, the police in this jurisdiction use radar speedmeters to measure the speed of cars. The technical theory underlying speedmeters has been accepted by scientists. Secondly, the speedmeter itself is a reliable instrument if it's in working order and operated correctly. You are to assume the validity of the theory and the general reliability of the instrument. I understand that we are about to hear some testimony about a particular radar speedmeter clocking of the speed of the defendant's car. I want to make it clear that I am not deciding whether this particular speedmeter was in good, working condition or whether the officer used the correct procedures. You will have to listen to the testimony and make those decisions. I am instructing you only that you must assume the validity of the scientific principle and the general reliability of speedmeters even though you won't hear any evidence on these topics.

The above hypothetical assumes a civil action. In a civil action, Federal Rule of Evidence 201(f) requires the judge to direct the jury to assume the existence of the noticed fact. However, Rule 201(f) prescribes a different rule for criminal cases: "In a criminal case, the court must instruct the jury that it may or may not accept the noticed fact as conclusive." Thus, neither the prosecution nor the defense can obtain an instruction worded in mandatory terms.

§ 11.04 JURY VIEWS

[1] THE DOCTRINE

Sometimes the attorneys want the jurors and judge to view an object or location that cannot feasibly be brought into the courtroom. In most cases, the attorney will be content to offer either a witness's oral description of the object, a diagram of the object, or a photograph. However, in some cases, the object is so complex and plays such a pivotal role in the case that the attorney wants the trier of fact to personally observe the object or location. This procedure is known as a jury view. The jury can view either parcels of real property or items of personal property that cannot conveniently be brought into the courtroom.

In most jurisdictions, the sense impressions the trier of fact gathers during a view do not qualify as substantive evidence in the case. However, there is a minority view. California Evidence Code § 140 defines "evidence" as including "things presented to the senses that are offered to prove the existence or nonexistence of a fact." The California Law Revision Commission comment explains that § 140 includes jury views. Hence, the information the trier of fact gains during a jury view constitutes independent, substantive evidence under the Code. Some federal courts have come to the same conclusion.[5]

[2] ELEMENTS OF THE FOUNDATION

The proponent of a jury view usually makes a pretrial motion for a view and submits affidavits or declarations in support of the motion. The declarations should show that:

1. Certain property exists.

2. The property is logically relevant to the pending case.

3. It is impossible or inconvenient to bring the property into the courtroom.

4. The features of the property are so complex or detailed that an oral description, diagram, or photograph would be inadequate.

5. The property is in substantially the same condition as at the time of the relevant event. If the property has changed materially, the judge usually exercises discretion by denying the motion. If the property has changed markedly, a view might mislead the jury. When there is potential for misleading the jury, Rule 403 cuts against granting the motion.

[3] SAMPLE FOUNDATION

The fact situation is a personal injury action arising from a collision in February YR-5 on a winding, rural road in Yolo County. The plaintiff moves for a jury view of the section of road where the collision occurred. In support of the motion, the plaintiff submits two declarations. Both declarations refer to the same section of road mentioned in the pleadings. For that reason, both declarations lay the first three elements of the foundation. The date of the hearing on the motion is August 1, YR-3.

---

[5] Lillie v. United States, 953 F.2d 1188 (10th Cir. 1992).

Form 11-3

DECLARATION[6]

1. My name is George Wasterson. I live at 1444 Court Street, Woodland, California.

2. I am a professional photographer. I am the proprietor of the Wasterson Photography Studio, 1456 Court Street, in Woodland. I have owned that company for 12 years. While I was on active duty in the United States Army between YR-28 and YR-19, I received formal training in photography. I have since taken seven photography classes at California State University in Sacramento.

3. On July 1, YR-3, an attorney, Ms. Eileen Richards, contacted me by phone. She asked me to meet her at the intersection of Rural Route 4 and Range Road outside the city limits of Woodland. (1), (2), (3) I met her there later that afternoon.

4. While we were at the intersection, Ms. Richards explained to me that she represented the plaintiff in a civil action arising from a collision at the intersection. She also explained that she was interested in showing the jurors the 200 yards of Range Road immediately to the west of the intersection with Rural Route 4. She asked whether I could photograph or videotape that section of road.

5. I carefully inspected the two hundred yards of road in question. I walked the stretch of road twice and drove it twice. I then advised Ms. Richards that in my professional opinion, neither still photographs nor a videotape would be adequate. The section of road in question is not only winding; the road surface is also extremely uneven—any car traveling that section of road is constantly riding up and then down and then up again. Even if I took 100 still photographs and submitted them to a jury, the stills would not adequately convey to the jury a realistic sense of traveling down that stretch of road. In addition, since the road is both curvy and uneven, even a videotape would convey only a limited sense of perspective of a driver on that stretch of road. I declare under penalty of perjury that the above statements are true and correct.

Executed this 14th day of July YR-3, in Woodland, Yolo County, California.

_____

/s/ George Wasterson

---

[6] California Code of Civil Procedure § 2015.5 permits the use of a declaration in lieu of an affidavit.

Form 11-4

DECLARATION

1. My name is Doris Kingman. I reside at 723 Range Road in Yolo County, California. I have lived at that residence for the past 37 years.

2. I am intimately familiar with the intersection of Range Road and Rural Route 4 outside Woodland in Yolo County. It is the intersection closest to my house. I have driven through that intersection thousands of times.

3. I can recall the condition of the 200 yards of Range Road immediately to the west of the intersection with Rural Route 4 as of February YR-5. I generally remember the condition of the road and the foliage on both sides of the road. I inspected that area again today. To the best of my recollection, the condition of the foliage and road today is substantially the same as the condition in February YR-5.

I declare under penalty of perjury that the above statements are true and correct.

Executed this 29th day of July YR-3 in Woodland, Yolo County, California.

_____

/s/ Doris Kingman

INDEX

[References are to sections.]

A

ANCIENT WRITINGS
Authentication of . . . 4.02[7]

ATTORNEY–CLIENT PRIVILEGE
Generally . . . 7.01 *et seq.*
Joint consultation exception . . . 7.05[3]
Work product protection
  Absolute . . . 7.06[2]
  Conditional . . . 7.06[1]

AUDIO RECORDINGS, AUTHENTICATION OF
Generally . . . 4.06[1]
Elements of foundation . . . 4.06[2]
Sample foundation . . . 4.06[3]

AUTHENTICATION
Generally . . . 4.01[1]
Animations and simulations, computer (See COMPUT-
  ERS, subhead: Animations and simulations, verifica-
  tion of)
Audio recordings (See AUDIO RECORDINGS, AU-
  THENTICATION OF)
Business writings (See BUSINESS WRITINGS)
Caller ID (See CALLER ID, AUTHENTICATION OF)
Cloud, electronic information stored in . . . 4.03[11]
Computerized courtrooms, in
  Generally . . . 4.01[3][a]
  Digitized exhibits on computer, presentation of
    . . . 4.01[3][d]
  Premarked exhibit presentation using document cam-
    era . . . 4.01[3][c]
  Unmarked hard copy presentation using document
    camera . . . 4.01[3][b]
Computer records (See COMPUTERS, subhead: Re-
  cords, authentication of)
Demonstrative evidence . . . 4.07[1]
E-mail (See E–MAIL, AUTHENTICATION OF)
Fax documents . . . 4.03[3]
Official writings (See OFFICIAL WRITINGS, AU-
  THENTICATION OF)
Oral statements (See ORAL STATEMENTS, AUTHEN-
  TICATION OF)
Photographs (See PHOTOGRAPHS, VERIFICATION
  OF)
Physical evidence (See PHYSICAL EVIDENCE, IDEN-
  TIFICATION OF)
Private writings (See PRIVATE WRITINGS, AUTHEN-
  TICATION OF)
Scientific evidence (See SCIENTIFIC EVIDENCE,
  VALIDATION OF)
Self-authenticating printouts
  Blockchain, printouts of records maintained on
    . . . 4.03[10]
  Data copies from electronic device, storage medium
    or file . . . 4.03[9]
  Records automatically generated by electronic pro-
    cess or system . . . 4.03[8]
Traditional courtrooms, in . . . 4.01[2]

AUTOMATED SURVEILLANCE CAMERAS
Verification of . . . 4.09[4]

B

BEST EVIDENCE RULE
Generally . . . 8.01
Copies
  Authenticated . . . 8.07[2]
  Duplicate originals (See subhead: Duplicate origi-
    nals)
Destroyed originals . . . 8.08[3]
Duplicate originals
  Generally . . . 8.06[1]
  Elements of foundation . . . 8.06[2]
  Sample foundation . . . 8.06[3]
"In issue," writings
  Generally . . . 8.03
  Collateral connection . . . 8.04
Lost originals . . . 8.08[2]
Non-production, excuses for
  Generally . . . 8.08[1]
  Destroyed originals . . . 8.08[3]
  Lost originals . . . 8.08[2]
  Official custody, originals in . . . 8.08[4]
  Refusal of party-opponent to produce . . . 8.08[6]
  Third-party possession, originals in . . . 8.08[5]
  Voluminous or bulky records . . . 8.08[7]
Official custody, originals in . . . 8.08[4]
Oral recollection testimony . . . 8.07[3]
Original evidence
  Generally . . . 8.05[1]
  Elements of foundation . . . 8.05[2]
  Sample foundation . . . 8.05[3]
"Original writing rule," as . . . 8.02
Private writings, authentication of . . . 4.02[1]
Refusal of party-opponent to produce . . . 8.08[6]
Secondary evidence, admissible
  Generally . . . 8.07[1]
  Authenticated copies . . . 8.07[2]
  Oral recollection testimony . . . 8.07[3]
Third-party possession, originals in . . . 8.08[5]
Voluminous or bulky records, non-production of
  . . . 8.08[7]
Writing requirement . . . 8.02

BOLSTERING OF WITNESSES
Generally . . . 5.02
Fresh complaint doctrine, use of
  Generally . . . 5.04[1]
    Elements of foundation . . . 5.04[2]
    Sample foundation . . . 5.04[3]
Prior identification testimony
  Generally . . . 5.03[1]
    Elements of foundation . . . 5.03[2]
    Sample foundation . . . 5.03[3]
Prohibition . . . 5.03[1]

BUSINESS WRITINGS
Authentication
  Generally . . . 4.03[1]

I-1

[References are to sections.]

BUSINESS WRITINGS—Cont.

Authentication—Cont.

Blockchain, printouts of records maintained on . . . 4.03[10]

Cloud, electronic information stored in . . . 4.03[11]

Computer records (See COMPUTERS, subhead: Records, authentication of)

E-mail (See E–MAIL, AUTHENTICATION OF)

Fax documents . . . 4.03[3]

Scanned writings . . . 4.03[5]

Self-authenticating printouts (See AUTHENTICATION, subhead: Self-authenticating printouts)

Self-authenticating writings . . . 4.03[7]

Web site information . . . 4.03[6]

Hearsay exception for business entries (See HEARSAY, subhead: Business entries exception)

C

CALLER ID, AUTHENTICATION OF

Generally . . . 4.05[5][a]

Elements of foundation . . . 4.05[5][b]

Sample foundation . . . 4.05[5][c]

CGA (See COMPUTERS, subhead: Animations and simulations, verification of)

CHARACTER EVIDENCE

Generally . . . 6.02[1]

Conduct, proof by specific . . . 6.02[4]

Cross-examination of character witness . . . 6.02[5]

Opinion evidence . . . 6.02[3]

Reputation evidence . . . 6.02[2]

CHILDREN

Witnesses - voir dire examination (See VOIR DIRE EXAMINATION OF WITNESS)

CLOUD STORAGE

Authentication of electronic information . . . 4.03[11]

COMPUTERS

Animations and simulations, verification of

Generally . . . 4.09[5][a]

Illustrative evidence . . . 4.09[5][b]

Immersive virtual environment (IVE) system . . . 4.09[5][c]

Substantive evidence . . . 4.09[5][c]

Authentication in computerized courtrooms (See AUTHENTICATION, subhead: Computerized courtrooms, in)

Hearsay rule, applicability of . . . 10.02[4]

Records, authentication of

Generally . . . 4.03[2]

Blockchain, printouts of records maintained on . . . 4.03[10]

E-mail (See E–MAIL, AUTHENTICATION OF)

Web site information . . . 4.03[6]

Social media profile page, authenticating printout of . . . 4.02[6]

CREDIBILITY EVIDENCE

Generally . . . 5.02

CREDIBILITY EVIDENCE—Cont.

Bolstering of witnesses (See BOLSTERING OF WITNESSES)

Impeachment of witnesses (See IMPEACHMENT OF WITNESSES)

Rehabilitation of witnesses (See REHABILITATION OF WITNESSES)

Rule 403 limiting . . . 5.01; 5.02

Significance of characterizing testimony as . . . 5.02

CROSS–EXAMINATION (GENERALLY)

Character witness . . . 6.02[5]

Foundation, laying of

Generally . . . 1.04[1]

Legal rules . . . 1.04[2]

Practical rules . . . 1.04[3]

Hearsay statement previously subject to cross examination (See HEARSAY, subhead: Prior testimony subject to cross-examination)

Impeachment of witness by inconsistent statements . . . 5.09[2]

D

DEAD PERSONS' STATUTE

Generally . . . 3.06[1]

Elements of foundation . . . 3.06[2]

Narrow construction of . . . 3.06[1]

Sample foundation . . . 3.06[3]

Waiver of . . . 3.06[1]

DEMONSTRATIVE EVIDENCE

Generally . . . 4.07[1]

Diagrams

Marking on . . . 4.07[3]

Verification . . . 4.07[2]

Models . . . 4.07[4]

Prejudice, risk of . . . 6.07; 6.08

DIAGRAMS

Marking on . . . 4.07[3]

Verification . . . 4.07[2]

DIRECT EXAMINATION (GENERALLY)

Foundation, laying of

Generally . . . 1.03[1]

Legal rules . . . 1.03[2]

Practical rules . . . 1.03[3]

DOCUMENTARY EVIDENCE

Best evidence rule (See BEST EVIDENCE RULE)

Writings, authentication of (See specific subject headings, e.g., BUSINESS WRITINGS)

E

ELECTRONIC RECORDS

Authentication of information stored in cloud . . . 4.03[11]

E–MAIL, AUTHENTICATION OF

Generally . . . 4.03[4][a], [4][c][i]

Chain of custody - testimony by employee of e-mail service . . . 4.03[4][c][ii]

[References are to sections.]

E–MAIL, AUTHENTICATION OF—Cont.
Digital signature, testimony regarding
  . . . 4.03[4][c][iii]
Elements of foundation . . . 4.03[4][b]
Reply letter doctrine . . . 4.03[4][b]

EXHIBITIONS, IN–COURT
Prejudice, risk of . . . 6.07

EXPERIMENTS, OUT–OF–COURT
Generally . . . 9.04[1]
Elements of foundation . . . 9.04[2]
Sample foundation . . . 9.04[3]

EXPERT TESTIMONY
Generally . . . 9.03[1]
Application of general methodology to case-specific
  information, proper . . . 9.03[5]
Case-specific factual bases for opinion
    Generally . . . 9.03[4][a]
    Assumed facts, hypothetically . . . 9.03[4][d]
    Independently admissible facts . . . 9.03[4][b]
    Personal knowledge of facts . . . 9.03[4][b]
    Secondhand reports . . . 9.03[4][c]
    Sufficiency of facts or data to support opinion
      . . . 9.03[4][e]
Competency of witnesses (See WITNESSES, subhead:
  Psychiatric testimony attacking competency)
Experiments, out-of-court (See EXPERIMENTS, OUT-
  –OF–COURT)
Explanation of opinion, importance of . . . 9.03[7]
Handwriting analysis . . . 4.02[5]
Qualifications of expert . . . 9.03[2]
Scientific evidence, validation of (See SCIENTIFIC
  EVIDENCE, VALIDATION OF)
Secondhand reports from third parties, reliance upon
  . . . 9.03[4][c]
Statement of opinion, form of . . . 9.03[6]
Theory or technique relied upon, statement of
  . . . 9.03[3]
Voice identification . . . 4.05[4]

F

FACEBOOK
Social media profile page, authenticating printout of
  . . . 4.02[6]

FAX DOCUMENTS
Authentication . . . 4.03[3]

FOUNDATION, LAYING OF (GENERALLY)
Cross-examination, on (See CROSS–EXAMINATION
  (GENERALLY))
Direct examination, on (See DIRECT EXAMINATION
  (GENERALLY))
Legal rules . . . 1.02[1]
Practical rules . . . 1.02[2]

FRESH COMPLAINT DOCTRINE
Bolstering of testimony (See BOLSTERING OF WIT-
  NESSES)

G

GOVERNMENT DOCUMENTS
Authentication of official writings (See OFFICIAL
  WRITINGS, AUTHENTICATION OF)
Best evidence exception, non-production of document
  warranting . . . 8.08[4]
Hearsay exception for official records (See HEARSAY,
  subhead: Official records exception)
Privileged communications (See PRIVILEGED COM-
  MUNICATIONS, subhead: Government privileges)

GRAND JURY TESTIMONY
Residual hearsay exception . . . 10.19[1]

H

HABIT EVIDENCE
Generally . . . 6.03[1]
Elements of foundation . . . 6.03[2]
Sample foundation . . . 6.03[3]

HANDWRITING
Expert testimony . . . 4.02[5]
Layperson's testimony . . . 4.02[3]

HEARSAY
Generally . . . 10.01
Admissions exemption
  Generally . . . 10.03[1]
  Adoptive admissions (See subhead: Adoptive admis-
    sions, exemption for)
  Personal admissions (See subhead: Personal admis-
    sions, exemption for)
  Vicarious admissions
    Civil cases . . . 10.03[4][a]
    Criminal cases . . . 10.03[4][b]
Adoptive admissions, exemption for
  Generally . . . 10.03[3][a]
  Express adoption . . . 10.03[3][b]
  Implied adoption . . . 10.03[3][c]
  Tacit admission . . . 10.03[3][c]
Assertive acts . . . 10.02[2][b]
Assertive statements . . . 10.02[2][a]
Bodily condition, declarations of
  External cause or source . . . 10.12[3]
  Past bodily condition . . . 10.12[2]
  Present bodily condition . . . 10.12[1]
Breathalyzer data, use of . . . 10.02[4]
Business entries exception
  Generally . . . 10.05[1]
  Elements of foundation . . . 10.05[2]
  Sample foundation . . . 10.05[3]
Computer printouts, use of . . . 10.02[4]
Confrontation of witnesses, right to . . . 10.14[2]
Contemporaneous statement doctrine
  Generally . . . 10.10[1]
  Elements of foundation . . . 10.10[2]
  Sample foundation . . . 10.10[3]
Data, use of . . . 10.02[4]
Declarations against interest
  Generally . . . 10.15[1]
  Elements of foundation . . . 10.15[2]

[References are to sections.]

HEARSAY—Cont.

Declarations against interest—Cont.
    Sample foundation . . . 10.15[3]

Defined . . . 10.02[1] *et seq.*

Discretion of court, residual exceptions at (See subhead:
    Residual exceptions)

Dying declarations
    Generally . . . 10.16[1]
    Elements of foundation . . . 10.16[2]
    Sample foundation . . . 10.16[3]

Emergency, statements made in course of ongoing
    . . . 10.14[2]

Excited utterances
    Generally . . . 10.09[1]
    Elements of foundation . . . 10.09[2]
    Sample foundation . . . 10.09[3]

Expert opinion, third-party reports as basis for
    . . . 9.03[4][c]

Forensic reports, admissibility of . . . 10.14[2]

Instrumentation data, use of . . . 10.02[4]

Learned treatises
    Generally . . . 10.08[1]
    Elements of foundation . . . 10.08[2]
    Jury, prohibition of physically submitting text or article to . . . 10.08[1]
    Sample foundation . . . 10.08[3]
    Scope of hearsay exception . . . 10.08[1]

Nonassertive acts . . . 10.02[2][c]

Official records exception
    Generally . . . 10.06[1]
    Elements of foundation . . . 10.06[2]
    Sample foundation . . . 10.06[3]

Operative fact or verbal act, statement as
    . . . 10.02[3][c]

Out-of-court declarant, effect of subsequent testimony
by . . . 10.02[5]

Past recollection recorded . . . 10.07[1]

Personal admissions, exemption for
    Generally . . . 10.03[2][a]
    Civil cases . . . 10.03[2][b]
    Criminal cases . . . 10.03[2][c]

Present recollection refreshed or revived . . . 10.07[2]

Present sense impression doctrine (See subhead: Contemporaneous statement doctrine)

Prior testimony subject to cross-examination
    Generally . . . 10.17[1]
    Elements of foundation . . . 10.17[2]
    Sample foundation . . . 10.17[3]

Private writings . . . 4.02[1]

Reliability exceptions . . . 10.04 *et seq.*

Residual exceptions
    Generally . . . 10.19[1]
    Elements of foundation . . . 10.19[2]
    Sample foundation . . . 10.19[3]

Startled utterances (See subhead: Excited utterances)

State of mind
    Declarant's statement as proof of . . . 10.02[3][b]; 10.11[1]
    Hearer or reader, effect of statement on
    . . . 10.02[3][d]

Subsequent conduct of declarant, statements indicating
    . . . 10.11[2]

HEARSAY—Cont.

Truth of matter asserted, statement made to prove
    . . . 10.02[3][a]

Unavailability, exceptions based on
    Generally . . . 10.13; 10.14[1]
    Constitutional requirements for showing unavailability . . . 10.14[2]

Verbal act or operative fact, statement as
    . . . 10.02[3][c]

Vicarious admissions, exemption for
    Civil cases . . . 10.03[4][a]
    Criminal cases . . . 10.03[4][b]

Wrongdoing, forfeiture of protection by
    Generally . . . 10.18[1]
    Elements of foundation . . . 10.18[2]
    Sample foundation . . . 10.18[3]

I

IDENTIFICATION EVIDENCE

Physical evidence (See PHYSICAL EVIDENCE, IDENTIFICATION OF)

Prior identification, bolstering of (See BOLSTERING OF WITNESSES)

Voice identification
    Expert testimony . . . 4.05[4]
    Layperson's testimony . . . 4.05[2]

IMMERSIVE VIRTUAL ENVIRONMENT (IVE) SYSTEM

Generally . . . 4.09[5][c]

IMPEACHMENT OF WITNESSES

Generally . . . 5.02

Bad acts, proof of
    Generally . . . 5.05[1]
    Elements of foundation . . . 5.05[2]
    Sample foundation . . . 5.05[3]

Bias, proof of
    Generally . . . 5.11[1]
    Elements of foundation . . . 5.11[2]
    Sample foundation . . . 5.11[3]

Competency, proof of deficient
    Generally . . . 5.12[1]
    Elements of foundation . . . 5.12[2]
    Sample foundation . . . 5.12[3]

Contradiction by other witness, proof of . . . 5.08

Convictions, proof of prior
    Generally . . . 5.10[1]
    Elements of foundation . . . 5.10[2]
    Sample foundation . . . 5.10[3]

Inconsistent statements, proof of prior
    Generally . . . 5.09[1]
    Cross-examination, eliciting through . . . 5.09[2]
    Extrinsic evidence . . . 5.09[3]
    Failure by witness to mention fact in prior statement
    . . . 5.09[4]

Polygraph examination, failure of
    Generally . . . 5.07[1]
    Elements of foundation . . . 5.07[2]
    Sample foundation . . . 5.07[3]

Prior convictions (See subhead: Convictions, proof of prior)

[References are to sections.]

IMPEACHMENT OF WITNESSES—Cont.
Prior inconsistent statements (See subhead: Inconsistent statements, proof of prior)
Untruthfulness, proof of
    Generally . . . 5.06[1]
    Elements of foundation . . . 5.06[2]
    Sample foundation . . . 5.06[3]

INFORMANTS
Identity, disclosure of
    Generally . . . 7.09[1]
    Elements of foundation . . . 7.09[2]
    Sample foundation . . . 7.09[3]

IN LIMINE MOTIONS
Generally . . . 2.02[1]
Elements of . . . 2.02[2]
Sample motions . . . 2.02[3]

IVE (See IMMERSIVE VIRTUAL ENVIRONMENT (IVE) SYSTEM)

J

JUDICIAL NOTICE
Generally . . . 11.03[1]
Sample foundation . . . 11.03[2]

JURY VIEWS, OUT–OF–COURT
Generally . . . 11.04[1]
Elements of foundation . . . 11.04[2]
Sample foundation . . . 11.04[3]

L

LEARNED TREATISES
Hearsay exception (See HEARSAY, subhead: Learned treatises)

LETTERS
E-mail, authentication of (See E–MAIL, AUTHENTICATION OF)
Reply letter doctrine
    Generally . . . 4.02[4]
    E-mail . . . 4.03[4][b]

LIABILITY INSURANCE
Relevance of evidence . . . 6.09

M

MISCONDUCT EVIDENCE
Generally . . . 6.04[1]
Civil actions, in
    Generally . . . 6.05[1]
    Elements of foundation . . . 6.05[2]
    Sample foundation . . . 6.05[3]
Elements of foundation . . . 6.04[2]
Sample foundation . . . 6.04[3]

MODELS
Foundations for use . . . 4.07[4]

MOTION PICTURES
Verification . . . 4.09[2]

MOTIONS (GENERALLY)
In limine (See IN LIMINE MOTIONS)
Strike, motions to (See STRIKE, MOTIONS TO)

MYSPACE
Social media profile page, authenticating printout of . . . 4.02[6]

O

OBJECTIONS (GENERALLY)
Pre-trial
    Generally . . . 2.01
    Motions in limine (See IN LIMINE MOTIONS)
Trial, during
    Generally . . . 2.03[1]
    Elements of . . . 2.03[2]
    Sample objections . . . 2.03[3]

OFFICIAL WRITINGS, AUTHENTICATION OF
Generally . . . 4.04[1]
Elements of foundation . . . 4.04[2]
Sample foundation . . . 4.04[3]

OPINION EVIDENCE
Generally . . . 9.01
Character evidence . . . 6.02[3]
Collective fact opinions . . . 9.02[2]
Expert testimony (See EXPERT TESTIMONY)
Lay opinion testimony
    Generally . . . 9.02[1]
    Collective fact opinions . . . 9.02[2]
    Owners' opinion regarding value of property . . . 9.02[4]
    Shorthand rendition doctrine . . . 9.02[2]
    Skilled lay observer testimony . . . 9.02[3]
Owners' opinion regarding value of property . . . 9.02[4]
Shorthand rendition doctrine . . . 9.02[2]

ORAL STATEMENTS, AUTHENTICATION OF
Generally . . . 4.05[1]
Caller ID, authentication of (See CALLER ID, AUTHENTICATION OF)
Expert testimony . . . 4.05[4]
Speaker's voice, layperson's testimony regarding . . . 4.05[2]
Telephone directory doctrine . . . 4.05[3]

OUT–OF–COURT EVIDENCE
Experiments (See EXPERIMENTS, OUT–OF–COURT)
Jury views (See JURY VIEWS, OUT–OF–COURT)

P

PHOTOGRAPHS, VERIFICATION OF
Generally . . . 4.09[1]
Automated surveillance cameras . . . 4.09[4]
Computer animations and simulations (See COMPUTERS, subhead: Animations and simulations, verification of)
Enhanced photographs . . . 4.09[6]
Motion pictures . . . 4.09[2]
Videotapes . . . 4.09[2]

[References are to sections.]

PHOTOGRAPHS, VERIFICATION OF—Cont.
X-rays . . . 4.09[3]

PHYSICAL EVIDENCE, IDENTIFICATION OF
Generally . . . 4.08[1]
Elements of foundation . . . 4.08[2]
Sample foundation . . . 4.08[3]

PHYSICIANS
Privileged communication exception . . . 7.05[4]

PLEA BARGAINING
Privileged communications in . . . 7.10[1]; 7.11[2]

POLYGRAPH TESTS
Impeachment of witness by failure (See IMPEACH-
    MENT OF WITNESSES)

PRIOR OFFENSES OR CONVICTIONS
Generally . . . 6.04[1]
Elements of foundation . . . 6.04[2]
Impeachment through (See IMPEACHMENT OF WIT-
    NESSES, subhead: Convictions, proof of prior)
Misconduct evidence (See MISCONDUCT EVI-
    DENCE)
Sample foundation . . . 6.04[3]

PRIVATE WRITINGS, AUTHENTICATION OF
Generally . . . 4.02[1]
Ancient writings . . . 4.02[7]
Best evidence issues . . . 4.02[1]
Execution, witness testimony regarding . . . 4.02[2]
Expert testimony regarding . . . 4.02[5]
Handwriting
    Expert testimony . . . 4.02[5]
    Layperson's testimony . . . 4.02[3]
Hearsay issues . . . 4.02[1]
Reply letter doctrine . . . 4.02[4]
Social media profile page, printout of . . . 4.02[6]
Witness testimony
    Execution of document, witness to . . . 4.02[2]
    Expert examiner . . . 4.02[5]
    Handwriting . . . 4.02[3]

PRIVILEGED COMMUNICATIONS
Generally . . . 7.01; 7.02
"Absolute" communications privilege . . . 7.02
Ad hoc need for privileged information does not defeat
    privilege . . . 7.05[1]
Attorney-client privilege (See ATTORNEY–CLIENT
    PRIVILEGE)
Compromise discussions
    Civil settlement negotiations, made in . . . 7.10[1];
        7.11[1]
    Plea bargaining, made in . . . 7.10[1]; 7.11[2]
Crime or fraud, communication to facilitate
    . . . 7.05[2]
Exception, proof of
    Generally . . . 7.02; 7.05[1]
    Ad hoc need for information does not qualify as ex-
        ception . . . 7.05[1]
    Burden of proof . . . 7.05[1]
    Crime or fraud, communication to facilitate
        . . . 7.05[2]
    Joint consultation exception . . . 7.05[3]

PRIVILEGED COMMUNICATIONS—Cont.
Exception, proof of—Cont.
    Patient-litigant exception . . . 7.05[4]
Government privileges
    Generally . . . 7.01
    Informant's identity (See INFORMANTS, subhead:
        Identity, disclosure of)
    Military and state secrets (See subhead: Military and
        state secrets)
    Minor government secrets
        Generally . . . 7.08[1]
        Elements of foundation . . . 7.08[2]
        Sample foundation . . . 7.08[3]
Informant's identity, protection of (See INFORMANTS,
    subhead: Identity, disclosure of)
Invocation of privilege
    Elements of foundation . . . 7.03[1]
    Sample foundation . . . 7.03[2]
Joint consultation exception . . . 7.05[3]
Military and state secrets
    Generally . . . 7.07[1]
    Elements of foundation . . . 7.07[2]
    Sample foundation . . . 7.07[3]
Patient-litigant exception . . . 7.05[4]
Physician-patient privilege . . . 7.05[4]
Plea bargaining, statement made during . . . 7.10[1];
    7.11[2]
Relationship requirement . . . 7.02
Settlement negotiations, statements made in
    . . . 7.10[1]; 7.11[1]
Special communications privilege . . . 3.05[1]
State secrets (See subhead: Military and state secrets)
Subsequent repair doctrine (See SUBSEQUENT RE-
    PAIR DOCTRINE)
Waiver, proof of
    Generally . . . 7.02; 7.04[1]
    In-court waiver . . . 7.04[2]
    Out-of-court waiver . . . 7.04[3]
Work product protection
    Absolute . . . 7.06[2]
    Conditional . . . 7.06[1]

PROOF, OFFER OF
Generally . . . 2.06[1]
Elements of . . . 2.06[2]
Sample offers . . . 2.06[3]

PSYCHIATRIC TESTIMONY
Witnesses, attacking competency of (See WITNESSES,
    subhead: Psychiatric testimony attacking competency)

R

REHABILITATION OF WITNESSES
Generally . . . 5.02
Consistency of statements, proof of
    Generally . . . 5.13[1]
    Elements of foundation . . . 5.13[2]
    Sample foundation . . . 5.13[3]
Truthfulness, proof of
    Generally . . . 5.14[1]
    Elements of foundation . . . 5.14[2]
    Sample foundation . . . 5.14[3]

ROUTINE PRACTICE EVIDENCE
Generally . . . 6.03[1]
Elements of foundation . . . 6.03[2]
Sample foundation . . . 6.03[3]

RULE 403
Credibility evidence, limiting . . . 5.01; 5.02
Historical merits of case, evidence relevant to . . . 6.01

S

SCANNED WRITINGS
Authentication of . . . 4.03[5]

SCIENTIFIC EVIDENCE, VALIDATION OF
Generally . . . 4.10[1]
Elements of foundation . . . 4.10[2]
Sample foundation . . . 4.10[3]

SETTLEMENTS, OUT–OF–COURT
Privileged communications in . . . 7.10[1]; 7.11[1]

SIMILAR HAPPENINGS EVIDENCE
Generally . . . 6.06[1]
Elements of foundation . . . 6.06[2]
Sample foundation . . . 6.06[3]

SOCIAL MEDIA PROFILE
Authenticating printout of social medial profile page of Facebook, MySpace or Twitter . . . 4.02[6]

SPOUSES AS WITNESSES
Generally . . . 3.05[1]
Elements of foundation . . . 3.05[2]
Sample foundation . . . 3.05[3]

STATE OF MIND (See HEARSAY)

STIPULATIONS
Generally . . . 11.02[1]
Elements of foundation . . . 11.02[2]
Sample foundation . . . 11.02[3]

STRIKE, MOTIONS TO
Generally . . . 2.04[1]
Elements of . . . 2.04[2]
Sample motions . . . 2.04[3]

SUBSEQUENT REPAIR DOCTRINE
Generally . . . 7.10[1]
Elements of foundation . . . 7.10[2]
Sample foundation . . . 7.10[3]

SUBSTITUTES FOR EVIDENCE
Generally . . . 11.01
Judicial notice
　Generally . . . 11.03[1]
　Sample foundation . . . 11.03[2]
Jury views outside courtroom (See JURY VIEWS, OUT–OF–COURT)
Stipulations (See STIPULATIONS)

SURVEILLANCE CAMERAS
Verification of . . . 4.09[4]

SURVIVORS' EVIDENCE ACTS (See DEAD PERSONS' STATUTE)

T

TELEPHONES
Caller ID, authentication of (See CALLER ID, AUTHENTICATION OF)
Telephone directory doctrine . . . 4.05[3]

TWITTER
Social media profile page, authenticating printout of . . . 4.02[6]

V

VIDEOTAPES
Verification . . . 4.09[2]

VIRTUAL REALITY TECHNOLOGY
Generally . . . 4.09[5][c]

VOICE IDENTIFICATION
Expert testimony . . . 4.05[4]
Layperson's testimony . . . 4.05[2]

VOIR DIRE EXAMINATION OF WITNESS
Generally . . . 2.05[1]
Children as witnesses
　Generally . . . 3.02[1]
　Elements of foundation . . . 3.02[2]
　Sample foundation . . . 3.02[3]
Sample request . . . 2.05[2]

W

WITNESSES
Bolstering (See BOLSTERING OF WITNESSES)
Character witness, cross-examination of . . . 6.02[5]
Children, voir dire examination of (See VOIR DIRE EXAMINATION OF WITNESS)
Competency, establishing
　Generally . . . 3.01
　Dead persons' statute (See DEAD PERSONS' STATUTE)
　Impeachment of competency (See IMPEACHMENT OF WITNESSES, subhead: Competency, proof of deficient)
　Personal knowledge (See subhead: Personal knowledge, establishing)
　Psychiatric testimony (See subhead: Psychiatric testimony attacking competency)
　Spouse as witness (See SPOUSES AS WITNESSES)
　Voir dire examination (See VOIR DIRE EXAMINATION OF WITNESS)
Dead persons' statute (See DEAD PERSONS' STATUTE)
Impeachment (See IMPEACHMENT OF WITNESSES)
Informant's identity, disclosure of (See INFORMANTS, subhead: Identity, disclosure of)
Personal knowledge, establishing
　Generally . . . 3.03[1]
　Elements of foundation . . . 3.03[2]

[References are to sections.]

WITNESSES—Cont.
Personal knowledge, establishing—Cont.
  Sample foundation . . . 3.03[3]
Private writings, authentication of (See PRIVATE
  WRITINGS, AUTHENTICATION OF)
Psychiatric testimony attacking competency
  Generally . . . 3.04[1]
  Elements of foundation . . . 3.04[2]
  Sample foundation . . . 3.04[3]
Rehabilitation (See REHABILITATION OF WIT-
  NESSES)
Spouses as (See SPOUSES AS WITNESSES)

WITNESSES—Cont.
Voir dire examination of (See VOIR DIRE EXAMINA-
  TION OF WITNESS)

WRITINGS, AUTHENTICATION OF (See specific
  subject headings, e.g., BUSINESS WRITINGS)

X

X–RAYS
Verification . . . 4.09[3]